STEPHEN H. SPURR, Ph.D., Yale University, is Professor of Botany and Public Affairs and President of The University of Texas at Austin. Professor Spurr formerly taught at Harvard University and the University of Minnesota, and was for many years Professor of Silviculture and Dean of the School of Natural Resources of The University of Michigan. He was editor of the periodical *Forest Service* and is the author of *Forest Inventory* and *Photogrammetry, Second Edition,* both published by The Ronald Press Company.

BURTON V. BARNES, Ph.D., The University of Michigan, is Professor of Forestry at the School of Natural Resources and Forest Botanist at the Matthaei Botanical Gardens of that institution. Professor Barnes served as a Research Forester at the Intermountain Forest and Range Experiment Station of the U. S. Department of Agriculture and a Postdoctoral Fellow of the National Science Foundation before joining the faculty at Michigan as silviculturist. He is an active contributor of research papers in his fields of specialization.

FOREST ECOLOGY

STEPHEN H. SPURR
UNIVERSITY OF TEXAS AT AUSTIN

BURTON V. BARNES
UNIVERSITY OF MICHIGAN

SECOND EDITION

THE RONALD PRESS COMPANY • NEW YORK

Library of Congress Catalog Card Number: 73–77862
PRINTED IN THE UNITED STATES OF AMERICA

Preface

Forest Ecology deals with the ecological basis of the management of forested land. It is designed for use as a textbook in courses in forest ecology, silvics, or principles of silviculture, for foresters, wildlife managers, and others interested in the ecology of forest land.

Since the appearance of the first edition in 1964, ecology has come into prominence popularly as well as scientifically. Increased ecological interest and concern present us with an opportunity and a challenge in managing our natural resources wisely. Ecological principles governing forest establishment, competition, succession, and growth are basic to managing trees and forests for whatever purpose and scale—from a city shade tree to a forested watershed. This book is devoted to providing an understanding of the basic ecological relationships of individual trees, forest communities, and forest ecosytems.

The book has four major subdivisions. "The Forest Tree" considers the variations between individual trees and the causes of diversity within and between species. "The Forest Environment" treats *autecology,* the influences of solar radiation, atmospheric conditions, climate, and soil on the individual forest plant. In "The Forest Community and the Ecosystem" *synecology* is covered as it relates to the factors that influence competition and survival in the forest and the forest ecosystem as it exists in time and in space. In addition, the comparatively new study of whole ecosystems is considered. Finally, "The Forest" explores *phytogeography.* Here, the actual historical development and distribution of the North American forest are briefly developed.

In this Second Edition we have attempted to retain the readable qualities of the First Edition while infusing new material and ideas. Due to the enormous volume of ecological literature, a rigorous selection was necessary. Although over 800 items of literature are cited, they constitute only a small sample of the many thousands of references in the authors' bibliographic collections. Preference has been given to major English-language works published since 1945. At the same time, though, an effort has been made to include a judicious selection of important earlier work, as well as representative papers written in languages other than English dealing with forests other than those in the United States.

We are indebted to many colleagues for their contributions and help in preparation of the revised edition. In particular we wish to acknowledge reviews by Robert Zahner, Willard H. Carmean, Margaret B. Davis, William S. Benninghoff, and James W. Hanover.

STEPHEN H. SPURR
BURTON V. BARNES

Austin, Texas
Ann Arbor, Michigan
    April, 1973

Contents

PART IV   THE FOREST

FOREST ECOLOGY

1

Concepts of Forest Ecology

A *forest* is a biological community dominated by trees and other woody vegetation. *Ecology* is the science of the interrelationships of organisms in and to their complete environment. *Forest ecology,* therefore, is concerned with the forest as a biological community, with the interrelationships between the various trees and other organisms constituting the community, and with the interrelationships between these organisms and the physical environment in which they exist.

Ecology

The broader the field of scientific inquiry, the more difficult it becomes to limit and define that field. Ecology, as the broadest of the biological sciences, is also the most indistinct. Since Ernst Haeckel in 1866 proposed the term *oecology,* from the Greek *oikos* meaning house or place to live, the term has been applied at one time or another to almost every aspect of scientific investigation involving the relationship of one organism to another, or to the relationship of an organism to its environment. Ecology, however, clearly is confined to a study of life at the plane of the individual whole organism and not at levels of portions of plants. In contrast, the study of the life processes of the various portions of plants falls within the discipline of *plant physiology;* the investigation of events within the cell is termed *cytology;* while the analysis of ultimate

3

chemical structure and life processes involves the science of *bio-chemistry*.

It is perfectly proper to investigate the life of an organism on any of these planes (Figure 1.1). The level-of-integration concept has great importance in the development of a logical approach to ecology (Rowe, 1961). As Decker (1959) illustrates the alternatives:

> A life history can be described as a chain of events, with each event involving a whole plant. For example, a seed germinates, the seedling grows to be a sapling, the sapling is killed by fire. The same life history can be stated in terms of several chains of organ events, that is, in terms of what happens to leaves, roots and stem. Or it can be described in terms of a still larger number of tissue events. The resolving can be done repeatedly down through cellular events, subcellular events, colloidal events and molecular events. That is, if information were available, a life history could be described as an incomprehensibly large number of molecular events. Environmental factors can be resolved similarly; for example, illumination of a mesophyll cell, a proton striking a chlorophyll molecule.

Investigations at each plane lead to an understanding of interrelationships at that plane. Ecological studies, therefore, may be expected to provide information as to observed correlations between whole organisms and their environment, and even as to cause-and-effect chains of events involving the whole plant or animal. Causality at other planes must be studied at the levels of other disciplines. It follows that ecological studies, involving as they do the complex of biotic communities, tend to lead to an understanding at the broad or integrative level; whereas the highly focused and localized attention of the biochemist, at the other extreme, proposes to understand the individual building blocks of life.

The term *ecology* was defined by Haeckel as the study of the reciprocal relations between organisms and their environments. A

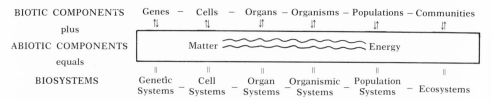

Fig. 1.1. Levels-of-organization spectrum. Ecology focuses on the right-hand portion of the spectrum, that is, the levels of organization from organisms to ecosystems. (After Odum, 1971.)

strict division of ecology into the study of individuals in relation to environment (autecology) and of communities in relation
to environment (synecology) is widely held by European scientists.
In their view the study of the development, composition, characteristics, and interactions of groups of plants or plant communities
is defined as plant sociology, or phytosociology. The contrasting
Anglo-American interpretation, and the one we follow, is that ecology is the study of the interrelationships of organisms to one another and to the environment (Hanson, 1962; Daubenmire, 1959,
1968).

The Forest

The forest is one of the basic physiognomic life forms by which
biotic communities may be classified. Characterized by the predominance of woody vegetation substantially taller than man, forests are widespread on land surfaces in humid climates outside of
the polar regions. It is with forests in general, and with the temperate North American forest in particular, that the present book is
concerned.

As with all biotic community types, the forest may be defined at
several levels. Most obviously, it may be considered simply in terms
of the trees, those plants which give the community its characteristic
physiognomy. Thus we think of a beech-maple forest, a spruce-fir
forest, or of other *forest types*, for which the naming of the predominant trees alone serves to classify the community.

A second approach to the definition of the forest takes into account the obvious interrelationships that exist between other organisms and forest trees. Certain herbs or shrubs are commonly
associated with a beech-maple forest while others are concentrated
in spruce-fir forests nearby. Similar interrelationships may be demonstrated for birds, mammals, arthropods, fungi, bacteria, etc. The
forest may be considered as an assemblage of plants and animals
living in a *biotic* association, or *biocoenosis*. The *forest association*,
or *forest community*, then, is an assemblage of plants and animals
living together in a common environment, and is thus a more explicit
and narrowly defined unit than the forest type, which is defined on
the basis of the trees only.

A forest community exists in a physical environment composed
of the atmosphere surrounding the aerial portions and the soil con-

taining the subterranean portions. This environment is not static but rather is changing constantly due to the rotation of the earth, the fluctuations in solar radiation, the changing atmosphere, the weathering of the soil, and indeed the effects of the forest community itself upon both the local climate and the local soil. The forest community and its habitat together comprise an ecological system, *ecosystem,* or *biogeocoenosis,* in which the constituent organisms and their environments interact in a vast and complex energy cycle. The *forest ecosystem,* taking into account both the organic and inorganic aspects of the energy cycle of life, is at the same time the most precise and the least comprehensible definition of the forest community.

An Approach to the Analysis of Forest Ecology

The scope of forest ecology, then, may be defined as the analysis of the forest ecosystem. Such an analysis is facilitated first by the segregation of the ecosystem into its organic and inorganic aspects and then by consideration of forest communities and entire ecosystems. The sequence of analysis is (1) the forest tree, i.e., the variation and diversity of forest species, (2) the forest environment, (3) the forest community and the forest ecosystem, and (4) forest history.

In a book such as this, designed primarily for those interested in forests and especially for forestry programs in a course on the ecological foundations of silviculture, the organic aspects must be concerned primarily with the forest trees themselves since these are the objects of management, and are the organisms with which the forest manager and the forest scientist are primarily concerned. While repeated references are made to the ground vegetation, the animals within the forest, and the complex biota of the forest floor and soil, these aspects of the forest community are dealt with only briefly in the present work and then only in connection with their interrelationships with the trees of the forest.

The forest tree owes its appearance, rate of growth, and size, in part, to the environment in which it has grown throughout its life. Put in modern biological language, the *phenotype,* the individual as it appears, is the product of the effect of the environment on its *genotype,* its individual hereditary constitution. This statement is basic to an understanding of the forest and, indeed, defines the scope of this book. An understanding of forest trees and communities in managed, exploited, or wilderness conditions is based in part upon the environment of the forest and the way it affects the trees making up the forest; but also in part upon the genetic nature of the trees themselves and the way in which this affects the response of trees to the environment they find themselves in. These genetic and environmental interactions are discussed in Part I.

The inorganic aspects of the forest ecosystem constitute the *physical environment*, or *habitat*, or *site*. Although the forest environment is the composite end product of many interacting factors, it is convenient to present and discuss separately each physical factor of the atmosphere surrounding the forest and of the soil in which the forest is grown.

The *habitat*, or *site* as it is more commonly called in the case of trees, is the sum total of the atmospheric and soil conditions surrounding and available to the plant. Among atmospheric factors, solar radiation, air temperature, air humidity, and carbon dioxide content all vary throughout the day, from day to day, month to month, and year to year, making up the complex we term *climate*. Below the surface, the supply of soil nutrients, the soil moisture regime, the physical structure of the soil, and the nature and decomposition pattern of the organic matter, i.e., factors pertaining to the soil—*edaphic* factors—all affect the growth and development of plants. Furthermore, the growing vegetation itself affects the climate and soil so that the site changes as the plants themselves grow and change. The study of environmental factors and their effects on plants constitutes the field of *autecology*. Part II summarizes those aspects of forest autecology most pertinent to an understanding of the forest ecosystem and its management by man.

The forest community (Part III) is produced by the interactions between forest trees and other forest organisms on the one hand, and the forest environment on the other, over a period of time. Together they constitute the forest ecosystem. Each community follows a definite life cycle in which it becomes established, develops, reaches maturity, and in turn gives way to another community either similar or different in composition. In the competition for growing space, many plants lose out while others thrive, either as a result of their ability to usurp space for themselves or to cooperate with other plants in establishing themselves in a niche. The structure and composition of the forest community change from time to time and from place to place. *Dynamic plant ecology,* emphasizing forest succession, is concerned with changes in time, while *plant sociology* stresses variations in space. The term *synecology,* referring to the study of biotic communities and the interaction of the organisms which compose them, is inclusive of both.

The physical environment and the community are components of the forest ecosystem and are operationally inseparable. Thus one must ultimately deal with the ecosystem in emphasizing the interdependence and causal relationships of plants and animals in their physical environment. The understanding of functioning forest ecosystems and the method of systems analysis in their study is considered in the final chapter of Part III. Because of the size and complexity of forest ecosystems, it has only been in recent times that the biological and mathematical skills, data processing methods, and funds (largely available through concern about overpopulation and endangered environments) have been available to conduct the comprehensive programs capable of determining how an ecosystem works. Such investigations have led to the creation of an exciting and entirely new level of ecological science.

Present-Day Forests

Although the principles of forest ecology may be presented by considering the forest as a complex ecosystem (Part III) arising out of the interactions of the forest trees and their environment (Parts I and II), so many factors are involved over so long a period of time that it is wise to conclude with a consideration of forests as they actually are and not necessarily as they should appear to be in accordance with our philosophy. Part IV brings together information on the present forest communities of the temperate portions of North America and on the past development of these communities as deduced from paleoecological studies or as recorded in the history of exploration by man, land settlement, logging, and farm abandonment. The forest of today is affected most strongly by the conditions that existed at the time the present individuals became established on that site, but it is also affected by all that has happened since that time. In the forest, the history of logging, land clearing, urban development, fires, windstorms, insect and disease epidemics, and other happenings that affect the life and growth of the trees all will influence the present forest stand.

Climatic fluctuations and the development of the soil profile also cannot be ignored. The more we can learn of the history of the land and of the plants and animals that occupy it, the better we can understand the present communities that we live and work with.

Here the biological historian must play the part of the detective, for written records are few and scanty, and precise measurements in the past are almost nonexistent. Fortunately, recent developments in the reconstruction of past forests through analysis of fossil pollen accumulations and other plant remains, in the dating of fossil organic matter through radioactive carbon analysis and related techniques, and in precise tree ring studies are all increasing our knowledge and understanding of the past.

Other Treatments of Forest Ecology

Such a complex subject as ecology may be approached in various ways, and no one approach has any inherent virtues outside of the clarity of its logic and the resulting understanding. Furthermore, no approach has any particular originality in modern times, all having evolved from man's long curiosity about his surroundings and from the gradual evolution of natural history into the science we know now as ecology.

Most texts dealing with the biological basis of silviculture have anticipated the present one in emphasizing the ecological approach, presenting first of all a single-factor discussion of the principal environmental factors and following up with a treatment of the forest community both as a static association and as a dynamic concept. Toumey's classic *Foundations of Silviculture* (1947) is an American statement of the classic German approach, including both autecology and synecology, the latter influenced in his day by the theories of F. E. Clements on plant succession. The present work differs from the pioneer effort of Toumey in its emphasis upon the ecosystem concept and the importance of genetic factors in the formation of the forest community, and in presenting a general synthesis of community dynamics less rigidly based and defined than that of Clements.

A physiological approach to the biological basis of silviculture also has its merits. An analysis based upon the life processes of the tree is just as valid as that based upon the organism itself. Thinking along this line has been greatly influenced by the English translation of Münch's revision of Büsgen's monograph on the *Structure and Life of Forest Trees* (1929), which remains a basic reference despite its age; the more recent and detailed revised German edition of this work (Lyr *et al.*, 1967) continues the physiological approach. Baker (1950) has attempted to synthesize the physiological and ecological viewpoints in his *Principles of Silviculture* while Kramer and Kozlowski (1960) and Kozlowski (1971) have summarized present-day information on tree physiology as such.

Recent and important European works include the two-volume revision of Dengler's famous treatment of the biological basis of silviculture (Bonnemann and Röhrig, 1971, 1972), a new two-volume study of environmental factors in relation to tree and forest growth (Mitscherlich, 1970, 1971), and a concise treatment of the forest as a living community (Leibundgut, 1970). Significantly, the thought of the famous Russian ecologist Sukachev and his school is now available in English translation (Sukachev and Dylis, 1968). This book, *Fundamentals of Forest Biogeocoenology*, provides an excellent introduction to Russian ecological thought and literature, is particularly strong in consideration of the animal and microorganismal components of the ecosystem, and above all stresses the ecosystem approach to silviculture.

Applicability to Silviculture

Although knowledge and understanding for their own sake are sufficient justification for the ecologist, forest ecology is taught in the professional schools of forestry and natural resources because of its importance in influencing silvicultural practice. *Silviculture* is the theory and practice of controlling forest establishment, composition, and growth (Spurr, 1945). Man's conscious motives for control of forests have changed drastically since the turn of the century and continue to change from a primarily timber-oriented management to multiple-use management where human and water resources play an ever-increasing role. Whatever the purpose, obviously, management based on knowledge and understanding is better than that not so based. It is almost trite to restate that a knowledge of forest biology, most frequently organized and taught with an ecological point of view, is as important to the resource manager as is a knowledge of business economics and a competence in the mathematics of forest measurements and estimates. Beyond this, opinions differ.

At one extreme, many foresters follow the classic viewpoint of the agriculturist in choosing his desired crop species and then growing it in formally planned and obviously man-made communities. Pure, even-aged plantations of such trees as pine, spruce, rubber, apple, and the date palm represent the type of arboriculture where the forester and the horticulturist differ only in that one is primarily concerned with the growing of timber while the other is similarly involved in the growing of fruit. Since such plantation crops are frequently grown on limited areas of carefully chosen site and since the value of the crops is usually high, management may be relatively intensive, and normal ecological trends may be countered successfully by fertilizers, herbicides, cultivation, and other measures. It does not follow, however, that a knowledge of these ecological trends and the consequences of herbicides, fertilizers, and cultivation is unnecessary to the plantation manager—quite the contrary.

At the other extreme, the "naturalistic" school of silviculture preaches that nature's ways are the best and the safest, and that the silviculturist should grow his forests in harmony with natural trends. While it is true that it is cheapest to sit back and allow the forest to develop in the absence of further interference, it does not necessarily follow that the greatest net return similarly will be realized either in tangible or in intangible values. The pines and Douglas-fir—indeed, most of our commercial timber species—require the aid of considerable effort on behalf of man if high yields are to be maintained year after year despite continual harvest of the timber crop by man. The more drastic the departure from the patterns and processes of the natural ecosystem, the more knowledge and understanding one must have of the ecosystem.

So, as with so many other things, the middle course is generally the best. As Lutz (1959) sums the matter up:

In conclusion, it seems to me that the silviculturist should seek to understand ecological principles and natural tendencies as they relate to the trees and forest communities with which he works. I do not infer that he is bound to follow them blindly but neither do I think that he can safely ignore them. Between the two extremes of passively following nature on the one hand, and open revolt against her on the other, is a wide area for applying the basic philosophy of working in harmony with natural tendencies.

To this we must also add that the consequences of our manipulation or non-interference must be considered by silviculturists, resource managers, and planners not solely on monetary or intangible benefits in the local ecosystem, but also on larger, interrelated terrestrial and aquatic systems. In most cases this means a change in our thinking to a systems approach—considering not only the effects of our acts on a single stand but on the ecosystem of which it is a part and also on the larger systems which in turn may be affected. Our understanding of forests as ecological systems and of the integrated functioning of all component parts must play a much greater role in the present and future than it has in the past.

THE FOREST TREE

2

Forest Tree Variability and Diversity

Too often and for too long in the past the approach to the ecological foundations of silviculture has been strictly environmentalistic. Most treatments have completely ignored the genetic basis which is equally important in determining the nature of the forest. In a sense, forest ecology has been too much a direct descendant of pre-Darwinian environmental naturalism.

Life, whether in a forest tree or in any other organism, cannot exist without a governing biochemical control mechanism which can be passed on from generation to generation to perpetuate the species; and the organism cannot exist independently of an environment. It is futile to argue whether genetic or environmental factors control the form and development of an organism. Both always together determine the nature of the phenotype. Environmental factors, being generally visible and readily accessible, are the most obvious, and it is natural that most ecologists have been preoccupied with their study. Genetic factors have been fully appreciated only in recent years, and their assessment in forest trees has lagged far behind their study in smaller and more tractable organisms.

The ability of organisms to live and reproduce in a given range of environments, termed adaptedness (Dobzhansky, 1968), had

15

been known since the days of Aristotle, and a convincing explanation was given by Darwin even though the causes of hereditary variation were then unknown. Darwin's theory of evolution by natural selection is an ecological theory based on ecological observations by perhaps the greatest ecologist (Harper, 1967). It is important for the forest ecologist to consider adaptiveness of forest species and their ability to adapt to changing environmental conditions. The long life and wide range of forest trees affect the stability and adaptive strategies of many associated plants and animals.

In the present chapter, the primary concern is variation: the sources of variation; the kinds and extent of variation within and between individuals, populations, and species; and how the environment and biotic factors elicit adaptive changes in tree populations. Although the evolutionary framework is briefly described, no attempt is made to discuss in detail physiological and population genetics; they are well treated in a number of texts (Stebbins, 1950, 1970; Grant, 1963, 1971; Solbrig, 1970; Mettler and Gregg, 1969). Treatments of forest genetics and tree improvement include those of Syrach-Larsen (1956), Wright (1962), and the FAO (1964, 1970).

COMPONENTS OF PHENOTYPIC VARIATION

As indicated in Chapter 1, the ecologist may work with organisms at various levels of complexity—the individual, the population, the community, the ecosystem. In general, the individual is the least arbitrary of these units. The genetic constitution of an individual is termed the *genotype*. We can never see a genotype because from the moment of fertilization the genotype is influenced by the plant's environment, the internal environment of cells, tissues, and biochemical reactions, and the external environment of temperature, moisture, and light. We see only the result—the *phenotype*—the observable properties of an organism produced by the genotype in conjunction with the environment. We may express this relationship for the entire organism or for individual characters by the simple formula $P = G + E + GE$. The phenotype or phenotypic character (P) is the sum total of the effects of three components, the genetic information coded in the chromosomes (G), the environment (E: all non-genetic factors including those of the plant and its physical and biotic environment), and the interaction of the genotype and environment (GE). Often the genotype-environment interaction is small and can be disregarded; in certain cases it is of special importance. Through complex pathways, the genes control physiological functions, and many of these influence the morphological and anatomical features of the plant. The interrelationship of the genotype, environment, and plant processes of the phenotype is illustrated in Figure 2.1.

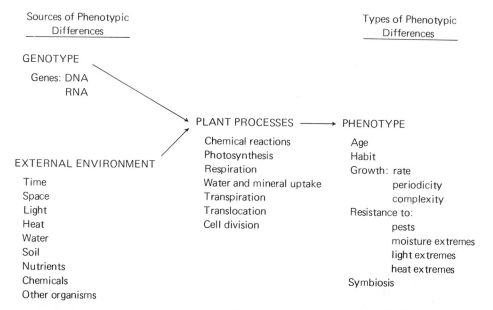

Sources of Phenotypic Differences

Types of Phenotypic Differences

GENOTYPE
  Genes: DNA
          RNA

PLANT PROCESSES ⟶ PHENOTYPE
  Chemical reactions
  Photosynthesis
  Respiration
  Water and mineral uptake
  Transpiration
  Translocation
  Cell division

EXTERNAL ENVIRONMENT
  Time
  Space
  Light
  Heat
  Water
  Soil
  Nutrients
  Chemicals
  Other organisms

Age
Habit
Growth: rate
       periodicity
       complexity
Resistance to:
    pests
    moisture extremes
    light extremes
    heat extremes
Symbiosis

Fig. 2.1. Relationship of an individual's phenotype to its genotype and environment. Differences in plant phenotypes have their origin in the genetic constitution or genotype of an individual and in environmental factors. Phenotypic differences of the individual become apparent as physiological processes occur in the internal environment of plant cells, tissues, and organs. (Modified from a diagram by J. W. Hanover, Michigan State University.)

A recurrent problem confronting the forest ecologist is the degree to which a phenotypic character is controlled by the genotype and by the environment. For example, to what degree are the cushion-like phenotypes of spruce trees at timberline due to wind, snow, and cold, and to what degree are they the result of genotypes that favor this growth form? If we set P in the formula equal to 100, do the environment and genotype contribute equally (50–50), or is one more important than the other? If so, how much? Or consider a dominant tree exhibiting excellent growth in an even-aged forest stand and an adjacent suppressed and dying tree of the same species. The dominant has a superior phenotype, but to what degree is the genotype responsible and to what degree does its microenvironment or such chance factors as better handling in the nursery account for the difference? Despite its poor phenotype the genotype of the suppressed tree may be superior to that of the dominant —or, of course, it may not.

The determination of the relative effects of genotype and environment is for the ecologist a recurrent and often unconscious feature in ecological studies. Both components are always involved and no two phenotypes are exactly alike. The important point is the relative degree of genetic and non-genetic influence on a given character.

Forest geneticists use the ratio between genetic variance (V_G) and total phenotypic variance (V_P) of a character, V_G/V_P, to estimate the strength of genetic control or *heritability* of that character. Strong genetic control (high heritability) has been shown for bole straightness, stem-wood specific gravity, monoterpene composition in certain conifers, susceptibility to leaf rusts, date of bud burst, and many leaf attributes. Low heritabilities have been consistently reported for height and diameter growth.

Plasticity of the Phenotype

A given genotype may assume one set of characters (exhibit one phenotype) in one environment and exhibit a markedly different phenotype in another environment. The degree to which a character of a given genotype can be modified (a non-genetic change) by environmental conditions is termed its plasticity or, in general, *plasticity of the phenotype* (Bradshaw, 1965).

For herbaceous species Bradshaw cites as plastic characters: size of vegetative parts, number of shoots, leaves, and flowers, and elongation rate of stems. Non-plastic characters include leaf shape, serration of leaf margin, and floral characteristics. There is good reason to believe this holds true for most tree species. In general, characters formed over long time periods of meristematic activity, such as stem elongation, are more subject to environmental influences and are more plastic than characters like reproductive structures that are formed rapidly or than traits such as leaf shape, whose pattern is impressed at an early stage of development.

Plasticity may have substantial adaptive value to plants in general and tree species in particular since trees are rooted in their environment and have life spans typically longer than annuals or herbaceous perennials. An example of plasticity of adaptive significance is the rooting habit of individuals of many tree species, particularly Norway spruce, white spruce, and balsam fir. The roots may be either shallow or moderately deep depending on the soil environment, e.g., a poorly drained swamp vs. a sandy loam upland soil. If individuals of a species exhibit a high plasticity for certain establishment and growth characters, they may be able to establish and maintain themselves in a variety of habitats and as adult trees endure decades or even centuries of fluctuating climate. Such a mechanism tends to decrease the need for specially adapted genotypes or races (genetically distinct populations of a species), each one fit for a special microhabitat.

We can summarize the differences in phenotypes by examining three hypothetical situations involving individuals of a given species:

Situation A	Situation B	Situation C
$P_1 = G_1 + E_1$	$P_4 = G_1 + E_1$	$P_7 = G_1 + E_1$
$P_2 = G_2 + E_2$	$P_5 = G_1 + E_2$	$P_8 = G_2 + E_1$
$P_3 = G_3 + E_3$	$P_6 = G_1 + E_3$	$P_9 = G_3 + E_1$

The phenotypes in A illustrate the typical situation in the field. All phenotypes have different genotypes, and the environments are also different enough to contribute to differences in the phenotypes. Situations B and C illustrate experimental situations where we can either hold constant the genotype (in B) or test different genotypes in a given environment (in C).

Situation B illustrates plasticity but would have to be related to a specific character. Different phenotypes of a single genotype (G_1) are the result of the environmental differences; modification has occurred. In nature, the degree of plasticity of a character cannot be measured precisely because each individual has a different genotype (as in A). The extent of environmental modification can only be inferred. For example, individuals of an even-aged stand in rolling terrain may occur from a dry ridge top to a moist, fertile valley. We observe a marked increase in height of the trees as we progress from ridge top into the valley. If it is unlikely that there are major changes in the genotypes along the gradient, we may infer that environment is the major factor controlling the phenotypic differences in height. To determine precisely the plasticity for representative genotypes we would have to conduct experiments based on model B.

In situation C we see that if the environment is the same for all individuals, phenotypic differences are due to differences among genotypes, and the amount of genetic variation can be estimated directly from the phenotypes. In practice the environment cannot be held constant. However, we may approach this ideal by using either growth chambers or relatively uniform field test plots and a replicated experimental design. This method is widely applied in determining genetic differences among selected individuals or populations.

SOURCES OF VARIABILITY

As we have seen, variation among phenotypes is attributable partly to the genotype and partly to the environment. The major sources of genetic variability are mutation and recombination of genes. Mutation is the ultimate source of variation and in its broadest sense includes both changes in the molecular structure of genes at individual loci (gene mutation) and chromosomal aberrations such as duplications, deletions, inversions, and translocations. Gene mutations have the effect of adding to the pool of genetic variability by increasing the number of alleles (the different forms of a gene) available for recombination at each locus. Two or more different alleles exist at 30 to 40 percent of the hundreds or thousands of gene loci possessed by each organism.

Continuous or polygenic variation is typical for most characters of trees. This is due to the simultaneous segregation and harmonious interaction of many genes affecting the character and the continuous variation arising from non-genetic causes. Only a few traits are controlled by a single gene with major effects (Wright, 1962). One prevalent trait controlled by one or a few genes is chlorophyll deficiency in seedlings of species of the Pinaceae (Franklin, 1970) and in many other conifers and angiosperms. The albino and yellow seedlings usually die soon after germination, but yellow-green types may turn green and survive in controlled environments.

Although mutation is the ultimate source of genetic variation, it is recombination that spreads mutations and extracts the maximum variability from them. Recombination is regarded as by far the major source of genetic variability of individuals in sexual systems. It makes available the raw material of variation which is acted upon by natural selection.

The exchange of genes between different populations is termed gene flow or migration and may also be considered a source of variation. Migrants, in the form of pollen and seed, bring to a population new genetic material from another population. When the populations involved are substantially different (such as species), the process is often termed *hybridization*.

The major sources of non-genetic variation are (1) the external or physical environment (biotic, climatic, and soil factors) and (2) the internal or somatic environment of the plant. Factors of the physical environment modify plants in many important ways and are discussed individually in Chapters 3–9. Much less appreciated is variation within individuals that is not directly related to factors of the external environment.

Although all cells of a tree have the same genetic constitution, the internal environment of the organism may affect the expression of genes and hence the traits we observe or measure. In the development of a seedling to an adult tree, striking physiological changes occur, and a series of developmental stages is recognized. Best known are the differences between the juvenile and adult stages. The characteristic features of these stages are apparently due to changes that take place in the apical meristems as they age. The most universal feature is the inability of trees in the juvenile stage to flower. Normally, floral primordia are formed only in trees attaining a certain size or age. Treatments that ordinarily stimulate flower production of adult trees have little effect when applied to trees in the juvenile stage.

Schaffalitzky de Muckadell (1959, 1962) investigated many other characters exhibiting differences in juvenile and adult stages. In European beech and oak, the brown and withered leaves are

retained over winter by trees in the juvenile stage; they are not retained in the adult stage. This feature is also observed in American
beech and many oaks. The entire portion of the lower trunk and
branches even of very old trees may remain juvenile. Reciprocal
grafting experiments of juvenile and adult branches show that the
juvenile stage consistently leafs out later than the adult stage of
European beech and ash. This juvenile trait may be of adaptive
value since late spring frosts can pose a serious problem in young
beech stands.

In many species, characters of adaptive importance are exhibited
by juvenile forms. The presence of thorns protects young trees
against animal damage, and greater shade tolerance increases the
chances of a young plant staying alive in a shaded understory.
Also, vegetative propagation is easier with juvenile material than
with that from the adult stage.

Juvenile foliage often differs greatly from that of the adult
stage and may cause difficulty in species identification. Even in
the adult stage most woody angiosperms exhibit substantial differences in leaf morphology for a given genotype. Morphological
and anatomical differences of sun and shade leaves are primarily
due to light conditions of the external environment. Nevertheless,
there are many differences in size, shape, venation, absence or
presence of glands and pubescence, and in other characters that
are essentially independent of the external environment. Such
differences are due to the time of primordia formation, type of
shoot (axillary or terminal, determinate or interdeterminate),
length of shoot, and position of the leaf on the shoot (Barnes,
1969).

In some species, two distinct kinds of leaves are produced.
In *Populus,* leaves flushing early in the spring (early leaves) are
preformed in the bud the year before they emerge (Critchfield,
1960). Late leaves may be produced on leader and terminal shoots
after the early leaves on those shoots have developed; they bear
little resemblance to early leaves (Figure 2.2). Even on a shoot
bearing only early leaves, leaf size and shape may vary greatly,
depending on their position along the shoot (Figure 2.3). The
different forms are all expressions of the same genotype and are
not attributable to the external environment. Rather, they are due
to the internal environment at the time and place of primordia
formation and development. Morphological analyses may be useful

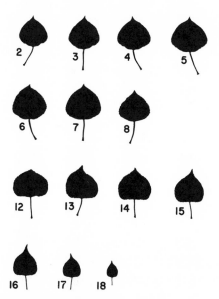

Fig. 2.2. Silhouettes of leaves from a leader shoot of trembling aspen. Leaves 2–7 are typical early leaves; 8 is a transition form to late leaves; and leaves 12–18 are typical late leaves. (After Barnes, 1969).

Fig. 2.3. Silhouettes of early leaves from a determinate shoot of bigtooth aspen. Leaf 1 was located at the base of the shoot, leaf 8 at the tip. (After Barnes, 1969.)

in ecological and taxonomic studies, but they may be misleading unless these kinds of variation are taken into account.

THE EVOLUTIONARY SEQUENCE

The starting point of evolutionary change is the formation of individuals with different genotypes. Without the heritable variation of these genotypes, natural selection cannot bring about evolutionary changes. Individuals, each usually a different genotype, may be grouped in populations for various reasons, and a general and non-restrictive definition is preferred: A population is any group of individuals considered together because of a particular spatial, temporal, or other relationship (Heslop-Harrison, 1956).

In evolutionary biology, the basic unit in sexual populations is no longer the individual, which by itself is usually a dead end; instead it is the local interbreeding population, a group of individuals that are potentially interbreeding and which constitute the gene pool for that population. Genes are sorted out and combined in genetically different male and female gametes at meiosis. Upon fertilization a new set of genotypes is produced, and the surviving phenotypes form the next generation having a new gene pool. Assuming the population is large enough (theoretically infinite), the frequencies of the respective genes will not change from generation to generation. They maintain an equilibrium or steady state, as shown by the Hardy-Weinberg law, and no evolution occurs. Evolution is the cumulative change in genetic make-up of populations of an organism during the course of successive generations —in simplest form a change in gene frequencies. Such changes are brought about by the guiding force of natural selection. Gene flow and genetic drift (chance effects that operate in small populations to make the new generation a random sample of the previous generation) may interact with natural selection to alter the way in which natural selection guides the course of evolution.

Natural selection is strongly associated with the nineteenth century naturalist's concept of differential mortality of individuals, Darwin's "survival of the fittest." Of the thousands or millions of zygotes of a species on a given site that might develop to maturity and contribute offspring to the next generation, only a few survive. Some individuals die as zygotes and fail even to develop as live embryos in seeds. Other ill-adapted plants fail to germinate or die soon after germination. Some individuals may die as a result of competition with existing vegetation for moisture and light. Diseases and insects may selectively take their toll. This is not to say that only the most highly adapted individuals survive, since chance factors are always operating. Some otherwise well-adapted seedlings may, by chance, become established in a moist microsite only to die later when the site dries out, whereas others may be eaten by animals along with less well-adapted types. Nevertheless, the continuous sifting and elimination of less well-adapted phenotypes occur throughout every phase of life, and are a very important part of natural selection. However, natural selection can take forms other than differential mortality of individuals, important as that may be. For example, surviving and otherwise fit plants may have differing abilities of reproduction. In certain tree species, vigorous individuals may be infertile year after year and may make little if any contribution to the succeeding generation. In addition, selection may act upon gametes as well as individuals. As a consequence the modern biologist defines *natural selection* as the differential and non-random reproduction of genotypes, stressing that ultimately it is the differential reproduction of genotypes, rather than just differential mortality of individuals, that brings about evolutionary change.

An example of the raw materials available to selection and the severity of selection comes from sugar maple. Curtis (1959) reported that of 6,678,400 potentially viable sugar maple seeds, 55.7 percent germinated, giving 3,673,100 seedlings per hectare. In late summer of the same year 198,740 remained, and two years later only 35,380 seedlings remained alive—less than 1 percent of those germinating. He estimated that the opening resulting from the death of a mature sugar maple tree (about 6 to 7 meters in diameter) would initially support about 15,000 seedlings. They would be reduced to about 150 during the first three years, and eventually one or two trees would occupy the opening. Although selection acts in every phase of the plant's life, it is most effective on young seedlings and in many plant species eliminates all that are not well adapted to their immediate environment (Harper, 1965).

Sexual and Asexual Systems

The sexual breeding system, dominated by cross-pollination, characterizes most woody species. Seedlings from self-pollination are consistently slower growing than outcross seedlings of the Pinaceae (Franklin, 1970) and are at a selective disadvantage in most natural environments. Evolution proceeds only in a sexual system where new genotypes are constantly generated. Nevertheless, most woody species have some form of asexual reproduction or *apomixis*—any means of reproduction, including vegetative propagation, which does not involve fertilization. In angiosperms, this includes sprouting from stems (oaks, chestnut) and roots (aspens, sweet gum, beech) following cutting or fire. Conifers rarely form sprouts (an exception is redwood), but the production of adventitious roots from branches (termed *layering*) in larch, white spruce, and firs is an important device in swamp or moist upland environments. Apomixis may even occur when seeds are formed asexually as in the hawthorns. Whatever the mechanism, asexual reproduction gives the plant immediate fitness in the prevailing environment; it is a uniformity-promoting device. A striking example is seen in the aspens of North America and Eurasia, which sucker from roots to form natural colonies termed *clones*. A clone is the aggregate of stems produced asexually from one sexually produced seedling. The clone is the typical growth habit of aspens throughout their worldwide range (Barnes, 1967), and their asexual proclivity may be the major factor in their ability to compete successfully in conifer-dominated landscapes. In parts of western North America, aspens occur in clones, some over 100 acres in size (Kemperman, 1970), and they may live for indefinite periods by recurrent suckering, barring major climatic changes.

GENECOLOGY

The foregoing review of the causes of changes in gene frequencies in populations leads to a consideration of genecology, a term the Swedish ecologist Turesson (1923) applied to the study of the variability of plant species and their hereditary habitat types from an ecological point of view. More specifically, genecology is the study of adaptive properties of any sexual population—race, species, subspecies, local interbreeding population—in relation to its environment (Langlet, 1971). Turesson, like others before him, demonstrated conclusively that ecologically correlated phenotypic variation among populations was typically genetically based rather than merely the result of environmentally induced modification of individuals. This concept has major practical implications for the silviculturist when introducing populations into a new environment. In tree-introduction attempts throughout the world, we have largely used the trial-and-error method—with some resounding successes and some dismal failures. Such a method is too arbitrary, costly, and time consuming as a general practice. Instead, we need to be able to predict how a given population will perform when grown in a new environment. To do this we need to know what environmental and biotic factors elicit a genetic response, how closely populations are adapted to these factors, and the patterns of adaptation along major environmental gradients. The basis of our knowledge of genecological adaptation and examples of it are presented below.

Comparative cultivation of seedling populations of forest trees, originating from environmentally different sites, was pioneered by Duhamel du Monceau about 1745 (Langlet, 1971), and the methods were continued and refined by other workers such as P. de Vilmorin (in the 1820's), Kienitz (1879), Cieslar (1887–1907), Engler (1905–1913), among others (Langlet, 1971). The careful historical documentation by Langlet (1971) makes it clear that the concept of genecological diversity, originating from an adaptational response to the environmental factors of the particular habitats, was known to forest botanists long before Turesson's work with herbaceous species. For example, Cieslar in Austria (1895, 1899) and Engler in Switzerland (1905, 1908) determined experimentally that forest trees in the Alps were genetically adapted to the climatic conditions of their respective environments. In 1895 Cieslar published evidence of a continuous gradient of juvenile height growth for Norway spruce demonstrating its genetic adaptation to growing-season conditions grading from low to high altitude. These results served to document observations of the previous century, published in 1788, that seedlings of lowland provenances proved worthless on mountain sites.

Unlike Cieslar and Engler, who used seeds for their experimental work, Turesson transplanted whole individuals from markedly different habitats and, like his predecessors, grew them under standard conditions of cultivation. This method of comparative cultivation is often termed the common garden technique. The phenotypes Turesson observed in nature were usually different in habit of growth (procumbent or erect) and in various morphological characters. These differences were usually maintained in the garden and hence indicated genetic differences between the populations studied.

The causes of the adaptive differences may be inferred by correlating the performance of the populations in the garden with the environmental and biotic factors of the original sites. Presumably, natural populations have been exposed to the factors of their respective environments for generations. Forces of natural selection have guided the genetic differentiation of each population so that it is more or less adjusted to the daily, seasonal, yearly, and even longer-term climatic, soil, and moisture fluctuations of its respective environment.

Because of the problems of preconditioning of whole plants (Rowe, 1964) and the difficulty in transplanting whole forest trees, forest scientists typically collect seeds from the desired populations, termed *provenances,* raise the seedlings in a common garden, and study the differences among the provenances. Such experiments are termed provenance, or seed source, tests. This type of testing determines (1) *if* there are significant genetic differences between populations in the characters chosen for study, and (2) the amount of genetic differentiation among provenances under the environmental conditions of the common garden. Provenance testing does not directly indicate what mechanisms caused the differences, although these may be inferred. Nor does it indicate whether such differences would exist or be of the same magnitude at another test site.

Patterns of Genecological Differentiation

A wealth of evidence has accumulated which confirms that genetically based ecological differentiation or divergence of populations, termed genecological differentiation, is a recurrent feature of plants in general. However, controversy has arisen over the pattern of differentiation—whether it is discontinuous or whether it is continuous or clinal in nature. Huxley (1938, 1939) introduced the term *cline* to designate a gradation in measurable characters, which might be continuous or discontinuous, stepped or smooth, or sloping in various ways. The term itself, as the definition indicates, does not mean or necessarily imply a genetically based gradation in a character. It could refer to a gradation of phenotypic characters observed along a natural gradient. If, however, a gradation in characters were found for populations in a common garden test, an adaptive cline would be demonstrated.

Genecological differentiation is a multidimensional response of individuals of a population to their environment. Although the response is unique for each species and population, we present the following generalizations as best summarizing current understanding of differentiation in forest species.

1. The total range of a species, the distribution pattern (continuous, discontinuous, mosaic) of a species within this range, and the way in which the conditioning environmental factors vary are three major determinants of the differentiation pattern. If a species is distributed continuously over a wide range, particularly in latitude or elevation, it is subjected to more or less continuously varying climatic factors, and adaptive variation tends to be continuous. If discontinuities occur in the species distribution or if the conditioning factors are discontinuous and sufficiently distinct, a discontinuous pattern may result. The variation pattern may be visualized as a series of contour lines whose spacing reflects the rate of change in the conditioning factors.

2. The results of a given genecological study tend to be related to the scale in which it is conceived and conducted (Heslop-Harrison, 1964). A wide-ranging investigation of a species along a north-south gradient may expose a clinal variation pattern that may mask other clines associated with elevation at a given latitude, or local discontinuities that might arise from a major change in soil type or soil-moisture conditions.

3. However continuous a cline may be, it is usually possible to show a seeming discontinuity by incomplete sampling and certain methods of data analysis (Langlet, 1959).

4. The dominant pattern of genetically based variation is more or less continuous; the discontinuous pattern is usually the exception. The clinal pattern has a fundamental basis in the genetic system of many forest trees favoring a high degree of recombination and outbreeding (cross-pollination) and the associated features of (a) long life span of individuals, (b) greater habitat and community stability, (c) high and selective seedling mortality, and (d) high physiological tolerance in the adult to fluctuating environmental conditions. Discontinuous variation, being favored by in-

breeding, low rates of gene recombination, short life span in ephemeral communities, and strongly fluctuating habitats, is more typical in herbaceous than in tree species. These and other evolutionary aspects of differentiation are discussed by Heslop-Harrison (1964).

The Ecotype Concept

Turesson (1922a,b) defined *ecotype* as the product arising as a result of the genotypical response of a population to a "definite habitat" or "a particular habitat." Controversy and confusion have arisen over the distinctness of ecotypes and over the related feature of their size—whether they are local or regional phenomena. The term ecotype is not only abused when applied in situations where genetic differences have not been proved, but it is also used in a number of different senses, each having a different genecological significance. Thus the convenience of classification by types is offset by the inadequacy of types to treat continuous variation.

The problem is traceable to two features of Turesson's ecotype concept. First, the definition as a genetical response of a species to a particular habitat has been interpreted to mean both local differentiation in specialized habitats (meadows, swamps, shifting sand dunes) and large-scale differentiation, such as climatic races embracing large portions of a species' range. Examples of the latter type are those described by Wells (1964) for ponderosa pine (Figure 2.4). Each regional ecotype occupies a large geographic area within which local differentiation undoubtedly occurs. For even a small part of the California ecotype, marked clinal differentiation along an elevational gradient has been demonstrated (Callaham and Liddicoet, 1961).

Turesson himself used "ecotype" not only to characterize local genecological differences but also in a much wider sense—"alpine ecotype," "coastal ecotype," etc.—applying to major habitat complexes. This usage implies that the term indicated populations adapted to types of environments and not to particular or special environments. Thus the term ecotype is ambiguous and fails to provide a useful concept except for the general fact of genetic adaptation to environment.

Second, Turesson's methods of sampling and cultivation culminated in his view of a species as a mosaic of populations, each

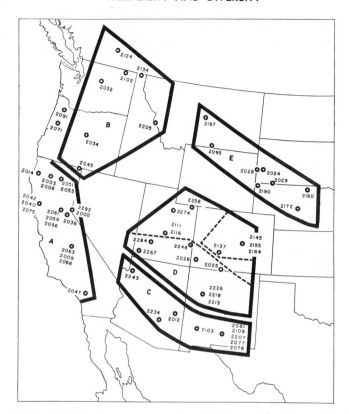

Fig. 2.4. Geographic ecotypes of ponderosa pine, based on 60 stand progenies grown for 2 years in East Lansing, Michigan: (A) California; (B) North Plateau; (C) Southern Interior; (D) Central Interior; (E) Northern Interior. (After Wells, 1964.)

adapted to distinct habitats. Each ecotype was shown to be morphologically different and distinct from others. Turesson's work in demonstrating ecotypes naturally led him to sample populations from distinctly different habitats, and the genetically based differences led him to stress the discontinuity of ecotypes. Subsequent investigations have indicated that the discreteness of ecotypes was exaggerated (Gregor and Watson, 1961). In general, by incomplete sampling or, as in Turesson's work, by ordering and analyzing the data in groups a seeming discontinuity may be demonstrated no matter how continuous the cline. Thus whenever the term ecotype is used, the user's precise definition of the term always should be sought. The trend today, however, is away from classification of populations by ecotypes and toward the study of the patterns of genecological differentiation in a species and of the mechanisms evoking genotypical response. Such patterns for the selected species described below illustrate the relative continuity and scale of adaptation and the kinds of physical and biotic factors of the environment evoking a genetic response.

Examples of Genecological Differentiation

The woody-plant literature abounds in references citing genetic differences in morphological and physiological characters among populations in a great variety of species. Much of the information comes from provenance tests established to meet the practical objective of finding the most suitable provenances for planting in the general area of the test site. Many of these tests are therefore not designed and cannot be expected to answer, except in a very general way, genecological questions of how and why populations are adapted to their environments. The term geographic is almost invariably associated with the literature surrounding these tests. The provenances are usually stratified by geographical regions, political units (country, state, or county), or varietal rank; genetic distinctions are then shown between these subdivisions. Ecological data on the origins are often sketchy, and genecological interpretations, if present, are as a result incomplete.

Despite inadequacies of many tests from a genecological standpoint, far-reaching provenance studies have uncovered major adaptive responses, primarily along latitudinal and altitudinal gradients. Scots pine, the most wide-ranging pine, has been investigated in many studies in Europe (dating from 1745) and in North America. Genetic differences in such diverse characters as height growth, foliage color, dry-matter content of seedlings, stem form, rooting habit, resistance to insect attack, fruitfulness, tracheid length, and time of bud set have been demonstrated (Langlet, 1959; Troeger, 1960; Wright et al., 1966; Wright et al., 1967). A clinal pattern is evident for most of these characters.

Portions of a cline, sometimes designated as "ecotypes" or "varieties," may be useful as the basis for selecting seed-collection zones, particularly where major differences in tree characteristics are important. American Christmas tree growers, for example, prefer Scots pine varieties from Spain and elsewhere in southern Europe, which remain green in winter, to those of northern Europe, which turn yellow (Wright *et al.*, 1966). The use of "varieties" in specifying such seed-collection zones may be convenient but may also convey a false impression of uniformity within the named group. The fact is that populations within a specified geographic area may be quite diverse. Obtaining seed from within the geographical boundaries of the "variety" seemingly best suited to a planting area is satisfactory only if the populations within the "variety's" boundaries are reasonably uniform.

Environmental Factors Eliciting Ecological Differentiation. Marked genetic differences in growth and other characters usually are expressed when populations are grown at latitudes or elevations substantially different from that of their native habitats. Limiting environmental factors affecting the length and nature of the growing season in the native habitat (such as temperature, thermoperiod, photoperiod, and amount and periodicity of rainfall) are important selective forces acting on growth rate and related characters.

Associated tree species and animals may play an important role in the evolution of some characters. The crooked stem form of lowland Scots pine sources in Germany may be attributed in part to competition of pine with European beech and oak. The hardwood species are highly phototropic and probably exert a much different selection pressure on juvenile pines than that encountered at high elevations with spruce and fir.

Coevolutionary systems have been reported for animals and reproductive traits of various woody-plant species. In studies of woody legumes in Central America, Janzen (1969) listed 31 traits that may act to eliminate or lower the destruction of seeds by bruchid beetles. The major defense mechanisms against these predators are deterrents, such as biochemical repellents (alkaloids and free amino acids), or an increase in the number of seeds to the point of predator satiation, probably requiring a decrease in seed size. Another important device is a dispersal system that effectively disperses seeds soon after maturation. In western North America, squirrels may act as important selective agents on the reproductive characters of conifers in the process of maximizing their own feeding efficiency (Smith, 1970). These studies emphasize the multidimensional nature of adaptation. Not only are characters influenced by many factors of the physical environment, but also by plant associates and the interrelated selective pressures of insects, mammals, and birds.

Survival and growth are closely related to the efficient use of the growing season. Plants must not grow too late in the fall or they will be damaged or killed by drought or early fall frosts. They must not cease growth too soon because longer-growing individuals may overtop and suppress them. In their native habitats, species anticipate seasonal fluctuations by responding to subtle and more reliable factors of the changing environment rather than being directly coerced by gross environmental factors, such as heat, cold, and drought (Hillman, 1969). In temperate regions, response to a photoperiodic signal of shortening days of summer and fall sets in motion a gradual and complex pattern of development which we call dormancy (Chapter 4). *Photoperiodism*, a response of plants to the timing of light and darkness (usually expressed as day length), is a biological clock enabling plants to adjust their metabolism to seasonal fluctuations. Unlike other environmental factors, day length changes everywhere in a regular yearly cycle, except at the equator. Plants apparently can measure these changes with remarkable precision.

Photoperiod largely controls the entrance into dormancy of many woody plants, particularly species with a northern range. These species are genetically adapted to a photoperiod that enables them to become dormant before the time when particular factors of their prevailing environment, such as cold or drought, become limiting. For trees in northern climates or at high elevations, early frosts in autumn and cold winters are factors of primary survival value. Hence a reliable mechanism, such as photoperiod, in triggering the dormancy sequence, may be highly developed. In other sites, moisture stress during the midst of the growing season may be a severe limiting factor. An adaptive system may evolve to promote dormancy and yet allow growth to resume again when moisture conditions are favorable.

In almost all genecological and provenance tests, populations are grown in day-length regimes different from that prevailing in their native habitats. In black cottonwood, for example, individuals of high-latitude provenances ceased height growth in June when planted at a low-latitude site near Boston, Massachusetts (Figure 2.5; Pauley and Perry, 1954; Pauley, 1958). Southerly provenances, moved north to the test site, continued height growth until Septem-

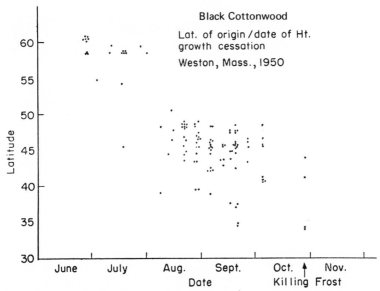

Fig. 2.5. Relation between latitude and time of height-growth cessation in black cottonwood. (After Pauley and Perry, 1954; from Kenneth V. Thimann, *The Physiology of Forest Trees* © 1958, The Ronald Press Company.)

ber and October; some individuals ceased growth only when their terminal shoots were killed by the first severe frost. Generally, movement from the natural habitat northward, into longer days, prolongs the active period of growth and results in greater plant size. However, it renders the plant susceptible to early frosts. Movement southward, into shorter days, shortens the active growth period in comparison to plants native at or south of the test site. In the black cottonwood examples, individuals of high-latitude provenances grew only about 15 to 20 centimeters, whereas those from southern localities grew about 2 meters (Pauley, 1958). When clones from the high latitude at the test site were given longer days by artificial light, they grew over 1.3 meters (Pauley and Perry, 1954), indicating a strong influence of day length in regulating growth.

Although a significant, genetically based, clinal response was shown in relation to latitude, the response is not simple and direct, as evidenced by substantial variation among provenances from 44 to 48 degrees (Figure 2.5). This group included a variety of sources sampled from the Pacific coast to western Montana and over an elevational range from sea level to 1525 meters. Although the difference in latitude is not great, there is known to be a marked difference in the length of growing season among these sources due to elevation, aspect, or microsite conditions. Clinal genetic adaptation to length of growing season was found within the narrow latitudinal range of 45–47 degrees (Figure 2.6) and probably explains

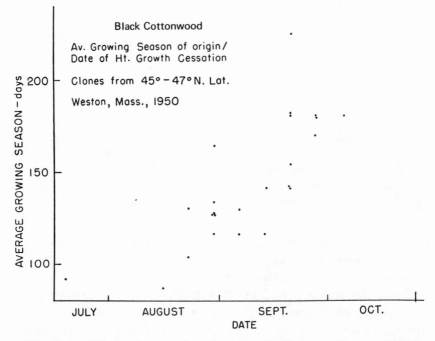

Fig. 2.6. Relation between length of growing season and time of height-growth cessation in black cottonwood. (After Pauley and Perry, 1954; from Kenneth V. Thimann, *The Physiology of Forest Trees* © 1958, The Ronald Press Company.)

much of the variability not accounted for by latitude. Thus populations at low and high elevations at a given latitude have growing seasons of different lengths and become adapted to different photoperiods accordingly, and in particular a photoperiod in autumn which is important in regulating their entrance into dormancy. High-elevation populations necessarily cease growth earlier than low-elevation populations due to earlier occurrence of killing frosts. Hence they adapt to relatively longer photoperiods (occurring earlier in the year) than those at low elevations.

Carrying this approach one step further, we see that a population at a high elevation may have the same length of growing season as a population at a lower elevation but several degrees of latitude farther north. Through equivalence in length of growing season, they would have a similar photoperiodic adaptation mechanism and, if interchanged, may show only negligible differences in date of growth cessation and growth rate.

This interrelationship between elevation and latitude has rarely been recognized in genecological studies. Almost without exception, correlations of cessation of growth or plant size and latitude of source are confounded by elevational differences. However, Wiersma (1962) modified a formula developed by Langlet (1936) for Swedish conditions, using growing season (number of days $\geqq 6°$ C) to relate latitude and elevation. He reported that a displacement of 1 degree of latitude north is equivalent to a displacement of 100 meters upward in altitude. Wiersma (1963) recomputed correlations of latitude of source and various characters from published papers using this adjustment and found greatly improved relationships. Sharik (1970) computed a corresponding value based on length of growing season (number of days $\geqq 0°$ C) for the Appalachian Mountains from New Hamsphire to North Carolina and found a relationship of 1 degree of latitude equal to a displacement of 189 meters. Adjustment of latitude by this factor substantially improved the correlation of latitude of origin and cessation of height growth for yellow birch and black birch populations, compared to the unadjusted relationships.

Genetic differences in plant size and growth cessation for numerous hardwood and conifer species have been related to latitude (Kriebel, 1957; Wright and Bull, 1963; Genys, 1968; Mohn and Pauley, 1969; Fowler and Heimburger, 1969; Clausen, 1968) and elevation of the source (Cieslar, 1895; Callaham and Liddicoet, 1961; Genys, 1968; Hermann and Lavender, 1968). These studies indicate that photoperiod is a timing device of major adaptive significance. The consistency with which given individuals of many species cease growth from year to year reinforces this conclusion. The clinal variation patterns of some growth traits are surprisingly regular despite interruptions of a species' range (Scots pine for example) and apparently reflect the strong adaptation of populations to the highly precise photoperiodic cycle.

The close association of various adaptive responses with different limiting factors of the native environment has been shown for

Douglas-fir seedlings grown near Corvallis, Oregon, by Irgens-Moller (1968). The late cessation of growth of coastal provenances (Vancouver Island) at the test site is related to the long growing season of their native habitat. In the northern Rocky Mountains, low summer precipitation and a short frost-free season apparently are responsible for early onset of dormancy of their provenances at Corvallis. Early dormancy was displayed, although soil moisture was kept in ample supply, indicating the lack of a direct effect by moisture stress. Photoperiod was again shown to be important since only long photoperiods could keep the plants actively growing. Sources from Arizona and New Mexico grew intermittently. They entered a short period of dormancy after which the majority resumed growth before entering winter dormancy. The distinct intermittent growth in the southwestern provenances and its lack in northern Rocky Mountains provenances may be explained by differences between the two areas in seasonal distribution of precipitation. A relatively high summer rainfall is received in Arizona and New Mexico as compared to Northern Idaho (64% of total annual rainfall compared to 29%). The intermittent growth may permit seedlings to go into early dormancy during periods of soil moisture stress and then resume growth quickly when moisture is abundant. Seasonal distribution of precipitation also may be an important factor affecting the adaptation patterns of ponderosa pine (Squillace and Silen, 1962) and slash pine (Squillace, 1966a).

The rate of change in a clinal variation pattern is well illustrated in an intensive study of the phenotypic and genetic variation of seedling slash pines by Squillace (1966b). This study revealed weakly defined or highly fluctuating gradients as well as distinct clinal trends. The reversal in the general cline, common to many of the twenty-five characters studied, is well demonstrated in the variation pattern of needle length (Figure 2.7). From a low of 16 cm in southernmost Florida, needle length of the progenies increased to its longest values, 19–20 cm, in south central Florida and then progressively decreased to the north.

Local Diversity. Natural situations may present local variation in soil and topography which cause specialized environments. Local adaptation to soil and climatic conditions within major climatic regions has been demonstrated repeatedly for herbaceous species (Heslop-Harrison, 1964; Jain and Bradshaw, 1966; Kruckeberg, 1969). The physical and chemical properties of soils can elicit

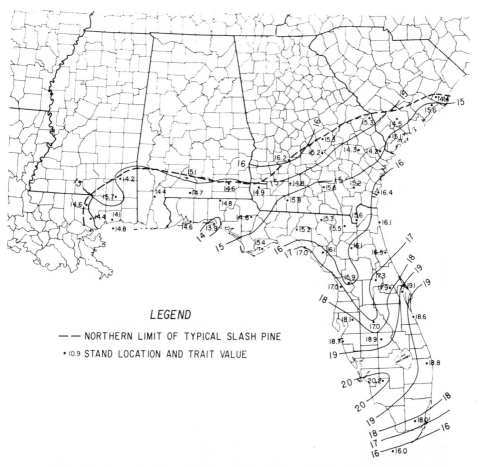

Fig. 2.7. The pattern of variation of needle length (cm) in seedling progenies of slash pine. (After Squillace, 1966b.)

sharp discontinuities in plant distribution, and woody-plant species showing marked edaphic preferences are not uncommon. However, infraspecific genetic adaptation to the local soil type or to soil-moisture differences has rarely been demonstrated. Although Kruckeberg (1951, 1958) demonstrated genetically different races of several herbaceous species on serpentine and non-serpentine soils, such differentiation was not immediately apparent for knobcone pine and digger pine seedlings originating from parents growing on serpentine and non-serpentine soils (McMillan, 1956; Griffin, 1965).

Genetic differences have been demonstrated between populations of northern white cedar from well-drained upland sites and those from frequently inundated swamps (Habeck, 1958). Root length of seedlings of the upland provenances was twice that of swamp seedlings grown in well-drained soils, but only about half as long in a poorly drained soil. Besides illustrating genetic sensitivity to soil-moisture conditions, this differential performance illustrates a genotype-environment interaction. An interaction occurs when different genotypes (or populations) do not respond in the same manner in different environments. It may often mean that the best genotypes in one environment are not the best in another environment. Genotype-environment interactions have often been reported (Squillace, 1970) and are to be expected whenever genetically diverse populations are grown in sites markedly different from their native habitats.

Localized ecotypic variation was reported by Squillace and Bingham (1958) for western white pine trees growing on a dry and on a moist site (0.8 kilometer apart, 15-meter difference in elevation). Differential germination percentages of the respective populations under simulated dry and moist conditions prompted this conclusion. They speculated that differences in seedbed moisture occurring between opposing north and south slopes might cause differences in selection pressures strong enough to evolve local races. Such aspect differences have been reported for Douglas-fir seedlings originating from north and south slopes in southern Oregon (Hermann and Lavender, 1968). In growth chamber experiments, north slope seedlings from 458-meter, 915-meter, and 1525-meter elevations had a longer growing season and greater dry weights of shoots and roots than seedlings from south-aspect parents of similar elevations. Additional and even more detailed investigations are needed to determine just how closely populations are adapted to aspect, soil-moisture differences, and soil type. Through longer-term field testing, we will also learn how small a difference in environment will require specially adapted genotypes.

Factors Affecting Differentiation: Gene Flow and Selection

The extent of differentiation depends on the amount of gene flow via pollen, seeds, and other propagules between populations and on the intensity of selection. Gene flow is a cohesive force acting to keep populations from diverging, and its role in differentiation was reviewed by Ehrlich and Raven (1969). Isolating factors such as spatial distance between populations, or ecological isolation (south versus north slopes, swamps versus uplands) act to disrupt gene flow. Selection is also important. Populations will tend to remain similar if subjected to similar selection forces but will differentiate if they are not. Over short distances gene flow is likely to be great and differentiation seems therefore unlikely. When it does occur in these situations, it is brought about chiefly by the impact of high selection pressures. First let us consider gene flow and then an example of intense selection.

Three important factors acting to restrict gene flow are (1) limited number of breeding trees, (2) differences in flowering times of individuals, and (3) limited dispersal of pollen and seeds. It is well known that there are marked differences among species in the age of seed bearing and periodicity of seed crops (Baker, 1950). Furthermore, within a species trees vary greatly in their reproductive capacity; some are highly fruitful, some moderately so, and others are completely barren year after year. Thus of the many trees in a population that could potentially exchange genes, only a few breeding trees may contribute appreciably to the next generation. For example, Schmidt (1970) found that in an 89-year-old Scots pine stand 30 percent of the trees produced 71 percent of the female strobili and 64 percent of the male strobili. For sugar maple Wright (1962) estimated that if there were 62 large fruiting trees per hectare, only 5 to 7 on the average would be breeding trees.

The time of pollen release and female receptivity (phenology of flowering) is vital in pollination and is closely related to air temperature and humidity. Trees within a given population are more likely to be synchronized with one another than with trees progressively farther away. Ordinarily the time of flowering is earlier at more southerly localities than at northerly latitudes, and at lower altitudes compared to higher altitudes. However, high-altitude variations in regional and local temperature and the advent of spring make the situation quite different in different years. For example, overlap in flowering time of Scots pine between southern and central Finland was observed to occur in four years in the 10-year period 1957 to 1966; in one year overlap was found between central Germany and central Finland (Koski, 1970). We may conclude that, although the timing of flowering on the average favors local gene exchange, the possibility of gene flow from distant sources definitely exists.

Although viable pollen may be transported many miles, it may reach another stand too early or too late to compete effectively with local pollen. This becomes even more important in Scots pine and probably other pines and conifers since the capacity of the pollen chamber is limited (Sarvas, 1962), and all grains do not have the same chance to fertilize the eggs. Of the many pollen grains reaching the micropyle only two, on the average, have the opportunity to fertilize the eggs of each ovule, one of which eventually develops into the embryo. Because of the greater probability of their being first to reach the micropyle, pollen grains of neighboring trees may have a higher probability of achieving fertilization than those of trees at more distant sites.

In forest trees, the range of seed dispersal is limited although there are exceptions in the willows, birches, and poplars. A mechanism favoring heavy seed has even evolved in island species, assuring that most of the seeds are not literally blown into the sea. In contrast, we know that pollen can be carried great distances (Lanner, 1966). Anderson (1963) reported that pollen was blown from Germany to southern Sweden, a distance of 72 kilometers, and that in Sweden one year the pollen crop was so heavy that clouds of pollen were mistaken for forest fires. The pollen-dispersal distance of Scots pine is at least in the tens of kilometers, and its transfer 600 to 700 kilometers in 10 to 12 hours has been reported (Koski, 1970).

The many reports of widespread dispersal might lead to the conclusion that populations over large areas are prevented from diverging because of widespread gene exchange. However, accumulating evidence indicates that in wind-pollinated species (most north temperate species) most individuals are pollinated and fertilized by trees of the surrounding stand or from adjacent stands. Studies of pollen dispersal from isolated trees indicate that most pollen that is recovered (not necessarily of the total pollen produced) falls within a relatively short distance from the source (ash, 17 meters, Douglas-fir, 19 meters, slash pine, 69 meters). These studies have tended to lead to the interpretation that trees are pollinated primarily by their neighbors. A study of Norway spruce showing effective pollination and fertilization within a 40-meter radius led Langner (1952) to conclude that fertilization of a given tree in a forest stand is effected by its immediate neighbors. However, detailed studies of pollen dispersal in extensive stands of Scots pine in Finland indicate that only half the pollen comes from trees growing less than 50 meters away (Koski, 1970). The remainder may come from trees more than 50 meters away in the same stand or from adjacent stands. Although long-distance transport of pollen occurs on a large scale, most of the pollen from afar ordinarily overflies the forests at an altitude of several hundred meters and only a small fraction of the grains that diffuse into the lower regions can participate in pollination in a stand. Due to the great difficulty of monitoring flow and destination of pollen from individual trees and from different stands, and considering the vagaries of environmental and biological factors, we can expect no generalized answer to the question of the extent of gene exchange. At times gene flow may be restricted to nearest neighbors, favoring inbreeding, whereas at other times some gene exchange may occur over considerable distances, thus enriching the gene pool of receptor populations. It is against this background of gene flow that natural selection guides the genetic make-up of populations.

The evidence available from many factors suggests that gene flow is limited in varying degrees in population systems. Thus selection pressures of the particular environment play a significant role and in herbaceous species may be effective over a distance of 2 to 4 meters (Aston and Bradshaw, 1966). The effect of intense selection was strikingly demonstrated by clinal changes in glaucous and non-glaucous (green) phenotypes of *Eucalyptus urnigera* in Tasmania (Barber and Jackson, 1957). Green phenotypes are typical of low elevations and more sheltered habitats, whereas glaucous individuals become more frequent in increasingly exposed environments along a gradient from low to high elevation. The change from glaucous to green types was essentially complete over a vertical distance of 122 to 152 meters (0.8–1.6-kilometer ground distance) in the adult populations. Glaucous seedlings may be produced from non-glaucous mother trees and vice versa, indicating gene flow via insect and bird pollinators. Nevertheless, intense selection eliminates glaucous seedlings as the forest matures in the lower elevations. At the higher elevations green seedlings are eliminated. The authors emphasize that strong selection can build up great genetic diversity even in the face of considerable gene flow.

ECOLOGICAL CONSIDERATIONS AT THE SPECIES LEVEL

As populations change through time and radiate into new areas, they typically become increasingly diverse in response to genecological differentiation. Also, due to geographic separation and other isolating mechanisms, some populations become less able to exchange genes with other populations; they become reproductively isolated in varying degrees. An important route of speciation involving geographic isolation followed by reproductive isolation is shown in Figure 2.8 (Stebbins, 1966). The isolating factors which act singly or, more usually, in combination, are presented in Table 2.1. The

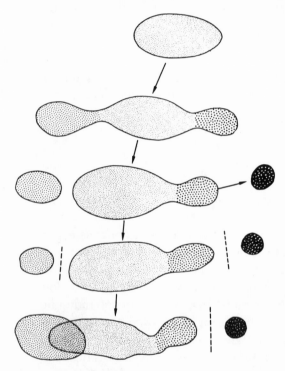

First stage.
A single population in a homogeneous environment.

Second stage.
Differentiation of environment, and migration to new environments produces racial differentiation of races and subspecies (indicated by different kinds of shading).

Third stage.
Further differentiation and migration produces geographic isolation of some races and subspecies.

Fourth stage.
Some of these isolated subspecies differentiate with respect to genic and chromosomal changes which control reproductive isolating mechanisms.

Fifth stage.
Changes in the environment permit geographically isolated populations to exist together again in the same region. They now remain distinct because of the reproductive isolating barriers which separate them, and can be recognized as good species.

Fig. 2.8. Diagram showing the sequence of events which leads to the production of different races, subspecies, and species, starting with a homogeneous, similar group of populations. (After Stebbins, 1966.)

various degrees of population differentiation (Figure 2.8) have been classified in a hierarchical system. Populations exhibiting minor differences are termed races, local or geographic. Populations that have more substantial differences in morphology and physiology, and are reproductively isolated, are classified as subspecies or species. These two classes are formal taxonomic designations while race is not.

Table 2.1. Major Isolating Mechanisms Acting To Separate Plant Species

---

Prefertilization Mechanisms: Prevent fertilization and zygote formation.
1. Geographical separation. Populations live in different regions (allopatric).
2. Ecological separation. Populations live in the same regions (sympatric) but occupy different habitats.
3. Seasonal or temporal separation. Populations exist in the same regions and may exist in the same habitat, but they have different flowering times.
4. Ethological separation. Pollination is accomplished by specific pollinators (as in some tropical species).
5. Gametic incompatibility. Pollination may occur but gametes are incompatible before or at fertilization.

Postfertilization Mechanisms: Fertilization takes place. Hybrid zygotes are formed, but they are inviable, or give rise to weak or sterile hybrids.
6. Hybrid inviability or weakness. Zygotes are formed but are unable to germinate or become established. If established, they break down before reproductive organs are formed.
7. Hybrid sterility. Hybrids are sterile because reproductive organs develop abnormally or meiosis breaks down due to chromosome incompatibilities.
8. F_2 breakdown. F_1 hybrids are normal, vigorous, and fertile, but F_2 generation contains inviable or sterile individuals.

SOURCE: Adapted from Stebbins (1966) and Solbrig (1970).

The assumptions that different species are of the same degree of differentiation and that individuals within a given species are uniform pose problems in forest ecology and management. In analyses of communities over wide areas, species are often entered into formulas or manipulated as if they were uniform units of comparable divergence. In physiological studies, results may be generated based on a few trees whose individual variation or genecological differentiation may or may not permit extrapolation of the findings as a general rule for the species. In management practice, examples are legion in Europe and North America where seed has been collected from genetically inferior trees or plantations established from ecologically inappropriate seed sources.

Forest species were named and described on the basis of morphological characters by the early taxonomists. They believed that species were specially created and morphologically uniform. Again, it is important to reiterate that the recognition of a class, such as a species, may convey a false impression of uniformity within the class.

Species are not all of the same degree of divergence. This can often be seen in the degree of morphological difference and in their reproductive isolation. For example, there is no gene exchange whatsoever between species such as loblolly pine and southern red oak or ponderosa pine and white pine. In other recognized species, however, such as Engelmann spruce and white spruce, there is considerable intergrading of populations and there may be considerable gene exchange. "Good" species, those that have full species status from the standpoint of reproductive isolation, are those that exist in the same geographic area (*sympatric* species) and yet maintain their distinctness, even though individuals of each are within effective pollinating range of one another and interbreeding would be possible (Figure 2.8, fifth stage). Sympatric species that are reproductively isolated by one or more of the isolating mechanisms include red pine and white pine, white oak and black oak, yellow birch and paper birch, and loblolly pine and shortleaf pine. These "good" species remain distinct even though they may interbreed and form hybrid individuals such as in loblolly pine and shortleaf pine and yellow birch and white birch. Isolating mechanisms operating at a later stage (stages 6–8 in Table 2.1) render hybrids sterile or act against hybrid or backcross progeny to prevent gene flow.

Where individuals of two species come together and hybridize, the species distinctions may be dissolved or swamped out in a flood of intermediates. In this situation, complete reproductive isolation has not yet occurred, and the populations may be more appropriately regarded as subspecies. This situation is indicated in Canada where the morphologically similar white spruce and Engelmann spruce, and balsam poplar and black cottonwood, intermingle. In both cases the recognition of subspecies has been suggested (Taylor, 1959; Brayshaw, 1965; Viereck and Foote, 1970).

Biologists recognize that no single definition of a species is entirely applicable to classify the enormous diversity of organisms nor serve the various purposes desired by different scientists. However, it is important to remember that although a system of populations is recognized as a "species," this in no way indicates that it is directly comparable in degree of divergence or morphological distinctness to other species. The problem of speciation has been considered concisely by Heslop-Harrison (1956), Stebbins (1966), and Solbrig (1970), and in detail by Stebbins (1950 and 1970) and Grant (1963, 1971).

Hybridization

Hybridization, the crossing between populations (races, subspecies, species) having different adaptive gene complexes, is frequent in natural populations of many woody-plant groups: in pines (Mirov, 1967), larches (Carlson and Blake, 1969), birches (Clausen, 1962), oaks (Tucker, 1961a, 1961b; Maze, 1968), poplars and aspens (Brayshaw, 1965), and many others. The great number of reports of hybrids during this century probably reflects the widespread disturbance of forest communities providing open sites for the establishment of hybrids.

Interspecific hybridization is probably of minor evolutionary significance (Wagner, 1968, 1970) although hybrids may act as evolutionary catalysts (Stebbins, 1969, 1970). However, they are of major ecological and practical significance.

Artificial hybridization has been pursued widely among species and races (Wright, 1962). Many hybrids are important in forest management and horticulture due to rapid growth, good form, disease resistance, or frost hardiness (Duffield and Snyder, 1958; Wright, 1962; Nikles, 1969).

Natural hybrids often occur in zones of contact between species (Remington, 1968; Brayton and Mooney, 1966) and in disturbed habitats. The disturbed area may be an intermediate or hybrid habitat (Anderson, 1948) where neither parent is well adapted. The common denominator of environments where hybrids become established, whether disturbed or not, seems to be lack of competition.

It has been popular to report natural hybrids, usually based on morphological characters, perhaps due to their presumed rarity, or as Wagner (1968) relates, seeking hybrids "was all part of the 'game,' and added to the thrill of the chase, like adding a new stamp to the collection." However, little detailed ecological study has been devoted to the comparative establishment of hybrids and their parents or the presumed differences between the so-called hybrid habitat and that of the parents.

Furthermore, little critical genecological study has been given the popular concept of *introgressive hybridization* or *introgression:* the gradual infiltration of germ plasm of one species into that of another as a consequence of hybridization and repeated backcrossing

(Anderson, 1949). After examining the variation of some thirty genera of flowering plants in the subcontinental area between the Great Plains and the Atlantic (including species of junipers, oaks, maples, and redbuds), Anderson (1953) reported: "For each of these genera, all the readily detectable variation can be ascribed to introgression." Introgression has been widely accepted, probably more out of faith and intuition than from fact. For example, a detailed reevaluation of Anderson's classic example of introgression, an iris complex in Louisiana, revealed hybrids in the populations but "no statistically significant effects of taxonomic or evolutionary importance attributable to introgression" (Randolph *et al.*, 1967).

Introgression is presumably achieved in three phases: (1) initial formation of F_1 hybrids, (2) their backcrossing to one or other of the parental species, and (3) natural selection of certain favorable recombinant types (Davis and Heywood, 1963; Figure 2.9). This is simply gene flow between species. If hybridization occurs between two closely related species, the probability of gene flow is higher than when the species have diverged sufficiently to have well-integrated, but different, gene pools. Genes from one population will

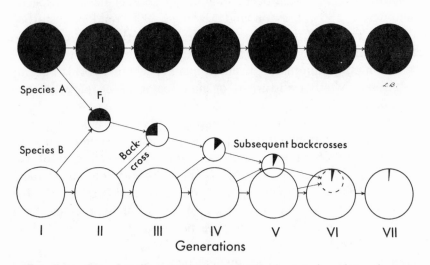

Fig. 2.9. Diagram illustrating introgression—the interbreeding of species, followed by backcrossing to one parent and ultimate absorption of some genes from one parent into at least some members of the population of the other. (After Lyman Benson, *Plant Taxonomy: Methods and Principles* © 1962, The Ronald Press Company.)

be incorporated into the gene pool of the other (regardless of rank —species, subspecies, etc.) if they improve the well-integrated harmony of the foreign gene pool. If they tend to disrupt the harmony, their frequency will be reduced; this is merely natural selection in action (Bigelow, 1965). Not surprisingly, we find frequent reports of introgression between the closely related spruces of western Canada (Horton, 1959; Daubenmire, 1968; Ogilvie and von Rudloff, 1968; Roche, 1969; Hanover and Wilkinson, 1970) and black spruce and red spruce of eastern North America (Morgenstern and Farrar, 1964).

In many instances introgression has been postulated or inferred rather than compellingly demonstrated. Often the range of variability of the parent species and the F_1 hybrids is not well known; F_1 hybrids may be mistaken for backcrosses (Dancik and Barnes, 1972) and backcrosses for a parent. In some cases we suspect that divergence caused by intense selection, as cited by Barbour and Jackson (1957), is misinterpreted as introgression. An example of the dilemma is a study of phenotypic variation of morphological traits of *Juniperus* (Van Haverbecke, 1968a,b). Upon finding two extremes types, Rocky Mountain juniper and eastern red cedar, connected by a series of intermediates in the Missouri River basin, the author first concluded that the data could be interpreted as evidence for introgression. He then stated that an even more tenable interpretation would be migration of junipers from west to east, bringing divergence of the populations.

In determining the amount of gene flow between species it is important to establish, through more than observations of morphological characters of phenotypes in nature, that (1) hybridization and backcrossing have actually taken place, and (2) increased variability of the parent species occurs outside the area of hybridization and is due to hybridization and not solely to intense selection.

Polyploidy

Polyploids are organisms with three or more sets of chromosomes. The ploidy level of a species (triploid = 3 sets, tetraploid = 4 sets, etc.) is measured in relation to the base or x chromosome number established for the genus or family, usually the lowest haploid (gametic) number for the group. For example, the base number for the genus *Pinus* is 12 ($x = 12$) and all pine species have 24 chromosomes ($2x = 24$, the diploid number). In *Betula* the base number is 14, and black birch has the $2x$ number of 28 chromosomes. However, other members of the genus are tetraploids (bog birch and European white birch, $4x = 56$), and yellow birch is a hexaploid ($6x = 84$). Paper birch is a complex population system with individuals having 28 ($2x$), 42 ($3x$), 56 ($4x$), 70 ($5x$), or 84 ($6x$) chromosomes (Brittain and Grant, 1967).

Conifers are almost exclusively diploid; only three species are known to be polyploids (Khoshoo, 1959), and the most important of these is redwood, a hexaploid with 66 chromosomes. Nearly 40 percent of the angiosperms are polyploids. Some woody angiosperm genera have no polyploid species (*Populus, Juglans, Robinia*), but many others each have species of various ploidy levels (*Prunus, Salix, Betula, Alnus, Magnolia, Acer*, and many others). Polyploidy in woody plants has been reviewed by Wright (1962), and the evolutionary aspects have been discussed by Stebbins (1950, 1970). Polyploids apparently arise most often by hybridization of related species followed by doubling of the chromosomes of the hybrids.

Polyploids are of considerable ecological significance. Compared to related diploids, they are more frequent in higher northern latitudes than in lower latitudes. Polyploids apparently are better able to colonize and persist on sites in the colder climates, particularly those resulting from Pleistocene glaciation. A major reason for the success of polyploids compared to related diploids under these severe conditions is that polyploidy is a uniformity-promoting mechanism. In general, polyploidy acts like a sponge, absorbing mutations but rarely expressing them. In diploids, mutations or new recombinations are more easily expressed due to the lower chromosome number and fewer of each kind of chromosome. Polyploids, however, have many chromosomes, often four to six of each kind, and new gene combinations are not likely to produce a major change in the phenotype. Mosquin (1966) reasoned that polyploids represent an efficient buffering system, resisting the effects of natural selection on particular genes and promoting and preserving phenotypic uniformity. According to Mosquin, the narrow adaptational limits of high latitude and weedy polyploids are an adaptive feature corresponding to the narrow and relatively uniform environments of boreal, arctic, and disturbed or weedy habitats. The range of polyploids is often great, as in high-latitude birches and willows, because such habitats are themselves widespread.

Polyploids, however, are not confined to recently disturbed boreal habitats, and some appear just as variable as diploid species. Temperate species such as American basswood and tulip poplar are apparently polyploids of ancient origin that have outlived their ancestors. High levels of polyploidy have also been reported for certain tropical floras, some of which are of very ancient origin. According to Stebbins (1970), newly opened habitats were available in ancient times for evolving angiosperms, and increasing polyploidy accompanied the establishment and spread of new groups of angiosperms during the early stages of their history. The ability of polyploids to colonize newly opened environments is apparently the common denominator of their success in diverse regions of the world, whether the time of their origin was ancient or modern.

The Fitness-Flexibility Compromise

To survive and persist through time a population must not only show adaptedness to its present environment, but have adaptability, the potential to change. Mather (1943) expressed this compromise between fitness for the environment as it exists and flexibility that will permit further adaptive change. Flexibility is favored by variability-promoting mechanisms such as cross-pollination and a high rate of recombination (Heslop-Harrison, 1964; Mosquin, 1966). Inbreeding, apomixis, polyploidy, and a low rate of recombination are uniformity-promoting devices that favor fitness in the given environment.

We have already cited polyploidy as a uniformity-promoting device, often in northern and glaciated or disturbed sites. Polyploidy may be coupled with cross-pollination, as in the willows and birches, adding to the flexibility side of the ledger. In most woody species, we see various mixes of uniformity- and variability-promoting devices giving the plants the best of both possible worlds. Selection through time has produced a different mix and different mechanisms, depending on the particular environmental situation. The proportion of each and the nature of the mechanism differ between species even within genera. The fitness-flexibility compromise is closely related to the limiting ecological factors of the species' environment.

For example, compare trembling aspen, widely distributed in northern, glaciated, and disturbed habitats, with eastern cottonwood, also wide ranging but primarily found in lower latitudes and growing in stream and river valleys. Both species are primarily dioecious (male and female flowers borne on different individuals), the most effective device for ensuring cross-pollination. Thus a great amount of variability is generated in these diploid species and then widely circulated through abundant seed production and excellent dispersal. Aspen has the remarkable ability of vegetative propagation by root suckers, which assures genetic uniformity; the clonal growth habit is pronounced throughout its range. Fire is probably the environmental factor that has most favored this adaptation. In contrast, cottonwood rarely produces root suckers in nature (in an essentially fire-free environment), but its branches and young shoots root easily in soil. This may be of considerable selective advantage and of immediate fitness in riverside sites subject to periodic disturbance through flooding. Thus both species have strongly developed mechanisms giving both fitness and flexibility.

Pines, typically cross-pollinating species, maintain a certain amount of self-pollinating ability in their breeding systems. In western white pine, for example, a great variation exists in self-fertility—from infertile individuals to highly self-fertile individuals (Bingham and Squillace, 1955). Since fire plays a major role in establishment of pines around the world, the ability of one or a few survivors of a severe fire to colonize the site, if necessary by self-fertilization, may be of selective advantage. Colonization is likely to be accompanied at first by an increase in the degree of inbreeding, but outbreeding will tend to be restored as the stand density increases (Bannister, 1965).

Selection pressures of this type have apparently been instrumental in promoting a very high degree of self-fertility in red pine (Fowler, 1965a). The species is highly self-fertile, and unlike most other pines, seedlings resulting from self-pollination are as vigorous as those from cross-pollinations (Fowler, 1965b). However, a high degree of self-fertility has been achieved, seemingly at the cost of variability, since red pine is one of the most uniform of all woody-plant species.

SUMMARY

Forest trees exhibit a great range of variation in morphological and physiological characters due to the interaction of their inherent genetic constitution residing in the chromosomal DNA (the genotype) and factors of their internal and external environment. Environmental influences may modify the expression of a genotype so that a number of different forms or phenotypes are assumed in different environments. The continuous variation pattern observed for most characters of trees is caused by simultaneous segregation of many genes affecting the character and variation arising from non-genetic sources. The major sources of genetic variation are mutation, the ultimate source of variation, and recombination of genes. Major sources of non-genetic variation are factors of the physical and biotic environment and the somatic environment of the plant itself. Considerable morphological and physiological diversity may be expressed in a given genotype essentially independent of influences of the physical environment.

Populations of forest trees are genetically adapted to the ecological conditions of their native habitats. Genecological adaptation patterns of tree populations mirror the patterns of physical and biotic environmental factors which elicit adaptive responses. Where the environmental factors are continuously varying and the organism exists over the gradient, the adaptation pattern is continuous or clinal; if the factors are discontinuous, the pattern also tends to be discontinuous. In general, the adaptation pattern for most characters of trees is more or less continuous, and the clines are usually parallel to the environmental factors that are responsible for them. The pattern of genecological differentiation tends to be related to the scale in which an investigation is conceived and conducted. Studies of large-scale continuous patterns of variation may fail to disclose local clines or discontinuities. Wide-ranging forest species are typically characterized by photoperiodic races. Shoot elongation and other characters of trees of such races typically exhibit a clinal adaptive response to the latitude, elevation, and growing season of their respective habitats. More rarely, local differentiation has been reported for specialized climatic and soil conditions.

Gene flow between populations and the intensity of selection control the extent of differentiation. Although pollen may be transported great distances, most trees are pollinated and fertilized by trees of the local population, thus tending to restrict gene flow. Intense selection may promote diversity despite considerable gene flow.

Forest species exhibit various degrees of morphological difference and reproductive isolation; they are not all of the same degree of divergence. Many tree species are able to retain their distinctness even though they may grow in close geographic association and even interbreed. In these cases one or more isolating factors prevents their replacement by a swarm of intermediates. Natural hybridiza- tion occurs frequently among forest species. Hybridization is of major ecological and practical significance and may play a catalytic role in evolution.

Polyploid species are common in angiospermous tree genera but are almost totally lacking in gymnosperms. Polyploidy is a uni- formity-promoting device which is apparently advantageous to tree species of northern, glaciated, and weedy environments. Tree species exhibit various uniformity-promoting and variability-promot- ing mechanisms, closely geared to their particular habitats, which respectively promote adaptedness to their present environment and yet provide potential to change with changing site conditions.

SUGGESTED READINGS

BARBER, H. N., and W. D. JACKSON. 1957. Natural selection in action in *Euca-lyptus. Nature* 179:1267–1269.

CRITCHFIELD, WILLIAM B. 1957. Geographic variation in *Pinus contorta.* Maria Moors Cabot Foundation Publ. No. 3. Harvard Univ., Cambridge, Mass. 118 pp.

DAVIS, P. H., and V. H. HEYWOOD. 1963. *Principles of Angiosperm Taxonomy.* (Populations and the environment, pp. 387–416; Evolution and the differentiation of species, pp. 417–461.) D. Van Nostrand Co., Inc., New York. 558 pp.

DOBZHANSKY, THEODOSIUS. 1968. Adaptedness and fitness. *In* RICHARD C. LEWON-TIN (ed.), *Population Biology and Evolution.* Syracuse Univ. Press, Syracuse, New York. 205 pp.

HESLOP-HARRISON, J. 1956. *New Concepts in Flowering-Plant Taxonomy.* (Eco-logical differentiation of populations, pp. 45–58; Geographical variation and re-productive isolation, pp. 59–78.) Harvard Univ. Press, Cambridge, Mass. 135 pp.

————. 1964. Forty years of genecology. *Adv. Ecol. Res.* 2:159–247.

KRUCKEBERG, ARTHUR R. 1969. The implications of ecology for plant systematics. *Taxon* 18:92–120.

LANGLET, OLOF. 1959. A cline or not a cline—a question of Scots pine. *Silvae Genetica* 8:13–22.

————. 1971. Two hundred years' genecology. *Taxon* 20:653–721.

LIBBY, W. J., R. F. STETTLER, and F. W. SEITZ. 1969. Forest genetics and forest-tree breeding. *Ann. Rev. Genetics* 3:469–494.

MIROV, N. T. 1967. *The Genus "Pinus."* (Physiology and ecology, pp. 396–464.) The Ronald Press Co., New York. 602 pp.

MOSQUIN, THEODORE. 1966. Reproductive specialization as a factor in the evolu-tion of the Canadian flora. *In* ROY L. TAYLOR and R. A. LUDWIG (eds.), *The Evolution of Canada's Flora.* Univ. Toronto Press. 137 pp.

ROCHE, L. 1969. A genecological study of the genus *Picea* in British Columbia. *New Phytol.* 68:505–554.

SQUILLACE, A. E. 1966. Geographic variation in slash pine. Forest Science Monog. 10. 56 pp.

WRIGHT, JONATHAN W. 1962. Genetics of forest tree improvement. (Geographic variation in forest trees, pp. 118–158.) FAO Forestry and For. Prod. Studies No. 16, Rome. 399 pp.

II

THE FOREST ENVIRONMENT

3

Solar Radiation

A facet of the forest community can no more be attributed solely to the forest environment than solely to the genetic or physiological make-up of the trees. It is not a question of one or the other, for the forest community is always the product of the two working together.

The forest environment divides itself naturally into the physical environment surrounding the aerial portions of the trees and that surrounding the subterranean portions of the trees. The sum total of these factors is the *forest site*.

These chapters on the forest environment fall within the subdivision of ecology known as *autecology,* the study of the organism—in this case the forest tree—in relation to its environment. Excellent coverages of forest autecology may be found in the writings of Toumey (1947), Daubenmire (1959), and Lundegardh (1957). German-language texts dealing with forest ecology include Gutshick (1950), Hartmann (1952), Rubner and Reinhold (1953), and Rubner (1960).

Site Factors

It is fairly easy to enumerate the factors making up the environment upon which the life and growth of the forest tree depends. It is exceedingly difficult, however, to understand and evaluate the sum total of the interactions among these environmental factors that make up the complex we term "site" or "habitat."

The tree grows with its crown in the atmosphere and its roots in the soil. To the crown come the warmth, light, carbon dioxide, and oxygen; and to the roots come the mineral nutrients and water necessary for photosynthesis and the other life processes. These are the basic factors which the site must supply. Their availability to the tree, however, depends upon an endless system of changing climate, day length, and soil development—changes that are in part related to the developing vegetation itself.

Classification of Site Factors

The single site factors, therefore, may be divided into broad groups, which may be considered separately. The site factors interact to yield the light, heat, water, etc., that are directly available and used by the plant (Figure 3.1). Climatic factors (Chapters 3–6) are those relating to the atmosphere in which the aerial portions of the trees grow. These include solar radiation, air tempera-

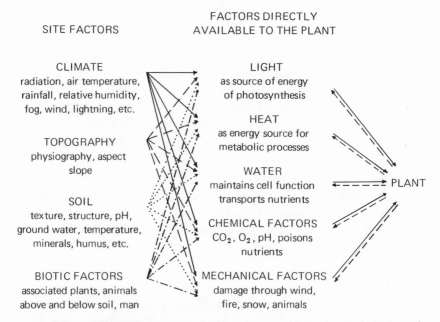

Fig. 3.1. Relationships between site or habitat factors and factors directly responsible for plant life. (After Ellenberg, 1968.)

ture, air humidity, wind, lightning, and carbon dioxide content of the air. Precipitation, whether rain or snow, is not a major direct climatic factor as it affects plant growth primarily through its indirect effect on soil moisture.

Soil factors (Chapters 7–10) include all the physical, chemical, and biological properties of the soil. The nature of the parent material, the soil profile, the nutrient cycle between the soil and the trees, the physical properties of the soil, soil-moisture relationships, and topography are particularly important in determining site quality.

Biological factors include the effects of plants and animals, both visible and microscopic, on the climate and the soil—and therefore on site quality. Large organisms (such as trees and grazing animals) create the most obvious changes in the microclimate and the soil, but small animals and plants occurring in great numbers (including fungi, bacteria, earthworms, rodents, and many others) can also bring about substantial changes in the site. Since the influence of plants and animals on site is exerted through changes in the climate and soils, the discussion of the biotic factor is integrated into the chapters on climatic and soil factors.

Fire is also a most important factor affecting forest site quality. The burning of organic matter on the soil and the heating of the top layers of the mineral soil result in changes in the physical and chemical properties of the soil. Since the effect of fire on site lies largely in the changed soil properties, this factor is discussed as a separate section on soil factors. The great importance of fires in affecting the composition of the forest community is considered in Chapter 14.

Once the individual factors affecting forest site have been considered, it becomes necessary to integrate them into a whole if the forest site is to be characterized simply and accurately. Forest productivity and the determination of forest site quality is considered in detail in Chapter 11.

Interrelations Between Site Factors

While it is both conventional and convenient to discuss the various factors of the forest environment one at a time, a word of caution must preface such a discussion. The presentation of the principal factors one by one may create a dangerous tendency to think of each factor as an independent force affecting the tree. We tend to think and talk in terms of simple direct relationships, and to make such statements as "at a temperature of 55° C, the plant suffers direct heat injury" or "precipitation is the limiting factor in determining the distribution of this species." Such statements have their value and even truth, but they *do* tacitly ignore the fact that the plant lives in the total complex of the environment—and a change in any one factor of this complex may well bring about a changed requirement of the plant for other factors. In other words, these individual environmental factors are not isolated independent forces operating on the plant, but rather interdependent and interrelated influences that must in the last analysis be considered together.

Much of this philosophy is embodied in the changing concept of the *law of the minimum*. As originally enunciated by Liebig in 1855, this law holds that the rate of growth of an organism is controlled by that factor available in the smallest amount. It has been demonstrated repeatedly, however, that such a law does not hold true—but that the rate of growth of a plant or tree can be increased by changes in the supply of more abundant factors that can compensate for the so-called "limiting factor." The law still retains much value and is part and parcel of the thinking of the forest biologist. In its modern form, though, it is usually restated to take into account the interactions existing between the various single factors. We may thus say with authority that "whenever a factor approaches a minimum, its relative effect becomes very great."

The changing concept of the law of the minimum has arisen from the natural development of ecological research methods. In early years, most ecological theories were based upon observations of trees and other plants under natural growing conditions. For instance, observations that seedlings die under dense forests may lead to conclusions that low light intensity is responsible for the mortality. On reflection, however, the ecologist will realize that many environmental factors are affected by a dense forest cover. Light intensity, of course, is low, but so also is the supply of moisture in a soil permeated by the roots of the many trees present. Under a dense forest, the temperature regime is greatly changed from that in the open or even that under an open forest. The humus type, too, will be greatly affected. In short, the whole environmental complex is related to forest cover density, and it is misleading if not downright incorrect to attribute changes in plant response to any single factor.

Through experimentation, however, it has become possible to grow trees under conditions where only one or two factors of the environment were varied, and these are varied by known amounts in comparable and replicated trials. In the forest itself, much has been learned from field experimentation, using treated sample plots and such devices as trenched plots and screen shades to vary given environmental factors. A higher degree of experimental control is possible in the nursery or the greenhouse where botanical research methods may be adapted to the testing of tree seedlings. In recent years, realization of the importance of controlling all environmental factors has led to the testing of trees under constant artificial environment in *phytotrons*—series of rooms for growing plants in which the air temperature, light, and sometimes humidity can be controlled at a series of given levels. These more precise experimental controls are adding much to our knowledge.

Importance of Site Factors in Forest Ecology

There is good reason for considering the site before one considers the vegetation. In the forest community, the site is more concrete, more stable, and more easily defined than the vegetation that occupies it. In a sense, therefore, the site constitutes a better basis for the description of the forest community than do the trees, other plants, and animals.

By site is meant the habitat of the forest community—a more or less homogeneous area as regards soil, topography, aspect, and climate; and one on which a more or less homogeneous forest type may be expected to develop. This homogeneity is strictly relative and must be defined with respect to the tree rather than to the lesser plants. A given forest site will inevitably contain many different microsites or niches where more restricted plant and animal communities will be found. The forest floor, the tree trunks, the crown, even the different levels within the forest all may contain specialized "layer communities"—subcommunities within the forest.

The forest site occupies a given geographical area and is capable of fairly precise definition. Depending upon chance, upon past history, and upon changing environmental conditions within that site, various types of forest communities may develop on that particular site. The likelihood of any given type developing may be given a statistical probability, but there is seldom any certainty that any given type will occur.

The superiority of site to plant species as a basic unit of plant community classification becomes apparent when consideration is given to the number of quite different communities that may be characterized by a given species or even by a given group of species. The frequent failure of a list of plant species to characterize a plant community is elaborated upon in a later chapter. Ideally, it is the combination of site and the biota, the ecosystem itself, that is necessary in describing, classifying, and, more significantly, understanding the forest.

SOLAR RADIATION AND THE FOREST ENVIRONMENT

Our climate arises from the interaction of solar radiation and the atmospheric blanket that surrounds the earth. From the sun come, directly or indirectly, the light that makes possible photosynthesis and the heat that warms the air and the soil to the point that permits the life processes of the plant to continue. From the atmosphere come oxygen, the carbon dioxide required for the photosynthetic process, and much of the moisture needed by the tree. Gases absorb very little solar radiation. Solids and liquids absorb many times more. Thus most heating of the atmosphere comes by conduction from the ground to the air at their boundary. Movement of the atmosphere profoundly affects the distribution of this heated air and the active gases—and wind is of course a prime factor governing both tree development and life span.

The sum total of these factors is climate. Climatic data obtained from standard weather stations are of the greatest importance in defining the macroclimate of a given region, and many valid generalizations can be drawn between the coincidence of broad climatic boundaries and the observed presence or behavior of forest trees. The climate in which a given tree or stand lives, however, may be entirely different from the regional macroclimate. In recent years, much has been learned about the microclimates—the climate near the ground, surrounding the tree, or affecting a critical part of the tree.

Nature of Solar Radiation Reaching the Earth

The energy making possible the growth of trees and other plants comes either directly or indirectly from the sun. Thus the nature and the amount of solar radiation received on the surface of the earth will affect the distribution and the growth of the forest. Photosynthesis, being a reaction that takes place only in the presence of light, is obviously affected by the quantity and quality of light. In addition, though, the structure, growth, and even the survival of the tree are affected in other ways by the light factor. The relative lengths of the day and night, too, are frequently prime factors in determining which plant can prosper best in a given environment. Finally, solar radiation ultimately governs air temperature and thereby indirectly determines the thermal conditions around and within the plant. The biological effects of radiation in all its phases have been summarized by Duggar (1936). Other major works treat energy exchange in the biosphere (Gates, 1962, 1968) and solar radiation in relation to forests (Reifsnyder and Lull, 1965; Reifsnyder, 1967).

The solar radiation that reaches the outside of the earth's atmosphere is dissipated in many ways, being in part reflected and in part absorbed by the atmosphere itself, by clouds and other masses of solid particles in the atmosphere, by the vegetation, and finally by the earth itself (Figure 3.2). The radiation reflected back into space amounts to about one-third of the total amount received, and this *albedo* gives a brightness to the earth that is similar to that of the planet Venus. Clouds, of course, reflect the most light, but atmospheric scattering and reflection from the surface of the earth are also important. Of the radiation absorbed by clouds, vegetation, and the earth, a substantial portion is reradiated. On cloudy days much of this radiation is retained by the cloud layer so that the days remain relatively warm. Night temperatures on the earth's surface also remain relatively mild, because of the thermal radiation of cloud layers.

Solar radiation reaches the outside of the earth's atmosphere at an average rate of about 1.95 gram-calories per square centimeter per minute. Actually this value, the so-called *solar constant*, is not constant, but varies about 1½ percent with variation in the activity of the sun, and about an additional 3½ percent depending upon the distance from the sun to the earth (List, 1958).

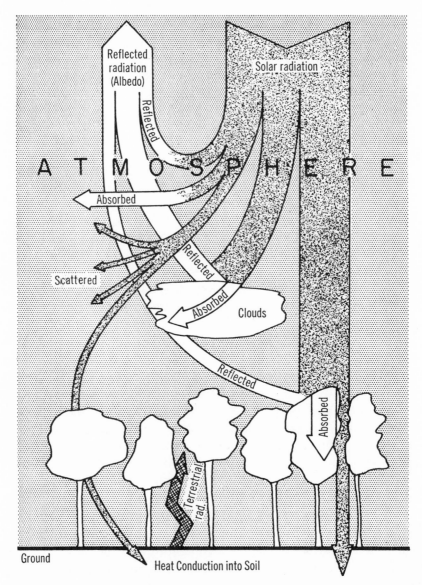

Fig. 3.2. Diagrammatic representation of the dissipation of solar radiation. The widths of the lines approximate relative amounts of energy. (Adapted from Geiger, 1950.)

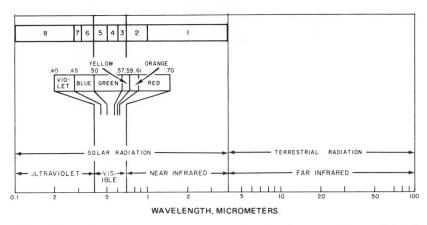

Fig. 3.3. Wavelength of solar and terrestrial radiation and spectral bands. (After Reifsnyder and Lull, 1965.)

The wavelengths of the bulk of solar radiation are divided into three regions, termed the *ultraviolet,* the *visible,* and the *near infrared* (Figure 3.3). The shorter ultraviolet rays are almost completely absorbed by the atmosphere. Radiation with wavelengths ranging from approximately 0.4 to 0.7 micrometers [1] is visible to the unaided human eye and is termed *light* (Figure 3.3). Approximately one-half of the total solar energy reaching the earth's surface is visible. The farther the sun is positioned from the zenith, however, and the greater the amount of atmosphere through which the sun's radiation must pass, the higher is the percentage of the solar radiation that is absorbed or scattered and not received on the earth's surface. When the sun is low on the horizon, therefore, very little ultraviolet radiation reaches the surface, and more infrared radiation reaches the earth than does light.

The total amount of solar energy that reaches the earth is substantially less than that which reaches the atmosphere (Figure 3.4). The atmosphere itself absorbs much. Representative values reported by Abbot (1929) for clear sky conditions with the sun directly overhead give the total solar energy received on Mt. Whitney in California (4,418 m) as 1.75 gram-calories per square centimeter per minute, as compared to 1.45–1.62 on Mt. Wilson (1,737 m), also in California, and 1.15–1.45 for Washington, D. C.—near sea

[1] One micrometer (μm) = 1000 nanometers (nm) = 1 micron (μ).

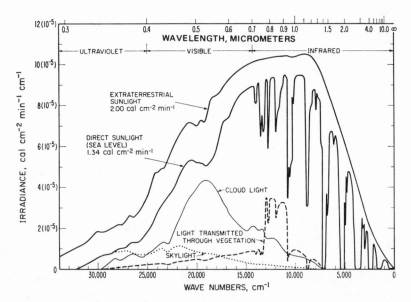

Fig. 3.4. Spectral distribution of the irradiance of extraterrestrial sunlight, direct sunlight at the earth's surface, scattered skylight, cloudlight, and light transmitted through a vegetation canopy. (After Gates, 1968.)

level. The lower the elevation, the smaller is the amount of radiation received.

As the sun departs from the zenith and the radiation is slanted through the atmosphere, the total amount is even further diminished. At a zenith angle of 20°, an additional 6 percent is absorbed over that absorbed when the sun is at zenith; at 40°, the loss is 30 percent more than the loss at zenith; at 60°, the loss is doubled; and at 88°, the loss is increased by 20 times.

Clouds, smoke, and other atmospheric impurities, of course, may intercept most if not all of the direct solar radiation. Values obtained for radiation on overcast days commonly range from one-quarter to one-half of those for cloudless days under the same conditions. Most of the radiation under such overcast conditions is scattered radiation—solar radiation that has been scattered by the atmosphere and other interceptors, and then reaches the ground more or less circuitously. Even on clear days, scattered radiation may amount to 10 to 15 percent of the total.

A distinction must be made at this point between total incident solar radiation per unit surface area and radiation only in the visible range, or *light*. These terms denote radiation measured in watts per square meter or in gram-calories per square centimeter per minute, also termed *langleys per minute*. These units are measurements of the ability of radiation to do work and create heat. Most ecological studies, however, have been based on measures of the ability of radiation to create visual response per unit area (lumens per square foot or per square meter), termed *illuminance*. Illuminance is commonly expressed in the English system in foot-candles and in the metric system in luxes. One foot-candle (F.C.) is equal to 10.764 luxes.

Illuminance, measured in foot-candles or luxes, is not a reliable indication of the energy in radiation in the visible range for biological processes (such as photosynthesis) other than vision, but it is widely used because of the availability of photoelectric light meters, which are calibrated to measure visual response. Total solar radiation and illuminance, however, are related, and approximate conversions are possible. These conversion factors vary with the atmospheric conditions. The average values of Kimball (List, 1958) are commonly used. On the average, 1 gram-cal/cm²/min supplies about 6,700 foot-candles of illuminance on cloudless days and about 7,440 on overcast days. The larger value for overcast days signifies that a high percentage of the non-visible radiation has been absorbed under such conditions and that a greater percentage of the energy reaches the ground as light, which can be converted to illuminance. Using an average value of 1.42 gram-cal/cm²/min, the maximum solar illuminance at sea level attained on a clear day with the sun at the zenith would be approximately 9,500 foot-candles. The figure of 10,000 foot-candles is commonly used for full sunlight. This value is lower than would be obtained at high altitudes with the sun overhead, but is higher than true values at low elevations or whenever the sun is at a considerable distance from the zenith.

All of the solar radiation values given above apply to radiation received by a horizontal surface. The slope and aspect of the ground also affect the amount of radiation received. In the Northern Hemisphere, south-facing slopes receive more radiation per unit area than north-facing slopes, the highest amounts being received by slopes most nearly facing the sun at its highest elevation during the day. The relative irradiance on a slope of any given slope and aspect may be approximated from standard formulae. The effects of these factors may be illustrated by curves computed by Byram and Jemison (1943) for north-, south-, and east-facing 100-percent slopes at north latitude 35°30′ on June 21, which show lower maximum irradiance levels on north slopes as opposed to south, a morning maximum for east and an afternoon maximum for west slopes (Figure 3.5).

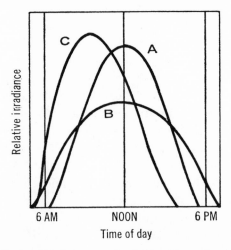

Fig. 3.5. Relative irradiance received throughout the day on a 100-percent slope in the southern Appalachians. (A) South. (B) North. (C) East. (After Byram and Jemison, 1943.)

The Energy Budget

The environment, through climatic factors, transfers energy to all living things. This flow of energy, which determines the energy budget of the plant and affects plant temperature, is accomplished primarily by solar and terrestrial radiation, convection, and transpiration. Each process by which energy is transferred between a plant and the environment can cause loss or gain of energy, but the sum total of all energy transferred must balance. Energy gained by the plant from the environment may be stored as heat or converted into photochemical energy by photosynthesis; it may be lost to the environment by radiation from the plant, by heat conduction or convection, or by evaporation and transpiration (evapotranspiration). The remainder of the arithmetic sum of energy flow to (+) and from (−) a surface is termed *net radiation*. The energy budget per unit area of an organism may be written as follows when net energy is neither gained nor lost:

$$Q_{abs} - \epsilon \sigma T_1^4 \pm C \pm LE \pm M = 0 \qquad \text{(Gates, 1968)}$$

where Q_{abs} = the total incident radiation of short- and long-wave radiation (always positive).

$\epsilon\sigma T_1^4$ = outgoing radiation dependent on the fourth power of absolute temperature and emissivity of the surface.

C = energy flow by convection and conduction.

LE = energy flow by water conversion (energy loss by evaporation or gain by condensation).

M = metabolic rate of the organism (negligible in plants).

If the plant is to survive, it can neither gain nor lose net energy over an extended period of time. If the net radiation at a point on the leaf surface is negative, then the energy arriving at the point is exceeded by the outflowing radiation, typical of forest conditions on cold, clear nights. Severe short-term energy deficits may lead to freezing injury of leaves and other plant parts. With a positive net radiation, the energy may heat the leaf surface (leading to injury if in excess), heat the air adjacent to the leaf, be transformed into latent heat through transpiration, or converted into photochemical energy by photosynthesis. Only about 2 percent of solar energy, however, is actually utilized in photosynthesis.

Plant foliage is beautifully adapted to handle solar radiation through its absorption, transmittance, and reflectance properties. These properties are remarkably similar for many species (Reifsnyder, 1967) and are illustrated for a leaf of eastern cottonwood (Figure 3.6). The curves indicate high absorptivity in the ultraviolet and the visible range, strikingly low absorptivity in the near infrared (the 0.7–1.5-μm range, high in energy—see Figure 3.4), and high absorptivity of far-infrared radiation where solar irradiance is very low (Gates, 1968).

Interception of Radiation

The effect of the forest itself in intercepting radiation is quite obvious. Only a small percentage of the incident sunlight reaches the floor of a dense forest. Many determinations have been made of the *relative illumination* (RI) within the forest, expressed as a percentage of total solar illumination.[2] Under leafless deciduous

---

[2] Ecologists may use relative illumination either to express the relative amount of radiation received in the visible spectral range (= *light irradiance,* measured in gram-calories per unit area) or the visual response of radiation (= *illuminance,* measured in foot-candles).

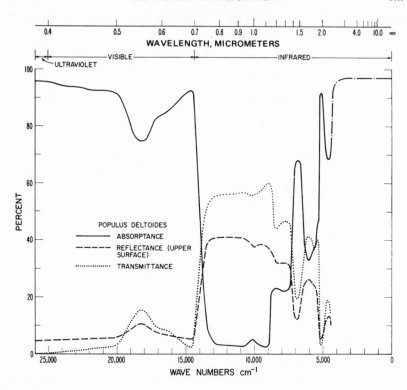

Fig. 3.6. Spectral distribution of the absorptance, reflectance, and transmittance of a leaf of eastern cottonwood, *Populus deltoides*. (After Gates, 1968.)

trees, the relative illumination may be as high as 50 to 80 percent of full sunlight; under open, even-aged pine stands, 10 to 15 percent represents a common range; under temperate hardwoods in foliage, values from 1 to 5 percent are common; while beneath the tropical rain forest (Carter, 1934), the relative illumination may be as low as ¼ to 2 percent. Among the densest temperate forests are those formed by pure stands of Norway spruce. Under high closed spruce canopies in Switzerland, total solar radiation may average only 2.5 percent of that in the open (Vézina, 1961).

The general relationship between percent forest cover and percent radiation transmission based upon conditions existing under conifers at high elevations in the Sierra Nevada of California during the spring melt season indicates a marked dropping off of relative illumination as crown density increases from zero to about 35 percent, with a more moderate decrease with further increases of density (U.S. Corps of Engineers, 1956). In this particular example, the relative insolation was 18 percent for 0.5 (i.e., 50 percent) density and only 6 percent for full crown density (Figure 3.7).

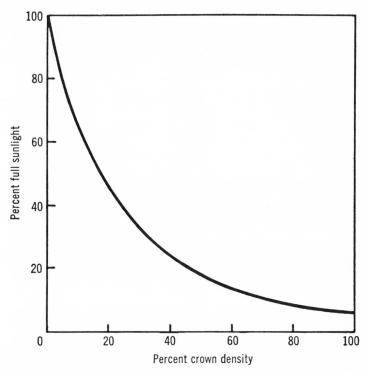

Fig. 3.7. Effect of crown density on penetration of solar energy into conifers in the California Sierra Nevada, during spring snow-melt conditions. (After U. S. Army Corps of Engineers, 1956.)

For western white pine, Wellner (1948) has developed a similar curve relating relative light irradiance to basal area per acre. At 400 square feet of basal area per acre, the mean light irradiance was 10 percent of that in the open. In a similar study for short-leaf pine in Georgia, Jackson and Harper (1955) found a strong inverse correlation between the logarithm of stand basal area and the logarithm of relative illumination.

It is somewhat misleading, though, to express radiation beneath the forest in such relative terms. Actually, much of the forest floor is in heavy shade most of the time, with relative illumination values under dense forest ranging from ¼ to 1 percent. Sunflecks sweep over the ground as the day progresses, however, bathing areas momentarily with radiation perhaps half as much as sunlight in the open (Figure 3.8). In a study of the Nigerian rain forest, Evans

Fig. 3.8. Sunlight penetrates the dense redwood forest canopy and sunflecks sweep over the ground, creating an important source of radiation for understory vegetation. (U. S. Forest Service photo.)

(1956) has estimated that from 20 to 25 percent of the ground is occupied by sunflecks at noon—and that these sunflecks account for 70 to 80 percent of the total solar energy reaching the ground. Under such conditions, it is likely that photosynthesis may occur only during the times that a leaf is in the sunfleck.

Light Quality Beneath the Forest Canopy

Leaves of the canopy transmit from 10 to 25 percent of the visible radiation they receive. The quality of radiation reaching the understory depends on the optical properties of leaves as well as incoming direct and scattered light penetrating openings in the canopy.

The broader transmission ability of conifers compared to the more selective absorption and transmission by deciduous canopies has been observed by many workers. In comparisons of light beneath sugar maple and red pine canopies Vézina and Boulter (1966) found far-red radiation to predominate in the sugar maple understory on a clear day, with lesser amounts of green, blue, and red light and ultraviolet radiation (Figure 3.9). Sunflecks were strikingly evident in the morning and early afternoon in Figure 3.9, and during these periods red light increases sharply. The red pine canopy was much less selective in transmission than sugar maple foliage, and for red pine no significant differences were found among the transmission values of the various wavelengths in the visible spectrum. On cloudy or overcast days, transmission of radiation by forest canopies is higher in general than on clear days, and the sugar maple canopy was not as selective as it was on clear days. Similar relationships for conifer and deciduous species and for cloudy and clear days were reported by Federer and Tanner (1966) in studies of scattered shade light. Under sugar maple, clearly defined minimums were found at 0.47 and 0.67 μm (probably resulting from high absorption by chlorophyll) on clear days but were not as well defined under overcast conditions.

The differential absorption and reflectance of wavelengths by forest species has been utilized in aerial photography and is the basis for new advances in remote monitoring of the environment, the subject of the following section.

Remote Sensing

Decreased leaf absorption and increased leaf reflectance in the wavelength region between 0.7 and 1.0 μm are more striking with broadleaved than coniferous species. This fact is the basis for the use of infrared-sensitive films for forest aerial photography when separation of broadleaved and coniferous species is desired. Figure 3.10 demonstrates that reflection from broadleaved and coniferous

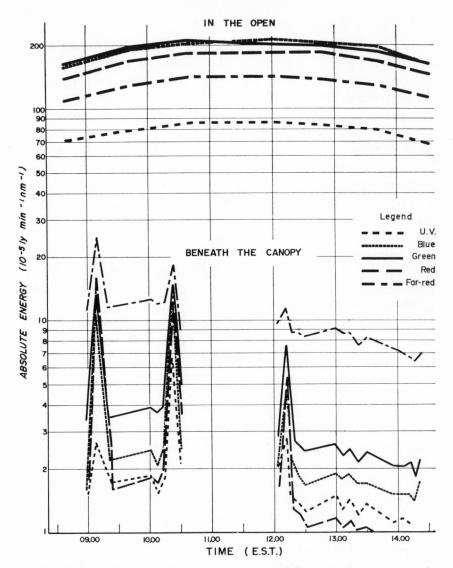

Fig. 3.9. Radiation quality in the open and beneath the sugar maple canopy. (After Vézina and Boulter, 1966.)

species is essentially the same in the visible spectrum (Figure 3.10A) but that the broadleaved species are significantly more reflectant than conifers in the near-infrared spectral band (Figure 3.10B; spectral range 0.7–0.98 μm). While aerial photography has been an indispensable part of forestry for many years (Spurr,

A   Visible spectral band (0.4–0.7 μm); hardwood plantations not distinctly different in tone from conifers in midsummer.

B   Near-infrared spectral band (0.7–0.98 μm); hardwoods markedly lighter in tone than conifers in midsummer.

C   Thermal infrared band (4.5–5.5 μm); small charcoal fires detected; conifers warmer (lighter tone) than leafless hardwoods in midwinter.

Fig. 3.10. Differences of reflectance of conifers and hardwoods in the visible and near-infrared spectral bands and emittance in the thermal infrared band, Saginaw Forest, Ann Arbor, Michigan. (Courtesy of University of Michigan.)

1948), new devices for recording energy over a broad spectrum of wavelengths now make it possible to monitor or "sense" environmental phenomena from remote stations, including aircraft and spacecraft. Thermal remote sensors capable of recording infrared energy with wavelengths too long to be recorded photographically (4.5–5.5 μm) can detect small fires from altitudes as high as 20,000 feet. For example, the eight bright spots in Figure 3.10C were caused by small charcoal fires with a surface area of approximately 1 square foot each. These hot spots are apparent in the 4.5-to-5.5-μm band because this is the wavelength of maximum emittance for an object whose temperature is approximately 304°C.

Remote sensors operating at still longer wavelengths (8.0–14.0 μm) can detect the effects of several kinds of insect and disease attacks, in some instances before visual symptoms appear. The affected trees are consistently one to three degrees Celsius warmer than unaffected trees (Weber, 1971). Once the visual symptoms appear, such insect-infested trees can easily be identified using color or black-and-white film, as illustrated in Figure 3.11 by a lighter tone

Fig. 3.11. Living (dark tone) and dead (light tone) ponderosa pine trees in a small stream drainage in the Black Hills of South Dakota. Trees recently killed by the mountain pine beetle (*Dendroctonus ponderosae* Hopk.) appear white whereas the older kills are grayish. (U. S. Forest Service photo.)

than that of the surrounding healthy individuals. Remote sensing has been successfully used in the inventory of big game animals whose body temperatures are several degrees warmer than their background (McMullough *et al.*, 1969). The many possible applications of remote sensing to forestry and natural resource problems make it one of the most significant and exciting fields in environmental science. Techniques and applications of remote sensing in forestry and ecology are presented in books by Johnson (1969) and Hildebrandt (1971).

Light and the Growth of Trees

The most obvious importance of solar radiation to forest trees lies in the dependence of life upon photosynthesis and the dependence of photosynthesis in turn on light. The term *light* is used here, because it is quite well established that it is the solar radiation in the visible bands of the spectrum that affects the photosynthetic process. We use *light irradiance* or *irradiance* to express the amount of radiation received per unit area in the visible spectral band.

Since chlorophyll is green, it follows that green foliage reflects a higher percentage of the green wavelengths than the blue-violet or the longer yellow-red wavelengths. Such indeed is the case (Figure 3.6). A corollary is that the blue-violet and the yellow-red wavelengths, being absorbed by the plant instead of being reflected, would exert a relatively greater influence on photosynthesis. This concept is confirmed in a classic study by Hoover (1937) with wheat, in which he found that the effectiveness of solar radiation on photosynthesis was almost entirely confined to the visible spectrum and that the most effective bands were the violet-blue and the orange-red. Similar relationships apparently hold for most plants and forest trees, although Burns (1942) found that, for Norway spruce, eastern white pine, and red pine, the orange-red wavelengths were most effective in stimulating photosynthesis, while the shorter violet-blue waves were relatively unimportant, a finding contrary to the earlier study of wheat by Hoover. Linder (1971), working with Scots pine seedlings, found absorption maxima in the red and the blue regions, but the photosynthetic efficiency of blue light was less than that of red light.

Since the growth rate of trees is obviously closely related to their rate of photosynthesis, and since the rate of photosynthesis can be measured under controlled conditions by measuring the uptake of carbon dioxide from the air by the plant, there have been many studies of the effect of varying amounts of light upon the rate of photosynthesis. At very low irradiance levels, photosynthesis takes place at such a slow rate that it fails to utilize all the carbon dioxide evolved by the plant in respiration. Under such conditions, carbon dioxide is actually given off by the plant rather than being absorbed by it from the atmosphere. The *compensation point* is that level of photosynthesis where carbon dioxide is neither given off nor taken up. In other words, it is the point at which photosynthetic gains balance respirative losses.

For forest trees under otherwise optimal conditions, the compensation point appears to occur at from 1 to 2 percent of full sunlight (RI). For example, Grasovsky (1929) found that this point for well-watered eastern white pine occurred at approximately 170 foot-candles. It thus appears that, in very dense forests, *net photosynthesis* (i.e., more photosynthesis than respiration) occurs only when the leaves are bathed in sunflecks. Similarly, many understory species in dense deciduous forests can make net gains in growth only during the leafless period of the overstory trees. Under dry conditions, the compensation point occurs at relatively higher light irradiance, so that more light is needed to permit an understory plant to hold its own where root competition limits its supply of soil moisture than when the plant is well watered (Takahara *et al.*, 1955).

The minimum light requirements vary for different species. In general, trees which are seldom found under dense canopies require more light at the compensation point than do those that commonly occur in the understory. In a test of fourteen species, Burns (1923) found that ponderosa pine and Scots pine required light irradiances at a compensation point three times as high as that of eastern white pine. At the other extreme, hemlock, beech, and sugar maple required the least amount of light to maintain themselves. Similar results were obtained for twelve species in the West, with redwood and Engelmann spruce having the lowest light requirements, and limber pine and pinyon the highest (Bates and Roeser, 1928). Redwood has one of the lowest light requirements of all species that have been studied, redwood seedlings having shown 90-percent survival and 66-percent increase in dry weight when grown for 55 days at 30 foot-candles (Shirley, 1929). For shade and sun plants in general, approximately 50 and 150 foot-candles, respectively, are required at the compensation point under natural conditions (Perry *et al.*, 1969).

Plants may live for a considerable length of time on stored food after environmental conditions develop to the point at which respiration exceeds photosynthesis. For example, Grasovsky found that white pine seedlings remained in good condition throughout the growing season under 65 foot-candles, even though 170 foot-candles is seemingly required at the compensation point. Sooner or later, though, such plants are bound to die. In studies with seedlings of several species, Grime (1966) observed the greatest height growth and least mortality in shade for species having large seeds. Mortality of black birch seedlings (0.7 mg dry weight of seed reserve) was four times that of red oak (1969.2 mg dry weight of seed reserve). The occurrence of one- or even two-year-old seedlings under dense forest stands does not demonstrate that light under those conditions is sufficient for growth; the seedlings may still be living on stored food material from the seed.

As the irradiance is increased above the compensation-point level, photosynthesis is increased proportionately. After reviewing the evidence of other workers as well as carrying out tests of his own, Shirley (1945a) concluded that, in the range from 1 to 15 percent of full sunlight, photosynthesis is directly proportional to irradiance if other factors are favorable. The increase in photosynthesis will continue until other factors combine to bring growth to a halt. At very high irradiances, such secondary factors as high respiration, water deficit causing stomatal closing, and overaccumulation of photosynthate in the leaves may result in decreased photosynthesis.

The relative effect of illumination upon photosynthesis in different species has been studied by a number of investigators. For example, both Kramer and Decker (1944) and Kozlowski (1949) have shown that seedlings of loblolly pine show increased photosynthesis for increased illuminance at all levels up to full sunlight, while associated hardwood species reach their maximum photosynthetic rate at 30 percent or less relative illumination. Such a finding tends to explain the better relative competitive ability of the hardwoods under open pine stands where the relative illumination is commonly in the neighborhood of 30-percent full sunlight (Figure 3.12).

Another factor affecting the relative ability of different species to compete under given light conditions is the color, shape, and arrangement of the leaves—factors which regulate the amount of light actually reaching the chlorophyll. Pines, for instance, characteristically have rounded needles in dense clusters. Such an ar-

Fig. 3.12. A conspicuous hardwood understory in an open 80-year-old loblolly pine stand, North Carolina. (U. S. Forest Service photo.)

rangement results in much scattering of light and much mutual shading (Kramer and Clark, 1947). Many hardwoods associated with pine in the eastern United States, on the other hand, have broad, thin leaves, arranged perpendicular to the direction of incident radiation and spaced so that shading of one leaf by another is at a minimum. It follows that the pine chlorophyll receives a much smaller fraction of the light incident to it than does the dogwood, to cite a specific example. This fact is at least one of the reasons why pine can maintain a high photosynthetic rate at high light irradiances which actually inhibit the growth of dogwood, while dogwood can carry on photosynthesis efficiently in low light conditions under a loblolly pine stand.

The failure of seedlings in shade is often associated with fungal attack. Compared to tree species intolerant of shade, shade-tolerant species are less susceptible to infection both above and below the compensation point (Grime and Jeffrey, 1965). The predisposition of shade-intolerant species to fungal attack may be due to characteristics arising from adaptation for survival in habitats of high light intensity. These characteristics are (1) attenuation of the stem and mechanical collapse when shaded, (2) inherently high rates of respiration, and (3) marked rise in respiration with increasing temperature (Grime, 1966).

The experiments detailed above have dealt with the rate of photosynthesis as measured by the uptake of carbon dioxide from the atmosphere. It is also possible, of course, to measure the actual height growth and weight growth of trees over a period of years under different degrees of irradiance. This has been done by a number of investigators, who for the most part have reduced the possible effect of soil moisture by watering the plants grown under all irradiances to keep the soil at a more or less optimum soil-moisture level.

In general, it has been found that at least 20 percent of full sunlight is required for survival over a period of years, the actual amount varying with the species and with growing conditions. For species that are usually found growing in full sunlight, growth commonly increases with irradiance up to full sunlight. Pearson (1936, 1940) grew ponderosa pine under various shade conditions in Arizona for periods up to 10 years and found the best growth under full sunlight, although the trees grown at 50 percent showed only slightly less height growth and about one-half the diameter growth. Shirley (1945b) and Logan (1966a) obtained similar results for red pine and jack pine.

Many other species, however, make as much or more height growth under partial light than under full light. Among conifers, white spruce and white pine provide examples (Gustafson, 1943; Shirley, 1945b; Logan, 1966a). Among hardwoods, this relationship seems to be the rule. Seedling height growth data for six hardwood species in Missouri (McDermott, 1954), showed that the maximum height growth of sycamore was measured at 20-percent relative illumination; of American elm, at 33-percent RI; and of winged elm, river birch, and alder, at 50-percent RI (Table 3.1). For five- to six-year-old hardwood seedlings in Ontario, Canada, Logan (1965, 1966b) reported the maximum height of white birch, yellow birch, and American elm was at 45-percent RI, whereas it was at 25 percent for basswood and sugar maple (both highly shade-tolerant). Few species, conifers or hardwoods, however, make better weight growth under partial light than under full light.

Regardless of whether or not height growth is increased or decreased by shaded conditions, there seems little doubt that root development of seedlings is sharply impaired. The lower the irradiance, the greater is this impairment, so that, at low irradiance levels, seedlings of most forest trees have relatively shallow and poorly developed root systems. The data of McDermott (Table 3.1) serve to illustrate this point. American elm may make the

Table 3.1. Seedling Height and Top/Root Weight Ratio of Newly Germinated Seedlings as Influenced by Amount of Sunlight

Species	20% RI Ht(cm)	T/R	33% RI Ht(cm)	T/R	50% RI Ht(cm)	T/R	100% RI Ht(cm)	T/R
American elm (*U. americana*) 13 weeks	73	3.1	81	3.2	69	3.0	37	1.7
Winged elm (*U. alata*) 13 weeks	59	5.2	71	3.9	76	4.4	28	1.9
Sycamore (*P. occidentalis*) 15 weeks	43	4.6	41	3.5	40	4.1	33	2.0
River birch (*B. nigra*) 10 weeks	26	13.4	33	9.3	52	8.3	41	3.6
Red maple (*A. rubrum*) 13 weeks	26	4.1	27	3.7	29	3.5	26	2.0
Alder (*A. rugosa*) 14 weeks	21	3.4	20	3.5	38	4.7	30	2.8

SOURCE: After McDermott, 1954.

tallest shoot growth at 33-percent RI, but the top is 3.2 times as heavy as the roots under these conditions. The shorter plant grown under full sunlight has a relatively better-developed root system, the top being only 1.7 times as heavy under these circumstances. Similar results have been reported for many other North American species (Baker, 1945; Shirley, 1945b; Logan, 1965, 1966b) and for European species (Harley, 1939; Brown, 1955; Leibundgut and Heller, 1960).

The marked effect of reduced light in reducing root growth is of major importance in explaining the growth and survival of plants in the understory. Under a growing forest, root competition substantially reduces the amount of soil moisture available to the seedlings (Chapter 9). The combination of reduced root size due to low light irradiances and reduced soil moisture due to root competition is frequently fatal to the seedlings. Frost-heaving, too, is increased for seedlings grown under low light irradiance (Hagem, 1947).

The fact that, under the forest canopy, both light and soil moisture are reduced makes meaningless any attempt to relate relative light intensity to survival and growth of seedlings under uncontrolled conditions. Curves showing the effect of light irradiance upon seedling development ignore the existence of variations in soil moisture and other environmental factors which also vary with different canopy densities. Nevertheless, such efforts have their value if the light measurements are considered to indicate merely the variation in the crown density and are not interpreted to mean the effect of light alone.

For example, Shirley (1932) found that red pine reproduction was uncertain under forest stands sufficiently dense to allow only 17 percent of the light to reach the ground, but that satisfactory reproduction became established when the stand was opened up to the point that the relative illumination on the ground was 35 percent. In France, Roussel (1948) found that Norway spruce seedlings could flourish for only the first one or two years under natural forest conditions where the relative illumination was less than 5 percent; at RI of 15 to 24 percent, plants ten to fifteen years old are still healthy; and at RI of 35 to 50 percent, conditions are optimum for seedling survival and growth. It should again be emphasized that, under such uncontrolled conditions, relative illumination merely measures the relative density of the forest and of all the environmental factors associated with this density. It does not measure the independent effect of light alone.

In studies where establishment and growth involve several environmental factors, compensating effects may be expected. In a study of yellow birch regeneration, Tubbs (1969) employed 64 different combinations of 3 major factors—light irradiance, soil moisture, and seedbed type—to assess germination, survival, and height growth. On well-drained sites good germination occurred under full sunlight on mineral soil, but on heavy and organic soils heavy shade was required. On mineral soil height growth was best in full sunlight on the well-drained site, whereas shade was necessary for maximum growth on the imperfectly drained site. Although partial shade has been found generally to promote better seedling development of yellow birch, full sunlight may be required under certain conditions. The study also demonstrated the remarkable phenotypic variability of the seedlings, all from one mother tree, in germinating and surviving over a wide range of environmental conditions.

Light and Tree Morphology

That plants grown under shade develop a structure and appearance different from the same plants grown under full sunlight is often noted. These morphological changes are of importance ecologically in understanding the capacity of a given species to become adjusted to shaded conditions and the reaction of such a plant when suddenly released, as by cutting of the overstory.

Since the leaf is the principal photosynthetic organ of the tree and therefore presumably most affected by changes in radiation and light, it has been the subject of many detailed investigations. The structure of leaves of typical understory plants has been compared with those of typical overstory plants; and sun leaves have been compared anatomically with shade leaves of the same plant. The findings are in essential agreement (Büsgen and Münch, 1929).

Some species exhibit but little plasticity in leaf anatomy with the result that there is but little difference between their sun leaves and their shade leaves. Such plants are usually found only in the overstory or only in the understory—their anatomy is suited for their survival under only one set of environmental conditions. Technically speaking, they are either obligate sun plants or obligate shade plants.

Most forest trees, however, have the faculty of developing different anatomical structures in leaves grown in the shade than in those developed in the sun (Hanson, 1917; Büsgen and Münch, 1929; Jackson, 1967). Typicaly, shade leaves are thinner and less deeply lobed, and have a larger surface per unit weight, a thinner epidermis, less palisade, more intercellular space and spongy parenchyma, less supportive and conductive tissue, and fewer stomata than comparable sun leaves off the same tree. Similar differences in leaf structure are found between species that characteristically grow in shaded conditions and those that grow under fully exposed conditions.

Presumably, the typical shade leaf is adjusted to carry on photosynthesis when efficiently protected from the detrimental effects of too much light. This seems to be the case. Working with Scots pine and Norway spruce, Stålfelt (1921) found that the shade leaves of both species carried out more photosynthesis per unit weight at all light irradiances. Furthermore, the shade leaves required less light at the compensation point, so they could survive and even add to the photosynthate with very little light.

Despite the assumption that shade leaves develop in response to a reduced light, it must be remembered that other factors may also be involved. The temperature is obviously different in sun and shade situations. Furthermore, leaves within the crown and in its lower portions are under less water stress on clear days than are the sun leaves at the top of a tree.

When shade leaves are suddenly exposed to full light, as commonly happens after partial cutting, they are frequently unable to survive. This failure may be due in part to excessive moisture loss and in part to excessive light reaching the chloroplasts. Under these conditions, the shade leaves commonly die and drop off, even in the case of conifers such as Norway spruce (Stålfelt, 1935). Survival of the branch depends upon the development of a new crop of leaves with anatomical characteristics suited to the new set of environmental conditions.

Much less work has been done on the effect of light upon bark thickness, the stimulation of adventitious buds, and upon root growth. Certain facts, however, seem to emerge from careful observation. For example, there is evidence that the bark of eastern white pine is substantially thinner, smoother, and more vulnerable to insolation when grown in the shade. Sunscald, a winter damage phenomenon apparently related to rapid temperature changes of the cambium (Huberman, 1943), occurs chiefly in thin-barked white pine whose shade bark is exposed to direct solar radiation of the sun by the removal of adjacent trees.

Adventitious buds in the bark may be activated to form epicormic branches when the bark is exposed to direct solar radiation. It does not follow, though, that there is a necessary cause-and-effect relationship between light and bud stimulation. The removal of surrounding trees, for example, will affect the environment of the remaining trees in many ways, and carefully controlled experimentation is required to determine which factor or combination of factors actually initiates the chain of physiologic circumstances that lead to the development of epicormic branches. It is known that the crown exerts a substantial control on sprouting; decapitation of the crown (Books and Tubbs, 1970) and pruning of live branches (Kormanik and Brown, 1969) stimulate sprouting. It is generally agreed that sprouting is triggered by a change in growth hormones within the tree. All that can be deduced from field observations is that epicormic branches form on the exposed boles of many trees, particularly those with poorly developed crowns, and that European foresters have been able to reduce the amount of epicormic branching on such species as oak by keeping the bole clothed with the foliage of understory trees such as beech and hornbeam. The occurrence of epicormic branches after thinning is particularly serious with many of the oaks, maples, birches, and other hardwoods where stem quality is of paramount economic importance. Under extreme conditions of change from shade to light, epicormic branches may develop in most forest trees, both conifers and hardwoods.

Photocontrol of Plant Response

The growth and development of all parts of the plant, including stem elongation, root development, dormancy, germination, flowering, and fruit development, are subject to the same causal photocontrol whereby light is absorbed by a reversible pigment system in the plant. This system is the physiological basis of photoperiodism, which has been repeatedly demonstrated to affect seasonal rhythm, timing, and amount of tree growth. *Photoperiodism* is the response of the plant to the relative length of the day and night and the changes in this relationship throughout the year.

The term photoperiodism was proposed by Garner and Allard (1920, 1923), who carried on extensive tests which demonstrated that both vegetative development and the initiation of reproductive processes in plants could be greatly affected by varying the relative length of day and night. Although many plants were not found to be especially sensitive to day length, others could be characterized as short-day plants because flowering could be induced under suitable conditions by exposure to days shorter than a certain critical length, while others could be termed long-day plants as these responded to days longer than a given critical length or even to continuous illumination. Responses to differing day lengths are clearly different for different species.

As we have seen in Chapter 2, photoperiodic requirements are not constant within a species, but vary with the latitude and altitude of the source. Thus genecological differentiation is characteristic of many tree species, having arisen as a result of natural selection for a particular photoperiod associated with the limiting factors of the growing season.

When plants respond to light they do so because light is absorbed by the phytochrome pigment system of the plant. The bluish protein phytochrome has been detected in all parts of higher plants and exists in two forms:

$$P_r \xrightleftharpoons[\text{far-red light 0.73 } \mu m]{\text{red light 0.66 } \mu m} P_{fr} \xrightarrow{\text{darkness}} P_r$$

One form, P_r, has an absorption peak (0.66 μm) in the red region of the spectrum; the other form, P_{fr}, biologically active, has an absorption peak (0.73 μm) in the far-red region. Absorption of light at the appropriate wavelength readily converts one form to the other; when the red-absorbing form receives red light, it is changed into the far-red-absorbing form (P_{fr}), and vice versa. Growth responses elicited by red light are reversed by far-red light. Besides reversibility, the system is characterized by a slow drift in darkness from the far-red-absorbing to the red-absorbing form. The detection of phytochrome, its properties, and effects in morphogenesis of plants are reviewed by Siegelman (1969) and Mohr (1969).

Growth cessation under short-day conditions and continuous growth under long days may be explained by the phytochrome system. At the end of the daily light period, in which red light predominates, more than 70 percent of the pigment is in the P_{fr} form. During the dark period that follows, the pigment slowly reverts to the P_r form, and if the dark period is long enough less than 10 percent remains in the P_{fr} form (Downs, 1962). If the pigment remains in the P_r form for a substantial time during each dark period, woody plants cease growth and enter dormancy, because the amount of biologically active P_{fr} form is inadequate. Thus it is the length of the night, rather than that of the day, that initiates through phytochrome the biochemical reactions controlling growth. Under long days or continuous light the pigment is in the P_{fr} form for an appreciable time and growth is promoted.

The control of bud-burst or leaf flushing is not as strongly controlled by photoperiod as growth cessation; chilling requirements and temperature play more important roles. Some species, European beech and birch, for example, resume growth in the spring once a photoperiodic requirement is satisfied: in beech when daylength exceeds 12 hours, but only after a certain chilling requirement is met and when temperature is adequate. The photoperiodic effect on flowering of trees is not well understood. It has not been possible to clearly establish long-day and short-day flowering types as has been done in herbaceous species, leading to the conclusion that most trees are day-neutral. The extreme difficulty of experimentation with trees in the adult stage under controlled light conditions has restricted our knowledge.

In recent years, photoperiodic treatment has been used increasingly as a tool to determine the nature of growth control within the plant. Such highly artificial treatment as a short period of light in the middle of the dark period has proved useful in understanding the nature of growth regulation. Such experiments, however, fall within the province of plant physiology rather than that of plant autecology.

SUMMARY

The discussion of climatic factors begins naturally with a consideration of solar radiation. The process of photosynthesis, involving the conversion of water and carbon dioxide into organic compounds, requires large amounts of light, particularly of the orange-red and the violet-blue portions of the spectrum.

Forest trees require at least 1 to 2 percent of full sunlight to hold their own. That much light is needed for gains from photosynthesis to offset losses from respiration. This "compensation point" differs between species, tolerant trees such as redwood, hemlock, beech, and sugar maple requiring less light to survive than intolerant trees such as ponderosa pine and Scots pine.

Above this minimum light requirement, plant growth is roughly proportional to light intensity up to perhaps 15 percent of full sunlight. In other words, a tree seedling receiving 10-percent full sunlight will grow twice as fast as another receiving only 5 percent. At higher light irradiances, however, growth levels off. Some relatively tolerant species, such as red oak, white oak, and dogwood, reach their maximum photosynthetic rate at as low as 30-percent full sunlight while intolerant species such as loblolly pine may require as much as 100-percent sunlight for maximum growth.

Under the forest canopy, light irradiances may vary from less than 1-percent full sunlight under the tropical rain forest to 10 to 15 percent under open, even-aged pine stands. In the coniferous forests at higher elevations in the Sierra Nevada of California, for example, 18 percent of the solar energy reaches the ground under a crown density of 50 percent, and this figure drops to 6 percent under a full canopy.

Leaves grown in the shade are thinner in cross-section and less resistant to heat and desiccation than leaves grown in the sun on the same plant. When shade leaves are suddenly exposed to full light, as commonly happens after partial cutting, they are frequently unable to survive. Survival of the branch thus exposed depends upon the development of a new crop of leaves with anatomical characteristics suited to the new set of environmental conditions.

The relative length of day and night (photoperiod) is in many ways as important to plant growth as the actual amount and quality of light. The phytochrome pigment system is the physiological basis for photocontrol of woody-plant growth and other processes. For many trees, the amount and duration of growth is related to the relative length of the day and night. Some species can be grown continuously throughout the year on artificially long days. Cessation of growth in the fall is usually conditioned by the shortening days. In many American cities, some types of shade trees will keep their leaves for days and weeks longer under street lights as contrasted with unlighted individuals of the same species down the street. Finally, once the trees have become dormant, this dormancy can frequently be broken by lengthening the day artificially under favorable temperature conditions. The photoperiodic requirement, a heritable characteristic, is not constant within a given species, but varies with the native latitude, altitude, and growing conditions of the individual tree.

SUGGESTED READINGS

Downs, Robert Jack. 1962. Photocontrol of growth and dormancy in woody plants. In Theodore T. Kozlowski (ed.), Tree Growth. The Ronald Press Co., New York. 442 pp.

————, and H. A. Borthwick. 1956. Effects of photoperiod on growth of trees. Bot. Gaz. 117:310–326.

Gates, David M. 1962. Energy Exchange in the Biosphere. Harper & Row, Inc., New York. 151 pp.

————. 1968. Energy exchange between organism and environment. In William P. Lowery (ed.), Biometeorology. Oregon State Univ. Press, Corvallis. 171 pp.

————. 1970. Physical and physiological properties of plants. In Remote Sensing, with Special Reference to Agriculture and Forestry. National Academy of Sciences, National Research Council, Washington, D. C. 424 pp.

Lowry, William P. 1969. Weather and Life, an Introduction to Biometeorology. (Chapter 2, Energy and ecology, pp. 9–12; Chapter 3, Radiation, pp. 13–30; Chapter 7, The energy-budget concept, pp. 113–121; Chapter 8, Energy budgets of particular systems, pp. 122–151.) Academic Press, Inc., New York. 305 pp.

Reifsnyder, William E. 1967. Forest meteorology: the forest energy balance. Int. Rev. For. Res. 2:127–179.

————, and Howard W. Lull. 1965. Radiant energy in relation to forests. USDA Tech. Bull. 1344. 111 pp.

Shirley, H. L. 1945. Reproduction of upland conifers in the Lake States as affected by root competition and light. Amer. Mid. Nat. 33:537–612.

Treshow, Michael. 1970. Environment and Plant Response. (Chapter 8, Light mechanisms, pp. 99–115; Chapter 9, Light stress and radiation, pp. 116–124.) McGraw-Hill Book Co., Inc., New York. 422 pp.

4

Temperature

Solar radiation is the source of the heat that controls the temperature regime near the ground of the earth. The great importance of terrestrial radiation and of air movements in affecting the level and distribution of temperature, however, makes it desirable to discuss solar heat and air temperature separately from solar radiation and light.

Basically, the mean annual temperature at any given spot on the earth's surface is a function of the incoming solar insolation at that spot modified by secondary heat transfer arising from terrestrial radiation and air movements. Heating up of the surface layers of air during the day is greatest under conditions where the greatest amount of infrared radiation is received, i.e., in tropical latitudes, at high elevations, and where the air is freest from water vapor, clouds, and atmospheric impurities.

Temperatures during the night, on the other hand, depend largely upon the amount of heat absorbed by terrestrial objects and atmosphere during the day and the rate at which this heat is given off as terrestrial thermal radiation. To cite an important example, the great capacity of large bodies of water to absorb solar energy and to reradiate it slowly and steadily results in greatly modified temperature extremes on lands subject to winds that have passed over the water. Thus the coastal areas of western North America and western Europe show little variation in temperature between day and night and even between winter and summer. This is the characteristic of maritime climates as contrasted with continental climates characterized by extreme changes in temperature between day and night, and between summer and winter.

Temperatures at the Soil Surface

The focal plane of temperature variation is the line of contact between the atmosphere and the ground (or, more accurately, the surface exposed to the sun). Both the surface of the ground and the adjoining surface layer of air heat up greatly under direct sunlight and cool off greatly at night as heat is lost through terrestrial thermal radiation. Direct solar insolation commonly produces a surface temperature at midday of at least 70°C, or 158°F, even in northern latitudes in the summertime (Baker, 1950; Vaartaja, 1954; Maguire, 1955).

The exact temperature reached at the soil surface depends upon the rate of absorption of solar energy and the rate at which it is dissipated once absorbed, which in turn is dependent primarily upon the amount of vegetation and litter cover, and only secondarily upon the color, water content, and other physical factors of the soil itself, if exposed.

The importance of soil color has been demonstrated by Isaac (1938), who found that charcoal-blackened soils will reach a temperature of 163°F when the air temperature was 100°F, at which time comparable grey mineral soil heated up only to 148°F and yellow mineral soil to 144°F. These values were obtained on bare soil in the Douglas-fir region of southern Washington.

The rate at which surface materials dissipate heat received was found to be highly important in determining surface soil temperatures by Smith (1951), who worked with white pine in Connecticut. A surface of white pine needle litter in a small clearing heated up to 68°C (154°F) on a day when the air temperature reached only 24°C (75°F). In contrast, the surface temperature of bare mineral soil reached 46°C (115°F) and that of polytrichum moss reached only 39°C (102°F). The specific heat and the conductivity of the surface materials are apparently the important physical factors involved. Wind speed, however, is most important of all.

Much of this variation in surface temperatures is due to the water content of materials. Moist material has a much greater capacity to dissipate heat through evaporation of water, while the evaporated water itself tends to reduce the amount of incoming solar energy.

Thus Maguire (1955), in California, sprinkled bare mineral soil with the equivalent of one inch of rain on May 17 and found that the watered soil was 41°, 26°, and 17°F cooler on the succeeding three days than on the comparable unwatered plot.

Temperature variations drop off sharply within the soil. Diurnal variations may disappear within a foot of the surface and annual variations within a very few feet. In fact, Shanks (1956) has argued that soil-temperature data from a 6-inch depth measured at weekly intervals serve as a useful integration of radiation and air temperature conditions during the preceding week. Indeed, temperatures measured deep in the ground, such as may be measured in caves, frequently remain constant throughout the year and may well measure the mean annual temperature of the area (Poulson and White, 1969). Such measurements may prove useful in measuring the extent of climatic fluctuation.

Temperatures Within the Forest

Within the forest, light crown cover and trees without foliage, as in the case of deciduous trees during the leafless season, tend to reduce air movement while allowing solar radiation to penetrate the canopy. Under such conditions, the mean air temperature may be higher within the forest than outside it. For example, Pearson (1914) found that the mean annual air temperature within the open ponderosa pine forest of northern Arizona was 2.7°F higher than in adjoining open parks, a phenomenon partly attributed to lower radiation losses from the forest and partly to the effect of the forest in deflecting cold air masses moving down from surrounding mountains. In the Copper Basin of Tennessee, Hursh (1948) found that air temperatures were 0.6 to 2.0°F higher in the deciduous forest than in the open during the winter months, although they ranged from 2.1 to 3.5°F lower during the summer months.

When trees are in full leaf, the extremes within the forest are generally less than outside, and the diminution of radiation within the forest may result in lower mean annual air temperatures. To cite one of many examples, data collected within and adjacent to a white pine plantation by Spurr (1957) gave a summer air temperature range within the forest of 28.6°F compared to 38.8°F in the open, and a winter range of 34.9°F within the forest compared to 42.3°F in the open (Table 4.1). Throughout the year, at a height of four feet from the ground, the maxima and means were lower and the minima higher within the forest as contrasted to the open station.

Table 4.1. Mean Weekly Maxima, Minima, and Mean Temperatures (°F) in the Open and Under a Dense 20-year-old White Pine Plantation[a]

	Winter	Spring	Summer	Fall
Open				
Maximum	41.1	73.1	85.4	57.5
Minimum	−1.2	28.1	46.6	18.8
Range	42.3	45.0	38.8	38.7
Mean	20.0	50.7	66.0	38.2
Under forest				
Maximum	36.8	67.9	78.0	51.8
Minimum	1.9	31.5	49.4	21.8
Range	34.9	36.4	28.6	30.0
Mean	19.3	49.7	63.8	36.8

[a] Petersham, Mass.; by 13-week quarters, 1943–44.

Higher up in the forest stand, temperature variations are less than they are near the ground. Fowells (1948) measured the temperature profile up to a height of 120 feet in a mature Sierra Nevada mixed conifer forest ranging up to 200 feet in height. He found that temperature variation decreased with increased distance from the ground. At 120 feet, minimum temperatures ranged up to 4°F higher than at 4.5 feet while maximum temperatures were similarly lower. At the top of the tree crown itself, however, surface conditions similar to those described for the forest floor exist. Consequently, extreme variation in temperature may be expected and has been described for the beech forest of Ohio by Christy (1952).

Temperature Variations with Topographic Position

The effects of local topography upon local temperature have been studied by a number of investigators (Pallman and Frei, 1943; Hough, 1945; Wolfe *et al.*, 1949; Spurr, 1957, among others). All have found that low concave landforms tend to radiate heat rapidly on still cold nights and to accumulate cold air which flows in from surrounding higher land. As a result, such sites will frequently have air temperatures near the ground as much as 15°F lower than that above surrounding terrain. The resulting condition is known as *inversion* in that the temperature increases with height in the layer of air near the ground in contrast to the usual decrease in temperature with height. The concave areas are known as *frost pockets* because the temperatures commonly occurring near the ground result in late spring frosts, early fall frosts, and consequent short growing seasons. The concave area need not be deep. Spurr (1957) found that minimum temperatures in a small depression only 3 or 4 feet deep were comparable to those in a nearby deep valley 200 feet below the general land level.

In contrast, relatively high convex surfaces will tend to drain off cold air as radiation from the ground proceeds, so that night minima remain fairly high. During the day, the low concave landforms tend to accumulate radiant energy and reach high maximum temperatures near the ground, while mounds, ridges, and other convex surfaces tend to remain cooler during the day.

A few examples will suffice. In a study of temperature variation 3 to 4 feet off the ground in the open, Spurr (1957) found that the weekly maximum temperatures on slopes with good air drainage averaged 5° to 6°F lower throughout the year than in nearby frost pockets. The weekly minimum temperatures, however, averaged 9° to 10°F higher on the well-drained slopes. The effect of this range on the growth of plants is indicated by the fact that on May 19, in the middle of the spring growing season, a frost dropped temperatures to 30°F at the top of the highest hill (1,383 ft. above mean sea level), while temperatures reached a low of 17°F in a small frost pocket. The effect of inversion in the frost pockets resulted in frost-free summer periods of only 77 and 104 days as compared to 161 days at stations with good cold air drainage. Despite the greater extremes in the concave areas, however, the mean annual temperatures remain essentially the same as on the upland sites with better air drainage.

Although variations in temperature due to local topography undoubtedly exert a strong influence on the distribution of plants, and almost certainly play a part in inhibiting tree growth in frost pockets, it must be remembered that soil water drainage is frequently an interacting factor. The same factors—especially the existence of convex surfaces—that make a soil very well drained are apt to insure good drainage of cold air and to indicate a site with lower maximum and higher minimum temperatures than would be indicated by a regional climatic average. Thus a very well-drained site is apt to have a moderated climate suitable to plants of a generally southern distribution. Likewise, a very poorly drained soil is apt to result from a concave land surface that inhibits the drainage of cold air as well as of water. Thus the very poorly drained sites are apt to be characterized by temperature extremes and a short growing season, and might prove suitable for plants of a generally northern distribution.

Finally, it should be realized that frost pockets can be created by the forming of a small clearing in a forest stand, the surfaces of the tree crowns of the surrounding forest functioning to channel cold air into the clearing as terrestrial radiation chills the surface layers of the air on still, clear nights.

Effects of Latitude and Altitude on Air Temperature

In general, temperatures decrease with increasing distance from the Equator toward the Poles and with increasing altitudes.

Many factors affect temperature other than latitude and altitude. Local topography, the direction and character of prevailing winds, storm patterns, and location relative to water bodies all contribute to the climate of a given place. It is both instructive and useful, however, to generalize the effect of latitude and altitude on temperature, holding these other factors as constant as possible.

Along the eastern seaboard of the United States, the mountains and uplands are oriented parallel to the coast. We would expect, therefore, a relatively uniform gradient in temperature from the crest of the Appalachians down to the Atlantic and from Canada south to Florida. Such indeed is the case. In a study of weather bureau data, mean annual temperature at sea level varied from over 70°F interpolated at latitude 30° North to 38°F at latitude 50° North. Mean annual temperatures for these latitudes and altitudes are given in Table 4.2. In this study (Spurr, 1953), mean temperature was used, as it tends to average out differences in local climate due to topography. In areas of good cold air drainage, as has been seen, maximum temperatures are lower and minimum temperatures are higher than in nearby areas of poor cold air drainage. The midpoint between the maximum and minimum (defined by meteorologists as the *mean*) is much the same, however, under both conditions.

From this study, it was estimated that 1 degree of latitude (69 miles) represents an average change of about 2°F, and that 1,000 feet of elevation represents a change of 3°F.

Table 4.2. Relation of Mean Annual Temperature to Latitude and Altitude in Eastern United States

Latitude	Mean Annual Temperature (°F)		
	Sea Level	2,000 ft.	4,000 ft.
35°	64	58	52
40°	54	48	42
45°	45	39	33

In the mountains of the American West, it is possible to utilize the climatic summaries of Baker (1944) and others to make similar generalizations. From the Pacific Ocean to the crest of the Cascade–Sierra Nevada chain, the prevailing on-shore winds are the dominant influence in the climates, and greatly diminish temperature variation from north to south. On the west side, there is a difference in mean annual temperature of less than one degree for each degree of latitude. The mean annual temperature on Puget Sound at the Canadian border in Washington (lat. 49°) is 49° F, compared to 60° F on the Pacific Ocean above the Mexican border (lat. 33½°). The overall change is ⅔° F per degree of latitude, or 1° F per 100 miles—only one-third of the change found on the east coast.

East of the Cascade–Sierra Nevada barrier, however, continental conditions generally prevail. At an elevation of 4,000 feet on the Canadian border in central Montana (lat. 49°), the mean annual temperature is 39° F; compared to 63° F for the same elevation on the Mexican border in Arizona (lat. 31½°). The overall change here in the interior is nearly 1.4° F per degree of latitude, or 2° F per 100 miles.

Temperature variation with altitude is similarly affected by prevailing wind patterns. In the maritime climate of California, the temperature decrease with each 1,000-foot rise in elevation is between 1 and 1½ degrees for the coastal ranges and 2½ to 3½ degrees for the Sierra Nevada. In the interior of the American West, the decrease for each 1,000 feet averages about 3.5° F, with the rate higher in July (3.5–4.0 degrees for each 1,000 ft.) than in January (3.0–3.5 degrees).

Temperature Variation with Time

It must also be realized that temperatures change with time, not only in geologic terms but also from year to year and from decade to decade. This fluctuation may or may not be cyclic—occurring at regular intervals or with a regular rhythm—but it does occur. The evidence comes in part from actual temperature records. The oldest and most complete set of data—from New Haven, Connecticut—dates from the late eighteenth century. From this it can be seen that the mean annual temperature was substantially lower in the early nineteenth century than at present, a fact confirmed by other meteorological records throughout the world and by indirect evidence such as the retreat of glaciers, the thinning of arctic and antarctic ice, and the changing distribution of plants and animals.

In New Haven, the coldest 10-year period since measurements were initiated in 1780 was that between 1812 and 1821, and the coldest 5-year period was between 1814 and 1819. The mean annual temperature there has risen from 47.6° F for the 10-year period ending in 1821 to a high of 51.6° F for the 10-year period ending in 1931, a rise of 4 degrees. Even a smooth curve drawn through the data indicates a rise of about 2½ degrees (Figure 4.1).

Kincer (1933) has demonstrated that this rise in temperature is significant, that it is duplicated in records from weather stations throughout the world, and that it is equally apparent at rural as well as at urban stations, obviating the possibility of city development having caused the trend. Recent studies further substantiate the warming trend of up to 4° F in the eastern United States from the middle of the nineteenth century to the 30-year period 1931–1960, but show a minor cooling trend in the western mountain states and Great Basin (Wahl, 1968; Wahl and Lawson, 1970). The general cooling trend in recent years indicates that we have passed the height of the warming episode (1880–1950) and are now reverting to climatic patterns established in the last century (Lamb, 1966; Wahl, 1968).

The long-term effect of climatic change upon forest migration and development is discussed in a later chapter. It is worthy of note here, however, that the rise in temperature from 1817 to 1950, nearly 3° F, represents a movement of the climate about 1,000 feet up in elevation, or about 100 miles north at the same elevation in

MEAN ANNUAL TEMPERATURE (°F)

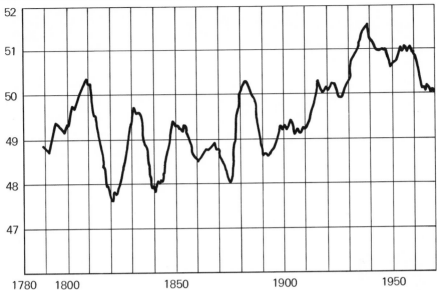

Fig. 4.1. Mean annual temperature at New Haven, Connecticut (ten-year moving average).

terms of the temperature gradient on the eastern seaboard of the United States (Table 4.2).

Quite obviously, such a change in temperature may exert a real influence upon the occurrence, natural regeneration, and growth of forest tree species, especially those growing near the limits of their natural range. Under far-northern conditions, temperature is the decisive climatic factor affecting the radial growth of trees (Mikola, 1962). For Scots pine in Finland the influence of summer temperature (mean July temperature) on tree growth increases from south to north, although the correlation is quite evident in both south and north. Radial growth increment increased sharply in the first part of the twentieth century, peaked in the mid-1930's, and declined with temperature thereafter.

Temperature and Plant Growth

Plants regulate their temperature by dissipating part of the energy they absorb and thus preventing death due to excessive temperature. Of the three major mechanisms, reradiation, transpiration, and convection, dissipation of energy by reradiation accounts for one-half of the energy plants absorb (Gates, 1965). Transpiration accounts for an additional heat loss as the leaf is cooled when energy is expended in changing water to water vapor. In addition, convection across the thin air zone that surrounds all surfaces in still air, the *boundary layer*, acts to transfer heat from the leaf to the cooler air. When the leaf is cooler than the air, as is typical at night, heat is transferred to the leaf from the air by convection and conduction. Through the interaction of these and other adaptations described below, the plant maintains a heat balance with its environment. These interactions tend to favor overall plant efficiency, tending to keep leaves warmer than cool air but cooler than warm air (Gates, 1965).

Plant activity and growth depend upon the availability of free water to the cells and thus are essentially limited to cellular temperatures above $0°$ C ($32°$ F). In forest trees, photosynthesis and respiration apparently can take place at air temperatures as low as $6°$ C ($10°$ F) below freezing (Freeland, 1944; Parker, 1953) because of the effect of solar and terrestrial radiation in warming the plant tissues to above-freezing temperatures.

As temperature increases, plant activities increase up to an optimum temperature and then decrease until at very high temperatures death occurs. The processes influenced most strongly by temperature are (1) the activity of enzymes that catalyze biochemical reactions, especially photosynthesis and respiration, (2) the solubility of carbon dioxide and oxygen in plant cells, (3) transpiration, and (4) the ability of roots to absorb water and minerals from the soil. Because different growth processes may require different optimum temperatures, one simply cannot characterize the growth or dry-weight production of a species by a certain optimum temperature. Actually, various phases of the temperature regime—day temperature, night temperature, heat sums, and the difference between day and night temperature (thermoperiodism)—all affect growth. Also, optimum growth requirements vary between species and populations within species and vary in a way related to the environmental conditions under which a population has evolved.

The experimental work of Hellmers and associates (1962, 1966a, 1970) and of Kramer (1957) has shown that seedlings of tree species may respond to one or more of these temperature conditions. Night temperature elicited the greatest growth response of Engelmann spruce and digger pine whereas redwood responded mainly to day temperature, reaching its maximum growth in the moderate range of 15–19° C (59–66° F). The low survival of Engelmann spruce under high day temperatures and cool nights perhaps explains in part the distribution of this species in cold climates, high altitudes, or in cold pockets and cold stream drainages at lower elevations. The finding that survival and growth of Engelmann spruce increase with increasing night temperature (Figure 4.2) seems to confirm

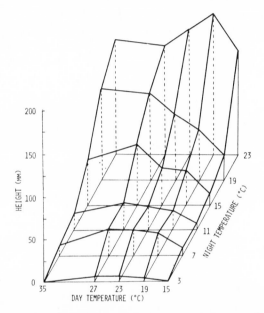

Fig. 4.2. Average height of 36 Engelmann spruce seedlings from each of 30 combinations of day and night temperature where the plants were grown for 24 weeks. (After Hellmers *et al.*, 1970.)

Wardle's (1968) suggestion that night temperature during the summer was an important factor in the survival of Engelmann spruce in Colorado. Although redwood and Engelmann spruce grew best with the same day temperature (19° C), spruce grew better under warmer nights and tolerated warmer days better than did redwood. Redwood grew best with slight differences in day-night temperature or at constant temperature, apparently reflecting the lower diurnal changes in its native coastal climate. In contrast, Engelmann spruce is apparently adapted to the greater diurnal changes of continental, mountain environments.

Several tree species are affected by total daily heat (heat sum = hours × temperature) irrespective of time of application. Although the biological significance of a heat sum is disputed, several species, including Jeffrey pine, erect cone pine, and eastern hemlock, show a marked growth response to total daily heat.

Although some species show a primary response to the heat sum, day temperature, or night temperature, many plants require nights considerably cooler than days for best growth. This reaction to various combinations of day and night temperature is termed *thermoperiod.* Low night temperatures coupled with moderate day temperatures are important in the flowering and fruit set, flavor, and quality of various crop plants and fruit trees (Treshow, 1970).

Seedlings of some forest trees respond strongly to thermoperiod. Maximum top growth of loblolly pine and Douglas-fir seedlings occurred under thermoperiods of 12° and 10° C (22° and 18° F), respectively, with night temperature colder than day temperature (Kramer, 1957; Hellmers and Sundahl, 1959).

Two effects of thermoperiod were observed for red fir (Hellmers, 1966a). First, maximum height growth on a warm day must be augmented with a cool night while a cool day must have a cold night. Second, maximum height growth was obtained when day and night differed by 13°C (23°F). The maximum growth under a 17°C (63°F) day and a 23°C (73°F) day was nearly equal. However, this growth occurred only when the cooler day was augmented by a 4°C (39°F) night and the warmer day with a 10°C (50°F) night. Not only was thermoperiod important but all four phases of the temperature regime affected growth and dry-weight production.

In contrast to the three species described above requiring cold nights and warm days, seedlings of ponderosa pine grow best with warm days and warm nights of 23°C (Larson, 1967), or with warm nights and cool days (Callaham, 1962). In the latter study the optimum growth of 6 provenances was with a thermoperiod of 5°C (9°F), with nights warmer than days. Furthermore, pines from diverse parts of the range showed significantly different responses to the temperature regime (Figure 4.3). Seedlings from east of the Rocky Mountains (Figure 4.3C) required a high night temperature for optimum growth. Seedlings from the Southwest grew remarkably fast under cold days and hot nights. Seedlings from the west slope of the Sierra Nevada Mountains in California

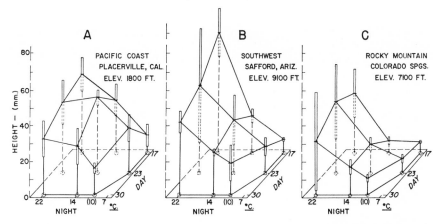

Fig. 4.3. Mean height growth of ponderosa pine progenies from three provenances in three regions. Treatment included 16-hr. days and 9 combinations of 3 day and 3 night temperatures. (The vertical bars show the range of the mean ± standard errors of the mean.) (After Callaham, 1962; from Theodore T. Kozlowski, *Tree Growth* © 1962, The Ronald Press Company.)

grew well with lower night temperature (14°C, 57°F). Root growth of ponderosa pine is more dependent on soil temperature and top growth more dependent upon air temperature (Larson, 1967). Optimum root growth occurred in 15°C (59°F) air and 23°C soil. Optimum root growth for red oak, basswood, and ash also occurs at relatively high soil temperatures (Larson, 1970).

The range of response in net photosynthesis of woody species to temperature has been demonstrated by Pisek and associates (Pisek *et al.*, 1969). Species were chosen to represent alpine, montane, and Mediterranean climates of central Europe. The high-elevation and alpine species exhibit lower temperature optima for net photosynthesis than Mediterranean and low-elevation species. The photosynthetic apparatus of the alpine species is more efficient in cold temperatures and less efficient in high temperatures than that of the Mediterranean species.

Studies with various tree species have shown that light interacts with air temperature in controlling growth rates. For example, the optimum temperature for photosynthesis is known to vary with light irradiance. Increasing temperature increases photosynthesis up to a point, and thereafter light irradiance must be raised if photosynthesis is to increase.

With increases of temperature above the optimum, the photosynthetic rate lessens. At about 30°C (86°F) many enzymes tend to become disrupted and if high temperature persists enzymes become non-functional, acting to slow growth processes. Furthermore, respiration increases greatly until at very high temperatures (perhaps 50°C, or 122°F) respiration exceeds photosynthesis. Finally, at even higher temperatures, death occurs. A number of studies (cf. Baker, 1929; Lorenz, 1939) seem to indicate that the lethal point occurs at about 55°C, or 131°F.

The temperature values referred to are those of the plant tissues themselves and not of the outside atmosphere. It stands to reason that air temperatures must be even higher to warm up the plant tissues to the lethal point. Thus prolonged exposure to air temperatures as low as 50°C may eventually induce death while the same plants might be able to withstand brief periods of exposure to outside temperatures as high as 66°C. This time factor has been demonstrated by a number of workers and is of considerable importance in seedling survival in that extremely high temperatures may be interrupted by even the lightest shade, such as is the case when cotyledons of the seedlings shade the basal portion of the seedling stem.

Leaf arrangement and orientation, a response to light intensity, may act to reduce the amount of solar energy absorbed and hence be of survival value by preventing overheating of the leaf. For example, when red maple seedlings are subjected to high light intensities the leaf blades are deflected downward until they hang in a vertical position; when shaded they return to the horizontal (Grime, 1966). Such a mechanism may explain in part why red maple is a versatile species, colonizing both dry exposed sites and shaded habitats.

Furthermore, the seedling may be able to maintain lower temperatures through the effects of transpiration and thus escape injury or maintain a better metabolic balance under very high outside temperatures. Shirley (1929) found that, for northern conifer seedlings in the Lake States, the killing temperature was higher in dry air, which favored seedling transpiration, than in moist air, which reduced it. In addition to the mechanisms of reradiation, transpiration, convection, leaf arrangement, and orientation already cited, leaf morphology, coloration, cuticle, pubescence, and degree of protein hydration may also act to enable the plant to function effectively at high temperatures (Treshow, 1970).

Since temperatures above 50°C are largely confined in forested regions to the ground-air boundary, direct heat injury in forest trees is most significant in its effect on small seedlings, which have relatively unprotected live tissues in this critical zone. However, leaves of many mature hardwoods and conifers suffer leaf damage due to water deficiency in cells, particularly along the leaf margin and the tip of conifer needles. For example, widespread leaf damage to a wide variety of woody species occurred in northern California when temperatures suddenly rose above 38°C in areas that had had an exceptionally cool spring (Treshow, 1970). Conifer needles may also exhibit a needle curl which has been reported for southern pines and lodgepole pine (Parris, 1967) and attributed to short periods of high temperatures, 37°–43°C, in the absence of moisture stress.

Cold Injury to Plants

Unlike lethal high temperatures, lethal cold temperatures occur periodically throughout the entire zone of tree growth in the temperate and boreal regions of the earth and thus affect to a greater or lesser degree the distribution and growth of trees in these zones.

Death of plant tissues, particularly of actively growing plants and succulent tissues, may occur from rapid freezing and formation of ice crystals within the protoplasm. Slow freezing also may kill many semihardy plants at temperatures of −15° to −45°C (5° to −49°F) at rates of cooling that commonly occur in nature (Weiser, 1970). According to Weiser, water between cells freezes, dehydrating cell contents until a point is reached when only "vital" water remains in the protoplasm. As temperature decreases further, vital water is pulled away from the protoplasm, initiating denaturation and ultimately causing death. In tropical plants death may occur at above-freezing temperatures ranging up to 5°C (41°F).

Most trees in the temperate and boreal zones, however, become increasingly inactive as the day length shortens and temperatures drop at the end of the growing season. As dormancy sets in, the water content of protoplasm is reduced and many species are able to survive subfreezing temperatures without damage. *Frost hardiness* is a function of this decreased moisture content and is developed by natural selection, so that local races of a given tree species are usually able to withstand normal cold periods in their locality. For example, Parker (1955) has shown that ponderosa pine and lowland white fir develop hardiness slowly in late summer and early autumn, with the final stages of hardiness developing rapidly when the temperature reaches near or below freezing for several nights. During January, needles of these species were able to withstand temperatures of at least −55°C (−67°F) without damage. Moreover, if the freezing rate to −30°C (−22°F) is relatively slow, numerous hardy species are known to withstand temperatures of −196°C (−323°F) (Weiser, 1970). The extreme of cold resistance is exhibited by the seeds of certain pine and spruce species which cannot be frozen at any normally occurring temperature when in a dry, dormant condition.

Acclimation or hardening are terms used to describe the change of plants from a succulent (tender) to a hardy or dormant condition. Three stages of dormancy are ordinarily recognized (Vegis, 1964; Perry, 1971): early rest (predormancy), winter rest (true dormancy), and afterrest (postdormancy). Short days act as an early warning system triggering growth cessation and initiating metabolic changes characteristic of the early rest or first stage of acclimation (Weiser, 1970; Figures 4.4 and 4.5). These changes facilitate further plant response in the second stage of acclimation (also accompanied by metabolic changes) that is triggered by frost (Figures 4.4 and 4.5). The final or third stage of acclimation and attainment of true dormancy is a purely physical process and is induced by low temperatures of −30° to −50°C. Truly dormant buds and seeds cannot be induced to immediate normal growth by any means. However, some species, birches, European beech, and some oaks, do not show true dormancy and hence pass readily from early rest to afterrest.

Buds and seeds of many woody species require a period of winter chilling or stratification (seeds) before growth is resumed in the spring. Temperatures near 5°C (41°F) are most effective (Perry, 1971). The nature of dormancy and the chilling requirement may vary with the local race of the species. For example, red maples from New York State attain true dormancy and require a month or more of chilling before resuming active growth (Perry and Wang, 1960). Red maples in south Florida cease active growth, drop their leaves but are unable to withstand freezing temperatures, and have no chilling requirement. As the afterrest period proceeds,

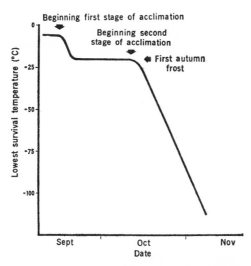

Fig. 4.4. A typical seasonal pattern of cold resistance in the living bark of red-osier dogwood *(Cornus stolonifera)* stems in Minnesota. In nature, acclimation in this hardy shrub and in a number of other woody species proceeds in two distinct stages as shown. The beginning of the second stage of acclimation characteristically coincides with the first autumn frost. (After Weiser, 1970.)

physiological changes take place enabling growth to resume once minimum-temperature and sometimes day-length requirements are met. An excellent review of acclimation is available (Weiser, 1970), and winter dormancy has been considered in detail by numerous authors (Romberger, 1963; Vegis, 1964; Wareing, 1956, 1969; Perry, 1971).

Life Forms

The importance of survival during the unfavorable periods has led to ecological classifications of life forms based upon the dormant condition of the plant under climatic conditions unsuitable for growth. The basic classification into evergreens, deciduous plants, perennials, and annuals is so well accepted that we almost forget it is a classification at all, so thoroughly have the terms been integrated into our vocabulary and thinking.

This classification was elaborated and systematized in 1907 by Raunkiaer (1937), who has suggested terms which have become widely accepted by ecologists. *Phanerophytes* include all plants, both evergreen and deciduous, in which the dormant buds are in

THE TIME	SPRING	SUMMER	EARLY AUTUMN	LATE AUTUMN	WINTER
THE PLANT	GROWING RAPIDLY	GROWING SLOWLY — FLOWERING - FRUITING	GROWTH SLOWS -- Photosynthates accumulate / GROWTH STOPS --- Rest period induced	LEAVES DROP — DORMANT	DORMANT
THE ENVIRONMENT	LENGTHENING DAYS ↓ RISING TEMPERATURES	LONG DAYS ↓ WARM TEMPERATURES	WARM DAYS — COOL NIGHTS	SHORT DAYS	PROLONGED SUB - FREEZING TEMPERATURE
ACCLIMATION — BIOCHEMICAL EVENTS	(HARDINESS INHIBITOR(S) PRODUCED IN LEAVES)	(HARDINESS INHIBITOR(S) PRODUCED IN LEAVES)	SHORTENING DAYS → PHYTOCHROME P_R ⇄ P_{FR} → (HARDINESS PROMOTER(S) SYNTHESIZED) → DNA DEREPRESSION →	(SYNTHESIS AND/OR INDUCTION OF ENZYMES) ← FROST → FROST INDUCED PROTEIN REARRANGEMENTS exposing new surfaces (ACTIVE METABOLIC CHANGES)	

108

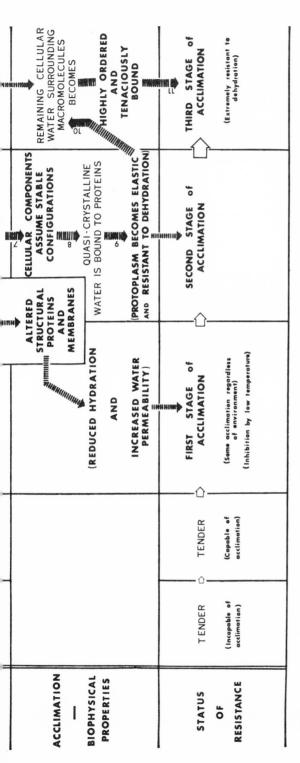

Fig. 4.5. A hypothesis to explain cold acclimation in hardy woody plants. Numbered arrows indicate the hypothetical sequence of events resulting in the most efficient and complete acclimation. Arrows without numbers identify sequential relationships and alternate acclimation pathways. Parentheses denote events which can be observed experimentally. (After Weiser, 1970.)

the atmosphere. All trees, of course, fall within this category. In *Chamaephytes,* the surviving buds are situated close to the ground; in *Hemicryptophytes,* the buds pass the unfavorable season in the soil surface, protected by the soil itself and by litter; while in *Cryptophytes,* the buds survive completely concealed in the ground or at the bottom of the water. Finally, the *Therophytes,* or annuals, complete their life cycle within a single favorable season and remain dormant in the form of seed throughout unfavorable periods.

Present-day plant ecologists have studied the correlations between the life-form spectra (i.e., percentage of plants in each of Raunkiaer's life forms) of plant communities and their distribution. In addition to their method of surviving unfavorable weather periods, so many factors affect the distribution of plants that such correlations as are found are generally weak; they usually end up merely confirming the fact that, the more severe the climate in the unfavorable period, the better adapted for survival are plants that lie dormant during this period in the seed or under the ground.

SUMMARY

Mean air temperature at a given place is a function of the incoming solar insolation modified by heat transfer from terrestrial radiation. The air heated by the sun during the day is kept relatively warm during the night by reradiation from the earth. The great capacity of large bodies of water to absorb solar energy and to reradiate it slowly and steadily results in greatly modified temperature extremes on lands subject to winds that have passed over the water. Thus the coastal areas of western North America and western Europe show little variation in temperature between day and night and not too great a contrast between winter and summer. Contrasted to such maritime climates are continental climates in the interiors of continents where temperature changes are extreme between day and night and summer and winter.

The major focal planes of temperature variation are the lines of contact between the atmosphere and the ground surface, and the atmosphere and the tree-crown surface. The forest floor or bare soil heats greatly under sunlight and cools rapidly at night through terrestrial thermal radiation. The heat conductivity of surface materials determines the temperature realized at the contact surface. Wet surfaces, a moist forest floor or leaf cells, are cooled by the process of evaporation in which heat energy is utilized. Various plant characters such as leaf orientation, morphology, and color may act to reduce the amount of heat energy absorbed.

Local topography, even that created by the top surface of the forest, may exert a great influence on air temperature. Low concave surfaces tend to radiate heat rapidly on still, cold nights and to accumulate cold air which flows in from surrounding higher land. As a result, such sites will frequently have air temperatures near the ground as much as 8°C lower than those above surrounding land. These low-lying areas—often termed frost pockets—typically have a shorter growing season than adjacent convex land forms which exhibit higher night and lower day temperatures than the concave forms. Mean annual air temperature decreases with increasing distance from the Equator and with increasing elevation. The rate of decrease, however, varies with the general climate of the region, especially as influenced by continental air masses, oceans, and other large bodies of water. Mean annual temperature shows gradual changes with time. The warming trend in the last part of the nineteenth century and first part of the twentieth century produced a rise of mean annual temperature in the eastern United States of about 1.7°C.

Plants regulate their temperature by dissipating part of the energy they absorb and thus preventing excessive heat accumulation and death; the three major mechanisms are reradiation, transpiration, and convection. Other mechanisms, such as leaf orientation, arrangement, coloration, and pubescence, allow the plant to function at high temperatures. When leaves are cooler than air temperature they may be warmed by the combined effect of convection and conduction.

Temperature strongly affects plant growth through its influence on plant biochemical reactions, transpiration, and the ability of roots to absorb water and nutrients. Tree species respond to different kinds of temperature conditions, some exhibiting maximum growth under high day temperatures while others grow best under conditions of high night temperature. Optimum growth of many plants occurs in fluctuating temperatures where day and night temperatures differ widely (*thermoperiod*). However, different growth processes require different optimum temperatures, and one cannot characterize height growth or dry-weight production of a species by a certain optimum temperature. Temperature requirements for growth vary among species and among races within species and are related to the genetic differentiation of a population under particular temperature conditions.

Plant activity and growth depend upon the availability of free water to plant cells, and this is essentially limited to cellular temperatures above freezing. Frost hardiness or acclimation is the change of plants from a succulent, growing stage to a hardy, dormant condition. These changes are initiated by shortening of day length in the fall. Frost brings on a second stage of acclimation causing further reductions in the water content of the protoplasm. Still lower temperatures bring on true winter dormancy, in which most buds or seeds cannot be induced to immediate normal growth by any means. However, not all woody species attain true dormancy. Before growth is resumed in the spring the shoots, roots, and seeds of many woody species require a period of winter chilling, the length of which depends on the local race of the species and the climatic conditions in which it has evolved.

SUGGESTED READINGS

GATES, D. M. 1965. Heat transfer in plants. *Sci. Amer.* 213:76–84.

HELLMERS, HENRY. 1962. Temperature effect on optimum tree growth. *In* T. T. KOZLOWSKI (ed.), *Tree Growth.* The Ronald Press Co., New York.

LOWRY, WILLIAM P. 1969. *Weather and Life, An Introduction to Biometeorology.* (Chapter 3, Environmental temperature, pp. 31–63.) Academic Press, Inc., New York.

PARKER, J. 1963. Cold resistance in woody plants. *Bot. Rev.* 29:123–201.

TRESHOW, MICHAEL. 1970. *Environment and Plant Response.* (Chapter 5, Temperature mechanisms, pp. 51–62; Chapter 6, Disorders associated with high temperatures, pp. 63–76; Chapter 7, Disorders associated with low temperatures, pp. 77–98.) McGraw-Hill Book Co., Inc., New York.

VEGIS, A. 1964. Dormancy in higher plants. *Ann. Rev. Plant Phys.* 15:185–224.

WAREING, P. F. 1956. Photoperiodism in woody plants. *Ann. Rev. Plant Phys.* 7:191–214.

———. 1969. Germination and dormancy. *In* MALCOLM B. WILKINS (ed.), *Physiology of Plant Growth and Development.* McGraw-Hill Book Co., Inc., New York.

WEISER, C. J. 1970. Cold resistance and injury in woody plants. *Science* 169:1269–1278.

WILSON, B. F. 1970. *The Growing Tree.* (Elongation and dormancy, pp. 47–67.) Univ. Mass. Press, Amherst. 152 pp.

5

Atmospheric Moisture
and Other Factors

Water is the inorganic substance most needed by plants and is present in plants in large amounts. The principal source of the water that reaches the tree is, of course, the soil, and soil moisture is treated in a later chapter. The amount of moisture in the atmosphere is important, however, because it is the source of most soil moisture, and in addition it affects the rate of water loss from the leaves through transpiration. Also, water may be supplied directly to the aerial portions of the plant through dew and other pathways.

Precipitation as such is not a factor directly influencing the growth of the plant under most conditions. Rain, snow, and other forms of precipitation are indirectly of the greatest importance in recharging soil moisture and thus influence plant growth indirectly through their effect on the soil. Situations do arise, though, where precipitation directly influences plant growth, and various types of precipitation—particularly snow, glaze, and sleet—are important causes of damage to trees. Because of the great importance of precipitation, even though its principal effect on plant growth is indirect, it must be accorded discussion at this point.

Nomenclature of Water Vapor

Water is always present in the atmosphere in the form of water vapor. The actual weight of water present per unit volume of air is termed the *absolute humidity,* while the percentage of vapor present relative to the maximum quantity that the air can hold is termed *relative humidity.* The vapor-holding capacity of the air is greatly affected by temperature. At 80°F, the air can hold twice as much water as it can at 60°F. In other words, the absolute humidity at 80° is twice that at 60° when the relative humidity is 100 percent at both temperatures.

Since the weight or pressure exerted by a given mass of air is increased as water vapor is added to it, absolute humidity can be measured in terms of *vapor pressure,* usually expressed in inches of mercury. Thus, saturated air at 60°F will elevate a mercury column 0.5220 inch over its height in vapor-free air; while at 80°F, with twice as much water being held by the saturated air, the elevation will be 1.0334 inches, or twice as much as at 60°.

The difference between the actual vapor pressure and the vapor pressure of saturated air at the same temperature is termed the *vapor pressure gradient,* and is a measure of the absolute amount of moisture that can be taken up by the air at that temperature. Thus, when the relative humidity is 70 percent and the air temperature is 80°F, the vapor pressure is 0.70 × 1.0334, or 0.7234 inch, and the vapor pressure gradient is 1.0334 − 0.7234, or 0.3100 inch.

Exchange of Water Vapor Between the Plant and Atmosphere

From the standpoint of tree growth, atmospheric moisture is important in changing the water relations of the plant tissues. Moisture will move from the plant into the atmosphere when the vapor pressure of the plant is greater than that of the atmosphere. This is the normal daytime situation when it is not raining. Moisture may also move from the atmosphere to the plant when the vapor pressures are reversed, as during a rain or when dew covers a plant that is not fully turgid. There is no exchange of water vapor between the plant and the atmosphere when the vapor pressures are equal as occurs when the air in both is saturated with water and the temperatures are the same within the plant and in the atmosphere, often the situation at night.

The actual rate of water movement is proportional to the vapor pressure gradient between the plant and the atmosphere. This, in turn, depends in large measure upon a thin layer of air surrounding the leaves, the thickness of which depends upon the wind velocity. Since the air within the leaf is normally saturated under growing conditions, vapor will normally move out from the leaves into the surrounding air unless the outside air is also saturated at the same or higher air temperature. Transpiration results. Even if the air is at 95-percent relative humidity, transpiration takes place. In the absence of actual precipitation, arid conditions and even deserts can develop in regions of characteristically high humidities. Braun-Blanquet (1964) cites as an example the dry cactoid-euphorbia-scrub along the coast of southern Morocco where the summer relative humidities average 90 percent.

The rate of transpiration, however, is directly dependent upon plant and air temperatures, relative humidity of the air, and air movement affecting the thickness of the air blanket surrounding leaf surfaces. The drier the air and the greater the air turbulence, the higher will be the rate of water loss, assuming that soil moisture is available.

Since the epidermis of many leaves and most fruits, stems, and other aerial organs is cutinized to a greater or lesser extent, most of the exchange of water vapor between the plant and the atmosphere takes place through the stomata. The rate of exchange, therefore, is further modified by the opening and closing of these stomata. Transpiration is similar to evaporation except that the movement of water vapor from plant cells is controlled to a substantial degree by leaf resistances that are not involved in evaporation. The cuticle and the stomata are the chief sites of leaf resistances.

Although most of the movement of water vapor is from the plant out into the atmosphere, the direction of movement may be reversed when the plant air has a lower vapor pressure than the outside air. This condition occurs during rains when the plant previously has been subjected to desiccating conditions, or more commonly occurs when the atmosphere is warmer than the plant tissues, resulting in the formation of dew on plant surfaces (Stone *et al.*, 1956).

Transpiration is the dominant process in water relations of plants because it provides the energy gradient that causes the movement of water into and through plants. Furthermore, transpiration causes water deficits to develop in the plant that may result in growth reduction or death. These and other aspects of transpiration are discussed in Chapter 9.

Precipitation of Water Vapor

The discussion of atmospheric moisture to this point has dealt with water vapor and its movement between the plant and the air. Equally important is precipitated water vapor—the main source of moisture upon which plant growth depends.

To summarize briefly the nomenclature and mode of formation of precipitation, precipitation occurs when warm moist air is cooled below the point of its water-holding capacity. This cooling may result from currents of air rising to higher elevations as occurs when cold air masses wedge under warmer air, or when warm air rides up over cold air (warm front); it occurs when moist air rises over warm land surfaces (convectional precipitation) and when air currents rise over elevated land masses (orographic precipitation).

If the condensation takes place below the freezing point, *snow* is formed; above the freezing point, *rain* ensues. Rain that freezes as it falls through subfreezing air layers becomes *hail* or *sleet;* if it freezes as it falls on a subfreezing surface, it forms *ice* or *glaze.*

Condensed water vapor in particles sufficiently small to remain suspended in the air forms *clouds* above the ground or fog in the layer of air near the ground. Finally, condensation of water vapor directly onto cooled surfaces gives rise to *dew.*

As has been pointed out previously, the greatest importance of precipitation to trees is not a direct one, but rather the indirect dependence of soil moisture supply upon replenishment by precipitation. The physical impact of precipitation, particularly glaze and snow, upon trees is a principal source of damage to forests. Indeed, in many areas, it is the most important factor determining the practicality of growing timber.

In a forest, much of the rainfall is intercepted by the crowns, whence it may drip to the ground, flow down the stems to the ground, be evaporated into the air, or be absorbed by the leaf surfaces. Reviews of interception studies conducted in the United States (Zinke, 1967) and elsewhere (Penman, 1963; Molchanov, 1963) indicate that forests often intercept a significant proportion of the annual precipitation ($\cong$ 20 percent). A few examples will indicate the results from typical interception studies: In second-growth ponderosa pine in California studied for a six-year period, the average annual precipitation was 47 inches, of which 84 percent reached the floor by penetration or drip and 4 percent through stem flow, leaving 12 percent that was intercepted and either absorbed by the foliage or evaporated (Rowe and Hendrix, 1951). In a young loblolly pine plantation in South Carolina, rainfall under the forest was only 86 percent of that in the open (14 percent being intercepted), with about one-fifth of the rainfall reaching the ground as stem flow (Hoover, 1953). In very light rains, as much as 93 percent may be retained by the crowns, while in heavy downpours as little as 6 percent may be intercepted (Ovington, 1954).

Deciduous species are reported to be similar in their ability to intercept rainfall during the growing season; conifers intercept more precipitation than deciduous species (Zinke, 1967). In a German example, the mean annual interception for European beech and Norway spruce was 7.6 and 26.0 percent, respectively (Eidman, 1959). In this study, more summer rainfall reached the forest floor through stem flow in beech stands (16.5 percent) than in spruce stands (0.7 percent).

There are few data available as to what proportion of the rainfall intercepted by the crowns actually enters the foliage and is utilized. Much evidence is accumulating, on the other hand, that the rain hitting the tree crowns actually removes substantial amounts of mineral nutrients and organic substances from the foliage and twigs.

Rain and Snow and the Forest

The amount and distribution of rainfall is related to meteorological conditions, season of year, topography, and many other factors. It may even be related in some local circumstances to the presence and structure of forests. For example, in the fume-denuded Copper Basin of eastern Tennessee, four-year (1936–1939) records were kept at two stations each in forest clearings (mean annual precipitation 57.4 inches), grassland (52.8 inches), and denuded land (50.3 inches). Hursh (1948) concluded that the forests in the area had a slight but statistically significant effect in raising the amount of precipitation. However, meteorologists now believe forest cover cannot exert any significant, large-scale influence on the amount of precipitation (Penman, 1963); increases brought about by the presence of forests are smaller than the errors in rainfall measurements (Stanhill, 1970).

The problem of measuring rainfall in the forest is complicated by the variability of precipitation from place to place, especially on rugged terrain (Hamilton, 1954), the effect of the clearing in which the rain gauge is placed upon local precipitation and catch, and the necessity of shielding rain gauges to reduce air eddies around the orifice. Because of the high variability in rainfall from place to place and from time to time, precipitation records from standard meteorological stations will only roughly approximate the rainfall in a given forest.

In the case of precipitation occurring as snow rather than as rain, interception is apt to be greater, but much of the snow intercepted will eventually drop off onto the ground (Hoover and Leaf, 1967), thus increasing the total amount of water that reaches the soil under the forest. For example, Kittredge (1953) found that from 13 to 27 percent of the seasonal snowfall on the west slope of the Sierra Nevada was intercepted by the forest canopies; but Rowe and Hendrix (1951), also working in California, found that an average of 4 percent more precipitation reached the forest floor during snow than during rain storms. In any event, it may be assumed that little snow moisture is directly absorbed by tree foliage.

Fog and Dew and the Forest

The interrelationship between condensed moisture and trees has been the subject of much speculation. Fog and dew may well be quite important in determining the growth and distribution of forests, but the extent and mechanism of the effect have proved difficult to demonstrate in precise experimentation. In addition to reducing transpiration losses, there can be no doubt that forests can condense appreciable amounts of moisture from fog—and also that appreciable amounts of moisture can be condensed on tree foliage during the night through dew formation. Whatever portion of this condensed moisture falls to the ground through fog drip or dew drip may be added to the soil and thus indirectly benefit the forest.

There is an obvious correlation in many parts of the earth between the distribution of certain trees and the presence of fog belts. Perhaps the most spectacular example occurs along the Pacific Coast of the United States and Canada where Sitka spruce (from Oregon north) and redwood (in California) characterize the very dense and fast-growing temperate rain forest (Figure 5.1).

The fact that the coastal zone of heavy summer fog more or less coincides with the Sitka spruce and redwood ranges, however, does not prove that a cause-and-effect relationship necessarily exists

Fig. 5.1. Redwood forest along California's coastal fog belt with luxuriant understory vegetation. (U. S. Forest Service photo.)

between the fog and the tree distribution, although such a relationship has been categorically stated on many occasions. The coastal zone differs climatically in many ways from adjacent forest zones, not only for its heavy summer fogs, but for its heavy winter rains and the general oceanic climate with little cold or hot weather but rather equable temperatures throughout the year. Furthermore, the summer fog itself may affect the tree climate in many ways. It may well have a direct effect in supplying summer moisture. In addition, however, it also has indirect effects in reducing the hours of summer sunshine, in reducing the summer daytime temperatures (Byers, 1953), and in increasing the supply of carbon dioxide (Wilson, 1948). Obviously, the relationship between fog and tree growth is too complex to conclude that redwood and Sitka spruce must owe their survival to the moisture-giving powers of summer fog along this coast.

Let us examine the actual evidence on hand. In the first place, there is no question but that forests can remove moisture from the air through condensing it from incoming fog. Fog may be collected and condensed by tree crowns and dripped to the ground in appreciable quantities when no moisture is caught by rain gauges in the open. For example, Isaac (1946) found that, on a ridge two miles from the Pacific Ocean in the Oregon fog belt, precipitation was one-quarter greater under trees than in the open because of fog drip; while in a valley five miles inland, precipitation was one-third less under the forest due to interception. In the San Francisco peninsula, Oberlander (1956) recorded up to 58.8 inches of fog drip under five trees during a rainless period of 40 days in mid-summer. In detailed studies of the "fog-preventing forest zone" on the southeast coast of Hokkaido (Hori, 1953), it was found that the forest could remove 300 gallons of moisture per acre of surface per hour under standardized conditions of fog density and wind movement. Under similar conditions, grassland captured not more than one-sixth to one-tenth this amount. The windward vertical edge of the forest captured as much fog water as a horizontal surface three times as large in area. At approximately 3,800 feet in the Bavarian Mountains of southern Germany, Baumgartner (1958) reported that 42 percent of the yearly total precipitation of 80 inches was received as fog. In the Green Mountains of northern Vermont a screened gauge, simulating the effect of coniferous needles in intercepting and collecting cloud droplets, collected 67 percent more water than an unscreened gauge (Vogelmann *et al.*, 1968). The needle-like foliage and twiggy character of the spruce-fir forests (above 2,500 feet) serve as effective mechanical collectors of wind-driven cloud droplets. A detailed review of mist precipitation and vegetation was given by Kerfoot (1968).

In arid and semi-arid regions, foliar absorption of water condensed as dew occurs primarily at night. Literature on the value of dew as a survival factor has been reviewed by Stone (1957) and found to be conflicting in the conclusions drawn by various investigators. The unanswered question is how much of this condensed moisture enters directly into leaves and benefits plants in this way.

In some studies it has been shown that water is taken up by branches in appreciable amounts, particularly through dew formation at night. For example, Gates (1914) found that severed black spruce and tamarack branches when exposed to moist air in Michigan summer conditions could take up moisture amounting to a 6-percent increase in weight in 4.5 hours. Later experiments by others confirm that considerable moisture may enter plants through either fog condensation or dew condensation. For ponderosa pine in the greenhouse, Stone and Fowells (1955) found that a fine mist, simulating dew, applied at night doubled the survival period of seedlings in soil dried to the wilting point. Artificial mists at night increased the survival of ponderosa pine, incense cedar, and white fir seedlings (but not of Jeffrey pine) although death ultimately occurred for all (Stone, 1957).

Geographical Variation in Precipitation

As with air temperature, precipitation varies with latitude and altitude. The distribution of precipitation over the face of the earth, however, depends primarily upon the interrelationships between air currents and large water bodies. The heaviest precipitation occurs when air currents passing over water bodies come into contact with cooler land masses or are caused to rise by elevated land masses, becoming cooler in the process. On windward coasts, over one hundred inches of rainfall per year are normal in such forest regions as the Pacific northwest of the United States and Canada, Hawaii, New Zealand, and India. To the leeward of major mountain ranges, *rainshadows* occur over which warming air currents depleted of moisture drop little on the land surface.

Elevated mountain masses, by causing air to rise, cause it also to cool, thereby increasing precipitation. Such orographic rainfall is essentially local, falling immediately on the windward side of the elevated land mass.

Precipitation, therefore, is not closely correlated with elevation above sea level as such. A major topographic feature such as the Mogollon Rim in Arizona may receive considerably more precipitation than is indicated by its altitude of 7,000 or so feet, while points on the Mogollon Mesa at the same elevation but remote from the rim may receive substantially less precipitation. An isolated mountain induces relatively slight orographic precipitation.

In very high mountains, the maximum precipitation is commonly reached somewhere along the slope, the air currents becoming too depleted of moisture to provide as much precipitation at higher elevations. Precipitation patterns are particularly affected by air currents and mountain barriers. Along the Pacific Coast, mean annual precipitation at the lower elevations increases sharply with altitude, at rates varying from 15 to 20 inches per thousand feet in the coastal range of Washington to 8 to 10 inches in the Sierra Nevada. The maximum precipitation occurs at the middle elevations—ranging from perhaps 3,000 feet in the Olympics to 5,000 feet in northern California and 8,000 feet in the southern Sierra Nevada. Above this elevation, precipitation decreases with altitude. East of the coastal mountain barrier in the mountains of the interior, the effect of elevation on rainfall is much more predictable, being approximately 4 to 5 inches per 1,000-foot rise in elevation (range 3,000 to 5,000 feet). These values seem to hold from the east side of the Cascade–Sierra Nevada east through the Rockies, and from Canada south to Mexico.

Carbon Dioxide

Although solar energy, including light and heat, and atmospheric moisture are the principal climatic factors affecting the distribution and growth of forest trees, other climatic factors must also be considered. Among these, the carbon dioxide content of the atmosphere, wind, atmospheric pollutants, and lightning exhibit the most important direct effects upon forest trees and are treated in the present chapter.

Carbon dioxide is present in low concentrations in the atmosphere, is required in large amounts for photosynthesis, and is given off in large quantities in both plant and animal respiration. Because of these factors, the amount of the gas in the air at any one time varies from time to time and from place to place. On the average, the air contains about 0.03 percent carbon dioxide by volume (0.57 mg per liter of air) but daily variations of 10 to 400 percent of this amount occur commonly. Rain and fog substantially increase the carbon dioxide content of the air (Wilson, 1948; Selm, 1952).

Carbon dioxide is being evolved continually by respiration of living organisms. The carbon dioxide level is therefore usually high in damp, calm air near the forest floor, where organic-matter decay by soil organisms is actively taking place. In such situations, the carbon dioxide percentage may rise to 0.18 percent by volume of the air (Fuller, 1948). Because respiration takes place during the night when photosynthesis ceases, and because of the prevalence of moist and calm air conditions during the night, carbon dioxide concentrations in the forest reach their highest levels toward the end of this period. However, the natural variation of CO_2 concentration at the crown level during the daylight hours, at most ±25 ppm, is not enough to influence photosynthesis significantly (Koch, 1969).

Photosynthesis requires large quantities of carbon dioxide that must be assimilated by trees from the atmosphere. Baker (1950) estimates that 12 tons of the gas are needed to generate the annual dry-matter production on an average productive acre of forest, more carbon dioxide than is present above that acre at any one time. It is obvious, therefore, that the carbon dioxide requirements of trees can be met only through the circulation of carbon dioxide in the ecosystem from oceans and land sources far removed from the local forest together with the rapid return of the gas from organic respiration and the circulation of this to the leaves through air movement. It follows that the carbon dioxide level in the forest will be lowest during the periods of maximum photosynthesis, i.e., at midday during the height of the growing season. Such appears to be the case (Mitscherlich et al., 1963).

The amount of carbon dioxide in the air surrounding tree crowns (from 0.03 to 0.04 percent) definitely limits photosynthesis. At such relatively low concentrations, photosynthesis tends to vary linearly with the carbon dioxide concentration (Decker, 1947). As CO_2 concentration is increased under artificially controlled conditions, the rate of increase of photosynthesis becomes less. After reaching a peak at from 5 to 8 times the normal concentration, photosynthesis decreases for various tree species, including Norway spruce, Scots pine, European silver fir, European beech, and European cottonwood. At the optimum concentration photosynthesis is increased up to 3½ times the normal rate (Koch, 1969; Stålfelt, 1924). According to Koch, closure of stomata at increasing levels of CO_2 above the normal concentration eventually causes photosynthesis to decrease.

Despite the fact that carbon dioxide content in the atmosphere apparently limits photosynthesis in tree leaves, it is difficult to see how this factor can be improved by silvicultural management. Nevertheless, the higher carbon dioxide content of moist, calm air may be related to the growth of forests under such conditions.

Wind

The turbulence and movement of air has many effects on the distribution and growth of tree species: (1) Air movement regulates in large measure evapotranspiration from leaf surfaces, thus exerting a major influence on the water regime of the plant and at the same time helping cool the leaves. (2) Air movement circulates the small quantities of carbon dioxide in the air to the leaf surfaces, making possible photosynthesis, and may also circulate salt and atmospheric pollutants that may damage or destroy forest and agricultural crops. (3) A minor biological effect of wind is the increased illumination within the forest resulting from the twisting and turning of foliage. (4) Continued winds from a single direction will exert a strong influence upon the morphology and size of tree crowns. (5) Sway caused by the wind will influence both the form of the tree, making for short boles and excessive taper, and the quality of the wood (Jacobs, 1955). (6) Wind is a major cause of breakage, windthrow, and subsequent mortality of stems. (7) Finally, wind is essential in the dissemination of pollen and seed for many forest species.

Air movement is deflected to a large extent by the exterior surfaces of a forest stand. Furthermore, movement near these surfaces is slowed by friction. It follows that wind velocity decreases with decreasing height above the stand and becomes markedly less within the stand. Wind velocity as affected by forest stands has been summarized for four separate studies by Reifsnyder (1955; Figure 5.2). Wind velocity is slowed in the vicinity of the crown and becomes negligible within the stand. In the case of forest clear of understory, however, wind velocity is somewhat higher in the trunk zone than near the ground or in the region of the tree crowns. In comparison, grass and brush vegetation affect wind velocity only through air friction on their surfaces, and this effect is marked only in the zone 10 to 20 feet above the vegetation (Fons, 1940). The small amount of air movement within a stand is indicated by a study in

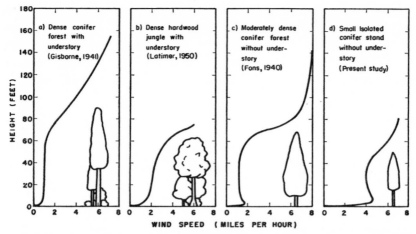

Fig. 5.2. Comparative wind profiles for four forest stands. (After Reifsnyder, 1955.)

a dense aspen stand in Utah, 12 feet in height (Marston, 1956). Over the summer, the mean wind velocity was only 1.76 miles per hour in comparison with 4.10 miles per hour in a clearing 70 by 200 feet in size. German research summarized by Geiger indicates that clearings in dense forests set up eddies that frequently reverse the prevailing wind within the clearing, while thinned stands will pass the air in the same direction as the prevailing wind but at a much slower rate.

Biologically, the chief importance of wind is its effect on evapotranspiration. When a plant is exposed to wind, leaf-water deficits develop more readily than in sheltered locations. A tree making all its development in an environment leading to water deficits will differ physiologically, morphologically, and anatomically from a tree sheltered from the exposure effects. The desiccating effect of wind on forests is demonstrated vividly in the dwarfed and deformed vegetation along windward ocean shores or in windswept mountain areas. The effects may be important economically within the forest. For example, on the north coast of Puerto Rico, the average growth is nearly twice as rapid on the west-facing leeward slope as on the east-facing windward slope (U.S. Tropical Forest Experiment Station, 1951).

It should not be assumed, however, that the drying effect of wind is the sole reason for such conditions. The mechanical shearing ac-

tion of snow is a chief factor in the development of the flag form
of many trees at timberline, where the prostrate portions are protected by a cover of snow in the winter months (Figure 5.3). The
prostrate tree form, termed *krummholz*, is a type of forest characteristic of alpine regions.

Fig. 5.3. Prostrate and erect forms of Engelmann spruce on the Snowy
Range, Medicine Bow National Forest, Wyoming. Snow driven by wind above
the winter snow line is responsible for keeping most trees sheared. (U. S.
Forest Service photo.)

In the critical stage of forest establishment, wind may be a crucial
factor, particularly for broadleaved species, for example black walnut
seedlings (Schneider *et al.*, 1970). Seedlings grown on level, windswept, open-field sites had less vigorous growth, reduced leaf area,
and greater foliage damage than those in forest openings or protected fields where similar soil conditions prevailed.

From a forest management viewpoint, wind is chiefly important
because of its great destructive potentialities. Few forests can stand
the devastating wind velocities and low air pressures of a hurricane
or tornado. In fact, such cyclonic storms have affected the forests
of much of the eastern half of the United States. In New England,
a region formerly considered relatively free from destructive wind-

storms, it is now known that occasional hurricanes and tornadoes have periodically blown down much of the older forests of the region.

Over and above the great destruction from major windstorms, however, is the immense amount of breakage and fall due to lesser winds, particularly around the edges of small holes, clearings, and cuttings in the forest. Local acceleration of wind due to the conformation of topography, the forest profile, and cutting boundaries may result in windfall under conditions where the unobstructed wind velocity is only moderate. Through the proper planning of harvest cuttings, windfall from these causes may be minimized. Indeed, much of the reason for the different silvicultural systems evolved in Germany and in the United States lies in the necessity for making partial cuts that will leave the residual stand as windfirm as possible. Often this involves cutting successive strips to eliminate vulnerable leeward boundaries by progressive cutting into the wind.

The prevailing direction of the *high velocity* winds must be known before any intelligent planning of cutting can be done. This is not necessarily the prevailing direction of *all* winds, and frequently cannot be determined from meteorological records. It can be determined, however, from existing windfalls. For instance, a tally of windfalls in the Fraser Experimental Forest in the Rocky Mountains of Colorado (Alexander and Buell, 1955) showed that most trees fell in an easterly direction, indicating that the destructive prevailing westerly winds were but little affected by the high mountain range four miles to the east or by local topography within the experimental forest.

The practical problems of wind behavior in mountainous forested country have been summarized by Gratkowski (1956) and Alexander (1964), who found that much windfall is due to local acceleration of wind currents by either topography or forest borders. Such acceleration can take place where the wind is speeded up (1) on ridge tops, upper slopes, the shoulders of a mountain, (2) on gradual and smooth lee slopes during severe windstorms, (3) in gaps and saddles of main ridges, (4) in narrow valleys or V-shaped openings in the forest that constrict the wind channel, and (5) where forest borders and cutting edges deflect wind currents, resulting in increased velocities where the deflected currents join others (Figure 5.4). The size of the clearing in the forest seems to be less important than its configuration.

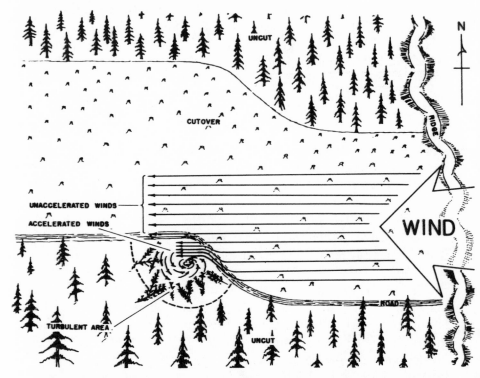

Fig. 5.4. Windthrow of standing timber following a harvest cut. A change in the direction of the cutting boundary that was parallel to the prevailing winds acts to funnel wind into standing timber, causing a pocket of blowdown. Routt National Forest, northwestern Colorado. (After Alexander, 1964.)

Windthrow is most apt to occur where the concentration of air currents causes high velocities at a particular spot. It occurs primarily in shallow-rooted species on shallow soils and those with impeded drainage. Thus it is possible to identify high-risk species, black spruce and Norway spruce for example, and high-risk sites (Godwin, 1968; Pyatt, 1968).

Atmospheric Pollutants

Civilization and industrialization have brought ever-increasing destruction of vegetation through diverse kinds of air pollutants. For at least 2,000 years sulphur dioxide has been evolved from the smelting of iron and copper ores, and emissions from coal burning, now accounting for approximately 60 percent of the pollution (Rohrman and Ludwig, 1965), have added to the problem. Treshow (1970) reviewed the major pollutants, sulphur dioxide, fluoride, ozone, harmful components of smog, and chlorine, as well as other, lesser-known pollutants, their effects on forest and agriculture species, and the relative resistance of many tree species to pollutants.

Smelter-fume pollution may cause striking patterns of vegetation damage, and sulphur fallout may change markedly the acidity of lakes near the source (Gorham and Gordon, 1960a; Gordon and Gorham, 1963). In a northern Ontario locality, vegetation was severely damaged by sulphur dioxide emissions downwind of an iron smelter (Figure 5.5). The number of species per 40-meter quadrat declined from 20–40 to 0–1 species between 10 and 2 miles from the pollution source (Figure 5.6). Along a northeast transect, seedlings of eastern white pine were not observed within 30 miles of the plant and those of white spruce, black spruce, and trembling aspen were not found within 15 miles.

Broadleaved species are generally more fume resistant than conifers. In their studies in Ontario, Gordon and Gorham (1963) found red maple, sugar maple, mountain maple, and red-berried elder (*Sambucus pubens*) quite fume tolerant. Highly sensitive conifers include western larch, Douglas-fir, ponderosa pine, and Engelmann spruce, while junipers are resistant (Katz, 1939).

Eastern white pine is highly sensitive to air pollutants, and serious disorders—chlorotic dwarf (Dochinger and Seliskar, 1970) and post-emergence tipburn (Berry and Hepting, 1964)—are caused by ozone, sulphur dioxide, and fluorine. The level of resistance of both disorders is apparently under strong genetic control (Dochinger and Seliskar, 1965), and selection of resistant phenotypes and breeding for genetic resistance are recommended.

Fluorides have been responsible for widespread mortality of coniferous trees near smelters, refineries, and power plants in the United States and Europe (Treshow, 1970). For example, needle burning and death of ponderosa pine over a 50-square-mile area near Spokane, Washington (Adams *et al.*, 1952), were caused by fluoride emissions of a local aluminum plant. More recently, fluoride emissions from an aluminum plant were shown to cause widespread foliar burn and terminal dieback in forests of northwestern Montana and to predispose conifers to insect attack (Carlson and Dewey, 1971).

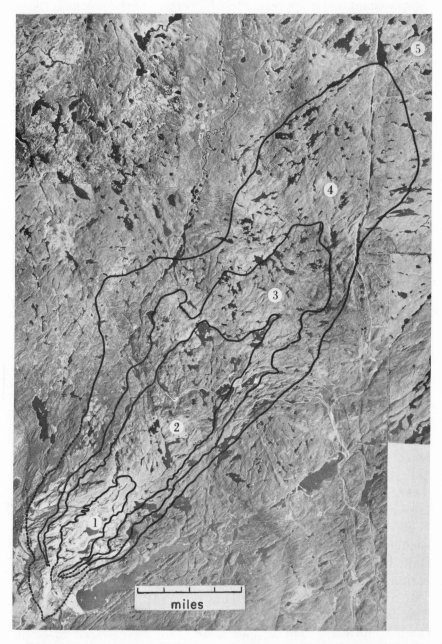

Fig. 5.5. Aerial mosaic northeast of Wawa, Ontario, Canada, showing emission source and boundaries of the categories of vegetation damage superimposed. 1—Very severe; 2—severe; 3—considerable; 4—moderate; 5—not obvious. (Courtesy of Dr. Alan G. Gordon, Research Branch, Ontario Ministry of Natural Resources.)

Fig. 5.6. Examples of damage categories shown in Fig. 5.5. 1—Very severe: overstory, shrub, and ground vegetation nearly all gone; erosion evident. 5—Not obvious: overstory with normal closed canopy. Normal understory, shrub layer, and ground flora. White spruce, balsam fir, white birch stand. (Courtesy of Dr. Alan G. Gordon, Research Branch, Ontario Ministry of Natural Resources.)

A widely known example of air pollution is that in forests of the San Bernardino Mountains of California, which receive ozone and other harmful components of smog blown 80 miles from the Los Angeles basin by westerly winds. Ozone is a natural component of the upper atmosphere, where it acts to absorb harmful ultraviolet radiation. It also forms and accumulates in urban environments, due to the many sources of combustion that emit nitrogen oxide and hydrocarbons. Ozone is known to cause a major needle disease of ponderosa pine (variously termed ozone needle mottle, chlorotic decline, and X-disease) resulting in decreased growth, needle drop, and death. In the San Bernardino National Forest, it is estimated that 1.3 million trees are affected by smog on an area covering more than 100,000 acres (Wert et al., 1970). In ponderosa and Jeffrey pines, the most sensitive of the dominant forest species, a yellow mottle of the normally green needles is followed closely by extensive needle drop, often leaving only the youngest needles on the tree (Miller, 1969). Although most pines are chronically affected, some trees remain green and healthy, suggesting a resistance of certain phenotypes to the disease. Most pines that are progressively weakened by smog injury are not killed by the disease itself, but by their natural enemy, the pine bark beetle (Cobb et al., 1970).

Lightning

No discussion of climatic effects on the forest can ignore lightning because of its great importance in terminating the life of trees and igniting fires, which play a dominant role in forest ecology. Since the earth experiences 44,000 thunderstorms per day and more than 8 million lightning discharges strike the earth each day (Taylor, 1969), it is not surprising that the effects of lightning on forests are widespread. Lightning has caused substantial mortality to ponderosa pine, Jeffrey pine, Douglas-fir, eastern hemlock, and loblolly pine (Taylor, 1969), and Reynolds (1940) reported that it was directly or indirectly responsible for 70 percent of the total volume loss in pine forests in southern Arkansas.

Exceptionally large trees, especially in exposed locations, become the ground terminals of lightning discharges. Lightning often strikes the tallest trees, killing them outright, or more often reducing their capacity to grow and increasing their predisposition to insect and disease attack. Not only are individual trees struck but entire groups of trees may be damaged by lightning alone (Taylor, 1971).

Species apparently differ in their predisposition to lightning damage (Treshow, 1970). For example, beech wood contains large amounts of oil while that of oak is free of it but high in water content. The high degree of hydration in oak may predispose it to lightning damage. Furthermore, since beech bark is smooth and constantly wet in thunderstorms, the electric current may be effectively conducted through the external water stream, minimizing injury.

Lightning-damaged conifers attract bark beetles, whose attacks on single trees may lead to mass attacks on surrounding healthy trees. Direct damage by lightning and wounds caused by lightning-induced fires present potential courts of disease, which may be of major significance in trees of all ages. In loblolly pine, lightning-struck trees are more susceptible to attack because of reduced oleoresin pressure, and they offer a more favorable brood environment for southern pine and *Ips* beetles (Hodges and Pickard, 1971).

SUMMARY

Water is the inorganic substance most needed by plants and is present in plants in large amounts. Precipitation is the major source of soil moisture—the principal source of water that reaches the tree. On the other hand some types of precipitation, particularly snow, glaze, and sleet, are important causes of damage to trees. Exchange of water vapor between plant and atmosphere takes place along vapor pressure gradients. *Transpiration* results when water is vaporized and moves out of the leaves (high pressure) into the surrounding air (lower pressure). Moisture may also move from the atmosphere into the plant when pressures in the plant are lower than those in the atmosphere, as in a rain or when dew covers a plant that is not fully turgid. The amount of moisture in the atmosphere significantly affects the rate of water loss from the leaves in transpiration. Transpiration is the primary process in the water relations of plants because it provides the energy gradient causing the movement of water and solutes into and through plants and may cause deficits to develop in the plant that adversely affect growth. In the process of transpiration, energy is utilized in the conversion of water from the liquid to the vapor form; in certain cases this cooling mechanism is important in dissipating heat energy accumulated by foliage during the daylight hours.

The greatest precipitation occurs where air currents passing over bodies of water come in contact with cooler land masses or are caused to rise by elevated terrain. Mountains cause air to rise and cause it also to cool, thereby increasing precipitation on windward slopes. Air currents depleted of moisture drop little precipitation at corresponding elevations on leeward slopes. Thus precipitation is closely correlated with elevation above sea level only when windward and leeward aspects are considered.

In forests, 20 percent of rainfall is commonly intercepted by the crowns, whence it may drip to the ground, flow down the stems, be evaporated into the air, or be absorbed by the foliage. Interception is of greater significance in coniferous than in broadleaf forests. In addition to rain and snow, fog may be an important source of moisture in certain forests located in fog belts. An obvious correlation exists in many parts of the world between certain species and the presence of fog belts. However, such coincidences do not prove that a cause-and-effect relationship necessarily exists between the moisture-giving property of fog and tree distribution. Other factors such as radiation, temperature, and carbon dioxide also may be involved.

Carbon dioxide is present in low concentrations in the atmosphere and yet is required in large amounts in photosynthesis. Carbon dioxide is continually evolved by respiration of living organisms and by the burning of organic materials, including fossil fuels. It is circulated in local ecosystems, across land masses, and from oceans to land masses by wind movement. In the forest, the carbon dioxide level is highest during the night when respiration is high and photosynthesis low; it reaches its lowest level at midday during the time of maximum photosynthesis.

Wind not only causes damage to the forest by stem breakage and windthrow but is instrumental in regulating photosynthesis and in circulating beneficial (carbon dioxide) and harmful (pollutants) gases. Lightning is a powerful atmospheric agent, not only responsible for destroying trees, but as the primary source of fire, which has greatly influenced the evolution, composition, and structure of many of the world's forests. Atmospheric pollutants may cause widespread damage to forests near smelters, industrial plants, and cities generating sulphur dioxide, ozone, and combinations of harmful gases such as smog. Conifers are particularly susceptible to fume damage. In the San Bernardino Mountains east of the Los Angeles Basin, wind-circulated smog has injured pines over thousands of acres, predisposing them prematurely to bark beetle attack.

SUGGESTED READINGS

ALEXANDER, ROBERT R. 1964. Minimizing windfall around clear cuttings in spruce-fir forests. *For. Sci.* 10:130–142.

GORDON, ALAN G., and E. GORHAM. 1963. Ecological aspects of air pollution from an iron-sintering plant at Wawa, Ontario. *Can. J. Bot.* 41:1063–1078.

KERFOOT, O. 1968. Mist precipitation on vegetation. *For. Abstracts* 29 (1):8–20.

PALMER, R. W. V. 1968. Wind effects on the forest. Suppl. to Forestry. Oxford Univ. Press, London. 93 pp.

STANHILL, GERALD. 1970. The water flux in temperate forests: precipitation and evapotranspiration. *In* DAVID E. REICHLE (ed.), *Analysis of Temperate Forest Ecosystems.* Springer-Verlag, New York.

TAYLOR, ALAN R. 1969. Lightning effects on the forest complex. *In Proc. Annual Tall Timbers Fire Ecology Conference, 1969,* pp. 127–150. Tall Timbers Res. Sta., Tallahassee, Fla.

TRESHOW, MICHAEL. 1970. *Environment and Plant Response.* (Chapter 10, Climatic extremes: lightning, hail, ice, and snow, pp. 125–137; Chapters 15–18 on atmospheric pollutants, pp. 245–353.) McGraw-Hill Book Co., Inc., New York.

6

Climate

The sum total of all climatic factors constitutes climate. We all can characterize climate in broad terms. When it comes to a precise description, however, our best efforts to date have left much to be desired.

Any usable climatic description must be based upon meteorological records, which are generally available for most localities. This limits us pretty much to precipitation and air temperature. Such data as we have on solar radiation, cloudiness, wind, and evaporation are available from relatively few stations.

CLIMATIC SUMMARIES

Actually, it is possible to characterize a climate reasonably well if the daily, monthly, and seasonal patterns of rainfall and air temperature are known. The difficulties arise from attempts to generalize from averages.

Climatic data for the United States are summarized in atlases compiled by Thornthwaite (1941) and Visher (1954) as well as in the 1941 U.S. Department of Agriculture *Yearbook*. Baker (1944) has brought together information available at that time on mountain climates of the western United States, while Pearson (1951) has compared climatic data in four widely separated portions of the ponderosa pine forest.

Let us consider a specific case. The meteorological station of the Southwestern Research Station of the American Museum of

Natural History is located in a broad valley within the Chiricahua Mountains of southeastern Arizona at an elevation of 5,400 feet. The vegetation consists of southwestern pines, junipers, and oaks. In 1957 rainfall records covered a seven-year span and temperatures a three-year span. The monthly temperatures and rainfall are summarized in Figure 6.1.

The quickest way to characterize the climate is in terms of the mean annual temperature and the mean annual precipitation. For this station, the former is 55°F and the latter is 17 inches. These figures convey a general picture of a warm climate with barely enough rain to support tree growth. Yet the mean temperature and rainfall for the San Francisco peninsula in California are almost the same as those for the Chiricahua Mountains of Arizona, while the climate is completely different.

These mean values do not indicate many important facts about the climate: in the case of the Chiricahua Mountain station, that the daily fluctuation in temperature is extreme, averaging 35 degrees; that killing frosts are common throughout all but the summer months; and that over half of the annual rainfall (9 out of 17 inches) falls during the growing season. In contrast, the San Francisco climate shows but little daily and seasonal difference in temperatures (an average of only 9 degrees difference between January and July), virtually no killing frosts, and virtually no rain during the summer months. In other words, San Francisco has a typical maritime climate with a summer dry season, while the Chiricahua Mountain station has a typical continental climate with a summer wet season.

Many attempts have been made to summarize climatic values graphically, in order to permit a visual comparison of the climates in different parts of the country. Obviously, the rather complete graphing of temperature and precipitation as in Figure 6.1, showing the monthly variability as well as the monthly averages, is too complex to permit the visual comparison of a large number of climatic stations.

Considerable simplification can be achieved by working with the mean monthly temperatures rather than with the average daily maximum and minimum temperatures during the month. Actually, "mean monthly temperature" is a misnomer. It is really the average between two temperatures only: the average daily high and the average daily low. The value does not take into account inter-

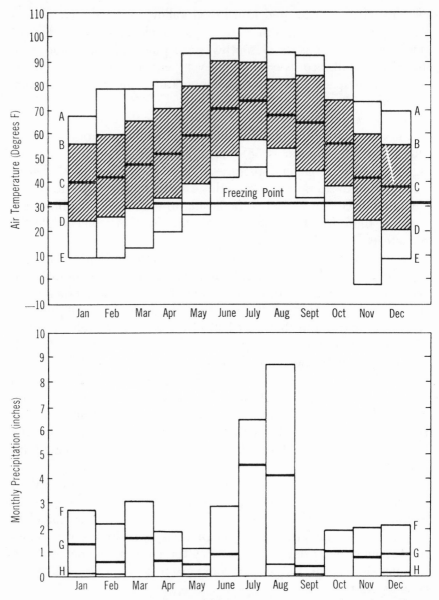

Fig. 6.1. Climatic summary of Painted Canyon Basin, Chiricahua Mountains, Arizona. Temperatures (1955–1958) include (A) extreme high recorded for month, (B) mean daily maximum for month, (C) mean daily, (D) mean daily minimum, and (E) extreme low recorded. Precipitation (largely rainfall, 1951–1957) includes (F) extreme high, (G) mean for month, and (H) extreme low.

mediate temperatures at all. Even so, and despite the fact that it
fails to give any indication of the daily fluctuation in temperatures,
the mean monthly temperature is a reasonably reliable guide to
the combined effects of solar radiation and air movement. In any
event, it has the virtues of both simplicity of concept and ease of
calculation.

In recent years, there has been a tendency among ecologists to
summarize climate for a given weather station by plotting mean
monthly temperature on the ordinate of a graph against mean
monthly precipitation on the abscissa. The resulting figure presents
an abstract picture of the climate, but one with little or no statistical
meaning (Figure 6.2). Nevertheless, it does follow that climates

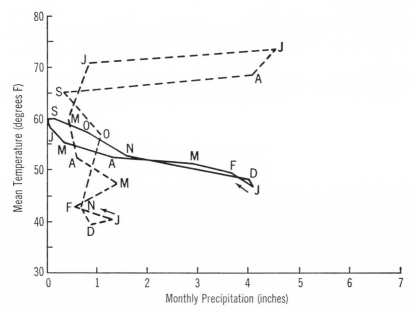

Fig. 6.2. Monthly precipitation–mean temperature relationship for San
Francisco (solid line) and Chiricahua Mountains (dashed line).

which in their graphed form present similar pictures are more or
less similar insofar as mean monthly temperature and precipitation
are concerned. The technique has little to recommend it, as it is
much more meaningful simply to graph the monthly trend in mean
annual temperature and precipitation. In Figure 6.3, our two illustrative climates with the same mean annual temperature and

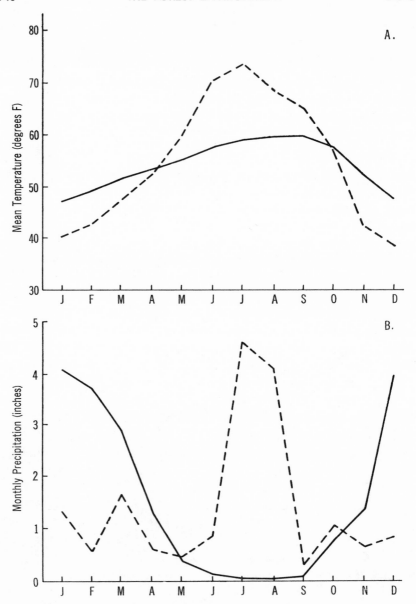

Fig. 6.3. Monthly trends in mean temperature (A) and precipitation (B) for San Francisco (solid line) and Chiricahua Mountains (dushed line).

precipitation are plotted on a monthly basis, and the differences between the two in temperature fluctuation throughout the year and in the pattern of rainfall are strikingly apparent.

Climatic Classifications

Many attempts have been made to classify climates. None has proved satisfactory in explaining to any degree the distribution of forests and other vegetation types. Yet the terminologies of several of our climatic classifications have crept into our literature and have, indeed, a certain value in characterizing a broad and approximate climatic zone.

Merriam's Life Zones. In 1898, C. H. Merriam published a classification of life zones that is still used by biologists, especially in the western United States. Theoretically based upon the summations of daily temperatures for the period of the year when the mean daily temperature exceeds 43°F, this basis has proved impractical in the field. As used at the present time, Merriam's life zones are not based upon climate but upon broad vegetational zones. Thus, the "Lower Sonoran" zone is a euphemism for the southwestern desert characterized by cacti, creosote bush, and the like. Similarly, the "Upper Sonoran" simply means that the vegetation consists of a woodland-savannah complex. Sagebrush, pinyon pines, desert junipers, oak savannah, and chaparral all fall within this zone. The "arid transition zone" refers to the ponderosa pine forest, and the "Pacific transition zone" to the Douglas-fir forest of the Pacific northwest. Finally, the "Canadian zone" includes the higher-altitude conifers, and the "Hudsonian zone" the alpine and boreal spruce-fir types.

Merriam's life zones have therefore lost much of their original climatic basis except so far as the broad vegetation types equated with them owe their distribution to climate. While it is true that climate is a prime factor in determining the distribution of these plant types, equally important factors are the soil, the past climatic and biological history of the locality, and the recent history of fire, grazing, logging, and other disturbances.

In short, although the terminology of Merriam is useful in briefly characterizing broad vegetational zones, there is little basis for attributing climatic implications. As for vegetational zones, it is often just as brief and far more accurate to be explicit—as for instance by referring to a "creosote bush desert" as such instead of the less definite "Lower Sonoran Life Zone."

Holdridge's Life Zones. Building on past attempts of climatic classification, Holdridge (1967) developed a system of life zones based on specific ranges of temperature and precipitation. This life zone system differs from Merriam's and other previous attempts in that the significant climatic factors of heat and precipitation are displayed in logarithmic progressions. The heat factor used, termed *biotemperature*, is the average annual temperature between 0°C and 30°C, which according to Holdridge is a measure of only the heat which is effective in plant growth. The resulting classification identifies a series of broadly defined life zones, such as rain forest, wet forest, dry forest, tundra, and steppe. Within each of the zones, plant and animal communities and their associated environmental features, such as topography, soils, and precipitation distribution patterns, are used to identify ecosystem units termed associations. Holdridge's life zones have found wide application in Central and South American countries in studies of land use planning.

Köppen's Climatic Provinces. Among geographers, the classification scheme of this German scientist has achieved considerable use. Basically, the climate is classified by three code letters, the first referring to one of five zones of winter temperature, the second to seasonal rainfall pattern, and the third to one of three zones of summer temperature. As with other worldwide schemes, this system is broadly related to major vegetation types, but shows little correlation with the actual distribution of the vegetation in a specific area. At least, that has been the finding in attempts to relate it to the distribution of American forest trees.

Thornthwaite's System. It has been known that the balance between water gain and water loss plays a dominant role in both the development of soils and vegetation. Where the annual addition of water to the soil through precipitation exceeds the annual loss through evaporation, a humid climate exists. Soils tend to be leached downward and a forest vegetation tends to develop in both temperate and tropical zones. Conversely, where the evaporative potential is greater than the supply of water from precipitation, arid conditions exist. Soil chemicals tend to move upward toward the surface and desert or grassland normally is found.

In the United States, a formalization of this concept by Thornthwaite has found widespread acceptance. The original basis of this scheme involved the recognition of five major climatic regions, based upon the ratio of precipitation to evaporation (superhumid, humid, subhumid, arid, and superarid). These zones are in turn subdivided. In more recent writings, Thornthwaite, recognizing the difficulty of amassing and analyzing actual evaporation data, has redefined his system in terms of potential evapotranspiration, a value that can be computed from temperature data (Thornthwaite, 1948; Thornthwaite and Mather, 1955).

By computing potential evapotranspiration from air-temperature data throughout the year, he has been able to express climate in a compound graph in which the contrast between the precipitation curve over time and the potential evapotranspiration curve over time indicates seasonal water surpluses or deficits. Thornthwaite's graphical method has found many applications in forest climatology, as illustrated by representative curves for a forest in southern Arkansas (Figure 6.4; Zahner, 1956). The Thornthwaite approach may be used, as in Figure 6.4, to analyze seasonal variation in climate or to show broad climatic relationships (Patric and Black, 1968). Patric and Black reported close relationships of potential evapotranspiration with broad vegetation types of Alaska, by Thornthwaite's method. They found that, even though temperature is recognized to govern growth of far-northern forests, i.e., precipitation is everywhere adequate to supply the needs of the growth possible under such cool conditions (Hare, 1950), potential evapotranspiration reflects forest distribution better than temperature data alone.

Multivariate Methods of Climatic Classification

Simple graphical methods, Köppen's classification, and multivariate statistical methods have been used to characterize the climates of British Columbia. Graphical or pictorial methods are satisfactory for demonstrating differences between a limited number of climates having major distinguishing features. For example, the precipitation, temperature, and growing season data clearly distinguish the climates of western British Columbia (*Cfb* of Köppen, marine west coast climate, Station 7), from that of the interior (*Dfb* of Köppen, humid continental cool summer climate, Station 59) (Figure 6.5; Krajina, 1959). However, multivariate methods offer the possibility to use a large number of variables to obtain the maximum differentiation and quantitative comparison of many climates (stations) simultaneously. By using the multivariate method of principal-com-

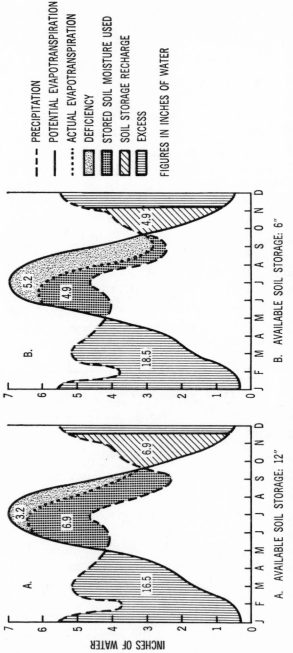

Fig. 6.4. Normal water deficiencies and excesses as influenced by soil-water storage capacities on the Crossett Experimental Forest. (After Zahner, 1956.)

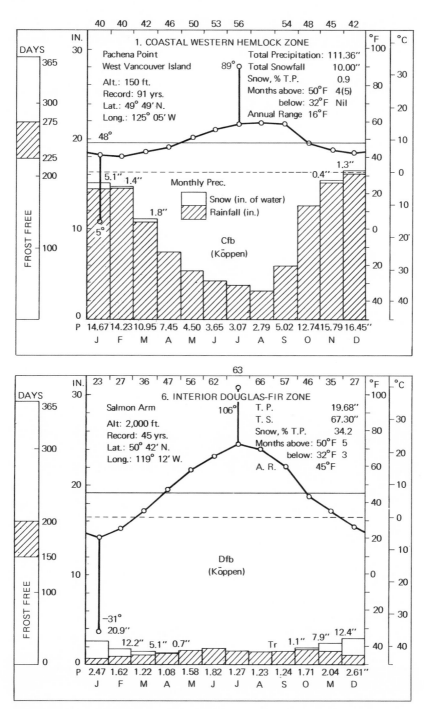

Fig. 6.5. Climatic characterization of stations representing coastal (1) and interior (6) climate. (After Krajina, 1959.)

ponents analysis, a large number of variables measured at each station may be replaced by one, two, or more synthetic variables, each of which is a combination of some or all of the original variables. For example, Newnham (1968) obtained climatic data for 19 variables (including seasonal temperature and precipitation data, length of growing season, elevation, and so on) for 70 stations in British Columbia (Figure 6.6) and subjected them to principal-components

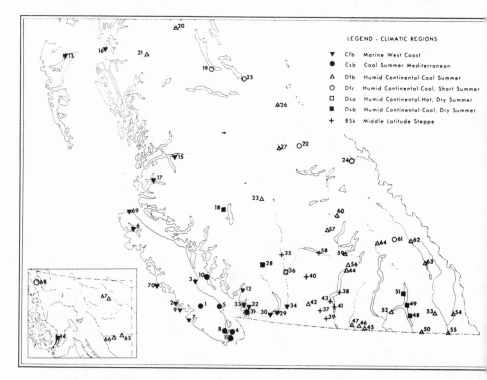

Fig. 6.6. Map of British Columbia showing the locations of the weather stations. (After Newnham, 1968.)

analysis (Figure 6.7). Three new variables were generated, the first, second, and third principal components, which accounted for 58, 29, and 5 percent, respectively, or together 92 percent of the total variation. The first principal component was primarily a combination of several factors related to length of the growing season while the second component was mainly determined by temperature and precipitation factors during the growing season.

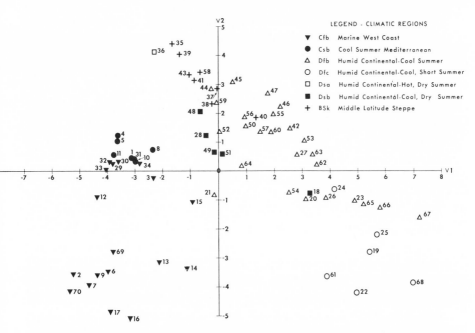

Fig. 6.7. The relationship between Chapman's (1952) climatic regions and the first and second principal components of climate. The coastal and inland stations of Figure 6.5 are 7 and 59, respectively.

The climates of the stations, as classified according to Köppen's system (Chapman, 1952), were reasonably well separated in the analysis (Figure 6.7). As in Figure 6.5, stations 7 and 59 and their respective *Cfb* and *Dfb* climates were widely separated in the principal components analysis. However, the *Csb* (humid continental cool, dry summer climate) stations were not well separated from one group of *Cfb* stations and station 18 seems to be misclassified.

The distribution of selected species, including coastal and interior races of Douglas-fir, Sitka spruce, Engelmann or white spruce, and ponderosa pine, was relatively well defined by the first two components of climate. Species distribution, however, was only generally related to climate.

Climate and Distribution of Vegetation

Climate is a major determinant of the distribution of vegetation on a broad or regional scale, and microclimate may significantly determine the local distribution of species and communities. The importance of climate as a determinant of vegetation distribution is closely related to the time and space scale under consideration. Viewed over thousands or millions of years or over a wide latitudinal gradient at a given point in time, climate is the predominant factor. Within a given region and point in time, however, climate may be less important than soil conditions and stand history. Thus, no single formula or universal classification scheme is adequate to explain or predict the existing vegetation distribution at regional and local levels. It is generally agreed that heat and water available to plants and the daily and seasonal fluctuations in these are the most critical climatic factors determining plant distribution. Daubenmire (1956) reviewed these factors in relation to the many attempts to combine them into formulas for classifying climates, classifications that might define the distribution of vegetation types. He found the classifications of Thornthwaite, Köppen, and Swain of little value in distinguishing areas of similar vegetation in the forests and adjacent grasslands of the northern Rocky Mountains. Furthermore the distinctions between grassland and forest climates could not be defined consistently by these classifications. However, a relatively high degree of correlation was achieved using graphs of mean monthly temperatures against median monthly precipitation.

Climatic factors may act directly to increase or decrease tree growth, which may change species distribution. Climate also may act indirectly by predisposing trees to insect and disease attacks and by intensifying an epidemic once it is initiated. For example, pole blight of western white pine, a disease reducing growth and causing substantial mortality in pole-sized stands in northern Idaho, has been linked to adverse temperature and moisture conditions for growth from 1916 to 1940 (Leaphart and Stage, 1971). These drought conditions on sites with shallow soils and severe moisture-stress characteristics led to root deterioration and rootlet mortality, crown decline, reduced growth, and ultimately the death of many trees. Recurrence of an adverse climatic pattern would increase the probability of the disease and would act to favor more drought-resistant species over western white pine on the sites with high moisture-stress characteristics.

The present distribution of species and communities is only generally related to climate. It also depends on physiography, on the age of the land and the nature of its soil, on the history of migration,

on competition and disturbances, and on chance (Rowe, 1966).
Obviously in specific situations climate is never the sole determinant,
nor does one factor of climate always play the major role. The
potential range of most species, based on climate and soil tolerances,
is typically much greater than the actual range. Interspecific competition greatly limits the range. For example, although the present
distribution of eastern white pine can be shown generally to follow
the zero line of precipitation minus potential evaporation (Bryson
et al., 1970), this pine when planted by man will grow far outside
this boundary. Many other examples could be cited demonstrating that, once established, woody species can survive and grow in
climates markedly different from their native habitat. The microclimatic, soil, and biotic factors (including competition) impinging
on seed germination and survival in the early years are neglected
aspects in our understanding of species' distribution in nature.
This, however, does not negate the fact that through climate's effect
on plant processes and soils, its effect on genetic differentiation and
interspecific competition, and as a causal factor of fires and windthrow, it is a major determinant of plant distribution.

Weather and Weather Modification

Weather is the current state of the atmosphere, the net effect of
numerous and variable meteorological factors. We have seen how
these factors influence tree growth, and that species distributions
bear a general relationship to climate, which is the long-term average of weather conditions. Being long-lived perennials, woody species must not only be adapted to the mean climate, but must be
able to withstand great fluctuations in weather from day to day,
month to month, and year to year. Genetically evolved timing
mechanisms, based on light, temperature, and moisture, enable them
to withstand these fluctuations and yet maintain enough variability
to meet the rate of long-term climatic change encountered in their
respective environment.

Technology may soon enable man to realize an age-old dream of
modifying weather to prevent monetary loss and personal suffering
from severe storms, frosts, and droughts. In their detailed study of
the ecological effects of weather modification, Cooper and Jolly
(1969) point out that modification will be desirable if, among other
reasons, significant options previously enjoyed by man are not lost.

These losses would include extinctions of plant and animal species, ruin of irreplaceable ecosystems, and destruction of valuable genetic material. If an increase of 10 percent in mean annual precipitation is achieved, changes in plant and animal communities are likely to be slow, but they could culminate in a rather extensive alteration of the original condition. No mass migration of communities is foreseen; rather, some plants will become regularly associated with species among which they were not commonly found in the past. Tree growth may be somewhat stimulated through partial alleviation of summer water deficits. The adjustment to an increase in precipitation leading to a changed community structure will normally take place more slowly in a region of highly variable weather than in one of relatively uniform weather.

SUMMARY

Every shortcut to climatic summarization involves a loss of precision and the elimination of data that may prove critical. The more detailed the climatic summary, the more likely it is that valid conclusions may be drawn. A complete graphing of the monthly means and extremes of both temperature and precipitation is probably the most satisfactory way of summarizing actual climate in reasonably brief terms. Multivariate statistical methods are useful if a simultaneous comparison is desired of many localities, each with a large number of climatic variables. The comparative precipitation–potential evaporation curves of Thornthwaite are perhaps most helpful in understanding those aspects of climate related to the all-critical moisture regime of plants. In many circumstances, the plotting of means only may prove to be a satisfactory shortcut. Further simplifications, whether in the form of graphics or as climatic classifications, are of only doubtful value to the forest ecologist concerned with specifics rather than with generalities.

Climate is a major determinant of the distribution of vegetation of the local and regional landscapes. However, many other factors, including soil, history of plant migration, competition, disturbance, and chance, also influence the distribution of species and communities. Although a given classification or formula based on climatic factors may provide broad patterns of the distribution that are useful at a general level, they are typically inadequate for the specifics required in many ecological studies.

SUGGESTED REFERENCES

DAUBENMIRE, R. 1956. Climate as a determinant of vegetation distribution in eastern Washington and northern Idaho. *Ecol. Monogr.* 26:131–154.

KRAJINA, VLADIMIR J. 1959. Bioclimatic zones in British Columbia. Botanical Series No. 1, University of British Columbia. 47 pp.

LEAPHART, CHARLES D., and ALBERT R. STAGE. 1971. Climate: a factor in the origin of the pole blight disease of *Pinus monticola* Dougl. *Ecology* 52:229–239.

NEWNHAM, R. M. 1968. A classification of climate by principal component analysis and its relationship to tree species distribution. *For. Sci.* 14:254–264.

PATRIC, JAMES H., and PETER E. BLACK. 1968. Potential evapotranspiration and climate in Alaska by Thornthwaite's classification. USDA For. Serv. Res. Paper PNW–71. Pacific Northwest For. and Rge. Exp. Sta., Portland, Ore. 28 pp.

WHITTAKER, R. H. 1967. Ecological implications of weather modification. *In* ROBERT H. SHAW (ed.), *Ground Level Climatology*. AAAS, Washington, D. C. Publ. 86. 395 pp.

7

Soil Factors

It is senseless to argue whether climate or soil is more important in governing tree distribution and growth. Both are important. The individual forest tree requires favorable soil conditions just as it needs favorable climatic conditions. From the soil through the tree roots come the water and the mineral nutrients required for life processes. The soil is also the medium of support that holds the tree upright and in place—at least most of the time. The roots themselves can thrive only under favorable conditions of air supply, water supply, soil nutrition, and warmth. Furthermore, certain soil fungi must infect the roots of many forest trees before the tree can grow normally and compete successfully for life.

Our concern here is with forest soils, but only those aspects of soils that are related to forest site quality. An understanding of forest ecology presupposes that the student has had, or will have had, exposure to the science of forest soils. We cannot here summarize this subject, but rather must confine ourselves to the relationship between certain soil characteristics and the definition of the forest site or habitat. Foremost among these are parent materials and the development of the soil profile (Chapter 7), the nutrient cycle (Chapter 8), the plant-soil water cycle (Chapter 9), and other soil factors affecting forest site quality (Chapter 10).

Contrasting American approaches on forest soil relationships are presented by Lutz and Chandler (1946) and Wilde (1958). Publication of the proceedings of two North American Forest Soils Conferences (Youngberg, 1963; Youngberg and Davey, 1970) offers a

152

wide array of papers summarizing recent information on soil, site, and tree growth relationships. For northern Europe, excellent treatments are those of Aaltonen (1948) and Tamm (1950). Tropical soil problems are summarized by Mohr and Van Baren (1954).

PARENT MATERIAL: GEOLOGY AND SOILS

The importance of the underlying rock material in determining the distribution of vegetation types is often obvious. When two completely different vegetations abut, investigation will usually disclose that each is growing on a different geologic material of differing mineral composition.

Residual Soils

These plant-rock correlations are more apparent when the soils in which the plants grow are derived directly from the underlying rock. In such cases, distinct bands of vegetation often serve to delineate equally distinct bands of parent material. Many examples may be cited.

In the Appalachian and Ozark Mountains, soils derived from underlying sandstones support trees entirely different from those growing on adjacent soils weathered from limestones. The former material results in a relatively coarse, porous, and acidic soil in which pines have a great competitive advantage. The latter rock weathers into a finer, richer, and neutral or basic soil suitable for the more demanding hardwoods—walnut, beech, ash, and so on—and for such conifers as red cedar. A study by Read (1952) of forest composition in relatively undisturbed forest sites on northerly slopes in northern Arkansas (Table 7.1) is illustrative of the situation. Red cedar is concentrated on the limestone soils, with elm and ash and other demanding species also indicating the presence of limestone either at the surface or in the subsoil. In contrast, the sandstone and chert soils were dominated by black and white oak, mockernut hickory, and black gum and other less abundant species. In the mountain country of the southeastern United States, a band of pine forest lying parallel to a band of hardwoods mixed with red cedar will commonly connote parallel layers of sandstone and limestone (Figure 7.1).

Across the country in the mountains of the Pacific Coast, as in many other parts of the world, soils derived from serpentine support

Table 7.1.   Tree Species in the Ozarks Ranked by Dominance Index on Soils Derived from Four Different Parent Materials

Rank	Chert	Limestone with Cherty Surface Soil	Limestone	Sandstone
1	Black oak	Northern red oak	Eastern red cedar	Black oak
2	White oak	White oak	Northern red oak	White oak
3	Flowering dogwood	Black oak	Winged elm	Black gum
4	Mockernut hickory	White ash	Chinquapin oak	Flowering dogwood
5	Black gum	Winged elm	Shagbark hickory	Ozark chinquapin

Source: Read, 1952.

Fig. 7.1.   Pines at higher elevation over hardwoods on lower slopes denote different geological strata in the Cumberland Plateau of Kentucky. (U. S. Forest Service photo.)

an entirely different vegetation than do surrounding areas (Whittaker, Walker, and Kruckeberg, 1954; McMillan, 1956). Serpentine is a mineral high in magnesium, and soils composed of its weathered fragments support only a poor and open plant life. In the ponderosa pine–mixed conifer forests, for example, serpentine soils are characterized by Jeffrey pine, a species otherwise restricted to higher elevations, and a distinct group of shrubs and other lesser plants. One subspecies of lodgepole pine is almost completely restricted to serpentine soils. These "serpentine barrens" play a similar part in the distribution of many other species and may elicit genetic differentiation in some species.

Differential chemical weathering of the same parent material may also affect tree distribution and growth. East of the Sierra Nevada in the semi-arid sagebrush or pinyon-juniper zones, Billings (1950) has found that outliers of ponderosa and Jeffrey pine are confined to volcanic rocks which had been hydro-thermally altered with resultant accelerated chemical weathering. Sagebrush and its associates have been unable to invade these mineral-deficient soils.

Transported Soils

Many of our forest soils, however, are developed from weathered rock fragments that have been moved to their present site by gravity, water, wind, or ice. During transport, a good deal of mixing usually occurs so that such soils are apt to contain fragments of many kinds of rocks and minerals. As a result, soils which have been transported are apt to differ more strikingly in their physical properties as these are related to the method of transport and the place of deposition rather than in their chemical properties.

Transported soils are characteristic of the Coastal Plains, the Great Plains, the valleys between the western mountain ranges, and the glaciated portions of Canada and the United States. Wherever differences in the mode of transportation and deposition occur, differences in composition of the vegetation may be expected.

For instance, in central New England, the native pines—white, red, and pitch—can usually compete successfully with hardwoods and form a major part of the plant community on sandy soils laid down by melt-water from the melting glaciers. On such sand *outwash plains* are found the best-developed and most persistent pine types. In contrast, *till*—the rock particles rolled out by the advancing glaciers—has evolved into a finer-textured and more fertile soil where the various hardwood species normally outgrow and suppress the pines. The latter grow on these till soils only when farming, fire, or other disturbances have held back hardwood development and growth.

In the northern tip of the Lower Peninsula of Michigan, the direction of the glacier advance is reflected in the vegetation. The next to the last ice sheets of the Wisconsin glaciation (Cary and Port Huron substage) advanced from the north, across the often-scraped and infertile Canadian shield of the Algoma section of Canada. Soils derived from the material carried by this ice are apparently coarser and less fertile than those in the same neighborhood derived from the last advance, which came from the northwest across the limestones and other rocks of the Upper Peninsula of Michigan.

In the Coastal Plain of the southeastern United States, finer-textured soils richer in organic matter are found in erstwhile lagoons rather than on the old beaches and beach dunes. The lagoons will often support a hardwood forest in localities where the latter grow longleaf pine. Other pine species may occupy the intervening sites.

Sometimes a soil change may be mistaken for an altitudinal relationship. For instance, in the Joshua Tree National Monument in California the upper limit of distribution of this giant yucca seems to be altitudinally controlled, whereas a more probable explanation is that the tree is restricted to the depositional soils in the valleys and is absent from the erosion surfaces on the sides of the mountains.

Very commonly, when two distinctly different forest or other natural vegetation types abut, and there is no obvious difference in their topographic situations, soil differences resulting from the abutting of two types of parent materials will be found to be responsible.

Physical Properties of Soils

Important physical properties of soils, particularly *texture* and *structure*, will be considered briefly as a basis for the discussion of related soil properties in succeeding chapters. Soils are made up of four major components: minerals and organic matter which together form the solid portion, and the soil solution and air which occupy the pore space. Texture, the relative proportions of mineral soil particles of various sizes, and soil structure, the arrangement of particles into groups or aggregates, largely determine the physical properties of the soil (Chapter 10).

The basic textural classifications are *sand, silt,* and *clay.* Sand particles are from 2.0 mm to 0.02 mm in diameter, silt particles from 0.02 to 0.002 mm, and clay particles less than 0.002 mm. Clay particles are particularly important since it is on their negatively charged surfaces (micelles) that most positively charged mineral cations (Ca^{++}, K^+, Mg^{++}, etc.) and hydrogen ions are adsorbed (Chapter 8).

The combination of the individual soil particles of different sizes into aggregates gives the soil its structure. The nature of soil structure affects the amount and size of the pores, which are filled by either water or air (Chapter 9).

Sandy soils (less than 15 percent silt and clay) are "light" in texture and can hold less water and minerals but more air than clays. In contrast, clay soils (more than 40 percent clay particles and less than 45 percent sand or silt) are "heavy" in texture and can hold more water and minerals but less air than sand soils. Soils containing generous proportions of silt particles, or about equal amounts of sand, silt, and clay, such as loam and silt loam soils, generally have the best balance between moisture, nutrients, and air.

SOIL PROFILE DEVELOPMENT

As the blanket of rock detritus weathers and is occupied by vegetation and animals, it differentiates into more or less distinct horizontal zones, giving rise to a soil profile. The type of profile that develops depends upon the interaction of (1) climate, (2) parent material, (3) plants and animals occupying the soil, (4) relief of the land, and (5) the amount of time that has elapsed. Soil formation is in part a geological process in that it results from the normal weathering of rock fragments exposed to air and water, and in part a biological process, since the presence of plants and animals in and on the soil affects the nature and the pattern of the weathering.

The Forest Soil Profile

Forests form the natural vegetation in many of the moister parts of the world—parts where the precipitation supplies more water than can be evaporated from the soil surfaces over the normal year. Under such conditions two factors dominate: the normal course of rain water is downward, thus tending to leach the upper soil horizons of the more soluble chemicals; and the deep-rooted trees remove both water and nutrients from the root zone, transpiring most of the former and eventually returning most of the latter to the soil in leaf-, twig-, and fruit-fall.

In temperate regions, the typical forest soil, therefore, can be roughly subdivided into four zones, or *horizons* (Figure 7.2). The

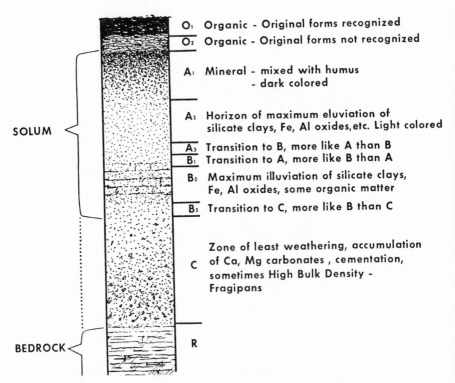

O₁ Organic - Original forms recognized
O₂ Organic - Original forms not recognized

A₁ Mineral - mixed with humus
   - dark colored

A₂ Horizon of maximum eluviation of
   silicate clays, Fe, Al oxides, etc. Light colored

A₃ Transition to B, more like A than B
B₁ Transition to A, more like B than A

B₂ Maximum illuviation of silicate clays,
   Fe, Al oxides, some organic matter

B₃ Transition to C, more like B than C

C Zone of least weathering, accumulation
   of Ca, Mg carbonates, cementation,
   sometimes High Bulk Density -
   Fragipans

R

SOLUM

BEDROCK

Fig. 7.2. A theoretical mineral soil profile showing the major horizons which may be present. (After Buckman and Brady, 1969.)

O or organic horizon is formed above the mineral soil and consists of an O₁ zone, containing recognizable litter from leaves, twigs, fruits, and dead plants and animals, and a lower O₂ zone, characterized by decomposed litter so that the original state of the organic material is unrecognizable. The decomposed litter is often termed *humus*. The A horizon is the surface layer of mineral soil that is leached of its nutrients by the downward-moving water. It, in turn, is subdivided into an upper A_1, in which organic matter is constantly being added to mineral soil through litter decomposition and mixing by animal activity, and a lower A_2 horizon, which is merely leached. The term *melanization* is sometimes applied to the process of organic matter incorporation into the surface of mineral soil.

Below is the zone of accumulation, the B horizon, characterized by the deposition of minute clay and organic particles derived from the leaching of the minerals and organic matter above. As a result the B horizon is usually finer-textured and darker in color than the parent material, while the A is coarser-textured and lighter in color. Occasionally the B horizon is so packed with clays that it forms a hardpan and becomes quite impermeable to water and even air movement.

Below the zone of clay deposition is the C horizon, composed of the same parent material as that from which the A and B horizons are formed. Commonly, the upper part of this zone is somewhat weathered, as air in the pore spaces will have resulted in oxidation of at least some of the rock minerals and as downward-percolating water may have leached calcium carbonates and others of the more easily soluble minerals. The soils specialist can often recognize several minor strata in the soil, characterized by minor differences in weathering, leaching, or accumulation. A subsoil horizon composed of a parent material different than that from which the A and B horizons are formed is termed the D rather than the C horizon. An example of the latter case is soil formed in a thin layer of glacial deposits over residual bedrock.

The typical layered forest soil profile is developed only under conditions of good drainage, when water can move down through the soil. The presence of a high water table in the soil, or of rock or soil layers impervious to water movement, will result in a truncated and modified profile. In the zone of a fluctuating water table, oxidation is periodically restricted, giving rise to a mottled soil profile of yellow or gray (unoxidized) and brown or reddish (oxidized) minerals. A permanent or stagnant water table will prevent any soil oxidation and may even result in the extraction of oxygen (i.e., *reduction*) from previously oxidized soil minerals, forming a *gley* horizon.

It should be noticed that the terms A, B, and C horizons refer to zones which have been leached, enriched, and unaffected, respectively. It does not necessarily follow that the upper mineral horizon is always the A. Following sheet erosion, the B or C horizon may be exposed at the surface. On the other hand, a soil may be superimposed on a fossil profile consisting of A, B, and C horizons. These and many other combinations are possible.

The development of a forest soil profile can be followed with particular ease when a sand dune composed of uniform unstratified sand grains is stabilized by the planting of forest trees. An example is provided by the afforestation of coastal sand dunes with Corsican and Scots pines at Culbin on the north coast of Scotland (Wright, 1955, 1956). By the time the pines had established a closed forest (22 to 80 years), their roots had dried out the sand considerably; but litter added to the surface had increased materially the moisture-holding capacity of the upper soil. A soil profile had begun to form in this brief period, as indicated by the downward distribution of the major nutrients through leaching, their recirculation through root absorption, and subsequent leaf-fall.

In Alaska, following the retreat of glacial ice, the establishment of an alder forest was found to reduce the reaction of the uppermost horizons of the glacial till from pH 8.0 to less than pH 5.0 within 35 to 50 years (Crocker and Major, 1955). During the same period calcium carbonate in the fine earth was reduced from about 5 percent to practically nothing. The total nitrogen content of the surface soils increases as long as the pioneer, nitrogen-fixing alder community persists, but decreases after about a hundred years when a spruce community replaces the alder in natural development.

Soil profile development may continue for many thousands of years. In the northern portion of the lower peninsula of Michigan, similar parent materials (both tills from advancing glaciers and sands from glacial melt-waters) can be dated from their position in relation to old lake levels of the Great Lakes (Spurr and Zumberge, 1956). One series, exposed for 3,500 years, shows only slight weathering and profile development. Even on sands, lime is available within a foot or so of the surface to the extent of favoring the growth of northern white cedar. On similar sand soils exposed for 8,000 and 10,000 years, the lime has been leached to a depth of about 3 feet and clearly segregated A and B horizons have been formed. On adjacent clay loams originating as till, however, soil profiles are still relatively immature after 10,000 years.

Non-Forest Soils

Quite different soil profiles normally develop under grass or brush vegetation than have been described for the forest. Ploughing, of course, mixes surface layers of the soil into a homogenized plough layer, below which the remains of the truncated soil profile may be detected. Under natural grassland, the dense fibrous root mass near the surface results in a higher surface content of incorporated organic matter and the retention of clays in this zone. Grassland soils, even in forested regions, develop a dark and rich topsoil which can be detected long after the natural vegetation has been destroyed by man. In lower Michigan, extensive areas of prairie soils stretching across the lower part of the state bear witness to an extension of the prairies existing there prior to settlement.

Grassland, brushland, and desert soils in regions of low rainfall differ from forest soils to an even greater degree. Under conditions where precipitation is insufficient to support a closed forest canopy, moisture entering the soil is pulled toward the surface and evaporated, leaving a layer of precipitated chemicals in its wake. The surface layer thus tends to become enriched in calcium and other readily soluble nutrients. Deeper in the soil there is little leaching and the soil is only gradually changed in depth by geological weathering. The result is that the vegetation often seems to be growing on a mass of weathered rock fragments rather than on a soil with a well-developed profile. In the mountains of southern Arizona, for example, the open woodlands are formed by the live oaks, junipers, and pinyon and other pines of the semi-arid country. The trees grow in rock detritus (colluvial slopes) at the base of outcropping bedrock.

Podzolization

Although any given soil profile is the product of many different weathering and other reaction-producing processes, two general types of soil formation have attracted particular attention from soil scientists because of the prevalence of these processes over large areas, and their importance in changing the capacity of the soil to grow vegetation. *Podzolization* refers to the process of acid leaching whereby clay and organic particles and mineral ions, primarily iron and aluminum, are carried downward, a process that, brought to its logical conclusion, will leave a leached A_2 horizon composed predominantly of silica and from which the iron and aluminum minerals have been removed. The term is from the Russian, meaning, "alkaline ash," and has become a part of basic soils vocabulary.

True podzolic profiles, termed *spodosols*, with a thick and impoverished A_2 horizon, are restricted to cool, damp climates and occur primarily under trees and shrubs that produce an acidic foliage low in content of calcium and other bases. The spruces and firs throughout Canada, northern Europe, northern Siberia, and in the high mountains of the North Temperate Zone generally create spodosols. So do heather, blueberry, and similar shrubs. For instance, in England, strong podzolic profiles under oak forest have been shown to have developed when the areas had been heathland prior to the invasion of the oak (Dimbleby and Gill, 1955).

Elsewhere in the Temperate Zone, podzolic soils tend to develop under the forest, the adjective implying that the process of podzolization is dominant, but that leaching has not or will not proceed to the point of reducing the A_2 horizon to a grayish and impoverished sand. Under pines and hemlocks, true spodosols may develop over a 50- to 100-year period, but if the forest is converted to hardwoods, the spodosol condition will often disappear in a similar span of time. When eastern white pine is planted on old agricultural land in central New England, a thin, leached podzolic horizon will normally appear in 40 to 50 years and may reach a breadth of an inch or two within 100. After the pines are harvested and are succeeded by red oak, red maple, and other hardwoods on till soils, the chemical effect of the hardwood foliage will gradually break down this grayish-white horizon until, after 30 to 50 years, it has been recolored and partially recharged with nutrients (Griffith, Hartwell, and Shaw, 1930). In England, it is estimated that 60 to 100 years will elapse after birch has invaded heath moorland before the spodosol profile formed under the acid raw humus of the moorland is destroyed (Dimbleby, 1952).

Podzolization is dominant in virtually all forest soils in moist temperate climates, and should be considered as a natural and inevitable soil-forming process under such climates.

Under certain conditions, intense podzolization may result in lowered productivity of the forest. The A_2 layer itself, severely leached of nutrients, especially of calcium, may act as an effective barrier to root penetration. A tree root cannot grow through a calcium-deficient zone to reach a more nutritious zone below.

More importantly, the extreme leaching characteristic of spodosol formation may result in the iron and aluminum minerals and other clay-forming materials effectively cementing the B horizon. Hardpans may develop that are impervious to air and water and which effectively seal off the tree roots from the soil moisture and nutrients below. Under such circumstances, the soil available to vegetation is the shallow zone above the hardpan, and this zone is very low in its supply of plant nutrients.

The classic example of soil deterioration due to podzolization is the heath and moorland of Great Britain and other parts of western Europe. Here, clearcutting and fires in bygone centuries have converted land that was originally forest to heather and related ericaceous species. Under the influence of the acid and indigestible foliage of these plants, podzolization was carried to the point of sealing off the B horizon with an iron pan. As a result, trees can no longer be grown to merchantable size on these sites. Yet, by breaking the iron pan with deep ploughs, by adding fertilizers, and by establishing trees and shrubs producing more nutritive foliage, the site can eventually be reclaimed for timber production. Oaks and birch are more effective in rehabilitating the soil than beech or Scots pine.

As early as the sixteenth century, and reaching a climax during the nineteenth century, many hardwood forests in central Europe were converted to stands of pure Norway spruce. Spruce was easier to regenerate than were hardwoods and became increasingly desirable because of its greater timber yields. Yet, in the second and third rotations of spruce, the yields in many cases fell off sharply. Although the decrease was attributed to the development of spodosols, such a generalization is unacceptable. The spruce monocultures do bring about marked physical and chemical changes in the topsoil, and on particular soils one or a combination of these, instead of or in addition to podzolization, may have evoked the decline.

The changes caused by spruce—even after one generation—include a reduction in the rate of organic matter decomposition, decreased earthworm and microorganism activity, decreased melanization, reduced water availability, and changed nutrient status in comparison to topsoil conditions under native hardwoods (Schlenker *et al.*, 1969). Under these conditions reductions in nutrient cycling may have in part led to the observed growth decline. In addition, on heavy clay soils spruce roots exist as a flat latticework in the topsoil, for they are much less effective in penetrating the lower horizons than are the roots of the native oaks and beech. In the first spruce generation following hardwoods, the soil is permeated by the old root canals of the hardwoods, and spruce roots may take advantage of these in penetrating deeper horizons and extracting quantities of water and nutrients. In succeeding generations of spruce, evershallower root systems are developed. The decreased ability of the root system to reach water and nutrients in lower horizons may therefore in part reduce growth in successive generations. Finally, on some sites spruce may accelerate the natural tendency of the soil to become watersoaked (Werner, 1964). However, spruce monocultures may suffer much greater damage from windthrow, disease, insects, and snow breakage than from the effects of podzolization or soil deterioration. For example, heart rot, caused primarily by *Fomes annosus*, may cause severe growth losses in spruce stands of the first and successive generations on specific sites formerly occupied by hardwoods (Werner, 1971; Schönhar, 1969). Current forest practice in central Europe shows a strong concern for identifying and mapping the kinds of sites where pure spruce may be grown with the least risk of injury or soil deterioration, sites where spruce should be grown in mixtures with other conifers (primarily silver fir) and hardwoods (primarily European beech), and sites where spruce should be excluded entirely.

So much has been written and argued about this particular soil problem that there is a tendency to think of podzolization as a "bad" or undesirable process. Actually, podzolization is the inevitable process of soil formation wherever moist, cool conditions exist. Furthermore, in most instances, there is no evidence that podzolization decreases timber growth rates or otherwise affects undesirably the characteristics of the forest. In some special situations, podzolization has resulted from mismanagement of the vegetation and has lowered the productive capacity of the soil. The danger of podzolization, however, has been overemphasized. Podzolization definitely benefits the water-holding capacity and nutrient build-up in B horizons of extremely sandy soils. For example, in northern lower Michigan, Hannah (1969) found 29 percent more volume and 20 percent more dry weight of stemwood in 35-year-old red pines growing on soils with moderate to well-developed, spodosol B_2 horizons than that of pines growing on soils in which podzolization was absent or weakly developed.

Laterization

Whereas podzolization reaches its greatest development in cool or cold climates, laterization characterizes the tropics and is primarily a process of hot, wet climates (Prescott and Pendleton, 1952). Through weathering and intense leaching under such conditions, the iron and aluminum minerals are changed to insoluble compounds which remain after the silicas and other minerals are carried downward, giving rise to *oxisols*. The soil is thus converted into a red or yellow body, a deep *oxic* subsurface horizon dominated by insoluble oxides of iron and aluminum, but impoverished of all else. Carried to the extreme, these minerals harden into a red rock or *laterite* (from the Latin word for brick or tile).

Laterization is essentially a geological weathering process in that it occurs with or without vegetation and that it may extend a hundred or more feet deep, far below the influence of plant roots. Vegetation, however, does influence the extent and nature of the process. Oxisols may develop under grassland, savanna, or forest. Under the forest, however, the concentration of iron and aluminum compounds occurs at some depth from the surface, while under grassland it occurs at the surface. Clearcutting the forest and converting the area to grassland, though, may result in accelerating the hardening of lateritic soils into laterite rock, a process which greatly lowers the productive capacity of the site (Griffith and Gupta, 1948). For this reason, the conversion of natural forest into teak or other tree-plantation crops is not recommended when the forest soils are highly lateritic.

Oxisols developed under tropical rain forest are subject to excessive leaching when the forest cover is removed. Frequently, virtually all nutrients are leached out by the heavy rains to a depth of six feet or more in six months or less. Only through the maintenance of a continuous cover of tree crops can soil nutrients be returned to the surface through litter-fall and the fertility of such soil be maintained.

SOIL CLASSIFICATION

The classification of soils presents many of the problems of classification of climates. So many separate factors enter into the formation of a given soil and so many different physical and chemical properties can be measured and evaluated that it is difficult to choose two or three values that adequately characterize the soil. Furthermore, all gradations of soils can be found between almost any two extremes, and any effort to divide the range into a set of classes becomes arbitrary and never more than partially successful.

Soils, however, are concrete in that they can be seen and described far more readily than the ephemeral and variable qualities of the atmosphere which we call climate. Furthermore, the importance of soils for agriculture and engineering is such that much attention has been given to the development of soil classification schemes, and much field work utilizing these schemes has been carried out.

A new system of soil classification, based largely on soil properties (soil morphology) rather than soil-forming processes (soil genesis), is widely accepted in North America although it is still being refined. This system and an earlier system, in use between 1938 and 1960, are described in detail by Buckman and Brady (1969). The primary advantage of the new system is that a soil profile itself, rather than a soil-forming process or presumed process, is classified. The system is modeled after the plant taxonomic system, with categories from "order" (the broadest group) to the "series" (roughly equivalent to a "species").

The main soil orders supporting forests in North America are *Entisols, Spodosols, Alfisols, Ultisols,* and *Inceptisols. Oxisols* are found in extensive areas of tropical and subtropical forests in Central and South America, southeast Asia, and Africa. Oxisols (from French *oxide,* oxide, and the Latin word for soil, *solum*) are highly weathered soils in which the subsoil is strongly oxidized. Entisols (recent soils) are mineral soils without, or with only the beginnings of, natural horizons. Examples of forested entisols are common: tallus slopes, flood plains (alluvium), sand dunes, and shallow bedrock soils. Spodosols (from Greek *spodos*, wood ash) are characterized by acid leaching in cold, temperate climates and reach their best development under boreal forests. Alfisols (from the chemical abbreviations for aluminum and iron) are characterized by less pronounced podzolic leaching and found mostly in humid regions under hardwood forests. Forest soils of the eastern and central United States, as well as those of the Rocky Mountains, the Cascades, the Sierra Nevada Mountains, and the Pacific Northwest are primarily Alfisols. The Ultisols (from Latin *ultimus*, last) are developed by podzolic processes in warm to tropical climates and are more highly weathered and acidic than Alfisols but not as acid as Spodosols. Ultisols are formed on old land surfaces, usually under forest vegetation, and most of the soils of the southeastern United States are of this order. Inceptisols (from Latin *inceptum*, beginning) are young soils not characterized by extreme weathering or major accumulations of clay or iron and aluminum oxides. Prominent among soils of this group are large areas of Oregon, Washington, and Idaho, where productive soils are derived from volcanic ash and loess.

Soil series are the basic taxonomic units used in field classification by the U. S. Soil Survey in the United States, and over 7,000 series have been described. In many cases subdivisions or "phases" of a series, based on specific factors such as stoniness, soil depth, or slope, are described and mapped. For example, the soil "Miami loam" is given a series name, Miami, for the Miami River Valley in Ohio, and a type name, loam, describing the texture of the surface soil. All soils of a given series are developed from similar parent material, by similar soil-forming processes, and have horizons of similar arrangement and general features. Thus Miami loam refers to a soil with general characteristics of the Miami series and a loamy surface soil and not necessarily to one with a loamy parent material, or C horizon.

Soil classification systems are developed by soil scientists primarily for description and mapping of agricultural soils. They are the basis of systematic soil surveys of agricultural, urban, and forested lands of the United States. The system in current use provides a taxonomic classification of forest soils but cannot be readily used without interpretation to characterize the productivity of forest stands.

SUMMARY

Soil, which provides the water, nutrients, and medium of support for tree growth, is derived from parent materials of differing mineral composition. These differences affect both the composition of forest vegetation and the rate of growth of forest trees. Soils may develop in place or be transported great distances by water, ice, or wind. The method of transport is significant in determining the physical properties of soils and their texture and structure, which also influence the composition and vigor of forest stands. As transported or residual rock detritus weathers, a soil profile develops, influenced not only by the physical factors of climate, physiography, and parent materials, but by the biota of the area and time. In temperate regions, four horizons comprise the typical, well-drained forest soil profile: an organic (O), a leached (A), an enriched (B), and an unaffected (C) horizon.

Two major types of soil-forming processes, podzolization and laterization, are important over large forested areas. These processes are particularly important in forest composition and growth because they affect the physical and chemical properties of soils in the rooting zone of trees. Podzolization is the leaching of organic particles and mineral ions from the upper horizon and the subsequent deposition of these materials in the subsoil. It is the inevitable soil-forming process in cool, moist climates, and the process is intensified under trees and other vegetation that produce an acid foliage. Laterization dominates in hot, wet climates. Soil is converted to a red or yellow body (oxisol) through weathering and intense leaching such that iron and aluminum minerals are changed to insoluble compounds and remain after other minerals have been carried downward.

Soils are classified in a taxonomic system based on soil morphology. The major forest soil order in the United States, the Alfisols, covers large portions of forested eastern, central, and western states. Other important orders of forest soils are: Entisols, Inceptisols, Ultisols, and Spodosols. Soils classified as Alfisols, Ultisols, and

Spodosols have developed by the process of podzolization. Spodosols are the result of severe podzolization and typically exhibit a highly leached A_2 horizon and hardpan formation in the B horizon. Within each order, soil "series" are the basic units used in field classification of agricultural, urban, and forest soils of the United States.

SUGGESTED READING

BUCHMAN, HARRY O., and NYLE C. BRADY. 1969. *The Nature and Properties of Soils*, 7th ed. (Chapter 12, Soil formation, classification and survey, pp. 293–354.) The Macmillan Co., Toronto. 653 pp.

8

The Nutrient Cycle

The forest and the soil together constitute an ecosystem in which each element of the community, both organic and inorganic, nurtures the others and in turn is affected by the others. The basic mineral nutrition of the vegetation is provided by the weathering of the soil minerals, and the soil itself is recharged and changed by the organic products of the vegetation. Other organisms form essential parts of the ecosystem. Bacteria are essential for the fixation of nitrogen, fungi are essential for the absorption of nutrients by tree roots, and a whole complex of soil biota is needed to effect the decomposition of organic debris to a state where it can be utilized over again by the vegetation. The cycling of organic matter, water, chemical elements, indeed of energy itself, is so basic that quantitative ecologists in recent years have developed concepts of the ecosystem based on them (Ovington, 1962, 1968).

To summarize such a complex ecological system requires a simplifying logic based upon a consistent point of view. One such view is the chemical approach, based upon following the movement of the basic mineral nutrients through the cycle from soil to the vegetation and back again. This is the theme of the present chapter. This cycling, however, is dependent in large measure upon the water cycle, which controls the availability of nutrients to tree roots, their rate of movement through the tree, the conditions under which the tree litter is decomposed, and the development of the soil profile which in turn affects the availability of nutrients to the tree roots as recycling is initiated. The water cycle is treated in the following chapter. Both approaches are valid and necessary. Only through an understanding of the ecosystem of the forest, involving both the chemical approach typified by the nutrient cycle and the physical approach illustrated by the water cycle, can the importance of soil factors in the forest environment be evaluated. As with so many ecological problems, it is not a question of which is the more important. Both are vital and cannot be overlooked. In some situations, the framework of soil chemistry may provide the clearest logical structure for the analysis of a problem. In others, thinking along the lines of soil physics may be the better method. In no case should either be ignored.

NUTRIENT UPTAKE

Although soil formation is in part a weathering process, it is also greatly affected by the circulation of soluble chemicals through the roots of plants into the stems and foliage; back to the surface of the ground in the form of leaves, fruits, and twigs; and into soluble compounds again by the decomposition of this litter through the combined action of bacteria, fungi, and soil animals. The relative amounts of the different nutrients taken up into the trees play a large part in determining the relative growth and competitive ability of the different species. Furthermore, the decomposition process will affect (and will also be affected by) the nature of the soil development and through this will exert an influence on succeeding vegetation.

Trees, like all other higher plants, require a whole list of chemical elements to live and grow. These include the gaseous elements (H, O, C), the macronutrients (Ca, K, Mg, N, P, S), and the micronutrients (B, Cu, Fe, Mn, Mo, Z). Carbon, hydrogen, and oxygen are obtained in large part from water and carbon dioxide. Phosphorus, potassium, and the other nutrients weather from rock material. The two major sources of available nutrients in the soil are the nutrients adsorbed on colloidal particles and the nutrient salts in the soil solution. Positively charged ions or cations, including NH_4^+, K^+, and Ca^{++}, are mostly adsorbed on the colloids. The negatively charged ions or anions, such as NO_3^-, Cl^-, SO_4^-, and some of the cations are found in the soil solution.

Nitrogen, phosphorus, potassium (these three constitute the NPK of the agricultural chemist), and calcium (commonly supplied in cultural practices as lime) are the chemicals most often in short supply in the soil. Sulphur, magnesium, and iron are seldom limiting in their availability in the soil. Minor elements are needed in minute amounts, and, rarely, a complete absence of boron, manganese, zinc, copper, or molybdenum may cause malnutrition of forest trees. For example, in parts of western and southern Australia, the addition of slight quantities of zinc—even the driving of a galvanized nail into a tree or the erecting of a galvanized rabbit fence—is sufficient to correct stagnation and dieback in Monterey pine and *P. pinaster* (Stoate, 1951). Stone (1968) observed that Stoate's finding of a kangaroo skeleton beneath the single green pine in an otherwise deficient plantation has somewhat limited implications for silvicultural practice. Over a wider area in Australia and New Zealand, as well as in flatwoods soils of the southeastern United States, phosphate additions have been demonstrated as essential for normal growth of pines, while additions of lime may be necessary for the establishment of conifers on many acid heaths in western Europe.

For optimum growth, trees require a balanced supply of these various nutrients. For example, good growth is obtained by supplying seedlings with artificial nutrient solutions commonly used in experimental studies. Trees do differ from most agricultural crops, though, in growing quite well on relatively small amounts of nutrients. Many forest sites with adequate tree growth test relatively low in nitrogen, phosphorus, potassium, or calcium. Wood has a low ash content and can be produced by trees using only small quantities of nutrients (Table 8.1). The leaves and fruit, wherein

Table 8.1. Nutrient Demands of Forest Compared with Agricultural Crops in Western Europe

Type of Management	Nutrient Removal from Site During 100-year Rotation or Cropping (kg per acre)		
	Ca	K	P
Pines	203	91	21
Other conifers	438	234	41
Hardwoods	879	225	50
Agricultural crops (oats, grass, potatoes, and turnips in rotation)	980	3000	430

Source: Rennie, 1955.

much of the mineral ash is concentrated, are annually returned to the soil. As a result, the recycling of a small quantity of mineral nutrients is often sufficient to keep a forest going well.

Accumulation of Nutrients by Trees

By analyzing the mineral content of the tree it is possible to determine the amounts of the various elements that have been taken up. The leaves are particularly responsive to nutrient supply, and foliar analysis has long been popular as a means of assessing soil fertility. In particular, the current year's foliage of the terminal shoot is especially indicative of soil conditions (Leyton and Armson, 1955; Leaf, 1968). For some species and nutrients, however, foliage from other portions of the crown, or other tissues such as bole wood, bole bark, live branches, or buds, may prove of greater diagnostic value (Leaf, 1968). The season of the year must also be considered, since the mineral content of the leaves changes as the season progresses.

Plants tend to take up soluble minerals as they are supplied to the roots. Nevertheless, the amounts of a given element in the leaves at a given time are not clearly related either to the amount available in the soil, as estimated crudely by conventional soil chemistry techniques, or to the nutritive requirements of the species, which takes up what it can and not necessarily what it needs. Rare metals in the soil, however, can frequently be picked up in foliar analysis, and this fact has been used to some extent in prospecting for minerals.

Nevertheless, there have been many comparisons between the mineral contents of the foliage of trees of the same species growing on different soils. In a study of white oak growing on different soil types in Illinois (McVickar, 1949), differences in the chemical composition of the leaf were significant only when trees growing on the poorest soils were compared to those growing on the best. Again, in New York State, when several hardwood species were compared on three soil types of varying limestone content, the calcium content of the foliage was found to be more dependent upon the inherent capacity of each species to absorb the nutrient rather than upon the calcium level of the soil itself (Bard, 1946).

The relative ability of different species to absorb nutrients has been studied in many parts of the world, particularly with reference to calcium uptake. In the northeastern United States, basswood, yellow-poplar, dogwood, and red cedar are among the trees that concentrate large amounts of calcium (and also phosphorus and potassium) in their foliage; while beech, red spruce, the pines, and hemlock are low in their uptake.

By putting together data for the mineral content of roots, stem wood, bark, branches, and leaves, it is possible to estimate the annual uptake of nutrients by forest trees. The accumulation and distribution of nutrients in three major kinds of European forests, deciduous, non-pine coniferous, and pine, show that calcium is always accumulated in the greatest quantities, especially in deciduous forests (Figure 8.1; Rennie, 1955). Pines have lower requirements than other ecosystems. The magnitude of accumulation by the three types seems closely related to the site conditions on which each naturally grows, deciduous forests on the more fertile sites and pines on infertile sites.

Effect on Tree Growth

When non-demanding trees are grown on their natural sites, little correlation is generally found between their nutrient uptake, as assessed by chemical analysis of the foliage, and their growth rate. For example, a Finnish study by Aaltonen (1950) showed no correlation between the chemical constituents of Scots pine and Norway spruce needles and four forest sites of different fertilities from which they were collected, and upon which these species demonstrated markedly different growth rates.

With more demanding species on poor sites, however, good correlations may be found. In the same Finnish study, European white birch leaves showed higher calcium and potassium contents (but lower phosphate contents) on the better sites than on the poorer. In a series of studies of coniferous plantations on poor heathland sites in Great Britain, Leyton (1955) found high correlation between the mineral content (nitrogen, phosphorus, and potassium) of the current year's foliage in the terminal shoot and the growth rate of the tree. On these degraded soils, Sitka spruce and Japanese larch seem to be more affected by the low mineral content of the soil than Corsican or Scots pine.

Undergrowth may compete with the tree overstory for the supply of tree nutrients. On the heath sites where the British experiments

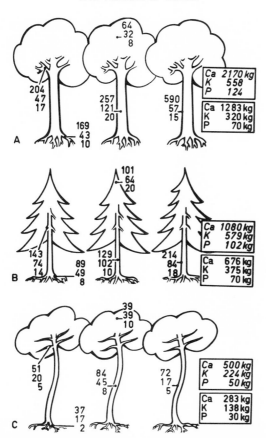

Fig. 8.1. Distribution (kg/ha) of calcium, potassium, and phosphorus in three major types of exploited forests. Total content in standing crop of 100-year-old forests (normal type) and total uptake (including output by thinnings) of the same elements over the century (italics). Values in boxes are for the total tree stand; various subtotals for leaves, branches, bark, wood, and roots are shown in the figures. (A) Deciduous hardwoods; (B) Conifers other than pines; (C) Pines. (Diagram from Duvigneaud and Denaeyer–De Smet, 1970; data after Rennie, 1955.)

were carried out, artificial shading of the ground vegetation to reduce the growth of the heather resulted in a substantial increase in the availability of nitrogen, ash, and manganese to the overstory of Sitka spruce (Leyton, 1955).

The effect of nutrients on tree growth has been intensively studied. Reviews of the nutrient requirements of forest stands

(Tamm, 1964), the deficiencies of potassium, manganese, and sulphur in forest trees (Leaf, 1968), and the microelement nutrition of trees (Fortescue and Marten, 1970; Stone, 1968) provide entry into the vast literature. Besides foliar analysis, other major methods of diagnosing the nutrient status of forests include experimental field, greenhouse, or hydroponic studies (Ingestad, 1962), visual deficiency symptoms (Hacskaylo *et al.*, 1969), and soil analyses (Tamm, 1964; Leaf, 1968). Despite the work involved, use of all the techniques may be justified in view of the large investments in forest fertilization that may be made on the strength of the diagnosis.

A useful analysis in field surveys to determine the nutrient status of stands involves sampling and analyzing the upper four centimeters of soil after removing the litter (O_1 horizon) (Evers, 1967). Since the soil zone is strongly influenced by the litter, this technique provides in effect a combination of soil and foliage analyses. Nutrient ratios, particularly C/P, C/K, and C/N, are then computed to describe the nutrient status of the stand. Ratios of C/P = 112, C/K = 92, and C/N = 20 characterized a Norway spruce stand of maximum growth in southwestern Germany, whereas nutrient disorders can be expected in pure and mixed stands of spruce with ratios higher than C/P = 400, C/K = 450, and C/N = 25. The method has proved inexpensive and simple, having no seasonal restrictions on sampling as in foliar analysis. Furthermore, the ratios are highly correlated with growth rate (Evers, 1971) and with the amount, availability, and cycling of nutrients (Evers, 1968).

Soil Acidity

The measurement of the available nutrient content of the soil or of the plant is a long and tedious operation. In the soil, the problem is further complicated by the fact that only those nutrient ions in solution or capable of moving into solution as others are removed can be absorbed by the plant. Much of the chemical content of the soil is held too tightly by the soil particles to be released to plant roots. Furthermore, the nutrient availability of the soil is constantly changing. Changes in the water content of the soil, the removal of nutrients by plant roots, and the chemical by-effects of soil organisms all constantly change the base-exchange balance.

To avoid both the tedious chemical analysis and the complexities of actual soil chemistry relationships, many workers with forest soils have emphasized the importance of soil acidity (Small, 1954).

This is usually measured in terms of pH, the logarithm of the reciprocal of the concentration of hydrogen ions in solution. The pH can be measured with reasonable accuracy in the field with a portable potentiometer employing a glass electrode or can be approximated with simple colorimetric tests. Many efforts have been made to relate soil pH to the distribution and growth of trees and other plants. Forest soils normally range from very acid, pH 4, up to slightly acid, pH 6.5. Only on calcareous soils does forest litter render soils neutral (pH 7) or slightly basic, pH 7.5.

Actually, soil acidity is far too complicated to be measured by a simple pH scale, and this measure of acidity must be accepted merely as an empirical number which provides a rough index to certain of the chemical properties of the soil. Approximate relationships may therefore be expected between soil pH and plant behavior, but cause-and-effect conclusions should not be drawn. The soil pH reflects both the chemical properties of the mineral soil as well as the chemical properties of the organic residue deposited as litter. Optimum growth of a tree may be associated with a narrow range in acidity. For instance, Sitka spruce in England has been demonstrated to grow better between pH 4 and 5 than under more acid or more alkaline conditions (Leyton, 1952). In general, lime-loving plants such as yellow-poplar and northern white cedar in the United States are found in neutral or alkaline soils, while acid-tolerant plants such as balsam fir and eastern hemlock are usually confined to highly acidic soils. Under various actual soil nutrient conditions, however, almost any species can be grown successfully under a wide range of soil pH conditions (Wilde, 1954).

The forest tree itself influences soil acidity. The general trend is for conifers such as the pines, spruces, hemlock, and Douglas-fir to intensify the increased acidity of the upper soil to a greater extent than hardwoods or cedars. Individual species, however, vary widely in their effect. An example is provided by soil pH on old fields in Connecticut where eastern red cedar and common juniper were growing side by side (Spurr, 1941). Under the cedar, soil pH was lowered in the root zone and raised in the topsoil where litter accumulated, indicating the high capacity of this species to remove calcium and other bases from the soil. In contrast, the juniper foliage increased the acidity of the topsoil, apparently because of the low base content of its foliage. Similar results have been reported elsewhere for other species.

Root-Inhabiting Fungi and Nutrient Uptake

When seedlings of forest tree species are grown in water cultures, root hairs develop. In the forest, however, root hairs are less conspicuous. Instead, the roots of forest trees are commonly ingrown with certain species of soil fungi. The association of plant root tissues and fungal mycelia is known as a *mycorrhiza* (meaning a fungus-root). In pines, birches, beeches, and oaks, *ectotrophic* fungi form a sheath or mat surrounding the rootlets, giving them a characteristic swollen appearance. The hyphae penetrate between the outer root cells but do not enter the cells. A less conspicuous group, *endotrophic* fungi, forms no sheath, but the filaments grow within and between epidermal and cortical cells and extend into the soil. They are associated with various cultivated crops, grasses, and some trees, including redwood, maples, yellow-poplar, and sweet gum (Buckman and Brady, 1969; Harley, 1969).

The symbiotic relationship that exists between tree roots and these mycorrhiza-forming fungi is exceedingly complex and is as yet but poorly understood. Whatever the mechanism may be, it is quite clear that the relationship is mutually beneficial (Rayner and Neilson-Jones, 1944; Kelley 1950; Harley, 1969). Even the presence of the fungi in the soil has been shown to benefit tree growth, presumably by their action in attacking soil organic matter and breaking it down into compounds available to the higher plant. The fungi themselves have been shown to grow better in the presence of tree roots than in their absence.

In fact, the presence of mycorrhiza-forming fungi is essential to successful growth of many species. In the case of many nurseries situated on non-forest soils and of many plantations situated on non-forest land, it has proved essential to introduce forest soil or litter infected with mycorrhiza-forming fungi. This has been necessary for all the extensive plantations of Monterey pine and other northern conifers in the Southern Hemisphere. To cite another example, when jack pine seedlings were grown in pot cultures with various types of fertilization and soil treatment, only the seedlings infected with humus from a healthy pine plantation developed mycorrhizae, and only these were normal in growth and appearance.

The importance of mycorrhizae to pines and other forest trees seems to be that they are highly efficient accumulators of nutrient ions which become available both to the host tree and to the fungus

(Melin, 1962). In fact, mycorrhizae do not form in trees growing in nutrient-rich soil, even when the soil is inoculated with the fungus (Harley, 1969). The ability of mycorrhizal roots to supply nitrogen to trees from nitrogen-poor soils has been much stressed. Investigations of beech in England (Harley, 1950 *et seq.*) and of Monterey pine in California (Stone and McAuliffe, 1954) also suggest that much of the benefit is due to the ability of mycorrhizal trees to take up phosphorus under soil conditions unfavorable to non-infected trees of the same species. Marx (1969 *et seq.*) has shown that mycorrhizae are beneficial in another way. They protect the host tree from root-rot pathogens by their antibiotic effects.

Fertilization of Forest Soils

Assuming that a forest soil contains mycorrhiza-forming fungi suitable for infecting the trees being grown, growth may in many cases be stimulated by adding the necessary fertilizers. Occasionally, fertilization may be essential in nutrient-deficient soils, as in the case of adding lime to certain heath soils being reforested in England and super-phosphate or zinc to soils deficient in that element in South Australia and being afforested to Monterey pine. More commonly, application of standard NPK (nitrogen, phosphorus, and potassium) fertilizers and lime in needed quantities and proportions will stimulate growth. Nitrogen has proved the most important single element generally in short supply in forest soils, and consequently addition of nitrogen fertilizers almost always stimulates forest growth.

In the past, fertilization of forest stands has been given only passing attention. However, under present economic conditions, which are much more favorable to intensive forest management, fertilization is becoming more and more practicable and is being carried out increasingly under specific site conditions in the Pacific Northwest (Gessel, 1968; Steinbrenner, 1968), the South (Broadfoot and Ike, 1968; Maloc, 1968), and parts of the eastern United States (White, 1968), at least on an experimental basis. Fertilizers are being increasingly used in hastening forest establishment, increasing forest growth in conjunction with thinning, and countering depletion of nutrients caused by intensive harvesting under short rotations. Fertilization has particular promise for the purpose of stimulating tree seed production.

Reaching far beyond increasing growth of trees are the complex effects of fertilization on forest ecosystems (Hilmon and Douglass, 1968). The positive effects of increased yield and quality of wild-life plant foods and cattle forage may be offset by animal damage to trees. The effects of forest fertilization on water quality and yield are under study. In upland forests, careful application of fertilizers apparently does not constitute a pollution hazard if water reaches the streams by moving through the soil.

NUTRIENT RETURN

The minerals that are taken up into the forest tree are eventually returned to the forest soil except for the amount carried out of the forest in logs and other forest products. Soil minerals are returned to the surface of the soil through leaf-fall and through the leaching effect of rain on the foliage. On the forest floor, a myriad of mammals, insects and other arthropods, earthworms, fungi, and bacteria attack the accumulating organic material, decomposing it and rendering it re-available for plant nutrition. The nature of the organic matter and of the soil plants and animals plays an important role in determining the nature of the soil profile and in limiting the vegetation that can thrive on the soil as the soil develops.

Litter-Fall

Leaves, small twigs, bark, and fruits add from 1,500 to 5,000 kilograms of oven-dry organic material to the surface of a fully stocked hectare [1] in a single year. Leaf litter accounts for roughly 70 percent of the total (Bray and Gorham, 1964). Under open conifer stands the weight of litter-fall may drop below 1,000 kilograms per hectare, and in the tropical rain forest as much as 10,000 kilograms may be accumulated (Lutz and Chandler, 1946; Bray and Gorham, 1964).

Climate exerts a predominant effect on litter-fall as seen in the annual production figures (kilograms per hectare) in four major climatic zones: arctic-alpine—900, cool temperate—3,100, warm temperate—4,900, and equatorial—9,700 (Bray and Gorham, 1964).

Considering a worldwide range of sites, total litter production of

[1] Kilograms per hectare is a relatively close numerical equivalent of pounds per acre: 1 kg/ha = 0.89 lb/acre.

evergreen forests exceeds that in deciduous forests by about 13 percent (Bray and Gorham, 1964). However, considerable variation exists for specific areas. European beech in Germany, for example, shows consistently greater litter production than pine or spruce, apparently reflecting the predominance of beech on the more productive soils. Substantial annual fluctuations in leaf-fall are possible under evergreen forests of temperate climates. Although evergreen conifers typically hold their needles for two years or more, the oldest needles normally drop off each year. In favorable seasons, older foliage may be retained in large part, whereas under the influence of drought or other unfavorable conditions several years' accumulation of leaves may be dropped.

Understory vegetation plays an important role in the circulation of nutrients that often has been ignored. Its contribution tends to be strongest in the early and late stages of stand development, when the amount of light reaching the understory is greatest. Under relatively open conditions understory vegetation may contribute up to 28 percent of the total litter (Bray and Gorham, 1964). Under white pine and mixed hardwood forests in Connecticut, Scott (1955) found that subordinate vegetation accounted for about 15 percent of the annual weight of the litter. The shrubs and herbs, however, contained higher percentages of many nutrient elements than did the tree foliage, so that as much as one-quarter of the annual return of nutrients to the soil came through the lesser plants. In an English sessile oak woodland, bracken fern (*Pteridium aquilinum*) contributed in both its litter and rainfall leachates nearly one-third of the total potassium reaching the soil annually (Carlisle *et al.*, 1967).

Rainfall

Precipitation of moisture plays an important part in adding to the supply of soil nutrients. It dissolves nitrogen and precipitates dust directly from the atmosphere. About 5 kilograms of nitrogen are added annually to each hectare of soil in the Temperate Zone.

In addition, rain washes materials from surfaces of plants and leaches from foliage substantial mineral nutrients which may be rapidly recycled through ecosystems. Washed-off materials include airborne dust particles, natural exudates, and materials released by the activities of damaging animals. Nutrients leached most easily from foliage include potassium, sodium, calcium, and magnesium (Tukey, 1962). In England, rainfall collected under forest canopies was found to have substantially (from two to eight times) more sodium, potassium, calcium, and magnesium than rain water collected in adjacent open locations (Madgwick and Ovington, 1959). The amounts of these nutrients contained in the precipitation were the same as or greater than the amounts of these nutrients taken up permanently in the tree crops. Phosphorus was present in rain water only in very small amounts. In an English oak forest, the contribution of precipitation (including washings from vegetation, stem flow, and incident rainfall) to the total of nutrients reaching the soil exceeded that of litter-fall for potassium, magnesium, and sodium (Carlisle *et al.*, 1967). In Monterey pine and Douglas-fir plantations in New Zealand, substantially more potassium and nearly as much phosphorus were returned to the soil by rainfall than by leaf-fall (Will, 1959).

The Forest Floor

The leaf-fall and other litter gradually accumulate on the forest floor until decomposition begins. Initially litter-fall may exceed decomposition but, sooner or later, an equilibrium will be reached between the yearly additions of organic matter and the yearly rate of decomposition. Later, in old, open forests litter decomposition may exceed litter-fall, and the surface layer becomes less. Under optimum conditions for soil biotic activity—with the forest floor being warm, moist, and well-aerated for much of the year—decomposition will keep pace with additions and no organic matter is accumulated. Where soil biotic activity is inhibited by cold, acid conditions, insufficient moisture, or insufficient oxygen, however, litter will accumulate indefinitely. Thick accumulations of raw (i.e., undecomposed) humus, peat, muck, and, eventually, coal beds thus arise.

The amount of time for the forest floor to reach near-equilibrium conditions of organic matter accumulation ranges from less than 10 years in fast-growing tropical forests to well over 100 years in the ponderosa pine type of the dry western United States.

Under such conditions, the forest floor will normally contain at any one time the equivalent of several years' litter-fall. Under upland oak forests in eastern Tennessee, where conditions are favorable for litter decomposition, the annual leaf-fall in one stand was found to be 2,915 kilograms per hectare as compared to a forest floor which contained 12,100 kilograms of organic matter after leaf-fall in the early winter and 9,420 kilograms at the end of the summer season of active decomposition (Blow, 1955). In a 27-year-old red pine plantation in Connecticut, annual needle-fall was 4,030 kilograms per hectare compared to the forest floor, which contained 31,170 kilograms per hectare.

In contrast to the eastern American forests, where the forest floor seldom contains more than the equivalent of 5 to 10 years' leaf-fall, the coniferous forests of the Pacific Coast may hold as much as the litter-fall of 50 years. The heavy accumulations of organic matter under the mixed coniferous forests of California and the Pacific Northwest result from the summer drought, which inhibits soil biotic activity.

In Britain conifer forests frequently develop a thick layer of organic matter, about three to five times the annual litter-fall, and Ovington (1962) assumes the annual litter-fall takes three to five years to decay. In deciduous forests on similar sites there is often little accumulation from year to year. Decomposition is frequently complete within twelve months and often virtually complete in six to nine months.

The Soil Biota

The surface of the forest soil supports one of the richest faunas and floras of all ecological niches—both in terms of numbers of species and their weight per unit volume of space. Plant litter forms the basic food supply, but interactions between plants that carry on photosynthesis, saprophytes that live on dead organic material, parasites, and predators are exceedingly complex. In a few paragraphs we can only indicate the complexity and some of the principal types of organisms responsible for the decomposition of organic matter. From the standpoint of forest site, their importance is their combined effect on the reduction of the litter into soluble compounds that can be taken up by the roots of the forest.

Under favorable soil conditions characterized by sufficient warmth, moisture, and oxygen, bacteria are not only the most numerous of all soil organisms but are also the heaviest. The bacteria inhabiting forest soil may weigh as much as 1,680 kilograms per hectare. In such quantities they are capable of processing much of the organic matter that is added annually to the soil. Bacteria are more abundant where other soil animals, particularly earthworms, are present. The main role of bacteria in decomposition is that of further breakdown of materials already ingested and excreted by macro-organisms. Soils worked by earthworms and millipedes contain about two-thirds more bacteria than unworked soils (Kollmansperger, 1956; Went, 1963). Acid soils limit bacterial populations probably because acid soils limit macro-organisms such as earthworms. A special group of free-living soil bacteria is particularly important in fixing atmospheric nitrogen into forms suitable for use by other plants and by animals.

The importance of fungi in forming mycorrhizae has already been discussed. The same fungi and many others are present in the soil in large amounts. Under conditions unfavorable to bacterial growth, fungi are better able to survive, grow, and become the dominant element of soil life. With the cool, wet, acid conditions characteristic of the forest floor under spruces and firs in boreal and high-altitude forests, fungi are the chief agent of humus decomposition. The fungi in such a soil may weigh a ton or more per acre.

The capacity of earthworms to cultivate the soil has been well known ever since the exploratory studies of Darwin. Earthworm populations in the temperate forest reach the hundreds of thousands per hectare (for example, 728,700 per hectare under mixed hardwoods in central Germany). Under the Nigerian rain forest, it has been estimated that 4,480 kilograms of soil per hectare are cast up upon the surface by earthworm activity.

Earthworms show marked preferences in their choice of litter for food supply. In central Europe, for example, they prefer alder and elm to oak and beech and cannot thrive at all on Norway spruce. In southern Germany, earthworms were studied in a series of paired plots stocked with hardwoods and Norway spruce, respectively (Schlenker, 1971). Stands of each pair grew on similar soils. Five times as many earthworms were found under hardwoods as under spruce, even in first-generation spruce stands following hardwoods. In the United States, earthworms show similar preferences for leaves rich in minerals (such as ash), a reluctant ability to handle the tough, leathery leaves of oak and beech, and a distaste for acid conifer needles.

Among the arthropods, the large division of jointed animals that includes insects, spiders and crustaceans, mites, and springtails (Collembola) is the most important (Birch and Clark, 1953; Murphy, 1953). Mites are microscopic or nearly microscopic relatives of the spiders that infest the surface layers of forest soils in immense numbers (Wallwork, 1959). Springtails are the most abundant of the many soil insects, as many as 60 species have been found in a single young white pine stand in Connecticut (Bellinger, 1954). Springtails live and feed in part on decaying plant material of the surface and in part on deeper-living microorganisms (Zachariae, 1962). Their role in the decomposition of organic matter is obviously great and is now being studied intensively (Edwards *et al.*, 1970). Termites and ants are also effective litter-decomposing agents, particularly in the Tropics. In the Nigerian rain forest study mentioned above, they were found to have deposited 1,120 kilograms of soil per hectare on the surface during the year.

Mammals, too, play a major role in the decomposition of organic matter. The smaller ground-inhabiting species—including the moles, shrews, voles, mice, and chipmunks—live upon plant materials and small animal life in the top soil layers. The tunnels and burrows they make aid materially in loosening compact soils, in incorporating organic matter in the deeper levels, and in providing passages for the downward movement of rain water containing soil nutrients. Because of their high metabolic work, their importance is great in proportion to their total weight.

Decomposition of Organic Matter

The total effectiveness of the bacteria, fungi, and animals of the soil in decomposing litter is shown by the fact that, sooner or later, the litter disappears from the soil in many forests as fast as it is added from above. Direct leaching by rain water must be added to the soil biota as an important factor in this disappearance. Complete decomposition may take from a few weeks to many years.

The nature of the decomposition process and the time it takes depend largely upon the forest tree species and upon the climate in which they grow. If the foliage is palatable to the soil organisms —and that condition seems to imply that it is rich in calcium and other nutrients and not excessively woody or leathery in structure —and if the forest soil is warm, well watered, and well aerated, organic matter is returned rapidly to the soil and litter does not accumulate. Such conditions characterize well-drained soils in the tropical rain forest and often occur in temperate zones in deciduous forests of the eastern United States on well-drained sites. Although more litter is deposited in tropical forests, the rich microflora and microfauna decompose it at a rate six to ten times as fast as in temperate forests (Madge, 1965, 1966). Also, in the pinyon-juniper woodlands of the southwestern United States, where summers are both hot and wet and litter-fall is relatively light, there is little or no humus accumulation.

Soft tissues of plants and animals are usually decomposed by soil microflora alone, while woody materials are typically broken down by the complex interaction of soil animals and plants. At the time of leaf-fall, leaves are already infested with an extensive external and internal microflora, and once on the forest floor they are also invaded by litter fungi. Leaf litter darkens as it weathers and the water-soluble substances, chiefly sugars, organic acids, and polyphenols, are leached out. Fragmentation of litter by soil animals, mainly earthworms in the temperate regions and termites in the tropics, provides a desirable physical substrate for microfloral growth, and the litter is invaded by omnipresent microorganisms. If fragmentation is retarded experimentally, the whole decomposition process is slowed (Edwards and Heath, 1963; Witkamp and Crossley, 1966). Tissue breakdown by microflora, in turn, favors attack by soil microfauna, and the cycle continues. Thus organic matter is gradually decomposed and incorporated into the soil through an intricate sequence of feeding by soil animals and growth of microorganisms.

If the foliage is palatable to soil organisms but the decomposition process is slowed down, the top layer of the mineral soil will gradually become mixed with finely divided, decayed organic matter. This mixture of mineral soil and humus creates what is known as a *mull* organic layer, a term taken from Middle English, meaning "dust." A mull humus layer is characteristic of much of the hardwood forest in the temperate zones.

If, on the other hand, the foliage is highly acid or is otherwise detrimental to soil biotic activity, raw humus tends to accumulate on top of the mineral soil. Rainfall then becomes the chief decomposing agent, and the acids dissolved from the foliage by the downward-percolating water have a high capacity for leaching the upper layers of the mineral soil of inorganic nutrients. This *mor* type of humus thus tends to favor the development of a podzolic soil condition. Mor humus conditions are typically found in cold climates in the boreal zones or at high altitudes, especially under spruces and other conifers that produce an acid foliage.

In the Temperate Zone forests of the northern United States and southern Canada and in similar zones in Europe and Asia, one tree species may favor the development of a mull condition while another may favor the mor. In central New England and Great Britain, pine plantations fall in the former category and natural hardwood stands in the latter. In the central hardwood region of the United States, oak litter is the slowest and elm the quickest to decompose (Kucera, 1959). In England, European beech litter has proved the most resistant to decomposition among major hardwood species; oak is relatively resistant, whereas elm, birch, and ash decompose completely within one year (Heath *et al.*, 1966).

The same species may favor the development of quite different humus types on different soils. Thus European beech in England and France forms a mull on calcareous soils in all conditions and also on non-calcareous soils, if not too acid, in a mild, moderately humid climate. In colder and wetter climates, or on poor and acid soils, the same species causes a mor humus layer, accentuated acidity, and accelerated leaching (Duchaufour, 1947; Ovington, 1968).

Many efforts have been made to classify forest humus types. All gradations between total decomposition and no decomposition, however, can be found. Actual humus conditions in the forest for the most part do not fall into clear categories, and the schemes proposed have little actual reality or interest save to the forest soils specialist.

The Nitrogen Cycle

In considering the cycling of nutrients from the soil to the tree and back again, a special word must be said for nitrogen, as this element comes largely from the air and not from the decomposition of soil minerals. The part that rainfall plays in the addition of nitrogen to the soil from the atmosphere has already been mentioned. This input by precipitation is in the form of ammonium and nitrate nitrogen.

Nitrogen-fixing bacteria living symbiotically in root nodules also contribute to supplying nitrogen directly from the air to plants. Legumes are the most important plants with nitrogen-fixing bacteria. Such species as black locust, honey locust, acacias, and mesquite are trees of the legume family in the North Temperate Zone. There are hundreds of similar species in the tropics. In addition, many herbs and shrubs of this family characteristically inhabit the forest floor throughout much of the world. In addition to the legumes, a number of other plants have been shown to increase soil nitrogen supply by their presence through the medium of nitrogen-fixing bacteria in their roots (Stewart, 1967). Among these are the alders (both in Europe and North America), casuarinas in the tropics, and shrubs of the genera *Ceanothus* and *Myrica*.

In many forests, free-living soil bacteria of the genera *Azotobacter* and *Clostridium* are the most important agents fixing atmospheric nitrogen into water-soluble compounds. In boreal forests with acid soils and no legumes, the only source of nitrogen is apparently from precipitation.

At any one time, the total amount of nitrogen in usable form in the soil is relatively small compared to that of other soil nutrients. Only the ammonium form, NH_4^+, and the nitrate form, NO_3^-, are taken up by higher plants. By far the greatest amount of nitrogen in any soil at any one time is in an organic form and not available in the soil solution. Furthermore, nitrogenous compounds are subject to losses by leaching and fire. The nitrate anion, NO_3^-, being very soluble, is subject to major losses by leaching, whereas the ammonium cation, NH_4^+, is much less affected, being retained by soil colloids through cation exchange. Being flammable, all forms of nitrogen are subject to loss by fire, and a hot fire can volatilize 50 kilograms per hectare or more of organic nitrogen to N_2 gas.

Successful tree growth, therefore, depends in large measure upon quick rotation of nitrogen. Most of the nitrogen taken up by the tree is returned to the soil, and the nitrogenous litter is quickly decomposed by bacteria and other soil organisms. Nitrogen constitutes from less than 1 to nearly 3 percent of the soil organic matter, and this small amount is used over and over again.

The nitrogen cycle of stable forest communities is diagrammed in Figure 8.2. The main cycle involves the production of NH_4^+ from decomposition of litter and its absorption again by the vegetation. The subcycle involving NO_3^- may be important under certain

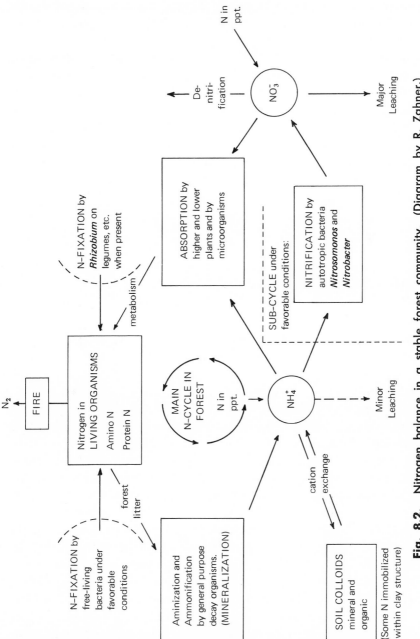

Fig. 8.2. Nitrogen balance in a stable forest community. (Diagram by R. Zahner.)

favorable circumstances when exchangeable bases are abundant. Tree species are known to have differing requirements for the different forms of nitrogen (Evers, 1964).

Any condition that causes raw humus to accumulate on the forest floor rather than decompose quickly tends to result in a shortage of nitrogen for tree growth. Under the cold, wet conditions in which peat forms, nitrogen is in particularly short supply. It is on such sites that pitcher plants and other plants that are able to obtain nitrogen by capturing insects thrive. An excessive development of the mor type of raw humus usually indicates poor nitrogen supply in the soil. Such a condition will result in lowered growth of many forest trees but usually not of the spruces and those other conifers for which a mor humus layer is a normal soil development.

OUTPUT OF NUTRIENTS

The End Products of Decomposition

As the decomposition of organic matter proceeds, mineral nutrients are gradually transformed to ions that can be absorbed by tree roots. Losses from leaching, fire, removal from the forest in the form of forest products and animals, and other sources must in the long run be balanced by additions from the weathering of soil minerals, additions in rain water, and by the fixing of atmospheric nitrogen. As a by-product, the evolution of carbon dioxide through the respiration of soil organisms plays an important part in replenishing the supply of this gas in the atmosphere.

Losses in Drainage Water and Timber Harvest

Nutrient losses from forested watersheds through drainage water seem not to be large. Using small undisturbed watersheds in the northern deciduous forest of New Hampshire under ideal topographic and bedrock conditions, Likens *et al.* (1967) reported that net losses of the minerals studied were counterbalanced by chemical weathering of underlying bedrock and till.

Nutrient losses from timber harvesting may seem minor because the boles of forest trees contain relatively small amounts of nutrients. On paper at least, losses appear small, particularly if expressed on an annual basis or when compared to the high amounts of nutrients removed in agricultural crops (Table 8.1). However, it is recognized that appreciable losses in nutrient capital may occur periodically, depending on the type and severity of the harvest (Ovington, 1968). Rennie (1955) also expressed concern that the nutrient drain through intensive harvesting might exceed the capacity of the ecosystem to replenish the losses.

Losses through harvesting are typically considered to be only the nutrients contained in tree boles. However, in addition to loss of nutrients in tree boles, which is easily determined, harvesting also causes disturbance to the site, and additional losses (their magnitude unknown at present) may occur due to the disruption of the normal cycling process, increased erosion, and runoff. Major disruptions such as clearcutting are more likely to accelerate nutrient losses than the annual removal of scattered trees. However, dense regrowth of herbaceous species, grasses, and woody vegetation following clearcutting on many forest sites may replace trees in the nutrient cycle and prevent major losses. Studies of the effects of timber harvest of various kinds and intensities on nutrient cycling are only now under way.

The magnitude of nutrient losses that may occur when the nutrient cycle is disrupted by complete removal of the forest has been forcefully demonstrated in studies of northern deciduous ecosystems at the Hubbard Brook Experimental Forest in New Hampshire (Likens *et al.*, 1970). On a small watershed all trees, saplings, and shrubs were cut, but not removed, and regrowth was inhibited by herbicide spray in each of two years following cutting. As a result, annual stream runoff increased and percolating rain water flushed substantial amounts of nutrients from the system during the two years following cutting (during the period vegetation was inhibited by spraying). Average stream water concentrations increased over 4 times for calcium and magnesium, over 15 times for potassium, and 1.7 times for sodium. Nitrate concentration increased 41-fold the first year and 56-fold the second above the undisturbed condition. Nitrification of NH_4^+ by bacteria increased manyfold when absorption of this cation by higher plants ceased (see Figure 8.2). This process led to a marked increase in nitrate and hydrogen ions. Then the mineral ions, Ca, Mg, K, and Na, were released into solution as hydrogen ions replaced them on soil particles. The total net export of inorganic substances from the treated system was 14 to 15 times that of the undisturbed watersheds.

The experiment is of great value in illustrating the response of an ecosystem to a disrupted nutrient cycle. Caution should be exercised, however, in extrapolating results of this experiment and citing them as a typical example of the clearcutting regeneration method. Contrary to what the name implies, clearcutting is rarely as severe as removing and suppressing all living vegetation. The study does provide an extreme case of complete artificial denudation.

MINERAL CYCLING IN THE ECOSYSTEM

The components of the nutrient cycle previously discussed may be combined to provide a general picture of the annual circulation of chemical elements in ecosystems (Figure 8.3). Nutrient cycling is essentially a polycyclic phenomenon consisting of two major cycles, the internal biological cycle of plant-soil exchanges and the external geological cycle of nutrient inputs from the atmosphere and from geologic weathering of parent material and losses through leaching. Within each are short-term (daily, seasonal) and long-term subcycles.

The uptake by the forest (sum of the retained and returned elements) comes partly from the products of organic matter decomposition and in part from minerals weathered directly from the parent materials. Not all the nutrients needed for annual growth and maintenance of tissues come from annual uptake from the soil; considerable amounts may be circulated within the trees themselves. In a 20-year-old loblolly pine stand, Switzer et al. (1968) estimated that 43 percent of the nitrogen needed by the stand was translocated within the trees, mainly from the foliage. Internal cycling is indicated by the seasonal variations found in the mineral content of leaves (Duvigneaud and Denaeyer-De Smet, 1970). Young leaves are richer in nitrogen, potassium, and phosphorus and poorer in calcium than mature leaves. In autumn nitrogen, potassium, and phosphorus contents of foliage decrease due to nutrient transport to other plant parts and to rainwater leaching, but calcium increases. Nutrient content of xylem sap of deciduous forests also varies seasonally, being higher in spring and fall than

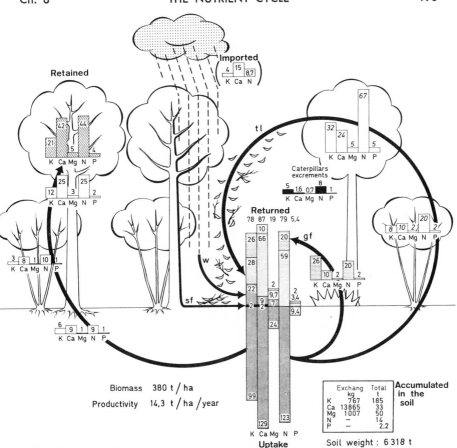

Fig. 8.3. Annual mineral cycling of potassium, calcium, magnesium, nitrogen, and phosphorus (in kg/ha) in a *Quercus robur–Fraxinus excelsior* forest with coppice of *Corylus avellana* and *Carpinus betulus* at Wavreille-Wève, Belgium. Retained: in the annual wood and bark increment of roots, 1-year-old twigs, and the above-ground wood and bark increment. Returned: by tree litter (*tl*), ground flora (*gf*), washing and leaching of canopy (*w*), and stem flow (*sf*). Imported: by incident rainfall (not included). Absorbed (uptake): the sum of quantities retained and returned. Macro-nutrients contained in the crown leaves when fully grown (July) are shown on the right-hand side of the figure in italics; these amounts are higher (except for calcium) than those returned by leaf litter, due to reabsorption by trees and leaf-leaching. Exchangeable and total element content in the soil are expressed on air-dry soil weights of particles < 2 mm. (After Duvigneaud, 1968, and Duvigneaud and Denaeyer–De Smet, 1968.)

in summer and winter, reflecting the seasons of greatest root absorption.

Nutrients used by the forest stand may be stored in the soil, the litter, or the trees themselves. In temperate forests accumulating litter contains a high proportion of the nutrients. In tropical regions of high rainfall, where evergreen forests occur on soil low in nutrients and where decomposition of litter is extremely rapid, storage of nutrients in the vegetation is necessary if excessive leaching is to be avoided. In a study of nutrient contents of a tropical forest in Ghana, Greenland and Kowal (1960) found most of the nutrients in the living trees. In the Belgian deciduous ecosystem over two-thirds of the nutrients, except phosphorus, are stored in the litter.

Nutrient transfers not illustrated in Figure 8.3 include nutrients leached out of leaves and quickly recycled and minerals released as a result of root exudation and annual mortality of fine roots. The amount of below-ground cycling is difficult to record, and there are conflicting reports of its significance.

Comparisons of ecosystems by their nutrient cycles show both similarities as well as striking differences (Duvigneaud and Denaeyer-De Smet, 1970). Oak ecosystems of Belgium and Russia were similar in their luxury consumption of calcium compared with the frugal turnover of calcium in spruce and pine ecosystems. The oak systems have significantly greater nutrient requirements, especially potassium and nitrogen, than beech, spruce, and pine forests of temperate Europe, and approach those of cultivated crops. Many differences between ecosystems in nutrient cycling, even forests of similar composition, not surprisingly, stem from basic differences in the chemical soil properties of the site.

Litter Removal

Just as the fertilization of forest soil may improve site quality, the removal of tree litter may lower it. Litter removal is essentially de-fertilization in that the nutrients in the litter are taken out of the nutrient cycle.

Since nutrients in the litter and even in the semidecomposed humus are not in a form immediately available to trees, the removal of litter or humus may have no immediate effect upon site quality. In parts of Europe where these have been removed repeatedly for livestock bedding, mulching, and other purposes, however, litter removal has resulted in severe deterioration of the site (Lutz and Chandler, 1946). German investigations indicate that the deficiency of nitrogen in soils subject to litter removal plays an important part in the impoverishment of the soil. The content of easily assimilable bases is also lowered.

In rare circumstances, the losses in nutrients resulting from litter removal may be more than counterbalanced by improved soil properties. Thus the removal of upland peat in northern Europe may result in warming the soil, reducing soil acidity, stimulating soil biota, and generally improving site conditions. The improvement of site through the burning or removal of accumulated litter and semidecomposed humus has been the subject of much investigation in northern Europe.

PLANT CHEMICAL PRODUCTS AND TREE GROWTH

The importance of soil fungi—particularly those fungi that form mycorrhizae on tree roots—in the mineral nutrition of forest trees has already been mentioned. On a site without necessary mycorrhiza-forming fungi, forest trees may not be able to survive or at best may grow but slowly. Simply by supplying the requisite fungi, however, excellent forest site conditions may be created. This relationship is but the most obvious example of plants and animals actually affecting forest site quality.

It is obvious that the great complex of plants that grow on and in the soil may well affect forest site quality in a similar fashion. Many examples are being discovered as research is conducted on the effect of chemicals produced by plants on the growth of other plants in the community (National Academy of Science, 1971). *Allelopathy*, the suppression of the growth or occurrence of some higher plants by chemicals released from another higher plant, has long been observed and discussed (Tukey, 1969) and is of widespread occurrence among woody plants and agricultural and wild species of many kinds (Whittaker and Feeny, 1971).

Allelopathic effects have been observed for rain-forest and temperate-forest species and for shrubs of the desert and the northern forest. Among forest tree species, the black walnut of the American northeast has long been known to affect markedly other plants through chemical exudate of its foliage and roots (Bode, 1958).

Many plants, including forest tree species, cannot grow if their root system comes into contact with that of a black walnut tree (Brooks, 1951). Others, such as Kentucky bluegrass, thrive and apparently grow better adjacent to the tree. Reduced growth of understory vegetation under cherrybark oaks was observed by Hook and Stubbs (1967) and confirmed by DeBell (1969) (Figure 8.4). The primary inhibitory substance in leaf extracts of cherrybark oak was found to be salicylic acid (DeBell, 1971). Leaching of this substance from oak crowns by rain presumably causes inhibition of vegetation beneath cherrybark oak. Other tree species known for allelopathic effects are ailanthus, eucalypts, Utah juniper, and sugar maple. In addition, nine woody species of western Washington, including Pacific madrone, western red cedar, Engelmann spruce, vine maple, and grand fir, were found to have a definite allelopathic potential (Del Moral and Cates, 1971).

Among the forest shrubs, particular attention has been given to the effect of bracken and heather on the growth of tree seedlings. Both are detrimental. For example, in Norway, roots of bracken were dried, ground, and an extract prepared with cold distilled water (Torkildsen, 1950). This extract, after being put through a bacterial filter, was used to water newly germinated Norway spruce seedlings growing in sterile sand. The plants so watered either died or were dwarfed. Three-year-old seedlings, however, were not affected by the treatment. Similarly, a water extract of heather has been shown to cause yellowing and abnormal growth of Norway spruce.

Various grasses have long been known to hold back the growth of many tree seedlings, particularly hardwoods. That the effect is in part chemical has been demonstrated by watering seedlings with the water extract of grass plants, a procedure which reduces the growth of potted hybrid poplars as compared to others treated with water only.

Substances that may potentially be involved in allelopathy are released from plants via litter-fall, leaching of foliage, volatilization from foliage, and root exudation. For example, leachates from eucalyptus leaves are known to inhibit the growth of grass and herbaceous species under natural conditions (Del Moral and Muller, 1970). In California shrub communities, volatile terpenes are released into the air from shrub species. They accumulate in the soil

Fig. 8.4. Vigorous development of vegetation beneath a sweetgum (A) in contrast with retarded development under a nearby cherrybark oak (B) four years after a seed-tree cut; coastal South Carolina. A sharp boundary between the affected and unaffected areas is evident in B. (U. S. Forest Service photo.)

during the dry season and inhibit growth of herbs causing bare belts, 1 to 2 m wide, devoid of herbs (Muller, 1966; McPherson and Muller, 1969). Root exudates have been implicated in the apparent inhibition of yellow birch seedlings by sugar maple (Tubbs, 1970).

That both the plants within the forest and the lower plants within the soil may directly affect the growth of forest trees, especially in the seedling state, is quite obvious. The mechanism by which this control is exerted, however, is only slowly becoming understood.

Several possibilities emerge. Most obviously, the various plants in the forest can, by absorbing moisture and soil nutrients, reduce the supply available to the tree and thus inhibit growth. Root competition is indeed a most important factor limiting growth in the forest and is discussed in detail in a later chapter. More is involved in the relationship. The growth of tree seedlings can be reduced even in the presence of ample water and nutrient supply by supplying an extract of plant substances as in the examples mentioned above.

The second possibility is that these plants produce chemicals which react with the chemicals of the soil in such a way as to change the supply of soil nutrients. Many soil bacteria and fungi attack and render available to tree roots the nutrients bound up in semidecomposed organic matter. Why should not they and other plants also react with and render unavailable other nutrients in the soil? Although the importance of nutrition is great, there is considerable evidence that it is far from the only factor involved.

The third possibility then is that the plants actually contain organic chemicals which, in minute amounts, may change the growth pattern of other plants that absorb them. This view finds increasing evidence in its support. The discovery that plants are regulated in many and diverse ways by auxins and other growth regulators; the practical use of growth regulators in killing plants and in stimulating abnormal growth; and the isolation of powerful antibiotics such as streptomycin and chloromycin from fungi that are found in the soil—all point to the tremendous potency of chemicals that may be present in the soil in minute amounts. The influence of certain plant extracts upon the development of other plants is undeniable. Indeed, as Whittaker and Feeny (1971) conclude, chemical agents are of major significance in the adaptation of species and the organization of communities.

SUMMARY

The mineral nutrition of the forest is provided primarily by the weathering of soil minerals and the mineralization of atmospheric nitrogen. The soil itself is recharged in nutrients by the decomposition of the organic products of vegetation. Thus a major cycle occurs with the movement of the basic macro- and micronutrients through the cycle from soil to vegetation and back again. Most nutrients are obtained by forest vegetation through root systems which absorb nutrient ions directly from the soil solution. In contrast to agricultural crops, many forests sustain satisfactory growth on relatively low quantities of nutrients. Forest tree species differ in their nutrient requirements, and in general the requirements are related to the fertility of the site conditions where the species normally grow and to which they have become adapted.

Soil fauna and flora form essential parts of the nutrient cycle. Fungal mycelia associated with plant root tissues, the mycorrhizae, are highly efficient accumulators of nutrient ions, supplying them to the host tree. Mycorrhizae also act as biological deterrents to the infections of feeder roots by pathogenic fungi. Soil organisms, particularly bacteria, fungi, mites, and earthworms, systematically reduce forest litter into soluble compounds that can be taken up by the roots of forest vegetation. Under favorable soil conditions bacteria are the most numerous soil organisms and process much of the organic matter. Under cool, wet, acid conditions which are unfavorable for bacteria, fungi become the dominant agents of decomposition. Earthworms and other soil animals fragment the litter, reducing it to a desirable substrate for microflora and microfauna.

A substantial portion of the nutrients utilized by forests is returned to the forest floor in litter-fall and recycled again through decomposition and absorption. Leaf litter and other litter gradually accumulate on the forest floor unless balanced or exceeded by decomposition. In tropical rain forests and in some temperate deciduous forests little or no accumulation of organic matter occurs, due to the rapid rate of decomposition. Heavy accumulations of organic matter may occur in coniferous forests of various climates due to conditions unfavorable for decomposition. Rainfall also may contribute significant amounts of nutrients to the forest ecosystem and in certain instances may exceed that contributed in leaf fall. Rainfall is also known to leach quantities of nutrients from the leaves of forest vegetation.

In contrast to other nutrients, nitrogen comes largely from the air and not from the weathering of soil minerals. In some forests, a major portion is contributed by nitrogen-fixing bacteria living symbiotically in root nodules of various plants, especially legumes. Once nitrogen is incorporated in organic materials, the main route of nitrogen recycling involves the production of NH_4^+ from decomposition of litter and its absorption again by the vegetation.

In undisturbed forest ecosystems, the nutrient losses in drainage water from watersheds do not appear to be large and may be balanced by weathering of soil minerals and inputs from the atmosphere. Complete forest denudation results in appreciable nutrient drain, but the amount of loss by controlled harvesting of timber crops is not well understood.

The effect of chemicals produced by some plants on the growth of other plants of the community may be considerable. Chemical substances that inhibit the growth or occurrence of competing plants are released via litter-fall, leaching of foliage, volatilization from foliage, and root exudation. Such allelopathic effects have been widely reported among plants, including various woody species of forest and range communities.

SUGGESTED READINGS

BRAY, J. ROGER, and EVILLE GORHAM. 1964. Litter production in forests of the world. *Adv. Ecol. Res.* 2:101–157.

DUVIGNEAUD, P., and S. DENAEYER-DE SMET. 1970. Biological cycling of minerals in temperate deciduous forests. *In* DAVID E. REICHLE (ed.), *Analysis of Temperate Forest Ecosystems.* Springer-Verlag, New York.

EDWARDS, C. A., D. E. REICHLE, and D. A. CROSSLEY, JR. 1970. The role of soil invertebrates in turnover of organic matter and nutrients. *In* DAVID E. REICHLE (ed.), *Analysis of Temperate Forest Ecosystems.* Springer-Verlag, New York.

FORTESCUE, J. A. C., and G. G. MARTEN. 1970. Micronutrients: forest ecology and systems analysis. *In* DAVID E. REICHLE (ed.), *Analysis of Temperate Forest Ecosystems.* Springer-Verlag, New York.

LIKENS, GENE F., E. HERBERT BORMANN, NOYE M. JOHNSON, D. W. FISHER, and ROBERT S. PIERCE. 1970. Effects of forest cutting and herbicide treatment on nutrient budgets in the Hubbard Brook watershed-ecosystem. *Ecol. Monogr.* 40: 23–47.

MULLER, CORNELIUS H. 1966. The role of chemical inhibition (allelopathy) in vegetational composition. *Bull. Torrey Bot. Club* 93:332–351.

Ovington, J. D. 1962. Quantitative ecology and the woodland ecosystem concept. *Adv. Ecol. Res.* 1:103–192.

———. 1968. Some factors affecting nutrient distribution within ecosystems. *In* F. E. Eckardt (ed.), *Functioning of Terrestrial Ecosystems at the Primary Production Level.* UNESCO, Natural Resources Research V, Paris.

Stone, Earl L. 1968. Microelement nutrition of forest trees: a review. *In Forest Fertilization.* Tennessee Valley Authority, Muscle Shoals, Alabama.

Switzer, G. L., L. E. Nelson, and W. H. Smith. 1968. The mineral cycle in forest stands. *In Forest Fertilization.* Tennessee Valley Authority, Muscle Shoals, Alabama.

Tamm, Carl Olof. 1964. Determination of nutrient requirements of forest stands. *Int. Rev. For. Res.* 1:115–170.

Whittaker, R. H., and P. P. Feeny. 1971. Allelochemics: chemical interactions between species. *Science* 171:757–770.

9

The Soil-Plant Water Cycle

The nutrient cycle, important as it is, is made possible only by the circulation of water from the soil through the roots to the foliage, to the atmosphere, and from the atmosphere back to the soil. Soil nutrients must be in an ionic state before being absorbed, and this requires the presence of soil water. The rising water column extending from the roots to the leaves carries the nutrients in solution and provides the means of transport within the tree. Transpiration of moisture from the leaf surfaces makes possible the movement of water to the tops of tall trees and in turn plays an important part in recharging the atmosphere with moisture. Finally, precipitation of moisture from the atmosphere is either directly or indirectly responsible for the recharge of the soil with moisture.

The water cycle thus constitutes a part of the forest ecosystem just as does the nutrient cycle. Furthermore, because the greater part of world forests is under moisture stress for at least part of the year, water often is a limiting factor in determining the distribution and growth of forests. In those areas of evenly distributed high rainfall or of shallow water tables where water is not a limiting factor, soil air frequently may be limiting because of its displacement by the excess water supply.

The water cycle is thus basic to an understanding of forest ecology. It affects the behavior and growth of trees to a very great extent and thus is of importance to the silviculturist concerned with the growing of these trees. It also affects stream flow and ground water supply and is thus of interest to the watershed manager. These two groups differ only in their outlook. To the silvi-culturist, water is either used by the trees or lost to the ground. To the forest hydrologist, water is either lost to the trees or used by humans, who obtain it indirectly from the ground. The basic data and principles, however, apply to both fields. A review of world literature relating vegetation and hydrology has been published by Penman (1963). Many aspects of the forest-water relationship are reviewed in the proceedings of the International Symposium on Forest Hydrology (Sopper and Lull, 1967), and an integrated and modern treatment of plant and soil-water relationships is presented by Kramer (1969).

SOIL WATER AND AIR

The supply of moisture to tree roots is inversely related to the supply of air to them. The pores in the soil may be filled with either air or water so that, as the supply of one increases, that of the other automatically decreases. For optimum tree growth, both air and water must be available to the roots at all times. This means that the larger soil pores should be occupied by air and the smaller by water. It is convenient to discuss and emphasize the water-holding capacity of soils. At the same time, though, we should remember that factors affecting the air-holding capacity are essentially the same, for any space in the soil not occupied by water will normally be occupied by air.

Water-Holding Capacity

Soil minerals have an average specific gravity of 2.65. An undisturbed soil sample, however, contains water, air, and organic solids, as well as minerals. Thus weight of minerals per unit volume of soil is called "bulk density," and varies between 1.0 and 1.6 depending on the amount of pore space. If the specific gravity of soil minerals is 2.65 and the bulk density 1.325, one-half of the oven-dry soil is composed of air. The pore volume is thus 50 percent. Most forest soils have pore volumes between 30 and 65 percent, distributed between both air and water when the soil is in its natural state in the field. Air and water relationships for soils of different textures are illustrated in Figure 9.1.

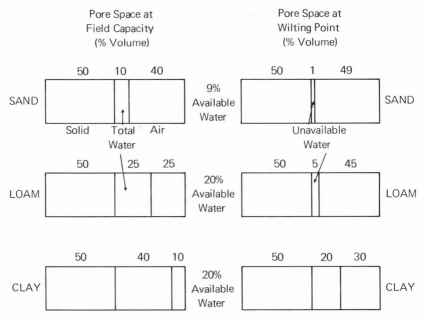

Fig. 9.1. Available water and aeration in different-textured soils, assuming 50 percent of the soil is mineral solid. Addition of organic matter increases capillary space in sand soils and air space in clay soils.

When soil is completely saturated, the contained water falls into three well-defined categories. *Free water* fills the larger pores (larger than about 0.05 mm) and drains off readily under the influence of gravity (Figure 9.2). This gravitational water is available but briefly to plant roots, and its direct effect on plant growth is transitory. It is, however, largely responsible for soil leaching.

After the saturated soil has been drained of gravitational water, it is said to be at *field capacity*. It holds all the water it can against the force of gravity. This force can be approximated in the laboratory by subjecting the saturated soil to a pressure of about 1/10 atmosphere over normal air pressure (Figure 9.2).

At field capacity, the free water remaining in the soil is known as *capillary water* and is held largely as thin moisture films around individual soil particles and aggregates. Capillary water will move very gradually from moister to drier portions of the soil. Thus, if tree roots and surface evaporation remove capillary water from the top soil layers, a certain amount of capillary water may move up into these layers from any moister soil beneath. The zone of capil-

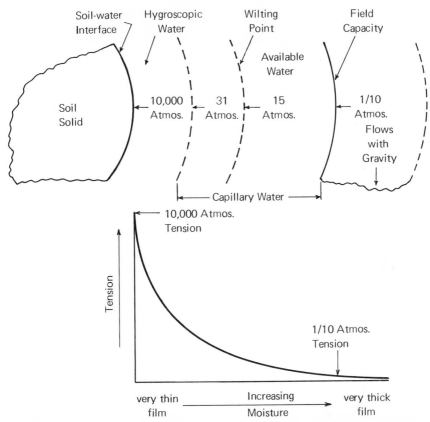

Fig. 9.2. Diagrams showing relationship between thickness of water films and the tension with which the water is held at the liquid-air interface. The tension is shown in atmospheres. (*Upper*) Sketch of water film thickness at several moisture levels. (*Lower*) Logarithmic change in tension with increase in thickness of moisture film. (After Buckman and Brady, 1969.)

lary movement beneath tree roots, however, is not great, varying from virtually nothing in coarse sands to a few feet in clay soils.

Finally, yet additional water is held quite strongly by soil particles and can be removed only by prolonged heating above the boiling point. Such *hygroscopic water* of the soil is unavailable to plant roots.

Water Available to Plants

Of the water that enters the soil, the only portion available to plants, then, consists of (1) gravitational water that comes momentarily into contact with roots on its downward journey, and (2) that portion of the capillary water held by forces slighter than hygroscopic water.

The mechanism of water absorption and rate of water flow from soil to plant are primarily controlled by water evaporating from the leaves. In transpiring plants, water moves from the soil→root cortex and free space→root xylem→stem xylem→leaf veins→leaf mesophyll and free space→atmosphere along gradients of decreasing *water potential*. Water in the plant-soil system has a chemical potential, a capacity to do work. By converting units of work to equivalent units of pressure, water potential may be expressed in bars or atmospheres. Pure free water is defined as having a potential of zero. The presence of solutes in plant cells or soil water reduces the chemical potential of the water in solution below that of pure free water. Likewise the adhesive forces holding water to the surfaces of soil particles reduce the potential of soil water far below that of free water.

As water evaporates from the free space of the leaf mesophyll, the water potential of the leaf is reduced and water flows from the stem xylem, where its potential is higher, into the leaf. This process is repeated for stem water and root water, finally reaching the interface between free space in the root and soil water itself. The solute content of living cells gives them sufficiently low water potential to resist desiccation by transpiration.

Movement of water takes place through the continuous water columns of the xylem elements. The roots act as passive absorbing surfaces across which water moves from the soil by mass flow. Although we may describe the absorption process in terms of the plant exerting tensions to overcome those of the water held in the soil, water transport, whether in rapidly or slowly transpiring plants, is controlled by differential water potentials developed in the soil and in various plant tissues. The mechanism of water absorption, the factors affecting it, and water movement in plants and soils are described in detail by Kramer (1969).

Water at field capacity can be easily absorbed by tree roots as it is held by only slight forces. As the soil dries out, however, the remaining water is more and more tightly bound to the soil particles, and can be removed with increasing difficulty by roots. Eventually, the point is reached where root water potential is equal to soil water potential and no more water enters the roots. This is termed the *permanent wilting point,* as plants maintained in such soil will wilt beyond recovery and die (Figure 9.2).

Originally, the permanent wilting point of a soil was determined by finding the lowest moisture level at which plants will remain alive. This method works only for succulent plants, however (sunflower is the classic test plant), as woody plants possess structure permitting the dried plant to hold its form; also, many woody plants can endure drought by going into dormancy. The permanent wilting point cannot be determined in this way for most forest tree species.

A great many studies have been directed at the problem of determining minimum soil moisture for the maintenance of plant life. In general, it seems that roots of most higher plants can extract water that is held by the soil at water potentials of greater than -15 bars. For example, Richard (1953) in Switzerland found no significant difference between the permanent wilting points of Scots pine, European alder, and dwarf sunflower. It follows that the soil-moisture content at the permanent wilting point can be best measured by subjecting the soil to an artificial water potential of -15 bars. The resulting moisture content will vary widely for different soils, ranging from perhaps 2 percent by volume for coarse sandy soils to as high as 35 percent for compact clay soils.

Although plants can exert energy sufficient to remove water from the soil down to levels of -15 bars, most of the water actually taken up is that portion that is more readily available. Many field studies have shown that water uptake by forest trees drops sharply when the energy required is greater than -1 bar of soil water potential. Water uptake in drier soils continues at a very slow rate (Zahner, 1967).

Due to the resistance of water movement into the roots, daily absorption, even in soil at field capacity, tends to lag behind transpiration. The resulting temporary, midday, internal water deficits tend to curtail growth but are not critical as the water in the tree is replaced overnight by continued absorption from the soil. The observation that growth of some crops and trees is greater at night than during the day (Kramer, 1969) may be, in part, a response to this pattern of water availability. In midsummer, when absorption is markedly reduced by lack of soil water and overnight absorption fails to regain turgor of the tree, serious water deficits develop in tissues of trees and cause major reductions in forest growth.

Evapotranspiration by the Forest

Evapotranspiration is the general term widely used for the transfer of vapor from land and water surfaces to the atmosphere. For evapotranspiration to occur from the forest both water and energy must be available at one or more of the following surfaces: external surfaces of leaves and plant stems, internal plant surfaces connected to the external atmosphere via the stomata, soil and litter surfaces, and snow pack surface (Goodell, 1967). Thus the entire water vapor exchange of a forest is concerned with evaporation, interception, and transpiration. Evaporation is used here for the physical process of vapor transport from soil or surfaces of vegetation and litter, and transpiration is used for the plant physiological processes. Interception originates on wet surfaces of plants and is principally derived from rain and snow (Chapter 5). Not all intercepted water may be evaporated to the atmosphere. Some may be absorbed by vegetation and utilized to recharge the internal water balance of the plants (Zinke, 1967). In addition intercepted water, while evaporating, may reduce the rate of transpiration, thus saving stored water in the soil. However, this effect appears to be slight (Hewlett, 1967; Rutter, 1968).

The soil moisture that enters tree roots passes up the stem into the foliage, bringing the nutrients to the growing organs of the plant, and is then transpired from the leaves, primarily through the stomata. Only a small amount of water is actually used in the photosynthetic process: about one-twentieth of an inch per year of water actually enters into the manufacture of cellulose and other organic products of the tree. The rest of the water that is taken up serves only as a mode of transport for nutrients, leads to some cooling of the leaves, and passes on into the atmosphere.

Allowed free access to unlimited water supplies, trees can transpire immense quantities of water. Willows, cottonwoods, and other phreatophytes growing on the banks of permanent watercourses and reservoirs have been shown to be capable of transpiring as much as 40 inches of water during the course of a single growing season. For a tree obtaining its moisture from one one-hundredth of an acre of land (assuming a fully stocked forest of 100 trees per acre), this amounts to a transpirational use of over 10,000 gallons per year for a single moderately sized tree.

Without access to the water table, forest trees will maintain maximum transpiration rates only as long as the soil water supply is excellent. Available water is first extracted from the zone of high root concentration in the upper two to three feet of soil. Later in the growing season extraction becomes nearly equal with depth, even down to 20 feet (Figure 9.3; Patric *et al.*, 1965). When soils are recharged

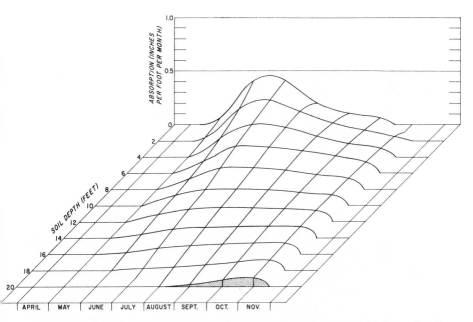

Fig. 9.3. The pattern of water absorption from the upper 20 feet of soil at a southern Appalachian Mountain site. Total absorption peaks in June and thereafter extraction of water comes more and more uniformly from the entire profile. (After Patric *et al.*, 1965.)

periodically by frequent rains, most transpiration by vegetation will come from the densely rooted surface soil. Studies in southern Arkansas by Zahner (1955) estimated a mean soil-moisture depletion of about 0.25 inch of water per day for the period of early summer when soil moisture was adequate. This estimate agrees closely with the computed theoretical evapotranspiration of the locality (Zahner,

1956). A maximum soil-moisture depletion rate of 0.2 inch per day was reported from a loblolly pine plantation in South Carolina (Metz and Douglass, 1959).

In well-drained soils, however, the amount of water transpired is much less. As has already been seen, water uptake is sharply curtailed when the energy required is more than −1 bar of soil water potential and ceases when more than −15 bars are required. As a result, the annual transpiration of forest trees is limited by the amount of annual precipitation that reaches the ground and the amount of water that moves upward into the root zones (especially from shallow ground water sources) less the amount that is lost to the trees by surface run-off and through gravitational drainage below the root depth.

In the hardwood forest of the southern Appalachians at the Coweeta research station, transpiration of forest trees has been determined on entire watersheds of 33 and 40 acres through measuring the effects on stream flow of clearcutting the forest. Of the annual rainfall of about 80 inches, about 20 (range 17–22) inches was shown to have transpired through mature undisturbed hardwoods. The phreatophytic undergrowth of laurel and rhododendron along the major streams alone accounted for about 2 inches of transpiration (Johnson and Kovner, 1956). Understory vegetation beneath a pine stand may account for as much as one-quarter of the total evapotranspiration loss (Zahner, 1958b).

In southeastern Ohio, white oak forests growing on loam soils transpired from 12 to 23 inches of water during the growing season. The annual rainfall here is about 40 inches (Gaiser, 1952). In cooler climates, transpiration is much less. For instance, aspen forests both in Utah (Croft and Monninger, 1953) and Russia transpired only 8 inches of water under the cooler conditions where these species occur.

From these and other determinations of transpirational use, it would seem that forests must take up at least 5 to 10 inches of water each year. Since transpiration from forests seldom accounts for more than one-third to one-quarter of the annual precipitation, annual precipitation must be at least three or four times greater, or 15 to 40 inches.

The water-use figures here presented actually include transpiration from the trees and in most cases also evaporation from the forest floor. The latter is, however, only slight where the soil is covered with tree litter and is shaded by tree crowns. The great preponderance of evapotranspirational loss in dense forests is attributable to transpiration. In open forests with exposed forest floors, evaporation from the soil and litter is also a major factor.

Marked differences are observed in total evapotranspiration among cover types. Listed in decreasing order of water consumption, they are: wet meadows, open water, forests, grasslands, vegetable crops, and bare soil (Baumgartner, 1967). Differences between the cover types may be explained quantitatively in part by energy considerations. Forests, due to their higher absorption of shortwave radiation, vaporize water more readily than other types of vegetation. Major differences in rooting habit and depth also account in part for the observed differences between forests and grasslands and also for differences among forest trees. The consumption by trembling aspen of 6 inches more water than Engelmann spruce from the surface 8 feet of soil in Colorado was attributed to rooting differences (Rocky Mountain Forest Experiment Station, 1959). Although annual evapotranspiration is not reported to differ appreciably between tree species grown at the same location (Douglass, 1967), more detailed investigations may reveal such differences, especially between conifers and hardwoods.

Seasonal Course of Water Uptake

The pattern of water uptake by trees varies widely. Water will be taken up in large quantities only when the soil is moist, the trees are growing, and the atmosphere is warm and dry.

A simple situation is represented by pines on deep sand dunes in north temperate climate (for example, the Culbin dune in northern Scotland, to which reference has already been made). Here, transpiration is great only during the growing season immediately after a rain. Thus large amounts of water are taken up immediately after a summer storm, water use tapering off and ending within a few days after the combined effects of gravity and root absorption have reduced the sands to near the permanent wilting point. Tree growth is largely concentrated in these brief periods.

In most forests, however, water is stored in the soil for longer periods of time. Wherever snow accumulates on the ground during the winter, and elsewhere in the temperate zones where precipitation is high during the dormant season, it is normal for the well-drained soil to be at or near field capacity at the beginning of the growing season. As the weather warms, growth of trees accelerates. Within a few weeks, the soil-moisture supply is depleted by transpiration to the point that tree growth begins to slow down. In the northeastern United States, growth is pretty much concentrated in the spring months—May and June—with growth tapering off in July and being maintained in August and September only in exceptionally wet years.

In the southern pine region, similar conditions prevail. With the onset of warm weather in the spring, transpiration reaches high levels until, in June, 0.2 to 0.25 inch of water is removed from the soil daily, as has already been seen. This maximum rate of transpiration loss, which continues as long as the soil can supply the moisture, agrees closely with the potential evaporation from the area as calculated with Thornthwaite's formula.

In the coniferous forests of the West, tree growth is largely concentrated in the spring months. The summer drought that characterizes the Douglas-fir region and much of the ponderosa pine region results in the soil becoming too dry for substantial tree growth during the summer months. A secondary growing season, however, sometimes occurs in the early fall, if substantial rainfall occurs while the weather is still warm.

From the evidence that has been gathered, it is apparent that forest soils reach field capacity or complete capillary water recharge only during dormant periods or exceptionally wet growing periods. Normally, during the growing season, light rains are largely intercepted by tree crowns, and the small proportion that reaches the ground goes to replenish the moisture in the surface soil only and is soon lost through absorption by surface roots and direct evaporation. Substantial rainfall is required to stimulate tree growth. Almost continual rain (or nearly 2 inches per week) is needed to maintain the soil at its field capacity during warm weather in temperate climates.

Ground Water and Trees

The presence of a water table available to tree roots has both beneficial and detrimental aspects. On the plus side, it provides additional water for transpiration. Often, though, transpirational use is partly luxury consumption as the tree may be already absorbing all the moisture it needs to transport the optimum quantity of nutrients and required water to the foliage. On the minus side, a permanent water table will normally prevent the downward development of roots (insufficient oxygen below the water line for root growth) and may even result in the development of a gley horizon in the subsoil, creating a nutrient-poor ground-water podzolic condition.

Where ground water is within reach of forest roots, the level of the water table is usually variable through the season, being highest just prior to the initiation of the growing season, and becoming depressed as transpiration by the forest depletes the water supply. The effective level of the water table, however, is pretty well marked by deoxidation or reduction that changes the affected soils to a grayish or whitish-gray color. This gley horizon is frequently mottled and easily detected. It is the upper limit of the reduced or mottled zone that should be taken as the effective height of the water table—not the actual height of the water at the time of measurement.

The great importance of the water table in affecting tree distribution and growth has led to the recognition of several different soil water conditions varying from completely drained to completely undrained conditions. A series of soils, alike in all respects except the position of the water table and its resulting effect on the profile, constitutes what is known as a *moisture catena* (from the Latin, meaning "chain"). The different members of the catena are arbitrarily defined, there actually existing a complete series of intergrading conditions. Since these classes can be defined to show a high correlation with forest site, however, it is worthwhile to consider them in some detail.

1. *Well-drained soils* are formed when the water table is permanently below the zone of tree roots and the A and B horizons. Since it is difficult to sample below 5 feet either with a shovel or an auger, the absence of mottling to a depth of 5 feet is normally considered evidence that the soil is well drained.

2. *Imperfectly drained soils* show evidence of a water table in the lower part of the B horizon or the upper part of the C. The A horizon and enough of the B horizon is well drained, however, to permit the normal development of the roots of shallow-rooted species

and the normal cycling of nutrients in this upper zone. In imperfectly drained soils, mottling is normally found at least 24 to 36 inches below the surface of the mineral soil.

3. *Poorly drained soils* are affected by a high water table into the lower part of the A horizon. Root development is consequently much restricted, and nutrients leached out of the surface zones may be lost to the forest. Mottling may occur within 6 inches or so of the surface.

4. Finally, in *undrained soils*, free water stands above the surface of the mineral soil for much of the year. As a result, tree litter is trapped in more or less stagnant water and tends to accumulate rather than to decompose completely. Organic layers of markedly decomposed plant material are termed *muck*, while layers only slightly decayed are known as *peat*. In the boreal forests of Canada, northern Europe, and northern Asia, peat bogs are a major feature of the landscape (Heikurainen, 1964). Peat may also accumulate on uplands where wet and cold summer weather normally inhibits the decomposition of certain types of litter. The formation of upland peat constitutes a serious forest problem in parts of Scotland and northern Europe.

The detrimental effects of high soil water tables arise in part from their capacity for dissolving and removing soil nutrients and in part from the shortage of oxygen in stagnant or anaerobic soil water. Moving soil water that carries substantial quantities of dissolved air and nutrients is hence far more favorable to forest growth than stagnant soil water low in oxygen and nutrient ions. Thus in the Lake States, the presence of northern white cedar in wet sites is indicative of seepage conditions where the water table is moving and relatively high in oxygen. With completely stagnant and oxygen-poor water, only black spruce and associated ericaceous species can grow.

Since forest trees may remove 20 inches or more of water a year from the soil, clearcutting the forest will result in raising a water table close to the surface. A rise in the water table of from 1 to 2 feet has been reported for such diverse forest types as loblolly pine in the southeastern coastal plain and aspen in the Lake States (Wilde *et al.*, 1953; Trousdell and Hoover, 1955). Such a rise will often convert an imperfectly drained soil into a poorly drained soil or even into an undrained condition.

WATER DEFICITS AND TREE GROWTH

Tree growth responds more to water stress than any other perennial factor of the forest site. Thus soil water is the key to forest site productivity for many species in many parts of the world. Apical, radial, and reproductive growth of trees, as well as seedling germination and establishment, are highly correlated with environmental moisture stress and have been reviewed in detail by Zahner (1968). In temperate climates moisture deficits during the middle of the growing season directly affect growth during both the current and succeeding growing seasons.

Indirect evidence of the marked effect of moisture stress on height growth is seen in the low heights that trees attain in dry climates or on dry sites, compared with trees growing on moist sites. Direct measurement of shoot growth of seedling and sapling trees under moisture stress confirms that growth is closely correlated with water potential within the plant and to environmental soil-moisture deficits.

The effects of moisture stress for a given species depend partly on the species' seasonal pattern of shoot flushing. Some species, such as birches, yellow-poplar, and loblolly pine, are capable of maintaining shoot elongation during the complete growing season and hence are affected by late season droughts. Other species, however, including red pine, white ash, and red and white oaks, complete height growth and set buds by midsummer, and their current year's growth is unaffected by late season water deficits. Their current growth is, however, affected by late summer drought of the preceding year. For example, Zahner and Stage (1966) accounted for 72 percent of the variation in annual shoot growth in five stands of young red pine by water deficits of the previous and current growing seasons together. The water deficit of the previous summer (June 15 through October) accounted for as much reduction in annual height growth as the deficit for May 1 to July 15 of the current year. As expected, tree species exhibiting continued shoot flushing (yellow-poplar) or recurrent flushing (loblolly, pitch, and Monterey pines) show little correlation between total annual height growth and the previous year's rainfall (Tryon *et al.*, 1957; Zahner, 1968).

Moisture stress plays an equally important role in the radial growth of trees. It affects the size of the annual ring, the proportion of earlywood and latewood, and various wood properties, particularly wood specific gravity. In conifers the transition from earlywood to latewood (from large, weak, thin-walled xylem cells to small, strong, thick-walled cells) may be directly affected by water deficits in the cambium (Zahner, 1968), as well as indirectly affected through reduction of auxin levels in the crown (Larson, 1963a, 1964).

Periodic changes (daily and annual) in radial growth of conifers and angiosperms have been repeatedly shown to be directly correlated with soil water availability (Figure 9.4). For several deciduous species over a 5-year period in Ohio, high air temperatures during periods of moisture stress in midsummer were consistently associated with temporary and sometimes permanent cessation of radial growth in all species (Phipps, 1961). Similarly, Fraser (1956,

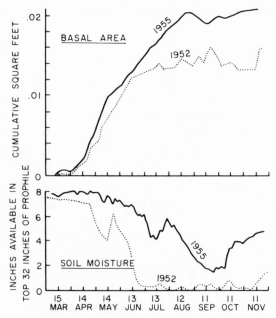

Fig. 9.4. Basal area growth per tree of shortleaf pine and trends of available soil moisture for relatively wet (1955) and dry (1952) growing seasons. Note that growth rate slowed in mid-June of 1952 but not until mid-August of 1955, at the time in each year when available soil water had been depleted to about 2 inches. (Redrawn from Boggess, 1956; after Zahner, 1968.)

1962) found the radial growth of the lower bole of northern hardwoods and conifers in Canada to be closely related to soil moisture. Zahner (1968) summarizes the typical response of trees growing in fully stocked stands on upland sites in temperate climates in this way:

> . . . water stresses are not serious prior to midsummer, at which time it is normal for absorption by roots to lag far behind transpiration, and the resulting dehydration of tissues in the crowns and stems causes important limitations in growth below the potential for that time of year. If the water stress is alleviated by late-season rains, radial growth usually resumes if the mid-season water deficit has not been severe.

Many studies demonstrate that water stresses normally occurring in fully stocked stands may be alleviated by silvicultural practices such as thinning or wide spacing of trees. Radial growth of residual trees is faster and more prolonged in thinned than in unthinned stands (Figure 9.5; Zahner and Whitmore, 1960). Furthermore, heavy thinning of loblolly pine stands may alleviate summer moisture stresses such that residual trees may continue to grow longer throughout the season (Bassett, 1964).

Drought years leave their record in the growth rings of trees, and the high correlation of ring width with summer water deficit is widely documented. Up to 90 percent of the variation in width of annual rings of conifers has been attributed to water stress in semi-arid climates (Douglass, 1919; Fritts et al., 1965) and up to 80 percent in humid temperate climates (Zahner and Donnelly, 1967). In the latter study 14 percent of the variation in ring width of young red pines in Michigan over a 10-year period was associated with moisture stress conditions of the previous season (July–September) and 68 percent with moisture conditions of the current season (May–September).

PRECIPITATION AND FORESTS

Soil moisture depleted through evapotranspiration must be replenished by precipitation or ground water. Since ground water itself originates from precipitation, however, and since soil-moisture relationships are most critical on well-drained soils where the root systems of trees do not reach the water table, we may confine our attention to the replenishment of soil moisture through precipitation.

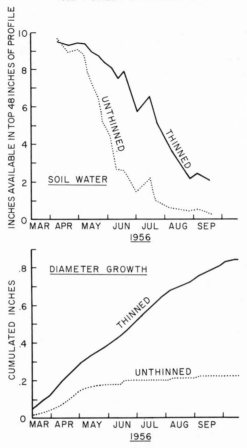

Fig. 9.5. Trends of soil water depletion and diameter increment per tree for average dominant loblolly pine during one growing season, thinned plots and unthinned plots. (Redrawn from Zahner and Whitmore, 1960; after Zahner, 1968.)

That the amount of water reaching the soil under a forest may differ considerably from the amount reaching a rain gauge in the open has already been discussed in Chapter 5. Considerable rainfall is intercepted by tree crowns and evaporated directly back to the atmosphere. On the other hand, considerable fog vapor is intercepted, condensed, and dripped to the ground by vegetation. The combined effects of interception and stem flow result in the concentration of rainfall into small openings in the canopy and in the immediate area of tree boles (Voigt, 1960; Eschner, 1967).

Surface run-off of rain water represents water lost to the plant. The useful water is that portion of precipitation that infiltrates the soil. The best infiltration is obtained with forest soils characterized by a good cover of litter and a low bulk density. Root and animal (worms, insects, mammals) tunnels are highly beneficial. A forest soil under hardwoods in southeastern Ohio, for example, was found to contain more than 400 large vertical channels per acre from decaying tap roots alone, an amount capable of handling most of the free water that reached the surface as precipitation.

In undisturbed forests, the infiltration rate is generally high. At Coweeta in the southern Appalachians, infiltration rates in such conditions generally are in excess of 10 inches of water per hour—far greater than observed maximum rainfall intensities. In sandy soils of Michigan, infiltration rates may be as high as 40 inches per hour.

When the surface litter is removed from fine-textured soils, however, permitting the striking energy of raindrops to destroy surface soil structures, the infiltration of rainwater is markedly inhibited. Compacting of the surface soil by cattle in grazed woodlots or by humans in forest park areas is even more destructive of infiltration capacity.

Forests and Water Yield

About 70 percent of the total precipitation falling in the continental United States is returned to the atmosphere through evapotranspiration, and forests contribute significantly to this loss. The management of forested watersheds for water is assuming an ever-increasing role since inadequate water supplies are no longer restricted to arid and semi-arid regions. In general, reduction of forest cover increases stream flow while establishment of forest cover on sparsely vegetated land decreases it. In a review of thirty experiments from various parts of the world on the effects of forest removal on stream flow, Hibbert (1967) reported the maximum increase for the first year was 18 inches per year with 100 percent of the forest cover removed, or 0.18 inch for each 1 percent of the forest cut. However, in two-thirds of the experiments the increase in water yield was less than half of this and in one-third of the studies negligible increases were recorded. Thus the response to treatment is highly variable and often unpredictable due to interactions of climatic, soil, and vegetative factors.

Increases in water yield typically show a decline soon after treatment. The rate of decline is positively correlated to the rapidity of revegetation. Clearcutting the forest overstory does not save all the water which otherwise would be transpired or intercepted. Evaporation from the soil and litter and use of water by understory vegetation mean the average increase will only be about 40 percent of the water used by the forest (Pereira, 1967).

The manner of cutting may affect water yield. For example, by removing 50 percent of the conifer cover on a watershed in Colorado in clearcut strips, Goodell (1958) recorded increases in stream flow of 10.8 and 8.6 inches in the 2 years following cutting. However, using a method of partial cutting removing 36 percent of the basal area of a mixed conifer stand in Arizona, large gaps were not created and stream flow was not increased significantly (Rich, 1959). Studies of snowpack accumulation in the central Sierra Nevada Mountains in California by Anderson (1967) suggest that snow accumulation would differ greatly under contrasting types of forest cutting—individual-tree selective cutting versus strip clearcutting. Assuming that both cuts remove 60 percent of the stand, the average percentage increase in accumulation over a 12-inch base for a dense forest would be 12 percent for the individual tree removal and 43 percent for the strip clearcutting (Anderson, 1970).

In montainous areas of high snowfall, the snowpack is an important consideration in influencing water yield. By manipulating forest stands in various ways, snow-water storage may be increased and snow melt may be delayed (Anderson, 1970). Besides an expected increase in snow accumulation and water yield following forest removal, increases in stream flow may also occur following cutting, through rearrangement of a given amount of snow. For example, in an experimental watershed in the Rocky Mountains of Colorado, alternate clearcutting of strips of timber resulted in an average increase of 25 percent in stream flow, most of which occurred in the spring (Hoover and Leaf, 1967). Comparisons of snow storage before and after cutting indicated no change in total snow on the watershed. Thus the increased stream flow was not attributed to decreased interception but to differential distribution of the same total snow pack over the watershed. Compared to the area before treatment, much more snow was trapped in the openings than in the forested portion. The integrated result of the increased snow in the clearcut openings and proportional decrease under forest was to increase the amount of stream flow from the same amount of snow pack.

Manipulation of forest cover is not only important in increasing water yield or decreasing peak discharges (in the case of floods) but in regulating the timing of water flow (Johnson, 1967; Dortignac, 1967) and decreasing erosion on denuded slopes (Margaropoulos, 1967; McClurkin, 1967). However, measures which increase water yield, cutting or fire, may adversely affect water quality by causing erosion and thereby increasing the amount of suspended sediment in stream water or by causing undesirable chemical changes. An undesirable circumstance is the occurrence of heavy rains following cutting and before vegetation has stabilized the soil. For example, the effect of complete clearcutting of all woody vegetation in a 455-acre watershed in north-central Arizona on water yield and other products was reported by Brown (1971). Three and six-tenths inches more water were produced the first summer than might have been expected without treatment, but a high sediment yield (27 tons per acre) was produced, much of it from a single, heavy summer rain one month following cutting. Sediment yields in the following two years, both wetter than average, dropped to 0.1 ton per acre. Strip clearcutting of ponderosa pine forests in the same area promises to give increased water, herbage, and wildlife yields and reduced losses in sediment compared to complete clearcutting.

Forest cutting may affect fish populations significantly. Although the indirect effects of timber harvest on fish populations may be minor compared to industrial pollution, it is of concern. The problem has been studied for many years (Chapman, 1962; Cordone, 1956) and is receiving increasing attention. For example, the physical effects of clearcutting on salmon habitat were investigated in two clearcut and one adjacent uncut watershed on the Prince of Wales Island in southeastern Alaska (Meehen et al., 1969). Massive clearcutting was conducted in the Maybeso valley from 1953 to 1957 and in the Harris River valley from 1959 to 1961 and encompassed a total area of approximately 10 square miles. The stream flow, suspended sediment, stream temperature, debris flow, log-debris jams, and the fish populations of the respective watersheds were studied and compared. Although changes were observed following clearcutting, the authors observed no obvious effects of clearcutting on salmon populations and concluded that the cutting as conducted apparently did not adversely affect salmon spawning habitat. The more subtle effects that may occur, and the less direct effects of logging on species having extended fresh water stages in their life histories, such as steelhead trout and coho salmon, need further investigation.

The total effects of watershed treatments on the forest, wildlife, and human consumers of water are essentially unknown and are only now being investigated through integrated studies of ecosystems.

Precipitation and the Distribution of Forests

Now that we have considered the place of precipitation in the soil-plant water cycle, we are in a position to summarize the relationships between precipitation and the distribution of trees. Precipitation is not a factor directly affecting tree distribution and growth, but rather is important because of its indirect effect in supplying moisture to the soil. It is thus discussed here under soil-water factors of the site rather than as a climatic factor.

For an area to support tree growth, enough water must be supplied to satisfy the minimum requirements of the trees for transpiration and photosynthesis. This amounts to about 5 to 8 inches of precipitation a year. For forests of moderate growth rates with tree crowns touching, the minimum supply approximates 15 inches a year. High growth rates require at least 20 to 30 inches a year. The precipitation must be sufficiently larger than these values to allow for interception, surface run-off, direct evaporation, and subsurface drainage.

In the far north, permafrost prevents drainage of water through the soil, no precipitation is lost during the long winter, and evaporation losses during the short summer are relatively slight. Under such conditions, good forest growth is possible with low precipitation. Vigorous forests grow in the vicinity of Fairbanks, Alaska, where the annual precipitation is only 12 inches (of which 5 fall during June, July, and August, however). Forests may grow in these latitudes with annual precipitation values as low as 7 or 8 inches.

In the eastern United States the *presence* of forests is nowhere limited by insufficient rainfall. In general, the soil is wet to or near the field capacity at the beginning of the growing season. Tree growth depletes the soil of moisture during the growing season and utilizes in addition water added by rain during this period. In the northern states, at least 25 inches of precipitation are needed for moderate forest growth, with 35 to 40 inches being similarly required in the southern states.

Across the Great Plains, the 20-inch precipitation line roughly delimits the boundary east of which it is possible to grow trees without irrigation or access to ground water. This line, which more or less coincides with the 100th meridian, passes through the Dakotas, Kansas, Nebraska, Oklahoma, and Texas. Actually, less precipitation is needed in the northern states and more in the southern; a range from 15 inches in North Dakota to 25 inches in Texas would probably be more accurate. It is this boundary that limits the western expansion of shelter belts in the Great Plains.

In the western states, transitions from forest to non-forest vegetation occur in all states, and many correlations have been made between these boundaries and mean annual precipitation. Generalizing, approximately 15 inches seem to be required to sustain an open woodland type of vegetation (pinyon-juniper, oak woodland, chaparral, etc.); about 20 inches for an open ponderosa pine forest; and over 25 for a closed-canopy mixed coniferous forest. Since the higher rainfalls occur at higher elevations (Chapter 5), temperature influences are interrelated with precipitation influences in these relationships. In the Southwest, the prevalence of summer rain tends to compensate largely for the greater heat of the summer sun. As a result, there seems to be less variation from north to south in precipitation requirements than in the east.

SUMMARY

Water is essential in every phase of the life history of forest trees and is probably the single most important substance cycled in the forest ecosystem. Much of the water that enters the soil is held as a thin film around soil particles and is available to tree roots as long as sufficient energy is available to extract it. Roots can extract only very little water held by the soil at water potentials greater than -15 bars, and most water is absorbed at water potentials between -0.1 and -3 bars. When water is readily available in the soil, its absorption and rate of flow from soil to the plant are largely controlled by transpiration. In transpiring plants, water moves from leaf to the atmosphere, to the leaves from roots through the continuous water columns of the stem xylem, and to the root xylem from the soil along gradients of decreasing water potential. Roots act as passive absorbing surfaces across which water moves by mass flow from the soil. Even when soils are saturated with moisture, absorption during the day tends to lag behind transpiration, and the resulting internal water deficit must be made up by continual absorption from the soil at night. In midsummer, when soil moisture is in low supply, absorption is significantly reduced, and serious internal water deficits develop at midday in plant tissues. This water stress greatly affects shoot elongation and radial growth of trees, yet may be alleviated somewhat by silvicultural practices of thinning and wide spacing of trees. The presence of a water table provides additional water for transpiration, but too shallow a ground water may hinder root development since oxygen is deficient for root growth below the water line. Soils are ranked in a moisture catena on the basis of their water table conditions from well-drained to undrained.

Most of the water absorbed by trees is transpired into the atmosphere. Forests are capable of transpiring large quantities of water, up to about one-third of the annual precipitation. Since forests may transpire as much as 20 inches per year, clearcutting the forest on some sites may result in raising the water table close to the surface and may adversely affect regeneration and development of the subsequent stand. On other sites clearcutting results in increased stream flow. Transpiration from vegetation and evaporation from the soil or surface layers of the soil, together known as evapotranspiration, may cause a substantial "loss" of water that might otherwise drain into streams and be used by man. Thus management of forest cover for water yield is of increasing importance due to inadequate water supplies. Removal of forest cover generally increases stream flow, and the amount of water obtained depends on both the severity and the manner of the cutting. Although heavy cutting of forest stands may increase stream flow, water quality may be adversely affected.

SUGGESTED READINGS

ANDERSON, H. W. 1970. Storage and delivery of rainfall and snowmelt water as related to forest environments. *Proc. 3rd Forest Microclimate Symp.*, pp. 51–67. Canad. For. Serv., Calgary, Alberta.

BUCKMAN, HARRY O., and NYLE C. BRADY. 1969. *The Nature and Properties of Soils*, 7th ed. (Chapter 7, Forms of soil water, their movement, and their plant relationships, pp. 161–189.) The Macmillan Co., Toronto, Ontario. 653 pp.

HIBBERT, ALDEN R. 1967. Forest treatment effects on water yield. *In* WILLIAM E. SOPPER and HOWARD W. LULL (eds.), *Forest Hydrology*. Pergamon Press, Inc., New York.

KRAMER, PAUL J. 1969. *Plant and Soil Water Relationships: A Modern Synthesis*. McGraw-Hill Book Co., Inc., New York. 482 pp.

MEEHAN, W. R., W. A. FARR, D. M. BISHOP, and J. H. PATRIC. 1969. Some effects of clearcutting on salmon habitat of two southeast Alaska streams. USDA For. Serv. Res. Paper PNW–82. Pacific Northwest For. and Rge. Exp. Sta., Portland, Ore. 45 pp.

PENMAN, H. L. 1963. Vegetation and hydrology. Bur. Soils, Harpenden. Tech. Commun. 53. 125 pp.

RUTTER, A. J. 1968. Water consumption by forests. *In* T. T. KOZLOWSKI (ed.), *Water Deficits and Plant Growth* II. Academic Press, New York.

SOPPER, WILLIAM E., and HOWARD W. LULL (eds.). 1967. *Forest Hydrology*. Pergamon Press, Inc., New York. 813 pp.

ZAHNER, R. 1968. Means and effects of manipulating soil water in managed forests. *In Forest Fertilization*. Tennessee Valley Authority, Muscle Shoals, Ala. 306 pp.

———. 1968. Water deficits and growth of trees. *In* T. T. KOZLOWSKI (ed.), *Water Deficits and Plant Growth* II. Academic Press, Inc., New York.

10

The Soil, Large Animals, and Fire as Site Factors

In forest ecology, soils are important insofar as their characteristics are related to those of the forest itself. Both the soil and the forest are a part of the forest ecosystem and as such are highly interrelated. The combined effect of geological material, climate, and vegetation in developing various characteristic types of soil profiles has been discussed briefly in Chapter 7. The nutrient cycle aspects of the forest ecosystem has been treated in Chapter 8, while the water cycle has been similarly discussed in Chapter 9. It remains to investigate those other aspects of the soil-forest system that have a direct bearing upon the composition, form, development, and productivity of the forest—in other words, upon the forest site quality. These include first, the topographic position of the site; second, the texture and structure of the mineral soil; third, the effect of large animals on the site; and fourth, the effect of fire on the site.

TOPOGRAPHIC POSITION

The nutrient supplies in the soil are not available to the forest tree unless tree roots are able to reach them and unless moisture is available to serve as a medium of transfer of the nutrients from the soil to the root. Root growth and soil moisture both depend in large measure upon the physical properties of the site, including the topographic position of the site, its slope, its aspect (the direction the slope faces), and also (to be discussed in the following section) its soil texture and soil structure.

Position on Slope

The location of the forest site with regard to surrounding land joins in importance the soil geology in determining the physical properties of the soil. High convex surfaces tend to be exposed to high winds, subject to erosion and weathering, and to be drier than is average for the region. (We have already noted that such sites also tend to have better cold air drainage and therefore cooler days and warmer nights than poorly drained concave landforms.) At the other extreme, low concave surfaces tend to be sheltered from high winds, subject to accumulation of soil rather than to erosion, and to be moister than is average for the region. Midslopes are generally intermediate in their characteristics. Level surfaces are very stable, their site properties being determined by the climate and the soil conditions.

The classification of forest site upon a basis of relative elevation (viz., high slope, midslope, low slope, basin, high level, and low level) is frequently one of the most useful and meaningful criteria of site classification. Practically, it has the advantage of being capable of classification on aerial photographs viewed stereoscopically. Many studies have found position on slope to be the single most useful factor in evaluating growth potential of forest trees (Ralston, 1964).

Slope and Aspect

The angle of repose of the soil is usually measured in terms of percentage (the vertical rise expressed as a percentage of the horizontal distance) or in terms of degrees. The greater the slope, the greater also is the surface area per acre or other area measured horizontally. For this reason, good forest sites of moderate slope usually contain more trees and produce greater yields per acre (measured horizontally as it always is) than do comparable level sites.

The great importance of slope, however, is in orienting the site with regard to the sun and wind. In the North Temperate Zone, the sun is to the south during the warmth of the day, and south-facing slopes receive more intense sunlight than any other. At any given latitude, then, the hottest and driest sites are those which most nearly face the sun during the middle of the summer day. Both steeper and more gradual slopes receive less insolation. The amount of insolation received on a site governs other related factors, air and soil temperature, precipitation, and soil moisture, all of which are important for establishment and growth of plants. In a detailed study of eight environmental factors of four southerly aspects in desert foothills of Arizona, Haase (1970) found the sequence of warmest and driest, based on annual means, was S, SSW, SW, and SSE. However, the warmest and driest aspect may change when the time of year is considered. For example, the SW aspect exhibited drought extremes during the arid spring but had the mildest drought conditions during all other seasons.

North slopes, on the other hand, receive less sunlight and are invariably cooler and moister in the Northern Hemisphere (these relations are, of course, reversed in the Southern Hemisphere). East and west slopes show similar but less extreme variation. East-facing slopes are exposed to direct sunlight in the cool of the morning and are normally somewhat cooler and moister than west-facing slopes. In mixed upland oak forests of the Appalachian Mountains northeast aspects were the most productive, being approximately 15 percent better than the south and west aspects, which were the least productive (Chapter 11).

The effect of sunlight on the different aspects may be accentuated or diminished by prevailing winds, which change the climate on windward slopes according to the nature of the wind. Thus, if the prevailing wind is off the ocean and is moist and cool, the windward slope will be moister and cooler than others, and vice versa.

SOIL TEXTURE AND STRUCTURE

Soil Texture

By soil texture is meant the size distribution of the soil particles, which range from gravel to sand, silt (microscopic and floury to the touch), and clay (submicroscopic and plastic to the touch). Near-equal mixtures of sand, silt, and clay are termed *loams*, with a modifying term indicating the dominant fraction (e.g., *silt loam*).

The texture of the soil parent material is determined in part by the mineralogy of the soil-forming minerals and in part by the degree of weathering. A coarse-grained granite will tend to weather into a soil composed dominantly of coarse sands, while a fine-grained diorite will tend to weather into find sands and silts. In the case of transported soils, the mode of transport is all-important. Rapidly moving waters will deposit only gravel or sand, while silt and clay will precipitate from very still water bodies. Ice, however, can move and leave all sizes of particles, so that glacial deposits may contain anything from large boulders to fine clays. Wind transports fine sand to form *dunes* and transports silt-size particles over much greater distances to form deposits termed *loess*.

As the soil profile develops, the different horizons tend to develop different soil textures. With podzolization, the leached A horizon becomes progressively coarser-textured (except at the surface, where fine-grained organic matter may serve to help maintain a fine texture) and may eventually become composed entirely of sand grains. In contrast, the B horizon receives deposits of clays and silts and becomes increasingly finer-textured, even to the extent of becoming cemented and impervious to water and air movement. Under arid and semi-arid climates, where evaporation moves water toward the surface, the surface horizons may become finer-textured than those lower down. In the process of laterization, the residual weathered material becomes progressively coarser-textured as time elapses. If the process proceeds to the end, however, this material forms into *laterite*, a dense and compact rock (Chapter 7).

Soil texture is extremely important in affecting site quality. It influences the chemical properties of the soil, soil moisture and air relations, and root development.

From a chemical standpoint, the minute clay particles are the most active and present the largest surfaces from which nutrients may be released to roots. The fertility of a forest soil is commonly correlated with the percentage of *fines* in the soil. These include the mineral silt and clay particles and similarly sized organic matter. Electrostatic properties of clay-size particles, both mineral and organic (humus), are responsible for the phenomenon of cation absorption in soils, a process that retains nutrient bases (Ca^{++}, Mg^{++}, K^+, Na^+) against leaching and thus enhances soil fertility. Soils high in sand content are normally low in fertility.

Physically, the texture of the soil regulates the pore space and consequently both the water and the air-holding capacity of the soil. Coarse-textured soils have much large pore space. They are easily drained, though, and are apt to be excessively dry. Fine-textured soils have very few large pore spaces but hold much water on the large surface area (i.e., their capillary pore space is large). Heavy clays are but little pervious to air and water. The best conditions for both absorption and retention of both water and air are mixtures of sands and fines. Well-balanced loams represent the most favorably textured soils under most forest climatic conditions (Figure 10.1).

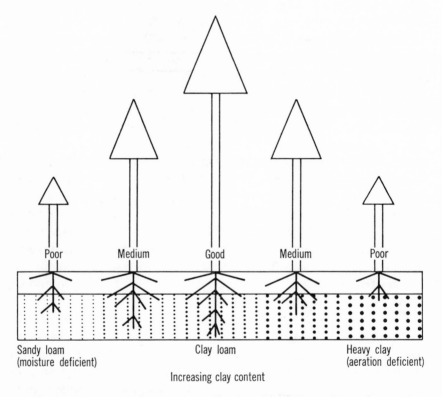

Fig. 10.1. How subsoil texture affects tree growth. (After Zahner, 1957.)

Soil texture affects root development primarily through the influence of texture on aeration and nutrient retention. Different species vary markedly in their ability to penetrate soils. The roots of red pine in the Lake States, for instance, can only penetrate soils with a high sand or gravel content. In medium sands, extensive and deep root systems are developed. Satisfactory root systems can also be developed in rocky soils where the interstices among the rocks are filled with relatively coarse soils. In poorly aerated tills and other heavier soils, however, red pine root development is largely confined to the A horizon that has been rendered coarse by leaching. Spruces, particularly black and Norway spruce, are widely known as shallow-rooted, blowdown-prone species on heavy and poorly drained and aerated soils. However, Norway spruce develops extensive and deep root systems in sandy and sandy loam soils.

Structure

Whereas texture refers to the actual size of soil particles, structure refers to the mode of grouping of these particles into aggregates. Thus a fine-textured soil may actually appear coarse—and may function in many ways as a coarse soil—because of the coalescing of particles into larger granules. Structure is most important in soils high in silt and clay content. The development of a granulated structure in such soils permits good percolation of both water and air, reduces erosion, and results in a soil that has many of the desirable physical and chemical properties of a good natural loam.

Favorable soil structure is promoted by the incorporation of organic matter deep into the surface horizons. Thus tree species and associated soil biota that promote a mull type of humus formation generally favor aggregation of the fines into crumbs or other types of larger particles. Earthworms are particularly beneficial in accomplishing this.

Favorable soil structure developed under forest conditions may be destroyed by removing the forest and exposing the soil surface to the direct striking of raindrops and to intensive leaching. In the Coweeta Experimental Forest in the southern Appalachians, a mountain slope cleared of its natural hardwood forest vegetation and put into agricultural use showed little erosion for the first 2 years because of the soil aggregates that permitted the rain to penetrate the soil rather than to run off the surface. After exposure and farming had reduced the number and size of the surface aggregates, however, more than 200 tons of soil were washed off the 23-acre tract in the following 11 years.

In the tropical rain forest, maintenance of favorable soil structure is even more important. Tropical downpours may leach the soil of nutrients to a depth of 6 or more feet within a year of clearcutting. Favorable site conditions are maintained only by a continuous forest in which the rapid turnover of organic matter results in the development of a granulated structure in an otherwise coarse lateritic soil. Following clearcutting, the combined effect of higher surface soil temperature, the drying of the surface soil under the direct rays of the sun, and the direct striking action of heavy rain results in the breaking down of the soil aggregates and consequent complete leaching of the surface soil. This process explains why tropical rain forest soils can only be cultivated for a few months after the forest is cleared before they must be abandoned and returned to forest growth. Under such conditions, only soil-protecting and deep-rooted plants can be grown for any period of time without soil deterioration.

LARGE ANIMALS AND COMPACTION OF THE SITE

The activities of man, deer, cattle, sheep, and other large animals result in substantial changes in the forest site. The hoofed grazing and browsing animals are the most effective, but logging equipment and other human implements are locally of the greatest importance.

The impact of herbivores on the forest site quality is both indirect and direct. Grazing and browsing animals change the vegetation through their selective feeding habits and the differential ability of different plants to survive and prosper. The changed vegetation in turn results in changed litter and soil biotic activity and thus in changed site conditions. The change may be for the better or worse, but is most apt to be the latter as the less palatable species are generally those with lower nutrient content, and the woody species are generally those with lower nutrient content, and more woody structure. The litter of such plants will generally decompose but slowly and will inhibit soil biotic activity. Thus changes in vegetation result in changes in soil organic matter, soil organisms, soil chemistry, and therefore soil productivity.

Heavy, single-species grazing pressure can cause entire changes in the structure of the plant community. For example, in the nineteenth century following white settlement of the intermountain

American West, grazing pressure from livestock, particularly cattle, depleted the bunch-grass vegetation (Wagner, 1969). As a result of the reduced competition from grasses, woody species such as big sage (*Artemisia tridentata*), junipers (*Juniperus osteosperma* and *J. scopulorum*), bitterbrush (*Purshia tridentata*), and service-berry (*Amelanchier alnifolia*) increased greatly and turned grassland into brushland. (The reverse is reported in Africa where elephants and other browsing animals may turn woodlands and brush types into grasslands [Wagner, 1969]). Then in the twentieth century widespread increases of the mule deer placed heavy pressure on the shrubs, causing them to slowly disappear. In many areas the vegetation is returning to the original bunchgrass type.

The direct effects of grazing on site result largely from the action of animal hoofs in compacting the surface soil and in breaking up the ground cover. Both are detrimental under most circumstances and often highly so. The pounding of animal hoofs results in a breaking down of the soil aggregates which give a crumb structure to the surface soil. The pore space of the surface soil is greatly reduced, often to the point of seriously reducing the supply of air in the soil, and of preventing the infiltration of rain water at a rate sufficient to prevent surface runoff. As a result, heavily grazed soils are apt to be poorly aerated, have a lessened water absorbing capacity, and become subject to sheet erosion. Biotic activity is minimized in highly compacted grazed soils. Site quality is often lowered substantially.

In a study of paired grazed and ungrazed woodlots in southern Wisconsin, Steinbrenner (1951) found that, in general, the highly compacted soils of the heavily grazed woodlots had a lower initial moisture content in the spring and dried out faster in the summer and late fall, evidently because of the lowered soil permeability and increased run-off. The grazed soils were so compacted that water permeabilities averaged about one-tenth those of comparable un-grazed woodlots. The organic matter content and the available potassium were significantly higher in the surface soils of the grazed woodlots, apparently due to the manuring action of livestock.

Grazing has greatly affected the forests and the site throughout most of the farm woodlands of the East, Central States, and South, and throughout most of the open woodland and ponderosa pine forests of the American West. Cattle do much damage because of their sharp hoofs, heavy weight, and tendency to congregate around water, salt, or bedding areas. Sheep may be harmful if run in excessive numbers, but, when herded from place to place so as to prevent overgrazing, usually leave the site in fairly good condition. Deer are generally not present in numbers sufficient to compact the soil excessively but have markedly changed the forest composition through the differential browsing of seedlings in many localities in the Appalachians, Lake States, western pine forests, and elsewhere. Where deer have been introduced into forests composed predominantly of palatable species previously unbrowsed, they may virtually eliminate all vegetation within reach. This has occurred in many indigenous forest areas in New Zealand. Other grazing and browsing animals such as elk, caribou, and bison have affected the site in local situations. *Around the world, grazing by livestock has probably been more important than any other factor in reducing the productive capacity of uncultivated land.*

A compatible relationship of plants, soil, and animals may be achieved by matching plant diversity and the diversity of grazing animals. For example, Holsworth (1960) reported that the major game populations of Elk Island National Park, Canada, were bison, elk, and moose. The three animals showed distinctly different habitat and food preferences such that their complementary feeding habits tended to maintain the vegetation, and thus the soil, in a form usable by all species. And in the East African savanna the specialization of feeding habits is strikingly seen. There herds of wild animals, composed mainly of 9 herbivores and 1 carnivore with a biomass of 70,000 to 100,000 pounds per square mile yearly, coexist, with no evidence of overgrazing or serious soil deterioration (Talbot *et al.*, 1965). This biomass is six times that of cattle, sheep, and goats supported in the same area under native herding with moderate to severe overgrazing and three times the biomass under European-type cattle ranching with slight to moderate overgrazing. According to Wagner (1969), the variety of herbivores is an important influence in maintaining the vegetative diversity and consequently the natural condition of the soil as well.

At the same time, the destructiveness of soil productivity by human activity should not be minimized. The effects of agricultural practices, both good and bad, on site quality are obviously great, but are outside the scope of the present work. It is equally obvious that the great changes in forest vegetation brought about by logging, burning, and other human activities have resulted in great changes in soil productivity.

Confining ourselves to direct effects, human activity is responsible for considerable site deterioration through soil compaction. Trucks, tractors, and other heavy equipment used in logging result in substantial soil compaction (Moehring and Rawls, 1970). In the Douglas-fir region in Washington, skid roads and other affected areas may occupy a substantial percentage of the logging area. Such compaction on skid roads has been shown to reduce the soil permeability 92 percent and the miscroscopic pore space by 53 percent, thus increasing the bulk density by 35 percent (Steinbrenner and Gessel, 1955). Similarly in the Atlantic coastal plain, soil compaction on skid roads was found to reduce soil infiltration rate and pore space by 84 and 34 percent, respectively, and to increase bulk density 33 percent (Hatchell *et al.*, 1970). Forty years may be required for infiltration to recover on severely compacted logging roads (Perry, 1964).

Compaction from logging traffic is much more pronounced on wet than on dry soils and more severe on clayey than on sandy soils (Steinbrenner, 1955; Moehring and Rawls, 1970). Severe skidding traffic on three or four sides of trees in wet weather significantly reduced growth of trees up to 60 percent of that of trees in an undisturbed stand (Moehring, 1970). Although this intensity is not normally encountered except at landings and along major skid trails, wet weather logging can cause soil compaction that may markedly reduce growth rates of established seedlings and significantly reduce seedling establishment on skid trails (Youngberg, 1959; Perry, 1964; Hatchell *et al.*, 1970). Hatchell and Ralston (1971) estimated that 18 years may be required for severely disturbed soils to attain normal tree densities.

The human foot itself is an effective compacting agent. The problem of soil compaction in forest parks and other recreational areas within the forest has been recognized for over 40 years (Meinecke, 1928) and is reaching serious proportions. Death of large and famous trees has been attributed to compaction, and decreased growth rate is frequently apparent. Because of compaction, it has been necessary to fence out tourists from the immediate neighborhood of famous trees, and to move public camp grounds out of old-growth areas as in the redwood and bigtree

localities in California. The increasingly intensive use of the forests
for camping and other recreation is giving added importance to the
dangers of site deterioration resulting directly from man and his
vehicles.

FIRE AND THE SITE

As with grazing, fire has affected a substantial portion of the
forests of the world at one time or other. In the United States,
virtually all of the upland forest in the South, the Lake States, in
the West, and much of that of the Northeast and Central States
has been burned over more or less frequently.

In early days, the tendency of forestry writers was to consider fire
as almost entirely a destructive agency, with few or no beneficial
aspects. The development of interest in prescribed or controlled
burning as a tool in silviculture, forest range management, and fire
hazard reduction, however, has caused a re-evaluation of the effect
of fire on the site—a re-evaluation that has led to the realization that
the effect of fire on forest land and its productivity is complex and
may often be entirely beneficial. Again as in the case of grazing,
we may distinguish between the indirect effects of fire on site quality
through its impact on vegetation and its direct effect on the properties of the soil.

The indirect effects of fire depend upon the changes in the vegetation. These are discussed in detail in a later chapter. Since fire
will kill most or all of the plant life above the soil surface, the
succeeding vegetation tends to be made up of light-seeded species
that can move in from outside the burned area, species with perennial root systems capable of sending up new sprouts, and species
with dormant seeds stimulated by heat. Many legumes fall in these
categories, and the abundance of these and other nitrogen-fixing
plants is often increased by burning. In such a case, although previously accumulated nitrogen is volatilized, there may shortly be a
net increase in available nitrogen and the overall site quality may
be improved. Unfortunately, though, in many parts of the world,
fire favors the development of a shrubby vegetation composed of
sprouting species with a characteristically tough foliage, low in
nutritive value, and slow to decompose when dropped to the forest

floor. Heather in northern Europe, blueberry species and bracken in many countries, junipers around the Northern Hemisphere, shrub oaks in an equally widespread region, and the many chaparral species of California and the Southwest—all are plants that become dominant after heavy and repeated fires. The heaths, the blueberry barrens, the juniper and oak woodlands, and the chaparral are fire types. In them the soil will usually deteriorate under the influence of woody and impoverished litter, until the soil can no longer support the original forest vegetation. The generalization is dangerous, for among the junipers, oaks, and chaparral species are some soil-building species, but the overall detrimental effect of most of these brushland fire types on the site cannot be denied.

To reclaim heathland back into forest, it is frequently necessary to break the hardpan with a deep soil plow, and to mulch and fertilize the planted tree seedlings. Even then, only trees such as Scots pine, black pine, and lodgepole pine that make little demand on the soil can be expected to thrive, and these will grow only slowly for many years.

The direct effects of fire on site quality arise from two principal sources: the burning of organic matter above and on the soil and the heating of the surface layers of the soil. The burning of organic matter results in the release of carbon dioxide and nitrogenous gases to the atmosphere and the deposit of the minerals in the form of ash. The wood and litter ash is more soluble than the organic matter from which it was formed. Thus the effect of fire is to increase the amount of available minerals, at least temporarily, to lessen the soil acidity, and to decrease the supply of nitrogen.

Two examples are indicative of many studies on these effects. In the ponderosa pine region of Arizona, burning was found to increase the soluble nutrients as a result of the ashing of the surface layer of *duff*, or unincorporated organic matter (Fuller *et al.*, 1955). This had the effect of causing an increase in the pH, available phosphorus, exchangeable bases, and total soluble salts and a decrease in organic matter and nitrogen to a depth of 8 to 12 inches. Microbiological activity, particularly of bacteria, increased as a result of burning. On the negative side, the surface was compacted by rains following the removal of litter with a decrease in the water penetration rate. In another study (Tarrant, 1956a), however, burning was found to be not detrimental and perhaps even slightly beneficial in its effects on permeability and associated physical properties in the soil in eastern Washington.

In the Douglas-fir region, Tarrant (1956b) has investigated the effects of slash burning on physical soil properties. Light burning increased the percolation rate of water within the surface 3 inches of soil, but severe burning confined to less than 5 percent of intentionally burned, logged-over sites did seriously impede water drainage about 70 percent.

Unfortunately, the same characteristics of small particle size and high solubility that render the ash minerals readily available to plants render the ash susceptible to leaching and erosion by rainwater. If the ash is washed down into the soil so that the roots can absorb the nutrient ions dissolved from it, site quality is usually improved by fire, at least temporarily. If, on the other hand, the ash is leached down below the tree roots, or is washed off the surface, then site quality is lowered. In general, the former occurs on level soils of sandy to loamy texture while the latter is apt to happen on heavy soils or very coarse sands, particularly those with considerable slope.

The loss of total nitrogen through volatilization is widely recognized and is related to the intensity of the fire. Knight (1966), working in the coastal Douglas-fir region, found no nitrogen loss in soils heated to 200°C (392°F), a 25-percent loss at 300°C (572°F), and a 64-percent loss at 700°C (1,292°F). The ability of the succeeding vegetation and soil bacteria to replace the nitrogen lost in burning is an important factor determining the effect of fire on the site. The higher pH due to release of mineral bases in the soluble ash can provide a more favorable soil environment for free-living, nitrogen-fixing bacteria, and thus result in a long-term net increase in soil nitrogen. Although the loss of nitrogen is widely cited as a deleterious effect of fire, the significance of the loss for the new regeneration and the overall nutrition of the ecosystem is not well known.

The actual heating of the soil is of relatively less importance than the action of fire on the organic matter. The heat of the fire does not penetrate far into the mineral soil. Even under a hot fire in logging slash, temperatures seldom exceed 79° to 94°C an inch down in the mineral soil. Light surface fires only heat the top fraction of an inch of the mineral soil to near the boiling point.

In this heated zone, soil aggregates may be broken down, first by the heat and later by the direct striking action of raindrops, resulting in loss of soil structure and in lowered infiltration capacity of the surface soil. In extreme cases—which are rare—clay soils may be baked hard, soil organisms will be destroyed, and small roots will be burned out, creating percolation channels. The chemical nature of the soil particles themselves may be altered by the heat, sometimes actually increasing the supply of soil nutrients.

Although the effects of direct heating on the mineral soil are many and varied, in general their sum total does not alter the site quality to any marked extent for any substantial period of time. Except in the rare burn that creates extreme heat within the mineral soil, the effects of fire on site quality are best interpreted in the light of its effect upon the soil through the destruction of organic matter.

There are some situations where fire is obviously catastrophic. These include cases where the soil is composed almost entirely of organic matter and those where the destruction of organic matter lays bare highly erodable soils to heavy rain.

The burning of a peat bog after drainage or a series of dry seasons literally results in the complete destruction of the soil and the return to swamp conditions. Thousands of years of peat accumulation are necessary to replace the lost organic soil, and such areas can be virtually eliminated from our productive sites. In the United States, many bogs in the Atlantic Coastal Plain and in the recently glaciated parts of the Northeast and the Lake States have been destroyed as forest sites by fire.

Similarly, the burning of humus lying directly on top of rock will eliminate the soil and destroy the site. In the glaciated portions of Canada and the northeastern United States, and in many mountain regions, thin accumulations of humus provide the only nutrition for forest trees. Fire in such cases often burns down to bedrock with disastrous results.

Still another bad situation occurs where highly erodable soil on steep slopes is exposed by fire burning the organic protection. The classic example is in southern California, where brush species and the organic matter from them protect heavy soils lying at approximately the angle of repose in steep mountains. If, after a fire, the heavy rainstorms characteristic of this semi-arid region strike before revegetation of the burn, whole slopes may wash downhill, not only lowering the growing potential of the soil, but frequently wreaking havoc on the valleys below.

The burning of litter and organic matter in the soil may be significant in indirectly bringing about erosion in many areas of the western United States where water-repellent soils have been reported (DeBano *et al.*, 1967). For a number of years California scientists were puzzled by the sight of "dusty tracks in the mud" in freshly burned watersheds after fall and winter rains. Now it is known that a variety of soils can become resistant to wetting. These are soils in which the particles repel water; droplets do not readily penetrate and infiltrate, but "ball up" and remain on the soil surface. This novel phenomenon appears to be widespread throughout wildland areas in the western United States and has also been detected in Florida, Australia, and New Zealand.

Plant species vary in their ability to induce soil wettability. Water-repellent layers are strongly expressed in brushland areas of southern California supporting juniper species, singleleaf pinyon pine, and big cone Douglas-fir as well as a number of chaparral brush species. The water-repellent layers are apparently formed when non-wettable or hydrophobic substances are vaporized as fire burns the litter and organic matter of an area. These substances then move downward in the soil and condense on soil particles (Figure 10.2, DeBano, 1969). The depth and thickness of the non-wettable layer probably depend on the kind and amounts of litter present and the temperature of the fire. Rain falling on the soil surface infiltrates readily until impeded by a non-wettable layer. After the wetting front encounters the repllent layer, infiltration is slowed, surface runoff begins, and erosion is likely to follow.

Just as there are cases where fire is catastrophic in its effects on site, so there are cases where it is clearly beneficial. Such is the case for sites in the far north where dampness and cold may prevent the decomposition of organic matter, giving rise to heavy mats of highly acid raw humus. In Norway, Sweden, and Finland, considerable success has been achieved by burning such sites to improve the site quality.

In most situations, however, the effect of fire on site quality is relatively less pronounced. Repeated burning—once haphazard and now more or less controlled—in the sand plains of the southern pine region has apparently had no major detrimental effect on site qual-

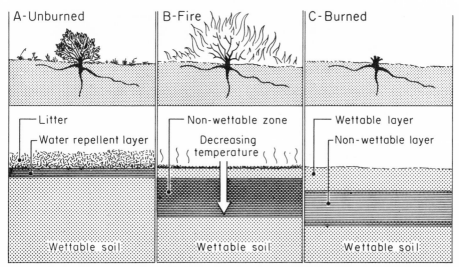

Fig. 10.2. Soil non-wettability before, during, and after fire. (A) Before fire, the non-wettable substances accumulate in the litter layer and mineral soil immediately beneath it. (B) Fire burns vegetation and litter layer, causing non-wettable substances to move downward along temperature gradients. (C) After a fire, non-wettable substances are located below and parallel to soil surface on the burned area. (After DeBano *et al.,* 1967.)

ity and in fact, has been shown locally to be beneficial to the soil (Metz *et al.,* 1961). In loess soils under even-aged shortleaf and loblolly pines on flat terrain in Arkansas, nine successive annual burns had little effect on the nutrient content or structure of the topsoil (Moehring *et al.,* 1966). Studies of soil microorganisms after 20 years of annual prescribed burning on a very fine sandy loam in the coastal plain indicated that burning had no effect on the total number of fungi per gram of soil, although it did reduce their total number through a decrease in weight of the organic horizon (Jorgensen and Hodges, 1970). The number of bacteria in the organic layer was reduced by annual burning but not in mineral soil. For the organisms studied, there was little indication that prescribed burning adversely affected soil metabolic processes. In the sand plains of the Lake States, organic matter provides the only source of colloids for soil nutrition. Burning the sand plains, therefore, may be undesirable and has been shown by Stoeckler (1948, 1960) to reduce site quality of trembling aspen. There seems no reason to fear site deterioration in burning the more level pinelands of the

Western states. When dealing with clay soils and steep slopes, however, fire may do no harm if gentle rains impound the ash and revegetation anchors the soil. And then, again, if this does not happen, the site may be greatly deteriorated, even destroyed.

SUMMARY

The composition, form, development, and productivity of the forest are affected by the physical soil factors, texture and structure, and the topographic position of the site. In addition, large animals (including man) and fire affect the physical and chemical properties of the soil and hence influence tree growth and productivity.

The position of the site on the slope is one of the most useful measures of the productivity of a forest because the relative position influences soil moisture and air drainage. The orientation of the site with regard to sun and wind (aspect) governs the amount of radiation received by the forest. This in turn affects many other site factors, such as air and soil temperatures and soil moisture, which affect establishment and growth of vegetation. Forest sites of east and north aspects are generally more productive than those of comparable soils on south and west slopes. Texture and structure of forest soils largely determine both water and air-holding capacity of the soil. Soil with a mixture of sands and clay particles permit extensive root development and provide the best conditions for water absorption and retention, and hence for growth. The development of a granulated structure of soils with a high content of silt and clay particles is essential for root development, aeration, and water infiltration.

Around the world, soil compaction by grazing animals has significantly lowered the productive capacity of forest sites. Compacted soils are poorly aerated, and their reduced water absorption capacity increases surface run-off, thereby promoting erosion. Through changes in the vegetation of the site, grazing indirectly causes changes in soil organic matter, soil organisms, rate of decomposition, and soil chemistry which ultimately may lead to decreased productivity. Compaction by man is a serious problem in overcrowded parks and recreation areas. Man's mechanization of timber harvesting has initiated locally serious tree establishment and growth problems on skid roads and trails where wet, clayey soils are compacted by heavy machines.

Wildland fire has long been a factor in many forests of the southern and western United States, and thus its wise use in these areas by man in prescribed burning is usually not detrimental to the physical and chemical properties of the soil. On certain sites fire may be entirely beneficial; on others it may be disastrous by destroying the thin layer of organic matter necessary for tree nutrition. On clay soils and steep slopes, fire may lead to soil compaction and erosion.

SUGGESTED READINGS

BUCKMAN, HARRY O., and NYLE C. BRADY. 1969. *The Nature and Properties of Soils,* 7th ed. (Chapter 3, Some important physical properties of mineral soils, pp. 41–63.) The Macmillan Co., Toronto, Ontario, 653 pp.

HAASE, EDWARD F. 1970. Environmental fluctuations on south-facing slopes in the Santa Catalina Mountains of Arizona. *Ecology* 51:959–974.

MOEHRING, DAVID H., and IKE W. RAWLS. 1970. Detrimental effects of wet weather logging. *J. For.* 68:166–167.

USDA Forest Service. 1971. Prescribed burning symposium proceedings. Southeastern For. Exp. Sta., Asheville, N. C. 160 pp.

11

Site

The forest ecosystem, then, functions as a complex energy cycle involving trees, ground vegetation, the atmosphere, and the soil, together with the multitude of plants and animals that inhabit it. The cycling of nutrients, of water, even of energy, is marked by losses and additions at the various stages.

The forest scientist, however, is primarily concerned with the forest tree segment of this ecosystem. He wishes to evaluate the suitability of various tree species or other genetic entities for a given locality, to rate the competitive ability of alternative species that are capable of growing in that locality, and to estimate the growth potential—particularly the productivity of wood substance—of the forest communities that occupy it.

With these points of view, the forest ecosystem may be divided into the forest trees and associated plants and animals (the biome or biocoenosis), the sites they occupy (defined by position in space), and the environmental conditions associated with these sites. Usually the term *site* (habitat) is assumed to include both the position in space and the associated environment and will be so defined and used in this chapter. The forest site quality thus is defined as the sum total of all of the factors affecting the capacity to produce forests or other vegetation. These include climatic factors, edaphic factors, and biological factors.

The forest scientist is faced with the problem of integrating all the various site factors so as to produce an estimate of the forest site quality. Statistically, the site factors are treated as independent variables and some measure of forest growth as the dependent variable. Yet, in fact, all are part of the same interacting ecosystem. The site factors are not only interdependent, but are also dependent in part upon the forest, which is itself a major site-forming factor. Because of these interactions, the simple regression technique of estimating site quality from an evaluation of a few important site factors, important as it is in practical forest ecology, can only be approximate. Only by considering the forest and the site together as a complex interrelated ecosystem can the true dynamic nature of both be fully understood.

Nevertheless, the estimation of forest productivity is of the utmost importance in both forest ecology and in silvicultural management. This productivity, or actual site quality, may be measured directly for a few forests where accurate long-term records of stand development and growth have been maintained. Generally however, it can only be estimated indirectly by one or more of these alternatives:

A. Vegetation of the forest
   1. Trees (site index)
   2. Ground vegetation (indicator species and species groups)
   3. Overstory and understory vegetation in combination
B. Factors of the physical environment
   1. Soil and topography
   2. Climate
C. Multiple factor or combined methods (using some or all of the foregoing factors and forest land-use history)

These are the alternatives discussed in the present chapter. Significant reviews of forest site quality have been published by Coile (1952), Rennie (1962), Ralston (1964), Jones (1969), and Carmean (1970a).

DIRECT MEASUREMENT OF FOREST PRODUCTIVITY

Actual forest productivity is generally measured in terms of the gross volume of bole wood per acre per year over the normal rotation. This gross mean annual increment (m.a.i.) may be computed from long-term permanent sample plot data. For instance, on pumice soil sites on the North Island of New Zealand, Douglas-fir has been computed to yield a gross m.a.i. of 439 cubic feet per acre per year, or 31 cubic meters per hectare per year (Spurr, 1963).

Yields of 516 cubic feet per acre per year may be expected from Monterey pine on similar sites (Spurr, 1962). In the United States, gross mean annual increments range upwards to perhaps 210 cubic feet per acre per year on the best sites (15 cubic meters per hectare per year). Average productivity in the temperate forest of North America and Europe is approximately 70 cubic feet per acre per year (5 cubic meters per hectare per year).

Actual gross productivity data, however, are scarce and in general are inadequately computed and presented from even such sample plot data as are available. Furthermore, it must be realized that actual yield is conditioned not only by site factors but also by genetic factors (of species, race, and individual), age or rotation, by the biotic history of the stand, and by stand density. Nevertheless, actual growth represents the proven productivity of a site and therefore may be taken as the closest available approximation of potential productivity.

It should be noted that growth is presented in gross values—the total amount of wood put on by all trees within a given unit of time without deduction for natural mortality, removal by man, or decrease in wood volumes by rot. By using such gross values, consistent increment measurements can readily be obtained.

Theoretically, a stand of a given species of a given age on a given site will produce the same amount of wood a year at various densities of stocking as long as the site is fully occupied. As long as the trees in the unthinned stands retain good crown development and vigor, they will fully occupy the site. Conversely, if the trees in thinned stands or even in open stands fully occupy the soil to the extent of being able to fully utilize available soil moisture, they will normally fully occupy the site even if excess crown space is available in the stand. These being the cases, thinned and unthinned stands, otherwise comparable, should give the same total increment. To make such a comparison, however, gross growth should be computed by adding back in mortality within a growth period, whether from man's cutting activity or from natural causes.

In recent years, forest ecologists have been attempting to estimate forest productivity in terms of all components of the forest ecosystem rather than of the tree boles alone. Researchers around the world have been sampling not only the stems but also the branches, the leaves, the organic matter in the forest floor, and even the animals inhabiting the forest, to provide a more exact appraisal of the entire forest ecosystem; their studies are considered in Chapter 16. For practical forest site evaluation purposes, however, the wood content of the boles or main stems of the forest trees remains the best-known and most useful measure of forest productivity.

HEIGHT AS A MEASURE OF SITE

The height of free-grown trees of a given species and of a given age is more closely related to the capacity of a given site to produce wood of that species than any other one measure. Furthermore, height of free-grown trees is less influenced by stand density than other measures of tree dimensions and may thus be used as an index of site quality in even-aged stands of varying density and silvicultural history.

The height of the dominant portion of a forest stand at a specified standard age is commonly termed *site index* even though tree height is but one of many indices of site quality used in forest ecological and silvicultural investigations (Figure 11.1).

In the United States, site index has long been defined as the average height that the dominant or dominant and codominant portion of the even-aged stand will have at a specified age. This standard age is generally 50 years in the eastern United States, and 100 years for the longer-lived species of the West Coast. Occasionally, other standard ages are specified for a particular species or region, for example, 35 years for pulpwood rotations in the South.

Measuring both dominant and codominant trees for height is not always satisfactory. In the first place, these tree classes are subjective, and two foresters may differ widely in their concept of what constitutes dominant and codominant trees. In the second place, many of the codominant trees will drop out of the main canopy as the stand ages and, therefore, perhaps should not be measured. Third, thinning and other cutting operations may artificially change the average height of the dominant and codominant trees without, of course, changing the actual site quality. Finally, it is often very difficult to see the tops of codominant trees in tall and dense timber, and it is therefore difficult to measure their heights accurately.

For these reasons there is a tendency to restrict more carefully the trees that should be measured for site determination. A preferable and growing practice is to measure the height of an ob-

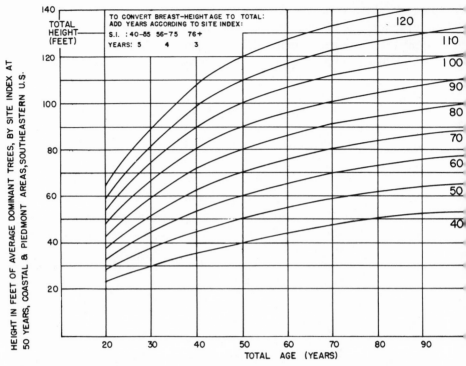

Fig. 11.1. Site-index curves for second-growth loblolly pine in the coastal plain and Piedmont areas of the southeastern United States. Example: If the total height of dominants in a second-growth loblolly pine stand averaged 55 feet (y-axis) at age 60 (x-axis), the site index is 50, indicating a relatively poor site. If the corresponding height and age values are 85 feet at 40 years in another stand, the site index is 95, indicating a relatively good site. (After Hampf, 1965. Source: U. S. Dept. Agr. Misc. Publ. 50, 1929; revised by Coile and Schumacher, 1953.)

jectively determined sample of the larger trees in the stand. In the British Commonwealth, the concept of *top height* is widely used. This refers to the arithmetic mean height of the 100 largest-diameter trees per acre. Since, however, it is seldom feasible to measure so many trees per acre for height, and since heavy thinning practices frequently reduce the stand to fewer than 100 trees per acre, the present tendency is to restrict top height to a smaller sample of the very largest trees. A mean height based on the largest 40 trees per acre (sometimes defined as mean *predominant height*) has the advantage in closely approximating the practice in metric-system countries of measuring the 100 largest-diameter trees per hectare. Top heights based upon the 25 largest-diameter trees per acre, the 3 to 5 largest trees, or even upon the 1 largest tree per acre are also used.

Although height is perhaps the single tree measure best related to the site productivity of a given species, it does not necessarily follow that it is completely unrelated to other factors, nor that a perfect correlation may be obtained between stand top height and site productivity. In particular, stand density, particularly extremes of stand density, may influence height growth. Under such circumstances, site-index curves should be developed separately for different stand density classes, as has been done for ponderosa pine in the Inland Empire (Lynch, 1958) and lodgepole pine in the Rocky Mountains (Alexander, 1966; Alexander *et al.*, 1967).

The genetic factors of a tree or population may well control height growth to a great extent on a regional basis. The many plantings of trees of different provenances testify eloquently to this (Chapter 2). Within a given region, however, the strength of genetic control (heritability) of height growth tends to be low and is demonstrated by the strong control of height growth by site factors such as soil moisture, topography, and temperature. Nevertheless, in a given stand, significant differences in individual genotypes may occur, primarily due to genetic factors. Naturally occurring aspen clones on sandy soils in northern lower Michigan have been found to differ greatly in height on the same site (Zahner and Crawford, 1965). Some clones are more than twice as high as adjacent clones of the same age. Such variations are more likely in species developing natural clones than in species where each stem is a different genotype. When stems of different genotypes compete in a stand (as in pines and maples), height growth is of survival value and slow-growing stems tend to be eliminated. In clones, however, competition is primarily between stems of the same genetic constitution, and slow-growing clones are more likely to survive.

Finally, the condition of the site at the time the stand is established as well as competition from other vegetation in early years may affect height growth markedly. Both naturally reseeding and planted pines will usually show different growth trends and amounts on old fields as contrasted with cutover sites.

Site-Index Curves

The usual method of determining site index on the basis of tree height depends upon the use of a height-over-age growth curve to estimate the height at a standard age. Most such curves for American species in the past have been based upon a series of regression curves, based upon a single guiding curve and harmonized to have the same form and trend (Figure 11.1).

The weaknesses of this approach are by now well known (Spurr, 1952b). First and foremost, the technique is sound only if the average site quality is the same for each age class. If, however, as is often the case, younger stands are found on generally better sites (perhaps because of early logging on these sites) while the remaining old growth stands are concentrated on the poorer sites, the average curve will be warped upwards at younger ages and downward at older ages. This seems to be the situation for the standard Douglas-fir site-index curves (Spurr, 1956c) when checked by the growth of permanent sample plots. The reverse situation can also occur.

A second major weakness of the conventional technique is the assumption that the shape of the height-growth curve is the same for all sites. Although this generalization gives good results in many instances, it does not hold for all soil conditions. For instance, if the depth of a soil is limited either by physical or physiological reasons, growth of a tree may be normal up to the point that the depth of the soil becomes a limiting factor (curve B; Figure 11.2). On another soil, the same species may grow slowly until the roots reach an underlying enriched horizon or a deep-lying water supply, after which growth will be accelerated (curve C). The shape of these two growth curves may differ markedly from the normal growth curve on a normal soil (curve A).

A corollary of this problem is the assumption in the standard technique that site differences are apparent at early ages. The process of harmonizing site-index curves assumes that, if a site produces a higher tree at age 50 or 100, that tree will be higher at all preceding and all subsequent ages. The assumption is in contrast to the fact that many plantations and even-aged natural stands on marginal sites may grow normally in youth and only in middle life exhibit sharply decreased growth. Planted black walnut trees on 7 contrasting sites in southern Illinois (Figure 11.3) show rapid early growth, even on the poorer sites, but may slow abruptly after 10 years (Carmean, 1970b). The polymorphic patterns are closely related to soil conditions. Trees on plot 1 are growing on a well-drained alluvial silt loam, while those on plots 4 to 7 are growing on a

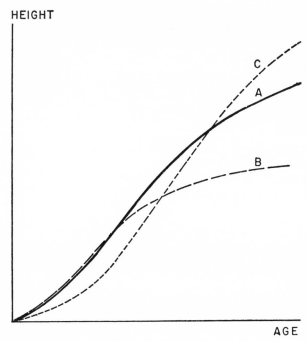

Fig. 11.2. Theoretical effect of soil profile on height growth. (A) Normal height growth in homogeneous soil. (B) Height growth on good but shallow soil. (C) Height growth on soil poor at surface but with rich horizon beneath.

bottomland silt loam soil underlain at 1 to 2 feet by a gravelly subsoil. A similar example is that of red pine plantations in the Saginaw Forest of the University of Michigan that were planted on glacial till soils of much heavier texture than those on which the species is generally found. Marked reduction in growth was noticed in the permanent sample plot data after 30 years. Concurrently, symptoms of malnutrition were noted that appeared to be similar to the little-leaf disease of shortleaf and loblolly pine in the southeastern states. Stem analysis revealed that a marked reduction in growth had occurred for 12 years before external symptoms had become evident. If, as seems to be the case, this reduction is due to commonly occurring soil conditions in the area, it should be taken into account in the site-index curves for red pine growing on those soils. Curves based on the premise of harmonization with a standard average curve cannot show such a plant-soil relationship.

Therefore, it is not surprising that polymorphic site-index curves have been repeatedly demonstrated to characterize the height-

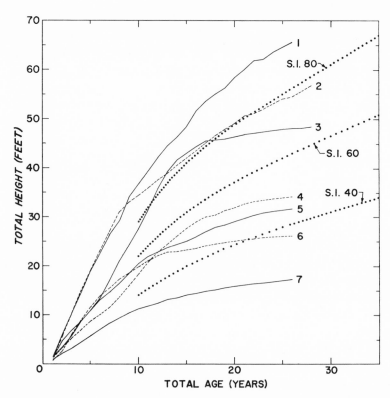

Fig. 11.3. Dominant black walnut trees from plantations in southern Illinois have marked polymorphic patterns of height growth. The height-age curves are averages from 36 sectioned trees growing on 7 contrasting-site plots. (Plot 1—deep, well-drained alluvial silt loam; plot 3—similar to 1 but with restricted internal drainage; plots 4–6—bottomland silt loam underlain at 1½ to 2 feet by gravelly subsoil; plot 7—bottomland silt loam underlain at 1 foot by a gravelly, cherty subsoil.) Also shown are the regional harmonized site-index curves for black walnut (Kellogg, 1939). (After Carmean, 1970b.)

growth pattern of forest trees better than the simple monomorphic pattern portrayed by regional harmonized curves (Carmean, 1970b). Height-growth patterns are known not only to vary in different parts of the range of a species but also in local areas of contrasting soil and topography. Height-growth patterns of oak, for example, not only vary between different soil texture groups, but also vary with aspect and slope within soil groups. Polymorphic site-index curves for different soil-site types have been obtained for many species, including red pine (Bull, 1931; Van Eck and Whiteside,

1963; DeMent and Stone, 1968), white pine (Beck, 1971), loblolly pine (Zahner, 1962), ponderosa pine (Daubenmire, 1961), Douglas-fir (Carmean, 1956), western larch (Roe, 1967), black spruce (Jameson, 1964), yellow-poplar (Beck, 1962), black oak (Carmean, 1965), and black walnut (Carmean, 1966).

Considering the weaknesses of the standard site-index curve techniques, height-growth curves should be based upon actual measured growth of trees on specific soils or site-types and not upon the harmonized method of averaging together height and age values from plots for the entire or regional range of sites upon which the species is found. Such a conclusion is not new. Most present-day European growth curves are based upon actual measured growth rather than upon temporary plots.

In studying height aspects of forest growth for correlation with soil characteristics, then, our basic objective should be to work with actual recorded tree growth and to collect our data in such a way that separate growth curves can be evolved for different soil-site conditions should evidence of differing curve shapes become apparent. There are three general sources of growth information that meet these requirements. The first and the best are the records of long-term permanent sample plots. Where enough plots have been established and measured for a considerable period of years, growth curves should be evolved from the data these plots provide.

In the absence of sufficient permanent plot data, recourse may be had to stem analysis. By sectioning trees from top to bottom, their course of growth can be reconstructed. This technique, too, has its pitfalls, but they are less serious and more easily overcome than those of the temporary plot techniques.

A third source of information is the internode distance on the boles of trees which put out distinct annual whorls. On Douglas-fir and many of the pines, the whorl pattern shows clearly the height of the tree each year in the past back to an early age. Careful measurements of such trees can be used to produce accurate height-growth curves (Bull, 1931; King, 1966; Beck, 1971). Growth curves can be produced by any of the above three techniques—or better yet by the combination of these techniques.

Comparisons Between Species

Just as trees of differing genetic character within a species may be expected to show variations in height response to a given forest site, different species growing on the same site will show the same variations but to a much greater degree. The height-over-age site-index curve may be quite different for two different species on the same site. Nevertheless, the site index as predicted from the measurement of height of one species may be used to give an estimation of the site index of the other (Foster, 1959; Curtis and Post, 1962; Carmean and Vasilevsky, 1971).

In a number of American studies, site indices of different species have been correlated statistically to permit the estimation of site index of one species on the basis of a knowledge of that of another. Most of these studies are limited in that they are based upon harmonized or generalized site-index curves rather than upon specific growth curves developed separately for the site in question. Nevertheless, these studies are useful in practical forestry provided that their limitations are understood. For example, in several studies in the southern United States, site indices for various species and species-groups have been correlated. A site-sensitive species such as yellow-poplar proved to have the highest site index of the best sites and the lowest on the poorest sites (Olson and Della-Bianca, 1959). In the southern Appalachians, site index of the oak group (excluding white oak) could be estimated with a standard error of 5.3 feet from a knowledge of the site index of other species (white oak, white pine, shortleaf and pitch pine grouped, and yellow-poplar; Doolittle, 1958).

Much more information is possible when the site-index comparisons are based upon stem analysis of paired trees, such as a study of white pine and red maple site index by Foster (1959). Here it was found that red maple height growth gave a better indication of potential white pine height growth than did a composite of 11 site factors based on soil and topographic characteristics. On sites that were average or poorer, the height of white pine sample trees at 50 years was superior to that of associated red maples. On the best sites, the height of red maple sample trees at age 50 was the greater. The only site characteristic that proved to have a differing effect on the two species was aspect. On northerly aspects, white pine grew relatively better than red maple with the opposite being true on southerly aspects. White pine site index could best be predicted by an equation based upon the independent variables of red maple height, red maple age, and aspect.

Height Growth for a Portion of the Life Span

Since the total height at a given age of a tree is an expression of all past growing conditions, such a measure may be influenced by conditions that prevailed for a few years—such as grass competition in the seedling state, absence of mycorrhizal infection in newly planted stock, insect attack, and drought. It is therefore sometimes preferable to estimate height-growth potential in terms of the measured growth over a period of a relatively few years in the history of the stand. This approach is particularly feasible for the white pines and other species which put on a single well-defined whorl of lateral branches each growing season.

The best indication of current growing conditions is, of course, current height increment, and this can usually be discerned readily from an inspection of the terminal part of a tree. For taller trees, of course, this is a difficult and time-consuming task.

For the middle part of the height-over-age growth curve, height growth is relatively constant, and the average annual distance between whorls may be assumed to hold true for a future short period. Thus Table 11.1 gives the expected annual height growth for white pine in the Harvard Forest on the various sites, site quality being determined by the parent material of the soil and the depth of the water table. Once a stand approaches maturity, however, height growth will diminish with the passage of time, and either present height or present age should be added as a second variable in the prediction of future heights.

The use of mean annual height increment over the middle period

Table 11.1. Height Growth of Immature White Pine (Central New England)

Site	Description	Annual Height Growth (feet)
A	Stratified drift with low water table	0.9
B	Stratified drift with medium to good water table; till with low water table	1.2
C	Till with medium water table	1.5
D	Till with high water table, but sufficiently aerated for good tree growth	1.8

NOTE: Restricted to stands 20 to 50 years old, with stocking of better than 50 percent.

of height growth as a measure of site quality is old and well established. In recent years, however, the method has been given the name of the *growth-intercept* method and has received renewed emphasis. For loblolly, shortleaf, and slash pines (but not for longleaf), the 5-year intercept above breast height has proved better correlated with site quality than total height in a test of trees from plantations about 20 years old (Wakeley and Marrero, 1958). The technique has been adapted to red pine, Douglas-fir, and other species on which the annual whorls are apparent.

VEGETATION AS AN INDICATOR OF SITE QUALITY

The presence, relative abundance, and relative size of the various species in the forest reflect the nature of the forest ecosystem of which they are a part and thus may serve as indicators of site quality. The correlation may or may not be apparent because the vegetation also reflects the effects of happenstance: plant competition; past events in the history of the vegetation such as drought, fire, and insect outbreaks; and many other factors in the ecological complex giving rise to the plant community. None the less, site characteristics are sufficiently reflected in the vegetation to make the use of the latter a successful index of site quality in many instances. The plants themselves are used as the measure of site: they are *phytometers.*

Tree species are useful indicators in that they are long-lived, relatively unaffected by stand density, and easily identified in all seasons of the year. Some species have such a narrow ecological amplitude that their occurrence is indicative of a particular site. Demanding hardwoods such as black walnut, white ash, and yellow-poplar reach their best development only on moist, well-drained, protected sites rich in soil nutrients and characterized by a well-developed forest floor. Most trees, however, have a wide ecological amplitude in that they may occur and prosper on a wide variety of sites. Their presence is thus of little indicator value. Their relative abundance and their relative size, however, may be. In the same eastern hardwood forests, the greater the proportion of red oak to black and white oak in the forest, the better will be the soil moisture conditions and the general site quality. The sizes of free-grown dominant oaks of these three species in even-aged stands of uniform density may all be used as an index of site quality.

Understory plant species in the forest—although more apt to be influenced by stand density, past history, and the composition of the forest than the tree species—have in many cases a more restricted ecological tolerance and may therefore be more useful as plant indicators. This is particularly true in the circumpolar boreal forest, where the dominant tree species—the spruces, firs, pines, birches, and aspens—are few in number and widespread in their distribution on various sites, thus having relatively poor indicator value. Under such circumstances, site classification schemes based upon indicator species in the understory have been markedly successful. They are most easily applied in regions where variations in altitude and precipitation are not great and man has not markedly altered the original vegetation.

The classic example is Cajander's system of site types for Finland (1926), designed to segregate minor quality classes in a forest characterized by spruce, pine, and birch in both pure and mixed stands. Height-growth curves of pine on four such site types are presented in Figure 11.4 These may be taken as indicative of the system.

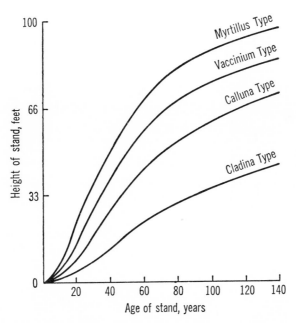

Fig. 11.4. Height-over-age curves of Scots pine on different site types in Finland.

The *Cladina* type is characterized by a lichen understory (*Cladonia alpestria* in particular) and occurs on dry sandy heaths of the poorest site quality. On the *Calluna* type, mosses and lichens are generally present, but heather (*Calluna vulgaris*) is typically the predominant species. *Juniperus communis* is also fairly common in the understory, while birches and spruce commonly occur with the dominant pine in the overstory. The *Vaccinnium* type is typified by the lingonberry, *Vaccinium vitis-idaea*, and occurs on moderately dry sandy ground and on glacial ridges. Mosses and lichens are of less importance and dwarf-shrubs of greater importance than in the preceding types. Finally, the *Myrtillis* type, named for the predominant *Vaccinium myrtillis*, is developed on a richer soil supporting a climax vegetation of spruce but frequently converted to pine by fires, felling, and silvicultural control. Lichens are unimportant and herbs more important and richer in numbers than in the other types cited.

At a more complex level, all of the resources of vegetation description may be brought in the segregation of forest site classes. It should be remembered, though, that site variation frequently takes the form of a gradient rather than of distinct and mutually exclusive site classes. The latter are found only when a distinct break in site factors occurs, such as a break between a sandstone-derived residual soil and a limestone-derived residual soil. Otherwise, site changes tend to be gradual, and the continuum may better be described in terms of an ecological gradient. Thus Rowe (1956), working with the mixed boreal forest in Manitoba and Saskatchewan, describes the changes in vegetation associated with a range of site varying from a very dry forest to a wet forest. Similarly, Whittaker (1954) categorizes the vegetation of the Great Smoky Mountains in terms of the interaction of ecological gradients of elevation and of moisture conditions, the latter being related to topographic site. This latter paper summarizes the present thinking of ecologists of plant indicators being an expression of the complex of the forest ecosystem rather than representing a specific effect of site quality. Again, in the Belgian Ardennes, Dagnelie (1957) has found it possible to characterize the site quality of beech forests in terms of the floristic and soil characteristics, although at a certain loss of precision when compared with site index based on tree height.

The understory plant-indicator concept has been adapted successfully to the spruce-fir forests of North America, in eastern Canada, the Adirondacks, Maine, the Great Smokies, and central Canada. Studies by Linteau (1955), Rowe (1956), Crandall (1958), Damman (1964), and Mueller-Dombois (1964) serve to refine and summarize competent earlier work along similar lines. In modern practice, however, even in Scandinavia understory plant indicators are not used exclusively (Fennoscandian Forestry Union, 1962). Increasingly, the overstory dominants and physical factors of the environment are used in conjunction with ground vegetation to classify sites and estimate site quality.

In the more complex and more disturbed forests to the south or at lower elevations than the spruce-fir forest, however, similar indicator site types based upon a relatively few understory species have proved less applicable. Here the vegetation approach to site classification has involved an evaluation of the total vegetation, including not only the species present in all layers of the forest, but also the abundance, size, and vigor of all elements of the flora.

Species Groups and Indicator Spectra

It is possible under certain conditions to characterize a site in terms of a very few species. However, the key indicator plants may or may not be present in a given locality because of chance, past forest history, or present competitive conditions. It is, for instance, subjectively difficult to classify a site as an *Oxalis-Cornus* site type if it contains no *Oxalis* and no *Cornus* because of past forest history or because of the flukes of local plant distribution. Yet the sum total of the vegetation and the growth characteristics of the forest may well fit the area into this category.

The disadvantages of the foregoing approach may be overcome by using many species either arrayed singly along an environmental gradient (indicator spectrum) or placed in groups, the species of each group having similar environmental requirements. A model of the indicator-spectrum approach was developed for spruce and fir in the northeastern United States (Table 11.2). The spectrum was modified by Marinus Westveld from a preliminary list of the senior author, and is presented here to indicate the method rather than a final listing. The indicator spectrum is simply a list of plants, including trees and shrubs as well as herbs and other vegetation, classified according to the sites they indicate. Plants denoting dry, infertile sites are placed at the top of the list and those character-

Table 11.2. Indicator Plant Spectrum (Northeastern Spruce and Fir)

Genus or Species	Site	Present	Common	Abundant
Myrica				
Vaccinium				
Gaultheria				
Hylocomium	A			
Hypnum				
Chiogenes				
Pteridium				
Coptis				
Bazzania	B			
Corylus				
Maianthemum		x		
Cornus		x		
Aralia			x	
Clintonia	C			
Oxalis				
Dryopteris				x
Acer saccharum			x	
Asplenium				
Smilacina				
Mitchella	D			
Viola				
Oakesia				

istic of moist and fertile sites are placed at the bottom. The forester takes the list into the field and checks the indicator plants as being present, common, or abundant. The center of the distribution curve produced by these checks denotes the site quality. In the sample, the site quality is clearly C although *Clintonia* and *Oxalis*, two characteristic plants of that site, are absent.

In one of the few trials of indicator plants in the southern United States, Hodgkins (1961, 1970) achieved limited success in predicting the site index of longleaf pine using a modified spectrum approach. The plant indicators failed to predict site index closely in deep soils with droughty surfaces since they do not utilize the deeper layers of soil tapped by pine roots.

A refinement of the spectrum technique is to group plants of similar ecological requirements together and use the groups to distinguish different ecosystems. Besides the example presented immediately below, the use of ecological species groups is described in conjunction with the multifactor site classification system used in Germany and presented later in the chapter.

In undisturbed coniferous forests of the Northern Rocky Mountains, Daubenmire (1952) and Daubenmire and Daubenmire (1968) used groups of understory species, termed *subordinate unions*, in combination with late-successional overstory species (*dominant unions*) to distinguish forest associations. The collective area of a given forest association, the *habitat type* (literally, the type of climax vegetation on a particular habitat or site), indicates similar environmental and biotic conditions, hence an ecosystem. The understory unions are composed of from 1 to 24 species, e.g., the *Physocarpus malvaceus* union of 6 species, the *Pachistima myrsinites* union of 24 species, and the *Xerophyllum tenax* union of 2 species. Different habitat types are distinguished by specific combinations of overstory and understory unions. In some cases the overstory union is the major determinant of the habitat type, whereas in other situations the understory union is definitive. The *Pinus ponderosa–Physocarpus* and *Pseudotsuga–Physocarpus* habitat types are distinguished by their respective overstory dominants. However, three habitat types with the same overstory, *Abies lasiocarpa–Pachistima, Abies lasiocarpa–Xerophyllum,* and *Abies lasiocarpa–Menziesia* occur on different sites and are distinguished by their understory unions. The polymorphic site-index curves of ponderosa pine in seven habitat types indicated that ecosystems delineated by vegetation are of substantially different site quality (Daubenmire, 1961).

ENVIRONMENTAL FACTORS AS A MEASURE OF SITE

Many situations exist where the forest vegetation, whether the trees or the understory plants, cannot be used to provide an index of forest productivity. Such are agricultural or other non-forested lands to be reforested; areas recently subjected to fire, logging, heavy grazing, or other disturbances; and areas to be converted from one forest type to another. In these and similar cases, site productivity must often be estimated from an analysis of the physical environment rather than from the vegetation.

Any factor of the environment may be used singly or in combination as an index of site quality. Included are all the climatic and edaphic factors discussed in the previous chapters. To be useful as an index, however, the factor should be capable of simple and inexpensive measurement and should furthermore be highly correlated to forest productivity. Many site factors are thus disqualified for index use because of lack of information concerning them or because of the difficulty or expense in obtaining this information. Others are not used because of their lack of sensitivity as a measure of site quality. In general, in accordance with the modern concept of the law of the minimum (Chapter 3), the most useful environmental factors for site-index purposes are those which are in short supply with regard to the demand by forest trees, so that small changes in the supply of the factor will result in measurable changes in the growth of trees. It follows that different environmental factors will prove useful in different forest situations. This is indeed the case.

Climatic site factors are generally useful in providing a rough index of regional forest productivity. In particular, rainfall and temperature data may be used to compare forest growth, both potential and actual, in various geographical regions, assuming similar soil conditions, or at least assuming soil conditions which in themselves are closely related to the climate.

Within a given climatic region, growth will vary greatly, depending upon the topographic site, aspect, and soil conditions. Edaphic site factors, therefore, are apt to be particularly useful in local studies of forest site quality.

Since the sum total of the climatic and edaphic factors define the site portion of the forest ecosystem, the more factors used as an index of forest productivity, the better will be the correlation. In recent efforts to construct universal environmental site classifications applicable to a wide area, multiple site factors are utilized so as to take cognizance of the greatest possible variety of combinations apt to influence forest distribution and growth.

The emphasis of the forest ecologist on environmental factors should not blind the forester to the realization that growth depends upon the genetic composition of the forest as well as upon the environment in which the forest grows. What constitutes a good site for one species may prove a poor site for another. To cite but one of many possible examples, Monterey pine in New Zealand and Australia makes phenomenal growth on sites that previously supported very slow-grown indigenous forests. Even within a species, genetic variations may be highly important. One genotype of aspen, growing in a clonal colony, may make twice the growth of another in an adjacent clone on exactly the same site. We should never forget that growth is a function of the effect of the environment on the genotype, and that site factors alone can never account for all the variation in growth rates found between different species or even between races or different sexually regenerated individuals within a single species.

Climatic Factors

Forest climate is obviously related to tree growth, since the crowns and boles live in the air and are affected by it. Although the average climate may not vary widely throughout a given forest region and is therefore usually ignored in the evaluation of site quality, local climate may vary significantly from place to place in a single locality.

Despite the obvious importance of local climate, however, it has seldom been used in site evaluation. For one reason, other variables such as land-use history, forest management history, and forest soils have obvious as well as masking effects on forest growth, and it has proved very difficult to obtain good correlation between local climate and growth. For another reason, local climate is often related to soils, or to local topography, and a site classification based upon soils and topography will also carry with it an implied classification with respect to local climate. Thus the same factors that make a soil very well drained are apt to insure good drainage of the cold air and to indicate a site with lower maximum and higher minimum temperatures than would be indicated by a regional climatic average. Likewise, a very poorly drained soil is apt to result from a topography that inhibits the drainage of cold air as well as of soil water. Thus the very poorly drained sites are apt to be characterized by temperature extremes and a short growing season.

Some general correlations between climate and forests have already been indicated. That both precipitation and the temperature regime influence the distribution and growth of the forests in a broad sense is illustrated by the rough correlation that exists between climatic classifications such as those of Merriam, Köppen, and Thornthwaite and the occurrence of forest types.

Many efforts have been made to relate rainfall to forest growth, and good relationships have been obtained in many cases since soil moisture is frequently a limiting factor in forest growth, at least during the hottest part of the growing season. For example, in the longleaf pine region of the deep south from Mississippi to Texas, the January–June rainfall, ranging from 24 to 34 inches, has proved more important than any soil factor in predicting site quality (Mc-Clurkin, 1953). In the mountains of the American West, the effect of rainfall is complicated by elevation, since precipitation normally increases with elevation; but temperature similarly decreases, so that site quality may sometimes be increased and sometimes decreased by the combined effects of increasing precipitation and decreasing warmth. Fog enters into the picture also. For instance, in the coast range of California, site quality of Douglas-fir and ponderosa pine increases with precipitation on interior sites. This increase in median site index for Douglas-fir is approximately 5 feet for each 10-inch increase in average annual precipitation, while for ponderosa pine it is about 5 feet for each 20 inches (Zinke, 1959). The reverse, however, is true for Douglas-fir in the fog belt, where an increase in precipitation is correlated with a decrease of site quality, apparently because of the diminishing effect of fog at the higher altitudes where the higher precipitation prevails.

Climatic summaries based upon a comparison of precipitation and evapotranspiration curves (Figure 6.4; Chapter 6), synthesizing as they do the combined effects of precipitation and temperature upon the water balance, have potential use in studying variation in site quality. Sites with large annual water deficits can be expected to produce less forest growth than sites with small annual water deficits.

An effort by Paterson (1956) to estimate potential forest productivity all over the world in terms of climatic factors of the site has attracted widespread attention. Based upon a cursory study of 41 permanent sample plots (27 in Sweden, 5 in Germany, 2 in Washington State, and 1 each from 7 other localities), Paterson proposed a "CVP index" (after the initials of climate, vegetation, and productivity) with the formula

$$CVP \text{ Index} = \frac{T_v PGE}{T_a 1,200}$$

where T_v is the mean temperature of the warmest month (in degrees Celsius), T_a is the mean annual range of temperature between the coldest and the warmest month, P is the mean annual precipitation (in millimeters), G is the length of the growing season in months, and E is the "evapotranspiration reducer," a factor based on latitude and giving the generalized total annual radiation received as a percentage of that at the Equator.

This obviously oversimplified formula assumes that the site quality improves linearly with the temperature of the warmest month, precipitation, the length of the growing season, and nearness to the equator, and that it decreases linearly with the range of mean monthly temperature from summer to winter. Few if any of these generalizations hold. Although site quality generally improves with increasing warmth up to a point, the rate of increase at higher temperatures is markedly less than it is at lower ones. Similarly, site quality increases with increased precipitation up to a point, but decreases with increased precipitation past this point because of the leaching effects on the soil of heavy and continued rain and the tendency for watersoaking and poor aeration of all but highly porous and steeply sloped soils. For instance, in New Zealand, growth of virtually all species is vastly better in the 50- to 70-inch rainfall belt than on the west coast of the South Island, where rainfalls range from 100 to 300 inches per year and where other climatic and parent material conditions are essentially similar.

It would be expected that any climatic—or indeed any environmental factor—index would show a high correlation with measured growth only for relatively homogeneous genetic material such as a single species or species group. Such indeed is the case. Different species may make markedly different growth rates on the same site. In New Zealand, Monterey pine produces a mean annual increment of over 520 cubic feet per acre per year and Douglas-fir produces 450 cubic feet per acre per year on sites where native podocarps and hardwoods produce less than 50. The difference can be lessened to some extent by expressing growth on a dry-matter production basis rather than in terms of volume. Nevertheless, differences in the response of different genotypes to climatic conditions are so great—both between species and between different individuals within a species—that it is certain that no really high correlations will ever be obtained between climatic factors and universal tree growth.

Paterson's *CVP* index is treated in some detail because it serves to bring in focus the combined effect of climatic factors upon tree growth. The treatments of the separate climatic factors as varying linearly with growth and varying independently of one another are statistically and biologically unsound. A similar attempt utilizing the growth records of a single species or species group and using a multiple correlation based upon curvilinear relationships for the site variables as well as interactions between them might produce better results. Although the simple *CVP* index, modified to suit local conditions, has proved useful in giving broad and approximate estimates of regional forest productivity in various European studies (Pardé, 1959; Paterson, 1959; Weck, 1960), an international commission (Weck, 1961; Nyyssönen, 1971) concluded that (1) the index does not offer a means of worldwide application for estimating even the average potential production of climatically homogeneous regions, and (2) in general, the quality of individual forest sites cannot be determined sufficiently accurately from a climatic index alone.

Soil Factors

The problem of relating soil to site has attracted many investigators. Of principal concern has been the determination of site quality for areas which are either unstocked, stocked with unwanted species, or stocked with trees unsuited for site-index measurements (Coile, 1952; Ralston, 1964).

Depending upon the nature of the specific site, many individual soil factors may serve as useful indices of forest productivity in that they may be correlated with the site index of the desired forest species. Before examining the problem in detail, however, two warnings are in order. First, the problem is one of correlation and not necessarily of cause and effect. Too many investigators have read into regressions based upon soil (or other) site factors causal relationships which are not justified or which merely reflect a causal relationship attributable to another and unmeasured soil characteristic. Second, frequently the dependent variable is site index read from harmonized site-index curves. As previously pointed out, such values are suspect by the very nature of the site-index construction method used. In any event, they are derived values read from a curve rather than actual values of forest productivity.

Generalizing from the many efforts to relate soil properties to forest site, the growth potential of forest trees is chiefly affected by the amount of soil occupied by tree roots and by the availability of nutrients and soil moisture in this limited space.

Of prime importance, then, is the *effective depth* of the soil—the depth of the portion of the soil that is either occupied or capable of being occupied by the roots of the tree for which the site index is desired. This effective depth may obviously be limited by the occurrence of bedrock near the surface. The position of the water table during the growing season likewise limits root penetration sharply. Less obviously but equally significantly, a coarse, dry stratum may prove an effective barrier to root penetration just as may a highly compact and impervious stratum such as a highly developed hardpan.

Consequently, many measures of effective soil depth have proved significant in correlating soil factors with site quality. Coile (1952) not only accomplished much of the basic work in this area but summarized earlier studies. Among the soil factors most frequently found important are the depth of the A horizon above a compact subsoil, the depth to the least permeable layer (usually the B_2 horizon), the depth to mottling (indicative of the mean depth to restricted drainage), and thickness of the soil mantle over bedrock. All these measures quantify the effective rooting depth of trees and are important when this value is low but are relatively unimportant when downward root development is unimpeded.

Next in importance are soil profile characteristics that affect soil moisture, soil drainage, and soil aeration. The physical nature in terms of soil texture and structure of the least permeable horizon (again usually the B_2) is here of principal importance.

By combining these and other physical factors influencing soil-moisture relationships, many useful formulas have been evolved by which site index can be estimated approximately (standard errors of the estimate range from 5 to 10 feet for trees 60 to 100 feet high at 50 years). For example, Zahner (1958a), restricting his regressions to soil groups within a limited geographical region, related the site index of two southern pines to the thickness of the surface soil, the percentage of clay of the subsoil, the percentage of sand of the subsoil, and the slope percentage. Many other studies, particularly with the southern pines on upland areas, can be cited.

Actually, however, the topographic position of the site is often closely related to the physical properties of the soil that govern soil-moisture and aeration relationships. Moreover, topographic site can be quickly recognized and evaluated, using aerial photographs and topographic maps, without the necessity of soil measurement. Many useful site relationships have been evolved based upon the relative topographic elevation, aspect, and degree of slope. Studies of oak site quality in the Appalachian Mountains and the Appalachian

Plateau (Trimble and Weitzman, 1956; Doolittle, 1957; Carmean, 1967) have found that relative position between ridge top and cove, aspect, and degree of slope are all closely related to site quality. Carmean (1967) found that equations based solely on topographic features explained more than 75 percent of the variation in total height of black oak in southeastern Ohio. These close relations between topography and site occur because topography is closely related to important soil features such as A horizon depth, subsoil texture, stone content, and organic matter content. The relationships of aspect, slope steepness, and site index are illustrated in Figure 11.5.

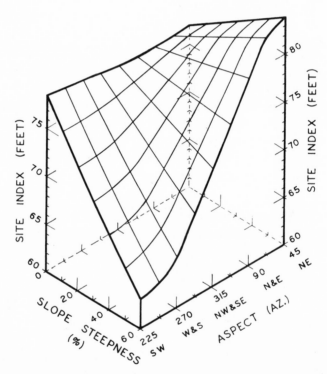

Fig. 11.5. Relation between aspect, slope steepness, and site index for black oak growing on medium-textured, well-drained soils. Site index increases from southwest-facing slopes to northeast-facing slopes. These increases are very pronounced for steep slopes, but site increases related to aspect are relatively minor on gentle slopes. For southwest-facing slopes, site decreases drastically with increased slope steepness whereas site increases slightly on northeast slopes as slopes become steeper. (After Carmean, 1967.)

The general relationship of site quality to aspect for mixed upland oak forests in the Appalachian Mountains resembles a cosine
curve (Figure 11.6; Lloyd and Lemmon, 1970). In hilly terrain,
the importance of topography and its close relationship with microclimate must be stressed. Northeast aspects and lower slopes usually
have cool, moist microclimates and thus are the better sites; southwest aspects and upper slopes and ridges have dry and warm microclimates and hence are usually the poorer sites.

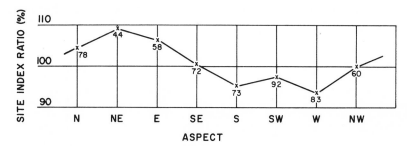

Fig. 11.6. Productivity curve with site-index ratio over aspect; based on
560 soil-site index plots on 27 soil series in mixed upland oak forests of the
Appalachian Mountains. Site-index ratio is the ratio of the plot site index to
the average site index of all plots of that soil series. (After Lloyd and Lemmon,
1970.)

The effective depth of the soil, however, remains highly significant,
along with topographic position. In the Douglas-fir region, Lemmon
(1955) listed effective soil depth, aspect, and position on the slope
as the most useful factors in delineating site quality. Minor variations in topography may be highly important in very flat locations,
reflecting the effective depth of the soil over poorly aerated lower
horizons. For instance, Beaufait (1956), working with southern
river bottomland oak sites, found that topographic features varying
only a few inches in elevation were correlated with marked differences in the silt and clay content of the soil, with flooding conditions,
and with soil aeration, and thus were highly related to site quality.
    Predicting site index using soil factors has worked well in some
upland areas for hardwoods and pine (Ralston, 1964). However,
it has proved discouraging for lowland hardwoods on alluvial soils
of the mid-south except for very small and uniform areas (Broadfoot, 1969). Working primarily on alluvial soils of the Mississippi

River over a six-state area, Broadfoot developed multiple regression equations for soil-factor relationships for each of seven hardwood species. None of the equations predicted site index with sufficient precision for investment planning. He concluded that over broad areas and complex land patterns the relationship between soil characters and height growth seems to defy quantification.

Although, under most American forest conditions, physical soil factors affecting the soil regime are of the greatest indicator value in site studies, deficiency situations exist where the nutrient levels in the soil markedly affect site quality. Experimentally, good results have been obtained in such circumstances by relating the available nutrients, measured from chemical analysis of the soil, of the humus, or from foliar analysis of tree material, to site quality. Practically, such determinations are time-consuming and expensive, although approximations of soil nutrition may be made on the basis of a thorough knowledge of soil geology.

Soil survey mapping, using soil series and phases (Chapter 7), provides a taxonomic classification of forest soils but has generally proved unsatisfactory for the precise estimation of tree site quality. Typically, the variation in forest productivity, as estimated by site index, within a given soil-taxonomic unit is too great to be acceptable. On soils of the Rustin series, loblolly pine site index ranged from 59 to 105 (Covell and McClurkin, 1967). In California, ponderosa pine site index ranged from 89 to 182 on the Shaver series; average annual precipitation in areas of Shaver soils ranged from 12 to 55 inches (Zinke, 1961). Excessive site variation within soil-taxonomic units also has been reported for numerous species in eastern hardwood forests (Carmean, 1970a).

It is now widely recognized (Coile, 1960; Rowe, 1962; Jones, 1969; Carmean, 1970a) that soil series alone are too heterogeneous to serve as a basis of site evaluation. They can prove satisfactory if they are refined to incorporate specific soil and topographic factors that are closely related to forest productivity (Richards and Stone, 1964; Carmean, 1967; 1970a). Carmean (1967) did this effectively in predicting site quality for black oak by combining existing soil series into two "woodland suitability" groups and subdividing them into phases based on topographic features known to be closely related to oak site quality. Because of their flexibility to provide phases or other subdivisions and their systematic and widespread application, soil surveys closely coordinated with soil-site research have a promising future in forest site evaluation (Byrd *et al.*, 1965; Bartelli and DeMent, 1970; Lemmon, 1970).

MULTIPLE-FACTOR METHODS OF SITE CLASSIFICATION

In the previous sections we have considered simple approaches to site quality, such as site index, and indicators such as soils and vegetation. However, these represent only individual elements of the ecosystem whereas site quality is the sum total of factors affecting the capacity of land to produce forests. The more factors taken into account, the better is the estimate of site productivity and site potential. Intensive methods involving multiple factors have been employed with success for over 45 years in Germany, and similar but more extensive methods have proliferated widely in Canada and the western United States.

The Baden-Württemberg System

Baden-Württemberg, a state in southwestern Germany of approximately 36,000 square kilometers (about the size of Connecticut, Massachusetts, and Rhode Island), has an enormous diversity of climatic, geological, and soil conditions. A mosaic of vegetation patterns exists, partly due to this variable environment and partly as a result of a long history of disturbance by man. To cope with the complexity of these problems a multiple-factor system, integrating geography, geology, climatology, soil science, plant geography and sociology, pollen analysis, and forest history, was developed to classify and map forest sites. Following classification and mapping, the growth, site index, and productivity in stem volume of the major tree species are determined for the major site units. Then silvicultural and management recommendations are made for each species and species mixture for each site. A model of this ecosystem approach is illustrated in Figure 11.7. Along with a similar system in eastern Germany, it is the most intensively developed and applied system of its kind. Although the system was developed for practical resource management purposes, it is one approach for describing and studying the structure, productivity, and processes of an ecosystem. It provides a framework of landscape ecosystems (Rowe, 1969) that have applications not only in forestry but also in the physical, biological, and social sciences.

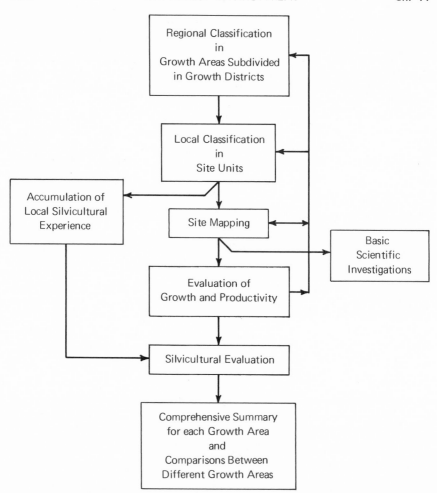

Fig. 11.7. Model of the site-classification system used in Baden-Württemberg, Germany.

The multifactor approach evolved from the pioneering work of G. A. Krauss who, beginning about 1926 in Tharandt, initiated a team approach to study complex site relationships. The method consists of a synthesis of important site factors at regional and local ecosystem levels (Krauss, 1936). The state is initially subdivided into major landscapes or *growth areas,* and each of these is then divided into minor landscapes termed *growth districts.* This feature acts to limit sweeping generalizations and practical prescriptions that were often made for a species over wide areas having vastly different environments, biota, and histories. On the local level a series of *site units*, each site unit identified by a particular combination of physical and biotic site factors, is distinguished for each growth district.

Parts of Baden-Württemberg have been settled for over 2,500 years, and the presettlement forest of beech and oak has been replaced by a monoculture, often several generations old, of Norway spruce. The system was initially employed to determine whether major site differences could still be distinguished in these areas, all of which appeared as one vast forest of spruce. Despite the homogeneity of the spruce stands and the changed ground flora induced by spruce, sites of markedly different productivity and silvicultural potential were identified (Arbeitsgemeinschaft, 1964). The concept and scope of the system as well as a brief discussion of methods, following the sequence shown in Figure 11.7, are present below.

Regional Classification. Seven broad forest landscapes, the growth areas, are distinguished by major differences in geology, climate, and soil (e.g., the Upper Rhine River Basin, the Black Forest, and Swabian Alb). The growth areas are not homogeneous and are subdivided into growth districts based on finer distinctions, in macroclimate especially, but also in parent material, soil, and vegetation. Each district is characterized by one or more dominant, indigenous forest types whose composition is determined largely by climate, e.g., lowland mixed-oak forest, montane beech-fir forest, boreal-montane fir-spruce-pine forest, etc. The natural forest vegetation is of major importance in determining the limits of growth districts, and since many of the stands have been disturbed by man, great attention is placed on pollen analysis, forest history, and studies of the ground vegetation. Through these studies the indigenous vegetation of the period beginning about 1,500 B.C. and ending in the Middle Ages is reconstructed.

Local Classification and Mapping. Each growth district is subdivided into site units, the number and character of which depend upon the conditions of the respective district. A site unit includes individual sites (the area occupied by a group of trees) which, though not identical, have similar silvicultural potential, growth rates, and productivity for the major tree species. The site unit is delineated in the field by local differences in topography, soil factors such as soil texture, structure, acidity, depth, and moisture-holding capacity, microclimate, and overstory and understory vegetation.

Each site unit is characterized by a local overstory type and in addition is floristically delineated through the use of *ecological species groups* (Table 11.3; Sebald, 1964; Schlenker, 1964; Dietrich, 1970). Each group is composed of several plant species, which, because of similar environmental requirements or tolerances, indicate certain site-factor complexes, for example, soil-moisture or soil-acidity gradients. Some species groups have a wide ecological amplitude, like the *Milium effusum* group, whereas others have a narrow amplitude, like the *Aruncus silvester* group (Table 11.3).

A representative sample of the 24 ecological species groups and 30 site units of the Upper Neckar Growth District (Sebald, 1964) illustrates the use of species groups to differentiate site units (Table 11.3). A site unit is characterized by the presence or absence of groups or the relative abundance of the species in the respective groups. The gradual trend of differences when site units are arranged along two moisture gradients (from moderately fresh to moderately dry, units 1 to 10, and from fresh to wet and imperfectly drained, units 11 to 15) is clearly seen. Units at opposite ends of the respective gradients are easily distinguished by the species groups. However, adjacent site units may be similar in their species groups and would be differentiated in the field by soil and topographic features. For example, site units 1 and 2 have similar vegetation, but 1 is a podzolized loamy sand on level terrain whereas 2 is a podzolized sand on a moderately steep slope of south or southwest aspect.

In field mapping, ecological species groups are used simultaneously with topography and soil characters to delineate site unit boundaries. The indicator value of each group is reliable only within the rooting zone of the species in the group. As seen in Table 11.3, certain site units are well defined by vegetation and could be mapped by vegetation alone. However, the combined technique, using soils and topography as well, is always faster and more reliable.

Mapping proceeds only after a detailed reconnaissance survey of the forest to be mapped and determination of a tentative list of site units. Mapping is conducted systematically over 100 percent of each major forest of a district, and the end result is a detailed map of the site units of each forest to a scale of 1:10,000. In addition, a

Table 11.3. Representative Ecological Species Groups and Site Units of the Upper Neckar Growth District [a]

Ecological Species Group	Site Unit Mod. Fresh → Mod. Dry										Fresh → Wet				
	1	2	3	4	5	6	7	8	9	10	11	12	13	14	15
Vaccinium myrtillus group	●	●	●	●	·						●	·			
Leucobryum glaucum group	●	●	·												
Bazzania trilobata group	●	·										·			
Deschampsia flexuosa group	●	·	●	●	·		·	·			●	•	•		
Pirola secunda group				·	·	·	●	·	·	·		·			
Milium effusum group	·	·	•	•	●	•	●	•	·	●	·	●	●	●	•
Elymus europaeus group						•	•		·						•
Aruncus silvester group														·	●
Ajuga reptans group				·	·	●	·					•	●	•	•
Stachys silvaticus group					·	·						·	·	•	●
Chrysanthemum corymb. group						·	●	·	·						
Carex glauca group						●	●	●	·						
Molinia coerulea group													·		·

SOURCE: After Sebald, 1964.

[a] Spaces between lines indicate major differences between species groups (13 of Sebald's 24 groups are shown). Two groups of site units are ordered along gradients from medium fresh to medium dry (units 1 to 10) and from fresh to wet and imperfectly drained (units 11 to 15).

Key: ● species of the group abundant
  • species of the group moderately abundant
  · species of the group rare

detailed report is prepared describing the major site features and the site units; for each site unit recommendations for choice of species, the risk of windthrow or fungus attack, rotation age, and other silvicultural and managerial features are presented.

Growth and Productivity. Growth rate, site index, and productivity are determined for the major species in a district or related group of districts upon completion of mapping. Using permanent sample plots and stem analyses, height-over-age curves are constructed for the major species of the most important site units. In a given site unit, substantial differences are often found between species. For a given species, polymorphic curves are prepared for the major site units within a growth district. This then is an example of how actual growth data on specific soil-site types have been used to resolve the major objections to site index listed earlier in the chapter.

The productivity in stem volume for the major species on each site unit can be determined, and the productivity of sites within a district or between districts can be compared (Moosmayer, 1955, 1957; Werner, 1962). Through such studies the site classification and mapping phases can be critically evaluated, and site units of similar yield classed together into "productivity groups." For example, Werner (1962) found more than threefold differences in stem volume of Norway spruce for the 13 major site units in the central Swabian Alb (Table 11.4). Obviously, the recognition of such differences in forest growth has great significance in forest management and land evaluation. Thus an intensive knowledge of soils, vegetation, climate, geology, and forest history are not academic exercises but can be integrated to give a meaningful and eminently practical result.

Table 11.4. Productivity of Norway Spruce in the Central Swabian Alb

Productivity Group		Site Unit	Average Mean Annual Increment [a]	
			m³	ft³
I		1	16.3	228
II		2	14.9	209
		3	14.7	206
III		4	13.9	195
	decreasing soil moisture	5	13.7	192
IV		6	12.9	181
		7	12.8	179
		8	12.4	174
V		9	10.5	147
		10	10.2	143
VI		11	9.0	126
VII		12	6.1	85
		13	5.1	71

[a] Volume in cubic meters per hectare per year at age 100.
Source: Werner, 1962.

Silvicultural Evaluation. The value of site classification lies not only in the ability to predict productivity but also in the silvicultural handling and the management of forested land. Differences in site units, i.e., local ecosystems, directly affect decisions as to the choice of species, establishment techniques, thinning regimes, and the risks of windthrow, soil degradation, disease, and insect attack.

The importance of distinguishing site units and knowledge of their characteristics may be illustrated by three examples. The culture of Norway spruce, the principal timber species in Baden-Württemberg, is undesirable on some site units because of high susceptibility to heart-rot fungi (*Fomes annosus*); on other units there is a high risk of windthrow or soil compaction. Douglas-fir is of increasing importance and is faster growing than Norway spruce on many site units. However, on certain site units with high concentrations of calcium in the topsoil its establishment is virtually impossible. On sites having heavy clay soils, European silver fir is recommended for planting in mixtures with spruce and beech due to its intensive root development in these soils.

Applications of Multifactor Methods in Europe and America. In Baden-Württemberg the intensive site classification system provides a framework for management of forested lands and is also used as a basis for research in forest genetics, growth and yield, silviculture, soils, and pathology. It has applications in regional planning, establishment of natural areas, watershed management, and in environmental education.

As desirable as it may seem, a system of this type is usually regarded as too intensive and impractical for American conditions. However, the model is a simple one and the level of intensity can be chosen to meet the level of management, extensive or intensive. The delineation of major and minor landscapes is certainly possible, has been in application for many years in Canada (Halliday, 1937; Rowe, 1959), and has been more recently initiated in the form of physiographic provinces in the Pacific Northwest (Franklin, 1965; Franklin and Dyrness, 1969), and in the northeastern (Committee on Site Classification, 1961) and the southeastern United States (Hodgkins, 1965). Within provinces multiple-factor classifications are appearing (Driscoll, 1964; Corliss and Dyrness, 1965; Franklin, 1966). For example, in the central Oregon juniper zone, vegetation, soil, and topographic features were used simultaneously to define nine units or ecosystems which are useful in range inventory, in evaluation of range conditions, and in designing range rehabilitation programs (Driscoll, 1964).

Multiple-factor methods employing soil, topography, and vegetation have been used extensively on the Pacific Coast. In California, soil-vegetation surveys of public land have been under way since 1947. Maps providing general information on soils and vegetation types for forest and range management planning have been prepared for 10 million acres (Wieslander and Storie, 1952, 1953; Zinke, 1960; Bradshaw, 1965). A site-index rating of the major species, where it can be determined from the existing stands, is indicated on the map units. In Washington and Oregon, the Weyerhaeuser Company has prepared detailed soil-vegetation maps of their tree farm system and find them extremely useful in many management decisions, from location of logging roads and fire-fighting access to timber production and recreation planning (Gehrke and Steinbrenner, 1965). The most active use of multiple-factor methods outside Europe has been in Canada, where, coupled with airphoto techniques, they promise site inventory and site-quality evaluation at any desired management level.

Forest Land Classification in Canada

Site classification in Canada, as in Europe, is characterized by many different systems and complex terminologies, but it is strikingly different due to its necessarily extensive scale. Because of the need to describe and classify Canada's immense land resources for multiple-use management, a combined approach of physiography and vegetation, relying heavily on aerial photo-interpretation, is being widely applied.

Much of the early attention in Canada was given to ground vegetation in site classification, due to the influence of Cajander's method and those of other European schools of plant sociology (Lemieux, 1965). Studies of vegetation-soil relationships and those emphasizing physiography have evolved into the combined use of vegetation and physiography in many of the province-wide programs. An important recent development is the nationwide program of Biophysical Land Classification (Lacate, 1969). Primarily reconnaissance in nature, the aim is to differentiate and classify ecologically significant segments of the land surface rapidly and at a small scale. An excellent review of the various Canadian approaches to forest site classification and evaluation has been presented by Burger (1972). Despite the diversity and dynamic state of these methods, two examples suffice to illustrate the design and practical features of major Canadian methods.

Hills' Method in Ontario. The "total site" classification system developed by Hills and his associates in Ontario (Hills, 1952; Hills and Pierpoint, 1960) since about 1940 is the most comprehensive and extensive system developed in a Canadian province. The method allows extensive application of airphoto interpretation in the classification, mapping, and evaluation of large, often inaccessible land areas. As in Baden-Württemberg, Hills has stressed the all-inclusive or holistic concept of site, defining it as the integrated complex of land and forest features within a prescribed area. Physiographic features are the basic frame of reference because "they remain most easily recognizable in a world of constant change." Thus *physiographic site types* and *forest types* (characterized by both overstory and ground vegetation) are combined to form the *total site types* (Figure 11.8).

To provide a framework for detailed classification, Ontario is subdivided into 13 site regions based on vegetation-physiography relationships reflecting major differences in climate. To gain addi-

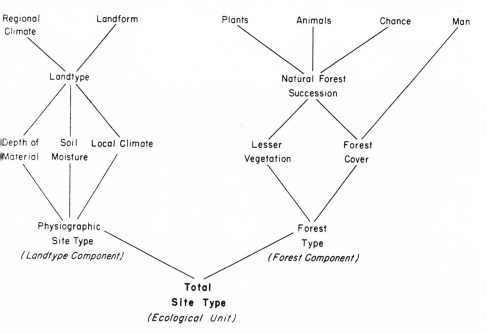

Fig. 11.8. Model of the classification of total site types by Hills' method. (After Hills and Pierpoint, 1960.)

tional homogeneity, a site region may be subdivided into site districts on the basis of relief and type of bedrock or parent materials. Details of classification are described by Hills (1952) and Hills and Pierpoint (1960), and examples of field application of the system are available in the works of Pierpoint (1962) and Zoltai (1965).

The present and potential production of tree species on the various physiographic sites are estimated, using ratings of I (very high) to V (very low). In addition, a capability rating of site types (A = excellent to G = extremely poor) is obtained by integrating the potential productivity and a rating of degree of effort required to achieve this production (Hills and Pierpoint, 1960). Such evaluations are much less precise than determinations of absolute productivity, as accomplished in the Baden-Württemberg system. However, they provide an important first step in extensive management by ranking sites in timber productivity and capability for a number of species or alternatively, providing wildlife or recreational capability ratings.

Extensive Land Classification in British Columbia. A method developed in British Columbia employs independent surveys of physiography and vegetation in mapping forest land for intensive or extensive management (Sprout et al., 1966). Segments of land, termed *land units*, are identified in the field and on air photos at a scale of 1:15,000 (Figure 11.9). Land units are relatively small, homogeneous segments of land having a similar soil and landform and have a good correspondence with independently mapped vegetation types. They have a characteristic physiographic location which is defined by slope steepness and position in the landscape. Soils of a given land unit are similar in parent material and profile development, i.e., a single soil series. For example, land unit A consists of bedrock devoid of soil and occupies ridge tops and steep sideslopes in excess of 30 percent, whereas land unit D is a loam overlying glacial till, imperfectly drained, and occupying middle slope positions with gradients between 5 and 30 percent. Eleven land units were recognized, and for mapping at the scale of 1:15,000, they were combined into eight map units (Figure 11.9). At scales of 1:30,000 and 1:60,000, land units were combined into four and three map units respectively.

The detailed interpretation and mapping at the 1:15,000 scale is most useful as a basis for intensive forest management. Land-

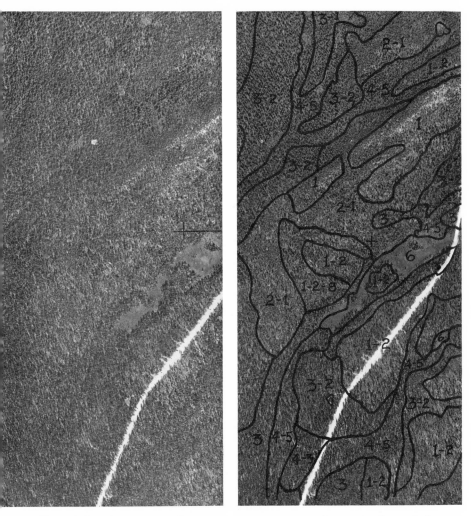

Fig. 11.9. Stereo-pair illustrating mapping units for a portion of the Niskonlith Provincial Forest, Kamloops District, British Columbia, Canada. (After Sprout et al., 1966.)

form features are mainly used to delineate map units at 1:30,000, and this scale is most practical for the management of large blocks of forest land (50,000 to 100,000 acres). Map units at the 1:60,000 scale, identified only by broad landform and geologic features (hills, valleys, plains, etc), are readily identified on airphotos, and large areas are quickly mapped. Mapping at this scale is most useful in planning regional resource surveys and inventories and in making regional comparisons.

The productivity of land units and vegetation types was independently estimated by the site-index method. In addition to productivity, land units and vegetation types were also used in providing ratings of trafficability, windthrow, and erosion and soil slump hazard.

In summary, site classification and forest land mapping from airphotos using physiographic and vegetation types can provide meaningful units for intensive or extensive forest resource management and more broadly for integrated resource planning (Rowe, 1971). The European methods illustrate that site classification and productivity evaluation can be developed to meet the most intensive management practices even in areas of highly variable soil, topography, and climate, and for sites which have been substantially disturbed by man. With the increasing refinement of airphoto techniques and methods of soil and vegetation classification, systematic site classification and mapping is becoming increasingly important in multiple-use land management and planning in the United States and Canada.

SITE AS A DYNAMIC CONCEPT

Since the forest ecosystem is a constantly changing dynamic complex with the environmental factors constantly affecting and being affected by the vegetation elements, it follows that site itself in the forest is in a constant state of change. Too often, site has been regarded as a constant in disregard of observed site changes within a few years. Second-generation forest plantations will frequently and even commonly exhibit growth rates different from first-generation stands of the same species planted on old agricultural or other non-forest land. In some forest ecosystems, the development of the soil profiles consequent to the development of the forest results in such great soil changes that the plants occupying the site lose their vigor and eventually become replaced by new forest communities. The development of spodosol profiles under spruce and fir forests is a case in point. The growth rate of the spruce-fir type and the forest succession itself are affected by the normal and inevitable development of the forest soil.

SUMMARY

The sum total of all factors affecting the capacity of land to produce forests or other vegetation is forest site quality. Forest ecologists and land managers are concerned with site quality because of its close relationship to the productivity of forest crops and to the suitability and competitive ability of alternative species that are capable of growing in a given locality. Because of past disturbances and lack of full vegetational stocking, rarely can site quality be estimated directly by the total stem volume of trees on an area. Usually site quality is estimated indirectly by the use of some characteristic of the trees themselves, the ground vegetation, or by one or more factors of the physical environment, such as soil, topography, and climate. Since we are really measuring the quality of a dynamic ecosystem with many interacting parts, the best estimates are those derived from an integration of the important factors of the ecosystem, including its land-use history.

The height of dominant, free-grown trees at a standard age, termed *site index,* is a convenient and widely used estimate of site quality. The site index of a given species for an area is determined from a family of harmonized curves, typically developed for a given region. Drawbacks in the construction of conventional and generalized site-index curves have led to the use of actual growth data of trees on specific soil-site types to generate polymorphic site curves. Using these curves, site quality may be estimated more precisely for local soil and climatic conditions than by using the regional site curves. The ground vegetation may be used to estimate site quality—either through individual indicator species or, more appropriately, through groups of species, each group indicating different soil-site conditions.

The independent use of soil properties in determining site quality has been widely applied. The effective depth of the soil and other characteristics that affect soil moisture and soil aeration are of primary importance. Topographic position is often closely related to local microclimate and to physical soil properties that govern soil moisture and aeration; topographic features usually can be quickly recognized and evaluated from topographic maps and aerial photographs. Soil survey techniques may be modified to aid in the determination of site quality.

Various drawbacks are inherent in the use of individual site factors in estimating site quality. Thus a more precise evaluation is achieved when the factors are integrated in a single system, usually employing a combination of soil, topography, vegetation, and sometimes other factors such as climate and land-use history. The trend today is toward systematic, well-planned site classification and mapping surveys, as evidenced by major programs in Europe, Canada, and the United States. These surveys provide information for a variety of alternatives in land-use management and may be designed either for extensive or intensive land management.

SUGGESTED READINGS

BURGER, D. 1972. Forest site classification in Canada, *Mitt. Vereins forstl. Standortsk. Forstpflz.* 21:20–36.

CARMEAN, WILLARD H. 1970. Site quality for eastern hardwoods. *In* The silviculture of oaks and associated species. USDA For. Serv. Res. Paper NE–144. Northeastern For. Exp. Sta., Upper Darby, Pa. 66 pp.

———. 1970. Tree height-growth patterns in relation to soil and site. *In* CHESTER T. YOUNGBERG and CHARLES B. DAVEY (eds.), *Tree Growth and Forest Soils.* Oregon State Univ. Press, Corvallis. 532 pp.

COILE, T. S. 1952. Soil and the growth of forests. *Adv. Agronomy* 4:330–398.

DAMMAN, A. W. H. 1964. Some forest types of central Newfoundland and their relation to environmental factors. For. Sci. Monogr. 8. 62 pp.

DAUBENMIRE, R., and JEAN B. DAUBENMIRE. 1968. Forest vegetation of eastern Washington and nortehrn Idaho. Washington Agric. Exp. Sta., Tech. Bull. 60. 104 pp.

FRANKLIN, JERRY F. 1965. Tentative ecological provinces within the true fir-hemlock forest areas of the Pacific Northwest. USDA For. Serv. Res. Paper PNW–22. Pacific Northwest For. and Rge. Exp. Sta., Portland, Ore. 31 pp.

HILLS, G. A. 1952. The classification and evaluation of site for forestry. Ontario Dept. Lands and For., Res. Rept. 24. 41 pp.

———, and G. PIERPOINT. 1960. Forest site evaluation in Ontario. Ontario Dept. Lands and For., Res. Rept. 42. 64 pp.

JONES, JOHN R. 1969. Review and comparison of site evaluation methods. USDA For. Serv. Res. Paper RM–51. Rocky Mountain For. and Rge. Exp. Sta., Fort Collins, Colo. 27 pp.

RALSTON, CHARLES W. 1964. Evaluation of forest site productivity. *Int. Rev. For. Res.* 1:171–201.

RENNIE, P. J. 1962. Methods of assessing forest site capacity. *Trans. 7th Inter. Soc. Soil Sci.*, Comm. IV and V, pp. 3–18.

ROWE, J. S. 1962. Soil, site and land classification. *For. Chron.* 38:420–432.

———. 1971. Why classify forest land? *For. Chron.* 47:144–148.

SPROUT, P. N., D. S. LACATE, and J. W. C. ARLIDGE. 1966. Forest land classification survey and interpretations for management of a portion of the Niskonlith provincial forest, Kamloops District, B. C. Dept. For. Canada, Publ. 1159. 34 pp.

WIESLANDER, A. E., and R. EARL STORIE. 1952. The vegetation-soil survey in California and its use in the management of wild lands for yield of timber, forage and water. *J. For.* 50:521–526.

YOUNGBERG, CHESTER T. (ed.). 1965. *Forest-Soil Relationships in North America.* Oregon State Univ. Press, Corvallis. 532 pp.

III
THE FOREST COMMUNITY
AND THE ECOSYSTEM

12

Competition and Survival

SYNECOLOGY

The individual organism, whether it is a forest tree or something else, is the product of its genetic constitution as affected by the environment. The study of the individual organism in relation to its environment falls within the scope of *autecology*.

The forest, however, is a complex of organisms, both plant and animal, mutually occupying a complex of environments. These organisms are in competition for the light, air, water, warmth, and nutrients necessary for life. Each, in its turn, creates part of the environment affecting the others. It is the study of the community and the interaction of the organisms which compose it that falls within the province of *synecology*. Synecology, thus, is broader than autecology, and a more integrative phase of ecology, dealing with living communities rather than with individuals (Weaver and Clements, 1938; Oosting, 1948; Braun-Blanquet, 1964; Daubenmire, 1968).

In the present text, the forest community is described and treated as being composed primarily of forest trees. We should not forget that many other plants and a host of animals of all sizes form an indispensable part of the forest community. The consideration of the forest as a community composed of a vast interdependent assemblage of plants and animals of all sorts and descriptions must await another treatment.

Scope of Synecology

When two forest trees occupy the same site in close proximity to one another, they inevitably come into competition for the same necessities of life. Furthermore, the presence of one will affect the life of the other as each is a part of the habitat in which the other lives. A consideration of competition for survival arises naturally out of autecology and is basic to an understanding of synecology, discussed in this chapter. The forest is never static, changing in its composition, structure, and general character continually; the dynamics of these changes over time is treated in Chapters 13 and 14, the former dealing with forest succession under disturbed conditions, and the latter with the effects of disturbances of various sorts. Not only does the forest vary continuously in time, but it varies continuously in space. The effect of variations in the forest site on the forest community is considered in Chapter 15.

In contrast to autecology, which is largely factual and scientific, synecology, because of its very complexity, tends to be subjective and philosophical. Our state of knowledge of the innumerable interrelationships between all the millions of organisms in any forest community and between these organisms and the physical factors of the site is so limited that we have no choice but to generalize and theorize without too many facts at our disposal. As a result, synecology has attracted many armchair philosophers who have concerned themselves with the use of deductive reasoning in the construction of elaborated structures of ecological systems, the building blocks of which are frequently a more or less private vocabulary of newly invented ecological terms. These efforts have added much to our appreciation of ecological problems. Unfortunately, they have also created a good deal of confusion and scepticism among the less than highly erudite students, a group which includes most biologists other than the ecological philosophers themselves. While it is the purpose of the present writers to eschew ecological philosophy as much as possible, some knowledge of the impact of the real contributions made in this area is essential and must inevitably be woven into the fabric of any discussion of community structure and dynamics.

Ecologists traditionally have tended to study the forest community separately from the forest environment, and with good reason. Through this separation, however, descriptive and classificatory studies of the community have flourished (community study was often seen as an end in itself) while studies of community processes and the interaction of communities and environment were neglected. The modern trend toward the ecosystem approach, the systematic study and modelling of community processes that are inseparable from environmental factors (Chapter 16), is shifting our thinking toward an understanding of the whole ecosystem, rather than just its component parts.

The consideration of the forest community and the ecosystem in Part III as a dynamic entity changing in time and in space, is illustrated in Part IV by reference to the historical development and present description of the present-day forests themselves, primarily those of the United States of America. This final portion of the book, dealing with historical forest geography, attempts to translate the theory of synecology to provide an understanding of the forest as it actually is.

THE FOREST COMMUNITY

No one will dispute the fact that trees occur with other plants and with animals in natural groupings that are more or less repeated from place to place over a period of years whenever similar conditions recur. Furthermore, an astute observer familiar with a forested region can usually identify the more distinct forest communities and can infer with reasonable probability the interplay of factors that have brought the vegetation into the conditions he sees before him. Consequently there exists a mass of valid descriptive data of specific forest areas that have been studied and written up by foresters and ecologists.

Our problem arises when one begins to generalize. The great complexity of ecological problems—involving the interaction of many organisms and many environmental factors over a long span of time, with much of the past history of the interaction virtually unknown—has resulted in a great gap between the description of given areas and the evolution of the laws and principles which are the ultimate goal of the scientist. Different individuals and groups, influenced by stimulating teachers and the problems in their particular geographical area, have assayed various paths to this goal and have developed languages of their own to express their thinking and progress. Nevertheless, an essential similarity of purpose exists between the different schools of ecological thought, a similarity indicated by the fact that most ecological textbooks end up with similar chapter headings, even though the order in which the subjects are presented may differ.

A community is a body of individuals. It follows, therefore, that a *forest community* is a body or group of individual trees of one or more species growing in a specific area and in association and mutual interaction with one another and with a complex of other plants and of animals.

Rarely, a forest community is unique. A mixture of Norway spruce and Asiatic spruce growing on abandoned farmland in the Harvard Forest in central Massachusetts, for example, is probably not duplicated or even approximated anywhere else in the world.

More commonly, however, the community is similar to other communities composed of the same or similar species and growing on the same or similar soil as a result of the same or similar sequence of events. Such a grouping of similar communities constitutes a vegetation type: in the case of forest communities, such a type is formed by jack pine, occurring in pure or nearly pure stands after fires on sand plains in the Lake States and eastern Canada. No two jack pine communities are alike in all respects; yet the vegetation complex occurring on these soils following fire is so characteristic that it can be immediately recognized and named by almost anyone.

The nature of a given forest community is governed by the interaction of three groups of factors: (1) the site, or habitat, available for plant growth; (2) the plants and animals available to colonize and occupy that site or habitat; and (3) the changes in the site and the biota over a period of time as influenced by changing seasons, climates, soils, vegetation, and animals—in other words, the history of that habitat.

Site

None of these three groups of factors is capable of precise definition or characterization. The habitat, or site, as it is more commonly called in the case of trees, is the sum total of the atmospheric and soil conditions surrounding and available to the community. Among atmospheric factors, solar radiation, air temperature, air humidity, and carbon dioxide contents all vary throughout the day, from day to day, month to month, and year to year, making up the complex we term *climate*. Below the surface, the supply of soil nutrients, the soil-moisture regime, the physical structure of the soil, and the nature and decomposition pattern of the organic matter all affect the growth and development of plants. Furthermore, the growing vegetation itself affects the climate and soil so that the site changes as the plants themselves grow and change.

Plants and Animals

The second broad group of factors concerns all the living organisms capable of migrating into an unoccupied habitat and becoming part of the community. Insofar as plants are concerned, this migration may be by means of seed or spore dispersal, or by vegetative growth.

Again the problem is exceedingly complex. First of all, we may begin by enumerating all the species of plants and animals having access to the unoccupied site and having the capacity to invade. Adjacent plants may not be able to invade the area, while seed from distant plants might well become successfully established. For example, in the northeastern United States, hemlock will seldom reproduce successfully on adjacent open areas, while birds will commonly bring in cherry seeds from afar.

It is not enough to confine our attention to species. Genetic variability within species must be taken into account. Some genotypes will have the capacity to become established in the unoccupied site; others will not. In the competition for survival, some will fare better than others.

History and the Time Factor

The community is not the result of a single interaction of the environment and the organisms that occupy it, but the end product of a long series of interactions over a period of time. The present community as we see it is affected most strongly by the conditions that existed at the time the present individuals became established on that site; but it is also affected by all that has happened since that time. In the forest, the history of logging, land clearing, fires, windstorms, insect and disease epidemics, and other happenings that affect the life and growth of the trees all will influence the present forest stand. Climatic fluctuations and the development of the soil profile also cannot be ignored. The more we can learn of the history of the land and of the plants and animals that occupy it, the better we can understand the present communities with which we live and work.

The Community and the Phenotype

As we have defined it, the forest or plant community is the product of the interaction of the living organisms and the site or habitat over a period of time. The biologist will at once recognize an analogy to the modern conception of the phenotype, the body of the individual plant or animal as we see it. The individual organism is the product of the interaction of its genetic make-up and its environment over its life. When we confine our attention to one individual, the problem becomes relatively concrete. We are confronted with a single set of genes and only those environmental conditions that have existed from the time that the gene combination was put together up to the present. At the community level, the same principles apply but in exponential proportions. Here we are confronted with many gene combinations representing many species of plants and animals and many gene combinations among the individuals of any one species. Our community is affected by all environmental conditions that have existed since the oldest plant invaded the habitat. Since conditions at that time were undoubtedly affected by the vegetation that existed then, we are concerned to some extent with even the earlier history of the site and the communities that occupied it in the past.

The community is infinitely more complex than the phenotype but the analogy is valid. Both are the product of the interaction of genetic and environmental factors over a period of time.

Is the Community an Individual Entity?

Some ecologists have carried the analogy of the community and the individual phenotype or organism to the point of classifying communities as individual organisms, even to the point of giving them binomial Latin scientific names. In such a holistic philosophy, there is a danger in forgetting that the individual community is only analogous to the individual plant or animal and not equivalent to it. Actually, the grouping of plants and animals on a given site into a community is a broader, more general, and less precise assemblage than the grouping of genes in a single body which exists in a single habitat. At the community level, we are dealing with an infinite and constantly changing number of gene combinations in a large and constantly changing number of organic bodies in a large and constantly changing number of microenvironments. *A given community exists only at a single point in space and time.* It seems futile to try to treat such a complex as a single individual and to try to define a series of more or less similar complexes with a single binomial Latin term.

We should rather consider the community for what it is: a rather indefinite and constantly changing grouping of plants and animals on a given site; a broader, less intelligible, and less definable category of classification than the individual phenotype.

CHANGE IN THE ECOSYSTEM

The forest community, then, consists of an assemblage of plants and animals living in an environment of air, soil, and water. Each of these organisms is interrelated either directly or indirectly with virtually every organism in the community. The health and welfare of the organisms are dependent upon the factors of the environment surrounding them; and the environment surrounding them is itself conditioned to a considerable degree by the biotic community itself. In other words, the plants, the animals, and the environment—including the air, the soil, and the water—constitute a complex ecological system in which each factor and each individual is conditioned by, and in itself conditions, the other factors constituting the complex. There is perhaps nothing really new in this concept of an ecological system, but in recent years, when we envisioned it more simply as an *ecosystem*, we have made considerable progress in understanding the complex interrelationships that exist. In contrast, in former years by trying to simplify particular elements of the ecosystem into simple cause-and-effect relationships, we too often drew misleading and inaccurate generalizations.

The *forest ecosystem*, then, is the complex of trees, shrubs, herbs, bacteria, fungi, protozoa, arthropods, other invertebrates of all sizes, sorts, and description, vertebrates, oxygen, carbon dioxide, water, minerals, and dead organic matter that in its totality constitutes a forest. Such a complex never does and never can reach any balance or permanence. It is constantly changing both in time and in space.

The changes of the forest ecosystem in time take many patterns. First, there are diurnal changes. The balance of the forest community at midnight—when the plants are taking up oxygen and giving off carbon dioxide, when some animals are dormant and others are active, when temperature is lowered, and when moisture and humidity are relatively high—is quite different from the forest ecosystem at midday when the reverse of all these processes is going on.

The forest ecosystem changes seasonally around the year. As the cycle of activity of each of the organisms changes, and as the climate changes, the balance of the ecosystem itself changes. The temperate forest is not the same biotic community in midwinter that it is in midsummer, or even in one week that it was during the previous week.

Nor should we ignore long-term climatic changes. Whether climatic fluctuation is cyclic or not is immaterial; the fact is that it does change from one set of years to another. The relative warmth of the 1940's is in sharp contrast to the relative cold of the early 1800's. The warm xerothermic times of four to eight thousand years ago are an even greater contrast to the late Pleistocene of sixteen to eighteen thousand years ago when the glaciers reached their last maximum. There is no such thing as a constant climate, and there can be no such thing as a constant ecosystem if that does not exist.

Finally, the plants and animals that constitute the ecosystem biota never remain the same for a given instant of time. There is a continual introduction of new species and the elimination of old, rarely when we consider the large and well-established trees, mammals, and birds, but frequently when we concern ourselves with the fungi, the bacteria, and the protozoa that far outnumber the larger organisms in the forest and approach them in overall importance. Even if we could prevent new organisms from constantly migrating into the forest and old organisms from constantly being eliminated from it, the organisms that remain there do not stay the same. Evolution is continual. The Douglas-fir of today is not quite the Douglas-fir of one hundred years ago and certainly not that of ten thousand years ago. The bark beetle is not the bark beetle of the previous decade. The blister rust of this year is not the blister rust of last year. Through mutation, through natural selection, and through new population distributions of the combinations of genes, the organisms constituting the forest ecosystem biota are continually in a state of flux.

Equally, the ecosystem changes constantly in space. At any given instant of time the forest ecosystems high in the mountains will be different from those in the lowlands. Even on a level plain the ecosystem will vary from north to south and from east to west. The extremes are obvious but the means are equally important. A distance of one hundred meters may not include any noticeable change in the distribution, size, and the vigor of the more visible components of the forest. The difference is there nonetheless. When one comes to consider the microorganisms in the forest floor which play such an important part in the total ecosystem production complex, changes in even one meter may be real, measurable, and important in affecting the total ecosystem.

In short, the forest ecosystem exists only at a given instant of time and a given instant in space. Regardless of appearances, the ecosystem is never the same on succeeding days, succeeding years, or succeeding centuries, up the slope 1,000 meters, north 10 kilometers, or east or west 100 kilometers. Change characterizes the forest ecosystem continuously. Stability is only relative and is only superficial.

If we adopt the biocentric concept of the ecosystem, we may draw some ecologic generalizations that modify substantially some long-standing and accepted ecological principles. Once we accept the fact that the ecosystem exists only at a given instant in time and at a given instant in space, we can take a fresh view of ecological theory.

First, it follows immediately that there is no meaning from a biocentric viewpoint to the contrasting concepts of native and introduced species. Characterizing a plant or animal as being exotic or endemic characterizes it only from the standpoint of man's relationship to it. Actually, all plants and all animals are introduced or exotic from a biocentric standpoint except at the very point in space where the particular gene combination was first put together. Whether the subsequent migratory pattern of that organism took place independently of man or with the help of man is important to man but not to the wilderness ecosystem itself.

Examples are many. It is of interest to man to know whether he carried the coconut to a given tropical island or not. To the coconut it is of little importance as to whether it floated by itself in an ocean current or was lodged in the hull of a native dugout canoe which in turn floated on the ocean current. To a maple growing in a given spot it is immaterial whether its seed flew there on its own wings or whether it was aided and abetted by the wings of an airplane. A wild cherry is unaffected by concern as to whether its seed was deposited by a sea gull who spotted a target below or by a human recreationist who brought it thither in a paper bag. The forest insect is just as much a member of the California ecosystem if it flew in as an endemic insect from Oregon or was brought in as an exotic insect from Aragon. In short, from the viewpoint of the forest, there is no distinction between native and introduced species. The ecosystem consists of all of the plants and animals that are there at a given point of space and at a given instant of time. All were migrants there: some recently, some from the dim geologic past, some carried in by wind, some by animals, some by water, some by man. Once they are there they are members of the local ecosystem from that time on until they or their descendants are eliminated. The true endemic, perhaps, is really that plant or animal that prospers in the local environment, that is competitive in the local ecosystem, and that can maintain and reproduce itself where it lives.

Second, it becomes clear in our philosophic approach that there is no such thing as a climax community in the sense of a permanent, stable condition. It makes no difference whether man has interfered or not. Change is perpetual and will go on at a rapid or at a gradual rate depending upon the rate of changes in the climate, the soils, the landforms, the fire history, and the biotic composition of the ecosystem. No matter how old the trees are, no matter how long fire has been kept out, the populations of the insects, the fungi, the plants, the animals all will change, and the ecosystem itself will as a consequence change. The concept of climax may have some residual value in referring to an old and superficially stable community of plants and animals. In actual fact, though, there is every reason to think that ecological change is going on as rapidly if less obviously under an old, established forest as on a freshly disturbed site.

Third, since the ecosystem exists only at a given instant in time and in a given instant of space, it follows that natural succession will never recreate an old pattern but will instead constantly create new patterns. After several hundred years the forest of Angkor

Wat resembles the surrounding jungle but is quite different in composition and in detail. The vegetation on Krakatoa is developing successionally, but it is already quite apparent that it will never equate itself with that of undisturbed islands nearby. After each retreat of the glaciers in the Lake States in the Pleistocene the forests moved back and reestablished themselves, but always in a new pattern with some new species present, some old absent, and the balance in many cases quite different. With widespread farm abandonment in New England the forests have reestablished themselves and have moved on into a new successional pattern with different balances of composition and different stand structures. In short, forest succession will lead to the development of a mature and long-lived forest community but one in which change under the surface is still going on and one which will never repeat exactly the pattern of a previous forest developed under a previous forest succession.

COMPETITION

Changes in the structure and composition of the forest result from the constant demand of each individual tree for more space and from the eventual death of even the most dominant individuals. The increasing size of the main story trees results in competition for growing space, with a few individuals gaining space, a few more holding their own, and an increasing majority losing space and eventually succumbing. The death of the dominants, due to lightning, wind, insects, diseases, and even to old age, releases from the main canopy a portion of the site for occupancy by a growing and developing understory.

Competition between the trees of the same species does not affect the composition of the forest type and therefore has no effect on forest succession. Competition between individuals of different species, however, results in a natural succession from one forest composition to another. The rate of species replacement slows as succession proceeds, and ultimately a group of species having complementary ecological roles characterizes the mature late successional forest. The severity of the physical and biotic factors of a habitat essentially controls the species diversity at any point in this process. Competition between species takes place both in the main canopy, or overstory, of the forest and in the understory.

Competition in the Overstory

The trees in the main canopy of the forest tend to increase yearly in height, bole size, length of each growing branch, and number of leaves. If the tree is to remain alive and vigorous, it must grow. To grow, it must increase its growing space—its utilization of the site.

In any fully stocked stand, then, it follows that competition between growing individuals in the overstory will result in the elimination of some trees, particularly of those species genetically less suited for survival under the particular environmental conditions that may exist. The result is a gradual change in the composition of the overstory and thus in the forest community. Examples are numerous.

In central New England, a mixture of hardwoods form a single-storied stand following the cutting or windthrow of old-field eastern white pine. These include long-lived "timber species" such as red oak, red maple, and white ash, as well as short-lived "weed" species such as gray birch, pin cherry, and aspen. The birches, cherries, and aspens (there are several species of each) seed into the former white pine site in tremendous numbers and dominate the sapling hardwood stand. In terms of the dominant tree species, the young stand may be termed a birch-cherry-aspen type.

Mortality due to the tent caterpillar, the gypsy moth, and simple inability to compete and survive, however, continually reduces the numbers of these species so that the pole-size stand becomes dominated with time by the more persistent oaks, maples, and the ash. Eventually, a red oak–red maple–white ash type will evolve characteristically with only an occasional black cherry, black birch, and a few of the other more persistent, earlier-dominant group.

Even within the developing longer-lived hardwood type, competition will favor one species against another. On the better hardwood sites in central Massachusetts referred to above, red oak continually expands its crown at the expense of neighboring white ash, with the result that the percentage of the stand basal area occupied by the former species increases with time while that of the latter species decreases.

The internal changes in a developing temperate forest are illustrated in Table 12.1, which summarizes the growth over 38 years

Table 12.1. Changing Composition After 38 Years in a Hardwood Stand on Sugar Island, St. Mary's River, Michigan

	1933	1938	1944	1949	1955	1960	1971
	Number of trees per acre						
Sugar maple	322	315	292	280	266	215	194
Red maple	125	118	81	72	69	63	55
Red oak	18	18	17	18	17	15	15
Paper birch	35	23	17	12	8	9	3
Yellow birch	16	9	7	6	6	6	4
Aspen	20	11	3	3	2	3	3
All trees	548	503	424	398	372	316	274
	Basal area in Square Feet per Acre						
Sugar maple	39.2	44.1	49.2	52.7	55.8	58.1	61.5
Red maple	29.6	32.5	30.7	30.6	33.2	34.1	33.7
Red oak	8.7	10.1	12.2	14.2	14.8	17.2	21.8
Paper birch	12.3	9.5	7.3	6.3	5.1	7.6	2.0
Yellow birch	4.4	8.0	2.9	2.8	3.1	3.3	2.6
Aspen	6.0	3.9	1.9	2.1	1.8	2.5	3.4
All trees	101.8	104.7	105.8	110.6	115.5	125.2	125.0

of a middle-aged, mixed hardwood stand growing on an island in St. Mary's River between Michigan and Ontario. During this period, the short-lived aspens have practically disappeared from the stand, while the slightly longer-lived birches have shown a steady decline both in number of stems and basal area. Red maple has also declined greatly in numbers, but the growth of the residual trees has been such that the basal area of this species has remained more or less the same. Sugar maple has also suffered mortality, but the growth of the residual trees has been great, with the result that the species has risen from 39 to 61 percent of the stand basal area over the period of the study. The few red oak have survived well and are making up a greater and greater proportion of the stand basal area. The better competitive ability of the sugar maple and red oak at the expense of the aspen and birches is bringing about major changes in the stand composition, although the total stand basal area is showing only moderate changes.

While permanent sample plot data record the changing composition of the overstory with time, they do not chronicle the cause of the death of the trees that disappear in the intervals between measurements. We generally assume that most of these trees simply are suppressed, i.e., their leaf area and feeding root area are reduced to the point that life can no longer be sustained and the tree dies.

In actual fact, death may be due to many causes. Even in the case of so-called natural mortality, the tree actually dies in all probability during some period of extreme stress, such as in a late summer, hot, dry spell or in a severe unseasonable frost, or in an extremely cold and open winter. In other cases, the tree becomes weakened to the point that it falls prey to some insect or disease. In many cases, several factors are interrelated and together account for death.

For example, black cherry seedlings are common in young hardwood stands in central Massachusetts. Yet, mature trees are seldom found in older stands on similar sites. Close observation of tagged cherry seedlings on sample plots revealed that the eastern tent caterpillar, *Malacasoma americana* F., typically defoliated the faster-growing dominant cherries year after year. As a result, these trees put on but little annual increment in height, soon becoming over-topped by competing oak, maple, and other species, and then dying because of inability to survive under shaded conditions as an under-story tree. Over a 4-year period, the dominant 6- to 8-foot high black cherry seedlings grew only 5 inches in an untreated plot as compared to 12 inches in adjacent plots where the egg clusters of the tent caterpillar were removed annually.

Again, Monterey pine in New Zealand and Australia is subject to mortality which has occasionally reached serious proportions. Present evidence indicates that epidemic mortality is primarily due to unusually dry years in which the trees are under severe moisture stress and readily succumb to attack by *Sirex noctilio* (F.), a wood wasp that oviposits in the bole cambium. If an unusually wet year precedes the dry period, *Phytophthora* fungi in the soil may cause substantial mortality to the feeding rootlets of the trees, predisposing the trees to even greater losses. Mortality in this instance may be due to a combination of wet and dry years, a fungus, and an insect.

Competition in the Understory

Whereas competition in the overstory involves relatively few individuals and is spread out over many years, competition near the forest floor involves not only trees but many shrubs and herbaceous plants, often in very large numbers and changing in relationships year by year.

Under a more or less fully stocked forest stand, the supply of light and soil moisture is limited. Light is available at a sufficient intensity for a net gain in plant weight through photosynthesis chiefly in the sunflecks that move over the ground as the angle of incidence of the sunlight is changed by the rotation of the earth, and as wind moves the foliage of the overstory. Moisture on well-drained sites may be largely restricted to current precipitation which reaches the forest floor partially through direct fall and partially through stem flow and drip from the overstory trees.

Many plants are adapted to spending their entire life cycle in the understory. Included are some herbs which carry on a major portion of their annual life activities before the trees reach full leaf. Included also are other herbs, many shrubs, and small trees which are "tolerant" of understory environmental conditions. Some trees can both thrive in the understory and also occupy the overstory itself when the opportunity occurs. Such species will normally succeed to dominance of the forest community.

In assessing competition within the understory, the problem of the successful plant attracts little attention. It is merely carrying on its growth under existing environmental conditions without incident. As Decker (1959) points out, it is with the failing and dying plant, the plant "intolerant" of understory conditions, that we must be concerned. The unsuccessful competitor loses vigor and dies, but the causes of death may be various. Starvation resulting from inadequate light and consequent inadequate photosynthesis is certainly a contributory factor. Inadequate soil moisture is another. Insects and diseases, too, play their role, particularly when the plant has reached a weakened condition. The factors of the environment relating to understory survival are discussed in some detail in the following section.

UNDERSTORY TOLERANCE

The problem of survival in the understory is basic to an understanding of forest succession, since those forest trees capable both of surviving as understory plants and responding to release to reach overstory size will inevitably form a major portion of the evolving forest community. A forest tree that can survive and prosper under a forest canopy is said to be *tolerant* while one that can thrive only in the main canopy or in the open is classified as *intolerant*.

This use of the term *tolerance* to refer to the relative capacity of a forest plant to survive and thrive in the understory is a restricted application of the general botanical meaning of the term, which deals with the general capacity of a plant to live under unfavorable conditions. Thus, a salt-tolerant plant is one that can grow in soil with a high salt content, and a fume-tolerant plant is one that can grow in the presence of gases noxious to most other plants. In forestry, however, the unmodified use of the term *tolerance* refers to a plant's vigor in the forest understory; understory tolerance is a more precise term.

Relative tolerance can be recognized and rated in general terms with little difficulty. An understanding of the nature of tolerance, however, has been the subject of much conjecture and controversy among forest scientists. If the term is used only in the sense of the ability of a plant to survive and prosper in the understory, then its nature can be investigated in terms of the ecology and physiology of understory plants and the understory environment (see below). Often many other characteristics of tolerants and intolerants are cited, and with their inclusion a broader understanding of the nature of tolerant and intolerant species is necessary.

Recognition of Tolerance

Since, by definition, a tolerant tree is one that grows and thrives under a forest canopy, it may be recognized by various values that relate to its vigor under such conditions. In contrast, an intolerant tree is frequently characterized by opposite extremes of the same traits. In addition, other characteristics have been cited as criteria or indicators for the determination of tolerance (Toumey, 1947; Baker, 1950):

Ocurrence in the Understory. Tolerant trees live for many years as understory plants under dense forest canopies. It should be noted that many trees may germinate and survive a few years under such conditions, but only tolerant trees will persist and continue to grow for decades.

Response to Release. The vigor of tolerant trees is indicated by the fact that, following removal of the overstory, they have the ability of responding by initiating immediate and rapid growth.

A tolerant tree may survive for years in the understory while putting on only 30 to 60 rings per inch of radius, and yet begin growing rapidly soon after release.

Crown and Bole Development. The lower branches on tolerant trees will be foliated longer and to a greater extent than those on intolerant trees. Consequently, tolerant trees will have deeper and denser crowns. It follows that tolerant trees will prune naturally at a slower rate, will maintain a greater number of leaf layers, and will maintain healthy and vigorous leaves deeper into the crown. The boles of tolerant trees tend to be more tapered than those of intolerant trees because of the greater depth of crown (Larson, 1963b).

Stand Structure. Tolerant trees persist over long periods of time in natural mixed stands, tend to be successful in mixture with other species of equal size, and consequently form denser stands with more stems per acre than do comparable intolerant trees.

Growth and Reproductive Characteristics. Tolerant trees frequently grow faster, particularly in height, than intolerant trees in the understory. In contrast, intolerants will normally outstrip tolerants under comparable conditions in the open. Tolerant trees typically mature later, flower later and more irregularly, and live longer than intolerant trees.

Although the understory tolerance of a species is defined on the basis of its ability to survive and prosper in the understory, it is not this attribute that causes the many other distinctive and important differences between tolerant and intolerant species. Populations of the respective types have evolved under different selection pressures of environment and plant competition and hence belong to two complex and markedly different adaptation systems. Tolerant species establish themselves, grow in, and have become adapted to conditions markedly different from that of intolerants. Although it is often instructive to compare the two extremes, we are dealing with species of varying degrees of intermediacy along a cline from very intolerant to extremely tolerant.

Intolerant species are typically pioneers that may colonize a wide variety of sites. They are successful because of two major types of adaptations. First, their capacity for rapid establishment on disturbed areas, fast growth in the open, early seed production, and widespread seed dispersal have enabled them to perpetuate themselves wherever burning, windthrow, cultivation, or other disturbances have eliminated or reduced the existing vegetation. In some climatic regions, disturbance alone may account for the perpetuation of intolerant species since they are replaced in time on most sites by more tolerant species.

However, intolerants have a second strategy—adaptation to extreme site conditions. They are typically adapted to some type of xeric (warm or cold) or infertile site as well as to the climatically extreme, initial conditions of the disturbed site. Thus they may form relatively permanent communities on extreme sites where more tolerant species are at a competitive disadvantage. For example, willows in annually flooded bottomlands, jack pine on sterile sands of the Lake States, Table Mountain pine on the driest and most sterile soils of the Appalachian Mountains are examples of intolerants occupying extreme sites of various kinds. Although fire contributes to the maintenance of Table Mountain pine, without fire and man-made disturbance the species would exist, but only on extremely dry and sterile rock outcrops and steep, shale slopes (Zobel, 1969). From such sanctuaries, especially in glaciated terrain with a mosaic of landforms and soil types, pioneer species are in a position to colonize readily adjacent mesic sites following disturbance.

In contrast, tolerant species occupy and are adapted to more moist, sheltered, and fertile sites (mesic conditions). They replace intolerant species and perpetuate themselves through adaptations favoring survival and growth in a shaded understory, establishment in undisturbed litter or duff layers, and a long life span.

Scoring Tolerance of Forest Trees

A relative tolerance rating for species in a given forest region and on a given site class may be obtained by arbitrarily scoring the various criteria of tolerance. Graham (1954) has evolved a technique of rating tolerance of forest trees in the Upper Peninsula of Michigan that may be used as a model for such an approach to an evaluation of tolerance. Graham's system is based on scoring a sample of trees, at least 10 dominant or co-dominant individuals, on (1) crown density, (2) ratio of leaf-bearing length to total length of branches, and (3) ratio of crown length to total height of trees growing in an unbroken forest. This basic score is modified by non-quantitative observations representing the opinion of the observer.

By thus scoring each species in a stand or locality it is a simple matter to arrange the trees in order of relative tolerance. The following listing gives the ratings so obtained for trees growing in Iron County, Michigan:

Tolerant	Score	Low Midtolerant	Score
Hemlock	10.0	Black cherry	2.4
Balsam fir	9.8	Black ash	2.4
Sugar maple	9.7	Red pine	2.4
Basswood	8.2		

High Midtolerant	Score	Intolerant	Score
White spruce	6.8	Jack pine	1.8
Black spruce	6.4	Paper birch	1.0
Yellow birch	6.3	Tamarack	0.8
Red maple	5.9	Aspens	0.7
White cedar	5.0		
White pine	4.4		

Tolerance Ratings of Species

While tolerance is relatively constant for a given species, it does vary with genetically different individuals and races, with different sites, with different plant associates, and with age. A given species may be more tolerant in one part of its range than in another, on one site in comparison to another, and in one forest type than in another.

For example, eastern white pine is more tolerant in Minnesota, where it is considered to be midtolerant, than in New England, where it is relatively intolerant. In central New England, it is more tolerant on dry sandy soils than on moister sandy loams—at least it occurs more consistently under the less dense stands on the former sites. Like many, if not most species, it is more tolerant as a seedling than a mature tree.

Tolerance, then, is not only a relative matter, but the relative ranking of a species with regard to tolerance will depend in part upon the locality, the site, and the associates. Tolerance ratings must be interpreted with this fact in mind.

At the same time, the approximate tolerance rating of the more important and characteristic American forest tree species (Table 12.2) should be known and understood by the practicing silviculturist as a general frame of reference and because it is related to many important attributes of tree species. Ratings of additional species may be found in Baker (1950).

Table 12.2. **Relative Understory Tolerance of Selected North American Forest Trees**

Eastern United States		Western United States
Gymnosperms	Angiosperms	
	Very Tolerant	
Eastern hemlock	Beech	Western hemlock
Balsam fir	Sugar maple	Western red cedar
	Basswood	
	Tolerant	
Spruces	Red maple	Spruces
	Silver maple	Firs
	Yellow birch	Redwood
	Intermediate	
Eastern white pine	Oaks	Western white pine
Slash pine	White ash	Sugar pine
	Elms	Douglas-fir
	Intolerant	
Red pine	Hickories	Ponderosa pine
Shortleaf pine	Black cherry	Lodgepole pine
Loblolly pine	Yellow-poplar	Junipers
	Very Intolerant	
Tamarack	Paper birch	Western larch
Jack pine	Aspens	Digger pine
Longleaf pine	Black locust	Cottonwoods

Nature of Understory Tolerance

Although the relative tolerance of a given species growing in a given community on a given site can be recognized with some degree of accuracy, the explanation of the nature of tolerance is much more difficult. This problem has intrigued silviculturists for many years and has been the subject for much controversy and semantic debates.

The nature of tolerance may be examined from the broad species-adaptation level, and as we have seen, the so-called tolerant and intolerant species belong to two complex and markedly different adaptation systems. Usually, however, the specific trait of survival in the understory is investigated by studying the environmental factors and the physiological processes involved.

Environmental Factors Relating to Understory Tolerance. The most obvious ecological feature of the understory environment is low light irradiance. In fact, many foresters to this day associate the capacity of a plant to survive in the understory solely with the capacity of a plant to survive under low light irradiances, equating the general concept of understory tolerance with the specific concept of shade tolerance.

As data have accumulated from studies of the effect of light irradiance on tree growth under controlled or semicontrolled forest conditions, however, it has become evident that the light irradiances under most forest canopies are more than sufficient to permit most forest trees to carry on photosynthesis at rates substantially higher than required to balance respiration losses (i.e., the *compensation point*). Under moderate covers, such as those created by pine and oak forests, ample light reaches the forest floor to provide energy for photosynthesis by many forest tree seedlings. Even under dense covers, such as those formed by spruce-fir and tropical rain forest species, light flecks sweeping through the forest permit occasional plants to survive and grow in the understory. Only in those forests where the relative illumination on the forest floor is less than about 2 percent is light obviously a single limiting factor in understory survival.

Light, though, is not the only environmental factor greatly modified by the forest canopy. Under a dense forest canopy, almost all the factors of the climate and soil differ from those characterizing similar open sites. Foremost among the affected environmental factors is soil moisture.

The importance of soil moisture in regulating understory occurrence and growth was demonstrated spectacularly in Germany in 1904 by Fricke, who cut the roots of competing understory trees by trenching around small, poorly developed Scots pine seedlings growing under a stand of the same species. These seedlings responded with vigorous growth, indicating that they had been inhibited principally by a shortage of soil moisture created by the competing roots of the overstory trees rather than by low light irradiances.

Trenched plots have been used with similar results under eastern white pine in New Hampshire (Tourmey and Kienholz, 1931), loblolly pine in North Carolina (Korstian and Coile, 1938), and others. Generally speaking, trenching a small plot a milacre or so in size under a pine stand so as to remove root competition by severing entering roots will result in a great increase in available soil moisture and the consequent appearance of luxurious vegetation. For example, soil moisture in a trenched plot under a red pine plantation in southern Michigan remained close to field capacity throughout the growing season whereas, outside the trenched plot but still in an area without ground cover, severe moisture stress was created by transpiration from the main canopy and existed throughout the growing season.

Usually, either trenching or watering understory plants will substantially increase their height growth whereas tying overstory tops back to allow greater amounts of light to reach their leaves will have but little effect.

It would be a mistake, however, to attribute tolerance solely to soil moisture just as it would to attribute it to light alone. Continued study of Toumey's trenched plot experiments (Lutz, 1945) indicated that the more intolerant species do poorly and eventually die even when root competition is kept low, so that the trenched plots gradually become dominated by tolerant plants. After 21 years, hemlock still survived and grew while white pine, which initially was the most abundant tree, had died out completely. Similarly, *Rubus hispidus* and other tolerant understory plants had completely replaced *Viola blanda* and other initial invaders of the trenched plot. Obviously, both soil moisture and light are involved in understory survival, and possibly other factors such as carbon dioxide content of the air as well.

A series of studies of the ecological nature of tolerance carried out with loblolly pine and associated hardwoods in North Carolina has done much to explain the cause of death of loblolly pine and other intolerant seedlings under loblolly pine overstories. In contrast to tolerant seedlings which are able to survive and even grow under pine canopies, the relatively intolerant loblolly pine seedling seems to photosynthesize more than enough to counterbalance respiration losses but not enough to permit its root system to expand and reach the deeper soil strata. Over the years, therefore, the loblolly pine seedling develops a somewhat etiolated top without a compensatory root system of sufficient extent and depth. Sooner or later, these seedlings will die during a period of unusually severe moisture stress under hot, dry midsummer conditions. In contrast, tolerant hardwood species under similar conditions will develop root systems big and deep enough to permit them to survive these droughts.

Ability to survive under the moderate light intensities and severe soil-moisture shortages characteristic of pine forests, then, appears to be dependent upon a plant's carrying on sufficient photosynthesis to develop a sufficient root system to survive midsummer drought in soils kept at low moisture levels by competing roots of overstory trees. Under other situations, either light or root competition may be relatively more important. Under dense Sitka spruce and western hemlock in the Pacific Northwest rain forest, light is at extremely low levels whereas the site is almost always wet or at least damp. Here, light is obviously the more important factor. Similarly, light was the most important factor influencing height growth and dry-matter production of planted red pine seedlings during their initial two years in competition with dense hazel brush (Strothman, 1967). The root systems were apparently well developed and in balance with the crown area so that, at least initially, moisture was not a limiting factor. Under open oak woodland types or under ponderosa pine in the drier parts of its range, light under the forest is well above any critical levels while moisture is always in short supply. Here, soil moisture is obviously the more important factor. Always, however, it is the interaction of light, moisture, and possibly other environmental factors as well which together determine understory survival and growth. It is the understory site *in toto*, viewed as an integrated whole, that determines the ability of a plant to survive in the understory and not any single factor of the site taken by itself.

Physiological Factors Relating to Tolerance. The very fact that some understory plants can develop structures necessary for survival under the site conditions of the understory while others cannot betokens a basic genetic difference between species which is exhibited in their physiological response to these environmental conditions. The surviving plants must exhibit some superiority over failing plants such as (1) in maintaining a greater photosynthesizing leaf area in the understory, (2) in photosynthesizing more efficiently per unit leaf area in the understory, (3) in maintaining lower rates of respiration per unit leaf area in the understory, (4) in converting a greater portion of their photosynthate into growth, or (5) in absorbing water more efficiently.

Present evidence from controlled laboratory experiments of shade tolerance indicates that plant characteristics leading to failure of a genotype or species in one environment may be an indirect consequence of adaptations necessary for survival in another (Grime 1965a). Thus the adaptation of photosynthetic and respiration mechanisms of intolerant species for full productivity under full sunlight is achieved at the cost of lowered efficiency under shade conditions. Although the rates of photosynthesis have been found closely associated with performance in shade (Logan and Krotkov, 1969; Logan, 1970), the differences in rates of respiration between tolerant and intolerant species may be the most important determinants of success or failure in forest shade, where the plant may spend many more hours below than above the light compensation point (Grime, 1965b; Loach, 1967). Intolerant species have high rates of photosynthesis, but they are offset by high rates of respiration and rapid conversion of photosynthate into growth. These species are highly productive in open environments but less adapted to shaded conditions. Tolerant species, according to Went (1957), are more competitive in shaded environments through selection for low respiration rates; they also tend to have lower photosynthetic rates and hence grow slowly in all environments.

A comparison of rates of photosynthesis and respiration for sun and shade leaves of several tolerant and intolerant species illustrates these relationships (Table 12.3; Loach, 1967). Striking differences

Table 12.3. Summary of the Major Differences in the Rates of Photosynthesis and Respiration of the Sun (100% Daylight) and Shade (17% Daylight) Leaves of Shade-Tolerant and -Intolerant Species

	Tolerant Species		Intolerant Species	
	Sun	Shade	Sun	Shade
P^{max}(mg CO_2/dm^2 hr)	7.0	6.4	18.0	12.2
P^{250}(mg CO_2/dm^2 hr)	0.9	2.0	0.3	1.4
R (mg CO_2/dm^2 hr)	1.2	1.0	2.5	3.2

P^{max} is the rate of photosynthesis at saturating light intensity and P^{250} the rate of photosynthesis at 250 ft-candles. R is the rate of respiration in darkness.
SOURCE: Loach, 1967.

occur between intolerants and tolerants at P^{max} (the maximum rate of photosynthesis attained by increasing illumination), indicating that intolerants can make more efficient use of strong light. Intolerant species, however, suffer the greatest proportional reduction in photosynthesis when grown in shade (P^{250}). Significantly, the respiration rates of tolerant species are consistently less than those of intolerants. Thus selection for a high rate of photosynthesis at high light irradiances and high growth rate in full sunlight may inevitably limit the plant in shade. It is clear that there are genetic differences between species in rates of photosynthesis and respiration and probably the other factors as well. It will remain, however, for careful physiological studies and modelling of the growth system of tolerants and intolerants, particularly under natural conditions where both moisture and light may be limiting, to determine the relative importance of photosynthesis, respiration, and other factors to survival and growth in the understory.

Examples of Tolerance in Forest Stands

A series of photographs, Figures 12.1–12.4, serves to illustrate various aspects of tolerance in four forest communities. Figure 12.1 depicts a young second-growth stand of intolerant yellow-poplar in a cove site of the Appalachian Mountains. Sufficient light and moisture reach the understory to favor development of a conspicuous and diverse community of midtolerant and tolerant species, such as oaks, maples, and beech, as well as a rich shrub and herbaceous flora.

The stand of midtolerant oaks of the Missouri Ozark Region (Figure 12.2) illustrates the dominant oak overstory and an open, partially shaded understory of oaks and associated vegetation. The shade cast by the overstory and the low soil moisture during the growing season combine to curtail growth of the understory. This is in contrast to the luxuriant understory of the yellow-poplar stand in the mesic cove site of Figure 12.1.

The dense shade from the overstory of sugar maples in a northern Michigan stand (Figure 12.3) favors the very tolerant sugar maple seedlings over all other species. In deep shade, they survive but grow slowly; in small openings where more light is available (background of Figure 12.3) they respond with accelerated growth and, barring disturbance, will perpetuate the dominance of sugar maple.

The western white pines of the northern Idaho stand in Figure 12.4 originally colonized the site following a fire. Now overmature, they form a dense stand and their crowns intercept most of the in-

Fig. 12.1. Young second-growth stand of yellow-poplar in a cove of the Appalachian Mountains, North Carolina. (U. S. Forest Service photo.)

coming light. However, they will be gradually replaced by the very tolerant species growing in the understory, western hemlock, grand fir, and western red cedar, in the absence of disturbances such as fire and logging.

OVERSTORY MORTALITY

The question of tolerance is associated primarily with understory survival. The trees in the overstory, too, have a more or less limited life span. There are many reasons for overstory mortality, among them being competition, senescence, and death caused by external

Fig. 12.2. Mature, uncut oak stand in the Ozark Mountains of southeastern Missouri. (U. S. Forest Service photo.)

factors such as insects, diseases, wind, and lightning. Examples have already been given.

Competition Among Overstory Trees

We have already seen that, as the surviving trees must inevitably expand and take up more growing space with the passage of years, other trees will become suppressed and will either drop from the overstory through failure to maintain growth, or will die; frequently

Fig. 12.3. Sugar maple stand in Michigan's Upper Peninsula. Unbrowsed sugar maple seedling shown on left and browsed seedling on right. (U. S. Forest Service photo.)

they will first drop from the overstory and then die after they have become overtopped.

The causes of death of suppressed overstory trees under severe competition are akin to those of intolerant smaller trees in the understory but have not been studied in detail nor thoroughly understood. Most obviously, the crowns of these trees recede because of lack of growth of the branch terminals coupled with the gradual lignification of the inner portions of the branch and associated loss of foliage. The friction of other tree crowns whipped back and forth in strong winds plays an important part in mechanically reducing crown size of those trees that have ceased to grow vigorously. Presumably, cessation of crown growth and reduction of crown size denote a comparable cessation of root growth and reduction of root extent, but few data are available on this aspect.

In any event, such trees will eventually die, as they are less able

Fig. 12.4. The overmature western white pines will eventually be replaced, barring disturbance, by very tolerant conifers that have become established in the understory; northern Idaho. (U. S. Forest Service photo.)

than the dominant trees of the stand to survive periods of unfavorable environmental conditions. Mortality will normally be concentrated in periods of extreme heat and drought, extreme cold, or other critical periods.

Senescence

As a tree grows larger, the distance between the feeding roots at the end of the root system and the active leaves at the top of the crown increases. Soil moisture and nutrients must move a greater and greater distance to reach the foliage, and food substances must move a greater and greater distance down to reach the roots. In short, the tree becomes less and less efficient as it becomes larger. Eventually, a given individual of a given species reaches a size at which it is barely able to maintain life without further growth, and further height increment becomes impossible. Thus, any tree has a maximum height which it can reach on a given site. Considerable variation will exist in this regard between various species. Even different individuals of the same species will vary in their genetic capacity to utilize a given site.

As a tree approaches its maximum size, the ability of its leaves to supply needed foods to the bole will decrease, particularly during periods of unfavorable growing conditions. Cells laid down by the bole cambium, therefore, tend with time to become fewer and somewhat smaller, thus increasing the inefficiency of the total organism.

The increasing inefficiency of a tree as it approaches maximum size is coincident with the declining growth curve of old age. During this period of senescence, the tree gradually becomes less and less able to withstand climatic extremes, just as do the aged of any other organism. Sooner or later it will be weakened to the point that it will succumb to some insect attack, fungal attack, or other external enemy, particularly following some extreme dry spell, wet spell, hot spell, or cold spell.

While it is obvious that trees become less efficient organisms with increasing size, it is less clear as to whether or not they also become senescent in the sense of actual aging and loss of vigor of the meristematic tissues and the living protoplasm of the cells that make up the functional tissues of the tree. Different physiological phases, such as the juvenile and adult stages described in Chapter 2, do exist. However, the deterioration of meristematic tissue, such that it itself is a primary cause of death, has not been demonstrated.

External Factors

In addition to mortality of overstory trees due to competition and senescence, many trees are killed by insects, fungi, and climatic factors. These external causes sometimes attack healthy, vigorous trees, and sometimes merely complete the process initiated by weakening of the tree as a result of competition and senescence.

In many parts of the world, lightning plays a prominent role in singling out and killing large dominant trees. Throughout much of the United States today, lightning is a major factor in removing one by one the largest trees in isolated residual old-growth stands of timber.

Among other climatic factors, snow and ice damage is particularly important, notably in dense, unthinned, even-aged stands. Trees of intermediate crown classes, the so-called "whips," are most apt to be bowed and broken down by snow and ice; but once a hole in the forest canopy has been opened, it frequently will be enlarged year after year by the bending and breaking of the exposed edge trees under the combined influence of snow, ice, and wind. Holes in Pacific Northwest stands of Douglas-fir and Norway spruce in Europe are continually being created and enlarged by this gradual process.

Winds, too, play a major part in removing the mature forest overstory. In the New England states, major hurricanes in 1635, 1815, and 1938, as well as many lesser storms, have blown down many thousands of acres of the taller forests. Tornadoes, thunderstorm fronts, and other storms have been destructive to forests throughout much of the country.

Although many insects and fungi do attack healthy, mature trees, the greatest number prey upon trees in a weakened condition. Oviposition in the cambium or phloem by insects is more frequent and more apt to be successful on trees under moisture stress, and low bole moisture content is a characteristic of a weakening and dying tree. Fungal attack is more frequent and more apt to be successful in trees whose bark and wood are opened or cracked by fire, ice, or wind so that both air and moisture are available to the attacking organisms. When a tree attains a weakened state, it is apt to fall prey to some insect or disease; which one may depend upon chance or local circumstances.

TRANSITION OF TREES FROM UNDERSTORY TO OVERSTORY

Forest succession under undisturbed conditions implies the development of understory trees into overstory. Several avenues are available for such movement.

Growth Up Through the Overstory

If the main canopy is not too dense, tolerant species may sometimes grow directly into it and penetrate it, becoming a part of the overstory or even forming a superior canopy over the former overstory.

Fig. 12.5. Shade-tolerant balsam fir and spruces penetrating and becoming part of the overstory together with the intolerant trembling aspen; northern Wisconsin. (U. S. Forest Service photo.)

In central New England, old fields are frequently restocked with gray birch and white pine, the former of which grows much faster in height and forms the initial overstory. The birch, however, maintains its vigor for only a few decades. As it declines, its utilization of the site diminishes, allowing the white pine to grow up through, suppressing it, and forming a pure white pine stand.

Similarly, white pine can grow up through a declining jack pine type in the Lake States; and balsam fir and black spruce can penetrate a decadent aspen canopy on the better sites in the same region (Figure 12.5).

Response to Release

Secondly, tolerant forest trees capable of occupying the overstory can persist in the understory for many years until death of one or more overstory trees creates a hole or opening which they can fill. Eastern hemlock in New England (Marshall, 1927) is notable for its capacity of living decades and even centuries as an understory tree and yet responding almost immediately to release with greatly accelerated growth. Yet the same species on the drier and hotter (in summer) sites of the northern Lake States will frequently deteriorate and die when released rather than respond with vigorous growth (Secrest *et al.*, 1941).

Although many understory trees can respond to release and assume overstory position through rapid growth, many others can not. Some tolerant understory tree species, such as flowering dogwood, hophornbeam, blue beech, and holly, simply do not have the growth potential to accelerate in growth upon release, or the genetic adaptation to grow as overstory trees. They are understory trees by nature and remain that way. Others persist in the understory but in such a debilitated condition that they have lost the capacity to respond, even though a seedling of the same species could germinate and grow successfully in the same forest clearing.

Colonization of Openings

A third avenue of access to the main canopy of an established forest is followed by species of intermediate tolerance which can colonize an opening quickly, and then proceed to outgrow competition to reach the overstory. Yellow birch in the northern hardwood forest of the eastern United States–Canadian border and white ash a few hundred miles to the south are such species. White pine in the East and Douglas-fir in the Pacific Northwest are also of this group. Such species have seed which is chiefly wind-disseminated and have the capacity of germinating on small patches of exposed mineral soil such as that created by the uptorn roots of a windthrown tree. Juvenile growth under conditions of partial shade and partial root competition is rapid so that the seedlings, or at least a portion of them, can outgrow the advance growth of more tolerant species already established in the openings; these may be, however, in more or less of a state of shock and therefore unable to respond quickly to the release.

Reaching the Overstory as Vines

Rarely in the North Temperate Zone but frequently in the Tropics and even in the South Temperate Zone, some trees can penetrate even a dense crown canopy as woody lianas or vines, and upon reaching the top of the overstory, expand and strangle their supporting tree, eventually forming a woody and self-supporting bole of their own. The strangler figs (*Ficus*) in the tropics and the northern rata (*Metrosideros robusta*) in New Zealand are examples of such vines that transform themselves into overstory trees.

SUMMARY

The forest is characterized by intense competition between trees for growing space at all stages. The concept of understory tolerance is descriptive and explanatory of the capacity to survive. Species may be ranked arbitrarily in a continuous series from highly tolerant to highly intolerant. Markedly different adaptation systems characterize the extremes of this series. Many important traits besides the ability to survive in the understory, such as response to release, crown and bole development, height growth, stand structure, and reproductive traits, characterize tolerants and intolerants. The dynamic changes resulting from the reduction in numbers of plants because of competition are basic to an understanding of forest succession, discussed in the following chapter. These changes involve competition of trees in the overstory, competition between trees in the understory, mortality of trees in the overstory with the passage of time, and the various means by which trees can reach the overstory from a subordinate position under the forest canopy.

SUGGESTED READINGS

Baker, Frederick S. 1950. *Principles of Silviculture.* (Tolerance and crown classes, pp. 60–78; The photosynthetic process, pp. 125–150.) McGraw-Hill Book Co., Inc., New York. 414 pp.

Daubenmire, Rexford. 1968. *Plant Communities.* (Introduction, pp. 3–35.) Harper & Row, Inc., New York. 300 pp.

Grime, J. P. 1965. Shade tolerance in flowering plants. *Nature* 208:161–163.

Korstian, C. F., and T. S. Coile. 1938. Plant competition in forest stands. Duke Univ. School For. Bull. 3. 125 pp.

Loach, K. 1967. Shade tolerance in tree seedlings. 1. Leaf photosynthesis and respiration in plants raised under artificial shade. *New Phytol.* 66:607–621.

13

Forest Succession

The bases of dynamic changes in the forest by which one community succeeds another have been detailed in the previous chapter. In synecology, *succession* refers to the replacement of the biota of an area by one of a different nature. Animals as well as plants are involved. Changes in the fauna, however, more often follow than lead the changes in the vegetation described in the present chapter. The development of the biota, beginning with unoccupied sites and proceeding in the absence of a catastrophic disturbance, is termed *primary succession* and is discussed in the present chapter. Succession which is subsequent to a disturbance that disrupts rather than destroys an existing biotic community is termed *secondary*. Primary succession is sometimes termed *autogenic* in that the displacement of one group of species by another results from the development of the ecosystem itself, being a part of the concomitant development of the vegetation, soil, and microclimate of the site. In contrast, secondary succession is *allogenic* in that it is induced by external forces which change the ecosystem (i.e., by forest destruction). Since disturbances are normal to the life of the forest, and since some disturbances such as changes in the microclimate and changes in the soil site are brought about in part by changes in the vegetation, the distinction between primary and secondary succession is more or less arbitrary rather than real. It is followed here simply as a matter of convenience in organizing material on dynamic changes in the forest composition and structure.

Succession is a continuing process marked by myriads of changes in the vegetation, the fauna, the soil, and the microclimate of an area with the passage of time. These changes occur together, mutually affecting one another, with seldom any simple cause-and-effect relationships becoming evident.

EVOLUTION OF THE CONCEPT OF FOREST SUCCESSION

The dynamic nature of the forest has been recognized at least from the time of the earliest observers who put their thoughts into writing. The formalization of the study of forest succession as a scientific discipline, however, has taken place in the last century.

Historical Antecedents

The origin of the concept of forest succession (Spurr, 1952a) can be traced back through the writings of eighteenth-century foresters in Europe and read, by implication at least, in the words of early Roman natural historians.

In America, Jeremy Belknap early recognized the transitory nature of forest types. Writing in his history of New Hampshire, which was published in 1792, he observed:

> There are evident signs of a change in the growth on the same soil, in the course of time; for which no causes can be assigned. In some places the old standing trees, and the fallen decayed trees, appear to be the same, whilst the most thriving trees are of a different kind. For instance, the old growth in some places is red oak, or white ash; whilst the other trees are beech and maple, without any young oak or ash among them. It is probable that the growth is thus changed in many places; . . .

The term "succession" was used in a letter by John Adlum included in a memoir of the Philosophical Society for Promoting Agriculture as part of material published by Richard Peters in 1806 on "Departure of the southern pine timber, a proof of the tendency in nature to a change of products on the same soil." In northwestern Pennsylvania, the occurrence of old red and white oak in northern hardwood stands suggested the succession to sugar maple, beech, and yellow birch in that area. In the mid-Atlantic states, oak and hickory were observed to follow the clearcutting of pitch pine, while white pine was noted as appearing "spontaneously" on old fields.

In Europe, beginning with Hundeshagen in 1830, observed changes in forest composition were the subject of specific articles by professional foresters and botanists. Hundeshagen pointed out instances of spruce replacing beech and other hardwoods in Switzerland and Germany, and of spruce and other species taking the place of birch, aspen, and Scots pine. Gand, in 1840, added other observations, quoting Michaux as having recognized that in America conifers spontaneously replaced overmature broadleaved trees and Bosc as having remarked in Baudrillart's *Dictionary* that when the American forests are cut for the first time, the new stand is totally different, oaks replacing pine, and walnuts (i.e., *Juglans* and *Carya*) replacing maple. He concluded "that the species are not all stable, that is to say that in the largest number of forests, they are not able to reproduce themselves indefinitely and there nearly always arrives a time more or less distant, after one or several rotations, when the trees which occupy the soil of a forest are replaced by trees of a different species."

Observations that forest trees were more apt to occur as an understory to trees of differing species, such as silver fir regeneration occurring under spruce and spruce regeneration occurring under fir, led about the same time to the theory of *alternation of species*. This theory postulates that a given niche in the forest will be occupied by one tolerant species and then another, with the first frequently returning and eventually replacing the second in the third generation. Couchon in 1846 credits the concept of alternation of species to the eighteenth-century scholar, Telles d'Acosta. This concept was well established in France in the nineteenth century, but was rejected by German foresters at the Congress of Baden in 1841.

The first detailed North American report of composition changes was apparently that of Dawson in 1847, dealing primarily with the Maritime Provinces of eastern Canada. He recognized the effects of windthrow and fire in the forests found by the original European settlers, and distinguished between successional trends in small clearings, following cutting, following a single fire, following repeated fires, and as a result of agricultural use of the land.

As early as 1863, Henry David Thoreau recognized that pine stands on upland soils in central New England were succeeded after logging by even-aged hardwood stands which today constitute the principal forest type of the region. He named this trend *forest succession*. A few years later, Douglas, in articles published in 1875 and 1888, discussed at some length the concepts of forest succession and pioneer species, and presented an explanation of how it is that short-lived, light-seeded pioneer species formed the first forest types on burned-over pine land.

The concept of forest succession, then, dates back well into the beginnings of forestry and ecological science. It evolved slowly, but was well established by the beginning of the twentieth century, when Cowles, Clements, and other American ecologists systematized its study.

Formal Ecological Theory

A general theory of plant succession, and indeed the foundations of plant ecology as a study of community dynamics, was initiated by Henry C. Cowles (1899) with an analysis of the succession on sand dunes of Lake Michigan, beginning with uncolonized sand and ending with a mature forest.

It remained for a contemporary, Frederic E. Clements, to fabricate an elaborate philosophical structure of plant succession (1916, 1949) which attempted to formalize all eventualities of plant community change. Specific examples of forest succession were early documented by William S. Cooper, with his studies of Isle Royale in Michigan (1913) and the colonization by plants following glacial retreat in Glacial Bay, Alaska (1923, *et seq.*). A detailed analysis of plant succession has been given by Daubenmire (1968).

Clements, in particular, evolved an elaborate nomenclature to describe plant succession, a system which has both facilitated and greatly complicated the efforts of his successors. Some of his terms have taken a permanent place in the vocabulary of ecologists, others have persisted but with broadened and changed meanings, while still others have been finding less and less general usage. In the belief that good general English usage is preferable to a formal, precisely defined vocabulary understandable only to the initiated, only the commonest and most widely understood ecological terms are introduced in the present text.

THE STAGES OF SUCCESSION

The simplest approach to an understanding of plant succession is to postulate an unvegetated substrate and then to deduce the successive plant communities that will occupy this site under the assumptions that (1) the regional climate will remain unchanged, and (2) catastrophic disturbances such as windstorm, fire, or epidemic will not occur. In view of the hundreds of years involved in most forest successions, these assumptions are completely unrealistic. Their adoption, however, does provide for an understanding of the development of vegetation on any area as an orderly, successional sequence depending upon the character of the original physical habitat and the climate.

The recognition of stages, too, is a matter of convenience rather than of their actual occurrence. Actually, the plant community on a given site is continually changing as new species invade the site and existing species either reproduce or disappear through failure to reproduce. The community is a continuum in time as it is also in space. Nevertheless, the arbitrary classification of this continuum into stages characterized by the dominance or presence of certain species or certain life forms of plants is a convenience worth maintaining.

Initial unvegetated sites range from pure mineral material (rock, soil, or detritus) to water, with mixtures of soil and water (i.e., moist, well-drained mineral soil) the most favorable for plant colonization and growth. Thus a continuous range in site exists. Nevertheless, it is convenient to select points along this range at which to postulate plant succession. Primary plant succession beginning with dry rock material (either as rock or as mineral soil) is termed a *xerarch succession;* that beginning with water is termed a *hydrarch succession;* while that beginning with moist but aerated soil materials is a *mesarch succession.*

Keeping in mind that many types of primary successions exist and that both the specific successions and the vegetational stages within each are more or less arbitrarily chosen, yet the general stages of primary succession are quite consistent and are worthy of detailed study. In Table 13.1, series of ten typical stages are given for each representative type of primary succession, following the general scheme of Graham (1955). Some stages are sometimes omitted under conditions where the next successional life form (as tree, shrub, herb, liana, etc.) is capable of directly colonizing an earlier vegetational type. In Clementsian terminology, these series of stages are termed *seres.*

Another useful delineation of stages in succession is that of Dansereau (1957), who recognizes four: (1) pioneer stage, (2) consolidation stage, (3) subclimax stage, and (4) climax stage. The

Table 13.1.   Stages in Primary Succession

Stage	Xerarch	Mesarch	Hydrarch
1	Dry rock or soil	Moist rock or soil	Water
2	Crustose lichens	(usually omitted)	Submerged water plants
3	Foliose lichens and mosses	(usually omitted)	Floating or partly floating plants
4	Mosses and annuals	Mostly annuals	Emergents
5	Perennial forbs and grasses	Perennial forbs and grasses	Sedges, sphagnum and mat plants
6	Mixed herbaceous	Mixed herbaceous	Mixed herbaceous
7	Shrubs	Shrubs	Shrubs
8	Intolerant trees	Intolerant trees	Intolerant trees
9	Midtolerant trees	Midtolerant trees	Midtolerant trees
10	Tolerant trees	Tolerant trees	Tolerant trees

only real difficulty with this terminology lies in the fact that, to some, subclimax refers to any of the developmental seral communities, while in Clementsian terminology, it refers to a relatively permanent stage that immediately precedes the last, or climax, stage.

The actual composition of the different stages will be dependent upon those species having access to the site in question either by virtue of their propinquity or by the capacity of their seed to reach the site by various avenues of dissemination. The actual plant communities on any given site, of course, depend upon the available plants as well as upon the site and will change from place to place and even in the same place from time to time.

It will be noted that the stages detailed in Table 13.1 are not mutually exclusive in that the various life forms and developmental stages may be characteristic of more than one stage, and, indeed, many persist through many stages. Some mosses, for instance, may invade a site early in the succession and persist through to the later vegetational stages characterized by tolerant trees. The term *forb* refers to an herbaceous non-grasslike plant such as violet, iris, or sunflower. It is ordinarily used in discussing grassland communities where the forbs are not dominant.

It may be inferred from Table 13.1 that the stages of the different primary successions become more and more similar as the succession develops, inasmuch as the last five stages are characterized by the same general terms. While this is true, and while one school of thought holds that, given indeterminate time, all successions in the same general climate will eventually lead to a vegetational community of the same composition and structure, in actual vegetation patterns this does not occur. Although the latest successional stage will usually be composed of tolerant trees in a climatic region characterized by forests, the identity and relative abundance of the different species will vary with the different sites within the region.

PRIMARY SUCCESSION

Complete sequences of vegetational development are initiated by disturbances that expose substrates which are essentially devoid of plant growth at the beginning. Primary successions may begin with water or mineral soil under a wide variety of climates. Mineral soil may be exposed in many ways: through glacial retreat, volcanic ash deposition, avalanches and landslides, spoils banks formation following strip-mining, extremely hot forest fires, sand dune formation, emergence of coastal strands, etc. Since the specific succession will vary not only with the type of site exposed, but also with the climate of the locality and the variety and abundance of plants accessible to the site for colonization, it is manifestly impossible to detail all the major types of primary forest succession. In the present section, therefore, attention will be focused on a few sample primary successions illustrative of the stages of vegetation development following different types of site exposure in various geographical regions and under differing climatic conditions.

Bog Succession in Eastern Canada

The succession beginning in shallow freshwater lakes of the spruce-fir boreal forest of eastern Canada and adjacent sections of the northeastern United States has attracted much attention. The lakes are of relatively recent origin, mostly being formed following the retreat of the last continental ice sheet from 6,000 or so to 10,000 years ago, so that succession is actively proceeding at the present time. The various stages in succession are obvious as concentric bands or zones of vegetation spanning the distance from open water in the middle of many lakes to mature forest at the borders growing on peat deposits that occupy what obviously was once open water. Finally, the area has long been accessible to plant ecologists from the heavily settled areas immediately to the south. As a result, many ecological studies have been concerned with bog forest succession in boreal North America (Rigg, 1940, 1951; Dansereau and Segadas-Vianna, 1952). In northern lower Michigan (Gates, 1942), for example, the most common typical sere is from open water through aquatic associations to the mat-forming sedge, *Carex lasiocarpa*, followed by *Chamaedaphne calyculata*, which invades the floating *Carex* sedge mat. Eventually, the *Chamaedaphne* is replaced by high bog shrubs (*Nemopanthus*, willow, alder, birch), and these eventually give way to swamp conifers such as tamarack, black spruce, and (under aerated seepage conditions) northern white cedar.

We should not infer that all bogs in the boreal forest are formed by the filling up of water bodies. Under cool and wet climatic conditions, bogs are also formed by the swamping out of previously well-drained forests. Either natural succession to a dense spruce forest, or secondary succession to heath (*Calluna* spp.), may bring about a type of vegetation whose litter forms an acid raw-humus mat sufficiently unfavorable to litter-destroying organisms that it will accumulate, retain more and more moisture, and eventually be transformed into upland peat, supporting a *Sphagnum* ground cover. As the upland peat builds up under cool, wet climates, it eventually develops a characteristic bog flora, so that bogs actually develop, even on steep slopes. This process is important in Scandinavia, Finland (Huikari, 1956), western Scotland and Ireland, and the wet Pacific Coast of southeastern Alaska and British Columbia.

Mangrove Succession in the Tropics

Coastal swamps of mangrove characterize shallow salt water bodies throughout the tropics. In these, plant succession is evidenced by zones of vegetation extending from the open sea to the interior high forest, just as in the case of the boreal bog succession.

The term "mangrove" refers to tropical maritime trees and shrubs, especially of the genus *Rhizophora*, but also including other plants similar in appearance and in ecological preference for coastal mudlands. With extensive aerial root systems, mangroves are important soil builders, becoming established in shallow water, where they obstruct currents, speed up the rate of deposition, and bind the soil with their roots and incorporated humus.

Mangrove swamps commonly show zonation of the dominant species more or less parallel to the shoreline, with each successive interior zone being characterized by less flooding and characteristic mangrove species (Richards, 1952). These zones may be considered to represent successive stages in a hydrarch succession originating with salt water mud flats and ending with tropical high forest.

In Florida (Davis, 1940), for example, continually submerged soil is first invaded by the red mangrove (*Rhizophora mangle*), the viviparous seedlings of which float in the sea and become established on shoals and sandbanks. With time, a mature *Rhizophora* forest develops to a height of 10 meters or more, resulting in substantial soil anchoring and accumulation. With better drainage conditions, *Avicennia* replaces *Rhizophora*, extending even to relatively dry sites. Further inland, in a zone seldom reached by tides, *Conocarpus* and other semimangrove species characterize the community.

In general, as the mangrove swamp extends seaward, the interior portions become denser and populated with a greater variety of species. Impedance of water movement from the sea by the mass of roots and accumulating debris, coupled with transpiration pumping of the water, permits fresh water to move seaward into the swamp, thus reducing the salinity of the water. With the gradual invasion of freshwater plants into the freshening site, a freshwater swamp forest is eventually developed in which mangroves are replaced by a variety of tropical swamp species. Under climatic conditions where the water table can be lowered by the high rate of transpiration possible in the tropics, the site can even be invaded by high forest species with the passage of time. Clearcutting of the forest or other destruction to the forest, however, will eliminate the transpiration pump, raise the water level of the site, and bring about a return to freshwater swamp conditions.

It should be pointed out that measurable rates of succession along the maritime strand can be obtained only under conditions where the coastline is actually advancing into shallow seas and the coastal marshes are actually filling in. In many, if not most, situations, these changes are not occurring and the different zones of vegetation lying parallel to the shore represent past succession that has ceased, so that the different types are each more or less permanent until the physiography of the site is changed again.

Following Glacial Retreat in Southeastern Alaska

The exposure of fresh deposits of moraines and outwash following retreat of glaciers provides one of the clearest and best studied examples of primary plant succession. In Glacier Bay, Alaska, studies of the development of pioneer plants on permanently marked plots established by Cooper in 1916 on surfaces left free by the ice on known dates as early as 1879 have made available much information about primary forest succession over a 75-year period in this particular locale (Lawrence, 1958). The stages run from pioneers through the establishment of alder thickets to a spruce-fir forest, followed by forest deterioration leading to muskeg and pit-pond development.

The pioneer plants, small and slow growing, invade as seeds or spores blown in by wind or carried in the digestive tracts of birds and mammals. On the nitrogen-deficient mineral deposits, willow and black cottonwood grow prostrate and slowly. Dryas forms a prostrate mat and is the most abundant pioneer plant.

The second stage is marked by the invasion of Sitka alder to form a thicket 11 feet high over a 7-year period. The alder, and probably the dryas as well, is nitrogen-fixing through symbiotic actinomycetes or fungi infecting root nodules, with the result that atmospheric nitrogen is fixed and accumulated in the soil, making possible the establishment and growth of more-demanding tree species.

In the next stage, the alder is mature—about 60 years after ice recession in the Glacier Bay region—with a maximum height of 25 to 35 feet and sagging stems 6 to 8 inches in diameter. First black cottonwood and later Sitka spruce and western hemlock infiltrate the alder thicket, giving the stand a "lumpy" appearance when viewed from a distance.

Maximum forest development is reached in the fourth stage with a dense spruce-hemlock forest, carpeted with mosses and litter 6 to 12 inches deep. About two centuries are required for the development of this stage after ice recession.

With the invasion by sphagnum mosses of the ground cover of the spruce forest, water retention is greatly increased. As aeration of the forest soil is impaired, the older trees gradually die, sphagnum mosses succeed one another in more and more luxuriant development, and the more level sites eventually are transformed into muskeg (a bog characterized by an abundance of sphagnum moss and tussocks). Forests maintain themselves, however, on the steeper slopes where lateral soil drainage is effective. Pacific Coast lodgepole pine alone is capable of surviving and growing in the developing muskegs. In the last stage of muskeg development on level and slightly sloping ground, pit-ponds develop, creating surfaces partially of water and partially of muskeg.

Bare Rock Succession

The classic xerarch succession beginning with bare rock surfaces is frequently cited in ecological texts. An example is provided by Oosting and Anderson (1939) for granitic rock in the Piedmont of the southeastern United States, in which the more or less level rock surfaces are invaded by a mat-forming moss (*Grimmia laevigata*) upon which a lichen (*Cladonia leporina*) becomes established. As the mat thickens, herbs come in with the eventual dominance by *Andropogon* spp. of bunch grasses. Shrubs, such as sumac (*Rhus copallina*), form the next successional stage, followed over the years by the development of an oak-hickory forest.

In detailing plant successions, we should remember that animals are equally involved in the succession of ecosystems. Not only do the species and relative abundance of the species change continually as the plant community changes, but the changes in the fauna play a part in causing changes in the flora as well as responding to such changes. An example of the interaction between animals and plants is provided by a detailed study of the contribution of rock ants to the afforestation of rocks in south Finland (Oinonen, 1956). This ant, *Lasius flavus*, reaches optimum development on rocks covered with lichens and mosses. The structure and location of its nests are favorable for the natural establishment of Scots pine and Norway spruce seedlings, whose roots can usually be retained by the nests for the first 5 to 10 years. The root aphids associated with the pines provide food for the ants, which in turn creates new sites for pine seedling establishment.

Forest Succession Following Landslides

In steep mountainous regions, earth slides caused by avalanches, excessive rain, destruction of anchoring vegetation by fire or grazing, seismic movements, and other causes create bare mineral soil upon which primary succession takes place. The more exposed landslides may remain relatively unvegetated for years. For example, 32 years after an avalanche had destroyed a subalpine forest in Switzerland composed of Mugo pine, with some European larch and Swiss stone pine, the site was still generally open, with only scattered Mugo pine (average height 1.7 meters), dwarf shrubs, and isolated trees of other species (Lüdi, 1954).

At the lower elevations under more temperate climatic conditions, however, colonization by tree species is relatively fast. In the White Mountains of New Hampshire, paper birch, yellow birch, pin cherry, and aspen come in almost immediately and rapidly develop a thicket (Flaccus, 1959). Succession to the more tolerant red spruce–balsam fir forest at the higher elevations or to the beech–sugar maple forest at the lower elevations takes place as the pioneer forest types mature and begin to open up through disintegration of the shorter-lived components.

Succession in landslide areas generally appears to involve the direct colonization of the site by shrub and tree species from undamaged forests on either side. Because of the steepness of the site, surface soil and rock particles tend to remain mobile for years, particularly in areas subject to annual freezing and frost action. Woody perennials appear best able to invade such open sites under climates favorable to forest growth.

Following Severe Fire

Fire normally initiates secondary succession. When the fire is sufficiently hot so as to destroy all higher plants, however, including their root stocks so that no sprouting occurs, all that is left is an ash-covered mineral soil, and the resulting invasion may accurately be described as primary succession.

Such a succession occurs following the destruction of a red spruce forest in northern New England, where the evergreen spruce foliage and the characteristic raw humus accumulation on the forest floor provide fuel for an extremely hot fire during warm weather droughts. Indeed, many such spruce forests have developed on bare rock following a classic xerarch succession so that a fire will remove the vegetation and organic soil, leaving only bare rock. The summit of Mt. Monadnock in southwestern New Hampshire was clothed with a red spruce forest until destroyed by fire in the eighteenth century, leaving only a rocky peak with a false timber line and primary succession slowly taking place in rock crevices and small patches of residual mineral soil.

The typical primary succession following complete destruction of red spruce forest on mineral soil (rather than rock) in northern New England involves six stages (Toumey, 1947): (1) moss meadow, (2) aster-fireweed meadow, (3) hairgrass-sedge meadow, (4) willow-birch thicket, (5) aspen forest, and (6) spruce forest. As with other primary successions, many variants are evident on different sites and with varying access of invading species.

In the Rocky Mountains of western United States and Canada, fire is similarly destructive of all vegetation in the coniferous forest zone. At the lower edge of this zone, where the climate is warmer and drier than at higher elevations, fire may so modify the local climate through destruction of all cover and exposure of the surface soil that plant succession may end to all intents and purposes with the colonization of the site by the grasses or desert shrubs characteristic of the next lower vegetational zone.

Dune Sands Along Lake Michigan

It was in the colonization of the dune sands along the southern margin of Lake Michigan that Cowles made his pioneering study of plant succession. The shifting sand dunes are first anchored by various dune grasses (*Ammophila, Calamouilfa, Andropogon*) and succession leads eventually to pine (jack and white) and black oak (Olson, 1958). The succession from barren dune sand to black oak forest requires about 1,000 years after stabilization, during which time the litter of the developing vegetation continually improves the soil. The changes and improvements slow down with time, however, so that there seems to be little prospect for continued change toward a more mesophytic forest or a better soil after this time. Although fire history on the drier sites plays an important role in holding back succession, yet the development of the more mesic basswood–red oak–sugar maple communities is restricted to the moister and more fertile sites on lower lee slopes and in dune pockets that are protected from drying and burning. Here the mesic community usually develops without passing through stages like those leading to the black oak–blueberry communities.

Mining Spoils

The waste of mining creates exposed mineral deposits that are suitable in many cases for colonization by vegetation. Abandoned rock quarries, slag from coal mines (pit heaps) in England, the dredgings of gold dredges in California and Alaska, and the spoils banks left by strip mining for coal from Pennsylvania to Illinois, and in Washington, Montana, and British Columbia—all are sites on which primary succession takes place (Schramm, 1966).

Frequently, the unweathered minerals in such deposits are so acid (as in the case of much coal overburden) or so basic (as in the case of limestone and chalk quarries) that they are unsuitable for plant growth until after years or even centuries of leaching and weathering. If barren after three or four years after exposure under climatic conditions favorable for plant growth, these sites are apt to remain barren for at least several decades, although grasses, shrubs, and some trees tolerant of exposure and unweathered soil conditions may eventually become established. Eventually, however, vegetation on the spoils may develop into communities similar to those on nearly undisturbed lands. On century-old iron-ore spoils in northern West Virginia, Tryon and Markus (1953) found no indication of significant differences in forest tree, shrub, or herb composition between spoils and undisturbed soils in a forest now characterized by red oak, chestnut oaks, red maple, and other central hardwoods.

Considerable effort has been put into the task of afforesting the spoils banks left by strip mining for coal in the northeastern United States, but the success of the plantations has been relatively limited. For all types of surface mining throughout the United States the reclamation success with vegetation has been poor; 71 percent of the disturbed lands have inadequate cover or are incapable of supporting vegetation (U.S. Department of Interior, 1967).

On Volcanic Ash

Fresh mineral exposures are created by vulcanism. Lava flows and volcanic ash both provide substrates for plant growth, although lava may take centuries and even thousands of years to weather sufficiently to support vegetation (cf. the Mesa basalt flow in Oregon and adjacent states). Ash deposits, however, are generally quickly colonized. For example, following the 1886 eruption of

Mt. Tarawera in New Zealand, new communities scarcely different from the old have evolved in the subsequent 70-year period (Nicholls, 1959). More generally, succession following older and more destructive ash showers in the North Island of New Zealand follows a well-defined pattern (McKelvey, 1953). A scrub community—probably *Leptospernum* spp.—apparently pioneered on the skeletal pumice soils, providing a nurse for the podocarps, the seeds of which were bird-disseminated into the devastated zone. Later, hardwoods invaded the podocarp forests, first as an understory, and eventually forming the overstory, with the more tolerant hardwoods gradually replacing the less tolerant species.

Within the tropics, the revegetation of Krakatau, a volcanic island in Indonesia where all the vegetation was destroyed by a spectacular eruption in 1883, has been summarized by Richards (1952); succession on the Soufrière of St. Vincent in the West Indies has been recorded by Beard (1945); and that on recent volcanoes in Papua was discussed by Taylor (1957). The vegetation in all these tropical situations trends toward the original undisturbed forest, but the progress is slow. On Krakatau, the terrain was a barren desert the year after the eruption of 1883 and was vegetated chiefly by ferns 3 years after, while the interior of the island was clothed by a dense growth of grasses 14 years after the eruption. Woodland zones were well developed after 23 years. By 1919, after 36 years, much of the savanna had been converted into woodland by trees spreading upwards and outwards from the ravines, and by 1931, after 48 years, a secondary forest had developed, similar to that elsewhere in the Malayan region. Many species, however, migrate very slowly into devastated areas. In Papua, even after 80 years, the number of species present on volcanic soils is only a very small proportion of those in nearby undisturbed forests (25 vs. 500).

NATURAL SUCCESSION WITHIN THE FOREST

In managing forested lands, the stages of succession from the exposure of the site to the appearance of a closed forest are of relatively less importance than the stages of succession from one forest type to another. Forest succession, in the limited sense, begins with the establishment of the pioneer forest trees and proceeds with their replacement by successor species which profit by the changing environment.

In general, the pioneer trees are intolerant, with midtolerant species characterizing the second tree stage, and tolerant species the late-successional forest types (Spurr and Cline, 1942). The correlation between tolerance and successional appearance, however, is not perfect. Some relatively tolerant species have the capacity of invading forest sites relatively early in the succession; while other tolerant trees, either because of a relatively short life span (as many of the true firs) or because of their inability to reach the overstory and survive in overstory environmental conditions (for instance, dogwood) may never form a major part of late-successional forest canopy. Nevertheless, it is true that pioneer forest communities are generally dominated by intolerant forest trees while late-successional types are characterized by tolerant species.

In the complex hardwood deciduous forest of the eastern United States, sugar maple, beech, and basswood continually invade midtolerant forests characterized by various oaks, ashes, and elms. The same relationships between genera occur in the deciduous forests of central Europe and far-eastern Asia.

Douglas-fir of the Pacific northwestern United States is a midtolerant. With time, pure Douglas-fir stands are gradually changed to communities dominated by the more tolerant western red cedar, western hemlock, or the true firs, depending upon the locality and site. A similar situation occurs in Tasmania, where the midtolerant eucalyptus forest is slowly replaced by mixed, tolerant, rain-forest species in the absence of disturbances.

Under certain conditions, however, intolerant species maintain themselves essentially without replacement by more tolerant species. Ponderosa pine in many parts of the Southwest, trembling aspen in parts of the Great Basin, and jack pine and black oak of the sand plains and dunes in the Lake States are examples. Thus, we cannot conclude that tolerant species always characterize late-successional forests. Many of these and other examples are presented in greater detail in the next chapter, dealing with the effect of disturbances upon forest succession.

THE CONCEPT OF CLIMAX

The process of plant and forest succession is incontrovertible and has been recognized from the earliest days of natural history study.

The question of what the last stage of succession is, if any, however, has been the subject of much discussion and debate, a controversy confused by semantic difficulties in that the participants have frequently used the same terms but with different shades of meaning.

Just as the soil is the product of the interaction of the surrounding climate, the supporting biota, the basic parent material, and the topographic relief over a period of time (Jenny, 1941), so the plant community can be considered as the product of the interaction of the surrounding climate, the interrelated biota, the underlying soil, and the topographic site over a period of time (Major, 1951).

Under specified site conditions—using site in its broadest sense to include geographic location, climate, soil, and topographic position—a series of stages of plant succession can be deduced which begins with the colonization of that site and proceeds to a stage typically characterized by tolerant and long-lived organisms that constitute a more or less balanced and relatively permanent community. Such primary plant successions have been detailed for illustrative situations in the preceding sections. In each case, the tacit assumption is that site is changed only through the interactions of the community and its environment, and not through any "external" factor such as fire, wind, human activity, or regional climatic change.

Under such an assumption—namely, that the site is constant except for changes brought about by the plant succession itself—then the last successional stage is termed the *climax*. It is theoretically a final, mature, stable, self-maintaining, and self-reproducing state of vegetational development that culminates plant succession on any given site.

Clements, who more than any other developed the theory and nomenclature of plant succession, believed that, given indefinite time without disturbance to the community or site, the plant communities in a given climatic region would approach the same composition and structure. In his so-called *monoclimax* theory, climate was the dominant community-forming factor, while the other factors (soil, topographic relief, and biota—time being another dimension and not a factor in the same sense), although important, were in some fashion of secondary importance. With such a philosophical frame of reference, one can theorize that, if disturbances such as fire, extensive windthrow, cutting of trees, and externally caused climatic change can be eliminated for thousands and even millions of years, the swamps will fill up, the hills will be eroded away, and the whole landscape will be a peneplane clothed with a uniform plant and animal community. The rationale of Clements' monoclimax represents an application to vegetation of the peneplane theory of Davis.

Be that as it may, the fact is that such conditions seldom if ever exist in nature. Furthermore, there seems to be no fundamental reason why climate should be a more important community-controlling factor than soil, topographic relief, and biota. If not, then it is equally possible to theorize a different climax community for each soil type, each topographic position, and indeed for each assemblage of plants and animals that through historical accident find themselves living and growing together. This is the *polyclimax* theory, a theory that holds that for any combination of organisms and environment, succession will take place toward a climax but that the specific nature of the climax will vary with the specific environmental and biotic conditions. The polyclimax theory has its roots in the contributions of Nichols (1923), who argued for a different *physiographic climax* on each site, differing more or less from the regional *climatic climax;* and of Gleason (1926), who maintained that plant communities were not individuals in themselves but more or less chance aggregations of the individuals which happened to have access to a particular site.

For example, in Cowles' classic studies of plant succession on the sand dunes of lower Lake Michigan, it was at first thought possible that succession on all sand dune sites would eventually reach the same mixed mesophytic hardwood forest stage. Yet, in a later study of the same area, Olson (1958) concluded that the drier and more exposed sites would never support such a community but would be more or less permanently clothed with a black oak–blueberry type because of the dryness and low fertility of the soil itself. Furthermore, he felt that although vegetational changes would continue with time, they would become slower and slower and never reach complete stability: "Vegetation, soil and other properties of the ecosystem usually change rapidly at first and more slowly later on. If they approach some limit asymptotically or fluctuate around it, this limit should describe the climax community on mature soil. . . . The limit itself may vary with time and place. Ideally, it describes a gradational 'climax pattern' of communities or eco-systems in any region—generally not a uniform 'climatic climax'."

Over the years, the concept of climax has become broader and more all-inclusive in line with the polyclimax approach. Tansley (1949) was instrumental in broadening the concept of climax by adopting a "dynamic" viewpoint in recognizing that "natural and semi-natural vegetation is constantly changing, that certain uniformities in the direction, methods, and causes of change can be detected, and that positions of relative equilibrium are reached in which the conditions and composition of the vegetation remain approximately constant for a longer or shorter time." The climax as a "position of relative stability" is a succinct and acceptable formulation of the climax concept. Furthermore, Tansley recognized that "these 'positions of equilibrium' are seldom if ever really 'stable'" and that they contained many elements of instability—as we have seen in the foregoing examples. Thus, as a result of the broadening concept of climax, many of the terms of Clements have fallen into disuse, while others have been used more and more in broader and less formal senses.[1] However, the polyclimax theory is also beset with its own terminology of climaxes: climatic, edaphic, topographic, topoedaphic, fire, zootic, salt, etc. (Tansley, 1935; Oosting, 1948; Daubenmire, 1968). Many of these are the same as or are merely more specific distinctions of Clemensian climaxes. For example, in polyclimax terminology the *monoclimax* of Clements becomes the *climatic* climax; Clements' subclimax may be either an edaphic or topographic climax; a disclimax becomes a fire or a zootic climax, etc. Many of the polyclimax terms will undoubtedly also fall into disuse. The major contribution of polyclimax theory, nevertheless, is in recognizing that factors other than climate may be determining in controlling community dynamics. However, it is not necessary or desirable to develop a new terminology for each factor or factor complex.

Phillips (1931, 1934–35), Tansley (1935), Cain (1939), Whit-

---

[1] Among the kinds of climax recognized and named by Clements are: *subclimax*, essentially equivalent to the physiographic climax of Nichols, being a more or less permanent but "imperfect" stage of development in which the vegetation is held indefinitely either by natural or artificial factors other than climate—such as grazing, burning, or cutting; *disclimax*, a replacement of the "true" climax, chiefly as a consequence of disturbance by man or domesticated animals; *postclimax*, the next more mesophytic climax to the local climax (i.e., the climax of a wetter and cooler climatic zone); and *preclimax*, the next more xerophytic climax to the local climax (i.e., the climax of a warmer and drier zone). All of these types are grouped as *proclimaxes*.

taker (1953), Daubenmire (1968), and Langford and Buell (1969) summarized differing viewpoints in the evolution of climax theory. Whether such a stable biotic community as a climax actually exists is the subject of the following section.

THE INSTABILITY OF THE FOREST

In humid climates where precipitation exceeds potential evapotranspiration, plant succession moves toward the development of a forest composed of tolerant tree species and associated understory tolerant plants and animals. In climax theory, the climax under such climates is a tree-dominated biotic community. Under climax theory, it is held that, following many years of changing community composition and structure, a stable or "climax" community is eventually attained which no longer changes.

True, secondary successions may be initiated by some "external" disturbance such as fire or human activity; but "internal" disturbances such as the killing of a single tree by lightning or bark beetle attack merely result in its replacement with a tree of the same species or another tree of the climax community from the understory.

It has long been recognized that such stability is seldom if ever actually attained in the forest. Secondary successions are ever present (see following chapter for discussion). Changes in both climatic and soil conditions vary from place to place within the forest, and from time to time, depending upon the evolution of the forest community itself as well as upon regional or worldwide climatic change. Species such as the American chestnut and American elm are eliminated from the forest community by disease while others such as Scots pine, the gypsy moth, and the chestnut blight fungus in northeastern United States are introduced—some by man and some by other forms of migration—and become part of the forest ecosystem.

More and more, it has become apparent that the forest is never stable, but remains a dynamic community in the later successional stages just as it was in the earlier stages of plant succession. A forest composed of tolerant tree species is constantly changing in composition and structure, and in associated fauna and flora as well, just as in a forest composed of pioneer intolerant tree species. The rate of change may be less, it may approach an asymptote or fluctuate around it, but change itself is still characteristic of the community.

If the concept of continual change is accepted, then the concept of the climax loses its meaning and validity, because the climax implies the existence of a stable and permanent community. True, the word does not disappear from our vocabulary, but it takes on a different meaning. Rather than referring to an ultimate and finite end stage of plant successions as it did in earlier ecological thought, it now becomes a term somewhat loosely applied to a more or less stable and long-lived community that develops late in plant succession in the absence of disturbance—a position of relative stability. In this modern sense, however, the climax is no longer considered final since changes are taking place within the biotic community all the time even if at a slower and less obvious pace.

Many examples may be cited pointing to the instability of all forest communities, even of the so-called climax types. The concept of a stable and enduring climax, developed in temperate vegetational zones, not only does not hold for these zones, but has even less reality in the arctic regions or in the tropics.

As Hewetson (1956) describes the tropical forest of India after many years of its study:

> I would describe the Tropical Forest as a continuum in which the parts are in unstable equilibrium. All the species can survive but some species are more closely adapted to the sum total of environmental factors and in average climatic conditions are more likely to be successful and to form the greater part of the growing stock. The average may, however, be deflected by exceptional events such as tornados or droughts or land clearance or fires. The effect of these exceptional events may be seen 200 or 300 years later, and the growing stock we see before us today can only be understood in the light of conditions in the past. The interplay of the individual speces extends from the trees in the top canopy down to the herb layer. The density and the composition of the lower strata may control what trees will succeed the present overwood as much as the potentiality for reproduction of the dominant species. It is quite possible the equilibrium may be maintained for a period in one forest and the same trees succeed their ancestors. Other forests may be in a condition of complete change with the present growing stock being replaced by different species. Between these two extremes, many variations are possible.

Raup (1957) has given examples of the basic instability of the site. A consideration of these results leads to the conclusion that repeated major disturbances by factors largely external to the vegetation should not be considered as unusual but as a part of the normal itself. As a result, actual succession should be considered as consisting of fragments of the theoretical complete succession, with the climax becoming a purely theoretical speculation. The grasslands of North America, as well as the forests, have had much the same history of oft-repeated disturbances (Malin, 1956).

The continual changes in the forest, which result in its common instability, are of many types. These include (Yaroshenko, 1946): (1) seasonal change, (2) annual changes due to year-to-year climatic variation, (3) short-term succession changes as discussed in this and the following chapter, and (4) long-term "historical" changes as discussed in Part IV. All result in a constantly changing forest ecosystem.

Boreal North American Forest

In the preceding portion of the chapter the primary succession following glacial retreat in southeastern Alaska is detailed, and it is indicated that a mature forest composed of Sitka spruce and western hemlock is eventually followed on many level and less sloping sites by muskeg formation leading even to the swamping out of much of the muskeg in pit-pond formation. The successional trends are clear, but, if one is attempting to apply the concept of climax to the succession, the question may be asked as to whether the conifer forest or the muskeg is the climax (Zach, 1950). In the Clementsian sense, the forest community qualifies as being mesophytic and composed of tolerant and long-lived species. Yet the fact remains that, given time, sphagnum invasion of the conifer forests on the more level sites will bring about the accumulation of upland peat, the deterioration of the conifers, and the development of a muskeg-pond type which could therefore be considered as the climax.

Similar situations occur elsewhere in the boreal forest of North America, although the species involved may differ. On glaciofluvial substrata in northern Manitoba, for instance, the sequence of vegetation moves from meadow to shrub to white spruce and tamarack forest, developing into a pure white spruce forest, which in turn swamps out to evolve into a black spruce forest with expanding bog and mound-hollow topography (Ritchie, 1957).

In the interior of Alaska, the effect of the development of a spruce forest canopy, according to Benninghoff (1952), is to decrease the amount of insolation reaching the ground, with the consequence that the ground becomes frozen throughout the year closer to the surface. Frozen ground acts as an impermeable stratum in the soil to perch the water table, with the result that the surface will sooner or later swamp out, leading again to muskeg and open-pond development.

The boreal vegetation, by and large, does not reach a stable and long-lived climax, but rather remains in a state of instability as a result of the complex interactions between vegetation, soil-water relationships, frost action, and permanently frozen ground. There is a basic instability in the environment and the vegetation (Churchill and Hanson, 1958). The concept of climax has little meaning in its original Clementsian sense. It may be used in a modified sense simply to identify the most mesophytic community that develops in a given succession on a given site. In the examples above, these would be the communities dominated by Sitka spruce on the coast or white spruce in the interior.

European Spruce—Fir—Beech

Within the Temperate Zone, the classic example of the instability of even the climax forest is provided by Norway spruce–silver fir–beech forests of central Europe, particularly in Switzerland and adjacent mountain areas in France, Germany, and Czechoslovakia. These species are all tolerant, long-lived, and capable of forming a many-aged, many-storied mixture which can be managed by single-tree selection methods of silviculture. By all conventional standards of the climax, this community qualified. Yet, on any given spot within this "climax" forest, the composition as well as the structure is unstable, with spruce replacing fir, fir replacing spruce, and similar changes taking place involving beech. This phenomenon of "alternation of species" has long been studied by European silviculturists (Nagel, 1950; Simak, 1951; Schaeffer and Moreau, 1958). In these mixed uneven-aged forests, all three tolerant tree species regenerate most commonly under one of the others rather than under the same species. Spruce regeneration, for instance, is far more common under fir than under spruce. The inability of spruce to regenerate under itself is presumed to be due to the fact that the shallow root system of the dominant tree reduces surface soil moisture to such a level that the even shallower root system of the seedlings cannot obtain moisture and dies of drought.

Lake States Tolerant Hardwoods

The climax forest of the northern Lake States is composed of tolerant, long-lived species capable of forming a long-enduring, mixed, uneven-aged community. Prominent among the components are sugar maple, basswood, beech (in the eastern portion of the region), and hemlock (Graham, 1941). In general, however, the forest never reaches an equilibrium but, because of the continual action of local windthrow, fire, drought, insect attack, and fungus infestation, consists of a mosaic of patches each of which is constantly changing in composition and structure (Stearns, 1949). Midtolerant species such as yellow birch and white pine are able to maintain themselves almost indefinitely in competition with the more tolerant species through exploitation of small gaps in the forest canopy. The term *gap phase replacement*, given to this process by Watt in a study of ecologically similar English beech forests (1947), can be applied to the Lake States forest as well (Bray, 1956). It is clear that the forests are instable, undergoing continual change. As Graham (1941) states it: "If by climax is meant those types of biota which are capable of reproducing themselves generation after generation on the same area, then the hemlock-hardwood forests do not, on the whole, represent a climax."

SUMMARY

Competition among organisms, the myriad changes within the forest ecosystem, and external disturbances bring about succession —the replacement of biota of an area in time by one of a different nature. Primary succession, the development and replacement of biota on unoccupied sites and proceeding without major disturbance, occurs on many substrates—open water, sand dunes, mining spoils, and bare rock, among others. Secondary succession follows a disturbance and disrupts rather than destroys an existing community. Succession may be described in a series of arbitrary stages proceeding from a position of relative instability to one of relative stability. Tolerant tree species typically characterize late-successional stages of relative stability. The rate of succession may be rapid on moist soils or very slow, seldom reaching the tree stage, on bare rock. The rate of change and the stage of succession reached (degree of stability achieved) are controlled by the prevailing site factors (regional and local climate, soil fertility and moisture), the degree of disturbance, competitive relationships of the species, and historical and chance factors. The forest is never stable, but remains a dynamic community in the later successional stages just as it was in the earlier stages.

SUGGESTED READINGS

BEARD, J. S. 1944. Climax vegetation in tropical America. *Ecology* 25:127–158.

CAIN, STANLEY A. 1939. The climax and its complexities. *Amer. Midl. Natl.* 21: 146–181.

CLEMENTS, FREDERIC E. 1949. *Dynamics of Vegetation: Selections from the Writings of Frederic E. Clements, Ph.D.* The H. W. Wilson Co., New York. 296 pp.

COOPER, W. S. 1913. The climax forest of Isle Royale, Lake Superior, and its development. *Bot. Gaz.* 55:1–44, 115–140, 189–235.

DAUBENMIRE, REXFORD. 1968. *Plant Communities.* (Plant succession, pp. 99–246.) Harper & Row, Inc., New York. 300 pp.

HEWETSON, C. E. 1956. A discussion on the "climax" concept in relation to the tropical rain and deciduous forest. *Emp. For. Rev.* 35:274–291.

LAWRENCE, DONALD B. 1958. Glaciers and vegetation in southeastern Alaska. *Amer. Sci.* 46:81–122.

OLSON, JERRY S. 1958. Rates of succession and soil changes on southern Lake Michigan sand dunes. *Bot. Gaz.* 119:125–170.

TANSLEY, A. G. 1935. The use and abuse of vegetational concepts and terms. *Ecology* 16:284–307.

WHITTAKER, R. H. 1953. A consideration of climax theory: the climax as a population and pattern. *Ecol. Monogr.* 23:41–78.

14

Disturbance Effects

Although primary plant successions are the most obvious manifestations of succession and consequently have attracted the most study by plant ecologists, it is with secondary successions that the silviculturist and forest ecologist are mostly concerned. Once established, the forest is seldom completely destroyed, and the areas of new soil or site being formed or created within a forested region are negligible compared to the areas of existing forest. Primary succession in forested regions is the exception, therefore, rather than the rule. Throughout any forest region, disturbances of one sort or another are constantly altering the course of forest succession, and initiating what is known as secondary succession.

Disturbances to the forest can be grouped into three classes; first, disturbances altering the structure of the forest; second, disturbances altering the species composition of the forest; and third, disturbances altering the long-term climate in which the forest grows. The first class includes fire, windthrow, logging, and land-clearing activities. The second involves the introduction of new plants or animals into the forest ecosystem or the elimination of plants or animals from that system. The third is concerned with climatic changes over a period of years as well as climatic extremes which affect the relative vigor and competitive ability of the species making up the forest.

FOREST DESTRUCTION

The most obvious disturbances to the existing forest are those which partially or completely destroy the forest structure by killing and overthrowing either the trees in the overstory or the trees and other plants in the understory. Prominent among the factors causing forest destruction and initiating secondary forest succession are: fire, windthrow, logging, and land clearing.

Fire

Fire is the dominant fact of forest history. The great majority of the forests of the world—excepting only the perpetually wet rain forest, such as that of southeastern Alaska, the coast of northwestern Europe, and the wettest belts of the tropics—have been burned over at more or less frequent intervals for many thousands of years. Even under present-day conditions, marked by a great awareness of forest fires in the United States at least, the separation of forest tracts by intervening tracts of farmland and settlement, and the crossing of the forest by many roads and trails, fire continues to be a major disturbing factor in much of the American forest. In the interior of Alaska (Lutz, 1956) and much of northern Canada, only the first rudimentary steps have been taken to curb the immense amount of annual burning.

The condition was quite different up to the present century. Primitive peoples throughout the world, and most civilized peoples as well, had until recently no compunction about burning the forest, and no desire or intent to put out existing fires, whether lit by man or lightning. In fact, throughout the world, fires have been set deliberately for thousands of years to clear the underbrush, improve grazing, drive game, without thought, or just for the hell of it. As more and more historical research is carried on into the ecological history of fire, the more it is realized that frequent burning has been the rule for the vast majority of the forests of the world as far back as we have any evidence. Fire has been a major force of natural selection resulting in many different, genetically controlled survival mechanisms and also inherent flammable properties that contribute to the perpetuation of fire-dependent communities (Mutch, 1970).

Within forest regions, fire has been primarily responsible for heathlands and moors of western Europe and the British Isles, for many of the savannas within the tropical forest belts, for upland meadows within the forests of the American mountains, and in general for the persistence of grassland areas on upland sites within forest regions. Around the world, the dominance of pine and oak forests of virtually all species and in virtually all regions is due predominantly to fire. So is the vast acreage of Douglas-fir in the Pacific Northwest and of eucalyptus in Australia. Even the vast areas of spruce in the boreal forest of North America and Eurasia are structured to a great extent by past fires (Bloomberg, 1950; Sirén, 1955). Closer to home, the present invasion of one-seed juniper into the grassland of northern Arizona is attributed chiefly to current practices of fire exclusion (Johnsen, 1962).

The foregoing statements are sweeping, cannot be proven because of the lack of evidence, and perhaps overstated. Nonetheless, they reflect the feeling of many silviculturists and forest ecologists who, wherever they have studied and worked, have come increasingly to realize the great importance of forest fires and secondary succession following forest fires in framing the local forest in its composition and structure (Cooper, 1961).

Out of the many examples that may be cited, a selection representing the most important North American temperate forest types together with one or two from other continents will serve to illustrate the great importance of secondary successions following forest fires.

Pine in New England and the Lake States. In the northeastern United States and southeastern Canada, the occurrence of the two- and three-needled pines (red pine, jack pine, and pitch pine) as well as of even-aged pure stands of white pine (but not of individual white pine in mixed forests) is largely controlled by the past occurrence of forest fires. In colonial days, many of the fires resulted from burning operations by white settlers in land-clearing operations, but the evidence is ample that fires were commonly set by Indians for many hundreds of years before the coming of the white man (Cline and Spurr, 1942; Day, 1953; Curtis, 1959). Lightning, because of the heavy precipitation commonly associated with summer thunderstorms, apparently has played only a minor role in causing fires in this region.

Ecological studies of a few relict old-growth pine stands have all shown that fire played an important part in their formation. In both northwestern Pennsylvania (Lutz, 1930b) and southwestern New Hampshire (Cline and Spurr, 1942), more or less pure even-aged stands of old-growth white pine have been shown to have originated from past forest fires, while nearby mixed types with occasional dominant white pine were relatively free from evidence of past burns. Stem and basal branch features can be used to determine whether old-growth pines originated in the open or under a partial forest canopy (Lutz and McComb, 1935). In northwestern Minnesota, the extensive even-aged stands of old-growth red pine clearly date from a series of forest fires, many of which antedate the advent of the white settler (Spurr, 1954). Each major age class of red pine owes its origin to a forest fire which can be dated through fire scars on occasional veterans which were not killed by the blazes.

Jack pine in the Lake States and Canada, and pitch pine on sand soils near the mid-Atlantic coast, are virtually completely fire-controlled. Jack pine, for instance, grows in nearly pure stands on dry sandy soils, forming a highly flammable vegetational type. At intervals of a few decades, the jack pine stands are burned during hot dry periods, with the fire characteristically crowning and killing all the vegetation above the surface of the earth. The next generation of trees arises from four sources: (1) in the case of jack pine, from seed stored in many years' accumulation of serotinous cones in the tree crown (Roe, 1963)—the cones being held closed by resin deposits which are melted at 122°F by the heat of the crown fire; (2) in the case of red pine, by seed from residual veteran seed trees with bark of sufficient thickness and clear bole of sufficient length to permit them to survive the fire without crowning out; (3) in the case of the hardwoods such as trembling and bigtooth aspen, red oak, and red maple, by sprouts arising either from roots or portions of the stem unkilled by the fire; and (4) in the case of pioneer hardwoods, by the dissemination of seed into the area from afar either by wind, as for aspens and paper birch, or by birds, as for the cherries. The composition of the postfire stand will depend upon the relative supply of seedlings by each of the above avenues.

Once a jack pine type has become established, however, it will persist over approximately the same tract of land as long as a fire occurs every few decades. If fire is excluded, however, the jack pine will begin to deteriorate and die out after 50 to 60 years, leaving the stand to associated longer-lived red pine; to white pines, which come in over a period of years and gradually infiltrate the overstory; and on mesic sites to tolerant species such as sugar maple, balsam fir, and black spruce, which come in slowly as understory plants and eventually form a late-successional stage.

Western Pines. The remarks made concerning the northeastern United States pines can be applied with but little modification to virtually all other pine species growing in the United States. In the interior of the western forest, lodgepole pine plays an analogous part to that taken by its close relative, jack pine, in the Northeast. It seeds in recent burns, largely from seed stored in serotinous cones of trees killed by the fire, to form dense, even-aged, postfire pioneer stands (Figure 14.1). Trembling aspen competes as a pioneer on the higher, cooler, and wetter sites, coming in as wind-disseminated seed in the northern Rocky Mountains and in western Canada but predominately as root suckers in the Great Basin and the central and southern Rocky Mountains of the United States. Given several hundreds of years free from forest fire, the lodgepole pine gradually will be replaced by tolerant Engelmann spruce and alpine fir, with white and black spruce also playing a part as late-successional species in Alberta, and Douglas-fir and other tolerant western conifers becoming prominent toward the Pacific Northwest. In subalpine and high foothills in Alberta, Horton (1956) estimates that from 225 to 375 years' exclusion from fire is required for succession to take place from pine to spruce and fir. On the drier southern slopes, the succession takes much longer, if indeed it ever takes place.

At lower elevations and in warmer, drier portions of the western forest of the United States, pure stands of ponderosa pine are commonly a product of a long and complex fire history (Figure 14.2; Cooper, 1960; see also Chapter 18). This is particularly true in the cooler and moister portions of the range of ponderosa pine where that species comes in as a pioneer following fire and is followed by more tolerant conifers such as Douglas-fir, incense cedar, and white fir. At the warmer and drier edge of the ponderosa pine range, it may be a late-successional, climax species (Chapter 15).

Southern Pines. Nowhere is the dependence of the pine forest upon recurring fires more evident than in the southern pine belt of the southeastern United States. Here, earlier travellers wrote

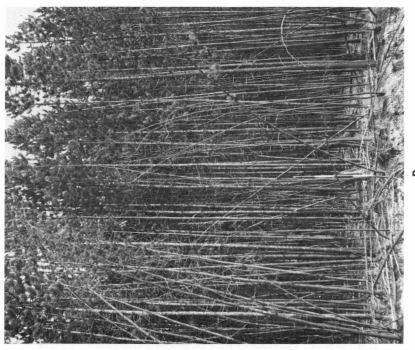

B

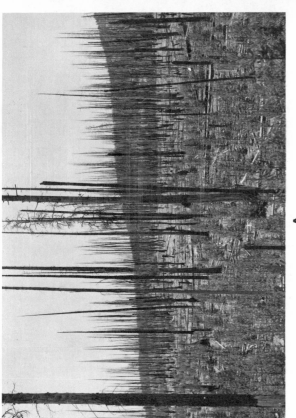

A

A—Lodgepole pine revegetates a large burn in central Oregon. Reseeding the area to grass after the burn delayed the establishment of pine.
B—Under ideal conditions of seedbed and seed supply, dense lodgepole
pine thickets develop following fire. This 65-year-old stand of about
25,000 stems per hectare in eastern Oregon averages only 8 meters in
height and 5 centimeters in diameter at breast height

Fig. 14.1. Lodgepole pine regeneration following fire in Oregon. (U. S. Forest Service photos.)

A light surface fire burns grass and litter of this stand in central Idaho.

Fires in pre-settlement times maintained open, grassy, parklike stands of ponderosa pine such as this one in western Montana.

Fig. 14.2. Fire and ponderosa pine. (U. S. Forest Service photos.)

of the open character of the "piney woods" due to Indian burning. Ever since settlements by whites, local farmers have periodically burned the woods to keep down the "rough" and bring about fresh postfire revegetation suitable for grazing by domestic stock. After many years of futile attempts at complete fire exclusion by foresters, the practice of "prescribed" or "controlled" burning by foresters has become well accepted in recent decades to reduce the hazard of a crown fire and to maintain the pine type without reversion to the hardwoods which otherwise would replace it through natural succession.

Of the four most common southern pines, longleaf pine is most clearly dependent upon recurring fires for its perpetuation (Chapman, 1932). Occurring primarily on seasonally dry sites, longleaf pine stands must be burned in the grass stage to control the brown spot disease (*Septoria acicola*) and repeatedly after a forest canopy is formed to prevent the establishment of understory hardwoods which invade the site and will gradually replace the pine in the absence of fire. Furthermore, the longleaf pine regenerates itself best in full light on mineral seedbeds created by forest fires which destroy all but scattered longleaf seed trees, the species being one of the most fire-resistant of all forest trees (Figure 14.3).

The other common southern pines—loblolly pine, slash pine, and shortleaf pine—as well as sand pine, Virginia pine, pitch pine, and other species of more or less local occurrence—all are pioneer species that become established after destructive forest fires and give way to tolerant hardwood mixtures in the long-continued absence of forest fires (Little and Moore, 1949; Wahlenberg, 1949; Campbell, 1955). The clearly established dependence of these species upon fire has given rise to extensive research and practical use of fire as a silvicultural tool or of alternative chemical and mechanical treatments that likewise will hold the natural succession in the pioneer pine stage.

Douglas-Fir in the Pacific Northwest. In the Douglas-fir region of northern California, Oregon, Washington, and southern British Columbia, the characteristic summer drought results in highly flammable conditions during the hottest period of the year with the result that extensive forest fires have not only been characteristic of the present century of forest management but also, and to a much greater extent, of the presettlement forest. On the west side of the Cascades and over much of the Coastal Range, Douglas-fir is the

Fig. 14.3. An excellent stand of natural longleaf pine seedlings in the Coastal Plain of South Carolina following a prescribed burn to prepare the seedbed. (U. S. Forest Service photo.)

pioneer species on burns, provided that adjacent Douglas-fir stands survive undamaged to furnish a source of seed. The commercially valuable pure Douglas-fir type, therefore, represents the first stage of a postfire secondary succession. More tolerant conifers such as western hemlock, Sitka spruce, and western red cedar invade the Douglas-fir type to form an understory and eventually achieve dominance after four or five hundred years with the decadence and death of the dominant Douglas-fir (Figure 14.4).

Eastern United States Hardwood Forest. Although the hardwood forests are less combustible than conifer forests, fire-controlled secondary successions seem to have been important factors in these as well. In the mixed hardwood forest complex of the eastern United States, many oak types on dry sites owe their existence to a past history of forest fires, frequently set by Indians for driving game (Cottam, 1949; Curtis, 1959; Brown, 1960). Throughout much of

Fig. 14.4. The dominant but overmature Douglas-fir (left) in this Western Washington stand in the absence of fire will eventually be replaced by more tolerant firs and western hemlocks of the understory. (U. S. Forest Service photo.)

the vast oak region, total exclusion of fire (together with grazing as well) usually results in the establishment of a tolerant hardwood understory characterized by beech, sugar maple, and basswood, with other species being important in addition, particularly in the southern oak types. It seems clear that the oak, under present climatic conditions, is a pioneer type following fire and maintained by recurrent disturbances of diverse sorts; while beech-maple represents the late-successional stage reached after long exclusion of such disturbances. This relationship, however, has undoubtedly been different in many respects in prior periods characterized by other climatic conditions.

Eucalyptus in Australia and Tasmania.   The tall-timber *Eucalyptus* species of the mountains of southeastern Australia occupy an ecological position very similar to that of Douglas-fir in the Pacific Northwest of the United States, in that they form tall, dense stands of high quality following fire under climatic conditions where more tolerant species would succeed in the forest succession if disturbance could be avoided. The eucalyptus succession is exemplified in a study by Gilbert (1959) of forest succession in the *Eucalyptus regnans* forest of western Tasmania. This species, the giant mountain ash (Victoria) or swamp gum (Tasmania) that reaches heights well in excess of 100 meters, forms dense stands following the burning of older eucalyptus forest—which is highly flammable during summer hot spells because of the flaky bark and the leaf oils characteristic of the genus. Where fire has been excluded for many years because of swamps, cliffs, or other natural barriers to its spread, however, an understory develops in which *Nothofagus* (antarctic beech), *Atherosperma*, and the *Dicksonia* tree fern are common components. Under rare circumstances where fire has been excluded for a century or two, the relatively short-lived eucalyptus tends to disappear from the forest and a late-successional, temperate Southern Hemisphere rain forest evolves through natural succession of the understory trees to dominance. Although the acreage of this rain forest in southeastern Australia is small because of the commonness and frequency of fires, it is clear that the predominant eucalyptus forest is but a pioneer community resulting from and perpetuated by frequent forest fires which prevent succession to the rain forest type.

Windthrow

Scattered windthrow of large, overmature trees is a prime cause of mortality in the old-growth forest and creates holes in the main canopy into which advance growth from the understory or newly germinated seedlings may develop. Such holes are frequently enlarged year after year by the attrition of surrounding trees under the weight of ice and snow and the pressure of high winds.

Occasional severe storms, particularly hurricanes and tornados, may destroy the timber on hundreds or thousands of acres, initiating secondary forest succession on a large scale. It is with such extensive windthrow that the present section is concerned.

The evidence of windthrow is preserved for many years in the forest by such signs as these: (1) hollows marking the holes made by uprooted trees; (2) ridges extending away from these hollows marking the remains of the fallen bole; (3) the frequent appearance of a row of younger trees along this ridge, particularly of species such as hemlock (both eastern and western) that characteristically seed in on rotten wood; (4) overturned soil strata in the mound created by the upturned roots at the edge of the hollow; and (5) evidence of release from suppression in the annual rings of the oldest adjacent trees, particularly of trees in the understory at the time of the storm which were released by the windthrow. The sharp release characteristic of hemlock in the eastern part of its range can easily be discerned in increment cores and used to date the time of windthrow. The dating of past windthrow by these techniques is a fascinating detective game and yields firm evidence of the prevalence of windthrow in the American forest for the past few centuries.

The great 1938 hurricane in New England created an awareness of the past occurrences of severe windstorms in this region at intervals ranging from a few to more than a hundred years. Other storms in the same region, including major hurricanes in 1635 and 1815, apparently inflicted similar damage to the forest. The study of natural regeneration following the 1938 hurricane provides an example of the effects of windthrow in initiating secondary forest succession (Spurr, 1956a).

In contrast to fire, which destroys the understory to a greater extent than the main forest canopy, windthrow damage is chiefly confined to the overstory. In forests where a tolerant understory is developing under a pioneer stage of succession, the effect of windthrow may merely be to end the pioneer stage and release the understory to form a new canopy. Thus in an old-growth white pine stand in southwestern New Hampshire blown down by the 1938 hurricane, the understory hemlock, beech, and red maple were simply released to form a low stand—but one of substantial age considering the great number of years these trees had existed in the understory prior to release. Together with the released hemlock and beech in the new stand, however, were mixed paper birch, yellow birch, and black cherry, all of which had seeded in on disturbed mineral soil upturned by the tearing out of the roots of the windthrown trees.

Although the more tolerant and vigorous understory trees may respond to release from windthrow, others will not have the crown development, the sun-foliage in the crowns, or the root development to so respond and will die, to be replaced by seedling sprouts from the living rootstock of the same dead stem, or by seedlings which invade the windthrown site, primarily on the exposed mounds of mineral soil upturned by the roots of the windthrown trees. In many cases, therefore, the secondary succession following windthrow will consist of a mixture of tolerant species from the released understory together with pioneers that have invaded the site.

Logging

Logging is similar to windthrow in that the cutting of commercially valuable trees tends to remove the overstory and release the understory. Many understory hardwoods that are cut in brushing or swamping operations connected with logging will resprout to form vigorous and fast-growing stems competing for overstory space in the developing new stand.

As a general rule, the intensity and pattern of the cut will affect the competitive ability of the new crop. Light partial cuts will favor tolerant species, particularly those already established in the understory, and thus will tend to push forest succession forward rather than initiate an earlier stage in the process (Figure 14.5). Moderately heavy partial cuts will favor midtolerant species as will the cutting of small groups of trees to create holes or gaps in the forest of approximately the same size that would be made by the death of an overmature dominant tree. Clearcutting, or the cutting of large holes in the forest with a diameter of at least twice the height of the stand, will favor the invasion of pioneer species, particularly if mineral soil is exposed by the logging operation. For these reasons, the silviculturist, by regulating the intensity, nature, and pattern of logging, can greatly influence subsequent forest composition and the rate of succession.

The effect of partial- versus clearcutting on forest succession is well illustrated by experience in the Douglas-fir region of the west side of the Cascades in Washington and Oregon. Much of the cutting in old-growth stands occurs in more or less even-aged stands composed predominantly of Douglas-fir and dating from past forest fires 150 to 500 years ago. Clearcutting in such stands at the time of, or immediately after, a seed year results in the reestablishment of even-aged Douglas-fir. Patches of Douglas-fir ranging from 1 to 30 or 40 acres in size will normally come back to Douglas-fir within a few years, with seed blowing in from surrounding uncut timber. On the lower and wetter sites in the coast range, red alder

Fig. 14.5. Partial cutting in this eastern white pine stand in Maine has favored advance regeneration of tolerant red spruce. (U. S. Forest Service photo.)

comes in prolifically as a pioneer species on clearcut sites. On any site, the new forest is composed of pioneer species which range from intolerant to midtolerant in their ability to compete in the understory in that region.

In contrast, partial cuttings in similar old growth Douglas-fir forests result in a quite different forest structure and composition (Isaac, 1956). Following cutting of from 20 to 50 percent of the gross volume in a variety of Douglas-fir types, mortality by windfall in the overstory has proven high in the first five years after felling, and often in the second five-year period. Felling and skidding also caused considerable damage to the residual stand. As the cutting was concentrated in the Douglas-fir, and since the residual Douglas-fir tended to be taller and slimmer than associated conifers of other species, the net result was to decrease the amount of Douglas-fir in the residual overstory and to increase the percentage of other species. In the openings created by the logging, few Douglas-fir seedlings appeared, but seedlings of the more tolerant species (western hemlock, grand fir, Pacific silver fir, and western red cedar) were well established in many stands. The end product of partial cutting in this type, then, is a deteriorating partial overstory with a vigorous understory composed of conifers more tolerant and less valuable commercially than the desired Douglas-fir.

Another effect of logging on forest succession results from the differential removal of one species and the leaving of another, thus changing the composition of the forest. The effect of logging a favored species on the composition of the forest is exemplified in the mixed-wood forests of Maine, where logging has been more or less continuous for a hundred or more years. Early logging was concentrated primarily on large white pines suitable for masts for wooden sailing ships, house construction, and floating down rivers from forest to the mill. Since the prime white pine trees grew as scattered old-growth dominants in a mixed conifer-hardwood forest, their removal by logging virtually removed the species from subsequent forest succession on those sites. Only following postlogging fires or on sandy and rocky sites did much white pine persist in the northern Maine forest.

The next stage of logging followed the building of sulphite and ground wood pulp mills and the large-scale cutting of red spruce to supply them. Since the red spruce grew in association with tolerant balsam fir, sugar maple, and beech, the logging of the spruce created a mixed wood of these species, a forest in which the proportion of spruce was drastically reduced. As the supply of red spruce became more limited and that of balsam fir increased, the latter species became more and more utilized in pulping operations. In softwood types, partial cuts for red spruce became transformed into more or less clearcuts in which both the spruce and balsam fir were taken. The heavy cutting has resulted in the swamping out of many of the wetter flats and the invasion of pioneers such as aspen and paper birch on many of the drier sites. In mixed-wood types, the removal of both red spruce and balsam fir has resulted in turning the site over to residual tolerant hardwoods. These in turn have formed extensive tracts of culled old growth which have been devastated in time by dieback of the yellow birch, beech, and sugar maple due to a combination of insects and disease attack, climatic conditions, and the low vigor of the residual old-growth trees. Thus successive waves of logging, each concentrating upon different species, have greatly modified the composition of the forests of central and northern Maine since the early part of the nineteenth century.

Logging, then, may exercise profound effects on forest composition and succession. Depending upon the intensity and pattern of the cut, and upon the species removed in mixed forests, the resulting forest community may be substantially altered from its previous structure and composition.

Land Clearing

Forested regions are moist regions and therefore eminently suitable for the raising of agricultural crops. Since the great majority of the world's population lives in forest regions, it is inevitable that much of the world's forest has been cut and the land cleared for agriculture. In the tropics, the use of forest land for agriculture is often transitory, with worn-out fields being allowed to revert to forest again after a few years of cropping. Even in the Temperate Zone, much land used for farming in the past has been found unsuitable for continued cropping, or has been supplanted by bringing better lands into production, with the result that it has been planted to forest or allowed to revert naturally to forest. In recent years, the trend of farm land abandonment has been intensified by the concentration of crop production on the best farm lands through the use of improved strains of plants, and better fertilization and cropping techniques.

Secondary forest succession following land abandonment, therefore, is an important process, taking place over many hundreds of thousands of acres in well-settled forest areas. The old-field succession in the eastern United States has been studied in particular detail, while the old-field succession in the tropical rain forest is of great long-term importance in the economy of tropical countries.

Old-Field Succession in the Eastern United States

Agricultural use of land was at its most extensive development in the New England states about 1815 to 1830, and began to decline with the opening of the West and its ready access via the Erie Canal (1815) and the trans-Appalachian railroads. In the Atlantic-facing Piedmont of the southeastern states, agricultural use of lands reached its peak at the beginning of the Civil War. Throughout the entire eastern seaboard, most upland sites were cleared and were farmed until the 1815–1860 period, when the industrialization of the Northeast, coupled with the opening of the farmlands of the

Midwest, initiated a long decline in agriculture acreage, a decline that is still in existence.

Secondary succession of forest on the abandoned upland fields and pastures has thus involved great acreages, and has been instrumental in reforesting much of the eastern landscape. Since Thoreau's essay on the topic in 1860, many ecological studies have described the major stages of forest succession on these sites.

In most cases, fields were abandoned as grass-bearing hayfields or pastures which had ceased to yield sufficient hay to justify annual mowing. In such cases, conifers form the initial old-field tree invaders. The old-field conifer in northern New England is red spruce, with white pine coming in on these sites in central New England and New York State, red cedar in southern New England and the mid-Atlantic states, Virginia pine in the upper South, and loblolly pine and shortleaf pine throughout most of the rest of the South. Only when fields have been abandoned as fallow cultivated croplands do hardwoods—such as gray birch in the Northeast and sweet gum in the Southeast—predominate in the pioneer stage of the secondary forest succession.

The greater ability of conifers to invade and establish themselves on old grasslands seems to be due to several factors, among them being: (1) the relatively heavy wind-disseminated seed, which can work down through the sod to make contact with the soil; (2) the presence of enough stored food in the seed to develop a seedling sufficiently large to compete with the grass; (3) the drought resistance of conifer seedlings, which permits them to survive summer droughts occasioned by root competition with grass; and (4) the probable presence of inhibiting substances associated with the grasses which retard the growth of invading hardwoods. Bormann (1953) studied this problem with particular reference to the relative ability of loblolly pine and sweet gum to colonize old fields in the Piedmont of North Carolina and found that the pine is not only better fitted for survival in the various manners outlined above, but also that its seed reaches old-field sites in far greater numbers due to the prevalence of adjacent seed sources.

The conifer forest is not usually pure but is mixed with varying proportions of hardwood pioneers which become established mostly on small bare patches, brush patches, or other non-grassy patches in the old field. In the North, gray and paper birch, pin and black cherry, and bigtooth and trembling aspen are the principal hardwood pioneers although some white ash, red oak, and other mid-tolerants will come in with the first wave of tree invaders. In the South, sweet gum, red maple, and many other hardwoods come in under these conditions.

Once the conifer forest is well established, it is itself invaded with midtolerant hardwoods which form a more or less abundant understory by the time the overstory is 20 to 40 years of age. In central New England, white ash, red oak, sugar maple, red maple, and black birch are the most common components; while in the Piedmont of North Carolina, sweet gum, black gum, dogwood, and sourwood are commonly present.

The overstory conifers seldom reproduce themselves under their own canopy except in the most open stands on the driest sites. As the years pass, some of these understory plants persist, others die back only to sprout again from the persisting root system, while others die back completely to be replaced in time with seedlings of more tolerant species such as hemlock, sugar maple, beech, and basswood.

The even-aged, old-field conifer stands are shorter-lived than mixed stands in which the same species is dominant because of over-growing, which results in time in tall, slender trees and in subsequent wind friction that whips the crowns back and forth past one another, abrading and reducing the crowns. In any event, the conifers tend to become overmature on these sites and in these stand structures before a century is up (in 50 to 60 years for red cedar to 70 to 80 years for loblolly pine and a little older for white pine). By the end of the second century, in the absence of any further disturbance, replacement by a tolerant community, consisting mostly of hardwoods, is complete. The late-successional stage is usually a beech–sugar maple–basswood type in northern New England, a hemlock–red oak–red maple type in central New England and New York, and an oak-hickory complex to the south. In the deep South, red gum, magnolias, and a great variety of tolerant hardwoods constitute the late-successional community.

The old-field white pine succession in central New England has produced much white pine of great commercial importance. It has been detailed in many studies at the Harvard Forest (Spurr, 1956b) and is pictorially depicted in the Harvard Forest models, which present in three-dimensional dioramas the history of land use in central Massachusetts (Figures 14.6–14.11).

Fig. 14.6.   The Harvard Forest models.   A reconstruction of the mixed pre-colonial forest, with hemlock, tolerant hardwoods, and occasional white pine. (Model 1, courtesy of Harvard Forest, Harvard University.)

Fig. 14.7.   The same view in central Massachusetts in 1740 shortly after settlement.   (Model 2, courtesy of Harvard Forest, Harvard University.)

Fig. 14.8. The same view at height of farming development, 1830. (Model 3, courtesy of Harvard Forest, Harvard University.)

Fig. 14.9. Farm abandonment and the seeding in of old-field white pine, 1850. (Model 4, courtesy of Harvard Forest, Harvard University.)

Fig. 14.10.   Harvesting the old-field pine in 1909 which seeded in after farm abandonment in the same view. (Model 5, courtesy of Harvard Forest, Harvard University.)

Fig. 14.11.   The young stand matures into the second-growth hardwoods characteristic of central New England of 1930. (Model 7, courtesy of Harvard Forest, Harvard University.)

The old-field red cedar succession has been studied by Lutz (1928) in Connecticut and Bard (1952) in New Jersey. The commercially important loblolly pine old-field succession has been the subject of many studies (Billings, 1938; McQuilken, 1940; Oosting, 1942; Barrett and Downs, 1943), particularly in the Piedmont of North Carolina. Successional trends in small mammals and birds in the hardwood old-field succession in southern Michigan is reported upon by Beckwith (1954).

Many of the old fields have been afforested by man rather than being allowed to seed in naturally. The resulting plantations represent the first stage of secondary succession just as do the natural stands and are similar in their ecological structure and subsequent development. The most successful planted species are the pines, which occur naturally as old-field species. In the eastern United States, however, the ranges of red pine in the north and of slash pine in the south have been greatly extended by extensive use as old-field planting species.

Abandoned Farmland Succession in the Tropical Rain Forest

Throughout the Tropics, the pattern of agriculture in the rain forest zones is one of shifting agriculture. Many names and many different tree species are involved, but the general story is much the same (Richards, 1952). The natives fell the trees (except for an occasional large tree here and there), burn the brush, and plant their crops. One or more crops (such as hill rice, cassava, maize, yams, or bananas) may be grown before leaching of the humus and compaction of the upper soil horizon of the oxisols reduce soil fertility and structure to the point where further cultivation is useless. Fertilizers other than wood ash from the burned forest are not used. In the higher rainfall areas it may take only six months to leach a cleared forest soil to an unproductive state.

With abandonment, a short-lived herb stage of the secondary succession is usually quickly followed by a dense stand of fast-growing, intolerant trees which form an even-aged stand composed of very few species as compared to the primary tropical rain forest. Balsa and various cecropias are characteristic of this pioneer forest community in tropical America, and various *Musanga* spp. commonly occur in tropical Africa. The trees in this stage are fast-growing, frequently have low-density wood, and commonly occur with many lianas, forming a tangled forest which is much lower, simpler in structure, and evener in crown canopy than the original forest.

The "low bush" or "fallow" may be replaced rapidly by many species of a transitional stage, followed by slow invasion of shade tolerant species that eventually form the primary rain forest. The last successional phase involves a long period of time, but the time scale is but little known. Richards (1952) has summarized the ecological investigations to date on secondary forest successions in the tropical rain forest.

The secondary succession following land clearing in the tropics is very similar, in the principal stages and the ecological characteristics of the trees composing each, to the forest succession following land clearing in the eastern United States. The chief difference is that this succession in the Temperate Zone is characterized by a coniferous pioneer stage, while that in the tropical rain forest is of necessity composed entirely of angiosperms.

Quantitative-Experimental Studies of Succession in the Rain Forest

Few quantitative studies of succession have utilized an experimental approach whereby a community of known composition is cleared and the progress of succession is followed over a period of years. Such a study by a team of English and Australian workers (Williams *et al.*, 1969) illustrates the experimental approach and the use of numerical methods of analysis. In a cleared portion of a moist, subtropical rain forest of eastern Australia, successional changes were studied over a 7-year period. A complete enumeration of all seedlings was made at 12 successive times; a total of 118 species were recorded. Using various numerical methods, they were able to distinguish important microsite differences in succession due to associated differences of litter cover, soil, and light. Just as major soil differences may influence the nature of late-successional vegetation within a climatic region (edaphic climax), so microsite differences influence the rate and course of succession in local areas. These effects contribute to a lack of orderliness on the local scale. Although they noted chance effects of density and availability of seeds and in meteorological conditions for their germination, overall they found that the processes they studied did not support the view that vegetation patterns are essentially due to chance.

Moreover, a major switch from a "temporal" organization to a "spatial" organization of the vegetation was revealed. During the first 6 sampling periods (up to 16 months after the area was cleared) the area behaved as a single unit. All 10 sample plots and the overall area exhibited an identical pattern of change. This temporal or pioneer stage was characterized by two successive influxes of annuals and short-lived perennials of wide ecological amplitude. The second stage was characterized by the persistence of two pioneer shrubs under which shade-tolerant plants of the mature forest will regenerate. At this stage the major differences between sites, plots 1 to 7 versus 8 to 10, asserted themselves, hence the change to a spatial organization. Plots 8 to 10 were nearly scraped clear of litter, were warmer, drier, and better lighted, and experienced more soil compaction, than plots 1 to 7. The different microsite of plots 8 to 10 favors invasion by a thicket-forming species, *Lantana*, and not the seed of the rain-forest species. An examination of the area 4 years after the last enumeration showed a relatively homogeneous stand of immature rain-forest species on sites 1 to 7 and on sites 8 to 10 a thicket of *Lantana* that had effectively blocked the normal succession.

Besides demonstrating the usefulness of numerical methods to detect early in succession temporal and spatial differences that were not qualitatively observable by eye, the problem of the introduced pest *Lantana* was clarified. In rain forests cleared for regeneration, the pioneer stage is critical in *Lantana*-sensitive areas. Since *Lantana* will not survive in shade, it is important to form a temporary canopy by artificially establishing other light-demanding species or even shade-tolerant species in the pioneer stage.

COMPOSITION CHANGES

Although secondary successions are considered to originate primarily from disturbances such as the factors of fire, windthrow, logging, and land clearing considered in the previous sections, the addition or subtraction of a species, whether plant or animal, will inevitably change the succession of the forest. Since these changes in the flora or fauna of the forest may result in considerable disturbance to the existing community, they may well be considered as initiating secondary successions in a very real sense.

Elimination of Species

When a species is eliminated or greatly reduced in abundance, its place in the ecosystem must be taken by other species. An outstanding example of this is the virtual elimination of the chestnut in the eastern hardwood forest by the blight caused by *Endothia parasitica*. This disease, introduced from Asia about 1904, killed most of the mature chestnut in New England within 20 years, and had completed its work in the southern end of the commercial range of the species in the southern Appalachians by the 1940's. Seldom if ever before in historical times has a major forest tree been so completely eradicated. Although the chestnut still sprouts profusely from root systems after a half-century, no trees survive long enough to reach the main canopy of a mature forest stand.

Succession following the elimination of the chestnut has resulted in the simple replacement of that species by its former associates (Korstian and Stickel, 1927; Keever, 1953; Woods, 1953; Nelson, 1955; Wood and Shanks, 1957). Chief among the succeeding trees in the southern Appalachians are the oaks (especially chestnut oak and red oak), along with various hickories and, on the better sites, yellow-poplar. Thus, the eradication of the chestnut in this region has resulted in the replacement of the former oak-chestnut type with an oak-hickory type. Similar changes, but involving some different species, previously occurred in the middle Atlantic states and southern New England.

More recently the Dutch elm disease, caused by the fungus *Ceratocystis ulmi* (introduced into Ohio from Europe about 1930), has in about 40 years, together with another disease, phloem necrosis, virtually eliminated mature American elm trees from mesic and lowland forests of the eastern United States. Studies of three Illinois woodlands (Boggess, 1964; Boggess and Bailey, 1964; Boggess and Geis, 1966) indicate that sugar maple is the species most likely to increase in dominance due to elm mortality, except where soils are too poorly drained. For example, in the Brownfield Woods, a 60-acre woodland remnant of a prairie grove in east-central Illinois, the most conspicuous change in the overstory of the forest from 1925 to 1960 was the 60-percent increase in basal area of sugar maple and the corresponding 70 percent decrease of elm (Boggess and Bailey, 1964). The maple understory was quite dense compared to trees of other species, indicating a continued or increased dominance of sugar maple. In addition to sugar maple, hackberry and ashes, particularly white ash, also show gains in Illinois woodlands, and their seedlings are abundant in areas of heavy elm mortality.

In the spruce-fir forest of eastern Canada and adjacent northeastern United States, periodic epidemics of the endemic spruce budworm have resulted in the killing of overmature and mature balsam fir over large areas together with lesser amounts of killing of the black and white spruces. The budworm apparently has played a major role in the mixed softwood forests in holding down the proportion of the very tolerant balsam fir as compared to that of the somewhat less tolerant spruces.

In the animal portion of the forest ecosystem, the virtual elimination of many predators—particularly the wolf, bear, cougar, and lynx—from much of the American forest has played a role in increasing the number of deer, rabbits, and other herbivores, with consequent effects upon the natural vegetation resulting from the greater browsing of the understory, including tree regeneration.

Addition of Species

The species occupying a given site are not necessarily those best adapted to compete and grow on that site, but merely the best of those that have access to that site at the time of its availability. Invasion of the site by better competitors often results in substantial changes in forest succession. It makes no difference whether this invasion occurs as a result of natural immigration or through introduction by man. The result ecologically is the same.

The chestnut blight fungus already cited in the previous section is an example of an accidental introduction that has greatly modified the forest. Other organisms may be trees, other higher plants, fungi, bacteria, and animals of all levels.

Of forest trees, many have become naturalized in new geographical areas in historical times to become a part of existing plant communities so as to modify successional trends. Beech has moved northward through England in the last two thousand years in response to postglacial revegetational trends. American beech may still be expanding northward and westward in the Lake States similarly. Coconut and *Casuarina* spp. are representative of many littoral species that have been widely disseminated throughout the Tropics, partly through human and partly through other forms of transport.

Important deliberate forest-tree introductions include American Douglas-fir, white pine, red oak, and black locust in Europe; Scots pine, Norway spruce, and European larch in the northeastern United States; and Monterey pine, patula pine, and slash pine in temperate zones of the Southern Hemisphere. These and many others have become vigorous and dominant species in the local flora and must be considered as natural parts of the present and future plant communities and succession.

Introductions to New Zealand.   A spectacular example of the rapid successional changes in both the flora and fauna of a region that can occur when better-adapted plants and animals are introduced is provided by the natural history of New Zealand. In this south temperate land, only Southern Hemisphere conifers (primarily podocarps) and hardwoods (primarily *Nothofagus* spp.) had access to the land prior to the coming of the Maoris a thousand years or so ago and of the white men in the past century or two. Birds— many of them without functional wings—constituted virtually all the higher animal life. The climate, however, is temperate, moist, and mild, ideal for many Northern Hemisphere plants and animals. Following extensive introduction by man in the last hundred years, the introduced flora and fauna are rapidly and effectively replacing their native counterparts (Figures 14.12, 14.13). Monterey pine, lodgepole pine, and Douglas-fir among the trees, gorse, blue grass, and ragwort among the smaller plants, and the European red deer, sheep, Australian possum, and Himalayan thar among animals are but a few examples of vigorous organisms better suited to the site than those isolated there by the accidents of geological history. The forest ecosystems and the successional trends within them will inevitably be more and more influenced by these new and vigorous plants and animals.

Increased Animal Use.   It is not necessary that a species be either added or eliminated in order to greatly affect forest succession. Change in the abundance of a species may have a considerable effect in itself. This fact is illustrated by the great changes brought about by the increase in number of herbivores in the forest through reduction of predators, burning of the woods to increase browse, and other activities of man. The herbivores may be domestic or wild—ecologically there is little difference in the end result.

Among domestic stock, goats are by far the most destructive of forest regeneration, followed by pigs, sheep, and cattle, in approximately that order. Long-continued overgrazing by any of these will result in the elimination of palatable species from the ground up to the browse line, compaction of the forest soil, and eventual conversion of the forest to an open scrub of unpalatable species or to grassland. This has been the history of much of the forest in the Mediterranean regions of Europe and Africa, virtually all of Asia Minor and the countries to its east, and of large areas in the U.S.S.R., China, India, and elsewhere. Jarosenko (1956) has detailed this history for Transcaucasia in a Russian book. Much of the scrub and grassland in the drier and warmer forest regions of the world owes its origin to the long-continued overgrazing by goats, sheep, and cattle. Many of these sites could support high forest if this were controlled.

This condition is not unique to the Old World, but is equally important in the New, particularly in Latin America. In the United States, the open character of much of the ponderosa pine forest, to cite but one example, and the holding of the succession at the pine stage instead of allowing it to move forward to the tolerant conifer stage, are attributable to heavy grazing by sheep, cattle, deer, and elk, coupled with periodic burning in the past (Arnold, 1950). In Mountain Meadows Valley, Utah (Cottan and Stewart, 1940), heavy grazing by cattle and sheep since 1864 has resulted not only in heavy erosion, but also in the replacement of grasses, rushes, and sedges by sagebrush, rabbitbrush, and juniper. With protection from heavy grazing, however, the range grasses can still successfully compete on the site.

In the eastern hardwood forests, deer may by themselves retard the forest succession to as great an extent as the combination of domestic and wild animals in the ponderosa pine. Overpopulation resulting from elimination of predators and restricted and inadequate hunting has resulted in the development of parklike forests virtually free from undergrowth in parts of the Appalachians, the Lake States, and in western Europe. Graham, Harrison, and Westell (1963) have detailed the effect of large deer populations in preventing regeneration in the aspen forests of lower Michigan, and the necessity of managing the deer herd concurrently with silvi-

Fig. 14.12. The original old-growth forest of New Zealand dominated by the podocarp *Rimu*, with characteristic understory of hardwoods and tree ferns. Under impact of logging and grazing, this forest is being replaced by North American conifers, both planted and naturally seeded. (New Zealand Forest Service photo by J. H. Johns, A.R.P.S.)

cultural treatment if yields both from the forest products and from the deer herd are to be maximized. The establishment of a tolerant understory is prevented, natural succession cannot proceed, and an open grassy woodland inevitably develops if the deer population is not substantially reduced for at least a period of years long enough to permit regeneration to grow up past the browse line (Habeck, 1960).

It is not only the larger herbivores that hold back forest succession; smaller mammals may play an equally important role. Squirrels in the eastern oak forest, deer mice in the Douglas-fir and sierra

Fig. 14.13. *Pinus radiata* (Monterey pine) forest in New Zealand, typical of the developing present-day forest there. These 47-year-old trees form a taller and higher-volume forest than the old-growth *Rimu*, several hundred years of age. (New Zealand Forest Service photo by J. H. Johns, A.R.P.S.)

forests, pocket gophers in the California red fir forests (Tevis, 1956), and many others may prevent the establishment of tolerant understory trees simply by consuming virtually all the available seed or by girdling the succulent seedlings that do manage to germinate.

CLIMATIC CHANGE

A third source of disturbance initiating secondary succession in the forest is climatic change. The change may be short and extreme such as a severe drought or cold spell that kills part of the existing forest, thus initiating a secondary succession with a different complement of potential competitors for space than existed previously; or it may be a long-term climatic change of lesser intensity, but one which changes the relative competitive ability of the competing species. The first type is obvious and well understood. The second is being increasingly realized as playing an important role in changing forest succession.

Evidence for long-term climatic change is presented in a later chapter, where its effect upon the distribution and composition of the forest is discussed in some detail. It would be inappropriate, therefore, to anticipate that discussion here without providing first the necessary background of fact and understanding. Suffice it to state that there is ample evidence that the climate of today is substantially different in many parts of the world from that of a hundred and fifty years ago, when many existing forest stands were formed. It follows that forest succession on the same site may have been quite different under differing climates from what it is now. Many examples can be cited. In the Lake States, for example, tree species near the southern edge of their natural range such as white pine, trembling aspen, and black spruce are much poorer competitors in the present warmer climate of the region, and thus form a substantially smaller proportion of newly forming forest communities. Islands of the more northern white spruce and balsam fir in the maple-basswood forest of northwestern Minnesota have been declining and dying out in recent years. In Wisconsin, the decrease of beech abundance near its western border and the consequent increase of sugar maple (Ward, 1956) may well be attributable to the warmer present-day climate of the area. Similarly, changes in water levels in swamps resulting from recent increased precipitation result in slower growth and general deterioration of tamarack on these sites in the same region (Isaak et al., 1959).

The effects of climatic changes upon forest succession are usually not clearly self-evident and are frequently confounded with other factors. For instance, in the ponderosa pine forests of the Southwest, it is difficult to separate out the relative effects of climatic changes, overgrazing, and past burning—all three are and have been important in determining the secondary forest succession. Nevertheless, major and continued climatic change is by now a well-established fact and must constantly be kept in mind in any study of forest succession. The Clementsian assumption of a long-continued stable climate simply does not hold for much of the forested regions of the world.

SUMMARY

Disturbance is a universal feature of forests around the world. Secondary succession is initiated and its rate variously modified by fire, windthrow, land clearing, grazing, logging, and climatic changes. Fire, from natural and human causes, has been the dominant fact in forest history. The most destructive fires have produced some of the most magnificent forests in the world. Pioneer species are primarily dependent on fire for their perpetuation; protection from fire invariably results in an increase of more tolerant species. Fire may be used as a tool to regenerate species that are economically important or aesthetically desirable. Windthrow and logging, unlike fire, favor the more tolerant species present in the understory. By controlling the intensity of cutting, the species composition of the next generation may be regulated. Land clearing and grazing in modern times are probably more important than fire in initiating, disrupting, and retarding succession. Major compositional changes may occur when new species are introduced into the ecosystem or when disease or insects eliminate species. Short- and long-term climatic changes may alter the relative competitive ability of associated species and hence also influence succession.

SUGGESTED READINGS

Auclair, Allan N., and Grant Cottam. 1971. Dynamics of black cherry (*Prunus serotina* Erhr.) in southern Wisconsin oak forests. *Ecol. Monogr.* 41:153–177.

Cooper, Charles F. 1960. Changes in vegetation, structure, and growth of southwestern pine forests since white settlement. *Ecol. Monogr.* 30:129–164.

———. 1961. The ecology of fire. *Sci. American* 204 (4):150–160.

Curtis, John T. 1959. *The Vegetation of Wisconsin.* (Pages 456–472.) Univ. Wisconsin Press, Madison. 657 pp.

Isaac, Leo A. 1956. Place of partial cutting in old-growth stands of the Douglas-fir region. U. S. For. Serv., Pac. Northwest For. Rge. Exp. Sta., Res. Paper 16. 48 pp.

Mount, A B. 1969. Eucalypt ecology as related to fire. *In Proc. Tall Timbers Fire Ecology Conference,* 1969, Tall Timbers Res. Sta., Tallahassee, Fla.

Mutch, Robert W. 1970. Wildland fires and ecosystems—a hypothesis. *Ecology* 51:1046–1051.

Spurr, Stephen H. 1956. Natural restocking of forests following the 1938 hurricane in central New England. *Ecology* 37:443–451.

Williams, W. T., G. N. Lance, L. J. Webb, J. G. Tracey, and M. B. Dale. 1969. Studies in the numerical analysis of complex rain-forest communities. III. The analysis of successional data. *J. Ecol.* 57:515–535.

15

Spatial Variation
in the Forest

The composition and structure of the forest differ not only with time but also in space. Both the site (including both climate and soil) and the geographical distribution of forest organisms determine in part the nature of a given forest stand. A forest on one site will obviously differ from that on a different adjacent site; a forest in one geographical area will also differ from a forest in another because of differing animal and plant populations in the two areas, differing histories, and, simply, different chance happenings.

The spatial variation within a forest may include abrupt changes from one type of forest to another as well as gradual changes in which the character of the forest alters with varying dominance or abundance of the component species, the appearance of new species, and the dropping out of others. That is, forest communities or types may change in composition either drastically or gradually over space. The concept of the forest community (association) is basic to an understanding of spatial variation in the forest.

CONCEPT OF THE FOREST COMMUNITY

It is common knowledge that certain patterns of forest composition characterize extensive areas of forest. A belt of spruce and fir forest extends around much of the boreal zone and has a characteristic physiognomy, composition, and structure which makes it immediately recognizable as a "spruce-fir" community, association, or forest type. Furthermore, many of the smaller plants and many of the animals found in one spruce-fir forest will be found occupying similar niches in other spruce-fir forests. True, the individual species of spruce, fir, other plants, and animals will vary from continent to continent and within the continent. Even within a forest characterized by the same species of spruce and fir, the races of these species will vary from place to place within the forest. Certain plants and animals will be found in one part of the community and not in others. Any one species of plant or animal may be present or absent and cannot be considered an organic part of the community. Even the spruces and firs themselves may grow just as well in pure stands or mixtures with other species as together with each other.

Nevertheless, it is clear that a common denominator exists, so that when we speak of the boreal or montane spruce-fir forest, we convey an immediately recognizable concept and picture to others. We identify a forest community with sufficient precision to be meaningful. We are speaking of a specific forest community or forest type.

Unfortunately, at this point, we become involved inevitably in nomenclature and in the semantic confusion which has beset the problem of identifying plant communities. Only a few of the many terms which have been proposed and deposed, however, have become an important part of our common vocabulary of community ecology.

Community is a general term of convenience used to designate sociological units of any degree of extent and complexity (Cain and Castro, 1959). Traditionally, ecologists have established a hierarchy of communities and assigned special names to distinguish them. Thus a *formation* is the largest and most comprehensive kind of plant community, such as the boreal or spruce-fir forest formation. Each formation is composed of various other distinctive communities termed *associations*. Thus the Deciduous Forest Formation is composed of many different associations—beech-maple, oak-hickory, maple-basswood, etc. In the Clementsian system and European schools of phytosociology, finer subdivisions of the association are recognized and named. The subdivisions of "association" or "community" most widely used by American ecologists are "layer," "union," or "synusia"—terms which are more or less synonymous (but which are defined differently by different ecologists). Thus the spruce-fir formation of northeastern United States and eastern Canada includes the red spruce–balsam fir association (community), which may in turn be subdivided into a tree layer, a shrub layer, and a ground cover layer.

An historical perspective given by Egler (1968) may be helpful at this point. Clementsian ecology was a very tidy and orderly science—far more orderly than nature itself. The analogy of the community with the organism was one of its key beliefs. At that time individuals of a species were thought to be more or less uniform; thus it was easy to believe in uniformity of plant communities. A special kind of community (corresponding to the species in plant taxonomy), the "association," was defined in a technical sense as a group of plants that has a definite floristic composition, presents a uniformity of physiognomy, and grows under uniform conditions of habitat. The term "association" was so completely aligned with its rigid classical definition and usage that it went into disfavor among many American ecologists, and many ecologists today read "community" in its place. The hierarchical system with "association" as its core is preferred by ecologists involved in describing and classifying vegetation. Other ecologists not so involved also may use the term "association" but often in a much more general sense without organismal overtones; in this sense the terms "community" or "climax community" appear synonymous with the term "association." The term "community" is not restrictive by itself, probably accounting for much of its modern popularity. Its particular meaning in a given study depends on the context in which it is used and the modifiers applied to it—oak-pine community, climax community, etc.

The community, of course, consists of plants and animals living in a physical environment. Together they form an *ecosystem* or *biogeocoenosis*. The plants and animals in an ecosystem may be termed a *biome*, or *biocoenosis*. Plant ecologists, however, tend to characterize communities in terms of their plant composition (*phytocoenosis*), only implying that certain animal patterns are usually associated with certain plant patterns.

Clements and ecologists who follow his rules of nomenclature have restricted the use of the term association to relate only to climax communities. This usage, in company with the concept of the climax as a permanent and stable community, is losing ground in favor of the more general and flexible uses of the term.

The term *forest type* refers to a forest community defined only by composition of the overstory. Since the community or association is or should be defined by the sum total of the ecosystem, its naming usually takes into account characteristic lesser plants as well, or, alternatively, its characteristic site. For instance, the ponderosa pine type in northern Idaho and eastern Washington has been subdivided into six associations according to whether the undergrowth is characterized by grasses on stony, coarse-textured soils (*Agropyron spicatum, Festuca idahoensis, Stipa comata*) or shrubs on heavier-textured, more fertile soils (*Purshia tridentata, Symphoricarpos albus,* and *Physocarpus malvaceus*) (Daubenmire and Daubenmire, 1968). A gradient exists from the associations on driest areas bordering grassland or semidesert containing the grasses (*Pinus ponderosa–Festuca, Pinus ponderosa–Agropyron, Pinus ponderosa–Stipa*) to dry areas containing the shrubs (*Pinus ponderosa–Symphoricarpos, Pinus ponderosa–Physocarpus*) and grading into a series of late-successional associations of Douglas-fir on moister sites.

Conceptions of the plant association by ecologists vary from organismic views in which the association is conceived more or less mystically as some sort of superorganism, to individualistic views which treat each of the species comprising the association as occupying its range, and sites within its range, independently of one another. There seems little justification in fact for either extreme viewpoint. Certainly, the association has no unifying control system similar to the genes and chromosomes of plants and animals which give unity to the individual. At the other extreme, though, it is equally obvious that the individual organisms in a community are not independent but are mutually interdependent in that each creates part of the environment in which the other lives. Furthermore, some interrelationships are so favorable that groups of organisms are far more likely to be found living in the same community than separately. The degree of interrelationship varies greatly, ranging from situations where two species have similar ecological requirements and are therefore apt to be found on the same site (such as spruce and fir; or beech and maple), to cases of obvious symbiosis (such as in mycorrhizae and lichens).

Communities are not composed of successive, mutually exclusive sets of species. It has been shown time and time again that individual species have different physiological and genetic tolerances and may exist in several different communities. A given species may be highly competitive in one community and hence predominate there. Although it may also exist in adjacent communities having different site conditions, other species may be more competitive in time and space and predominate in this different environment. Most forest species of a given climatic region probably have their optimal development under similar environmental conditions. Hence it is competition in space and time, coupled with adaptation of species to particular site conditions, that elicits differentiation of what we may recognize arbitrarily as distinct communities. For example, in a large part of central Europe many forest species reach their optimal development under similar environmental conditions of moisture and acidity (Figure 15.1; Ellenberg, 1963). However, because of the enormous competitive ability of European beech in space and time, the other species are competitive only in restricted portions of their potential range.

Although plants may have similar ecological requirements, they occur together in recognizable communities not because they react

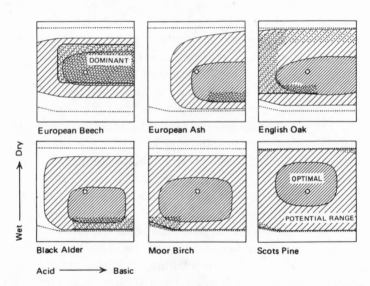

Fig. 15.1. Physiological amplitude of selected tree species of Central Europe of the submontane zone. Ordinate = moisture level from very wet to very dry. Abscissa = soil reaction from very acid to basic. Above dotted line at top is too dry for forest. Below dotted line at bottom is too wet for forest. Widely spread diagonal lines = potential range of species; closely spaced diagonal lines = optimal range; dotted area = portion of range in which through natural competition a given species attains a dominant position. (Modified from Ellenberg, 1963.)

in the same way, but because they compete successfully in various ways due to differences in their genetic makeup and physiological responses. Different tree, shrub, and herb species may exist in a given arid, cold, or wet environment, and seemingly have similar requirements, but they occupy different *niches*. That is, they occupy different sites or microsites (spatial niche), or they utilize a given site differently through their physiological responses and life history traits (functional niche) such as time of germination, amount and timing of shoot and root growth, and adaptive mechanisms for obtaining water and retaining it. Thus species are co-adapted to one another and their physical and temporal environment. Actually, we know very little about the multiple dimensions of the niches of forest species and the interactions of these organisms with one another and with their environment. If the degree of integration in communities is to be understood, the ecosystem must be increasingly the focus of study and the community and species seen as integrated parts of the system.

The forest community, then, cannot be precisely defined. It varies in composition and structure. It has no genetic or other basic biological unity. Nevertheless, some plants and animals do "associate" commonly in that they have similar ecological requirements and that they themselves tend to create environmental conditions suitable to the existence of one another. In general terms, a forest community can be identified by the occurrence of one or more characteristic plant indicators. Accurate identification, however, must involve a description of a much larger segment of the ecosystem. Because vegetation is only one component of the ecosystem, Rowe (1961, 1966, 1969) maintains that it alone is an incomplete and unsatisfactory object for scientific study.

A word about nomenclature might be in order at this point. Any nomenclature involves abbreviation in the sense that a few words are used to define a relatively complex structure. Thus, the association described as *Pinus ponderosa–Agropyron* above is in reality a complex and variable community. The two plants named, one a tree and the other a grass, both occur commonly in other communities, and many other plants occur in the community being described.

Many plant sociologists go further and give the association a binomial Latin name modeled on taxonomic nomenclature rules. In the above example, the name would be *Pinetum agropyronum*, or, more fully, *Pinetum ponderosae agropyronum*. The giving of binomial names to plant communities implies belief in the organismic conception of the plant community and is a particular fetish of European and European-influenced plant sociologists.

The Zürich-Montpellier School of Phytosociology

The most important and influential European school of phytosociology is the Zürich-Montpellier school of phytosociology; its principal exponent is J. Braun-Blanquet (Poore, 1955; Becking, 1957; Whittaker, 1962; Braun-Blanquet, 1964). In this system the association is seen as an organism and is comparable to the species of plant taxonomy. The association is the basic unit of a hierarchical system of vegetation classification which has become the primary goal of the school identified with Braun-Blanquet. The association has a type specimen complete with author, date, and description analogous to that of a plant species: for example, "*Abieti-Fagetum* Oberdorfer 38"; and the "*Galio-Carpinetum* (Buck-Feuct 37) Oberdorfer 57 em. Th. Müll. 66." As we have indicated earlier, however, the association is not an organism and there is no single genetic control determining the nature of the association. Thus, there is little justification for the naming of communities as if they were species.

In the Braun-Blanquet method, the association, an abstraction, is determined by the comparison of a number of lists of species made in selected sites in the field. It is not defined by site factors, but entirely by floristic composition. The field plots are subjectively selected for uniformity, which cannot be defined with precision (Poore, 1955). At each of the plots a complete vegetation list is made of species from all layers. One of the major advantages of the method is the completeness of the species list; many North American studies appear incomplete by comparison.

The plant lists from the plots are grouped into association tables, from which the associations are determined (Ellenberg, 1956; Poore, 1955; Becking, 1957). Although associations are the cornerstone of the system, it is recognized that they intergrade extensively (Becking, 1957). However, erection of seemingly discrete classes, due primarily to the non-random method of plot selection, has conferred a false sense of uniformity within associations and discontinuity between them.

Many English and American ecologists have either been alienated by the system or have adopted an attitude of critical disinterest

(Poore, 1955). This has been due to the questionable modelling on the plant taxonomic system, the seemingly rigid classification, and subjective methods. One result has been that many ecologists have hesitated to use the terms "association" and "phytosociology" and renounced for a time the use of classification, in part, at least, because of the close relationship of these terms and methods with this school. Criticism from without and within has led to a proliferation of modifications in the approach until today a single and dominant school cannot be clearly recognized. At one time hierarchical classification was a major feature of the method. Now, however, many workers find it more practicable for most purposes to establish and map associations as equals, regardless of rank in a hierarchical scheme.

Despite its shortcomings, this approach has made and continues to make important contributions to the description and classification of vegetation. A major advantage for those versed in the method is the rapidity with which major associations can be described. The approach is widely applied in continental Europe in one variety or another and used by many plant sociologists throughout the world. Detailed considerations of this and related European phytosociological methods are given by Kershaw (1964) and Küchler (1967).

SPATIAL CONTINUITY OF THE FOREST COMMUNITY

Accepting the concept of the forest community as a group of interrelated plants and animals that occur together more frequently than can be ascribed to chance—and as neither a superorganism nor a chance aggregation of species, each of which reacts independently to its environment—the question then arises as to how the forest varies spatially with changing conditions of site and geographical location.

One can readily find cases where one community is separated from an entirely different community by a sharp boundary. A field is distinct from an adjacent woods; and a pine plantation from an adjacent natural hardwood stand; and a tamarack bog from an adjacent upland conifer type. One can just as readily, though, find cases where the nature of the community changes gradually. A redwood type grades into a Douglas-fir-type upslope; a slash pine type near the border of a cypress-gum bottom grades into a loblolly pine type; and a good white oak type into a poor white oak type.

In nature one observes all degrees of change between communities—from abrupt to imperceptible. Yet a major controversy developed around the abstract conception of the distinctness or continuity of communities. The concept of continuous change in vegetation, the continuum concept, was conceived and developed in reaction to the organismal concept of the plant association as a discrete unit of vegetation and its use as the basis for a seemingly rigid classification of vegetation. Unfortunately, the controversy has usually been framed in terms of two opposing viewpoints: the association-unit (community-type) approach versus the continuum approach. However, this is a serious oversimplification of viewpoints and concepts. Having polarized ecologists for a time, the controversy today is largely academic. All parties agree that floras [1] are continuous and that abrupt as well as gradual changes exist between communities on the ground. Furthermore most ecologists agree that the community is not as well integrated as an organism nor are species making up the community completely independent of one another. What is not well known is the rate of change between communities and the degree of integration and mutual interdependence of species of a community.

Perhaps the most significant viewpoint in light of the controversy has been the approach of English workers who have seen neither the concept of discrete classes nor the continuum as a useful basis for investigation (Lambert and Dale, 1964). They have developed objective, numerical methods and have applied them in studying vegetation and associated habitat conditions in a variety of temperate and tropical ecosystems.

The continuum concept will be discussed in the next section. Thereafter, discrete and merging forest communities of the "real world" will be considered giving specific examples of the continuum and community-type approaches.

The Continuum Concept

The concept of a vegetational continuum was introduced in the United States by John T. Curtis and co-workers at the University of Wisconsin (Curtis and McIntosh, 1951; Bray and Curtis, 1957; Curtis, 1959). The continuum was defined as:

---

[1] Many ecologists distinguish between flora, the basic unit of which is the species, and vegetation, of which the community is the basic unit.

An adjectival noun referring to the situation where the stands of a community or large vegetational unit are not segregated into discrete units but rather form a continuously varying series.

The continuum meant that all communities of a vegetation type, e.g., forest or grassland, could be ordered or ordinated [2] in an abstract series whose species composition changed gradually—typically along one or more environmental gradients. Thus although distinct, adjacent communities were encountered in the field (Curtis, 1959), they could be fitted into their respective position in the abstract continuum. Thus according to Curtis (1959):

> It is not possible to erect a classification scheme which will place the plant communities of any large portion of the earth's surface into a series of discrete pigeonholes, each with recognizable and describable characteristics and boundary limitations. The plant communities, although composed of plant species, are not capable of being taxonomically classified, as are the species themselves.

The strong position against a taxonomy of vegetation is not surprising since the continuum concept was directed primarily to a different facet of vegetation study—the relationship of species and communities to one another and to environmental factors. The major contributions of the approach have been the demonstration of considerable variability within stands and communities, the impetus it has given for the use of more objective techniques in vegetation analysis, and the demonstration of coordinated patterns of species and community variation along environmental gradients. Continuum theory and methods have been widely applied; McIntosh (1967) cites over forty publications whose authors consider that such diverse vegetation as tropical rain forests, the Sonoran desert, and tundra of Alaska, constitutes a continuum. Gradient analysis has been a popular continuum method in mountainous terrain and the subject of extensive work by Whittaker (1956, 1967b, 1970).

The continuum approach has been criticized on the merits of its methods and on a variety of other accounts. It is beyond the scope of this chapter to review the history and details of the controversy; many viewpoints have already been expressed (Daubenmire, 1966; McIntosh, 1967; Dansereau, 1968; Langford and Buell, 1969; and Whittaker, 1970; among others). Some ecologists prefer the community-type approach exclusively, but many of the recent studies employ a descriptive phase of the study using community types

---

[2] An ordination is an arrangement of species, communities, or environments in sequence along axes with their respective properties determining their position.

(associations) and then gradient anlysis or ordination in the causal-analytical phase. Curtis himself subjectively recognized major vegetation types in Wisconsin. Within each then he was able to show continua, using ordination methods.

There is no question even by continuum critics that vegetation or floras are continua (Daubenmire, 1966; Daubenmire and Daubenmire, 1968). This is true for a number of reasons: (1) environmental conditions change in space at varying rates affecting the establishment and, through competition, the composition of the vegetation; (2) genecological variation of tree species is typically clinal, and in addition a given genotype often has a wide environmental tolerance; (3) historical and chance events reinforce points 1 and 2 so that no communities are exactly alike; and (4) a continuum of successional changes in time is superimposed upon changes in composition in space.

Continuum ecologists were opposed to classification, but according to McIntosh (1967) agree that "if classification is urged simply as a desirable convenience for mapping or information storage (Daubenmire, 1966) for practical ends and specific purposes, the classification being arbitrary and directed to these specific ends (Rowe, 1960), there is no contest." Much of the controversy falls within this realm.

Concerning classification and ordination, Lambert and Dale (1964) summarize the alternatives:

> . . . There seems to be a common misconception that classification is only properly applicable to "discontinuous" data, while ordination techniques are more appropriate to continuous systems. In contrast, it cannot be too strongly emphasized that there is no *a priori* reason why the use of either method should be restricted in this way: continuous systems can be efficiently classified if classification is desired, while "discontinuous" (i.e., markedly heterogeneous) systems can be ordinated if ordination is thought more useful for the immediate purpose in hand. Moreover, there is in principle no reason why classification and ordination techniques should be mutually exclusive: classified units can be ordinated, and ordinated units classified. Which method to adopt at a given stage of the investigation is entirely a matter for the user, irrespective of any subjective concept of the "real" nature of vegetation.

To further reconcile the viewpoints we call attention to McIntosh's citation of numerous authors who recognize that the two views are not incompatible. Major (1961) wrote, and we agree, that the differences between the viewpoints are a question of degree: "All users of continua do recognize some units; all users of associations do recognize some transitions." Leith (1968), who has worked with both methods, finds that the character of nature itself may dictate the appropriate methods.

However, there are substantive objections to the continuum approach. The vegetational continuum is the product of a continuum in space (species and communities influenced by environmental and biotic factors) *and* a continuum in time, i.e., succession. A major objection to continuum methods is that the continuum typically cited is an artifact of sampling vegetation as it exists. When vegetational samples in different successional stages are included, the result necessarily may be a more gradual change in the series of communities than if late-successional stands only were sampled. In the studies of Curtis and associates in Wisconsin, stands of varying successional stages were used and the resulting continuum is, to an unknown degree, partly temporal and partly spatial. This aspect of continuum methods has important theoretical and practical implications.

Studying vegetation as it exists, regardless of successional stage, will tend to give one picture of gradually changing communities. Sampling only late-successional stands throughout the same spectrum of sites might show an abrupt rate of change in some places and gradual rates in others. Thus both Daubenmire (1966) and Langford and Buell (1969) have argued that if climax stands were used one might find more or less discrete associations connected by ecotones (transition zones between communities). The crux of the problem according to Daubenmire (1966) is:

There is no denying that vegetation presents a continuous variable by virtue of ecotones; the argument hinges on the existence or absence of plateau-like areas exhibiting minor gradients separated by areas of steper gradients, with the plateau-like areas being of sufficient similarity to warrant being designated as a class.

In studies of stands in essentially pristine forests of the northern Rocky Mountains, Daubenmire presented evidence to substantiate the reality of these "plateau-like areas" (Daubenmire and Daubenmire, 1968). He found the associations, determined subjectively, extended across hundreds of kilometers without losing their identity. Although he indicates that these types intergrade, he believes the discontinuities become important enough to "compel the segmentation of the landscape into categories that are objective in that different workers commonly recognize the same discontinuities independently." He credits part of the distinctness to the use of both overstory and understory vegetation, a combination that has not been a major determinant of continua in most investigations by continuum workers.

From a practical standpoint the forest land manager is concerned with the site potential. Neither an existing forest-type classification nor a continuum based on a mixture of successional stages may be useful in decision making. We agree with Rowe's (1962, 1969) recommendation in forest mapping that the landscape pattern first be broken into geomorphological parts, each relatively constant as to surface materials, which in turn can be subdivided into relatively homogeneous forest-land patches or ecosystems. Then late-successional vegetation for each ecosystem may be determined (as in the Baden-Württemberg system) or environmental factors may be used directly in determining site quality.

In summary, it is possible, then, to approach the problem of the spatial relationships of vegetation either from the viewpoint of communities as separate units of vegetation which may be idenitfied as a type and delineated on maps; or to consider the vegetation as a plastic community which changes gradually from place to place, without any specific point of maximum change. Both approaches, the community-type approach and the continuum approach, have widespread application in forest community studies. After considering in great detail diverse approaches to the classification of communities, Whittaker (1962) concluded that quite dissimilar approaches may be equally justified and may to some extent complement one another.

Numerical Analysis of Vegetation

English workers, predominantly Williams, Lambert, and associates, have developed an alternative system of vegetational analysis (Lambert and Dale, 1964). More objective than any previous approach, there is much to recommend it from ecological and mathematical standpoints. They found neither the approach using discrete communities nor that of a vegetational continuum particularly useful in extracting maximum ecological information from given areas. Making no assumptions except that vegetation was heterogeneous, they developed and adapted various classification techniques and used computer methods to describe and analyze vegetation-site relationships.

On the grounds of general efficiency they prefer to use qualitative information (presence-and-absence data) rather than quantitative measures (Lambert and Dale, 1964). Where many species are involved, the increase in information gained from using quantitative data rather than qualitative data is likely to be very small. Results of studies have demonstrated that, for most ecological purposes where phytosociological issues are concerned, presence-and-absence data for all species are adequate.

In one of the earlier studies, a particular form of association analysis termed *nodal analysis,* meaningful vegetational units were extracted by routine mathematical methods independent of previous experience on the areas studied (Lambert and Williams, 1962). Since selection of stands by eye introduces a subjective element, an arbitrary system of systematic sampling was used, with a sample size appropriate to the size of the plants themselves. Lambert and Williams pointed out, however, that what they obtained by computer methods the trained ecologist could determine by study in the field. Nevertheless, the computer has certain advantages besides speed in data processing. Above all, no preconceived ideas gained from experience which may be inappropriate to the new areas of study are brought to the analysis. Computer analysis has been consistently found to disclose features of importance that can be overlooked in subjective analyses.

The English group has used both classification and ordination methods in studying species-site relationships in complex rain-forest communities (Webb et al., 1967a, b). In one study (Webb et al., 1967a) ordination was found the single most informative method, but the larger part of the information was recovered by classification, which is simpler and faster. Thus they recommended classification first, followed by ordination only if classification proves unprofitable. Other workers agree; for example, Greig-Smith et al. (1967) indicate that classification is more satisfactory at high levels of variation in composition of vegetation and ordination more satisfactory at lower levels. Thus, a combination of the two approaches will be more informative than either alone.

In further studies, Williams and colleagues used numerical methods to analyze local forest-environment patterns (Williams et al., 1969), secondary succession (Williams et al., 1969; see Chapter 14), and the floristic-versus-physiognomic classification of complex rain forests (Webb et al., 1970). Although their studies have been primarily methodological, their ecological contributions have been substantial as well.

DISCRETE FOREST COMMUNITIES

Wherever one type of forest community abuts on another distinctly different type of forest community, it will be found that this abrupt change is related to an abrupt change in site conditions or to a completely different vegetational history of the two communities. The existence of discrete communities, therefore, is evidence of the existence of discrete differences in growing conditions, either now or in the past.

The boundary betwen two communities is usually a belt rather than a sharp line. It is a belt or zone, though, which may vary widely in width. In the forest-grassland transition, there will always be an outer belt of forest which will be modified by the adjacent open areas, and an inner belt of grassland which will be modified by the adjacent forest. As mentioned above, the transition zone between two communities is termed an *ecotone*. It usually embodies some of the ecological features of the two communities, but has a characteristic ecological structure of its own.

Many persisting, abrupt site differences can give rise to sharp forest-type boundaries. Among these are: (1) a sharp boundary between two geological formations, giving rise to a sharp boundary between two soil types which differ markedly in the mineral sites they provide to vegetation; (2) a sharp boundary in soil-moisture conditions, such as between a poorly drained swamp and a well-drained upland; (3) a sharp boundary in topographic position affecting local climate, such as a knife-edged ridge separating a north from a south slope or an air dam impeding cold air drainage so that frost pocket conditions exist below the level of the dammed air; and (4) a sharp boundary in the structure of the vegetation affecting the local climate and soil conditions, such as a forest edge facing grassland or a shrub community impinging upon open rock surfaces. Among the historical accidents that may give rise to sharp boundaries between plant communities are fires, tornados and other windstorms, salt spray from the sea, fumes from smelters, logging, and agricultural development of land. Many examples could be cited, but these are, in general, obvious. Abrupt changes in vegetation associated with changes in the parent geological material are dealt with in Chapter 7. Such changes may be found at the contact between sandstone and limestone outcrops, serpentine and adjacent soils, and organic and mineral soils. Relationships between vegetation and soils around the world are summarized by Eyre (1962).

The ecotones between forest and adjacent low-vegetation types have long attracted the attention of ecologists, particularly the forest-grassland ecotone and the alpine timberline.

Forest-Grassland Ecotone

Abrupt changes between forest and grassland in the tropical and temperate zones may or may not be associated with abrupt changes in site. Once the forest edge has been established, such as by fire or land clearing, site conditions—both climatic and edaphic—within the forest may differ so substantially from those in the grassland as to perpetuate the forest border.

This is not to say that abrupt site changes cannot be found in many instances. In moist climates, forests are frequently found on well-drained upland soils, with grasslands becoming dominant on poorly drained sites. In the American tropics, all types of climate in the lowlands are adequate to support woody growth of some kind, but savannas occur upon ill-drained country of little relief such as an old alluvial plain or reduced upland (Beard, 1953). In semi-arid regions, forests may be confined to coarse-textured or rocky soils while grassland occurs on the finer-textured soil types. For instance, in the Black Forest of Colorado, arborescent communities occur under the same climatic conditions as grasslands, but on sites where coarse-textured soils result in more rapid infiltration of the limited precipitation, reduced run-off, and lower wilting percentages in the soils (Livingston, 1949).

Often, however, the grassland originates in forested country as a result of a fire which destroys the forest and creates an environment at the ground more suitable for the development of grasses than for the reestablishment of the forest. Once established, the grassland persists because of the inability of the adjacent forest trees to invade the site—whether due to the recurrent incidence of fire (Wells, 1965; Rowe, 1966); to the failure of the tree seeds to penetrate the sod and reach a medium suitable for germination; to biochemical antagonisms between the grasses and the tree seedlings; to excessive root competition for soil moisture provided by the grasses; to the absence of mycorrhizae (Langford and Buell, 1969); or to the damage of direct insolation to the seedlings on the exposed open sites. The alpine meadows of the western American mountains, the balds of the Appalachians, the fingers of prairie extending up into the Black Hills of South Dakota, and the extension of the Prairie Peninsula east into Michigan, Indiana, and Ohio, all are examples of fire-caused grasslands that have persisted for hundreds of years under climates suitable for tree growth.

This does not imply that the forest-grassland border is ever static. Invasion of one type by the other does occur. In the present century, grasslands within forested regions are being invaded by forest throughout the world, partly because of the improvements in modern fire-suppression techniques and, in some cases, partly because of a change in climate. In northwestern Minnesota, to cite one case, the maple-basswood forest has been recently invading adjacent prairie (Buell and Cantlon, 1951; Buell and Facey, 1960).

Alpine Timberlines

The upper edge of forest in mountain ranges provides another spectacular forest edge. Many ecologists, ignoring the biotic aspects of the plants forming the timberline and their history, have attempted to define timberlines purely in terms of the site, and have tried to evolve rules defining the height of the timberline for a given latitude, aspect, and other physical aspects of the timberline position.

As with all ecological phenomena, the timberline is a result of the interaction of the trees and the site over a long period of time. The position of the timberline may differ greatly with the species available to form it. In New Zealand, where only *Nothofagus* spp. form the temperate tree flora at high altitudes in the mountains of the South Island, the timberline is much lower than would be the case if North American conifers had been in the local plant population. In fact, it seems that lodgepole pine—both planted trees and seedlings from seed blown in from planted trees—will eventually form a new timberline type a thousand or more feet higher than the present *Nothofagus* type.

Naturally enough, the timberline tends to rise toward the Equator, but the greatest height at which trees grow occurs in warm-temperate belts (about 30° latitude in the Northern Hemisphere and 25° in the Southern) rather than in the deep tropics. Generalized data on American timberlines are summarized by Daubenmire (1954), who has brought together theories concerning the distribution of American timberlines.

Many causes have been ascribed to timberline formation. Above the *forest line* (the upper edge of continuous forest), trees grow up to the *tree line*, the altitude of the highest stunted tree. Within this zone of stunted and recumbent trees, wind, snow blown by the wind, snow pack, and other factors produce an exposed and rigorous climatic zone near the ground through which trees cannot grow. Other causal factors of timberline formation that have been cited include excessive light, carbon dioxide deficiency, desiccation during temperature inversions in the winter, precipitation deficiency, solufluction, and light deficiencies in certain mountain regions commonly clouded over. After reviewing the evidence, Daubenmire concluded that one of the principal factors determining timberline location (as contrasted with climatic factors that cause dwarfing and recumbent growth) is heat deficiency during the growing season at high altitudes, which prevents trees from surviving and growing. Wardle (1968) found that summer temperature data bore out this conclusion in a study of timberlines in Colorado which are among the highest in the world despite desiccating wind and low winter temperatures. He also found a strong correlation between the distribution and growth form of Engelmann spruce and exposure to wind. Wind also kept sites blown free of snow so that there was a lack of protection for seedlings during the winter and an absence of melt-water in the spring to moisten the rocky, coarse-grained soils. In the Austrian Alps, Aulitzky (1967) reported that only the highest tree line was governed by the 10°C (50°F) line of July temperature. In most situations, growth of trees was lower than this level due to other unfavorable factors, wind, snow depth, and snow duration.

MERGING FOREST COMMUNITIES

While distinct plant communities, separated by transitional belts or ecotones, reflect abrupt changes in site or land history, gradual changes in site or vegetational history result in similar gradual changes in the composition and structure of the forest. Such gradual changes are characteristic of forests of a generally similar history over a geographical stretch of many miles (such as north to south or east to west), over a slope, from one aspect to another, or over a gradual change in soil fertility.

Continua characterize the composition and structure within forests in the absence of an abrupt change in site or vegetational history. The great deciduous hardwood forest of the eastern United States stretching from the Gulf of Mexico to Canada is, in its broader aspects, a great continuum within which distinctive communities may be recognized. Such also is the conifer forest of western United States and Canada, although here the intrusion of large areas of desert and grassland, the presence of abrupt superficial geological changes, and the lasting effects of past severe forest fires all tend to emphasize the discreteness of forest associations rather than the gradual sequence of change that is superimposed over these local influences.

Eastern Deciduous Forest

The forest of the eastern United States—characterized by deciduous hardwood species, but containing evergreen hardwood species in the deep south and conifers such as white pine, hemlock, and red cedar in much of it—constitutes a single great vegetational complex that shows many gradual changes from place to place and from site to site in any given place. Related to similar hardwood forests in Mexico, it reaches its greatest complexity and size of individual trees, however, in the southern Appalachian region and may have spread out in postglacial times from that center of distribution (Braun, 1950).

Within this great forest complex, ecological studies in the southern Appalachians, central New England, and Wisconsin may be taken as illustrations of the principle of gradual change resulting in continua, or merging forest communities, and of how in each case specific types of communities of the continuum have been distinguished. It should be emphasized that in all these studies tree species have received either major or exclusive emphasis.

Southern Appalachians. The old eroded slopes, valleys, and ridges of the southern Appalachian Mountains and the Cumberland Plateau to the west in Kentucky and Tennessee provide ecological gradients on which forest composition is similarly graded. Detailed studies by Braun in the Cumberland Mountains (1942) and Whittaker in the Great Smoky Mountains (1956) illustrate many of these changes.

Extensive surveys of uncut, old-growth, mixed deciduous forest in the Cumberland Mountains have resulted in a series of papers by Braun which present the general picture of an "undifferentiated" complex marked by gradients in composition occurring with changes in elevation, aspect, and soil-moisture relationships. For instance, around the head of a west-facing stream valley in the Log Mountains, sugar maple, basswood, and buckeye constituted the major portion of the forest canopy on the north-facing slopes, and diminished in abundance toward the west, being absent on the south. Similarly, yellow-poplar, chestnut, and red oak varied in numbers with the aspect, reaching their maximum abundance on the west slopes; while chestnut oak and white oak were most abundant on the south slopes. In the upper mountain slopes, hemlock–beech–yellow birch forest in the ravines was found to grade gradually into chestnut oak–chestnut–hickory forests on the upper slopes. No sharp line dividing two quite different forest types could be drawn. Rather, the transition from one to another is indicated by declining numbers of one species and expanding numbers of another.

In the Great Smoky Mountains, Cain, in a series of papers, analyzed the vegetational communities in considerable detail, followed by Whittaker, who studied gradients in composition with altitude and with "moisture gradients" within altitudinal belts. This latter term refers to the complex gradient from valley bottoms to dry slopes without any assumption as to its causation. In such a gradient, the most numerous trees (counted as the total number of stems one inch and larger in diameter) vary from mesic species in the valley bottoms to xeric species on the driest and most exposed portions of the slope. For instance, between, 2,500 and 3,500 feet in elevation, hemlock was most numerous in the bottoms, with silver bell, red maple, chestnut, chestnut oak, scarlet oak, pitch pine, and Table Mountain pine each entering the transect and becoming more numerous toward the drier end of the gradient. Similarly, altitudinal gradients were constructed for a given site moisture. On the mesic sites, hemlock and red maple were most numerous at low elevations (2,000 to 3,000 feet) with silver bell, yellow birch, sugar maple, and basswood reaching maximum abundance in the 3,000- to 4,000-foot zone, and buckeye, mountain maple, and beech being most common at higher elevations. The species named are only a few of the many species present, but are those occurring in the greatest numbers.

Some tree species show multinodal distributions indicative of the existence of two or more populations, some of which, like red maple and yellow birch, overlap, and some, like beech and white oak, are separated by an altitudinal zone of a thousand feet or more.

Combining the two gradients, Whittaker synthesized a general vegetation pattern of the Great Smokies (Figure 15.2). He found

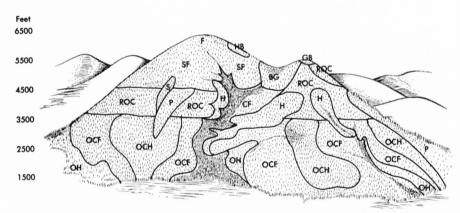

Fig. 15.2. Topographic distribution of vegetation types on an idealized west-facing mountain and valley in the Great Smoky Mountains. Vegetation types: *BG*, beech gap; *CF*, cove forest; *F*, Fraser fir forest; *GB*, grassy bald; *H*, hemlock forest; *HB*, heath bald; *OCF*, chestnut oak–chestnut forest; *OCH*, chestnut oak–chestnut heath; *OH*, oak-hickory forest; *P*, pine forest and pine heath; *ROC*, red oak–chestnut forest; *S*, spruce forest; *SF*, spruce-fir forest; *WOC*, white oak–chestnut forest. (After Kormondy, 1969, based on diagram by Whittaker, 1956.)

the forest pattern one of continuous gradation of stands along environmental gradients. Certain relatively discontinuous types were found that showed continuous gradation within themselves and usually intermingled with other types in directions other than those where discontinuities were found. As described by Whittaker (1962):

The whole pattern was conceived to be a complex continuum of populations, with the relatively discontinuous types confined to "extreme" environments and forming a minor part of the whole. Allowing for discontinuities produced by disturbance and environmental discontinuity, the vegetation pattern could be regarded as a complex mixture of continuity and relative discontinuity.

It is noteworthy that, while he disavowed the concept of the association, he did recognize the existence of abrupt discontinuities as between cove forests and beech stands on south-facing slopes, between grassy balds and forests, and between heath balds and spruce-fir forests. Also, he treated the boreal forest characterized by red spruce and Fraser fir as being a separate entity from the eastern forest, thus accepting the principle of the existence of two major forest formations in the mountains. The synthesized vegetational pattern portrays tacit acceptance of the convenience of community-type designations whether or not the investigator accepts their existence as discrete units.

Whereas Whittaker emphasized a modified continuum approach, Hack and Goodlett (1960), working in similar Appalachian hardwood forests but in the upper Shenandoah Valley region, found that species assemblages were generally coincident with topographic units and often change abruptly with changes in the form of the slope. Pine-oak forests were found to be generally restricted to noses, ridges, and other convex slopes; yellow birch–sugar maple–basswood forests were found to be generally restricted to hollows and other concave surfaces; while oak forests were found generally on straight slopes. The strong coincidences between the local distribution of species and groups of species are modified by: (1) the size of the valleys, a minimum area being essential for the establishment of the northern hardwood type in a hollow; (2) the orientation of the valleys and side slopes, north and east slopes being commonly forested with northern hardwoods, and south and west slopes being characteristically oak; and (3) the nature and attitude of the bedrock, formations favoring moisture accumulation and retention being more favorable for the more mesophytic species.

New England. In central New England the different successional stages of the old-field white pine succession occupy much of the forested landscape. It has occurred on soils of glacial origin ranging from poorly to excessively drained. As a result, the composition of the forest varies in response to two major ecological gradients: one gradient, in time, covering the development of old-field succession, and one, in space, covering the range of site conditions from wet to dry. In this region of moderate elevations and rolling topography, neither absolute elevation above sea level nor aspect is as important in affecting the composition of the forest as the two gradients named.

In the Harvard Forest in central Massachusetts, Spurr (1956b) classified all existing stands according to both relative position on the successional-development gradient (pioneer, transitional, or late-successional) and relative position on the soil-moisture gradient (from very well to very poorly drained.) The frequency of occurrences of the individual tree species was found to vary consistently with the two gradients. Table 15.1 summarizes the change in the

Table 15.1. Occurrence of Species as Major Components in Harvard Forest "Transitional" Middle-Aged Stands

Site	Red Oak	Red Maple	Paper Birch	White Oak	White Ash
	Frequency (percent)				
Very well drained	67	0	0	33	0
Well drained	95	61	14	13	3
Imperfectly drained	81	81	9	6	19
Poorly drained	42	100	8	0	8
Very poorly drained	20	100	0	0	0

transitional type associated with changes in the moisture gradient. Two species were found to be practically omnipresent. Red oak and red maple were prominent in all successful stages, and one or the other was prominent on all sites. Both exhibited marked relationship to soil moisture, red oak being most frequent on the well-drained and red maple on the most poorly drained sites. Other species proved more specific in their site associations. White oak was most frequent on very well-drained, paper birch on well-drained, and white ash on imperfectly drained sites.

Everything considered, all the forest communities found in the Harvard Forest seem to represent a continuous gradational series correlated with successional stage and soil moisture (Table 15.2). Thus, the old-field white pine and the pioneer hardwood types are pioneer communities which vary in composition according to the site where they occur. Among the transitional types, the white pine–hardwoods type on the driest sites grades into the transitional-hardwoods type on the intermediate sites, which in turn grades into the swamp-hardwoods type on the wettest sites. Among the late-

Table 15.2. Tree Species Characterizing Communities in the Harvard Forest

Site	Pioneer Communities	Transitional Communities	Late-Successional Communities
Very well drained	WHITE PINE GRAY BIRCH Red maple Paper birch Red oak Black cherry	RED OAK WHITE PINE *White oak* Red maple	HEMLOCK WHITE PINE RED OAK Red maple White oak
Well drained	WHITE PINE (old fields) RED MAPLE RED OAK *Gray birch* *Black cherry* White ash Paper birch	RED OAK RED MAPLE *Paper birch* *White oak* Black birch	HEMLOCK RED OAK RED MAPLE *White pine* *Yellow birch* Paper birch Black birch
Imperfectly drained	Insufficient data (Red maple, white ash, and birches predomi- nate.)	RED OAK RED MAPLE *White ash* *Yellow birch* Paper birch	HEMLOCK RED MAPLE *Red oak* Yellow birch
Poorly drained	Insufficient data (Red maple and birches pre- dominate.)	RED MAPLE *Red oak* *Yellow birch*	HEMLOCK RED MAPLE *Yellow birch*
Very poorly drained	Insufficient data	RED MAPLE *Red oak* *Black birch* *Elm*	HEMLOCK RED MAPLE *Spruce* White pine Tamarack Yellow birch Black gum

NOTE: Relative importance is indicated by CAPITALS, followed by *italics,* followed by regular type.

successional types, the white pine–hemlock–hardwoods type on the driest sites grades into the softwood-swamp type of the wettest sites. A similar gradational series is found on each site as between the different successional stages. In general, the pioneer hardwood communities (but not pioneer white pine) are less than 30 years old, the transitional communities from about 30 to 60 years old, while the late-successional communities are older.

Wisconsin. In Wisconsin and adjacent areas of the Great Lakes region, J. T. Curtis and his students developed the continuum concept of variation in the composition of the forest (Curtis and McIntosh, 1951; Curtis, 1959; Maycock and Curtis, 1960; *et al.*) Curtis' classic book, *The Vegetation of Wisconsin*, is a definitive treatment of the vegetation in relation to environment, glacial history, and man, as well as the presentation of his concept of the vegetational continuum.

The state was classified into two floristic provinces (southwest and northeast halves), and within each intergrading vegetation types (forests, savannas, and grasslands) were recognized on the basis of physiognomy. Finer subdivisions within vegetation types were based on floristic composition. The techniques of sampling and stand analysis used are open to question, but the results have clearly indicated the existence of compositional gradients, i.e., vegetational continua, in both provinces. Each continuum could be arbitrarily divided into segments emphasizing the relationship between the community and a major environmental gradient, primarily soil moisture. Thus in the southwestern mixed hardwood forest, five segments of the continuum were recognized as communities: dry, dry-mesic, mesic, wet-mesic, and wet southern hardwoods. In all, 21 communities were identified.

In the Wisconsin studies, the forest stands chosen for sampling have typically been those of natural origin at least 15 acres in size, on upland landforms not subject to inundation, and free from recent disturbances within the lifetime of the stand as far as could be determined. From sampling at a number of points within each stand, the *relative frequency* (percentage of samples in which a species occurs), *relative density* (number of individuals of a given species per unit area as a percentage of the total of all species), and *relative dominance* (basal area represented by individuals of a given species as a percentage of the total basal area) of each tree species were determined. The value obtained by arbitrarily adding together the three separate measures of a given species, without exploring the interrelationships between them, is termed the *importance value*. It has the merits of quickness and simplicity and the demerits of unproven assumptions, subjectivity, and the absence of analysis. Lambert and Dale (1964), in reviewing the use of statistics in phytosociology, state that there is little to be said for such mixed quantitative values and view the importance value as a sum of non-additive numbers. Langford and Buell (1969) cited instances where use of composite indices such as importance values may tend to obscure differences between communities. In these cases artificial populations were generated having marked differences in relative density and relative dominance compared to a natural population yet having exactly the same importance values.

In early studies, the importance value was multiplied by an arbitrary climax adaptation number varying from one to ten (essentially the same as the tolerance rating discussed in Chapter 12) and when summed for all species gave a *continuum index*. This index was then used to position stands in a linear continuum (Curtis, 1959). Later attempts were made to segregate out more complex patterns by the ordination of stand data on three interrelated axes (Bray and Curtis, 1957; Maycock and Curtis, 1960). Improved computer methods of ordination are replacing the early methods, and their relative merits are under study (Gauch and Whittaker, 1972).

In the 1951 study of the upland (i.e., on well-drained soils) forests of the prairie-forest floristic province of southwestern Wisconsin, Curtis and McIntosh found that black oak, white oak, red oak, and sugar maple were the most important species. Relatively undisturbed forest stands in that region could be arranged in accordance with arbitrary and synthetic continuum index values, characterizing an ecological gradient which runs from communities containing bur oak, aspens, and black oak at one end to those including hop hornbeam and sugar maple at the other. Since ordination was in terms of vegetation composition, the gradients could not be used to relate vegetation as the dependent variable to environmental or successional gradients as independent variables. It seems evident, however, that the vegetational continuum described is in part a successional continuum from pioneer to climax species and in part a response to a site or geographic continuum. In sampling stands in Wisconsin or the western Great Lakes region, inclusion of stands of different stages of succession apparently cannot be avoided. Since the methods used in the analysis cannot separate temporal and environmental gradients, the nature of the continuum across changing environments cannot be precisely determined by floristic methods.

In an extensive study of the boreal conifer-hardwood forests of the northern Great Lakes region, Maycock and Curtis (1960) did establish a moisture gradient broken into five arbitrary classes from dry to mesic to wet. Without taking into consideration the successional development of the stands, the occurrences of the various species were found to vary significantly with this moisture gradient. White pine and white spruce are of major importance on dry sites; sugar maple, red maple, yellow birch, and hemlock on mesic sites; and balsam fir and northern white cedar on wet sites. Jack pine and black spruce are found commonly on both dry and wet sites, but are poor competitors under intermediate moisture conditions.

Western Coniferous Forest

The discontinuities created by geographic separation, abrupt topographic changes, geological unconformities, and forest fires have resulted in many distinct vegetational zones within the forests of the mountains of the American West. Indeed, it is here that much of the important early work on the zonation of vegetation, particularly with reference to altitude, has been done (Merriam, 1890; Shreve, 1915, 1922; Daubenmire, 1943).

Nevertheless, recent ecological studies in the western coniferous forests have demonstrated the existence of vegetational gradients with altitude, soil-moisture conditions, parent materials, climate, and other ecological factors which create a gradual sequence of changes in forest composition and structure as well as some relatively abrupt transitions from one community to another. These may be illustrated with examples from the Inland Empire in northern Idaho and the mountains of Arizona.

Northern Rocky Mountains. The vegetation of relatively undisturbed stands of the conifer forest of eastern Washington and northern Idaho has been investigated intensively by Daubenmire (1952, 1966; Daubenmire and Daubenmire, 1968). Daubenmire recognized, in contrast to continuum methods, more or less distinct associations separated by relatively narrow ecotones. The major differences of approach are in data gathering and manipulation and Daubenmire's use of climax tree and understory dominants in defining his associations (Chapter 11).

In general, the approach was to identify late-successional community types subjectively in the field and then sample the vegetation, the environments, and the biotic features within these types. The first stage of classification was to determine the climax tree species—those that were demonstrating reproductive success in the face of intense competition. On this basis, eight late-successional forest types (all but one defined by a single tree species) were recognized along a macroclimatic gradient from warm and dry lowlands to cool and moist highlands (Figure 15.3). At a second level of classification, most of the eight forest types were subdivided on the basis of shrubs and herbs dominant in the understory. Distinctions at this level reflect primarily soil microclimatic variation within a macroclimatic zone. In total, 22 associations were distinguished. They can be identified even in the early stages of secondary succession following fires, due to the persistence of climax herbs and shrubs

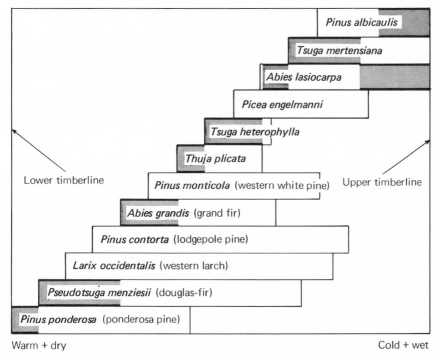

Fig. 15.3. Coniferous trees in the area centered on eastern Washington and northern Idaho, arranged vertically to show the usual order in which the species are encountered with increasing altitude. The horizontal bars designate upper and lower limits of the species relative to the climatic gradient. That portion of a species' altitudinal range in which it can maintain a self-reproducing population in the face of intense competition is indicated by the heavy lines. (After Daubenmire, 1966.)

many of which sprout back after burning. This layer approximates stability long before it is achieved in the overstory.

Each kind of association indicates a different kind of ecosystem. This is indicated by correlations that can be shown between these vegetational units and specific edaphic and climatic conditions, differences in tree growth rate, and disease susceptibility. Thus, the ecosystems recognized, termed *habitat types*, can be identified by and are named by the plant associations. For example, the *Pinus ponderosa–Symphoricarpos* association identifies an ecosystem termed the *Pinus ponderosa–Symphoricarpos albus* habitat type. The habitat types are similar in principle to the site units of the Baden-Württemberg system (Chapter 11) although they differ in scale and though vegetation is used to a much greater extent in their identification.

Using continuum methods of sampling and importance values, which give all species equal weight regardless of successional status, Daubenmire (1966) demonstrated that a continuum could be shown for his data. In regard to his classification based on late-successional species he stated:

A basic aim of synecology is to predict the potentialities of disturbed areas from inspection of their current, usually disturbed, plant cover. To do this, any units of classification or ordination must emphasize trends rather than take a static view that emphasizes only current vegetation composition (Daubenmire and Daubenmire, 1968).

Daubenmire's purpose is in classifying and describing ecosystem units and is clearly different from that of the continuum workers in studying the similarity of existing stands and drawing inferences of species relationships to environmental factors. Similar in the type of terrain of their study areas, the respective approaches of Daubenmire and Whittaker are also similar in their desire to identify ecosystem units. Whittaker's approach emphasizes the environmental factors of the gradient in relation to the distribution of individual species and the pattern of communities, although he does recognize community types and discontinuities. Daubenmire emphasizes the distinctness of types based on late-successional species and the characteristics (environment, biota, dynamics) of the community rather than continuity of species along gradients. As in the Wisconsin and Great Smokies studies, the conifers he studied had individualistic ranges so that contiguous communities tended to share many of the same species (Figure 15.3). Nevertheless, only in one segment of this range does a given species achieve climax status. This is well illustrated in three associations all dominated in the understory by the Pachistima union—*Abies grandis–Pachistima, Thuja-Pachistima; Tsuga-Pachistima*. The respective associations can be distinguished reliably only by the reproductive success of their characteristic climax tree species.

Regarding the continuity of the habitat types, Daubenmire stated:

> As with other biologic classifications, we do not imply that intergrades do not exist. Not only is variation within types recognized, but a deliberate attempt has been made to document as much of this variation as possible. The ecotones of the eight primary divisions based on overstory are relatively sharp, but those of the subdivisions based on undergrowth sometimes intergrade to a considerable extent (Daubenmire and Daubenmire, 1968).

Thus, despite differences in various continuum approaches and this community-type method, different degrees of distinctness are typically found in natural environments. This is particularly noteworthy in the work of Daubenmire where by studying communities independently of secondary succession he has found varying degrees of continuity—neither the perfectly distinct association nor the completely continuous continuum.

Arizona.   The mountains of Arizona, rising abruptly out of the cactus desert to an elevation of 11,000 feet and more, provide unusual opportunities for the study of vegetational change with altitude. It was here that, in 1890, C. Hart Merriam evolved his concept of life zones in the course of a survey of the biota of the San Francisco Mountains northwest of Flagstaff. Although he was concerned chiefly with the fauna of the region, he did take notes on the altitudinal distribution of the different tree species. For purposes of classification, he recognized in descending order an alpine zone, timberline zone, spruce zone, fir zone, pine zone, pinyon zone, and desert zone. His sketch (Figure 15.4), showing diagrammatically the effects of slope exposure on the altitudinal distribution of these zones, has been widely reproduced in subsequent ecological works. Although this study formed the basis for Merriam's life zones, it is noteworthy that Merriam himself clearly recognized the arbitrary nature of his groupings and the many factors that disturb their orderly distribution on the mountain range.

Working out from the old Carnegie Desert Laboratory, Forest Shreve concerned himself (1915) with the distribution of vegeta-

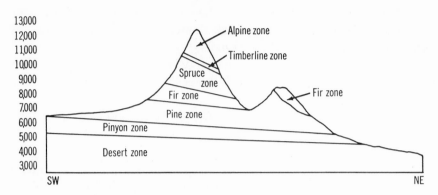

Fig. 15.4. Diagrammatic profile of San Francisco and O'Leary Peaks from southwest to northeast, showing the several life zones and effects of slope exposure. (After Merrian, 1890.)

tion on the south face of the Santa Catalina Mountains, lying northeast of Tucson. Although he relied heavily upon the altitudinal distribution of the various plant species, he emphasized the effects of aspect and site on this distribution. Shreve was impressed with the independence of each species—the associated members of a plant community were not able to follow each other to a common geographic and habitat limit. He observed that the most closely associated species were not alike in their life requirements. The members of many diverse biological types or growth forms in a community found their soil moisture at different levels, procured it at different seasons, and lost it through dissimilar foliar organs, at the same time that they reacted differently to the same temperature conditions. Thus they did not live in the same climate but in different spatial or temporal sections of it.

In a comparative study of the vegetation and site conditions of north and south slopes of the Santa Catalina Mountains, Whittaker and Niering (1964, 1965, 1968a, b) have amplified Shreve's studies and further described the remarkable vegetational gradient from subalpine forest to Sonoran desert (Figure 15.5). Besides the vertical zonation of communities, one observes the effect of aspect on the altitudinal distribution of the communities. A more complex vegetational pattern existed on the north slope than on the south slope. This may be largely due to the mosaic of parent materials on the north slope (including both an acid granite-gneiss complex

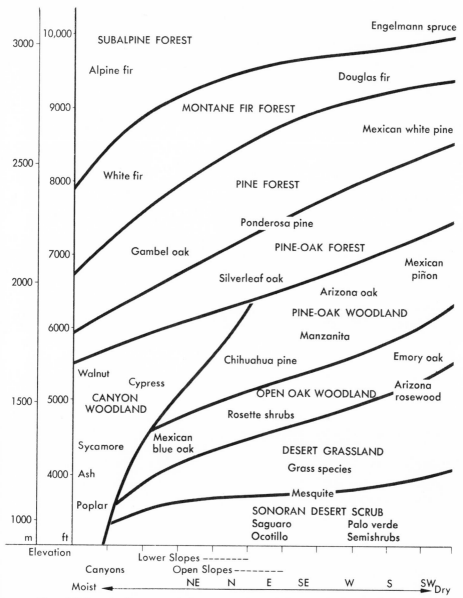

Fig. 15.5. A diagram of the vegetation of the south slope of the Santa Catalina Mountains in southeastern Arizona. (The vegetation above 9,000 feet is for the nearby Pinaleño Mountains.) Major species are indicated by their centers of maximum importance. (After Whittaker and Niering, 1965.)

and basic limestone) in contrast to the dominant granite-gneiss complex of the south slope.

As was also found in the Siskiyou Mountains of Oregon (Whittaker, 1960) and in the Coast Range of central California (Mc-Millan, 1956), species did not form distinct groups adapted and restricted to one parent material or another; they showed all degrees of relative restriction. Rasmussen (1941) made similar findings in his studies on the Kaibab Plateau in the northwestern portion of Arizona. He included the altitudinal distribution of tree species in his survey of the biotic communities of the area. His work is noteworthy in that he found it impractical to recognize different forest zones except in a very broad sense. Rather, he emphasized that each species had a different altitudinal range and different abundance at each altitude so that a series of intergrading forests occurred with the various species appearing, gaining abundance, and dropping out, more or less independently of one another. Similarly, the altitudinal distribution of forest trees on the mountains of southern Arizona is illustrated diagrammatically in Figure 15.6, based upon unpublished work by the senior author. The individualistic nature of the distribution pattern of each species is clearly shown, ranging from the high-altitude fir to low-altitude oaks. Although Douglas-fir is more abundant at higher altitudes than ponderosa pine and has a generally higher altitudinal range, there is such a broad range of overlap that both species may be expected to occur together in the absence of a disturbance, such as a fire, that might eliminate the fir. Similarly, the pinyons, oaks, and juniper share a low altitudinal range, but each species shows different affinities, so that the characteristic community might vary widely and more or less continuously in the absence of abrupt changes in aspect, soil moisture, parent material, or land history that might result in equally abrupt changes in the vegetation pattern.

The foregoing relationships provide evidence for the often cited principle of species individuality, originally set forth by Gleason (1926, 1939) as the "individualistic concept of the plant association." Rephrased by Whittaker and Niering (1968a), it states that "each species responds to the various environmental factors involved differently from any other species, according to its own genetic structure, range of physiological tolerances, and population dynamics including effect of competition and other relations to other species." Paradoxically, it is probably due to species interrelationships—interaction of species through competition and co-evolution, that tree

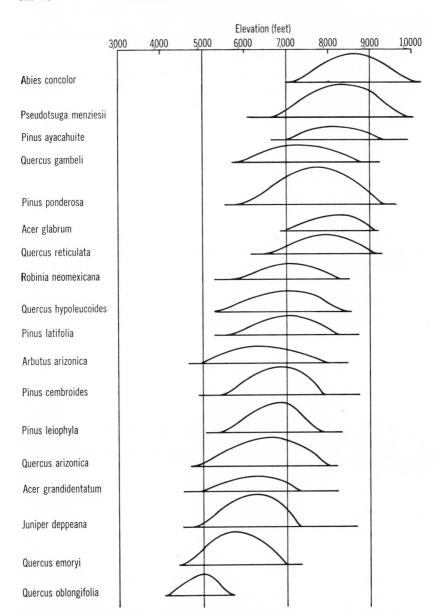

Fig. 15.6. Ecological range of mountain trees in southern Arizona.

species show the individual distributions invariably found along gradients. Community studies typically have been directed toward describing communities and their species composition. The more complex questions of the degree of mutual interaction of species within a community and of community stability shift the emphasis of study from the community itself to the ecosystem. Such investigations involve the construction of models and testing of hypotheses of how ecosystems work and, ultimately, the kinds of genetic and non-genetic interrelationships of organisms to one another and to their physical environment. This important and difficult task of understanding ecosystems is undertaken in the following chapter.

SUMMARY

Spatial variation in the composition of forest communities may be more or less gradual and continuous, or it may involve abrupt and distinct transitions from one community to another. Quite commonly, the forest varies in space at an uneven rate, so that communities characterized by a low rate of change are separated from other communities by ecotones in which the rate of change is very high.

Discrete communities easily separable by a line or narrow zone occur because of such factors as these:

1. Abrupt changes in parent soil material.
2. Abrupt changes in soil drainage or in soil-moisture relationships.
3. Abrupt changes in aspect, such as from north to south slope in steep terrain.
4. Abrupt climatic borders, such as from a frost pocket to a slope of good air drainage, the alpine timberline, or the prairie edge.
5. Destructive forest fires.
6. Land clearing.
7. A fence line on either side of which differential grazing has long existed.
8. Windfall.
9. Logging.

In contrast, ecological gradients involving gradual changes in forest composition and structure occur in response to gradual alterations in the forest site occasioned by changes associated with the following:

1. Geographical locations—such as from north to south or east to west.
2. Altitude.
3. Soil moisture.
4. Local climate.

5. Forest succession.

6. Long-term climatic changes.

Thus plants sort out along environmental gradients, whether natural or artificial. At times the subtle shift in species composition may make it difficult or impossible to designate community types. At other times the environmental gradient is steep and contrasting community types can be identified and sampled. Following natural or artificial disturbances, changes in species composition in time may tend to mask spatial change. In these situations, ecologists and silviculturists interested primarily in site potential should study environmental features of topography, soil, and microclimate as well as the existing vegetation.

SUGGESTED READINGS

CURTIS, JOHN T. 1959. *The Vegetation of Wisconsin*. Univ. of Wisconsin Press, Madison. 657 pp.

DANSEREAU, PIERRE (ed.). 1968. The continuum concept of vegetation: responses. *Bot. Rev.* 34:253–332.

DAUBENMIRE, R. 1966. Vegetation: identification of typal communities. *Science* 151:291–298.

———. 1968. *Plant Communities*. (Chapter 4, Vegetation and ecosystem classification, pp. 249–273.) Harper & Row, Inc., New York. 300 pp.

———, and JEAN B. DAUBENMIRE. 1968. Forest vegetation of eastern Washington and northern Idaho. Washington Agric. Expt. Sta., Tech. Bull. 60. 104 pp.

HACK, JOHN T., and JOHN C. GOODLETT. 1960. Geomorphology and forest ecology of a mountain region in the central Appalachians. U. S. Geol. Surv. Prof. Paper 347. 66 pp.

LAMBERT, J. M., and M. B. DALE. 1964. The use of statistics in phytosociology. *Adv. Ecol. Res.* 2:55–99.

LANGFORD, ARTHUR N., and MURRAY F. BUELL. 1969. Integration, identity and stability in the plant association. *Adv. Ecol. Res.* 6:83–135.

McINTOSH, ROBERT P. 1967. The continuum concept of vegetation. *Bot. Rev.* 33: 130–187.

ROWE, J. S. 1961. The level-of-integration concept and ecology. *Ecology* 42:420–427.

———. 1969. Plant community as a landscape feature. *In* K. N. H. GREENIDGE (ed.), *Essays in Plant Geography and Ecology*. Nova Scotia Museum, Halifax, N. S.

SPURR, STEPHEN H. 1956. Forest associations in the Harvard Forest. *Ecol. Monogr.* 26:245–262.

WHITTAKER, R. H. 1956. Vegetation of the Great Smoky Mountains. *Ecol. Monogr.* 26:1–80.

———. 1967. Gradient analysis of vegetation. *Biol. Rev.* 42:207–264.

———. 1970. *Communities and Ecosystems*. The Macmillan Co., New York. 158 pp.

16

Analysis of Forest Ecosystems

In the preceding chapters the classical ecological approach of autecology and synecology has been followed. The treatments of autecology and synecology are distinct, and information from one approach has had little effect on the development of principles from the other. However, it is clear that communities and individuals are interrelated with one another and their environment through the cycling of water and nutrients, the circulation, transformation, and accumulation of energy and matter, and the multiplicity of regulatory mechanisms which limit the numbers of plants and animals and influence their physiology and behavior. The term *ecosystem* is the most concise formulation of this concept of an interacting system comprising living organisms together with their non-living habitat. Although the idea of the ecosystem is of great antiquity and is recognized universally among mankind (Major, 1969), it is only in the electronic and atomic age that we are able to deal with the ecosystem as a whole on a firm scientific basis.

The goal of ecosystem analysis is to understand ecosystems and ecosystem processes. In forest systems, the goals may be directly related to a knowledge of the biological limits of productivity and the influence of such management practices as fertilization, timber harvest, grazing, irrigation, and drainage on the health, growth, and reproduction of the forest. Disturbances in the forest ecosystem and its breakdown through overgrazing, air pollution, and over-cutting have made us aware that we know too little about the functioning of the system and its interrelationship with adjacent terrestrial and aquatic systems. In the present chapter an overview of the approach to the analysis of ecological systems is given, energy cycling and productivity of ecosystems are discussed, and examples of the ways in which forest ecosystems are currently being studied are presented.

ECOSYSTEMS AND SYSTEMS ANALYSIS

An ecosystem is a special case of a general system—a collection of interacting entities or collection of parts, together with statements on the relationships between these parts (Dale, 1970). A system is termed *open* if there are inputs into and outputs from the system. An ecosystem is an open system in which at least one of the entities is living. In the system displayed in Figure 16.1, solar energy and precipitation are inputs into the system, and water, mineral substances, matter, and energy are outputs. In a managed forest system, timber, animals, water, aesthetics, and recreational values are the outputs that are utilized by man.

Various kinds of ecological systems may be recognized and studied, depending on the level at which life is examined. The biosphere with its total environment is a gigantic ecological system. Within the biosphere are ecosystems of forests, grasslands, swamps, and cultivated fields, all of which fit the general scheme of Figure 16.1, i.e., a biotic community together with its physical environment. At a lower rank each plant or animal individual, with its particular microenvironment, constitutes a biological system. Within the individual we can cite a further series of systems: organ—tissue—cell—organelle. An ecosystem can be broken into a hierarchy of subsystems based on processes. For example, subsystems of an ecosystem depicted by Figure 16.1 would include among others: the energy transfer system, the precipitation-evapotranspiration system, and the mineral cycling system.

The principal common denominator of terrestrial ecosystems is the food chain linking the physical environment with the three major living components, producers, consumers, and decomposers (Figure 16.1). Producers are usually green plants which produce carbohydrates and accumulate other organic substances. They are

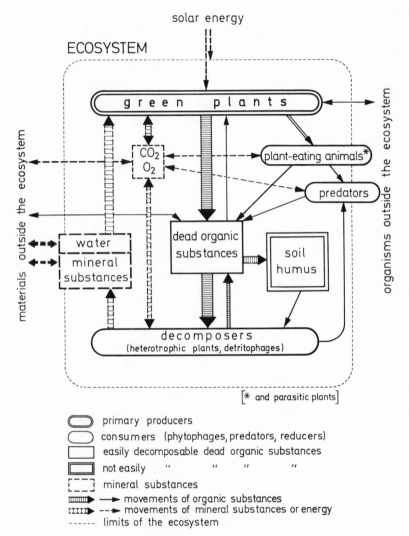

Fig. 16.1. General scheme of an ecosystem. (After Ellenberg, 1971b.)

termed *autotrophic* (self-feeding) since the carbohydrates they produce satisfy their own nutritional requirements.

Herbivores, carnivores, and parasites are the consumers that feed on plants and are termed *heterotrophic* (other-feeding) because they derive their nutrition from other organisms. Decomposers (also heterotrophs), especially fungi and bacteria, live on dead organic material and are essential in the processes of mineral cycling, which many consider the heart of ecosystem dynamics. In contrast to nutrient flow, which is cyclic, energy transfer is unidirectional, and energy is lost irretrievably from a system in several ways.

Systems analysis is the method which allows us to handle the great complexity of ecosystems. It is simply the conscious application of scientific method to complex organizations in order that no important factor be overlooked (Dale, 1970). It may be described as an explicit statement of what goes on, and in what order, in a system. Systems analysis is similar to problem solving in that the same phases are characteristic of both (Dale, 1970): (1) identification of all significant components that are of interest, (2) definition of the relationship between the selected components, (3) specification of the mechanisms by which changes in the system (the distribution of properties across the components) take place, and (4) solution and validation of the model outputs by comparing them to real system outputs. This approach allows us to examine large segments of nature as integrated systems.

DEVELOPING A SYSTEMS MODEL

Once the level and purposes of the analysis have been determined, the boundaries of the ecosystem must be established and the components of interest identified. The boundaries are arbitrary except that the area must be large enough to contain all ecosystem components, processes, and their interactions. In addition, the boundary should be placed where inputs and outputs across it are most easily measured.

A good example of an ecosystem for studying the nutrient cycle–hydrological interaction is the small watershed approach at Hubbard Brook, New Hampshire, described by Borman and Likens (1969). The ecosystem is a forested watershed of uniform geology which is underlain by a tight bedrock. The inputs of water and minerals in precipitation could be measured. Since the watershed is watertight, all geological output (water, sediment, and dissolved minerals) can be measured as all drainage water flows over a notch in a weir at the mouth of the stream draining the watershed (Figure 16.2). The nutrient balance for a single element in the ecosystem is then: geological input + meteorological input + biological input − (geological output + biological output) = net loss or gain. Bi-

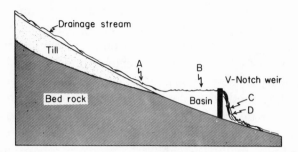

Fig. 16.2. Sampling design for measurement of output components in stream water of a terrestrial watershed ecosystem. A, water sample for dissolved substances; B, sediment load dropped in basin; C, water sample for millipore filtration; D, net sample. Total losses = dissolved substances (A) + particulate matter (B + C + D). (After Bormann and Likens, 1969.)

ological components would be animals and plants entering and leaving the system.

Once the boundaries and components of interest are identified, the relationships between the components may be modelled diagrammatically in a flow chart (Figure 16.3). Alternatively, a tabular format may be used to formalize a system; we will follow closely the one described by Smith (1970). First, assume the Hubbard Brook watershed has n components, each of which can be described quantitatively by many criteria, such as amount of calcium, nitrogen, and phosphorus, water content, caloric content, and so on. The components could be the individual plant and animal species, or, more conveniently, trees, shrubs, herbivores, carnivores, fungi, and bacteria. For each variable (such as calcium) a set of tables can be used to describe the system. For example, Table 16.1 shows the amounts (x_i) of calcium in each component

Table 16.1. The Amounts (x_i) of Calcium in Each of the n Components of an Ecosystem, and the Rates at Which Calcium Is Entering (a_i) and Leaving (z_i) the System via Each Component

Component	1	2	3	•	•	•	n
Amount	x_1	x_2	x_3	•	•	•	x_n
Inflow	a_1	a_2	a_3	•	•	•	a_n
Outflow	z_1	z_2	z_3	•	•	•	z_n

NOTE: In any real system many of the rates will be virtually zero.
SOURCE: Smith, 1970.

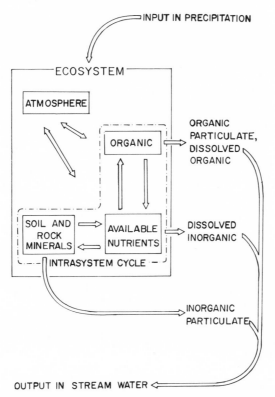

Fig. 16.3. Nutrient relationships for a terrestrial watershed ecosystem. Sites of accumulation, major pathways, and origins of chemical losses in stream water are shown. (After Bormann and Likens, 1969.)

of the system; also shown are the inflow (a_i) and outflow (z_i) of calcium for each component of the system. The total amount of calcium in the system is the sum of the first row (x_n); the total inflow is the sum of the second row (a_n); and the total outflow is the sum of the third row (z_n). This table esentially summarizes the nutrient budget for calcium for each component and for the ecosystem as a whole. The budget for calcium, based on input and output data from Hubbard Brook, is illustrated in Figure 16.4.

Calcium may be transferred from one component to another in the ecosystem in addition to inflow and outflow. This is illustrated in Figure 16.4 in the reciprocal transfer of exchangeable calcium between soil and trees and between components of the soils and rock minerals. Again a tabular presentation may be used to show trans-

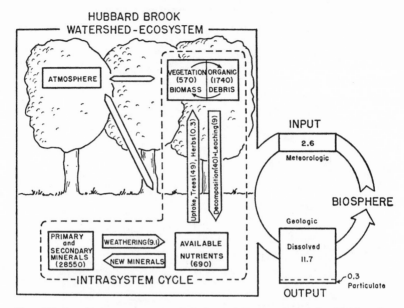

Fig. 16.4. Major parameters of the calcium cycle in the Hubbard Brook watershed ecosystems. All data in kg/ha and kg/ha/yr. (After Likens and Bormann, 1972.)

fer to and from each component (Table 16.2). Each row shows losses from a given component, and the row sum is the total rate of loss to other components. Each column shows gains to a particular component, and the column sum is the total rate of gain from all other components. Many entries in such a table may be negli-

Table 16.2. Transfer Rates of Calcium Among n Components of an Ecosystem

		Transfer to Each Component							
		1	2	3	4	•	•	•	n
Transfer from Each Component	1	—	y_{12}	y_{13}	y_{14}	•	•	•	y_{1n}
	2	y_{21}	—	y_{23}	y_{24}	•	•	•	y_{2n}
	3	y_{31}	y_{32}	—	y_{34}	•	•	•	y_{3n}
	4	y_{41}	y_{42}	y_{43}	—	•	•	•	y_{4n}
	•	•	•	•	•	•	•	•	•
	n	y_{n1}	y_{n2}	y_{n3}	y_{n4}	•	•	•	—

NOTE: In any real system many of the rates will be zero.
SOURCE: Smith, 1970.

ible or zero. An advantage of this format is that it can handle any degree of complexity within the system. Following Smith's (1970) description of the method, it is possible to write an equation for the rate of change of each variable (calcium, nitrogen, water, etc.) for each of the components with this information. Thus, the equation for component 3 would be:

$$dx_3/dt = a_3 - z_3 + (y_{13} + y_{23} + \ldots + y_{n3}) - (y_{31} + y_{32} + \ldots + y_{3n})$$

If component 3 were leaf litter, the equation might represent the rate of change with time in the amount of calcium due to: litter moved inward across the ecosystem boundary, minus that moved outward, plus litter received from various plant components (other y_{i3} terms may be zero), minus litter removed by consumers or decomposers, and minus litter transformed into humus (other y_{3j} terms may be zero).

If a study of the Hubbard Brook ecosystem had been made using the tabular format, Tables 16.1 and 16.2 could be filled with numbers representing amounts and rates. One would learn where activity does and does not occur, an important gain in information for most ecosystems. The system could then be set into a computer and, beginning with all the x_i's at their estimated levels, allowed to change through time according to the equations dx_i/dt.

Although we have learned many new things about the ecosystem, we will discover at this point that the data are inadequate to describe the functioning or dynamic nature of the ecosystem. Under computer simulation each component changes in the same direction at the same rate indefinitely. Because we are using average rates, the system we have modelled cannot respond to change with changes in rates. It is these responses that characterize the real-world ecosystem which we wish to simulate. For example, if the growing season is exceedingly dry, the rates of calcium transfer from litter to soil and soil to plants may be markedly reduced and the output from the system substantially different from the average estimate. Thus the use of an average rate (a simple number), rather than a variable rate (a mathematical function) corresponding to changes in environmental factors, destroys the dynamic properties of the system.

Smith (1970) describes what is necessary as follows:

It turns out in fact that the new problem is an order of magnitude more complicated than the estimation of averages. In particular, the rates must be expressed as *functions* of the system, and not as simple numbers, if we wish to learn anything about the system. Each transfer rate, y_{ij}, and each outflow, z_i, is a *set* of functions, an equation, which relates the rate to all those direct causal factors that govern it. It is only then that we can predict how each rate will change if the system is changed. Furthermore, if all of these are combined in the computer, we can predict how the system will respond to change. This is the only way that we can discover how ecosystems operate.

This development means that a great amount of experimental research that is relevant in the system, much of it physiological ecology, must be conducted. The expression of rates as sets of functions requires the estimation of many parameters other than the amounts and rates of calcium transfer. In simplified form, these can be arranged as shown in Table 16.3. In addition to x_i, a_i, and y_i, for each component, additional properties or attributes are usually needed. These w_{ij}'s may include the average size, age, and number of individuals in a component, distribution in space, growth habit, etc. Like the y_{ij}'s and the z_i's they may be sets of functions. In addition, a set of additional inputs (A_i) to the system, shown at the bottom of Table 16.3, is necessary. These are external variables, such as

Table 16.3. Additional Descriptors Needed for the Specification of Functional Relations in an Ecosystem of *n* Components

Component	Component Attributes (Open List)					
1	w_{11}	w_{12}	w_{13}	•	•	•
2	w_{21}	w_{22}	•	•	•	
3	w_{31}	w_{32}	w_{33}	w_{43}	•	•	•
•						
•						
•						
n	w_{n1}	w_{n2}	w_{n3}	•	•	•

External Attributes (viz., climate, weather; open list): A_1, A_2, A_3, A_4, etc.
SOURCE: Smith, 1970.

climatic factors and season, that affect the system as a whole. These and the inflows, a_i, are externally controlled variables that influence the system but are not affected by it. The rates, y_{ij} and z_i, measure system processes that may be functions of the external variables and any or all of the other amounts and rates that have been presented.

The immediate goal of system research workers is to find appropriate mathematical functions for the effect of external variables and for relationships among internal variables. The initial phase of ecosystem modelling is adequate once a satisfactory set of these functions is developed. The validity of the model can be assessed starting with an initial distribution of amounts, x_i, and a program through time of the input variables (A_i and a_i) and then comparing the amounts of the components predicted by the computer with observations in the field. This is the validation phase of the systems procedure, and the primary interest lies in how well the model outputs mimic those of the real system. To obtain a high fidelity to a real system requires a process of successive approximation, with the model progressively changed until the desired fidelity is achieved. The effects on the system of a treatment such as fertilization may be simulated by increasing the inputs of mineral nutrients and following the computer program. The results may be compared with field trials and further adjustments made in the model as necessary. Once a satisfactory model has been constructed, it becomes a powerful tool of management for predicting treatment effects. At the same time it has extended biological and other knowledge of the system and thus provided an understanding of certain portions of an ecosystem.

PRODUCTIVITY

The greatest contribution of research on ecological systems is the elucidation of the functional processes of forests such as photosynthesis, respiration, and the cycling of water and nutrients, and the bearing of these processes on forest productivity (Ovington, 1962). With progressively fewer exceptions most of the world's forests are man-made or man-modified through management or mismanagement. Thus forest processes must be understood in detail to predict not only production but the other potential effects of manipulations. The first step in studying the processes as they relate to productivity is essentially an inventory of the levels of dry matter (gm/m^2) in each component of the ecosystem. The most widely studied aspect of forest ecosystems in a systems context has been the flow of energy into photosynthate, its partition into dry-matter production of plants, and energy flow through the food chain of consumers and decomposers. Studies of production, although not currently applicable in site quality estimation, provide new ways of characterizing and comparing forest communities and also gross estimates of the average productivity of major portions of the earth. The terminology of production and examples of productivity attributes of several forest communities are considered in this section.

A small fraction of the radiant energy reaching the earth's surface, about 2 percent, is converted by green plants into chemical energy in photosynthesis and is termed their *gross primary production*. This gross production may be utilized in the formation of plant tissues (biomass) or used in respiration. Thus gross primary production minus respiration of green plants (the primary producers) equals a biomass termed *net primary production*. The energy of net primary production may be partitioned in several ways. A portion is accumulated in the community in plant and animal tissues (biomass accumulation) and part is used in the respiration of animals and plants that feed on the green plants. These relationships are seen clearly when diagrammed:

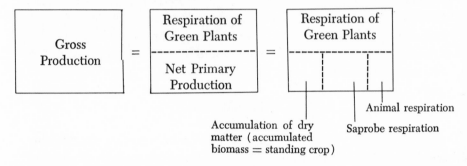

Productivity may be expressed either as an amount for a given period or an amount per unit time (rate), usually a year. The energy or dry matter in plants that is left after subtracting plant respiration per unit area and time is net primary productivity, which may be expressed either as energy ($cal/cm^2/yr$) or dry organic matter ($gm/m^2/yr$). The energy equivalents of dry-weight production are based on bomb calorimetric measurements for different tissues. Land plant tissues average about 4.25 kCal per dry gram. For example, the productivity of an oak-pine forest on Long Island, New York, has been estimated (Whittaker and Woodwell, 1969; Whittaker, 1970) and is partitioned as follows:

Gross productivity = Net primary productivity + Respiration

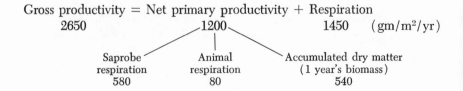

Most of the gross productivity goes to ecosystem metabolism, and less than half the net primary productivity and only 20 percent of the gross productivity remains in the standing crop of trees, under-story plants, and animals.

The biomass, the weight of all organisms (usually expressed in dry-matter content), per unit area in an ecosystem at a given moment in time is termed the *standing crop*. In a forest com-munity, standing crop is biomass accumulated to the time of measurement, whereas net primary productivity is but a fraction of this, the amount of dry matter produced in a given time period, usually a year. For example, the standing crop per acre in a red-wood forest 1,500 years of age may be enormous compared to its present net productivity per year, which may be very low. An ecosystem supporting a fast-growing 15-year-old stand of eastern cottonwood, however, may have only a fraction of the biomass of the redwood ecosystem, but a net primary productivity many times that of the redwood system. The ratio of standing crop to net primary productivity, the biomass accumulation ratio, is typically low in young, fast-growing stands, where most energy is used for growth. It is higher in old stands, where most of the energy is used to maintain the high existing biomass.

Consumers (herbivores and carnivores) feeding directly or in-directly from primary producers create a secondary production (Figure 16.5). As energy flows or is dragged forcibly from one trophic level to the next, from primary producer to herbivore and from herbivore to carnivore, energy is lost and production decreases. Herbivores in the forest community utilize only a small part of the total gross production of green plants. Part of it is utilized in respiration of primary producers, and much material is simply unavailable in roots, stem wood, bark, and branches. Even much of the available leaves, shoots, fruits, and seeds may be of a quality not acceptable to mammals, birds, and insects. Similarly, at the next trophic level secondary production by carnivores is substan-tially less than that of herbivores. Thus the energy entering the system is dissipated to the environment by respiration and biologi-cal activity and must be constantly replenished from the external radiation source.

Secondary production may be significant in a grassland or aquatic ecosystem where the herbivore-carnivore system (grazing chain) is especially well developed. However, in forest ecosystems,

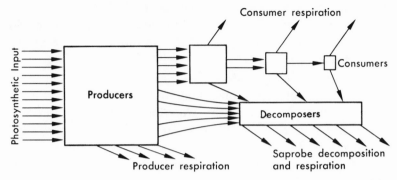

Fig. 16.5. Flow of energy in a natural community. In a steady-state community the intake of photosynthetic energy on the left, and the dissipation of energy back to environment toward the right, are in balance; and the pool of energy of organic compounds within the community remains constant. (After Whittaker, 1970.)

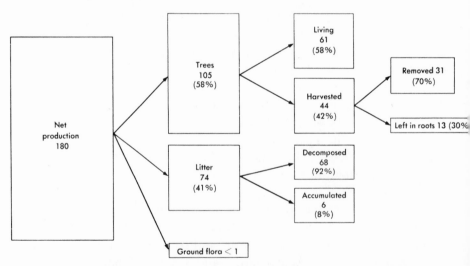

Fig. 16.6. Fate of energy in a Scots pine (*Pinus sylvestris*) plantation over 18 years, in 10^7 kilocalories/hectare. (Based on data of Ovington, 1962; after Kormundy, 1969.)

and especially plantations, litter decomposition and decomposers are primary sources of energy dissipation. Figure 16.6 illustrates the partition of energy in a young plantation of Scots pine. In an 18-year period most of the net production was stored in trees or in the litter or was decomposed by soil organisms. Instead of passing from herbivores to carnivores, much of the energy of net production was harvested by man.

Summaries of standing crop biomass and net primary productivity data (Art and Marks, 1971; Newbould, 1967; Ovington, 1962; Rodin and Bazilevich, 1968) show increasing productivity with increasing radiation (from arctic to tropical areas), decreasing elevation, and increasing moisture. Productivity estimates provide a a very general comparison of ecosystems of various kinds (Table 16.4). The estimates must be viewed with caution. For example, it would seem that temperate forests are about twice as productive as agricultural land in terms of net primary productivity (Table 16.4). However, this does not necessarily indicate that forest land is more fertile than agricultural land or that forests are more efficient than crop plants in producing organic matter. Actually, these productivities are not entirely comparable since that of agricultural crops is typically based on plants using only part of one growing season while annual production of forests is based on a growing stock that may have 30, 50, or more than 100 years of accumulated biomass. In Table 16.4, for example, the mean biomass accumulated in temperate forests is 30 times that of agricultural land.

The standing crop is not a measure of potential site productivity, but rather a function of age. Stem biomass accumulates year by year and becomes an increasingly greater part of the total biomass of the community. The change of biomass with age in a natural stand of oaks and pitch pine (Figure 16.7) illustrates the increase in dry weight of trees and the declining biomass of the undergrowth as the trees become dominant.

Community or stand comparisons of biomass must also take stand density and past stand history into account, in addition to age. For example, markedly different estimates of biomass were found for three 100-year-old stands of lodgepole pine of different densities and past treatment in western Alberta, Canada (Table 16.5; Johnstone, 1971). The site conditions were similar for all stands, and the ground vegetation was negligible in the three stands. Stand 2 had been thinned at age 70, but the dry weight of the material removed is unknown. A major problem in using biomass to compare potential productivity of natural forest communities over large portions of North America is that their densities

Table 16.4. Net Primary Production and Plant Biomass for Major Ecosystems for the Earth's Surface

	Area [a] (10⁶ km²)	Net Primary Productivity, per Unit Area [b] (dry gm/m²/yr)		World Net Primary Production [c] (10⁹ dry tons/yr)	Biomass per Unit Area [d] (dry kg/m²)		World Biomass [c] (10⁹ dry tons)
		Normal Range	Mean		Normal Range	Mean	
Lake and stream	2	100–1,500	500	1.0	0–0.1	0.02	0.04
Swamp and marsh	2	800–4,000	2,000	4.0	3–50	12	24
Tropical forest	20	1,000–5,000	2,000	40.0	6–80	45	900
Temperate forest	18	600–3,000	1,300	23.4	6–200	30	540
Boreal forest	12	400–2,000	800	9.6	6–40	20	240
Woodland and shrubland	7	200–1,200	600	4.2	2–20	6	42
Savanna	15	200–2,000	700	10.5	0.2–15	4	60
Temperate grassland	9	150–1,500	500	4.5	0.2–5	1.5	14
Tundra and alpine	8	10–400	140	1.1	0.1–3	0.6	5
Desert scrub	18	10–250	70	1.3	0.1–4	0.7	13
Extreme desert, rock and ice	24	0–10	3	0.07	0–0.2	0.02	0.5
Agricultural land	14	100–4,000	650	9.1	0.4–12	1	14
Total land	149		730	109.		12.5	1,852.
Open ocean	332	2–400	125	41.5	0–0.005	0.003	1.0
Continental shelf	27	200–600	350	9.5	0.001–0.04	0.01	0.3
Attached algae and estuaries	2	500–4,000	2,000	4.0	0.04–4	1	2.0
Total ocean	361		155	55.		0.009	3.3
Total for earth	510		320	164.		3.6	1,855.

a Square kilometers × 0.3861 = square miles.
b Grams per square meter × 0.01 = t/ha, × 10 = kg/ha, × 8.92 = lbs/acre.
c Metric tons (10⁶ gm) × 1.1023 = English short tons.
d Kilograms per square meter × 10 = t/ha, × 8922 = lbs/acre, × 4.461 = English short tons per acre.

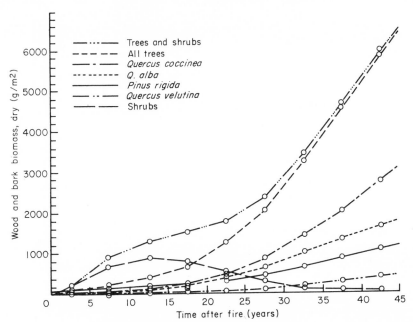

Fig. 16.7. Accumulation of wood and bark biomass in living trees above ground since a fire 45 years ago in the Brookhaven Forest, Long Island, New York. (After Whittaker and Woodwell, 1969.)

vary greatly and their past histories, often including harvesting, burning, grazing, or windthrow, are unknown.

The measurement of biomass and net annual productivity of the plant component of the ecosystem is an enormous task. In a plantation of trees of the same age, a sample of trees and other

Table 16.5.   Stand Attributes and Standing Crop of Biomass for Three Stands of 100-year-old Lodgepole Pine

	Stand 1	Stand 2 [a]	Stand 3
Number of living stems per acre	1,020	290	4,960
Mean diameter (in.)	6.4	9.8	2.2
Mean height (ft)	55	66	19
Stem volume per acre (cu ft)	6,356	5,107	2,594
Dry weight (of needles, branches, stem, and roots) (lbs/acre)	242,115	197,404	99,514

[a] Had been thinned.
Source: Johnstone, 1971.

vegetation may be harvested and the dry weight per unit area of roots, stems, branches, and leaves determined to give the biomass of the existing community. In a 70-year-old stand, the total biomass divided by 70, plus corrections for annual production of leaves, flowers, and fruits as well as root, stem, and branch mortality, would give an estimate of average net productivity per year. In natural forest communities that have many species of different ages, complex sampling and analysis procedures are required (Newbould, 1967; Whittaker, 1966; Whittaker and Woodwell, 1968), and they are constantly being improved.

Net primary productivity changes with age, probably not unlike the curve of mean annual increment of stem wood (Bruce and Schumacher, 1950), and hence, as with the standing crop, comparisons of community net productivity must consider age. The change in net productivity in a Scots pine plantation in England is illustrated in Figure 16.8 (Ovington, 1962). The mean productivity of trees increases to a maximum at about 35 years and decreases slightly thereafter. The current productivity of trees rises

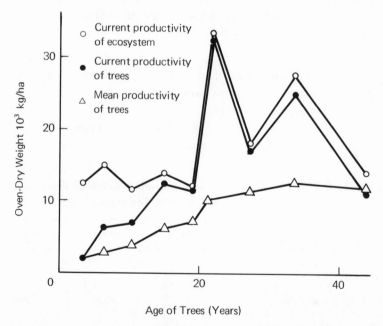

Fig. 16.8. Annual net production of organic matter by the trees and ecosystem (trees + understory vegetation) in plantations of Scots pine. (After Ovington, 1962.)

rapidly until about age 20, is maintained for several years, and declines rapidly after age 35. The understory vegetation makes its greatest contribution when the plantation is young and its least when tree dominance is greatest (dense crown cover and greatest root development). At later stages, particularly after age 35, thinning creates openings in the canopy that are not entirely closed so that additional light and moisture are available for undergrowth.

The productivity of a young oak-pine community on a poor site in central Long Island, New York, has been studied intensively by Whittaker and Woodwell (1968, 1969), and a comparison with a mixed hardwood cove forest in Tennessee (Table 16.6; Whittaker,

Table 16.6. Net Production and Biomass in Temperate Zone Forests

	Oak–Pine Forest [a]		Cove Forest [b]	
	Net Production	Biomass	Net Production	Biomass
Totals, net production (gm/m^2/yr) and biomass (kg/m^2), dry matter, for trees	1,060	9.7	1,300	58.5
Totals for undergrowth	134	0.46	90	0.135
Percentages of totals for trees in				
Stem wood	14.0	36.1	33.3	69.3
Stem bark	2.5	8.4	3.7	6.3
Branch wood and bark	23.3	16.9	13.1	10.3
Leaves	33.1	4.2	29.1	.6
Fruits and flowers	2.1	.2	1.8	.03
Roots	25.0	34.2	19.0	13.5
Biomass accumulation ratio	8.5		43.5	
Total respiration/gross productivity	0.80		1.0	
Age of canopy trees, years	40–45		150–400	
Mean tree height, m	7.6		34.0	

[a] Young, oak-pine forest at Brookhaven, Long Island, New York.
[b] Climax deciduous cove forest, Great Smoky Mountains National Park, Tennessee.
SOURCE: Modified from Whittaker, 1970.

1970) illustrates several new ways in which different ecosystems may be characterized. Small white, scarlet, and black oaks, along with scattered pitch pines, dominate the Long Island forest. They grow on well-drained podzolic soils derived from outwash sands and gravels. The authors characterize the community as floristically simple, spatially homogeneous, and of small stature. In contrast, the cove forest is rich floristically and spatially heterogeneous, with mature trees of large dimensions. The youth and small stature of the oak-pine forest is evident from the low standing crop of biomass, high proportion of biomass in branch, bark, and leaves, and the low biomass accumulation ratio.

The biomass of the root system of the oak-pine forest is about 2½ times as great as that of most mature forests (Whittaker and Woodwell, 1969) and exceeds that of the cove forest by a similar amount. The oaks and many shrubs of the oak-pine forest are adapted to fire and the shoots of the present stand arose from root systems which survived a fire about 1918. The roots have undoubtedly grown through more than one generation of shoots and are massive in comparison to the shoots they currently support (Table 16.6).

The oak-pine forest is atypical in the low percentage of stem wood of the total biomass compared with most of the forest communities for which estimates have been published. In general, the proportion of stem wood is particularly high (usually over 50 percent of above-ground biomass) in closed stands of conifers and for pioneer conifers and hardwoods in particular. Even the intolerant pitch pine of the oak-pine forest, due to its open-grown, branchy form, had only 19 percent of stem wood in the total above-ground biomass. Oaks and more tolerant species such as beech and maple have a greater proportion of branch, bark, and leaf dry matter than intolerants, due to their inherent branchiness and slow natural pruning. For example, the stem wood percentage of the total tree biomass of aspen and birch species in Japan was 47 to 64 percent while that for beech (*Fagus crenata*) was 34 percent (Satoo, 1970).

Although studies of productivity may be employed to compare different ecosystems, using the new dimension of dry-matter production, their primary purpose lies in providing basic information for understanding dry-matter, carbon, and nutrient cycling in ecosystems, i.e., in function rather than description. Moving beyond the current inventory stage of productivity estimates, the dynamics of biomass (carbon) transfer can be elucidated (see below) and the effect of external factors, such as drought, flooding, or fertilization, on biomass transfer in various systems can be evaluated. This will not only provide information on how ecosystems respond to treatments, but insights into the adaptation and integration of communities with their environments.

Productivity studies have generated increasing interest in the utilization of the total dry-matter content of stands as opposed to the traditional use of wood volume in tree boles (Keays, 1971; Young, 1964, 1971). The possibility of obtaining 40 to 50 percent more dry matter from a given stand is attractive to forest managers even if the quality yield (from leaves and bark) is lower. Total utilization might also open up for management many marginally productive or so-called "unmerchantable" stands, like the low-grade oak-pine stands on Long Island. The potential of complete-tree utilization is high, but the ramifications are many and complex (Keays, 1971). In particular, the massive biological problems of the effects of complete-tree utilization on the nutrient cycle, soil erosion, subsequent growth, natural or artificial regeneration, and the aesthetic-recreational problems await exploration.

EXAMPLES OF ECOSYSTEM ANALYSIS

Analysis of forest ecosystems calls for investigators of many disciplines to work together in constant communication, exchanging ideas and data, and studying that which is relevant in the system (Smith, 1970). Although many individual investigators may study the separate components of a system, unless there is overall planning, integration, and synthesis, we have merely a series of more or less related studies. Each may be very useful in its own right, but collectively they do not add up to an understanding of system dynamics. For this reason scientists in many parts of the world, recognizing the fragility of many natural systems and the ever-increasing demands of man on his environment, have planned and initiated ambitious and impressive programs known collectively as the *International Biological Program.*

A major goal of the International Biological Program (IBP) is to broaden our understanding of productivity in nature. This aim not only demands an inventory of the productivity of the world's ecosystems, but more significantly it implies an understanding of the dynamics and functioning of processes of these systems. If sufficiently profound, this can serve as an effective guide to prediction of the changes that are likely when ecosystems are subject to stresses and manipulations. In addition, systems-oriented studies allow us to perceive and resolve environmental problems in a new way. As stated by Reichle (1971):

Ecologists cannot continue to respond to each new environmental crisis by simplistic "cause and effect" studies of isolated ecosystem components. The totality of environmental systems must be recognized and an understanding developed of the interactions and interdependencies of systems components. Only in this way can the effects of perturbation upon individual components be interpreted in the total context of the system.

Research in some European programs (most IBP programs are country-oriented), notably in Belgium and Germany, began in the mid-1960's. In North America, programs of a wide scope were organized to study six major biomes: the deciduous forest (eastern United States), the coniferous forest (parts of the western United States), the grassland, the desert, the tundra, and the tropical biomes. The purpose of this section is to illustrate and briefly describe the scope and approach of two programs on different levels of complexity.

The Solling Project

The major German program is the intensive investigation of four ecosystems: deciduous European beech forest, evergreen Norway spruce forest, grassland under different fertilizer treatments, and cultivated field with annual plants under different fertilizer treatments (Ellenberg, 1971b). All four ecosystems, of similar climates and soils, are in a 25-sq-km area of the Solling plateau of north-central Germany. The general model applicable for all systems is that of Figure 16.1, and each compartment is under detailed study by teams of scientists.

In species composition, the forest ecosystems are representative of major forested areas of Germany and Central Europe. Beech communities are the most abundant deciduous forest communities in Germany. Although the beech forest is native in Solling, like most others in Germany, beech stands are carefully regenerated by man using natural seed crops. Norway spruce is not native in the Solling area but has been introduced and artificially cultivated in large plantations.

The Solling project illustrates what might be termed the intensive single-site approach. At one locality and for each ecosystem, detailed studies of all possible ecosystem processes are conducted. The four ecosystems will be characterized and compared with regard to:

Basic data on ecosystems:

1. Inventory of species and structural descriptions of the communities;
2. Variations in the abundance of important species and subspecies over time;
3. Biomasses and effective surfaces of the main components;
4. Biotope (climate, weather, topography, soil profile, human influences, etc.).

Magnitude of production by important partners in the biological communities:

1. Photosynthesis in the various layers of the stand;
2. Dry-matter production of the plant and animal populations;
3. Composition and quality of plant and animal products.

Exchanges and cycles:

1. Energy exchange in the ecosystems;
2. The water cycle (over the period of one year and over shorter periods of time);
3. The carbon cycle;
4. The cycling of primarily soil-related elements (N,P,Ca,K,Na, etc.).

Correlations:

1. Life cycles and environmental factors;
2. Magnitudes of production and environmental factors;
3. Magnitudes of production and easily obtained population data.

The model, the interrelationships, and the responses are therefore specific to the local community and its environment. It is a classical study of the total features of a terrestrial system, independent of a watershed system or a regional landscape. It has the advantage of developing an understanding of a specific ecosystem to an unparalleled degree. The approach has the possible disadvantage of limited application of the quantitative model derived at Solling to other ecosystems of different communities and environments. However, the scientists have chosen the most important forest communities of Central Europe so that results of the intensive single-site studies at Solling have good potential for extrapolation. Coupled with smaller-scale studies in beech and spruce stands under environmental conditions different from those at Solling, the specific process models may be generalized for use under a variety of European soil and climatic conditions. Methods and initial results have been presented by Ellenberg (1971a).

The Deciduous Forest Biome

In marked contrast in scope and approach to the Solling project, the Deciduous Forest Biome of the United States International Biological Program seeks to understand the dynamics and functioning of ecosystems in the eastern third of the United States. The forests of the deciduous forest biome region, 350 million acres, are predominantly native deciduous forests but also include substantial areas of pine and other conifers in the southeast, south, and north. Almost all of the forests have been subjected to disturbance by man. Approximately two-thirds of the population of the United States resides in the region, and it is the major area of man's impact through pollution, recreation, transportation, and use of food and wood products.

The deciduous forest biome program is directed at all aspects of complexity of the ecosystem—biotic and abiotic, structure and function, interaction and synthesis; the explicit goals are:

1. To develop and provide a synthesis of knowledge of ecosystem processes;
2. To derive from this knowledge a scientific basis for resource management, including the basis for long-term utilization of land and water resources in ways that maintain or improve environmental quality.

As in the German program, the objectives are oriented toward ecosystem processes, a comparison of the actual and potential efficiency of production in natural versus managed ecosystems (forested versus agricultural or aquatic), and the productivity of natural and managed systems as influenced by treatments such as fertilization, harvesting, and fire. The deciduous forest biome program, as contrasted to the intensive study of four local terrestrial ecosystems at Solling, is more comprehensive (understanding the ecosystem at several levels of area and complexity), and for this reason alone certain differences in objectives and approach necessarily arise.

Two important differences characterize the objectives of the deciduous forest biome in contrast to the Solling project. First, major emphasis in the deciduous forest biome is placed on development of *general models* of productivity and related ecosystem processes of natural forested and man-modified agricultural landscapes on a regional as well as a local basis. In other words, emphasis will be placed on increasingly more generalized mathematical models with wide biome applicability that can be then adapted to many different local ecosystems. Nevertheless, these models must be developed from data gathered at specific sites; they are then integrated into a general model, i.e., the general model is built from the bottom up. A totally different approach has been taken in the grassland biome. The grassland ecosystem model is built from the top down, beginning with a conceptual plan of the whole ecosystem. The more detailed submodels are then designed to fit into the overall model. Due to the much wider scope of both American biomes, general models are of more concern than they are in the Solling project.

Second, the deciduous forest biome project seeks an understanding of the influence of terrestrial ecosystems on the biological productivity of aquatic ecosystems and the quality of water in these systems. Herein lies a major contribution of the deciduous forest biome project, the *coupling of the terrestrial system and its trophic dynamics through the hydrologic system with the aquatic system.* This approach is also being followed in other North American Biome projects, particularly the coniferous forest and tundra biomes. Figure 16.9 illustrates the trophic-level approach of the deciduous forest biome program and particularly the linkage of the terrestrial and aquatic systems through the land-water interaction. The Solling model (Figure 16.1) is essentially comparable to the upper left-hand compartment, labeled "terrestrial ecosystems," of the deciduous forest biome (Figure 16.9).

The strategy in developing the generalized models requires first an intensive study of a given process at one site. Once functional expressions have been derived for the process, a computer model will permit prediction of future states of the system when the initial levels and inputs are specified. In order to provide for generalized application of the model, complementary but less detailed studies of the same process and the environmental factors affecting it are conducted at a number of different sites. The five major sites at which the process, modelling, and validation studies are being conducted are: (1) Oak Ridge site, eastern Tennessee; (2) Coweeta site, southwestern North Carolina; (3) Triangle site, Piedmont plateau, North Carolina; (4) Lake Wingra, southern Wisconsin; and (5) Lake George, northeastern New York.

In addition to the five major sites, biome-wide studies on a large geographical scale ("biome and regional analysis" of Figure 16.9)

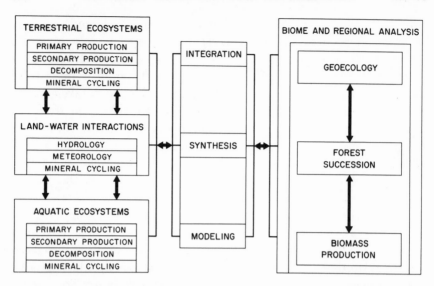

Fig. 16.9. Diagram of the interrelated parts of the deciduous forest biome program, a modified trophic-level approach. (After Auerbach, 1972.)

are designed to provide the kinds of information needed for the ecosystem models being developed at the major sites. These studies are of three kinds: (1) of the key environmental and vegetative variables most likely to vary across the biome, such as climate, soils, and differences in species composition; (2) of macroecological processes, such as forest succession, that operate at the level of entire landscapes or regions; and (3) of biomass production. Thus studies of productivity, climate, and species composition are being studied along transects connecting the major sites. For example, if models of productivity and chemical budgets are developed based on the vegetation and climate at the Oak Ridge site, information on biomass levels and climatic gradients are needed in the model to predict productivity along geographic gradients radiating from Oak Ridge.

Through an example of the kinds of studies conducted at one site, the Oak Ridge National Laboratory, Oak Ridge, Tennessee, and their integration, we can gain an overview of the approach at a key site. The Oak Ridge site program mirrors the objectives of the total biome program in requiring development of mathematical models at three levels: I—the individual forest and aquatic ecosystems, II—the watershed ecosystem, and ultimately, synthesis at level III, the regional drainage basin.

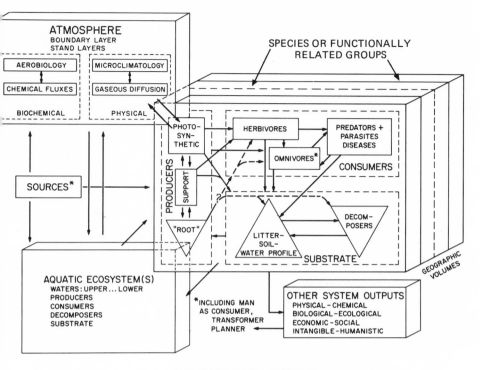

LAND ECOSYSTEM MODULE

Fig. 16.10. Model of levels I, II, and III of system complexity, Oak Ridge Site. The processes and components of terrestrial and aquatic ecosystems (level I, upper left and center) are shown coupled (lower left) in a watershed which is part of a regional drainage basin system (level II). The coupling of aquatic and terrestrial ecosystems in a number of watersheds, or "geographic volumes," constitutes the regional drainage basin system (level III). (Courtesy of Oak Ridge Site, Eastern Deciduous Forest Biome, US–IBP.)

A model of the individual forest and aquatic ecosystems (level I) and their coupling in a small-scale watershed of a regional drainage basin system (levels II and III) is shown diagrammatically in Figure 16.10. Research at the Oak Ridge site emphasizes (1) models of processes of a forested ecosystem and the manner in which nutrients and water affect forest growth and production and (2) direct manipulation of a small watershed system by fertilization with nitrogen and phosphorus. The manipulation permits expansion of the initial model and provides data relevant to management. The ability to predict watershed responses enables the watershed to serve as the validation site for the coupling of detailed forest and aquatic ecosystem models developed in level II. This is illustrated in the lower left portion of Figure 16.10 with the coupling of the aquatic system to a terrestrial system of one of the "geographic volumes." A practical objective of this modelling is to seek a balance which maximizes wood fiber production and minimizes eutrophication of the aquatic system.

The processes are being studied through intensive investigations at one research site, an ecosystem supporting a yellow-poplar community. This is at a level analogous to the beech and spruce ecosystems of the Solling project, but only selected processes are studied intensively. The initial model of the terrestrial forest system will consider the standing crop of dry matter or its carbon equivalent and the flow of the basic ecosystem components, water and nutrient elements. The generalized model for these key processes is shown in Figure 16.11. Research will determine the levels of each constituent

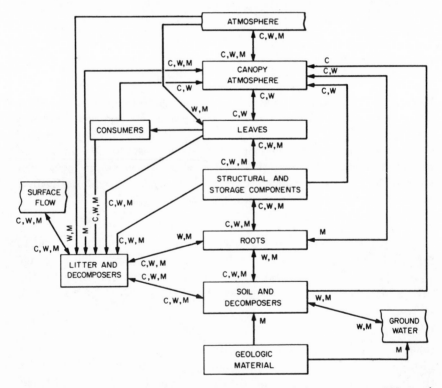

Fig. 16.11. Basic compartment model for carbon (C), water (W), and minerals (M), in a forest ecosystem. (After Reichle et al., 1971.)

in the system and transfer rates of these constituents between compartments. From the measurements, functions which describe transfers can be postulated. A quantitative model that describes the
temporal behavior of the system is the result, and the effects of
changes or perturbations on the system can be predicted.

An example of a model of organic matter (Figure 16.12) in the
yellow-poplar (tulip-poplar) ecosystem, derived in part from studies
using radioactive cesium, illustrates the compartments, their respective levels of organic matter, and the annual transfers between them.
Through the use of these data and the diagrammatic model, a mathematical model of organic matter transformation is being developed

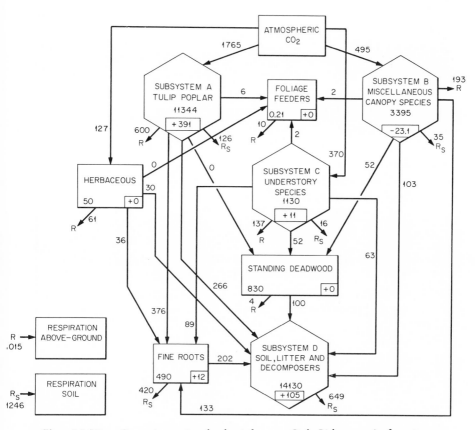

Fig. 16.12. Organic matter budget for an Oak Ridge mesic forest ecosystem. Compartment values in grams of dry weight per square meter; flow
values (on arrows) in grams of dry weight per square meter per year. (After
Sollins, 1972.)

that can vary with season or stage of stand development (Sollins, 1972). The transfer values show total transfer during one year but are not meant to imply even distribution throughout the year. Litter-fall is concentrated in about a three-week period, and almost every flow is greater during the growing season as a result of both biological and climatic factors. In this system, the rapid decomposition rate and substantial release of carbon through soil respiration is apparent (Figure 16.12). As in most forest systems, very little transfer occurs through herbivores (foliage feeders); large amounts of carbon are stored, particularly in the stem, litter, and soil.

The coupling of the terrestrial processes (developed from intensive site studies) with the aquatic ecosystem through the hydrologic cycle (Figure 16.10) will be studied at the Walker Branch Watershed. The Walker Branch drains a 241-acre forested watershed having two subwatersheds and underlain by dolomitic rock. The two main forest communities on the watershed are oak-hickory and chestnut oak. Part of each watershed was cleared for agriculture prior to 1942, but since then the area has been virtually undisturbed and natural succession has returned these areas to a well-stocked forest condition.

The Walker Branch study is aimed at synthesis of an empirical model which will:

1. Relate the productivity and water quality of the stream to the productivity and nutrient balance of the adjacent terrestrial subsystem;
2. Establish the relationship between the hydrologic cycle and nutrient flow;
3. Provide benchmark information of natural terrestrial-aquatic ecosystems for comparison with man-modified systems;
4. Enable the measurement of environmental degradation caused by man's cultural practices.

Diverse kinds of aquatic, terrestrial, and hydrologic studies are necessary to characterize the aquatic and forested ecosystems (including study of biomass, net productivity, soil-moisture movement, and runoff yield) and the flow of water and minerals through the watershed. Once the input and output relationships have been characterized (a 3- to 5-year period) for each subwatershed to establish its own peculiar response to mineral and water input, one subwatershed will be fertilized. Then by monitoring posttreatment terrestrial and aquatic processes and the flow of water and minerals through the watershed, the effects of fertilization on components of the system may be evaluated.

In summary, the Oak Ridge site program is one of intensive characterization of certain ecosystem processes, integration of process-level studies through development of generalized mathematical models at the ecosystem level, an extensive study of the land-water interaction of these processes, and validation of ecosystem models in a small watershed under treated (fertilized) and natural conditions. The strategy of this site program, like that of the Deciduous Forest Biome as a whole, is to build the ecosystem model from the bottom up. That is, after some 10 to 15 models of fundamental processes have been constructed they will be integrated into an overall model.

The series of studies and biome projects of the International Biological Program now under way is the most significant event in the history of ecological research. The study of whole ecosystems is in effect the creation of a whole new level of ecological science (Smith, 1970). Whether the large interdisciplinary approach of the Biome projects based on greatly simplified models will lead to major improvements in the scientific understanding of ecosystems remains to be seen. Despite problems, however, it is increasingly clear that we cannot wait for more detailed and basic studies before initiating studies of entire ecosystems. The payoff lies in predicting long-term changes, and in understanding how man can manage the fundamental processes of ecosystems for his greatest advantage in an age of shrinking environmental resources and environmental quality.

Computer Simulation of Forest Growth and Succession

In addition to projects involving the modelling of entire ecosystems, models simulating specific forest processes are being developed and tested. Such a computer simulation, which successfully reproduces the population dynamics of trees in a mixed conifer-hardwood forest of northeastern North America, has been developed by Daniel Botkin and co-workers in conjunction with the Hubbard Brook ecosystem study in New Hampshire (Borman and Likens, 1967; Borman et al., 1970). Details of the model, development of formulas, and the results of the simulation are given by Botkin et al. (1972a).

The goal was to produce a dynamic model of forest growth and succession in which changes in the state of the forest are a function of its present state (including general species characteristics) and random components. The conditions of the forest in its present state were determined from a study of vegetation and site characters on 10-by-10-meter plots throughout a range of elevations from 458 to 1,068 meters in the Hubbard Brook Watershed. Each of the 13 tree species (11 hardwoods and 2 conifers) was defined in the simulator by nine characteristics, such as maximum age, maximum diameter and height, relationship between total leaf weight and diameter, relationship between rate of photosynthesis and available light, and so forth. Site conditions were defined by seven attributes, including elevation, soil depth, soil-moisture holding capacity, temperature, and precipitation.

The assumptions necessary to define competitive relationships between the species and generate a reasonable model of succession were incorporated into three basic subroutines in a computer program. In the simulation program these were titled "grow," "birth," and "kill." These subroutines were developed to obtain reasonable growth rates for each species (grow), to determine the probability of the ingrowth of saplings of each species into a plot (birth), and to determine the probability of the mortality of stems of a given species on a given plot (kill). Using these equations and the initial plot data, the species composition (number of each species present), basal area by species, and total basal area per unit area were computed at yearly intervals. The successional changes in species composition in plots at the various elevations shown by the simulator could be verified by observations in forests of the Hubbard Brook watershed and the model modified as necessary.

The assumptions made in the simulator define the strategies of the different species. For example, red spruce is the slowest-growing yet longest-lived species. It is shade-tolerant and enters the shaded understory in small numbers. In contrast, white birch is fast-growing, short-lived, shade-intolerant, and colonizes open areas in large numbers. The competitive strategies of the species in the simulator mimic natural conditions whereby birch occupies open sites, grows rapidly to maturity, and produces abundant seed to initiate colonization of other available sites. Spruce enters the shaded site, persists in the understory, and eventually succeeds birch in the overstory. In this way, at least the more obvious strategies of successional and climax species can be simulated by a few comparatively simple assumptions.

Simulated succession following clearcutting resulted in a rapid decline in numbers of pin cherry and a continuous decline of white and yellow birch, from the first 10-year period to 100 years. Shade-tolerant, slow-growing beech (and other tolerant species) increased gradually with time elapsed from clearcutting. In addition to reproducing general characteristics of forest succession, the model also demonstrated the changes in vegetation that accompany changes in elevation (Botkin *et al.*, 1972b).

Long-term behavior of the forest was also simulated and demonstrates relationships that invite verification. Figure 16.13 illustrates

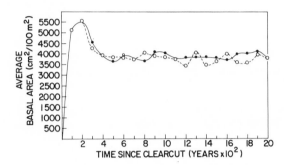

Fig. 16.13. Two long-term predictions of average basal area per plot of the model at 610-m elevation. Each line represent the average of 100 plots with identical site conditions including a deep, well-drained soil and constant climate, but starting with different pseudorandom numbers. (After Botkin *et al.*, 1972b.)

the average total basal area per plot for 2 groups of 100 identical plots at 610 m at 100-year intervals for 2,000 years. The basal area is nearly identical for both groups for years 100 and 200. Thereafter, random events bring about the fluctuating curve pattern of the sets of plots. The climax state following clearcutting is reached at about 400 years, whereas the maximum standing crop in basal area occurs at about 200 years. Following clearcutting, according to Botkin *et al.* (1972b), species diversity increases to a peak at approximately 70 years at 610 m and then decreases thereafter. The simulation also indicated that the late-successional forest is dynamic, and suggests that what is generally called a climax state is the most probable but not the only state of a small forested area in a stable climate. Early-successional conditions equivalent to clearcutting occur on about 1 percent of the plots even at 200 years, allowing the intolerant species to enter the stand and grow. Although the results must be treated with caution, the simulation technique illustrates that the general development and successional behavior of a complex forest community can be reproduced from relatively few characteristics.

SUMMARY

The goal of the study of whole ecosystems is to understand their processes and functioning. Such an understanding is urgent because we need to predict the long-term as well as the short-term consequences of man's actions in an ecosystem. A typical terrestrial ecosystem consists of all organisms of a forest community together with its physical environment. It receives inputs of energy, water, and nutrients, and yields to man outputs of timber, animals, water, aesthetics, and recreational values. To understand the functioning of an ecosystem, the method of systems analysis enables us to break the ecosystem down into its component parts and processes (such as energy transfer, mineral cycling, water cycling) so that no important factor is overlooked. In the first step of analysis, descriptive work is employed to identify all the significant components of the system that are of interest. In a forest ecosystem, a partial list would include the atmosphere, the forest trees, the understory plants, the litter, and the soil. Next, a model is constructed showing relationships between the components for some property of the system. Then the rates of transfer of the property between components are specified—such as the rate of nutrient exchange from atmosphere to forest, forest to soil, and soil to forest. Furthermore, the mechanisms by which changes in these rates occur (changes in temperature, precipitation, cloud cover) must also be specified and built into the model. Based on the trial model of interrelationships between components, the exchange rates, and the factors affecting them, inputs may be entered and run through the system. The outputs of the model are then compared with those of a real-world system and changes to the model are made as necessary. Once a model mimics a natural ecosystem reasonably well, a disturbance such as fertilization, fire, or clearcutting may be simulated and its effect on all components of the system determined.

In forest ecosystems, the greatest emphasis has been placed on the processes of photosynthesis and respiration, on the cycling of water and nutrients, and on the bearing of these to forest productivity. The flow of energy into photosynthesis and its partition into dry-matter production of plants (the producers) and energy flow through the food chain of consumers and decomposers is under intensive study. Only about 2 percent of the radiant energy is converted by green plants into chemical energy in photosynthesis, and this is termed gross primary production. Gross production may be utilized in formation of plant and animal tissues (biomass) or may be used in plant, animal, and saprobe respiration. In forests, most of the biomass is stored in the standing crop of trees and in the litter. In young forests, gross production is high, respiration is moderate, and as a result there is rapid biomass accumulation. In old forests, respiration takes a proportionately greater part of the gross production. Although the standing crop of biomass is high, the rate of new biomass accumulation is relatively low.

Recognizing the need to understand whole ecosystems, comprehensive ecosystem studies have been initiated in many countries of the world. In the Western Hemisphere, interdisciplinary studies of six major biomes are under way: the tundra, the coniferous forest, the deciduous forest, the grassland, the desert, and the tropical biomes. In the deciduous forest and the coniferous forest biomes, process models are being built from ecosystem studies at specific sites and then integrated into an overall biome model. A major contribution of these large-scale projects is studies of nutrient and water cycling which link terrestrial forest systems with aquatic systems. Through such studies, the effects of cutting, fertilizing, or fire in a forest ecosystem on adjacent streams and lakes can be monitored. This kind of integrated study will increasingly provide the basis for management of both terrestrial and aquatic ecosystems.

SUGGESTED READINGS

BOTKIN, DANIEL B., JAMES F. JANAK, and JAMES R. WALLIS. 1972. Some ecological consequences of a computer model of forest growth. *J. Ecol.* 60:849–872.

DALE, M. B. 1970. Systems analysis and ecology. *Ecology* 51:2–16.

KORMONDY, EDWARD J. 1969. *Concepts of Ecology.* (Chapter 1, The nature of ecosystems; Chapter 2, Energy flow in ecosystems; Chapter 3, Biogeochemical cycles and ecosystems.) Prentice-Hall, Inc., Englewood Cliffs, N. J. 209 pp.

ODUM, EUGENE P. 1969. The strategy of ecosystem development. *Science* 164: 262–270.

OVINGTON, J. D. 1962. Quantitative ecology and the woodland ecosystem concept. *Adv. Ecol. Res.* 1:103–192.

SMITH, FREDERICK E. 1970. Analysis of ecosystems. *In* DAVID E. REICHLE (ed.), *Analysis of Temperate Forest Ecosystems.* Springer-Verlag, New York. 304 pp.

WALTERS, CARL J. 1971. Systems ecology: the systems approach and mathematical models in ecology. *In* Eugene P. Odum, *Fundamentals of Ecology.* W. B. Saunders Co., Philadelphia. 574 pp.

WHITTAKER, ROBERT H. 1970. *Communities and Ecosystems.* (Chapter 4, Production.) The Macmillan Co., New York. 158 pp.

———, and G. M. WOODWELL. 1969. Structure, production and diversity of the oak-pine forest at Brookhaven, New York. *J. Ecol.* 57:157–176.

THE FOREST

IV

17

Historical Development
of Forests

PHYTOGEOGRAPHY

In this final part, we are concerned with providing a brief description of the present-day forests of the world with particular reference to the forests of temperate North America. Description, however, is not enough. An understanding must be provided also by summarizing briefly what is known of the historical development of present-day forests (this chapter), and, in the description of these forests, bringing in as much as possible of the climatic, edaphic, and dynamic relationships which go far toward explaining why a particular type of forest is growing on a particular site.

That phase of botany in which geographical problems of plant distribution are emphasized is termed *plant geography,* or *phytogeography.* Although much of the concern and knowledge is shared with plant ecology, it differs in that it has arisen from studies of the distribution of particular taxa of plants, rather than from studies of the environment. In other words, plant geography basically is floristically oriented whereas plant ecology is environmentally oriented, although both are concerned with the interrelationship of plants and their environment.

Plant geography is concerned with historical and present-day distributions of plant taxa, the location of their origins, studies of dispersal and migration, and in general with the evolution and present distribution of our flora. Only those phases pertinent to a brief survey of the present distribution of the world's forests can be summarized here. Excellent textbooks (Wulff, 1943; Cain, 1944, Good, 1965; and Polunin, 1960) are available for those wishing to delve more deeply.

PALEOECOLOGY

In order to understand the present-day distribution of the forests of the United States and Canada—and indeed of the world—it is essential to know something of the evolution of modern forms of trees through geological times, the widespread changes in their distribution during Pleistocene glaciations, the changes in forest composition in postglacial times, and the effects of the development of civilizations on the distribution and character of forests.

The historical development of plants is known variously as *historical plant geography* if the emphasis is on geographical distribution of the various elements of the flora, and as *paleoecology* if environmental changes are of primary concern. Plant geographical knowledge with particular emphasis upon its historical development is covered by Cain (1944) while European literature and viewpoints are presented by Firbas (1949, 1952), Frenzel (1968), and Straka (1970). Recent advances in paleoecology are reported in the excellent and comprehensive treatment of the Quaternary of the United States (Wright and Frey, 1965) and in several symposium volumes (Cushing and Wright, 1967; Hopkins, 1967; Dort and Jones, 1970; and Turekian, 1971).

EVOLUTION OF MODERN TREE SPECIES

Aside from a few tree ferns and cycads which reach tree proportions, modern trees may be grouped as *gymnosperms* and *angiosperms*. The appearance of their prototypes and the gradual development of modern forms are recorded in fossils with which the study of paleobotany is concerned (Arnold, 1947). A few salient points may be summarized briefly.

The oldest lineage of modern trees is possessed by the conifers, which can be traced back to late Paleozoic. Some prototype conifers had leaves and branches very like those of modern species of

Araucaria, a Southern Hemisphere genus which persists today with species such as Norfolk Island pine (*Araucaria excelsa*), hoop pine of Queensland (*A. cunninghamii*), Parana pine of Brazil (*A. angustifolia*), and the monkey-puzzle tree of Chile (*A. araucana*). These primitive conifers, however, constituted but a small part of the forests which formed the coal beds of Carboniferous (Mississippian and Pennsylvanian) times. Tree fern (Pteridosperms), horse-tails (Calamites), club-mosses (Lepidodendrids), and an extinct line of primitive conifers (Cordaites) formed the dominant tree flora. These lowland, mild-climate plants were largely eliminated during the continental uplift and large-scale glaciation of the Permian times, leaving the land open to colonization by the developing modern arborescent groups.

In Mesozoic times, the conifers evolved into many forms and achieved great abundance. By Jurassic times, forms similar to modern *Libocedrus, Thuja, Sequoia,* and *Agathis* (the kauri of New Zealand and nearby lands) had appeared. Since identifications must be made frequently on impressions made by fragments of leaves and other vegetative parts, many are highly tentative. The general predominance of conifers in the fossil record of Mesozoic times is clear, however, as is the fact that most present-day genera of conifers are much less widely distributed than they apparently were in late Jurassic and early Cretaceous times (Li, 1953). The genus *Sequoia,* for example, is known from fossil records across Europe, central Asia, and North America as well as from Greenland, Spitsbergen, and the Canadian Arctic, but is restricted today to one species with local distributions in California. *Metasequoia,* also, was abundant at high northern latitudes during Cretaceous and early Tertiary times, but now exists only locally over a very restricted range in the interior of China (Chaney, 1949). *Cupressus* is still another once widespread coniferous genus, which now occurs only in widely scattered relict stands. The now widespread pines were less abundant during the Mesozoic. However, a Cretaceous pine recently described from the Cretaceous of Minnesota is closely similar to red pine (*Pinus resinosa*), which occupies the same region today (Chaney, 1954). In Australia and Tasmania, conifers similar to present-day podocarps of the area have been described from the Tertiary (Cookson and Pike, 1953).

One of the earliest and most primitive forms that has survived in a closely related form to the present day is the ginkgo (*Ginkgo biloba*), the sole surviving member of a once numerous group of gymnosperms. Species with leaves similar in form and in the structure of the epidermal layer to the present-day tree, which occurs naturally only in western China but which is widely introduced, are common in Triassic floras.

The angiosperms developed later than the conifers, but by the middle of the Cretaceous had become common and well represented in fossil floras. Pollen and macrofossil evidence indicates that the early angiosperms of the lower Cretaceous or possibly the late Jurassic showed little taxonomic diversity and were probably not closely similar to modern flowering plants. The first angiosperms apparently developed slowly on temperate tropic uplands of the ancient landmass of Gondwanaland (Axelrod, 1970). Thereafter angiosperms evolved during periods of great environmental change which probably elicited increasing diversity in plant forms. Continents changed in position, configuration, size, and altitude through ocean-floor spreading, continental rafting (drift), and the fragmentation and joining of plates of the earth's crust. Mountains elevated as the plates collided (Himalayas and American Cordillera), and some desert lands became moist tropics; climates changed drastically. As summarized by Axelrod (1970):

The great diversity of taxa in numerous families in the tropics and subtropics, as well as the evolution of unique floras of arid to semiarid regions and those of the temperate climates as well, seems directly related to the breakup of Gondwanaland following the medial Cretaceous and subsequent evolution in isolation.

During the Tertiary, flowering plants became widely distributed and well differentiated throughout the world. In Eocene times, the warmest Tertiary epoch, tropical types of plants were intermingled with warm temperate types as far north as London, England, and the coastal plain of eastern United States. In the Eocene London coal beds, Nipa palm was one of the commonest species—it is now a salt-water swamp species of southeastern Asia. The vegetation around the north Pacific basin from Oregon to Alaska and southwest to Japan was tropical to subtropical in character. Then a major deterioration in climate took place in the Oligocene with broadleaved deciduous forests replacing subtropical forests. Except for minor fluctuations, the cooling trend continued in the Miocene and Pliocene and culminated in the Pleistocene ice age.

In Miocene times, a forest of temperate mesophytic species (ancestor of the modern Mixed Mesophytic Forest) replaced the warm temperate and subtropical types in much of the Northern Hemisphere. A continuous band of this broadleaved deciduous forest existed around the north Pacific from Oregon to Japan. The resemblance of forests in these areas is remarkable even on the species level. Furthermore, as late as 15 million years ago (middle Miocene) floristic continuity existed between eastern North America and eastern Asia. The Mixed Mesophytic Forest included several species that ranged across the broad land bridge in the Bering Sea area. This land bridge, open throughout much of Cenozoic times, aided in securing a broad interchange between Asiatic and American floras and faunas (Hopkins, 1967a).

By late Miocene, coniferous forests began to occupy large upland areas in Siberia and northern North America as the mesophytic hardwoods retreated southward (Wolfe and Leopold, 1967). A coniferous forest of spruce, fir, and hemlock for the first time extended from the uplands of Oregon northward through British Columbia into Alaska. The Mixed Mesophytic Forest of the northwest gradually became extinct with the coming of a cooler climate and the rise of the Cascades, which brought dry and even arid conditions to vast areas of the interior. A southern extension of the eastern American forest, represented by such trees as sweet gum, white pine, blue beech, American beech, the sugar maple group, and black gum in the cloud forest of Mexico and Central America (especially in the Sierra Madre Oriental), apparently originated about this time (Martin and Harrell, 1957). In Europe, the mesophytic flora was largely eliminated. Examples of genera that became extinct in Europe with progressive cooling are the following (Van der Hammen *et al.*, 1971):

At the End of	Extinct Genera of Europe
Miocene	*Castanopsis, Clethra, Libocedrus, Metasequoia*
Pliocene	*Aesculus, Diospyros, Elaeagnus, Liquidambar, Nyssa, Palmae, Pseudolarix, Rhus* (and probably *Sequoia* and *Taxodium*)
Pleistocene	*Carya, Castanea, Celtis, Juglans, Liriodendron, Magnolia, Ostrya, Tsuga*

That many of these genera survived in North America and eastern Asia is ascribed to the north-south orientation of the mountain chains of these areas, permitting the temperate species to migrate southward to warmer areas and then expand northward in the interglacial intervals. In Europe, the Pleistocene continental glaciations, combined with east-west chains of the glaciated mountains (Alps, Pyrenees, Carpathian and Caucasian Mountains), are thought to account for the extinction of these elements in Europe and western Asia.

The extensive glaciation of the Pleistocene denuded much of the northern portions of the Northern Hemisphere. The distribution of trees as it is believed to have been during the maximum extent of the latest Pleistocene glaciation and the revegetation of the glaciated terrain are discussed in the following section.

GLACIAL AND POSTGLACIAL FORESTS

One of the major scientific advances of recent decades has been the unraveling of much of the complex history of the vegetation and climates of the world from the time of the last great glacial advance to the present. By bringing together data from archeological sources, fossil studies and in particular pollen analysis, tree-ring analysis, and radio-carbon dating, it has become possible to spell out in considerable detail the overwhelming of the forests before the advancing Pleistocene ice, and their migration back onto the glaciated terrain as the ice melted. The irrefutable evidence that vegetation has been in an almost constant state of instability and adjustment due to an almost constantly changing climate over the past ten thousand years, and even over the past several hundred years, has done more than anything else to demonstrate the necessity for recognizing that present vegetation patterns are closely related to events in recent geological history.

In considering glacial and postglacial forest history, it is well to first summarize the techniques by which the various lines of evidence have been accumulated, then the geological history of ice advance and retreat, and then the evidence of changing forest composition over the last ten thousand years, which is one of the major proofs of rapid and continuing climatic changes extending up to and including the present.

Lines of Evidence

The dating and ecological interpretations of the prehistoric past are made possible only by the combination of many lines of evidence. Archaeological stratigraphy, geomorphological evidence such as glacial varves and stream-terrace studies, dendrochronology or tree-ring studies, peat analysis, pollen analysis, carbon-14 and other types of radio-isotope dating, and many other research techniques all contribute bits of information and evidence which add together to give a picture of past vegetation and climate. The most important lines leading to a picture of the historical development of forests are outlined briefly below.

Fossil Wood.   Since wood rots only under moist, aerobic conditions, wood may be preserved many years under anaerobic (i.e., without air) or under very dry conditions (without water). Wood may thus be preserved for many thousands of years in acid peat bogs, buried under glacial drift deeper than surface air can penetrate, or in the desert, particularly under protected cliffs. Charcoal, being carbonized wood, is chemically inactive under ordinary conditions of exposure and may be preserved for thousands of years in the soil, giving evidence of past fires. It can be frequently identified as to genus and dated as to age.

Important deposits of preserved wood are many. Buried under glacial till in the Lake States, the Two Creeks buried spruce forest dates the time of a late ice advance in northeastern Wisconsin, while spruces and larches buried under older tills in Indiana and elsewhere in the Central States give evidence both of the vegetation at the time of glacial advance and of the time of advance. Inundated forests in the Columbia River gorge date a prehistoric flooding of that river by a landslide in the Cascades; while similar inundated forests standing *in situ* below the tide level in Alaska record recent lowering of the land with consequent rising of the sea. Wood preserved in the pyramids of Egypt and in old Pueblo dwellings in the southwest American desert can be used as evidence of the vegetation at the time of construction and of the date of construction. Tree-ring analysis and carbon-14 dating are the chief methods of analysis of these and other fossil woods.

Tree-Ring Analysis.   The science of dendrochronology owes much of its impetus and achievement to A. E. Douglass, his successor, Edmond Schulman, and the continuing work of Harold Fritts and co-workers at the tree-ring laboratory at the University of Arizona (Schulman, 1956; Fritts, 1965, 1966, 1971). Through the comparison of tree-ring widths from old living trees growing on sites where they are sensitive to annual changes in limiting soil-moisture supply, and similar sections taken from prehistoric ruins, it has been possible to establish tree-ring chronologies extending over the past 2,000 years for the American Southwest. From these, the dates of growth of timbers found in pueblo ruins and elsewhere usually can be established. For example, tree-ring materials from Mesa Verde National Park, Colorado, definitely indicate that a severe local drought was evident in the thirteenth century (Fritts *et al.*, 1965). At this time the prehistoric cliff dwellings of Mesa Verde were apparently abandoned, and the severe drought from 1273 to 1285 was probably one of the factors in a chain of events which led to the disappearance of prehistoric Indian dwellers of Mesa Verde. Even earlier information is provided by ring-width studies of 4,000-year-old bristle-cone pines, 2,000-year-old limber pines, and 3,200-year-old giant sequoias. From studies of relative width of rings, it is possible not only to date past severe droughts, but tree-growth response also can be used to reconstruct the occurrence of past climatic cycles (Fritts *et al.*, 1971).

Carbon-14 Dating. The actual age of fossil wood and of much other old organic material can be dated within the past 20,000 or so years by measuring the ratio of radioactive carbon-14 to stable carbon-12 in the sample. Carbon-14 is produced by the action of cosmic rays on the earth's atmosphere, and recently synthesized wood will have approximately the same proportion of it as will the atmosphere. As time goes on, however, the amount of carbon-14 in wood will decline until, at approximately 5,568 years, one half of the radioactive carbon-14 atoms will have decayed to carbon-12. By computing the ratio of carbon-14 to carbon-12 as determined by careful analysis of radioactivity in a wood or other organic sample, and comparing this ratio with the disintegration curve of carbon-14 based on a half-life of 5,568 years, the approximate age of the sample can be computed. Spruce wood of the Two Creeks forest in northeastern Wisconsin has been dated many times by several different carbon-14 laboratories as being 11,850 ± 100 years old, thus dating the last major glacial advance of the Wisconsin period affecting the continental United States. It is through carbon-14 dating, developed by W. F. Libby and refined by others since World War II, that the absolute chronology of late-glacial and postglacial events rapidly is being established.

Peat Analysis. Acid peat bogs preserve plant remains in great abundance. Through studies of these fragmentary remains, it is possible to isolate fossil wood in the various levels and date them by carbon-14 dating. It is also possible to evaluate the relative abundance of various types of peat-forming bog plants and from these to derive some knowledge of past climatic fluctuations. As the bog builds up, different strata of peat indicate the kinds of vegetation present in the bog at different times. Peats may be derived from mosses (including Sphagnums), sedges, and woody plants. Sphagnum peats are indicative of cool and humid times while alternating ligneous or woody peats in the same bog denote milder climatic conditions. Prominent ligneous peat horizons in European bogs are found over large areas and seem to date from the same period of formation. Volcanic ash horizons, such as commonly occur in the Pacific Northwest, can frequently be dated. The Katmai ash from the 1912 eruption on the Alaska peninsula provides a datum from which the current rate of peat accumulation may be dated. It is from the study of trapped pollen rain, however, that the greatest information is obtained by means of peat bog analysis.

Pollen Analysis. Lake sediments are rich reservoirs of fossil pollen and plant remains. Lakes are common in glaciated areas, and the pollen of their sediments reflect the regional character of the vegetation. In addition, the cold, wet, anaerobic environment provided by acid peat bogs constitutes a perfect preservative for hard plant parts. None is preserved better than pollen, whose hard outer coats, or *exines*, are extremely resistant to decay. However, trees growing on the bog surface are likely to contribute disproportionately large amounts of pollen. Thus lake sediments are the chief source for pollen analytical studies. Many pollen grains can be identified as to genus and some as to species.

Pollen analysis, although perhaps the most useful single tool in the deciphering of past vegetational history, is fraught with many dangers of misinterpretation. The pollen rain falling on a lake, open bog, or other repository in which the pollen may be enclosed in sediments and preserved will contain an over-representation of species which produce pollen abundantly and whose pollens are disseminated by wind, and an under-representation of species which produce pollen sparsely and whose pollens are disseminated by insects or other means.

A major problem in interpretation of the fossil pollen record has been the nearly universal reliance on percentages of pollen of the various genera (or species) in a sample to determine the composition of past vegetation. Such compositional percentages tell us which types of pollen were represented better than others, but there is not necessarily a high correlation between the forest composition indicated by the percentages and the actual composition of the forests at that time. This problem has been resolved in part by the geographical study of modern pollen rain and a comparison of the pollen assemblages of modern forest types, whose composition is known, with fossil pollen assemblages.

Pollen grains, being produced in various quantities by different species and carried by the wind, are related in a complex way to the vegetation from which they came. Once this relationship is understood for modern forest communities, the fossil pollen record can be more accurately interpreted. To accomplish this task, the pollen content of sediment surfaces from lakes and peat bogs in various forest and tundra regions has been determined. Distinct pollen assemblages (Figures 17.1 and 17.2) characterize regions of distinct vegetation such as tundra, boreal conifer forest, mixed conifer-deciduous forest, and deciduous forest. The same pollen assemblages that are recognized over a climatic gradient in modern forest communities may be recognized in a vertical sequence in

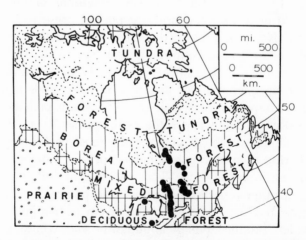

Fig. 17.1. Major vegetation regions in eastern and central Canada modified from Rowe (1959). The black dots represent sites where surface samples have been collected along a north-south transect. (After Davis, 1969.)

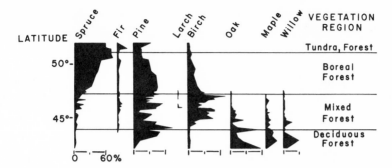

Fig. 17.2. Pollen assemblages in surface samples collected along the north-south transect through Canada shown in Figure 17.1. The percentage value for each type of pollen is shown on the abscissa. The latitude at which the sample was collected, and the forest region, are indicated on the ordinate. (After Davis, 1969.)

deposits of ancient pollen. For example, fossil pollen assemblages from southern New England and from the Great Lakes resemble characteristic but different modern vegetation types of the tundra and of forests of eastern, central, and west-central Canada (Davis, 1967). Although this method has become widely used for interpreting pollen data, it cannot be used everywhere because some fossil pollen assemblages occur that have no modern counterpart (Davis, 1969). In addition to the use of percentage composition values of various genera, the absolute numbers of pollen grains deposited at different times in the past give an idea of which pollen types actually increased in numbers through time (Davis, 1969).

Through these and other refinements, pollen analysis has evolved from a highly intuitive and speculative field to an exciting and expanding science; it is one of the most powerful methods of modern paleoecology. Detailed reviews of the methods and progress of pollen analysis related to forest vegetation of the late Tertiary and Quaternary (Davis, 1963, 1969; Leopold, 1969; Wright, 1971) and an excellent book on palynology (Tschudy and Scott, 1969) are available.

Pleistocene Glaciation

The advance of glaciers during the Pleistocene into the present temperate zones of the earth, while apparently less disruptive to vegetation than the Permian glaciation, is, of course, the major event in late Cenozoic forest history. At its maximum, ice covered approximately 32 percent of the land area of the world as compared to the 10 percent covered at the present time.

There were at least four major glaciations in the Pleistocene, each separated by a warm interglacial period of considerable length during which climates as mild and often milder than those of today existed. The last glaciation itself, insofar as the Great Lakes region is concerned, can be subdivided into four or more substages. The next to the last (the Cary, or Woodfordian, substage in North America) apparently began to melt northwards about 16,000 to 18,000 years before present (B.P.) while the final ice advance to reach the continental United States reached maximum extent in the Lake Michigan basin about 11,850 years ago and began to retreat shortly thereafter.

Obviously, forests were eliminated from the land under ice, and since these lands constitute some of the most important forest areas of the earth today, it is equally obvious that their present vegetation dates from the last retreat of the Pleistocene ice.

Not all the northern world, however, was under ice. A large area in the interior of Alaska and adjacent Yukon escaped glaciation, possibly because of low precipitation in that region, and apparently supported a tundra flora, probably because summers were too short and too cold to support forests (Hopkins, 1967a). Unglaciated areas on the islands off the Northwest Pacific coast such as the Queen Charlotte Islands of British Columbia likely served as refugia for Sitka spruce and western hemlock during glacial maxima. *Nunatuks*—isolated mountain peaks surrounded by ice— were far less likely to support tree growth of any kind during the Pleistocene.

Considerable controversy exists as to the extent to which forests were displaced south of the glacial border. The difficulty arises from the fact that no comparable conditions exist today. Existing continental glaciers such as in Greenland, Baffin Land, and Antarctica are confined to high latitudes; while existing temperate zone glaciers are of limited extent and therefore exert relatively little influence on climate beyond their borders. One school holds that the forests were displaced relatively little south of the glacial border, citing such instances as the west coast of New Zealand, where podocarps and tree ferns grow adjacent to glaciers coming from the Southern Alps. Others, citing the evidence of fossil spruce pollen from Georgia and eastern Texas, hold out for a major southward displacement of forest types. Another point of controversy concerns the extent and persistence of any tundra or other nonforest zone between the edge of the ice and the edge of the forest. Some believe that in what is now the United States, forests could have existed right up to the edge of the ice and even on mineral detritus covering the ice, as can be seen in some of the glaciers of southeastern Alaska. Others, arguing by analogy with the Arctic today, believe in the existence of a broad band of tundra between the forest and the ice in the Temperate Zone. Neither analogy, of course, is valid.

Although many of the details have yet to be worked out, considerable literature is accumulating on these problems (Heusser, 1960; Davis, 1965, 1967; Whitehead, 1965, 1967; Wright, 1970, 1971). The truth seems to be that the forests were displaced considerably southward, but not to a distance comparable with the advance of the ice. A conifer forest dominated by spruce and pine (presumably jack pine), which are boreal species today, occupied much of the area south of the ice in main Wisconsin times. Furthermore, pollen and macrofossil records indicate that a forest of jack pine and some black spruce, together with aquatic vegetation, occurred in the piedmont region of northern Georgia 23,000 to 15,000 years ago (Watts, 1970). This vegetation, typical of modern forests 1,100 kilometers to the north, indicates a major climatic change (Wright, 1971). Boreal forest also occupied parts of the Middle West. However, in southern Illinois, the full-glacial vegetation apparently was not a true boreal conifer forest, but a mosaic of stands (composed of oak, spruce, and pine) and open areas (E. Grüger, 1972). Further west in northeastern Kansas, pollen assemblages of 24,000 to about 15,000 years ago indicate a spruce forest with no pine and little oak (J. Grüger, 1973). Thus the full-glacial conifer forest differed considerably in composition from east to middle west in contrast to the relatively uniform boreal forest of spruce, fir, and pine across Canada today.

We have only sketchy and inconclusive evidence concerning the distribution and composition of temperate deciduous forests during the main Wisconsin glaciation (Whitehead, 1965; Wright, 1971). Oak pollen has been reported from the full glacial of northern Georgia (Watts, 1970), and it is likely that temperate deciduous trees existed on the more favorable sites in the southeast.

Presumably, the subtropical and south temperate species were able to persist along the Gulf Coast and on the peninsula of Florida.

As for the tundra or grassland zone, it undoubtedly occupied a wide zone adjacent to glaciers for several thousands of years in Alaska, and there is evidence of a narrower, moderately long-lived tundra zone in Nova Scotia, New England, and in Europe. In Europe, polar or cold rock deserts existed near the ice front, and bands of tundra were characteristic of the last glacial maximum. One of the main reasons for their development was the presence of the Alps, which helped maintain the zone of high pressure that spread out from the continental ice sheet; much of the warm air of the westerlies was thus diverted south of the Alps. During warmer interglacial periods, forests expanded to reoccupy areas previously covered by ice, polar desert, tundra, and steppe.

Late-Glacial and Postglacial Forests and Climatic Changes

Late-glacial history begins with the fluctuating retreat of the last glacial maxima (16,000 to 18,000 B.P.) and ends with a major and abrupt climatic change which took place about 10,000 years ago. The exact dates involved are being modified as additional evidence comes to the fore. Furthermore, there still exist many minor discrepancies both in correlation and in interpretation. Nevertheless, the general story of changes in forest and climate outlined below are well established even though subject to modification of detail. The various events can be traced more or less contemporaneously throughout the world although the mass of evidence concerns the changes in western Europe and eastern North America.

With the melting back of the Cary ice in the Great Lakes region, the open land was first colonized by tundra-forming sedges and other plants or by boreal trees. A readvance of ice about 11,850 years ago extended as far south as the middle part of the Lake Michigan basin. It prolonged the spruce period in the forests of the surrounding area but had little effect on the revegetation patterns to the east (New England) and west (Minnesota and the Great Plains). This minor readvance is now regarded by some as a regional surge of ice and apparently was not associated with a major climatic change.

During the past 10,000 years or so, pollen studies have given a detailed picture of the appearance and disappearance of many forest genera and some other plants and at least an approximate idea of their relative abundance at any one time. In general, a warming trend is seen up to a time when the climate was considerably warmer and drier than it is today. This has been followed by a general cooling up to the present time. However, much regional variation is seen in this overall pattern. The warmer-drier period in postglacial times seems to have occurred relatively early in the Southeast (10,000 to 6000 years B.P.), from 8000 to 4000 B.P. in the Middle West, where part of the deciduous forest changed to prairie and back again, and still later in New England (4000 to 1500 B.P.) (Wright, 1971). These variations are not surprising in view of recent climatological evidence that a shift in air mass distribution does not have a uniform effect over continental North America.

The changes in pollen percentages with time may be considered a continuum, although abrupt as well as gradual changes have been observed. The appearance in large numbers of some tree genera and the disappearance of others may be taken as demarcating zones in the postglacial chronology. At least three such arbitrary zones are frequently recognized: an initial cold period, a second warm period, and a final cooler period. Five zones are recognized in New England, seven in Great Britain, and eleven to twelve in northern Europe. It is obvious that different genera, or the same genera occurring in different relative numbers, will characterize different sites at the same time in the past. These vegetation changes may be summarized for various parts of the world for which pollen chronologies have been prepared.

Britain. Western Europe has long been the center for palynological research. Early in the century, von Post recognized the three major postglacial stages of increasing warmth, maximum warmth, and decreasing warmth. In more recent studies, the details of vegetational changes are represented by pollen spectra. The postglacial history of Great Britain is representative (but not necessarily typical) of this work. Here, pollen sequences have been given absolute datings through carbon-14 determinations so that a well-defined history is available in the English language (Godwin, 1956; Godwin, Walker, and Willis, 1957; Godwin and Willis, 1959).

An excellent book on the history of British vegetation is available (Pennington, 1969), and the effects of Neolithic and modern man on the forests is especially well documented.

New England. Throughout much of the Northeast, peat bogs and pond deposits consistently yield a maximum of spruce and fir pollen in the oldest and deepest stratum (A zone), followed by a pine maximum (B zone), and that by a hardwood zone (C zone) (Deevey, 1949). Each may be subdivided according to relative dominance of species, particularly of hardwood species in the top zone. These zones are not necessarily contemporaneous from one area to the next. Obviously the spruce zone will occur earlier and end earlier in the south than in the north under comparable conditions of ice retreat.

In southern New England, the period of increasing warmth following the retreat of Wisconsin ice was characterized by a long interval of tundra lasting until about 12,000 years ago, followed by a shorter period in which a transitional, open, spruce-hardwood woodland was succeeded by an open, spruce woodland (Davis, 1969). Then a dramatic change occurred about 9,500 years ago as mixed deciduous-coniferous forest replaced the spruce woodland. The transition from spruce woodland to mixed deciduous-coniferous forest took place before a closed boreal forest could develop. Except for this missing community, the boreal forest, which today separates subarctic woodland and the mixed deciduous-coniferous forest, the march of vegetation in time closely resembles the arrangement of modern vegetation regions from north to south in Canada (Figure 17.3). The oldest pollen assemblages resemble those deposited in the modern pollen rain in tundra regions far from any forest. The spruce woodland of 10,500 years ago resembles modern open woodland north of the boreal forest in Quebec, and the deciduous-coniferous forests of 9500 B.P. are similar to modern forests of Canada and the northern Great Lakes region south of the present boreal forest. The resemblance of the late-glacial forest of New England to modern vegetation of central Canada indicates the climate was drier, cooler, and more continental than at present (Davis, 1967).

The period of maximum warmth (now termed Hypsithermal, but formerly termed xerothermic or climatic optimum), about 4000 to 1500 B.P., is marked in southern New England by a drier type of flora with less hemlock and more oak and hickory than either in

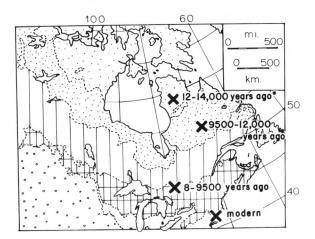

Fig. 17.3. Localities in Canada where surface pollen assemblages resemble fossil assemblages in southern New England. The sites are indicated by crosses. The age of the analogous fossil material is indicated for each locality. The location in the tundra indicated by an asterisk (*) is extrapolated from the resemblance of fossil material to assemblages from northernmost Quebec (Bartley, 1967). Surface samples are not yet available from the precise locality shown. (After Davis, 1969.)

earlier or later pollen levels. The increase of hemlock and other conifers, beech, maple, and other cool-climate species following the warm period is usually attributed to a change of climate. Alternatively, it may be due to the activities of Indians and Europeans prior to the major forest clearings of the early nineteenth century. The effects of land clearing are well documented in the pollen record by the rise of non-arboreal pollen (grass, composites, plantain, ragweed, maize, and cereals) and pollen of certain tree species such as poplars, red maple, spruce, and fir.

Western Great Lakes Region. In much of the western Great Lakes region, tundra was absent in late-glacial times. It has only been identified in northeastern Minnesota. Farther south, spruce forest apparently extended to the edge of the ic and may have covered a zone of stagnant receding ice (Wright, 1971). Wright believes that some temperate deciduous trees, probably oak and ironwood, together with the boreal species birch and alder, were minor components of this late-glacial spruce forest; pine was generally absent from the area from Manitoba to northern Ohio.

Birch and alder were the first species to invade the spruce forest as a warming climate affected its outer portions, beginning about 12,000 B.P. in southern Minnesota (Wright, 1971). The rapid rise of pine pollen 10,000 years ago in eastern Minnesota marked a swift expansion of the jack pine–red pine type (jack pine and red pine are often considered together because of the similarity of their pollen) from the east. The westward expansion had been blocked by dense spruce forests in Ohio and by ice and glacial lakes in the Lake Michigan basin until about 11,000 B.P. Whereas pines migrated into the Great Lakes region from the east, deciduous elements moved in from the south. In Ohio, oak replaced spruce about 10,500 years ago (Ogden, 1966), and elm, oak, and associated hardwoods entered southern Minnesota about 9500 B.P. and spread rapidly northward.

As the climate warmed and mean circulation of the westerlies increased, a wedge of air, dried by subsidence on crossing the Rockies, was driven eastward by the westerlies bringing with it dry conditions and an associated biota. In turn, oak savanna and true prairie expanded eastward. Fire was also a major associated factor in pushing back and maintaining the prairie-forest border. Reaching into Minnesota, Illinois, Indiana, southern Michigan, and Ohio, prairie openings apparently gradually replaced mixed pine-deciduous forests to the north and elsewhere deciduous forests and oak savannas. This *Prairie Peninusla* (Transeau, 1935) is evidenced by the widespread occurrence of prairie soils, remnants of oak savannas, and by the persistent fragments of the prairie until the initiation of farming by white man. The boundary dates of this period of maximum warmth and dryness are placed from 8,000 to 4,000 years ago; the peak of the warm period was apparently about 7000 B.P. The deterioration to a cooler, moister climate was slower than the rapid onset of the warm period had been. Pines and temperate hardwoods gradually replaced prairies, although prairie openings probably survived in east central Minnesota until 4,000 years ago (Wright, 1971). The Prairie Peninsula posed a barrier to the northward migration of upland mesophytic species such as beech, hemlock, and yellow-poplar. These species migrated into the central and southern portion of Lower Michigan from the east, entering these areas before reaching the eastern edge of the prairie in Indiana (Benninghoff, 1963).

White pine, which may have had its refuge in the Appalachian highlands during full glacial times, migrated more slowly than jack pine and red pine. It arrived in New England about 9,000 years ago and ultimately reached eastern Minnesota in quantity about 6800 B.P., just several hundred years after the prairies had arrived from the southwest (Wright, 1971). White pine was apparently halted here during the warm prairie period, but with the change toward cooler, wetter conditions, it renewed its westward migration. The uplands, although dominated by white pine, gained more mesic species, such as sugar maple and red maple as well as basswood, elm, and oak, that had survived the warm period. With the onset of cooler times, the jack pine–red pine type expanded out of its prairie-period refuge in northeasternmost Minnesota and reached the Itasca Park area about 2,000 years ago. On lowland sites, macrofossil analysis indicates the cooler, wetter trend by a marked increase of remains of spruce, larch, and ericaceous bog vegetation. More recently, the arrival of man on the scene brought extensive cutting of the pine forests and their replacement in many areas with birch and aspen. Detailed accounts of vegetational history of the western Great Lakes are found in the works of Cushing (1965), McAndrews (1966), and Wright (1971). An excellent collection of papers on the Pleistocene and recent environments of the central Great Plains, especially the interrelationships of climate, vegetation, animals and man, is available (Dort and Jones, 1970).

Pacific Northwest. Postglacial history in the Pacific Northwest (from Oregon north to Alaska) is complicated by the fact that the Cordilleran ice radiated east and west from the high mountain ranges extending north and south rather than simply moving southward as in eastern North America; that maritime climatic conditions originating from the Pacific Ocean moderated at least some of the postglacial climatic fluctuations found elsewhere; and that refugia for various plants and animals, including Sitka spruce and western hemlock, along the Pacific Coast served to restock much of the glaciated terrain rather than simple migration from the south as in the case of the eastern part of the continent (Hansen, 1947, 1955; Heusser, 1960, 1965). An extensive refugium in unglaciated interior Alaska existed for forest trees such as spruce and birch, along with shrubs and herbs of the arctic tundra.

The Pacific Northwest has a late-glacial and postglacial history similar to that of eastern North America in that ice had begun to recede as early as 14,000 B.P., and that a late-glacial cold period was followed by a warmer and drier trend which ultimately gave way to a cooler, more humid climate. Following retreat of the glaciers, a lodgepole pine parkland developed in the Pacific Northwest and northwestward as far as southeastern Alaska. As the climate ameliorated, alder, birch, and more tolerant coniferous species replaced pine. Douglas-fir became the dominant species of the Pacific Northwest during the warmer and drier times. Where rainfall was heavy, western hemlock replaced pine and mountain hemlock, and Sitka spruce became well represented from British Columbia to southeastern Alaska. In the Willamette Valley, the succession following pine was to Douglas-fir and Oregon oak, and east of the Cascades grassland achieved dominance on the dry plateaus. The approximate boundary dates of this period of maximum warmth and dryness are 8000 to 4000 B.P.

Reversal of the warming trend brought shifts to western hemlock in northwest forests as far north as southeastern Alaska. Coastal areas too dry for hemlock supported Douglas-fir, as do these areas today. In eastern Washington, open ponderosa pine forests succeeded grasslands.

To the northern interior, records from lakes in Glacier National Park in northern Montana show that lodgepole pine and western white pine dominated the earliest forest; Engelmann spruce and alpine fir were also present. A trend to warmer and drier conditions is indicated (coincident with volcanic ashfall from Mount Mazama —now the remnant Crater Lake in Oregon) about 6600 B.P. by the rapid increase of pollens of Douglas-fir and ponderosa pine and a decrease in that of western white pine and lodgepole pine. Thereafter, a cooler and more humid climate ensued with western white pine, Engelmann spruce, and alpine fir becoming dominant. Lodgepole pine is also strongly represented in pollen spectra, and its abundance is attributed to a greater incidence of severe fires in more recent times (Hansen, 1948).

Around the World. The examples cited above from England, New England, the western Great Lakes region, and the Pacific Northwest are but a few of similar pollen sequences throughout the world. Elsewhere, the broad picture is much the same. The Pleistocene glaciers reached their last maximum extension about 12,000 to 18,000 years ago. The end of Pleistocene glaciation was marked by a clear, worldwide climatic change which was unidirectional in its major effects. For many thousands of years afterward, the climate in the ice-free areas ameliorated, and wave after wave of forest tree species migrated into the former glaciated sites. Not all postglacial changes were synchronous around the world since they were influenced greatly by regional air mass distributions. For example, the time of maximum warmth varied considerably from region to region in continental United States, depending on regional climatic patterns. From the warm period up to historic times, the climate has been becoming colder and in many places wetter. Many minor changes and stages are interpreted locally, but the general outline holds for the northern, southern, eastern, and western hemispheres.

RECENT EVIDENCE OF CLIMATIC CHANGES

The continuing instability of vegetation as a result of continuing climatic change and continuing migrations of tree species becomes more and more apparent as we examine the more plentiful evidence of recent times (Dolf, 1960). Norsemen settled Greenland a thousand years ago, raising many head of cattle on what is now permanently frozen ground and traversing sea lanes blocked with floating ice but a century ago. Glaciers in Iceland were far less extensive from 900 to 1300 than they have been since. Glaciers in the Alps reached their maximum development during the period from about 1600 to 1850 and have since been receding, as indeed have the glaciers throughout all the rest of the world.

The evidence from the fluctuations of lakes, from tree rings, and from other sources point to the fact that the first millenium of the Christian era was relatively warm, but that a period of increasing cold set in about 1300 which culminated about 1800. During this latter period, mesophytic forest trees in many parts of the world were invading sites occupied by other species better suited to drier and warmer climates. European beech moved northward in Britain, American beech and sugar maple expanded their distribution in the Lake States, invading oak-hickory sites just as the oak and hickory were encroaching upon the eastern sections of the prairie. In New Zealand, evidence from existing old-growth stands is that *Nothofagus* was similarly invading podocarp forests (Holloway, 1954).

The best evidence to date is that these marked climatic fluctuations are not cyclic or periodic. Whether the recent long trend toward cooler climates or the even more recent but short trend toward warmer climates will prevail in the future cannot at present be predicted. It is clear, though, that our climate is unstable and that changes are to be expected both in future climates and in the forests as a result of the response of various species to changed environmental conditions.

SUMMARY

The historical development of modern forests may be traced back to fossil remains of plants in deposits of late Paleozoic times resembling the modern genus *Araucaria*. In the Mesozoic era, conifers evolved many forms and achieved great abundance. Angiosperms arose much later than the conifers, probably in the Cretaceous period. They evolved a great diversity of forms, apparently associated in part at least with the break-up of Gondwanaland and the major environmental changes caused by continental drift and mountain building. However, deciduous forest species similar to modern ones were not recorded in the fossil record until late Cretaceous times.

Forest trees became widely diversified and distributed in the Tertiary. In warm Eocene times, tropical and subtropical trees grew with warm temperate species as far north as London, England. A major cooling of the climate then occurred and temperate broadleaved deciduous tree species (ancestor of the modern Mixed Mesophytic Forest) came to dominate much of the Northern Hemisphere in Miocene times. The climatic deterioration continued, and although marked with warming episodes, culminated in the Pleistocene ice age. Many temperate deciduous species were eliminated from western North America, Europe, and western Asia shortly before or during the Pleistocene. Today remnants of the once widespread Mixed Mesophytic Forest are found only in parts of eastern North America and eastern Asia.

At least four separate periods of glaciation occurred during the Pleistocene, initiating a series of migrations of tree species in response to alternating cold and warm periods. The history of plant migration following the fluctuating retreat of Wisconsin ice (the last glaciation) is being unraveled through many lines of evidence —glacial geology, pollen analysis, studies of macrofossil remains of plants and animals, archeology, radiocarbon dating, tree-ring dating, and volcanic ash chronology.

In full-glacial times, Wisconsin ice displaced forests far south of their present ranges in eastern North America; jack pine and spruce apparently grew as far south as Georgia. A worldwide warming trend marked the end of the Wisconsin glaciation and was unidirectional in its major effects. A generalized climatic sequence together with an associated vegetative change is apparent in the last 12,000 to 16,000 years for many parts of the world. A cold late-glacial period was followed by a warming trend in postglacial times culminating in a period several thousand years long of warmer and drier conditions than exist at present. Thereafter, a trend to cooler and usually more humid conditions has prevailed to the present. Considerable variation, however, has been recorded in the specific times of these periods in North America. For example, due to the effect of differential regional air mass circulation, the warmer-drier period occurred at different times in the Southeast, Middle West, and Northeast of the United States.

Following retreat of the glaciers, either tundra or boreal forest vegetation was first to occupy open land. In much of North America an open spruce or pine parkland was the prominent forest vegetation of late-glacial times. As the warming trend continued, waves of increasingly temperate species replaced boreal spruce forest or pine. In the western Great Lakes region, deciduous forest changed to prairie and back again during the warmer interval 8,000 to 4,000 years ago. The trend to a cooler, more humid climate has been recorded in more recent times, but not without local warmer and drier episodes. The history of vegetation, especially during the last 12,000 years, illustrates enormous changes in vegetation, some seemingly gradual through time and others abrupt. It emphasizes that climate is not stable, not necessarily gradually changing, and that forests are to be expected to change in the future as their environment changes.

SUGGESTED READINGS

AXELROD, DANIEL I. 1970. Mesozoic paleogeography and early angiosperm history. *Bot. Rev.* 36:277–319.

BRYSON, REID A., DAVID A. BAERREIS, and WAYNE M. WENDLAND. 1970. The character of late-glacial and postglacial climatic changes. In WAKEFIELD DORT, JR., and J. KNOX JONES, JR. (eds.), *Pleistocene and Recent Environments of the Central Great Plains.* Univ. Press of Kansas, Lawrence.

DAVIS, MARGARET B. 1967. Late-glacial climate in northern United States: a comparison of New England and the Great Lakes region. In E. J. CUSHING and H. E. WRIGHT, JR. (eds.), *Quaternary Paleoecology.* Yale Univ. Press, New Haven.

———. 1969. Palynology and environmental history during the Quaternary period. *Amer. Scientist* 57:317–332.

FRITTS, HAROLD C. 1971. Dendroclimatology and dendroecology. *Quaternary Res.* 1:419–449.

HEUSSER, CALVIN J. 1960. Late-pleistocene environments of North Pacific North America. Am. Geog. Soc. Special Publ. 35. 308 pp.

―――. 1965. A Pleistocene phytogeographical sketch of the Pacific Northwest and Alaska. *In* H. E. WRIGHT, JR., and DAVID G. FREY (eds.), *The Quaternary of the United States.* Princeton Univ. Press, Princeton, N. J.

HOPKINS, DAVID M. 1967. The Cenozoic history of Beringia―a synthesis. *In* DAVID M. HOPKINS (ed.), *The Bering Land Bridge.* Stanford Univ. Press, Stanford, Calif.

McANDREWS, J. H. 1966. Postglacial history of prairie, savanna and forest in northwestern Minnesota. *Torrey Bot. Club Mem.* 22 (2). 72 pp.

PENNINGTON, WINIFRED. 1969. *The History of British Vegetation.* English Universities Press, London. 152 pp.

WHITEHEAD, DONALD R. 1965. Palynology and pleistocene phytogeography of unglaciated eastern North America. *In* H. E. WRIGHT, JR., and DAVID G. FREY (eds.), *The Quaternary of the United States.* Princeton Univ. Press, Princeton, N. J.

WOLFE, JACK A. 1971. Tertiary climatic fluctuations and methods of analysis of Tertiary floras. *Palaeogeog., Palaeoclimatol., Palaeoecol.* 9:27–57.

―――, and E. B. LEOPOLD. 1967. Neogene and Early Quaternary vegetation of northwestern North America and northeastern Asia. *In* D. M. HOPKINS (ed.), *The Bering Land Bridge.* Stanford Univ. Press, Stanford, Calif.

WRIGHT, H. E., JR. 1971. Late Quaternary vegetational history of North America. *In* KARL K. TUREKIAN (ed.), *The Late Cenozoic Glacial Ages.* Yale Univ. Press, New Haven.

18

The American Forest Since 1600

In the United States, written historical records of forest description and forest history date from the seventeenth century and settlement by the white man. Evidence from contemporary naturalists, surveyors who parceled off the wilderness, and from analysis of old-growth forest relics still or recently extant have done much to give us an understanding of the pre-settlement forest in the United States and the many changes that have taken place since settlement. A brief survey of the nature of the pre-settlement forest and of the effects on it of land clearing, logging, fire, and land abandonment is essential to an understanding of the present forests of temperate North America. A brief discussion of the effects of human activity on the European and near-east Asian forest is also included.

THE PRE-SETTLEMENT FOREST

The question as to what constituted the original, or virgin, forest is an intriguing one. We have already seen that the forests in the glaciated region of the Northern Hemisphere have been in an almost constant state of instability and change over the past ten thousand years. Furthermore, most of this region has been inhabited by man since the retreat of the glaciers, and it is now well established that

extensive burning by primitive man has been widespread throughout this period and throughout the world.

Actually, there is no such thing as an original forest or even a
virgin forest. Our concern is often with the nature of the forest at
the time of colonization of the land by white man. In eastern North
America, we thus are interested in the composition and structure
of the sixteenth-century forest. Farther west in the Central States,
our interest is in the eighteenth-century forest; while in many of the
more mountainous regions of the West we can still see the pre-
settlement forest, simply because the land has never been settled
and the forests have never been logged.

A further word about the concept of the virgin forest is in order.
The terms "virgin forest" and Longfellow's "forest primeval" conjure
up an image of great and old trees standing undisturbed and
changeless for centuries. Specifically, any disturbance by man is
ruled out. They must be uncut and unharmed by man-set fires and
the understory must be ungrazed by domestic stock. In other
words, we conceive of the virgin forest as being simply an unharmed old-growth forest.

Such stands simply do not exist. We have already seen that
forests of any age are in a constant state of change, arising from the
growth and senescence of the trees themselves, from consequent
changes in the microclimate and edaphic site, from normal forest
succession, and from regional climatic and geologic changes. Inter-
ferences with normal growth and development are common, and
it is a meaningless semanticism to try to distinguish between "natural" disturbances and "artificial" disturbances caused by man. To
the tree, it makes little difference if a fire is set by lightning or by
a human incendiary, if the soil is upturned by a plough or by a tree
uprooted in a storm, if a leaf is eaten by an insect that came by
wind or one that came by airplane, or if cellulose is consumed by
a fungus bred on the roots of a neighboring tree or one introduced
on a piece of lumber from overseas. Disturbances to tree development and growth are normal, instability of the forest is inevitable,
and the changeless virgin forest is a myth.

The forests which confronted the colonizing white man on the
Atlantic seaboard of North America were in a state of constant
change wrought by forest succession, climatic change, fire, wind,
insects, fungi, browsing animals, and Indian activity. Nevertheless,
since they are now vanished, it is worthwhile to reconstruct their

composition and structure as an aid in understanding the present-day forests of the same region. It is less necessary to do this for the western American forest, where extensive old-growth stands still antedate in their history the presence of the white man in that region.

Contemporary Observers

In a sense, it is surprising how little is recorded of the forests by the sea captains, explorers, first settlers, and travelling naturalists who saw and travelled in the pre-settlement forest. Their chronicles are almost inevitably concerned with their own comings and goings, with the Indians, and with human affairs generally. Nevertheless, here and there are preserved fragmentary comments that cast some light upon the early American forests. Early historical accounts have been put together in the greatest detail for the New England states, although the writings of such early eighteenth-century travellers as John Bartram in the American South and Alexander Mackenzie in the Canadian Northwest were notable for their description of the terrain and vegetation of the regions they traversed.

In most cases, comparisons of the present forest with early descriptions show that the forests of the two eras do not differ substantially, as in the case of Martha's Vineyard as reported by Ogden (1962). A description of the coastal New England forests between 1629 and 1633 is given by William Wood in his *New England Prospect*, published in 1634. As quoted by Hawes (1923), he said in part:

> The timber of the country grows straight and tall, some trees being twenty, some thirty foot high before they spread forth their branches; generally the trees be not very thicke, tho there be many that will serve for mill posts, some being three foote and a half o're. And whereas it is generally conceived that the woods grow so thicke that there is no cleare ground than is hewed out by labour of man; it is nothing so; in many places divers acres being cleare, so that one may ride a hunting in most places of the land, if he will venture himself for being lost; there is no underwood saving in swamps, and low grounds that are wet in which the English get osiers and Hasles and such small wood as is for their use. Of these swamps some be ten, some twenty, some thirty miles long, being preserved by the wetness of the soile wherein they grow; · for it being the custom of Indians to bourne the wood in November when the grass is withered and leaves dryed, it consumes all the underwood and rubbish, which otherwise would overgrow the country, making it impassable, and spoil their much affected hunting; so that by this means in those places where the Indians inhabit there is scarce a bush or bramble, or any combersome underwood to be seene in the more Champion ground.

In Jeremy Belknap's history of New Hampshire (1792), he describes both the original forest and its clearing by the settlers:

Another thing, worthy of observation, is the aged and majestic appearance of the trees, of which the most noble is the mast pine. This tree often grows to the height of one hundred and fifty, and sometimes two hundred feet. It is straight as an arrow, and has no branches but very near the top. It is from twenty to forty inches in diameter at its base, and appears like a stately pillar, adorned with a verdant capital, in form of a cone. Interspersed among these are the common forest trees, of various kinds, whose height is generally about sixty or eighty feet. In swamps, and near rivers, there is a thick growth of underwood, which renders travelling difficult. On high lands, it is not so troublesome; and on dry plains, it is quite inconsiderable.

. . . .

In the new and uncultivated parts, the soil is distinguished by the various kinds of woods which grow upon it, thus: white oak land is hard and stony, the undergrowth consisting of brakes and fern; this kind of soil will not bear grass till it has been ploughed and hoed; but it is good for Indian corn, and must be subdued by planting, before it can be converted into mowing or pasture. The same may be said of chestnut land.

Pitch pine land is dry and sandy; it will bear corn and rye with plowing; but is soon worn out, and need to lie fallow two or three years to recruite.

White pine land is also light and dry, but has a deeper soil, and is of course better; both these kinds of land bear brakes and fern; and wherever these grow in large quantities, it is an indication that ploughing is necessary to prepare the land for grass.

Spruce and hemlock, in the eastern parts of the state, denote a thin, cold soil, which, after much labor in the clearing, will indeed bear grass without ploughing, but the crops are small, and there is a natural tough sward commonly called a *rug*, which must either rot or be burned before any cultivation can be made. But in the western parts, the spruce and hemlock, with a mixture of birch, denote a moist soil, which is excellent for grass.

. . . .

When the white pine and oyl-nut are found in the same land, it is commonly a deep moist loam, and is accounted very rich and profitable.

Beech and maple land is generally esteemed the most easy and advantageous for cultivation, as it is a warm, rich, loamy soil, which easily takes grass, corn and grain without ploughing; and not only bears good crops the first year, but turns immediately to mowing and pasture; the soil which is deepest, and of the darkest color, is esteemed the best.

Black and yellow birch, white ash, elm, and alder are indications of good soil, deep, rich and moist, which will admit grass and grain without ploughing.

Red oak and white birch are signs of strong land, and generally the strength of land is judged of by the largeness of the trees which it produces.

. . . .

In the spring, the trees which have been felled the preceding year, are burned in the new plantations. If the season be dry, the flames spread in the woods, and a large extent of the forest is sometimes on fire at once. Fences and buildings are often destroyed by these raging conflagrations. The only effectual way to prevent the spreading of such a fire, is to kindle another at a distance, and to drive the flame along through the bushes, or dry grass, to meet the greater fire, that all the fuel may be consumed. In swamps, a fire has been known to penetrate several feet under the ground, and consume the roots of the trees.

From such sources as the above as well as from the writings of Thomas Morton (1632), Peter Whitney (1793), and Timothy Dwight (1795–1821), we may conclude that the precolonial forests of New England were made up of the same species that characterize the region today. Furthermore, specific kinds of sites were occupied by forest types generally similar to those occupying them today. The importance of any given species, or the composition of any given type within the original forest, cannot be more than roughly approximated from early descriptions, and any attempt to reconstruct such evidence must of necessity be highly subjective in nature.

Survey Records

Much more specific information is available from the notes of original land surveys where trees were commonly used for corners, bearing trees, and witness trees. Such records of the kind and size of trees at surveyed corners do not constitute a random sample of the forest, for the surveyor naturally chose trees having a durable wood, and of a size suitable for scribing and likely to be found again years later. Nevertheless, they do provide an important guide to the nature of the pre-settlement forests in areas where old-growth forests are virtually non-existent today.

Metes and Bounds Surveys. Along the Eastern Seaboard, and throughout colonial times generally, American surveys were by metes and bounds, with the surveyor recording the compass bearing and distance of each line bounding a tract of land. The technique is well illustrated by the still-extant surveying notes of George Washington (Spurr, 1951) and a study of the original forest composition in northwestern Pennsylvania based on survey notes of 1814–1815 (Lutz, 1930).

The job of the frontier surveyor was to lay out land for settlement as quickly and as inexpensively as possible. The surveying techniques of Washington were therefore of the rough-and-ready sort. He used a staff compass and chain. Magnetic bearings were recorded to the nearest degree and distances were measured to the nearest rod (termed "pole" by Washington). No corner stakes were set; rather, a convenient tree was chosen as a corner, blazed, and inscribed. It is this practice of the frontier surveyor of tying in to trees rather than stakes that provides the information concerning the forests of the time. A sample survey chosen at random from Washington's notes illustrates the type of survey and the nature of the information supplied:

April 24th 1750   Plat drawn

   Then Surveyed for Thomas Wiggans a certain tract of Waste Land Situate in Frederick County & on Potomack River about ½ mile aboe ye Mouth of great Cacapehon & bounded as followeth beg: at a white Oak a white Hickory & White Wood Tree just on ye Mount of Wiggan's Run & opposite to a nob of ye Mountains in Maryland & run thence S° 25 W^t Two hund^d & twenty Eight Poles to a white hickory an Elm & Mulberry about 30 Pole from Cacapehon thence N° 75 W^t One hund^d & forty Poles to a Chestnut Oak & white Oak thence N° 25 E^t Two hund^d & Sixty Poles to a white Oak red Oak & Iron Wood on ye Riverside thence down ye several Meanders thereof S° 67½ E^t 37 Po S° 58½ E^t 74 Po S° 55 E^t to ye beg Con^g 210 Acres—
John Lonem
Isaac Dawson
William Wiggans

There seems to be no reasonable doubt that Washington knew the trees of the middle Appalachian regions. His reputation as a surveyor would naturally depend in part upon the accuracy of his description of corners, and this in turn depended upon the correct naming of the corner trees. Furthermore, there is a wealth of internal evidence in the surveying notes confirming this knowledge. For example, he was very precise in his identification. He names separately seven oak species, including such a relatively uncommon and confusing species as swamp white oak. He readily distinguished the two *Juglans* from each other as he did also between the two maples. In all, he listed some thirty-five different tree species, all of which are known to occur in the area and on the sites and in the communities where he placed them.

The descriptive phrases are particularly convincing as to Washington's knowledge of trees. How very typical are the descriptions "three Lynn [basswood] trees growing from one stump," "a Black Walnut in a Poysoned Field by a Limestone Rock," and "2 Sycamores & a White Wood [yellow-poplar] tree Standing in ye Fork." Certainly, Washington was a qualified observer of the forest.

The most commonly cited trees in Washington's surveying notes are listed in order of abundance in Table 18.1. These were listed from lot surveys in the valleys of the Shenandoah, the Cacapon, and the South Branch of the Potomac Rivers. White oak, red oak, and

Table 18.1. Trees Cited in George Washington's Surveying Notes in Northwestern Virginia and Northeastern West Virginia, 1751–1752

Species	Number
White oak	366
Red oak	181
Hickory	142
Pine (Virginia?)	132
Chestnut oak	51
Black oak	37
Black locust	36
Spanish oak (pin or scarlet?)	28
Others	141
Total	1,114

hickory were the characteristic species with considerable pine growing on the hills and mountain sides in the latter two areas.

On the hills and mountain sides, above the Cacapon and South Branch rivers, pines, hickories, chestnut oak, and other oaks were the characteristic species. The implication frequently is that the trees were generally small and not overly valuable. This is especially true of hickory. Typical descriptions are of "a Pine & two hickory bushes on the Top of a clear hill," "two Chestnut Oaks and a red Oak in amongst very steep pine Hills," "2 Chestnut Oaks and a black in Piney Ground," and "two Chestnuts and one Chestnut Oak near the side of some Large hanging Rocks on the side of a Mountain."

All in all, the picture of the colonial forest of the central Appalachians as reconstructed from Washington's notes is a very believable one, and one that shows relatively little change in the forest of this area over the last two hundred years.

Lutz (1930a) was able to compare data from an 1814–15 survey in Warren and McKean Counties, Pennsylvania, with information from an intensive study of the Heart's Content old-growth forest in the same part of northwestern Pennsylvania (Table 18.2). The similarity of forest composition, as regards dominant species, between the two sets of data is remarkable, both indicating a beech-maple-hemlock forest with smaller amounts of chestnut and white pine.

Rectangular Surveys. As the inadequacies of metes and bounds surveys became appreciated, they were supplanted by various types

Table 18.2   Percentages of the Most Common Forest Trees in the Old-Growth Forests of Northwestern Pennsylvania

	Dale Survey, 1814–1815	Heart's Content Old Growth, 1930
Beech	30.8	24.0
Hemlock	26.8	36.1
Maple (red and sugar)	13.0	10.9
Birch (black and yellow)	6.1	2.8
White pine	6.0	11.1
Chestnut	5.6	8.8
Others	11.7	6.3
Total	100.0	100.0

From Lutz (1930a).

of rectangular surveys. In the eastern United States, various un-official types of rectangular grids were used; but in the nineteenth century, these were supplanted by the United States public lands survey in which most of the country was laid out into townships six miles square, these being subdivided into sections one mile square. Since witness trees were required to be blazed, measured, and recorded at each section and quarter-section corner, and since the surveyors were required to record the point at which their lines crossed rivers, prairies, swamps, peat beds, precipices, ravines, and tracks of fallen timber, it is possible to reconstruct the forest cover of the time of the original survey with some confidence and precision.

There are many pitfalls inherent in interpretations of forest cover from early General Land Office Surveys (Bourdo, 1956). The procedure of the survey was not standardized until 1855, and even then practices varied according to the personnel involved. Some surveys are unreliable and some are strictly fictitious. Individual surveyors had their own preference in selecting trees for bearing and witness trees. In general, they were partial to medium-sized trees of species capable of attaining large size. Tree diameters were estimated by the surveyors, usually to the nearest 2-inch class. Distances were also sometimes estimated. Nevertheless, if the modern investigator acquaints himself with the survey procedure of the area he studies and studies the work of the particular surveyors involved, he can interpret much about the nature of the pre-settlement forest.

Reconstructions of pre-settlement forest composition from public land survey records have been particularly fruitful in the American Midwest, where various investigators have constructed maps of pre-settlement vegetation for given districts, counties, and even states. In northern Lower Michigan, for instance, Kilburn (1957) recorded the trees cited in the 1840 and 1855 surveys and found hemlock the most abundant species, although today, after complete clear-cutting and extensive burning, the species is virtually absent in that area. The most extensive pre-settlement forest type was hemlock-beech-maple, with pine forests (red, white, and jack) being common on the sandier soils and swamp conifers (northern white cedar, tamarack, spruce, and balsam fir) in the bogs. Today, aspens (big-tooth and trembling) are the dominant tree species in the area with red oak and red maple the commonest hardwoods. Only the swamp conifers and the jack pine on the sand plains still occupy for the most part their presettlement sites.

Old-Growth Remnants. In areas long cut-over, and consisting largely of second growth, occasional remnants of old-growth forests can be found, the detailed study of which provides valuable information on the forests at the time of settlement. Many of the more spectacular of these remnants are preserved as parks or as wilderness areas. Among those which have been studied in detail in the northeastern United States are the Heart's Content stand (Lutz, 1930b) and East Tionesta Creek forest (Hough, 1936) in northwestern Pennsylvania, the Pisgah forest in southwestern New Hampshire (Cline and Spurr, 1942), and the Itasca red pine stands in northwestern Minnesota (Spurr and Allison, 1956). Others can be cited.

Similar studies have been made of small residual old-growth stands in western Europe. One example is the survey of the native Scots pine stands of Scotland by Steven and Carlisle (1959). The three dozen or so remnants were found to have a principal age class of from 140 to 190 years old and were lacking in the younger age classes. The low stocking of the overstory had had the consequence of giving rise to a rank growth of an understory so as to make natural regeneration difficult. Since most Scots pine do not survive more than 250 years in that region, positive action is needed to regenerate and protect the few residual woodlands.

A survey of the residual old-growth red pine stands in Lower Michigan similarly turned up about a dozen small tracts with a scattering of pine (Collins, unpublished). They were confined exclusively to sandy glacial outwash soils with similar frequencies of particle-size distribution. The pines ranged up to nearly 300 years in age and 123 feet in height and seemed to occur almost entirely in even-aged groups dating from pre-settlement fires.

In Itasca State Park, Minnesota, the old-growth stands similarly occur in even-aged but intermingled age-classes, each dating from past forest fires (Spurr, 1954). On a single tree, fire scars indicate major conflagrations in 1714, 1772, 1803, 1811, 1820, 1865, and 1886. The last two are recorded also by nineteenth-century travellers to the headwaters of the Mississippi River.

Second Growth Stands

As long as the forest itself is old, it is not necessary that it contain old trees in order to reconstruct the past forest history and cover of the tract. Many second-growth stands can yield valuable information on the pre-settlement forest.

The essential is that the land has never been completely cleared, ploughed, and farmed. If it has merely been logged from time to time, considerable evidence remains. Even in areas once largely farmed, careful surveys of land deeds indicate that certain areas have been described as woodlots back to the period of settlement (Raup and Carlson, 1941). Other evidence obtainable from the forest itself involves stump sprouts, root suckers, species that characteristically seed in on rotten wood, evidence of past windfalls, soil structure studies, and the occurrence of charcoal in the soil.

In the eastern hardwood forest of the United States, many species have a high coppicing ability throughout their life. A large percentage of the present oak forest, for instance, consists of stump sprouts which have arisen from stump sprouts which in turn can be traced back in time to the period before settlement and land clearing. In such a case, it is obvious that the same species—and indeed the same genotype—occupied the same site several hundreds of years ago. The same is true for root-suckering species such as aspen, where the size of the clonal colony may indicate the length of time that a particular clone has grown on that particular spot.

In the case of species that characteristically seed in on rotten wood, the history of the forest can be traced well back. In the coastal Sitka spruce–western hemlock forests of British Columbia and Southeastern Alaska, these species habitually become established on the elevated rotten wood of dead trees, the only sites in the forest dry enough for seedling establishment. Here, it is common to see a giant western hemlock growing ten feet from the ground on the stump of a prior western hemlock which itself rises out of the rotten wood of still another gigantic tree of the same species. Assuming that each lived a life span of 400 years, a record of 1,200 years is thus provided during which that particular spot always had a western hemlock growing on it.

The presence of old windfalls is indicated by a mound marking the former position of upturned roots and by a ridge marking the position of the former bole. Careful soil excavation of the mound will reveal upturned soil strata, a disturbance of the minute structure of soil particles, and a displacement in the distribution of heavy minerals. Species such as eastern hemlock frequently line the site of the fallen bole where they seeded in on the rotten wood. Their age can be used to date the windfall. Sudden release of nearby trees as indicated by an abrupt widening of the annual rings is also indicative of windfall.

Finally, charcoal can be found in the soil, old fire scars can be found on old-growth trees, and these can be used to date prehistoric forest fires. The charcoal can be dated by carbon-14 techniques and the fire scars by tree-ring analysis.

Reconstruction of past forest composition on the basis of such lines of evidence is entirely possible, but it is time-consuming. The pleasure arising from the detective work necessary to unearth the clues and run them down, however, may be added to the value of the information obtained in order to justify the task.

HUMAN ACTIVITY

In the United States and Canada, the persistence of large areas of pre-settlement forest, particularly in the mountains of the West, is due primarily to the short span of time that the white man in large numbers has been present on the scene. Undoubtedly, considerable changes in the forest cover had previously resulted from Indian fires. Evidence in Alaska is certainly indicative of this (Lutz, 1956) as is fragmentary evidence from the rest of North America. For instance, the use of thousands of ponderosa pine timbers in pueblos in the American Southwest located 60 or more miles from any present timber of the same species certainly points to widespread destruction of the ponderosa pine forest by Indian cutting and burning.

It is impossible to overestimate the effect of human activity on the forests of the world, whether by civilized or by prehistoric uncivilized man. The character of the vegetation of a large part of the world has been greatly altered by extensive burning, logging, land clearing for agriculture, and grazing by domestic stock. Although there is neither time nor space here to detail the historical evidence, illustrations from Europe and the United States are indicative of the story of the forests of the rest of the world.

Europe and Adjacent Lands

Throughout the Mediterranean regions, in Asia Minor, throughout southern Europe, and to a lesser extent in northern Europe, the forests have been completely altered by hundreds of thousands of years' habitation by man. Everywhere, the evidence of fossil plant remains and fossil soil horizons indicates widespread destruction of the forest by repeated logging, burning, and continued grazing, particularly by goats. Climatic change is also involved, and it is impossible as yet to allocate responsibility for forest destruction between human activity and climatic change. Yet, there is no reason to doubt but that the barren nature of much of southern Europe—and of adjacent portions of Africa and Asia—is in large measure due to the destruction of forests in antiquity by human mismanagement (Darby, 1956).

Extensive forests once occurred in Greece, North Africa, Asia Minor, the northern or forest steppes of Russia, and elsewhere. In these regions today, the climate is favorable for tree growth once a forest is reestablished, but the eroded condition of the soils, the adverse microclimate of barren planting sites, and the difficulty of controlling browsing by goats and other domestic stock make reforestation extremely difficult if not impossible.

Forest deterioration in Europe, however, is not confined to the Mediterranean and dry eastern regions. In northern Europe, Neolithic activity about 5,000 years ago probably was associated with the abrupt fall in *Ulmus* pollen, marking the Elm Decline. Upon reaching northern Europe, Neolithic peoples encountered continuous forest and no large pastures. Therefore, leafy branches of forest trees, primarily elms, whose leaves are most nutritious for this purpose, were repeatedly gathered and fed to stalled domestic animals. This repeated pruning would reduce significantly the pollen production of elms. Furthermore, the development of polished stone axes led to deliberate clearance of all trees in limited areas by Neolithic agriculturists. Experiments in Denmark have indicated that three men equipped only with Neolithic axes could clear about 200 square meters of forest in four hours. Cereal crops, including Emmer wheat (*Triticum dicoccum*), were grown in woodland soil and the ashes resulting from slash burning. When soil fertility declined, in about three years, fields were abandoned and agriculture shifted to a new forested site. Abandoned lands reverted to scrub and through succession to forest again.

In England, many of the present moors were once deciduous forest. Pollen analysis of moorland in Yorkshire, for instance, establishes the presence of deciduous forest cover during Bronze Age human occupation (Dimbleby, 1952). Moor formation is apparently due in large measure to repeated woods burnings by primitive man. In the wet climatic regions of Ireland, Scotland, and Scandinavia, upland peat bogs owe their origin to a combination of climatic deterioration (the cold and wet conditions in the second millennium of the Christian era) and prehistoric farming methods (Morrison, 1956). The pre-bog woodland was frequently pine which degenerated into open woodland or scrub with a greater percentage of birch due to repeated burning, grazing, and the development of acid-humus forming ericaceous plants (*Calluna* heath and others). Under cold, wet climatic conditions of the past thousand years, raw humus profiles over strongly leached spodosols have gradually developed into blanket upland peats which have eliminated the forests on many sites. In lower Provence in France, human activity in recent centuries, particularly in repeated cutting, burning, and domestic grazing, has led to a regression of the natural oak forest and its replacement by scrub (Nicod, 1951). Many other examples could be cited.

United States

Extensive forest change, due to human activity of recent vintage in the eastern United States, is much easier to trace than in Europe, where higher levels of population have prevailed for a much longer period of time. Indians had a significant effect on forest composition, due primarily to the fires they set, both accidentally and intentionally. Curtis (1959) estimated that 50 percent of the land surface of Wisconsin was directly influenced by Indian fires. The only important forests to escape Indian fires were the mesic forests of both the south and north. Open communities of prairies, oak savannas, and pine lands were favored by burning. Although fire was by far the most important Indian influence on forest history, Indians also introduced various crop and tree species. An interesting example is the Kentucky coffeetree, whose large, hard seeds were used in a kind of dice game by various tribes. Apparently many seeds were lost in the vicinity of villages since reports in Wisconsin and from New York show the species has a very local distribution, in each case at or near an Indian village site.

Granting the undoubted effects of Indian burning on the forests, and in particular the effects of this practice on the distribution and abundance of the various pines, much has happened since extensive settlement by the white man.

In central and southern New England, much of the land was cleared for crops, hay, and pasture by the middle of the nineteenth century. In central Massachusetts, the virgin forests were almost completely cut before the end of the eighteenth century and much of the area cleared for farming. For a generation or two in the first portion of the ninetenth century, the area was largely agricultural. To illustrate this with a specific example, the senior author prepared an agricultural land-use map of the Prospect Hill Block (Figure 18.1). Areas which apparently have been always forested were mapped out on the basis of the Raup and Carlson study and of original field checks in which the ages of standing trees were determined and in which stumps and other evidence of former tree growth were noted. Nine percent of the tract fell into the continuously forested category. Less than one acre previously described is still covered with old-growth trees. The rest is occupied by hemlock, red spruce, red maple, and other species in stands less than one hundred years old, although an occasional older hemlock and spruce can be found which originated under the previous stand and which was subsequently released by logging.

The remaining 91 percent has been cleared for agricultural use at one time or another, but not necessarily all at one time. Much of this has obviously never been cultivated repeatedly or thoroughly, but rather has been primarily for upland pasture. To estimate how much land has been cultivated, the stone walls were followed and

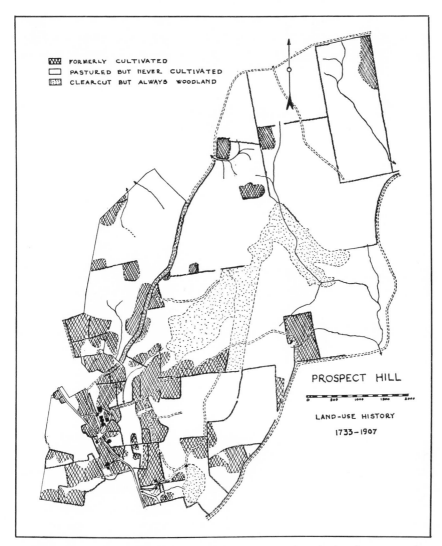

Fig. 18.1. Reconstruction of maximum agricultural development of a 1,000-acre forest in central Massachusetts.

studied (Figure 18.2). Stone walls made up of boulders taken from cultivated fields are typically larger and contain a greater variety of stone sizes and a greater number of stones than do simple stone walls that were erected merely to mark property lines or to fence in cattle and sheep. By correlating the nature of the stone wall with the character of the ground surface on either side, it was possible to

Fig. 18.2. Stone walls and former grist-mill site with grindstone still in place under middle-aged hardwoods in central Massachusetts. (Courtesy of Harvard Forest, Harvard University.)

delineate those areas that had very likely been cultivated repeatedly or thoroughly. These areas covered 16 percent of the tract, the remaining 75 percent being mapped as having been cleared for upland pasture but not having been intensively cultivated. The proportions of land in the other two tracts that have been continuously in forest, cultivated, or which have been cleared for pasture are apparently of the same general order of magnitude as in the Prospect Hill Block, but were not determined.

Following the opening of western and northern lands to settlement, much of the cleared land was abandoned, and seeded in to even-aged stands consisting largely, but by no means entirely, of white pine. These old-field pine stands became characteristic of the region, and by 1900 gave rise to a substantial logging industry. However, as Thoreau first noted and as professional foresters have since rediscovered to their sorrow, these pine stands on upland soils were succeeded after logging by even-aged hardwood stands which today constitute the principal types in the region.

Much the same history of extensive land clearing followed by large-scale farm abandonment, revegetation with old-field pines, and subsequent hardwood invasion holds for the southeastern United States. Here, the economic consequences of the Civil War coupled with soil deterioration resulting from erosion and lack of adequate fertilization have resulted in the abandonment of millions of acres of tobacco, cotton, and other cropland.

In the Georgia Piedmont, the original forests seem to have varied from pure hardwoods on red lands through mixed pine and hardwoods on the gray, sandy lands to predominantly pine on the sandier and drier granitic lands (Nelson, 1957). Early settlers soon cleared the forest and developed an agricultural economy based on cotton which began to decline with the onset of the Civil War. Loblolly pine seeded in most commonly on abandoned farm lands, but the pine stands, if unburned or otherwise left untreated, develop dense hardwood understories which may develop with time to convert the pine forests to hardwood forests, particularly on the moister and richer soils.

Extensive changes in the forest due to human activity in the eastern United States are not confined to areas formerly farmed. In lands that have always been forested, the effects of repeated cutting, burning, and heavy domestic grazing have been equally marked. Prior to the development of the coal resources of Pennsylvania and West Virginia, extensive areas of hardwood were clearcut at frequent intervals to provide fuel wood for domestic use, brick yards, iron works, railroad engines, and other purposes. Wooded hillsides in southern Connecticut, in northeastern Pennsylvania, and elsewhere adjacent to long-settled industrial areas have been cut and burned so much that tolerant and fire-susceptible species such as hemlock and beech have been virtually eliminated except in protected ravines.

In northern Maine, the forests were logged over in the first half of the nineteenth century for white pine which was floated down the Androscoggin, Penobscot, Aroostock, and other waterway systems to sawmills down river, of which Bangor was the capital and logging center. Subsequently, late in the century, ground wood and sulphite pulp mills were established along the larger streams which were fed first with spruce only, and later with an increasing percentage of balsam fir. In recent years, the development of sulphate, cold soda, neutral semi-chemical and other processes have made possible the exploitation of many hardwoods. As a result, the forests are being logged over for still other species. The net result of these many waves of logging is that the present forest differs substantially from the pre-settlement forest in its composition and structure, even though it is made up of the same species.

In the Ozarks, extensive burning in the last century and before had resulted in the development of extensive tracts of open, parklike forest and grassland (Beilmann and Brenner, 1951). With better fire control in recent years, coupled with an increase in human population, the forests have been reestablishing themselves widely. Eastern red cedar aggressively invades old fields and grasslands. Fire-resistant oak woodland types of blackjack oak and post oak are being invaded by the more mesophytic red oak, white oak, and hickories.

In the southwestern United States, pre-settlement ponderosa pine forests were open, parklike stands of predominantly mature pine (Cooper, 1960). According to Beals (1858):

We came to a glorious forest of lofty pines, through which we have travelled ten miles. The country was beautifully undulating, and although we usually associate the idea of barrenness with the pine regions, it was not so in this instance; every foot being covered with the finest grass, and beautiful broad grassy vales extending in every direction. The forest was perfectly open and unencumbered with brush wood, so that the travelling was excellent.

Surface fires at regular intervals of three to ten years maintained the clumped pattern of all-aged stands in even-aged groups and reduced excess fuel. Fires set naturally by lightning and by Indians thinned out young pine reproduction and counteracted the tendency of trees to take on a random distribution. The most important changes brought by white man were the attempted exclusion of fire, which was accomplished by an intense fire prevention program, and the introduction of livestock that reduced the inflammable grasses. With few fires, dense pine thickets developed and with them accompanying problems of slow growth and stagnation.

SUMMARY

The few examples briefly described above are merely indicative of the vast changes in forest vegetation wrought by human activity.

Man's role in changing the face of the earth is indeed tremendous (Thomas, 1956) and can be elaborated in great detail. The chaparral belt in the Sierra Nevada foothills of California, the maquis of the Mediterranean, the manuka scrub in New Zealand, the vast areas of deforested land in Africa and China—all point to the fact that a great deal of forest has been eliminated, and even more has been greatly altered and rendered derelict by human activity, particularly through indiscriminate burning, logging, farming, domestic grazing, highway and power line construction, and home building.

Man's continued destruction of the environment has brought great concern for the establishment of various kinds of protected natural ecosystems such as parks, natural areas, and wilderness, for scientific and amenity purposes. In Germany, where man has managed and mismanaged forests for thousands of years, the lack of natural areas is so severe that lands formerly under management are now set aside as protection forests (Dieterich *et al.*, 1970). These forests will revert to natural conditions in time. Protection or preservation, however, is no guarantee that the presettlement condition or a vegetational status quo will be maintained. Silvicultural management of even wilderness areas, including use of fire and judicious cutting, will be important in maintaining forest ecosystems in the "natural" condition for which they were set aside.

SUGGESTED READINGS

CURTIS, JOHN T. 1959. *The Vegetation of Wisconsin.* (Chapter 23, The effect of man on the vegetation, pp. 456–475.) Univ. Wisconsin Press, Madison. 657 pp.

IVERSEN, J. 1949. The influence of prehistoric man on vegetation. Geol. Survey of Denmark. N. series 3, No. 6, 25 pp.

LUTZ, H. J. 1930. The vegetation of Heart's Content, a virgin forest in northwestern Pennsylvania. *Ecology* 11:1–29.

PENNINGTON, WINIFRED. 1969. *The History of British Vegetation.* (Chapter 7, The Neolithic revolution; man begins to destroy the forests, pp. 62–77; Chapter 9, Later changes in vegetation, and species introduced into the flora by man, pp. 88–99.) English Universities Press, London. 152 pp.

SPURR, STEPHEN H. 1951. George Washington, surveyor and ecological observer. *Ecology* 32:544–549.

————. 1966. Wilderness management. The Horace M. Albright Conservation Lectureship, Univ. California, School of Forestry, Berkeley, Calif. 16 pp.

19

Forests of the World

The description of the forests of the world on either a physiog-nomic-structural or a floristic basis involves the adoption of some type of classification within a geographical framework. The choice is large, for there are approximately as many classifications of vege-tation types as there are writers on the subject. The fact that no single approach has achieved anything like widespread recognition and adoption testifies to the arbitrariness and artificiality of most classifications. The fact is that each geographical area has its own peculiar history, that each species and each genus have their own particular distributions, and that there is and can be no compart-mentalized classification scheme of vegetation types that can set up mutually exclusive divisions. Nevertheless, there are broad floristic provinces which have a general validity and usefulness in denoting geographical areas that are characterized by given groups of plants. Within these provinces, various communities occur which show less variation within the communities than between different communi-ties. On this basis, the general forest patterns of the world are described in this chapter.

Before entering upon a description of the forests of the world, however, it is well to note briefly those vegetational classification schemes which have achieved greatest recognition and usage.

CLASSIFICATION OF VEGETATION

As noted above, within a geographical setting, vegetation may be described either on a physiognomic-structural or a floristic basis. Since the end result of vegetational classification frequently is a map of the vegetation of a district or region, geographical, climatic, physiognomic, and floristic considerations must eventually be integrated in order to prepare it. Much more than in the past, vegetational classification and maps are designed so that vegetation units designate similar site conditions. Thus there is a continuing evolution from strictly vegetation classification to the classification of all elements of the ecosystem, even though vegetation may be used to name each type of ecosystem recognized.

Geographical-Climatic Classification

To even the most casual observer, the vegetation of the North Temperate Zone is characterized by common genera that set it apart from the South Temperate Zone. Similarly the tropical flora of the New World is quite different floristically from that of the Old World. Most plant geographers, therefore, recognize four plant kingdoms: (1) *boreal* and north polar (North Temperate Zone); (2) *paleotropical* (Old World Tropics); (3) *neotropical* (American Tropics); and (4) *southern oceanic and subantarctic* (South Temperate Zone).

These "kingdoms" are subdivided into geographical subkingdoms, or regions, which represent major subdivisions of continents on the basis of broad floristic differences. Here there is less consistency, but North America, for example, can be divided into: (1) arctic or tundra zone; (2) boreal conifer forest; (3) western temperate conifer forest; (4) eastern temperate pine-hardwood forest; (5) central prairie belt forest; (6) subtropical forest; and (7) tropical forest.

The regions can be further subdivided into provinces, the provinces can be further subdivided into sectors, and these into districts. The further the subdivision is carried, the more arbitrary and artificial it becomes and the less is the agreement between plant geographers on the classification of vegetation. The floristic province, however, characterized by a general coincidence of distributions of a group of species over a geographical range, has considerable validity and usefulness.

Physiognomic-Structural Classification

The outward appearance of vegetation, i.e., its physiognomy (closed forest, open woodland, grassland), and structural features (evergreen forest, deciduous forest, thorn forest) have been widely used to describe and map vegetation on a world scale. The classification by Ellenberg and Mueller-Dombois (1970) is a good example, and a modified portion of this classification is shown in Table 19.1. As seen in Table 19.1, the physiognomic-structural

Table 19.1   A Portion of a Physiognomic-Structural Classification of Forest and Related Woody-Plant Ecosystem

I. *Closed Forests*
   A. Mainly Evergreen Forests
      1. Tropical rain forest
      2. Tropical and subtropical evergreen seasonal forest
      3. Tropical and subtropical semideciduous forest
      4. Subtropical seasonal rain forest
      5. Mangrove forest
      6. Temperate and subpolar rain forest
      7. Temperate evergreen seasonal broadleaved forest
      8. Winter-rain hard-broadleaved (sclerophyll) evergreen forest
      9. Coniferous evergreen forest
   B. Mainly Deciduous Forests
      1. Drought-deciduous (monsoon) forest (tropical, subtropical)
      2. Cold-deciduous forest with evergreens
      3. Cold-deciduous (summergreen) forest
   C. Dry Forests
      1. Hardleaved forest
      2. Thorn forest
      3. Mainly succulent forest

II. *Open Woodlands*
   A. Mainly Evergreen Woodlands
      1. Evergreen broadleaved woodland
      2. Evergreen needle- or scale-leaved woodland
   B. Mainly Deciduous Woodlands
      1. Drought-deciduous woodland
      2. Cold-deciduous woodland with evergreen
      3. Cold-deciduous woodland
   C. Dry Woodlands

Modified from Ellenberg and Mueller-Dombois (1970).

classification is closely related to environmental factors, especially temperature and precipitation. For example, "Closed Forests" are not exclusively characteristic of any one geographic region, but are further subdivided on the basis of geographic differences of temperature and moisture. Webb (1959, 1968) has provided a useful physiognomic-structural classification of the forests of eastern Australia. The change in structural types along three environmental gradients is clearly depicted in Figure 19.1.

Physiognomic-structural features are not only suitable for classification at the broad reconnaissance level but have proved useful at lower levels as well, as in the tropical rain forests of eastern Australia (Webb *et al.*, 1970). Here they were demonstrated to be as efficient as floristic classification in assessing the environmental conditions of an area. Structural classification is particularly useful in areas such as tropical rain forests where the flora is not well known and structural data may be rapidly collected, even by inexperienced personnel.

Floristic Classifications

Plant sociologists have long attempted to develop systems for classifying plant communities along lines similar to those that have been evolved for plant individuals. Starting with the analogy between the plant species and the plant association, elaborate schemes of community classification and their binomial nomenclature have been proposed. In western Europe, where the greatest effort at systematization has occurred, the schools of Braun-Blanquet, Schmid, Du Rietz, Gaussen, and Aichinger (Küchler, 1967) are in conflict on many points. In northern Europe, classification of the forests is greatly influenced by Cajander's reliance upon the occurrence of characteristic ground-cover species, whereas in Russsia, the work of Morosov, Sukachev, and others has led to quite different schemes of classifying the boreal forest.

Braun-Blanquet, for example, recognizes the *circle of vegetation* as the highest and broadest unit of community classification. This is subdivided into a *class*, which is more or less synonymous with Clements' *formation*. Further breakdowns include the *order*, the *alliance* (analogous to the *genus*) and the *association*. In binomial nomenclature, the suffix *-etalia* denotes an order, *-on*, an alliance, and *-etum*, an association. In the terminology of Braun-Blanquet, the *association* refers to any plant community described at the level of the species, whereas Clements restricts the term (and the term *formation* as well) solely to climax communities. Hierarchical ranking of vegetation groups, similar to that of the plant taxonomic system, is less popular in Europe than it once was. At Montpellier in France, where Braun-Blanquet enjoyed his greatest success, vege-

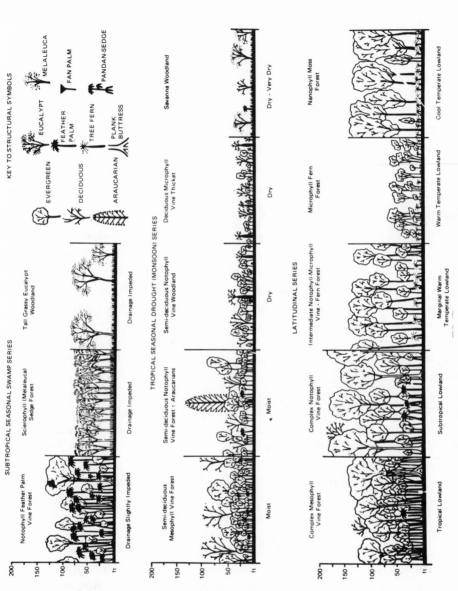

Fig. 19.1. Forest profile sketches illustrating structural changes along different environmental gradients for forests of eastern Australia. (After Webb, 1968.)

tation maps are prepared floristically but with much more attention to habitat conditions than pure floristic relationships with hierarchies (Küchler, 1967).

A Classification of Forests

Since it is necessary to espouse some system of classification in order to discuss logically the forests of the world, the following loose and approximate scheme will be followed:

As a basic major division, forests characteristic of frost-free regions (i.e., the Tropics) will be considered separately from those annually subject to frequent and severe frosts (i.e., the Temperate Zone and temperate belts within the Tropics).

Within the Tropics, forest formations are recognized on the basis of soil-water relationships arising from the amount and seasonal pattern of precipitation and upon drainage conditions in the soil.

Within the Temperate Zone, forest formations are recognized on the basis of dominant tree genera. Within these formations, forest types are recognized as characterized by dominant tree species. These in turn may be subdivided into communities on the basis of total floristic composition.

TROPICAL FORESTS

In the frost-free tropical zone, many species of trees live and thrive, forming a great complex of vegetational formations and associations. The species are numbered in the hundreds and even in the thousands, and classification of forests on the basis of floristic composition is not only extremely difficult but results in the recognition of hundreds of taxa. Forests on similar sites, however, tend to have a similar physiognomy and structure regardless of their species composition. An ecological classificaiton of vegetation based on site has proved much simpler and more useful than one based upon species. Such an approach will suffice for the present brief description of tropical forests.

A few tropical plants occur in habitats protected from frost north of the Tropic of Cancer and south of the Tropic of Capricorn. These are almost entirely confined to windward ocean sites where moderating maritime influences create a frost-free—but not necessarily a warm—climate. Palms are grown in Devon and Cornwall in southwestern England. Both the southern half of the Florida peninsula and the southern coast of California support frost-susceptible plants in large numbers and can be considered at least as subtropical if not actually tropical. Similar conditions occur in North Africa, northern New Zealand, and other areas of mild oceanic climate.

Classification of Tropical Forests

Within the frost-free zone of the world, the physiognomy of vegetation varies primarily according to the amount and seasonal pattern of rainfall and secondarily in response to human activity, primarily land clearing, burning, and plant introduction. Many classifications of tropical forests have been proposed (Beard, 1955; Haden-Guest, 1956; Cain and Castro, 1959; Webb, 1968). All recognize a gradation ranging from swamp forests to tropical desert, a moisture cline which may be divided arbitrarily into few or many vegetational types. The following is perhaps the simplest possible classification:

Swamp forest
  Salt water swamp
  Fresh water swamp
Rain forest, climate wet the year around
  Lowland rain forest, grading with increasing altitude into
  Montane rain forest and cloud forest
Monsoon forest, alternating wet and dry seasons
Dry forest, no pronounced wet periods
  Closed dry forest, grading with decreasing precipitation into
  Savanna woodland

Swamp Forest

Poorly drained and undrained sites in the Tropics support the most hydrophytic formations. These range from salt-water swamps and low beaches through brackish water swamps to fresh-water swamps. Swamp forests may be classified further according to the depth of the water, aeration of the water, the type of substrate, and the seasonal variation in the water level.

Salt-Water Tropical Shorelines. The vegetation closely associated with seawater is quite distinct from that associated with fresh water. The nature of the vegetation differs with geographical location, nearness to the shore, and soil—whether mud, sand, or coral.

Mangroves are evergreen trees and shrubs belonging to several unrelated families which form communities very similar in physiognomic appearance on tidal mud flats throughout frost-free climates of the world. Mangrove swamps grow to latitude 32° north as far as Bermuda, the Gulf of Aqaba in the Red Sea, and southern Japan; and in the Southern Hemisphere as far as south Natal and northern New Zealand. *Rhizophora* is the commonest and most widespread genus of mangroves. The species occurring in mangrove swamps of the Indian and western Pacific Oceans differ from those of America, the West Indies, and Africa, but the two formations are very similar in appearance and ecological relationships.

Mangroves are of considerable local importance for fuel wood, tannin, and even for timber. The strongly developed zonation in mangrove swamps is strongly indicative of primary succession and has already been discussed (Chapter 13).

In brackish swamps inland, other species occur. Nipa palm, important for thatch, is widespread in occurrence in southeastern Asia and the western Pacific.

On sandy beaches, still other species are found. Species of *Barringtonia* (Indian and Pacific Oceans), *Pandanus* (Asia and Africa), and *Coccoloba* (New World) are particularly widespread genera of trees and shrubs. *Casuarina* is a characteristic littoral tree that has been planted even more widely throughout the tropics for its shelter-belt and fuel value. Most important, of the shoreline trees, however, is the coconut, a species so widely spread by man that its "natural" range is still in dispute.

Fresh-Water Swamps. Both the site and the vegetation of fresh-water swamps grade into upland tropical rain forest as the soil drainage improves. The swamp vegetation, because of limiting soil aeration, however, is more open and irregular in structure, and consists of fewer species than nearby upland types. Various palms reach their optimum development and abundance in fresh-water swamps and are perhaps the most characteristic plants of these sites. Cabbage palm (*Sabal palmetto*) is such a tree in the fresh-water swamps of Florida. Others are *Euterpe* and *Mauritia* in South America, *Phoenix* in Africa, and sago palm (*Metroxylon*) in the western Pacific. Various *Cecropias* are important in developing forest successions in tropical America, where the largest late-successional fresh-water swamp species is the huge emergent, *Ceiba pentandra*.

Rain Forest

Under conditions of adequate precipitation, lush rain forests develop in the Tropics. The extent, however, is limited by climatic
patterns, much of the Tropics being too dry. The rain forest is concentrated in three broad regions: (1) northern South and adjacent
Central America, particularly in the Amazon Basin; (2) western
Equatorial Africa from Sierra Leone to the Congo Basin; and (3)
the Indo-Malayan region, including the west coast of India, much
of the Indo-Chinese Peninsula, Indonesia, New Guinea, and the
northeast coast of Australia. The vegetation differs greatly not only
between the three main belts of tropical rain forest but in different
portions of each belt. The number of species represented is not
known. Individual regions such as the Congo and Borneo have
been estimated to contain about 10,000 species of phanerogams each.
In the Malay Peninsula alone, about 2,500 species of trees are
known, while the great rain forest or *hylaea* of the Amazon contains
at least that many species of large trees. Richards (1952) has
brought together and interpreted our knowledge of the tropical
rain forest. His book is an indispensable reference to those interested in the subject.

Fortunately, the general appearance and structure of the tropical
rain forest is much the same everywhere. Its description in tropical
Africa by Aubréville in *A World Geography of Forest Resources*
(Haden-Guest *et al.*, 1956) is typical and worth quoting:

The rain forest is very dense, with a tightly closed canopy. Three stories
may be distinguished. The upper story is discontinuous, composed of a relatively few gigantic and usually isolated trees with mighty crowns rising 40 to 45
meters above the ground. At a height of about 25 to 30 meters a continuous
middle story of crowns pressed one against another gives the forest, as seen
from an airplane, a characteristically undulating and unbroken appearance and
hides the trunks from view. The lowest story is made up of small trees and
bushes whose crowns fill almost all of the remaining space.

Not much light penetrates to the undergrowth through the higher levels of
foliage, and the sun's rays seldom reach the ground. Nor can one, from the
ground, see the crowns of the biggest trees, hidden as they are by those of the
lower stories. Indeed, because of the dimness in the undergrowth and the
clutter of small trees and lianas, one cannot see even the trunks of the largest
trees, except from close at hand. Hardly ever does the rain forest offer those
beautiful vistas of great columns that are presented by some of the mature
forests of temperate lands. The ground, however, is bare, or garnished with a
few sporadic herbaceous plants. It is easy enough to walk through the forest,
but creepers frequently hinder rapid progress. The humidity is high, but the
air seems fresh by contrast with that of sun-baked clearings unprotected by

the forest screen. The secondary forests, on the other hand, are difficult to penetrate because of the density of the stems, which are often spiny, and the great quantity of lianas and herbaceous plants.

Lianas of all kinds also abound in the primary rain forest: filiform lianas, stretched like strings; huge woody lianas that curl around the tree trunks; rope-like lianas that hang to the ground from branches. Some of the lianas ramify out into the sunshine in the crowns of larger trees, joining the upper stems and branches one to another, and making the forest canopy yet more dense. Epipyhtes are equally abundant, gripping tree trunks and branches. Palms are infrequent except for those of the genus *Raphia,* which grows in stands in marshy bottoms, and the creeping rattan palms. The latter proliferate on the banks of streams and climb to the highest tree tops with the help of leaves provided with hooks along their rachises.

In the mountains and in humid ravines there are sometimes clumps of beautiful arborescent ferns. Here and there one finds the strangler fig. Springing from seed lodged in the crook of treetop branches, it grows into a small epiphytic bush; its roots reach the ground by spiraling down around the trunk and then grow into powerful tentacles that anastomose and stifle the supporting tree. After the latter's death, the fig may live on independently as a large tree. Some trees are cauliflorous: first their flowers and then their fruits—some of which may be huge—are produced directly from the tree trunk itself.

The crowns of the trees seldom have any one characteristic shape. Some are wide and strongly sculptured; others, where compressed by neighboring crowns, may be ovoid and astonishingly narrow. Yet more remarkable are the tabular crowns composed of the verticils of horizontal branches (e.g., of *Terminalia superba* and *T. ivorensis*). Other crowns—notably Mimosaceae—spread out like parasols.

Many tree trunks are remarkably free of branches to great heights. Standing almost perfectly upright, they look like narrow cylinders and give the impression, when they are seen from a distance, that they are inordinately tall and thin, although their actual diameters may be large. Indeed, some trees, free of branches up to a great height, have cylindrical trunks that seem technologically perfect (*Entandrophragma utile, Mimusops heckelii, Terminalia superba*). Others have trunks of irregular cross section or are fluted at the base. Trees with really large diameters (i.e., more than 2 or 3 meters) are exceptional. Eighty centimeters at the larger end of the utilizable portion of the trunk is about average diameter of the timber trees now being exploited.

The most remarkable physiognomic characteristic of many of the great trees of these forests is the buttress structure at their bases. Usually triangular these buttresses serve as firm anchors for very tall trees that are otherwise attached to the soil by shallow root systems only. The buttresses rise several meters above the surface and sometimes stretch out 10 meters or more along the ground in the shape of winding flattened roots. Some of them are spectacular indeed. Their presence and in some cases their form characterize different species. Some species have no buttresses, but merely trunks thickened at the base, as in temperate-forest trees. The degree to which the buttresses are developed in individual trees depends on the depth of the soil. Sometimes parts of them are raised completely off the ground to form true aerial roots that let one see clear under the tree (*Tarrietia utilis,* many *Xylopia, Musanga smithii,* etc.). Other trees, yet more curious, are upheld by systems of adventitious curving and ramifying roots (which may be as thick as a man's arm), in such a way that each tree appears perched upon a network of intertwined roots. Among trees of this type are the mangroves (genus *Rhizophora*), found in marshy soil, and trees of genus *Uapaca*, which grow in dry soil.

Buttresses and aerial roots naturally make felling difficult. Cutting is commonly done above the buttress, and the woodsmen build a platform around the tree on which to work.

All types of bark are represented in the tropical rain forest: smooth, thin, thick, fissured, gnarled, prone to come off in sheets, and so forth. Some barks are conspicuously colored yellow or even bright red (*Distemonanthus benthamianus*, some of the *Copaifera* and *Xylopia*). The fragrance of certain barks is equally distinctive: the cedar smell of mahogany, *Guarea*, *Lovoa;* the garlic smell of *Scorodophloeus zenkeri*. Latex, appearing in a gashed bark, and dripping gum likewise give valuable clues to the forester, who can thereby recognize certain tree families (Moraceae, Sapotaceae, Apocynaceae, etc., with latex; Guttiferae and Hypericaceae, with dripping gum).

The great number of tree species and the complexity of tropical rain forests have long intrigued biologists. Their very complexity and relative inaccessibility have limited detailed analytical studies of their nature. Nevertheless, the large number of species and the low density of adults of each species in the rain forest as compared to the temperate forest may be explained at least in part by several interacting factors: (1) favorable temperature, precipitation, and soil conditions permitting expression of many and varied mechanisms of plant growth and reproduction, i.e., relatively free release and expression of genetic variability; (2) proportionately greater interspecific competition as individuals approach maturity (contrasted to greater intraspecific competition in temperate forests) leading to the evolution of mutually avoiding, hence ecologically complementary, species (Ashton, 1969); (3) environmental conditions favoring a rich fauna, particularly insect, bird, and bat pollinators which, being many and specialized, promote speciation of plants; and (4) the action of predators destroying seeds and seedlings, which tends to increase the distance between adult breeding trees of many species, leaving more space in the habitat for other species (Janzen, 1970). Summarizing his work in the species-rich southeast Asian mixed dipterocarp forests, Ashton (1969) stated that the complexity of the rain forest can be explained in terms of:

(i) The seasonal and geological stability of the climate which had led to selection for mutual avoidance, and through increased specialization, to increasingly narrow ecological amplitudes, leading to complex integrated ecosystems of high productive efficiency. As the complexity increases, the numbers of biotic niches into which evolution can take place increase but become increasingly narrow.

(ii) Their great age.

Commercially important rain forest trees include: mahogany (*Swietenia* spp.), rosewood (*Dalbergia* spp.), Spanish cedar (*Cedrela* spp.), balsa (*Ochroma* spp.), and rubber (*Hevea brasilensis*) in the American forest; African mahogany (*Khaya and Entandrophragma* spp.), okoume (*Aucoumea klaineana*), and ebony (*Diospyros* spp.) in Africa; and Philippine mahogany (*Shorea* and *Parashorea* spp.) and yang (*Dipterocarpus alatus*) among the dipterocarps of the southeast Asia–western Pacific area.

The tropical rain forest in any one geographical area represents a multidimensional continuum with gradual changes in composition and structure occurring with distance from the ocean, distance from rivers, increasing altitude, and changing geographical position. A given acre may contain fifty species; a hectare perhaps one hundred species, while another hundred species may be found by extending the search over several hectares. Riparian forest communities are usually rather different from the forest communities away from streams, but even here the ecotone between communities is apt to be broad and indistinct.

With increasing altitude, the rain forest becomes shorter in stature, simpler in floristic composition, and increasingly characterized by luxuriant epiphytes, particularly mosses and lichens. At elevations above about 2,000 meters (6,600 feet) in the equatorial Tropics, this trend culminates in the *montane rain forest*, also termed the *cloud forest* or *mossy forest*. If dwarfed, it may be called *elfin woodland*. As the names imply, the mountain climate around such forests is apt to be mostly cloudy with the air saturated with moisture and fog-drip providing daily precipitation. The climate is cool, constantly damp, and persistently misty. Whereas tree heights in the lowland rain forest frequently exceed 30 meters (maximum 84 meters for *Koompassia excelsa* in Borneo), heights in lower montane belts commonly are only 20 to 25 meters, and in the high mossy forest may be only 6 meters. The number of tree stories and the number of tree species become fewer with increasing elevation, but the number of individual trees increases.

Monsoon Forest

Since evapotranspiration in the Tropics (outside of the cloud zone in the mountains) is extremely high, evergreen broadleaf forests are confined to the rain belts, where at least 10 centimeters of rain normally fall each month of the year and 200 centimeters or more of rain fall during the year at least. In regions with 100 to 200 centimeters' annual precipitation that are characterized by a dry period of a month or more, some of the dominant trees tend to lose their leaves, especially toward the end of this period. The term *monsoon forest* is given to the deciduous and semi-deciduous forests of southeastern Asia developed under a climate characterized by a very dry period of two to six or more months, broken by the very wet monsoon which comes in June or thereabouts depending upon the locality. Not too accurately, the term has been extended to refer to smaller areas of deciduous and semi-deciduous forests elsewhere.

Changes in the seasonal foliation of forests tend to occur gradually with climatic gradients in the Tropics. A marked deciduous period occurs in forests growing in areas with an equally marked dry season. A general lowering of annual precipitation without a strongly marked dry season, however, results in the forest being simpler in structure, smaller in size, and more xerophytic in character, but not necessarily deciduous.

The tropical deciduous forest is extremely important in southeast Asia, both for its extent and for the commercial importance of its tree species. Dipterocarps constitute the most important genus. In the wetter zone, the dipterocarps are tall and shed their leaves annually only after the new leaves are expanded. In drier zones, the dominants may have a leafless period while the understory shrubs and trees may remain evergreen. Teak (*Tectona grandis*) is commercially the most important of the monsoon forest trees. *Xylia xylocarpa*, a deciduous leguminous tree, however, is more abundant. *Terminalia* and *Shorea* are other common genera, sal (*Shorea robusta*) being a commercially important monsoon forest tree in India.

Dry Forest

With less than about 100 centimeters of rain, forests in the Tropics tend to be very xerophytic. Depending upon the amount and distribution of annual precipitation, such forests vary from low and rather simply structured closed forest to open woodland, thorn woodland, and open wooded savannas. These dry forests occupy most of tropical Africa south of the Sahara except for the equatorial rain forest, much of tropical Australia, and a good deal of South America both north and south of the Amazon Basin.

As with other tropical vegetation types, composition and structural changes are graded to climatic changes, there being no sharp cleavage between dry closed forest, dry open forest, and savanna forest. Fire is the dominant factor in these dry tropical types, having been widespread and frequent for many thousands of years. Vast areas of forest have been degraded by repeated burning into sparsely wooded savannas (Bartlett, 1956). On the driest sites, thorny shrubs and small trees with thin parasol-like crowns replace the larger arborescents. *Acacia* is a particularly common dry tropical genus of wide distribution.

FROST-HARDY FORESTS

As with the tropical forests of frost-free climates, frost-hardy forests subject to annual freezing temperatures are marked by discontinuity. The distribution of temperate genera and species is broken, however, not only by oceanic barriers, but by the barrier of the equatorial belt as well. Although high elevations with temperate or near-temperate climates occur in the tropics of all continents, these areas are not continuous, and relatively few forest trees have ben able to migrate across them from one temperate zone to another, particularly in recent historic times.

In many cases, however, closely related *"vicarious"* species occupy similar sites in widely separated areas. In still other places, vicarious species are missing through historical factors governing their distribution, their place in the ecological scheme being taken by unrelated trees which can occupy the site in the absence of better competitors.

The other major factor governing the distribution of frost-hardy forests is the existence of a circumpolar boreal forest belt populated around the world with various closely related species of spruces, firs, larches, birches, and aspens. This belt is of relatively new origin, much of it growing on sites that have been glaciated up to within the last ten thousand years. As a result, it is inhabited by northward migrants of various populations that survived the Pleistocene in cool moist refugia. Most of these were located in lower-latitude highlands, but some were located in coastal areas and other unglaciated portions of the higher latitudes (Chapter 17). Many tree genera are represented in several of the temperate forest centers in the

Northern Hemisphere, and others are similarly represented in temperate forest centers of the Southern Hemisphere. Since the species of each genus tend to occupy similar ecological habitats or niches wherever they occur, the homologous nature of the temperate forests of the world can perhaps best be approached by considering the world distribution and ecological habits of the most important tree taxa. These may, for convenience, be considered in two groups: boreal trees which comprise the circumboreal forest of the high latitudes and which also occur at high altitudes in the temperate zone; and temperate forest trees which form discontinuous distributions between the boreal forest and the Tropics.

Boreal Forest Taxa

The principal boreal forest groups include the spruces, firs, larches, birches, and aspens (section Leuce of *Populus*). Of these, the spruces are the most widespread in distribution and the most characteristic of the boreal forest.

Spruces. The circumpolar forest is characterized by spruces, except for eastern Siberia, where larches are more numerous. The principal species in North America are white and black spruce, which have similar ranges from Alaska to Newfoundland. Norway spruce in western Europe and the closely related Siberian spruce (*Picea obovata*) in Russia and Siberia occupy similar sites in similar latitudinal belts from Norway to eastern Siberia.

South of the boreal belt, about 25 species of spruce occur in isolated mountain ranges as far south as the 25th parallel in Mexico (*P. chihuahuana*) and the 23rd in Taiwan (*P. morrisonicola*) (Wright, 1955). All are similar in appearance and in ecological habit and show close taxonomic relationships between widely spaced species in the different continents. Characterized by a shallow root system, often largely confined to the organic humus layers of the typical mor-type soils which develop under all spruces, the genus is particularly well adapted to grow in cold soils and even on permanently frozen ground and on glaciers covered with detritus, for it is this shallow top layer which warms up and dries out sufficiently under arctic climatic conditions to make tree growth possible. On lighter-textured and warmer soils, however, spruces, particularly Norway spruce and white spruce, develop moderately deep root systems. This suggests considerable plasticity in their rooting depth, depending on the local soil and humus environment. Being characterized by sharply conical crowns, the spruces are well suited to bear winter snows and to shed them when slight warming or wind occur. Partly because of their shallow root systems, and partly because of their low nutrient requirements, spruces are tolerant of acid, undrained soil conditions and are able to survive and even grow in northern bogs and (as in the case of Sitka spruce) in cold, wet, rain forest or cloud forest conditions. It is not by accident, therefore, that spruce is the characteristic genus of the northern forest, and that its world distribution may be taken as approximately delineating both the circumpolar forest and its outliers in the high mountains of the Northern Hemisphere.

Firs.   Being similar to the spruces in general form and appearance, and occupying much the same ecological niche, it is not surprising that the genus *Abies* has much the same distribution as the genus *Picea*. The fact that spruces and firs are frequently lumped together as characterizing the boreal forest, however, should not obscure the fact that the firs are less tolerant of poorly drained conditions, less tolerant of fire, and more tolerant of warmer and drier climates. While firs are common upland species in the boreal forest of North America, therefore, they do not occur to any extent in the boreal forests of Eurasia. Also, they occur farther south and in somewhat drier mountain ranges than the spruces.

The principal boreal forest firs are the balsam fir of eastern North America and the alpine fir of western North America. In Eurasia, fir is primarily a high mountain genus of the Temperate Zone, important species being European silver fir (*A. alba*) in the mountains of central Europe and as far south as the Pyrenees, where it is the major tree species, *A nordmanniana* in the mountains of the Caucasus and the Black Sea region of Turkey, and silver fir (*A. pindrow*) in the Himalayas. The genus occurs in several high mountain ranges far south, with *A. guatemalensis* and *A. religiosa* growing in the mountains of Mexico and Guatemala, *A. pinapso* and *A. numidica* in the mountains of North Africa, *A. cilicia* in the mountains of Asia Minor, and *A. pindrow* in the mountains of northern Indo-China.

Larches.   In contrast to *Abies*, which is more a boreal group of the New World than of the Old, *Larix* is the principal boreal genus in Siberia, and occurs in the American boreal forest only as tamarack, a species typically restricted to swamps by its relatively poor competitive ability. Being deciduous, the larches are better adapted to survive in cold, dry climates than the spruces and firs, which are better suited to cold, wet climates. Being highly intolerant as a group, however, the larches require an open site and a dominant crown position throughout life and cannot compete successfully with spruces, firs, and other trees under moister climatic conditions.

Larch is the principal forest genus in eastern Siberia, forming extensive stands from longitude 90 to 150 and almost as far south as the southern border of the U.S.S.R. In fact, larch (chiefly *L. sibirica*) is by far the most widespread tree of the U.S.S.R., occupying some 43 percent of the total forest area of the country, mostly in the cold, dry region described.

Elsewhere, with the exception of the boreal swamp-inhabiting tamarack, larch is primarily a mountain tree of cold, dry climate. Such are *L. occidentalis* in the Inland Empire region of northern Idaho and western Montana, *L. decidua* in the mountains of central Europe, *L. griffithii* in the Himalayas, *L. gmelini* in Korea, and *L. leptolepis* in Japan. None of these species, however, extends as far to the south as species of spruces and firs in the same localities, nor do they occur as far down the slopes when they do occur in the same latitudes.

Birches and Aspens. Associated with spruces and firs, but growing into drier climates than the conifers, are the birches and aspens. Both are light-seeded pioneer trees which can colonize even large burns, and which can regenerate from undamaged rootstocks after fire has killed their above-ground portions—the birches by stump sprouts and the aspens by root suckers. These are the fire species of the boreal forest *par excellence,* and their abundance is a direct measure of the severity and frequency of past forest fires.

Birches form a circumpolar population composed of separate migrations from various Pleistocene refugia which have merged and interbred to form a complex of closely related species. The *Betula papyrifera* complex in North America and the *Betula alba* complex in Europe (*B. pubescens* and *B. verrucosa*) form a single species-group of white birches which are similar in morphology and ecological habitat and closely related genetically. The birches and aspens extend farther east in Siberia than the spruces and larches, and are the principal forest trees of Kamchatka. Birches and aspens occur abundantly throughout the dry larch forests of eastern Siberia and commonly though less abundantly in the moist spruce-fir forests of Europe and western Siberia. In North America, birches and aspens are most abundant in the drier sections of the Canadian north and in the most heavily burned sections of the Lake States.

In the Arctic tundra, dwarf birches form a characteristic part of the vegetation, while south of the boreal forest, outliers of birch occur in major mountain ranges of the eastern United States, the Pyrenees, the Himalayas, and the Korean mountains. These temperate species vary from midtolerant to intolerant and in their site preferences from riverain to mountain-slope species. They perhaps reach their optimum development in the northeastern United States, where yellow and black birches form a minor but important part of the forest complex.

The aspens similarly form a circumboreal complex made of intergrading populations that have migrated north from various Pleistocene centers of refuge. *Populus tremula* in Europe and Asia, *P. suaveolens* in eastern Siberia, and *P. tremuloides* in North America are the names given respectively to the Old and New World portions of this complex. In contrast to birches, which have only a limited distribution in the western United States, aspen extends southward at high elevations down the Rockies and Sierra Nevada to the mountains of northern Mexico. In the eastern United States, *P. grandidentata* has a range which overlaps the eastern portion of the *P. tremuloides* range, but the former species grows better on drier and warmer sites than the latter. In Eurasia, outliers of *P. tremula* occur in the Himalayas, China, Korea, and Japan. *Populus alba* is another poplar of section Leuce which is native to moister and riverain sites from central Europe through the Balkans as far west as Iran.

Summary. The spruces, firs, larches, birches, and aspens, then, each consist of a group of boreal forest species of widespread distribution together with a number of isolated relict species in cool temperate mountain climates at lower latitudes. The cool-temperate forest throughout the Northern Hemisphere is dominated by these five groups, the composition of any one place depending upon historical factors governing the present distribution and the differing climatic and site tolerances of the different species. The spruces, aspens, and birches are the most widely distributed in the boreal forest zone as larches are relatively unimportant in boreal North America and firs the same in boreal Eurasia. The wetter cool cli-

mates are apt to support spruce-fir types while the drier sites are best
suited to dominance of larches, birches, and aspens. The latter two
are particularly well adapted to regenerate both sexually and
vegetatively after forest fires, which are frequent, severe, and extensive in much of the northern world. The spruce-fir, larch, and
birch-aspen forests everywhere have a similar physiognomy, similar
ecological relationships, and respond to similar silvicultural treatment.

Temperate Forest Taxa

The belt of frost-hardy forests that occupies the temperate zones
of the Northern Hemisphere between the boreal forest and the
frost-free forest of the Tropics, and all of the Southern Hemisphere
south of the Tropics (there being no austral equivalent of the boreal
forest) consists of many disjunct tree populations separated by
oceanic and desert barriers of long geologic standing. In both the
Northern and Southern Hemispheres, however, closely related species of the same genera (i.e., *vicariads*) frequently occupy similar
ecological niches in the different regions, so that a discussion
of the temperate forest on the basis of the dominant forest taxa
serves to indicate the large common denominator of these forest
stands throughout the world. Pines, oaks, beeches, and eucalypts
are the principal forest-forming trees, but other conifers and angiosperms must be included in the discussion.

Pines. The genus *Pinus* is the most important of all forest-tree
genera. There are approximately one hundred species and most of
them are locally or nationally important in the timber economy.
They occur from the boreal forest to south of the Equator in the
equatorial mountains of Sumatra and Java (*Pinus merkusii*). An
excellent monograph on the genus *Pinus* has been prepared by Mirov
(1967).

Despite the taxonomic variety and the wide distribution of pines
in the Northern Hemisphere, however, all have a great deal in common in their ecological place in the world's forest. Virtually all are
characteristic of coarse dry soils, especially sands, gravels, and rock
outcrops; and most owe their dominance to the frequent burning
of such sites and their ability to regenerate abundantly in the ashes
of the blackened site. The closed-cone pines are the most dependent
on fire, but even the five-needled white pines, the most mesophytic

of the group, are commonly found in pure, even-aged stands most often after destruction of the prior forest by fire.

As a group, the pines have a deep root system, with the growing root tips requiring large soil interstices for penetration. Because of the deep root system, they do not grow well on frozen or poorly drained soils, and because of the poor penetrating ability of the roots, they grow best on deep coarse soils. They have a high ability to withstand hot, dry conditions, whether in the Tropics or in northern continental climates as in the interior of Canada and Siberia. The closed cone "serotinous" habit of many of the two- and three-needled pines is well adapted to supply seed after the passing fire has melted the resin, causing the cone scales to reflex. The bark of most of the pines (but not the white pines) is thick, and insulates the cambium well against the heat of passing surface fires.

The pines, then, are the characteristic trees of coarse soils subject to frequent burning, and have a wide tolerance for temperature variation. They are widely used for lumber, naval stores (resin and turpentine), and edible nuts (pinyons and stone pines) throughout much of the Northern Hemisphere.

In the boreal forest, the vicariads, Pacific coast lodgepole, Rocky Mountain lodgepole, jack pine, and Scots pine form a circumpolar belt of forest across North America, Europe, and Asia. These species do not extend far into the northern zones of permanently frozen soils, but do extend quite far south along high mountain ranges, lodgepole occurring as far south as southern California and Scots pine growing in Spain, Italy, Greece, and Turkey.

Also north temperate for the most part are the five-needled white pines, of which closely related vicarious species occur in relatively cool, moist temperate zones around the world. The subsection Strobi include: sugar pine and western white pine in the western United States; eastern white pine in eastern North America and Chiapas; Mexican white pine (*P. ayacahuite*) in Mexico; Japanese white pine (*P. parviflora*); Formosan white pine (*P. formosana*); Macedonian white pine (*P. peuce*); and Himalayan white pine (*P. griffithii*) in the Himalayas. The other groups of white pines include the stone pines and the limber pines, both also widely distributed.

The hard pines, usually with two or three needles in a cluster, are more xerophytic than the white pines and generally grow in warmer drier sites (except for the boreal pines mentioned above which do, however, endure a hot, dry continental summer in much of their ranges). These pines have a similar physiognomic appearance and occupy similar sites whatever their name and wherever they grow.

In western North America, ponderosa pine is the principal hard pine, with lodgepole, and Jeffrey pines being also of major importance. The closed-cone relict pines of the Pacific Coast, particularly *P. radiata* and *P. muricata*, however, thrive extremely well when transferred to maritime climates elsewhere.

In eastern North America, red pine (*P. resinosa*) and the four principal southern pines (*P. taeda, P. elliotii, P. palustris,* and *P. echinata*) are the major hard pines, but, as in the west, many other species occur locally.

The Mexican and Central American pines are little known to the North American forester, although *P. caribaea, P. hondurensis,* and *P. patula* have proven well suited for extensive planting in other continents. A considerable number of other species also occur, occupying chiefly gravelly and sandy soils at high elevations. *Pinus caribaea,* however, reaches the seacoast as far south as Honduras and Nicaragua.

The dry mountain ranges of southern Europe, the Mediterranean region in general, and Asia Minor shelter many species of pines, although their ranges and quality have been severely limited by centuries of grazing and burning. Perhaps the most important is *P. nigra,* which grows in moderate temperate climates from the Pyrenees east to Greece, Turkey, and Cyprus. Several populations have been distinguished, the most important in world forestation being var. *corsicana* or Corsican pine and var. *austriaca* or Austrian pine. Other species of the region of widespread distribution are French maritime pine (*P. pinaster*), an important sandy coastal species growing from Portugal to Italy and reaching its optimum development along the Bay of Biscay in northern Spain and southwestern France; Aleppo pine (*P. halepensis*), which occurs from Spain on both sides of the Mediterranean into Jordan, Israel, and Turkey, enduring hot, dry climates in many sites; Calabrian pine (*P. brutea*) in the mountains of the Near East from Turkey to Iraq; and Italian stone pine (*P. pinea*), a nut or pinyon pine that provides edible fruits from Spain to Turkey. A purely tropical European pine is the Canary Island pine (*P. canariensis*), found only on those islands.

In Asia, aside from the great northern extent of Scots pine, temperate pines occur in the mountains of India and Pakistan, China, Korea, and Japan. In the Himalayan region chir pine (*P. roxburghii*) grows in the hot and dry lower elevations, with Himalayan white pine (*P. griffithii*) being the principal species of the higher zones. In China, *P. massoniana* and *P. tabulaeformis* are the principal pines; while in Japan, Japanese black pine (*P. thunbergii*) and Japanese red pine (*P. densiflora*) are both important species. Two of the important Asiatic pines are tropical, growing widely in the southwest Pacific in the same regions as podocarps and other south-temperate genera. *Pinus merkusii* occurs in the mountains of Burma, Thailand, the Indo-Chinese peninsula, the Philippines, and one locality in Sumatra, where it extends south of the equator. *Pinus khasia* has a very similar range and frequently grows in conjunction with it but at higher elevations. The geography of each pine species is discussed by Mirov (1967).

Oaks. The members of the genus *Quercus* are the angiosperm equivalents of the pines, being a Northern Hemisphere, widely distributed group of deep-rooted, xerophytic trees that occupy dry sites from the southern edge of the boreal forest well into the Tropics. As with the pines, oak bark is thick and fire-resistant. When the bole is killed, the root system remains alive almost indefinitely, sending up generation after generation of coppice stump sprouts that perpetuate both the individual tree and the dominance of oaks in the forest. Throughout the North Temperate Zone and much of the high country of the north Tropics, oaks are the characteristic late-successional dominants on the drier forest zone and occur also as mid-successional species on the more mesic sites. Oaks do not extend as far north as the pines, and thrive on drier sites in southern latitudes. Otherwise, their ecological requirements are much the same as those of the pines. Fire-induced pine types in much of the world will be succeeded in the absence of repeated fire by oaks, which invade as understory plants and assume dominant position when the pines die or are overthrown by wind. In other words, the oaks are more tolerant of understory conditions than the pines as a group, and follow the pines in natural succession. On the warmer and drier sites, they will thus replace the pines in the forest community in the absence of severe disturbances.

The oaks show a great deal of genetic variation. More than five hundred species have been recognized, but the merging of morphological characteristics between adjacent populations makes species identification difficult and nomenclature uncertain in many instances. With this wide diversity in morphology goes a similar wide tolerance of ecological conditions. Although primarily xerophytes, there are species of oaks that have become adapted to mesic and even hydric conditions. In the eastern United States, for instance, cherrybark oak (*Q. falcata* var. *pagodaefolia*) is but the most important of many bottomland oaks in the Mississippi Valley flood-plain; the red oaks (*Q. rubra* and *Q. falcata*) range over a wide range of sites and regions but reach their best development under mesic conditions; white and black oaks (*Q. alba* and *Q. velutina*) similarly have a wide ecological amplitude but are most characteristic of drier sites; chestnut oak (*Q. prinus*) is dominant on very dry hillsides and mountain slopes; while a whole series of scrub oaks (such as *Q. ilicifolia, Q. laevis,* and *Q. marilandica*) grow on the very driest and most infertile sand plains, sites often too poor for good pine growth.

In the North Temperate Zone, the oaks are deciduous, but in the South Temperate Zone, oak species are frequently evergreen or have but a brief leafless season. Most oaks are *sclerophylls,* having a hard leaf with thick-walled structures suitable for preventing wilting or withering of the leaves, even under protracted drought conditions. Mesophytic species of oaks, however, may have quite succulent leaves, particularly under shade-grown conditions. On the very driest sites, on the other hand, oaks tend not only to be highly sclerophyllous, but also to have narrow or deeply-cut leaves with small leaf surfaces.

The Temperate Zone has dry forest ranging from dry closed through dry open to dry scrub just as in the Tropic Zone. Oaks are frequently the characteristic species of these zones. Open oak woodlands are widespread in the South Temperate Zone from California east throughout the Southwest to Texas, throughout the Mediterranean region, Asia Minor, and southern Asia to New Guinea in the south of eastern Asia and Japan in the north. Scrub woodland stands, frequently with oak as a major species, occur similarly distributed on the drier sites. The *chaparral* ("little oak") of California, the *scrub oak* of the southeastern United States, and the *maquis* of the Mediterranean are examples. *Arbutus* and *Pistacia* are common associates of oak in the Mediterranean scrub.

Some of the major oak species around the world may be mentioned. In eastern North America, oaks are the most abundant and widely distributed tree genus, with red oak (*Q. rubra*), black oak (*Q. velutina*), and white oak (*Q. alba*) being perhaps the most important. Along the Gulf Coast, in the Southwest, and in Mexico, many of the oaks are evergreen or have but a brief leafless period. These live oaks include several species in both the Southeast (*Q. virginiana*) and the Southwest (*Q. agrifolia, Q. chrysolepis, Q. emoryi, Q. wislizenni*). As far south as Costa Rica, *Q. copeyensis* forms magnificent stands in the mountains of Central America, while other species occur as far south as Colombia and Ecuador.

White oak is the most important and widely distributed hardwood in Europe with two closely related species, *Q. robur* (= *Q. pedunculata*) and *Q. petraea* (= *Q. sessiliflora*) extending from Portugal and Ireland on the west to central Russia and the Caspian Sea on the east and from southern Scandinavia south to the Mediterranean (Schoenicher, 1933). The Mediterranean forests are dominated by other oak species including cork oak (*Q. suber*) in the west from southern France to Morocco; holm oak (*Q. ilex*) in the maquis of the entire Mediterranean; and *Q. macrolepis* or Vallonia oak, important for the tannin from its acorn cups in the eastern Mediterranean. In Asia Minor, *Q. aegylops*, is important; while *Q. aegylops, Q. castaneaefolia*, and *Q. infectoria* occur widely in Iraq, Iran, and surrounding regions. Farther east, the Himalayan oaks are numerous and range widely both in elevation and extent. To the north, oaks are important in China, Korea, and Japan; while to the south they grow in Assam, Indo-China, Indonesia, and the mountains of New Guinea. The Mongolian oak (*Q. mongolica*) is widely distributed throughout southeastern Siberia, Mongolia, Manchuria, and Korea.

Beeches and Maples. Several genera of angiosperms typically occupy the more mesic sites in the Temperate Zone of the Northern Hemisphere. Of these, the beeches and maples are particularly widespread and important. The species of these genera are commonly highly tolerant, as a result of which they frequently succeed oak in the absence of fire by seeding in to the understory and growing slowly many decades until they are released by the death or decadence of the oaks. In the moister and cooler sites, beech and maple occur in all stages of the forest succession and characterize the hardwood forest.

The principal beeches include *Fagus grandifolia,* which grows in eastern North America from Cape Breton Island and Ontario to Florida and east Texas on the Gulf of Mexico, with outlying relict colonies in Mexico; *Fagus silvatica,* which occurs from England and southern Sweden south to northern Spain, the Italian mountains, and Greece; the closely allied *Fagus orientalis* from Greece through the high mountains of Asia Minor and the Caucasus to the Caspian forest of northern Iran; and five species in eastern Asia. These are all very similar in appearance and in ecological requirements, characterizing the moist, cool, temperate forest, and forming late-successional communities whether in pure stands or mixed with other tolerants in areas long unburned.

The maples have similar ecological preferences to the beeches, but being more variable and consisting of many more species (70 as against 8 or 9), have a wider distribution and a wider ecological amplitude. Some are large trees but others are primarily shrubs. In eastern North America, the sugar maple group (*Acer saccharum et al.*) has a very similar distribution to beech from Canada to Mexico and occurs in mixed beech-maple stands on the rich, cool, moist, undisturbed sites. The red maple group (*A. rubrum et al.*) has even a wider range and a wider ecological amplitude, growing on virtually all sites, and frequently forming pure stands in swales and swamps.

In western North America, bigleaf and vine maples (*A. macrophyllum* and *A. circinatum*) are fire-susceptible tolerants that form a minor part of the conifer forest of the Pacific Northwest, especially in the moist ravines and draws; while in the Rocky Mountains, the bigtooth maple (*A. grandidentatum*) occurs in similar sites.

In Europe, the maples are less important than beech, but do occur widely as minor components of the forest. Sycamore maple (*A. pseudoplatanus*), Norway maple (*A. platinoides*), and field maple (*A. campestre*) occur throughout much of central Europe with Norway maple extending as far north as southern Norway and Finland, and field maple as far south as North Africa and Turkey.

Other maples are associated with the oak forests throughout Asia, forming minor portions of the stand, especially on the cooler moister sites in the Middle East, the Himalayas, China, southern Siberia, Korea, and Japan. They extend into the tropics and south of the equator in the mountains of Indonesia.

Miscellaneous Hardwoods. The distribution of the birches, aspens, oaks, beeches, and maples has already been discussed. Other hardwood or angiosperm tree taxa are also widely distributed in the North Temperate Zone. As with the more abundant genera, these are frequently represented with vicarious species in North America, Europe, southwestern Asia, the Himalayan region, and eastern Asia. The mixed hardwood complexes of the eastern United States, western Europe, the Himalayas, eastern Siberia, Manchuria, and Japan have much in common. Genera that occur with disjunct species pretty much around the Northern Hemisphere include the lindens and limes (*Tilia*), elms (*Ulmus*), ashes (*Fraxinus*), walnuts (*Juglans*), hornbeams (*Carpinus*), chestnuts (*Castanea*), planes or sycamores (*Platanus*), willows (*Salix*), and alders (*Alnus*). Still others are common to both the eastern American and east Asian forest, including *Liriodendron, Liquidambar, Magnolia,* and *Nyssa;* while only a few are confined to a single continent.

The extent of the southern temperate land zone is very limited and what there is is sparsely forested. Relatively few hardwoods, therefore, are abundant or widespread south of the Tropics. *Nothofagus,* the antarctic or southern beech, is by all means the most important, with deciduous and evergreen species characterizing the cool wet forest of southern Chile and Argentina, and evergreen species the similar zones of New Zealand and southeastern Australia. In New Guinea, *Nothofagus* occurs with *Quercus,* this region forming a bridge between the north-temperate and south-temperate Fagaceae.

The other southern hemisphere hardwood genus of great importance is *Eucalyptus,* with several hundred species in Australia and the islands to its north. It occurs both in tropical and temperate climates, and in both xeric and mesic moisture zones. In fact, there is in Australia a eucalyptus community in every type of forest niche from cool, wet, rain forest through closed mesic forest to open xeric forest and sparsely wooded semidesert. The large, fast-growing eucalypts, however, grow in the higher rainfall belts under temperate climatic conditions. These include blackbut (*E. pilularis*) and flooded gum (*E. grandis*) in the east, alpine ash (*E. delegatensis*), mountain ash (*E. regnans*), and messmate (*E. obliqua*) in the southeast, and jarrah (*E. marginata*) and karri (*E. diversicolor*) in the far west. These trees reached heights of 60 to 98 meters and are among the fastest-growing trees in the world.

Miscellaneous Conifers. The principal north temperate conifers mentioned thus far—the spruces, firs, larches, and pines—belong to the pine family, the Pinaceae. There are others of the pine family of local importance. These include Douglas-fir of western North America, hemlock in western and eastern North America and western Asia, and the true cedars (*Cedrus libani*, Lebanon cedar, in the near east; and *C. deodar* in the Himalayas).

The members of the family Cupressaceae are also of great importance in the Northern Hemisphere, with some genera occurring locally in the southern. The junipers, in particular, occur around the Northern Hemisphere, occupying dry and infertile sites and forming open woodlands at the drier edge of the forest. Other members of the family of local importance include sha mu, or Chinese fir (*Cunninghamia lanceolata*), the most important timber tree of China; sugi (*Cryptomeria japonica*) in Japan; *Cupressus lusitanica* in the mountains from Mexico to Honduras; cypress pine (*Callitris cupressiformis*) in the dry interior of Queensland; southern bald cypress (*Taxodium distichum*) in the swamps of the American Southeast and redwood (*Sequoia sempervirens*) in coastal northern California.

In the Southern Hemisphere, however, Araucariaceae and Podocarpaceae are the two important gymnosperm families. The former includes *Araucaria* and *Agathis*, and the latter, *Phyllocladus*, *Podocarpus*, and *Dacridium*.

The araucarias are important timber trees in Australia, islands east and north of Australia, Chile, and Argentina. *Agathis*, including the kauri of New Zealand (*Agathis australis*), is a tropical genus of the southwestern Pacific with a number of commercially important species, frequently reaching gigantic size (Figure 19.2), extending from Borneo and the Philippines on the North to Queensland and northern New Zealand on the South. The kauris as a group are important not only for their lumber but for their gum, used in the manufacture of varnish.

The various podocarps are widely distributed in the Southern Hemisphere, occurring in Africa, southern Asia, and the southwest Pacific, and the Americas from the West Indies to southern Chile. They constitute the native conifers of east and south Africa, and also occur in Indo-China, New Guinea, the Philippines, Australia, and New Zealand. In the latter country, rimu (*Dacrydium cupressinum*), totara (*Podocarpus totara*), and kahikatea (*P. dacrydioides*) are the principal native conifers. Among the American species is *P. coriaceous* in the uplands of the West Indies, Venezuela, and Colombia.

Fig. 19.2. Giant kauri in Waipoua Forest, North Island, New Zealand. Diameters exceed 3 meters with little stem taper. (New Zealand Forest Service photo by J. H. Johns, A.R.P.S.)

SUMMARY

Forests of the world have traditionally been classified on a floristic or on a physiognomic-structural basis. Physiognomic-structural classifications have been widely applied on global bases whereas floristic classifications have been particularly useful on regional and local levels. In tropical rain forests however, where the flora is not well known, physiognomic-structural classifications may be especially valuable on regional and local levels and can even reveal considerable information about habitat conditions.

Tropical non-seasonal rain forests may contain hundreds of species per hectare whereas the more abiotically restrictive boreal and cool temperate forests are by comparison species poor. Species of these tropical forests show highly specialized adaptations to their biotic and physical environments.

In this brief discussion, the forests of the world have been summarized briefly on the basis of the distribution of the principal tree genera. The occurrence of the same genera in various portions of the world emphasizes the similarities between forests growing in similar climates and on similar soils in different geographic zones. One familiar with the spruce-fir forests in eastern Canada can learn much from and contribute in turn to the knowledge of the spruce-fir forest of northern Europe, the Himalayas, or eastern Asia. Forest ecology is a worldwide subject and must be studied as such.

SUGGESTED READINGS

BEARD, J. S. 1955. The classification of tropical American vegetation-types. *Ecology* 36:89–100.

ELLENBERG, H., and D. MUELLER-DOMBOIS. 1970. Geographical index of world ecosystems. *In* DAVID E. REICHLE (ed.), *Analysis of Temperate Forest Ecosystems.* Springer-Verlag, New York.

HADEN-GUEST, STEPHEN, JOHN K. WRIGHT, and EILEEN M. TECLAFF (eds.). 1956. *A World Geography of Forest Resources.* Amer. Geog. Soc. Spec. Publ. 33. The Ronald Press Co., New York. 736 pp.

KÜCHLER, A. W. 1967. *Vegetation Mapping.* (Part V. Application of vegetation maps, pp. 307–402; Vegetation classification, pp. 438–451.) The Ronald Press Co., New York. 472 pp.

MIROV, N. T. 1967. *The genus "Pinus."* (Chapers 1–3, pp. 1–320.) The Ronald Press Co., New York. 602 pp.

RICHARDS, P. W. 1952. *The Tropical Rain Forest: An Ecological Study.* Cambridge Univ. Press, London. 450 pp.

WEBB, L. J. 1959. A physiognomic classification of Australian rain forests. *J. Ecol.* 47:551–570.

———. 1968. Environmental relationships of the structural types of Australian rain forest vegetation. *Ecology* 49:296–311.

Scientific Names of Trees

Acacia	*Acacia* spp.
Ailanthus or tree of heaven	*Ailanthus altissima* (Mill.) Swingle
Alder, European or black	*Alnus glutinosa* (L.) Gaertn.
Alder, red or Oregon	*Alnus rubra* Bong.
Alder, Sitka	*Alnus sinuata* (Reg.) Rydb.
Alder, speckled	*Alnus rugosa* (Du Roi) Spreng.
Ash, black	*Fraxinus nigra* Marsh.
Ash, European	*Fraxinus excelsior* L.
Ash, mountain (Australia)	*Eucalyptus regnans* F. Muell.
Ash, white	*Fraxinus americana* L.
Aspen, bigtooth	*Populus grandidentata* Michx.
Aspen, quaking or trembling	*Populus tremuloides* Michx.
Balsa	*Ochroma pyramidale* (Cav.) Urban
Basswood	*Tilia americana* L.
Beech, American	*Fagus grandifolia* Ehrh.
Beech, Antarctic	*Nothofagus antarctica* (Forst.) Oerst.
Beech, blue	*Carpinus caroliniana* Walt.
Beech, European	*Fagus sylvatica* L.
Bigtree, or giant sequoia	*Sequoiadendron giganteum* (Lindl.) Buchholz
Birch, black or sweet	*Betula lenta* L.
Birch, bog, swamp, or low	*Betula pumila* L.
Birch, European	*Betula pendula* Roth.
Birch, gray	*Betula populifolia* Marsh.
Birch, moor	*Betula pubescens* Ehrh.
Birch, paper	*Betula papyrifera* Marsh.
Birch, river or red	*Betula nigra* L.
Birch, yellow	*Betula alleghaniensis* Britton
Buckeye, Ohio	*Aesculus glabra* Willd.
Buckeye, yellow	*Aesculus octandra* Marsh.
Butternut	*Juglans cinerea* L.
Cedar, Alaska	*Chamaecyparis nootkatensis* (D. Don) Spach
Cedar, eastern red	*Juniperus virginiana* L.
Cedar, incense	*Libocedrus decurrens* Torr.
Cedar, northern white	*Thuja occidentalis* L.
Cedar, Port Orford	*Chamaecyparis lawsoniana* (A. Murr.) Parl.

523

Cedar, southern white	*Chamaecyparis thyoides* (L.) B. S. P.
Cedar, western red	*Thuja plicata* Donn
Cherry, black	*Prunus serotina* Ehrh.
Cherry, choke	*Prunus virginiana* L.
Cherry, pin	*Prunus pensylvanica* L. f.
Chestnut, American	*Castanea dentata* (Marsh.) Borkh.
Chinquapin, Ozark	*Castanea ozarkensis* Ashe
Coconut	*Cocos nucifera* L.
Cottonwood, black	*Populus balsamifera* ssp. *trichocarpa* (Torr. & Gray) Brayshaw
Cottonwood, eastern	*Populus deltoides* Bartr.
Cottonwood, European or black poplar	*Populus nigra* L.
Cypress, Arizona	*Cupressus arizonica* Greene
Cypress, southern bald	*Taxodium distichum* (L.) Rich.
Dogwood, flowering	*Cornus florida* L.
Douglas-fir	*Pseudotsuga menziesii* (Mirb.) Franco
Elm, American	*Ulmus americana* L.
Elm, Siberian	*Ulmus pumila* L.
Elm, slippery	*Ulmus rubra* Mühl.
Elm, winged	*Ulmus alata* Michx.
Eucalyptus	*Eucalyptus* spp.
Fir, alpine	*Abies lasiocarpa* (Hook.) Nutt.
Fir, balsam	*Abies balsamea* (L.) Mill.
Fir, Douglas-	*Pseudotsuga menziesii* (Mirb.) Franco
Fir, European silver	*Abies alba* Mill.
Fir, Fraser	*Abies fraseri* (Pursh) Poir.
Fir, grand or lowland white	*Abies grandis* (Dougl.) Lindl.
Fir, noble	*Abies procera* Rehd.
Fir, Pacific silver	*Abies amabilis* (Dougl.) Forbes
Fir, red	*Abies magnifica* A. Murr.
Fir, white	*Abies concolor* (Gord. & Glend.) Lindl.
Gum, black	*Nyssa sylvatica* Marsh.
Gum, southern blue	*Eucalyptus globulus* Labill.
Gum, sweet	*Liquidambar stryaciflua* L.
Hackberry	*Celtis occidentalis* L.
Hawthorne	*Crataegus* spp.
Hazel	*Corylus cornuta* Marsh.
Hemlock, eastern	*Tsuga canadensis* (L.) Carr.
Hemlock, mountain	*Tsuga mertensiana* (Bong.) Carr.
Hemlock, western	*Tsuga heterophylla* (Raf.) Sarg.
Hickory, bitternut	*Carya cordiformis* (Wangenh.) K. Koch
Hickory, mockernut	*Carya tomentosa* Nutt.
Hickory, pignut	*Carya glabra* (Mill.) Sweet
Hickory, shagbark	*Carya ovata* (Mill.) K. Koch
Holly, American	*Ilex opaca* Ait.
Hophornbeam, or ironwood	*Ostrya virginiana* (Mill.) K. Koch

Ironwood, or hophornbeam	*Ostrya virginiana* (Mill.) K. Koch
Juniper, alligator	*Juniperus deppeana* Steud.
Juniper, common	*Juniperus communis* L.
Juniper, one-seed	*Juniperus monosperma* (Engelm.) Sarg.
Juniper, Rocky Mountain	*Juniperus scopulorum* Sarg.
Juniper, Utah	*Juniperus osteosperma* (Torr.) Little
Kentucky coffeetree	*Gymnocladus dioicus* (L.) K. Koch
Larch, European	*Larix decidua* Mill.
Larch, Japanese	*Larix leptolepis* (Sieb. & Zucc.) Gord.
Larch, western	*Larix occidentalis* Nutt.
Laurel, mountain	*Kalmia latifolia* L.
Locust, black	*Robinia pseudoacacia* L.
Locust, honey	*Gleditsia triacanthos* L.
Madrone, Pacific	*Arbutus menziesii* Pursh.
Magnolia, sweetbay	*Magnolia virginiana* L.
Mahogany, West Indies	*Swietenia mahagoni* Jacq.
Mangrove, black	*Avicennia nitida* Jacq.
Mangrove, red	*Rhizophora mangle* L.
Maple, bigleaf	*Acer macrophyllum* Pursh.
Maple, mountain	*Acer spicatum* Lam.
Maple, Norway	*Acer platanoides* L.
Maple, red	*Acer rubrum* L.
Maple, silver	*Acer saccharinum* L.
Maple, striped	*Acer pensylvanicum* L.
Maple, sugar	*Acer saccharum* Marsh.
Maple, vine	*Acer circinatum* Pursh.
Mesquite	*Prosopis juliflora* (Sw.) DC.
Mountain-ash, American	*Sorbus americana* Marsh.
Mulberry, red	*Morus rubra* L.
Oak, bear	*Quercus ilicifolia* Wangenh.
Oak, black	*Quercus velutina* Lam.
Oak, blackjack	*Quercus marilandica* Muenchh.
Oak, bur	*Quercus macrocarpa* Michx.
Oak, California live	*Quercus agrifolia* Née
Oak, canyon live	*Quercus chrysolepis* Liebm.
Oak, cherrybark	*Quercus falcata* var. *pagodaefolia* Ell.
Oak, chestnut	*Quercus prinus* L.
Oak, chinquapin	*Quercus muehlenbergii* Engelm.
Oak, Emory	*Quercus emoryi* Torr.
Oak, English or European	*Quercus robur* L.
Oak, interior live	*Quercus wislizenii* A. DC.
Oak, live	*Quercus virginiana* Mill.
Oak, Oregon	*Quercus garryana* Dougl.
Oak, pin	*Quercus palustris* Muenchh.
Oak, post	*Quercus stellata* Wangenh.
Oak, pubescent	*Quercus pubescens* Willd.
Oak, red	*Quercus rubra* L.

Oak, scarlet	*Quercus coccinea* Muenchh.
Oak, sessile	*Quercus petraea* (Mattuschka) Lieblein.
Oak, southern red	*Quercus falcata* Michx.
Oak, swamp white	*Quercus bicolor* Willd.
Oak, turkey	*Quercus laevis* Walt.
Oak, white	*Quercus alba* L.
Palm, cabbage	*Sabal palmetto* (Walt.) Lodd.
Palmetto, saw	*Serenoa repens* (Bartr.) Small
Pine, Caribbean	*Pinus caribaea* Morelet
Pine, Corsican or Austrian	*Pinus nigra* Arnold
Pine, digger	*Pinus sabiniana* Dougl.
Pine, eastern white	*Pinus strobus* L.
Pine, erect cone or Calabrian	*Pinus brutia* Ten.
Pine, jack	*Pinus banksiana* Lamb.
Pine, Jeffrey	*Pinus jeffreyi* Grev. & Balf.
Pine, knobcone	*Pinus attenuata* Lemmon
Pine, limber	*Pinus flexilis* James
Pine, loblolly	*Pinus taeda* L.
Pine, lodgepole	*Pinus contorta* Dougl.
Pine, longleaf	*Pinus palustris* Mill.
Pine, maritime	*Pinus pinaster* Ait.
Pine, Mexican pinyon	*Pinus cembroides* Zucc.
Pine, Monterey or radiata	*Pinus radiata* D. Don
Pine, mugo or mountain	*Pinus mugo* Turra. [*P. montana* Mill.]
Pine, patula	*Pinus patula* Schl. & Cham.
Pine, pinyon	*Pinus edulis* Engelm.
Pine, pitch	*Pinus rigida* Mill.
Pine, ponderosa	*Pinus ponderosa* Laws.
Pine, red	*Pinus resinosa* Ait.
Pine, sand	*Pinus clausa* (Chapm.) Vasey
Pine, Scots	*Pinus sylvestris* L.
Pine, shortleaf	*Pinus echinata* Mill.
Pine, slash	*Pinus elliottii* Engelm. var. *elliottii*
Pine, sugar	*Pinus lambertiana* Dougl.
Pine, Swiss stone	*Pinus cembra* L.
Pine, Table Mountain	*Pinus pungens* Lamb.
Pine, Virginia	*Pinus virginiana* Mill.
Pine, western white	*Pinus monticola* Dougl.
Pine, whitebark	*Pinus albicaulis* Englem.
Poplar, balsam	*Populus balsamifera* L.
Redbud, eastern	*Cercis canadensis* L.
Redwood	*Sequoia sempervirens* (D. Don) Endl.
Rhododendron	*Rhododendron maximum* L.
Sagebrush	*Artemisia tridentata* Nutt.
Sassafras	*Sassafras albidum* (Nutt.) Nees
Sequoia, bigtree	*Sequoiadendron giganteum* (Lindl.) Buchholz

Silver bell or Carolina silverbell	*Halesia carolina* L.
Sourwood	*Oxydendrum arboreum* (L.) DC.
Spruce, black	*Picea mariana* (Mill.) B. S. P.
Spruce, Engelmann	*Picea engelmannii* Parry
Spruce, Norway or European	*Picea abies* (L.) Karst.
Spruce, red	*Picea rubens* Sarg.
Spruce, Sitka	*Picea sitchensis* (Bong.) Carr.
Spruce, white	*Picea glauca* (Moench) Voss
Sumac, smooth	*Rhus glabra* L.
Sycamore, American	*Platanus occidentalis* L.
Tamarack	*Larix laricina* (Du Roi) K. Koch
Tamarisk, five-stamen	*Tamarix pentandra* Pall.
Teak	*Tectona grandis* L. f.
Tree of heaven or ailanthus	*Ailanthus altissima* (Mill.) Swingle
Tupelo, swamp	*Nyssa aquatica* L.
Walnut, black	*Juglans nigra* L.
Willow, black	*Salix nigra* Marsh.
Yellow-poplar	*Liriodendron tulipifera* L.

Bibliography

AALTONEN, V. T. 1948. *Boden und Wald, unter besonderer Berücksichtigung des nordeuropäischen Waldbaus.* Paul Parey, Berlin. 457 pp.

———. 1950. Die Blattanalyse als Bonitierungsgrundlage des Waldbodens. Commun. Inst. For. Fenn. 37(8). 41 pp.

ABBOT, CHARLES GREELEY. 1929. *The Sun.* Appleton-Century-Crofts, Inc., New York. 447 pp.

ADAMS, D. F., D. J. MAYHEW, R. M. GNAGY, E. P. RICHEY, R. K. KAPPE, and I. W. ALLEN. 1952. Atmospheric pollution in the ponderosa pine blight area. *Ind. Eng. Chem.* 44:1356–1365.

ALEXANDER, ROBERT R. 1964. Minimizing windfall around clear cuttings in spruce-fir forests. *For. Sci.* 10:130–142.

———. 1966. Site indexes for lodgepole pine, with corrections for stand density; instructions for field use. USDA For. Serv. Res. Paper RM–24. Rocky Mountain For. and Rge. Exp. Sta., Fort Collins, Colo. 7 pp.

———, and JESSE H. BUELL. 1955. Determining the direction of destructive winds in a Rocky Mountain timber stand. *J. For.* 53:19–23.

———, DAVID TACKLE, and WALTER G. DAHMS. 1967. Site indexes for lodgepole pine, with corrections for stand density: methodology. USDA For. Serv. Res. Paper RM–29. Rocky Mountain For. and Rge. Exp. Sta., Fort Collins, Colo. 18 pp.

ANDERSON, EDGAR. 1948. Hybridization of the habitat. *Evolution* 2:1–9.

———. 1949. *Introgressive Hybridization.* John Wiley & Sons, Inc., New York. 109 pp.

———. 1953. Introgressive hybridization. *Biol. Rev.* 28:280–307.

ANDERSON, H. W. 1967. Snow accumulation as related to meteorological, topographic, and forest variables in Central Sierra Nevada, California. Int. Ass. Sci. Hydrol. Publ. 76:215–224.

———. 1970. Storage and delivery of rainfall and snowmelt water as related to forest environments. *Proc. 3rd Forest Microclimate Symp.*, pp. 51–67. Canad. For. Serv., Calgary, Alberta.

ANDERSSON, ENAR. 1963. Seed stands and seed orchards in the breeding of conifers. World Consult. For. Gen. and For. Tree Imp. Proc. II FAO-FORGEN 63–8/1:1–18.

ARBEITSGEMEINSCHAFT "OBERSCHWÄBISCHE FICHTENREVIERE." 1964. *Standort, Wald und Waldwirtschaft in Oberschwaben.* Verein forstl. Standortsk. Forstpflz., Stuttgart. 323 pp.

ARNOLD, J. F. 1950. Changes in ponderosa pine bunchgrass ranges in northern Arizona resulting from pine regeneration and grazing. *J. For.* 48:118–126.

ART, H. W., and P. L. MARKS. 1971. A summary table of biomass and net annual primary production in forest ecosystems of the world. *In Forest Biomass Studies.* Misc. Publ. 132, Life Sci. and Agr. Exp. Sta., Univ. Maine, Orono.

ASTON, J. L., and A. D. BRADSHAW. 1966. Evolution in closely adjacent plant populations. II. *Agrostis stolonifera* in maritime habitats. *Heredity* 21:649–664.

AUERBACH, STANLEY I. 1971. Analysis of the structure and function of ecosystems in the deciduous forest biome. Oak Ridge National Laboratory research proposal, Oak Ridge, Tenn. 133 pp.

————. 1972. Analysis of the structure and function of ecosystems in the Eastern Deciduous Forest Biome. Continuation Proposal 1972–74. Volume I. Proposed research, sites and facilities, and subproject abstract. EDFB–IBP 72–2, Oak Ridge National Laboratory, Oak Ridge, Tenn. 324 pp.

AULITZKY, HERBERT. 1967. Significance of small climatic differences for the proper afforestation of highlands in Austria. *In* WILLIAM E. SOPPER and HOWARD W. LULL (eds.), *Forest Hydrology.* Pergamon Press, Inc., New York.

AXELROD, DANIEL I. 1970. Mesozoic paleogeography and early angiosperm history. *Bot. Rev.* 36:277–319.

BAKER, FREDERICK S. 1929. Effect of excessively high temperatures on coniferous reproduction. *J. For.* 27:949–975.

————. 1944. Mountain climates of the western United States. *Ecol. Monogr.* 14:223–254.

————. 1945. Effects of shade upon coniferous seedlings grown in nutrient solutions. *J. For.* 43:428–435.

————. 1950. *Principles of Silviculture.* McGraw-Hill Book Co., Inc., New York. 414 pp.

BANNISTER, M. H. 1965. Variation in the breeding system of *Pinus radiata. In* H. G. BAKER and G. LEDYARD STEBBINS (eds.), *The Genetics of Colonizing Species.* Academic Press, Inc., New York.

BARBER, H. N., and W. D. JACKSON. 1957. Natural selection in action in Eucalyptus. *Nature* 179:1267–1269.

BARD, G. E. 1946. The mineral nutrient content of the foliage of forest trees on three soil types of varying limestone content. *Proc. Soil. Sci. Soc. Amer.* 10:419–422.

————. 1952. Secondary succession on the Piedmont of New Jersey. *Ecol. Monogr.* 22:195–215.

BARNES, BURTON V. 1967. The clonal growth habit of American aspens. *Ecology* 47:439–447.

————. 1969. Natural variation and delineation of clones of *Populus tremuloides* and *P. grandidentata* in northern Lower Michigan. *Silvae Genetica* 18:130–142.

BARRETT, L. I., and A. A. DOWNS. 1943. Hardwood invasion in pine forests of the Piedmont Plateau. *J. Agr. Res.* 67:111–128.

BARTELLI, LINDO J., and JAMES A. DEMENT. 1970. Soil survey—a guide for forest management decisions in the southern Appalachians. *In* CHESTER T. YOUNGBERG and CHARLES B. DAVEY (eds.), *Tree Growth and Forest Soils.* Oregon State Univ. Press, Corvallis, Ore.

BARTLETT, H. H. 1956. Fire, primitive agriculture, and grazing in the tropics. *In* WILLIAM L. THOMAS (ed.), *Man's Role in Changing the Face of the Earth.* Univ. Chicago Press.

BARTLEY, D. D. 1967. Pollen analysis of surface samples of vegetation from arctic Quebec. *Pollen & Spores* 9:101–105.

BASSETT, J. R. 1964. Diameter growth of loblolly pine trees as affected by soil moisture availability. USDA For. Serv. Res. Note SO–9, Southern For. Exp. Sta., New Orleans, La. 7 pp.

BATES, C. G., and JACOB ROESER, JR. 1928. Light intensities required for growth of coniferous seedlings. *Amer. J. Bot.* 15:185–244.

BAUMGARTNER, ALBERT. 1958. Nebel und Nebelniederschlag als Standortsfacktoren am grossen Falkenstein (Bayr. Wald). *Forstw. Centralbl.* 77:257–272.

————. 1967. Energetic bases for differential vaporization from forest and agricultural lands. *In* WILLIAM E. SOPPER and HOWARD W. LULL (eds.), *Forest Hydrology.* Pergamon Press, Inc., New York.

BEARD, J. S. 1945. The progress of plant succession on the Soufrière of St. Vincent. *J. Ecol.* 33:1–9.

————. 1953. The savanna vegetation of northern tropical America. *Ecol. Monogr.* 23:149–215.

————. 1955. The classification of tropical American vegetation-types. *Ecology* 36:89–100.

BEAUFAIT, W. R. 1956. Influence of soil and topography on willow oak sites. U. S. For. Serv., Southern For. Exp. Sta. Occ. Paper 148. 12 pp.

BECK, DONALD E. 1962. Yellow-poplar site index curves. Southeastern For. Exp. Sta. Res. Note 180. 2 pp.

————. 1971. Polymorphic site index curves for white pine in the southern Appalachians. USDA For. Serv. Res. Note SE–80. Southeastern For. Exp. Sta., Asheville, N. C. 8 pp.

BECKING, R. W. 1957. The Zürich-Montpellier school of phytosociology. *Bot. Rev.* 23:411–488.

BECKWITH, S. L. 1954. Ecological succession on abandoned farm lands and its relationship to wildlife management. *Ecol. Monogr.* 24:349:376.

BEILMANN, A. P., and L. G. BRENNER. 1951. The recent intrusion of forests in the Ozarks. *Ann. Mo. Bot. Gdn.* 38:261–282.

BELLINGER, P. F. 1954. Studies of soil fauna with special reference to the Collembola. Conn. Agr. Exp. Sta. Bull. 583. 67 pp.

BENNINGHOFF, WILLIAM S. 1952. Relationships between vegetation and frost in soils. Proc. Permafrost International Conference, pp. 9–13.

————. 1963. The Prairie Peninsula as a filter barrier to postglacial plant migration. *Proc. Indiana Acad. Sci.* 72:116–124.

BENSON, L. B. 1962. *Plant Taxonomy: Methods and Principles.* The Ronald Press Co., New York. 494 pp.

BERRY, CHARLES R., and GEORGE H. HEPTING. 1964. Injury to eastern white pine by unidentified atmospheric constituents. *For. Sci.* 10:2–13.

BIGELOW, R. S. 1965. Hybrid zones and reproductive isolation. *Evolution* 19:449–458.

BILLINGS, W. D. 1938. The structure and development of old-field pine stands and certain associated physical properties of the soil. *Ecol. Monogr.* 8:437–499.

————. 1950. Vegetation and plant growth as affected by chemically altered rocks in the western Great Basin. *Ecology* 31:62–74.

BINGHAM, R. T., and A. E. SQUILLACE. 1957. Phenology and other features of the flowering of pines, with special reference to *Pinus monticola* Dougl. Intermountain For. and Rge. Exp. Sta. Res. Paper 53. 26 pp.

BIRCH, L. C., and D. P. CLARK. 1953. Forest soil as an ecological community— with special reference to the fauna. *Quart. Rev. Biol.* 28(1):13–36.

BLOOMBERG, W. J. 1950. Fire and spruce. *For. Chron.* 26(2):157–161.

BLOW, F. E. 1955. Quantity and hydrologic characteristics of litter under upland oak forests in eastern Tennessee. *J. For.* 53:190–195.

BODE, HANS ROBERT. 1958. Beiträge zur Kenntnis allelopathischer Erscheinungen bei einigen Juglandaceen. *Planta* 51:440–480.

BOGGESS, W. R. 1956. Weekly diameter growth of shortleaf pine and white oak as related to soil moisture. *Proc. Soc. Am. Foresters,* 1956, pp. 83–89.

————. 1964. Trelease Woods, Champaign County, Illinois: woody vegetation and stand composition. *Trans. Ill. Acad. Sci.* 57:261–271.

————, and L. W. BAILEY. 1964. Brownfield Woods, Illinois: woody vegetation and changes since 1925. *Am. Mid. Nat.* 71:392–401.

————, and J. W. GEIS. 1966. The Funk Forest Natural Area, McLean County, Illinois: woody vegetation and ecological trends. *Trans. Ill. Acad. Sci.* 59:123–133.

BONNEMANN, ALFRED, and ERNST RÖHRIG. 1971. *Waldbau auf ökologischer Grundlage. I. Der Wald als Vegetationstyp und seine Bedeutung für den Menschen.* Verlag Paul Parey, Berlin. 229 pp.

————, and ————. 1972. *Waldbau auf ökologischer Grundlage. II. Holzartenwahl, Bestandesbegrundung und Bestandespflege.* Verlag Paul Parey, Berlin. 264 pp.

BIBLIOGRAPHY

Books, David J., and Carl H. Tubbs. 1970. Relation of light to epicormic sprouting in sugar maple. USDA For. Serv. Res. Note NC–93. North Central For. Exp. Sta., St. Paul, Minn. 2 pp.

Borchert, J. R. 1950. The climate of the central North American grassland. Ann. Assoc. Amer. Geog. 40:1–39.

Bormann, F. H. 1953. Factors determining the role of loblolly pine and sweetgum in early old-field succession in the Piedmont of North Carolina. Ecol. Monogr. 23:339–358.

———, and G. E. Likens. 1967. Nutrient cycling. Science 155:424–429.

———, and ———. 1969. The watershed-ecosystem concept and studies of nutrient cycles. In George M. Van Dyne (ed.), The Ecosystem Concept in Natural Resource Management. Academic Press, Inc., New York.

———, T. G. Siccama, G. E. Likens, and R. H. Whittaker. 1970. The Hubbard Brook Ecosystem Study: composition and dynamics of the tree stratum. Ecol. Monog. 40:373–388.

Botkin, Daniel B., James F. Janak, and James R. Wallis. 1972a. The rationale, limitations and assumptions of a computer model of forest growth. IBM J. Res. Dev. 16:101–116.

———, ———, and ———. 1972b. Some ecological consequences of a computer model of forest growth. J. Ecol. 60:849–872.

Bourdo, Eric A., Jr. 1956. A review of the general land office survey and of its use in quantitative studies of former forests. Ecology 37:744–768.

Bradshaw, A. D. 1965. Evolutionary significance of phenotypic plasticity in plants. Adv. Genetics 13:115–155.

Bradshaw, Kenneth E. 1965. Soil use and management in the national forests of California. In Chester T. Youngberg (ed.), Forest-Soil Relationships in North America. Oregon State Univ. Press, Corvallis, Ore.

Braun, E. Lucy. 1942. Forests of the Cumberland Mountains. Ecol. Monogr. 12:413–447.

———. 1950. Deciduous Forests of Eastern North America. McGraw-Hill Book Co., Inc., New York. 596 pp.

Braun-Blanquet, J. 1964. Pflanzensoziologie, 3rd ed. Springer-Verlag, Vienna. 865 pp.

Bray, J. R. 1956. Gap phase replacement in a maple/basswood forest. Ecology 37(3):598–600.

———, and J. T. Curtis. 1957. An ordination of the upland forest communities of southern Wisconsin. Ecol. Monog. 22:217–234.

———, and Eville Gorham. 1964. Litter production in forests of the world. Adv. Ecol. Res. 2:101–157.

Brayshaw, T. C. 1965. Native poplars of southern Alberta and their hybrids. Canada, Dept. of Forestry Publ. No. 1109. 40 pp.

Brayton, R., and H. A. Mooney. 1966. Population variability of Cercocarpus in the White Mountains of California as related to habitat. Evolution 20:383–391.

Brittain, W. H., and W. F. Grant. 1967. Observations on Canadian birch collections at the Morgan Arboretum. V. B. papyrifera and B. cordifolia from eastern Canada. Canad. Field-Naturalist 81:251–262.

Broadfoot, W. M. 1969. Problems in relating soil to site index for southern hardwoods. For. Sci. 15:354–364.   ,

———, and A. F. Ike, Jr. 1968. Research progress in fertilizing southern hardwoods. In Forest Fertilization. Tennessee Valley Authority, Muscle Shoals, Ala.

Brooks, M. G. 1951. Effects of black walnut trees and their products on other vegetation. West Va., Agr. Exp. Sta. Bull. 347. 31 pp.

Brown, Harry E. 1971. Evaluating watershed management alternatives. J. Irrigation Drainage Div., Proc. Amer. Soc. Civil Engineers. 97:93–108.

Brown, J. H., Jr. 1960. The role of fire in altering the species composition of forests in Rhode Island. Ecology 41:310–316.

Brown, J. M. B. 1955. Ecological investigations: shade and growth of oak seedlings. Rep. For. Res. Comm., London, 1953–54.

BRYSON, REID A., BRUCE HAYDEN, VAL MITCHELL, and THOMAS WEBB III. 1970. Some aspects of the ecological climatology of the Jornada experimental range New Mexico. In R. G. WRIGHT and G. M. VAN DYNE (eds.), Simulation and Analysis of Dynamics of a Semidesert Grassland. Colorado State Univ., Fort Collins, Colo.

BUCKMAN, HARRY O., and NYLE C. BRADY. 1969. The Nature and Properties of Soils, 7th ed. The Macmillan Co., Toronto, Ontario, Canada. 653 pp.

BUELL, M. F., and J. E. CANTLON. 1951. A study of two forest stands in Minnesota with an interpretation of the prairie-forest margin. Ecology 32:294–316.

———, and V. FACEY. 1960. Forest-prairie transition west of Itasca Park, Minnesota. Bull. Torrey Bot. Cl. 87(1):46–58.

BULL, H. 1931. The use of polymorphic curves in determining site quality in young red pine plantations. J. Agric. Res. 43:1–28.

BURGER, D. 1972. Forest site classification in Canada. Mitt. Vereins forstl. Standortsk. Forstpflz. 21:20–36.

BURNS, GEORGE P. 1923. Studies in tolerance of New England forest trees IV. Minimum light requirements referred to a definite standard. Univ. Vermont Agr. Exp. Sta. Bull. 235.

BURNS, G. RICHARD. 1942. Photosynthesis and absorption in blue radiation. Amer. J. Bot. 29:381–387.

BÜSGEN, M. and E. MÜNCH. 1929. The Structure and Life of Forest Trees, 3d ed. Trans. by THOMAS THOMSON. Chapman & Hall, Ltd., London. 436 pp.

BYERS, H. R. 1953. Coast redwoods and fog drip. Ecology 34:192–193.

BYRAM, GEORGE M., and GEORGE M. JEMISON. 1943. Solar radiation and forest fuel moisture. J. Agr. Res. 67:149–176.

BYRD, H. J., N. E. SANDS, and JACK T. MAY. 1965. Forest management based on soil surveys in Georgia. In CHESTER T. YOUNGBERG (ed.), Forest-Soil Relationships in North America. Oregon State Univ. Press, Corvallis, Ore.

CAIN, STANLEY A. 1939. The climax and its complexities. Amer. Midl. Nat. 21:146–181.

———. 1944. Foundations of Plant Geography. Harper & Row, Inc., New York. 556 pp.

———, and G. M. DE OLIVEIRA CASTRO. 1959. Manual of Vegetation Analysis. Harper & Row, Inc., New York. 325 pp.

CAJANDER, A. K. 1926. The theory of forest types. Acta For. Fenn. 29. 108 pp.

CALLAHAM, ROBERT Z. 1962. Geographic variability in growth of forest trees. In THEODORE T. KOZLOWSKI (ed.), Tree Growth. The Ronald Press Co., New York.

———, and A. R. LIDDECOET. 1961. Altitudinal variation at 20 years in ponderosa and Jeffrey pines. J. For. 59:814–820.

CAMPBELL, R. S. 1955. Vegetational changes and management in the cutover longleaf pine-slash pine area of the Gulf Coast. Ecology 36:29–34.

CARLISLE, A., A. BROWN, and E. WHITE. 1967. The nutrient content of tree stem flow and ground flora litter and leachates in a sessile oak (Quercus petraea) woodland. J. Ecol. 55:615–627.

CARLSON, CLINTON E., and GEORGE M. BLAKE. 1969. Hybridization of western and subalpine larch. Montana For. and Cons. Exp. Sta. Bull. 37. Univ. Montana, Missoula, Mont. 12 pp.

———, and JERALD E. DEWEY. 1971. Environmental pollution by fluorides in Flathead National Forest and Glacier National Park. USDA For. Serv. Northern Region, Missoula, Mont. 57 pp.

CARMEAN, WILLARD H. 1956. Suggested modification of the standard Douglas-fir site curves for certain soils in southwestern Washington. For. Sci. 2:242–250.

———. 1965. Black oak site quality in relation to soil and topography in southeastern Ohio. Proc. Soil Sci. Soc. Amer. 29:308–312.

———. 1966. Soil and water requirements. In Black Walnut Culture. U. S. For. Serv., North Central For. Exp. Sta., St. Paul, Minn.

———. 1967. Soil refinements for predicting black oak site quality in southeastern Ohio. Proc. Soil Sci. Soc. Amer. 31:805–810.

————. 1970a. Site quality for eastern hardwoods. *In* The silviculture of oaks and associated species. USDA For. Serv. Res. Paper NE–144. Northeastern For. Exp. Sta., Upper Darby, Pa. 66 pp.

————. 1970b. Tree height-growth patterns in relation to soil and site. *In* CHESTER T. YOUNGBERG and CHARLES B. DAVEY (eds.), *Tree Growth and Forest Soils.* Oregon State Univ. Press, Corvallis, Ore.

————, and ALEXANDER VASILEVSKY. 1971. Site-index comparisons for tree species in northern Minnesota. USDA For. Serv. Res. Paper NC–65. North Central For. Exp. Sta., St. Paul, Minn. 8 pp.

CARTER, G. S. 1934. Reports of the Cambridge expedition to British Guiana, 1933. Illumination in the rain forest at the ground level. *J. Linn. Soc., London. Zool.* 38:579–589.

CHANEY, R. W. 1949. Redwoods—occidental and oriental. *Science* 110:551–552.

————. 1954. A new pine (*Pinus clementsii*) from the Cretaceous of Minnesota and its palaeoecological significance. *Ecology* 35:145–151.

CHAPMAN, D. W. 1962. Effects of logging upon fish resources of the west coast. *J. For.* 60:533–537.

CHAPMAN, H. H. 1932. Is the longleaf pine a climax? *Ecology* 13:328–335.

CHAPMAN, J. D. 1952. The climate of British Columbia. *Trans. 5th Brit. Columbia Natur. Resour. Conf.*, pp. 8–54.

CHRISTY, H. R. 1952. Vertical temperature gradients in a beech forest in central Ohio. *Ohio J. Sci.* 52(4):199–209.

CHURCHILL, E. D., and H. C. HANSON. 1958. The concept of climax in arctic and alpine vegetation. *Bot. Rev.* 24(2/3):127–191.

CIESLAR, ADOLF. 1887. Über den Einfluss der Grosse der Fichtensamen auf die Entwicklung der Pflanzen nebst einigen Bemerkungen über schwedische Fichten und Weissfohrensamen. *Centbl. gesam. Forstw.* 13:149–153.

————. 1895. Über die Erblichkeit des Zuwachsvermögens bei den Waldbäumen. *Centralbl. gesam. Forstw.* 21:7–29.

————. 1899. Neues aus dem Gebiete der forstlichen Zuchtwahl. *Centbl. gesam. Forstw.* 25:99–117.

CLAUSEN, KNUD E. 1962. Introgressive hybridization between two Minnesota birches. *Silvae Genetica* 11:142–150.

————. 1968. Variation in height growth and growth cessation of 55 yellow birch seed sources. *In Proc. Eighth Lake States For. Tree Imp. Conf.*, pp. 1–4, USDA For. Serv. Res. Paper NC–23. North Central For. Exp. Sta., St. Paul, Minn.

CLEMENTS, FREDERIC E. 1916. Plant succession: an analysis of the development of vegetation. Carneg. Inst. Wash. Publ. 242. 512 pp.

————. 1949. *Dynamics of Vegetation: Selections from the Writings of Frederic E. Clements, Ph.D.* The H. W. Wilson Co., New York. 296 pp.

CLINE, A. C., and STEPHEN H. SPURR. 1942. The virgin upland forest of Central New England. Harv. For. Bull. 21. 51 pp.

COBB, FIELDS W., JR., and R. W. STARK. 1970. Decline and mortality of smog-injured ponderosa pine. *J. For.* 68:147–149.

COILE, T. S. 1952. Soil and the growth of forests. *Adv. Agronomy* 4:330–398.

————. 1960. Summary of soil-site evaluation. *In* P. Y. BURNS (ed.), *Proc. Eighth Annual Forestry Symposium.* Louisiana State Univ. Press, Baton Rouge, La.

————, and F. X. SCHUMACHER. 1953. Site index of young stands of loblolly and shortleaf pines in the Piedmont Plateau region. *J. For.* 51:432–435.

COMMITTEE ON SITE CLASSIFICATION, NORTHEASTERN FOREST SOILS CONFERENCE. 1961. Planting sites in the Northeast. Northeastern For. Exp. Sta. Paper 157. 24 pp.

COOKSON, I. C. and K. M. PIKE. 1953. The Tertiary occurrence and distribution of Podocarpus (section *Dacrycarpus*) in Australia and Tasmania. *Aust. J. Bot.* 1:71–82.

COOPER, CHARLES F. 1960. Changes in vegetation, structure, and growth of southwestern pine forests since white settlement. *Ecol. Monogr.* 30:129–164.

————. 1961. The ecology of fire. *Sci. American* 204(4):150–160.

————, and WILLIAM C. JOLLY. 1969. Ecological effects of weather modification:

a problem analysis. Univ. of Michigan, School of Natural Resources, Ann Arbor. 160 pp.

COOPER, W. S. 1913. The climax forest of Isle Royale, Lake Superior, and its development. *Bot. Gaz.* 55:1–44, 115–140, 189–235.

———. 1923. The recent ecological history of Glacier Bay, Alaska. *Ecology* 4:93–128, 223–246, 355–365.

CORDONE, ALMO J. 1956. Effects of logging on fish production. Calif. Dept. Fish and Game, Inland Fish. Admin. Rep. 56–57. 98 pp.

CORLISS, J. F., and C. T. DYRNESS. 1965. A detailed soil-vegetation survey of the Alsea area in the Oregon Coast Range. *In* CHESTER T. YOUNGBERG (ed.), *Forest-Soil Relationships in North America.* Oregon State Univ. Press, Corvallis, Ore.

COTTAM, G. 1949. The phytosociology of an oak woods in southwestern Wisconsin. *Ecology* 30:271–287.

COTTAM, WALTER P., and GEORGE STEWART. 1940. Plant succession as a result of grazing and meadow desiccation by erosion since settlement in 1862. *J. For.* 38:613–626.

COVELL, R. R., and D. C. MCCLURKIN. 1967. Site index of loblolly pine on Ruston soils in the southern Coastal Plain. *J. For.* 65:263–264.

COWLES, HENRY C. 1899. The ecological relations of the vegetation on the sand dunes of Lake Michigan. *Bot. Gaz.* 27:95–116, 167–202, 281–308, 361–391.

CRANDALL, DOROTHY L. 1958. Ground vegetation patterns of the spruce-fir area of the Great Smoky Mountains National Park. *Ecol. Monogr.* 28:337–360.

CRITCHFIELD, WILLIAM B. 1960. Leaf dimorphism in *Populus trichocarpa.* *Amer. J. Bot.* 47:699–711.

CROCKER, R. L., and J. MAJOR. 1955. Soil development in relation to vegetation and surface age at Glacier Bay, Alaska. *J. Ecol.* 43:427–448.

CROFT, A. R., and L. V. MONNINGER. 1953. Evapotranspiration and other water losses on some aspen forest types in relation to water available for stream flow. *Trans. Amer. Geophys. Union* 34(4):563–574.

CURTIS, JOHN T. 1959. *The Vegetation of Wisconsin.* Univ. Wisconsin Press, Madison. 657 pp.

———, and R. P. MCINTOSH. 1951. An upland forest continuum in the prairie-forest border region of Wisconsin. *Ecology* 32:476–496.

CURTIS, R. O., and B. W. POST. 1962. Comparative site indices for northern hardwoods. Northeastern For. Exp. Sta., Sta. Paper 171. 6 pp.

CUSHING, EDWARD J. 1965. Problems in the Quaternary phytogeography of the Great Lakes Region. *In* H. E. WRIGHT, JR., and DAVID G. FREY (eds.), *The Quaternary of the United States.* Princeton Univ. Press, Princeton, N. J.

———, and H. E. WRIGHT, JR. (eds.). 1967. *Quaternary Paleoecology.* Yale Univ. Press, New Haven. 433 pp.

DAGNELIE, P. 1957. Recherche sur la productivité des hêtraies d'Ardenne en relation avec les types phytosociologiques et les facteurs écologiques. *Bull. Inst. Agron. Gembloux* 25(1/2):44–94.

DALE, M. B. 1970. Systems analysis and ecology. *Ecology* 51:2–16.

DAMMAN, A. W. H. 1964. Some forest types of central Newfoundland and their relation to environmental factors. For. Sci. Monogr. 8. 62 pp.

DANCIK, BRUCE P., and BURTON V. BARNES. 1972. Natural variation and hybridization of yellow birch and bog birch in southeastern Michigan. *Silvae Genetica* 21:1–9.

DANSEREAU, PIERRE. 1957. *Biogeography, an Ecological Perspective.* The Ronald Press Co., New York. 394 pp.

——— (ed.). 1968. The continuum concept of vegetation: responses. *Bot. Rev.* 34:253–332.

———, and FERNANDO SEGADAS-VIANNA. 1952. Ecological study of the peat bogs of eastern North America. I. Structure and evolution of vegetation. *Can. J. Bot.* 30:490–520.

DARBY, H. C. 1956. The clearing of the woodland in Europe. *In* WILLIAM L.

THOMAS, JR. (ed.), *Man's Role in Changing the Face of the Earth.* Univ. Chicago Press, Chicago.

DAUBENMIRE, R. F. 1943. Temperature gradients near the soil surface with reference to techniques of measurement in forest ecology. *J. For.* 41:601–603.

————. 1952. Forest vegetation of northern Idaho and adjacent Washington, and its bearing on concepts of vegetation classification. *Ecol. Monogr.* 22:301–330.

————. 1954. Alpine timberlines in the Americas and their interpretation. *Butler Univ. Bot. Stud.* 11:119–136.

————. 1956. Climate as a determinant of vegetation distribution in eastern Washington and northern Idaho. *Ecol. Monogr.* 26:131–154.

————. 1959. *Plants and Environment,* 2d ed. John Wiley & Sons, Inc., New York. 422 pp.

————. 1961. Vegetative indicators of rate of height growth in ponderosa pine. *For. Sci.* 7:24–32.

————. 1966. Vegetation: identification of typal communities. *Science* 151:291–298.

————. 1968a. *Plant Communities.* Harper & Row, Inc., New York. 300 pp.

————. 1968b. Some geographic variations in *Picea sitchensis* and their ecologic interpretation. *Can. J. Bot.* 46:787–798.

————, and JEAN B. DAUBENMIRE. 1968. Forest vegetation of eastern Washington and northern Idaho. Washington Agric. Exp. Sta., Tech. Bull. 60. 104 pp.

DAVIS, J. H. 1940. The ecology and geologic role of mangroves in Florida. Carneg. Inst. Wash. Publ. 517.

DAVIS, MARGARET BRYAN. 1958. Three pollen diagrams from central Massachusetts. *Amer. J. Sci.* 256:540–570.

————. 1963. On the theory of pollen analysis. *Amer. J. Science* 261:897–912.

————. 1965. Phytogeography and palynology of northeastern United States. *In* H. E. WRIGHT, JR., and DAVID G. FREY (eds.), *The Quaternary of the United States.* Princeton Univ. Press, Princeton, N. J.

————. 1967. Late-glacial climate in northern United States: a comparison of New England and the Great Lakes region. *In* E. J. CUSHING and H. E. WRIGHT, JR. (eds.), *Quaternary Paleoecology.* Yale Univ. Press, New Haven.

————. 1969. Palynology and environmental history during the Quaternary period. *Amer. Scientist* 57:317–332.

DAVIS, P. H., and V. H. HEYWOOD. 1963. *Principles of Angiosperm Taxonomy.* D. Van Nostrand Co., Inc., New York. 558 pp.

DAY, G. M. 1953. The Indian as an ecological factor in the northeastern forest. *Ecology* 34:329–346.

DEBANO, LEONARD F. 1969. The relationship between heat treatment and water repellency in soils. *In* LEONARD F. DEBANO and JOHN LETEY (eds.), *Water-Repellent Soils.* Univ. Calif., Riverside.

————, JOSEPH F. OSBORN, JAY S. KRAMMES, and JOHN LETEY, JR. 1969. Soil wettability and wetting agents . . . our current knowledge of the problem. USDA For. Ser. Res. Paper PSW–43. Pacific Southwest For. and Rge. Exp. Sta., Berkeley, Calif. 13 pp.

DEBELL, DEAN S. 1969. An evaluation of phytotoxic effects of cherrybark oak (*Quercus falcata* var. *pagodaefolia* Ell.). Ph.D. diss., Duke Univ., Durham, N. C. Univ. Microfilms, Ann Arbor, Mich. Microfilm No. 70–10368. 107 pp.

————. 1971. Phytotoxic effects of cherrybark oak. *For. Sci.* 17:180–185.

DECKER, J. P. 1947. The effect of air supply on apparent photosynthesis. *Plant Physiol.* 22(4):561–571.

————. 1959. A system for analysis of forest succession. *For. Sci.* 5:154–157.

DEEVEY, EDWARD S., JR. 1949. Biogeography of the Pleistocene. *Bull. Geol. Soc. Amer.* 60:1315–1416.

DELFS, J. 1967. Interception and streamflow in stands of Norway spruce and beech in West Germany. *In* WILLIAM E. SOPPER and HOWARD W. LULL (eds.), *Forest Hydrology.* Pergamon Press, Inc., New York.

DEL MORAL, ROGER, and REX G. CATES. 1971. Allelopathic potential of the dominant vegetation of western Washington. *Ecology* 52:1030–1037.

———, and C. H. MULLER. 1970. The allelopathic effects of *Eucalyptus camaldulensis*. *Amer. Midl. Nat.* 83:254–282.

DEMENT, J. A., and E. L. STONE. 1968. Influence of soil and site on red pine plantations in New York. II. Soil type and physical properties. Cornell Univ. Agric. Exp. Sta. Bull. 1020. 25 pp.

DENAEYER-DE SMET, S. 1967. Recherches sur l'écosystemes forêt. La chênaie à *Galeobodolon* et *Oxalis* de Mesnil Eglise (Ferage). Contribution à l'étude chimique de la sève du bois de *Corylus avellana* L. *Bull. Soc. Roy. Botan. Belg.* 100:353–372.

DIETRICH, HERMANN. 1970. Die Bedeutung der Vegetationskunde für die forstliche Standortskunde. *Der Biologieunterricht* 6:48–60.

———, SIEGFRIED MÜLLER, and GERHARD SCHLENKER. 1970. *Urwald von Morgen.* Verlag Eugen Ulmer, Stuttgart, Germany. 174 pp.

DIMBLEBY, G. W. 1952a. The historical status of moorland in north-east Yorkshire. *New Phytol.* 51:349–354.

———. 1952b. Soil regeneration on the north-east Yorkshire moors. *J. Ecol.* 40:331–341.

———, and J. M. GILL. 1955. The occurrence of podzols under deciduous woodland in the New Forest. *Forestry* 28:95–106.

DOBZHANSKY, THEODOSIUS. 1968. Adaptedness and fitness. *In* RICHARD C. LEWONTIN (ed.), *Population Biology and Evolution.* Syracuse Univ. Press, Syracuse, New York.

DOCHINGER, LEON S., and CARL E. SELISKAR. 1965. Results from grafting chlorotic dwarf and healthy eastern white pine. *Phytopathology* 55:404–407.

———, and CARL E. SELISKAR. 1970. Air pollution and the chlorotic dwarf disease of eastern white pine. *For. Sci.* 16:46–55.

DOLF, ERLING. 1960. Climatic changes of the past and present. *Amer. Sci.* 48:341–364.

DOOLITTLE, W. T. 1957. Site index of scarlet and black oak in relation to southern Appalachian soil and topography. *For. Sci.* 3:114–124.

———. 1958. Site index comparisons for several forest species in the Southern Appalachians. *Proc. Soil Sci. Soc. Amer.* 22:455–458.

DORT, WAKEFIELD, JR., and J. KNOX JONES, JR. 1970. *Pleistocene and Recent Environments of the Central Great Plains.* Dept. Geol., Univ. Kansas Special Publ. 3, Univ. Press of Kansas, Lawrence. 433 pp.

DORTIGNAC, E. J. 1967. Forest water yield management opportunities. *In* WILLIAM E. SOPPER and HOWARD W. LULL (eds.), *Forest Hydrology.* Pergamon Press, Inc., New York.

DOUGLASS, A. E. 1919. Climatic cycles and tree growth; a study of the annual rings of trees in relation to climate and solar activity. Carnegie Inst. Wash. Publ. 289.

DOUGLASS, JAMES E. 1967. Effects of species and arrangement of forests on evapotranspiration. *In* WILLIAM E. SOPPER and HOWARD W. LULL (eds.), *Forest Hydrology.* Pergamon Press, Inc., New York.

DOWNS, ROBERT JACK. 1962. Photocontrol of growth and dormancy in woody plants. *In* THEODORE T. KOZLOWSKI (ed.), *Tree Growth.* The Ronald Press Co., New York.

———, and H. A. BORTHWICK. 1956. Effects of photoperiod on growth of trees. *Bot. Gaz.* 117:310–326.

DRISCOLL, RICHARD S. 1964. Vegetation-soil units in the central Oregon juniper zone. USDA For. Serv. Res. Note PNW–19. Pacific Northwest For. and Rge. Exp. Sta., Portland, Ore. 60 pp.

DUCHAUFOUR, P. 1947. Le hêtre est-il une essence améliorante? *Rev. Eaux For.* 85(12):729–737.

DUFFIELD, J. W., and E. B. SNYDER. 1958. Benefits from hybridizing American forest trees. *J. For.* 56:809–815.

DUGGAR, BENJAMIN M. (ed.). 1936. *Biological Effects of Radiation*. 2 vols. McGraw-Hill Book Co., Inc., New York. 1343 pp.

DUVIGNEAUD, P. 1968. Recherches sur l'écosystème forêt. La Chênaie-Frenaie à Coudrier du Bois de Wève. Aperçu sur la biomasse, la productivité et le cycle des éléments biogènes. *Bull. Soc. Roy. Botan. Belg.* 101:111–127.

———, and S. DENAEYER-DE SMET. 1968. Biomass, productivity and mineral cycling in deciduous mixed forests in Belgium. *In* H. E. YOUNG (ed.), *Symposium on Primary Productivity and Mineral Cycling in Natural Ecosystems.* Univ. Maine Press, Orono, Maine.

———, and S. DENAEYER-DE SMET. 1970. Biological cycling of minerals in temperate deciduous forests. *In* DAVID E. REICHLE (ed.), *Analysis of Temperate Forest Ecosystems.* Springer-Verlag, New York.

EBELL, L. F., and R. L. SCHMIDT. 1964. Meteorological factors affecting conifer pollen dispersal on Vancouver Island. Canada, Dept. For. Publ. No. 1036. 28 pp.

EDWARDS, C. A., and G. W. HEATH. 1963. The role of soil animals in breakdown of leaf material. *In* J. DOEKSEN and J. VAN DER DRIFT (eds.), *Soil Organisms.* North-Holland Publishing Co., Amsterdam.

———, D. E. REICHLE, and D. A. CROSSLEY, JR. 1970. The role of soil invertebrates in turnover of organic matter and nutrients. *In* DAVID E. REICHLE (ed.), *Analysis of Temperate Forest Ecosystems.* Springer-Verlag, New York.

EGLER, FRANK E. 1968. The contumacious continuum. *In* PIERRE DANSEREAU (ed.), The continuum concept of vegetation: responses. *Bot. Rev.* 34:253–332.

EHRLICH, PAUL R., and PETER H. RAVEN. 1969. Differentiation of populations. *Science* 165:1228–1232.

EIDMANN, F. E. 1959. Die Interception in Buchen- und Fichtenbeständen; Ergebnis mehrjähriger Untersuchungen im Rothaargebirge, Sauerland. *In Proc. Hannoveresch-Münden Symposium, Eau et Forêts,* pp. 8–25. Publ. Inter. Assoc. Sci. Hydrol. 48.

ELLENBERG, HEINZ. 1956. *Aufgaben und Methoden der Vegetationskunde.* Eugen Ulmer, Stuttgart. 136 pp.

———. 1963. *Vegetation Mitteleuropas mit den Alpen.* Eugen Ulmer, Stuttgart. 943 pp.

———. 1968. Wege der Geobotanik zum Verständnis der Pflanzendecke. *Naturwissenschaften* 55:462–470.

———. 1971a. *Integrated Experimental Ecology.* Springer-Verlag, New York. 214 pp.

———. 1971b. Introductory survey. *In* H. ELLENBERG (ed.), *Integrated Experimental Ecology.* Springer-Verlag, New York.

———, and D. MUELLER-DOMBOIS. 1966. Tentative physiolognomic-ecological classification of plant formation of the earth. *Ber. gebot. Forsch. Inst. Rübel* 37:21–55.

———, and ———. 1970. Geographical index of world ecosystems. *In* DAVID E. REICHLE (ed.), *Analysis of Temperate Forest Ecosystems.* Springer-Verlag, New York.

ENGLER, ARNOLD. 1905. Einfluss der Provenienz des Samens auf die Eigenschaften der forstlichen Holzgewächse. *Mitt. schweiz. Centralanst. forstl. Versuchsw.* 8:81–236.

———. 1908. Tatsachen, Hypothesen und Irrtümer auf dem Gebiete der Samenprovenienz-Frage. *Forstwissenschaftliches Centralblatt* 30:295–314.

ESCHNER, ARTHUR R. 1967. Interception and soil moisture distribution. *In* WILLIAM E. SOPPER and HOWARD W. LULL (eds.), *Forest Hydrology.* Pergamon Press, Inc., New York.

EVANS, G. G. 1956. An area survey method of investigating the distribution of light intensity in woodlands with particular reference to sunflecks. *J. Ecol.* 44:391–428.

EVERS, FRITZ HELMUT. 1964. Die Bedeutung der Stickstofform für Wachstum und Ernährung der Pflanzen, insbesondere der Waldbäume. *Mitt. Vereins forstl. Standortk. Forstpflz.* 14:19–37.

———. 1967. Kohlenstoffbezogene Nährelementverhältnisse (C/N, C/P, C/K,

C/Ca) zur Charakterisierung der Ernährungssituation in Waldböden. *Mitt. Vereins Forstl. Standortk. Forstpflz.* 17:69–76.

―――. 1968. Die Zusammenhänge zwischen Stickstoff-, Phosphor- und Kalium-Mengen (in kg/ha) und den C/N-, C/P- und C/K- Verhältnissen der Oberböden von Waldstandorten. *Mitt. Vereins forstl. Standortk. Forstpflz.* 18:59–71.

―――. 1971. Untermauerung der Standortsgliederung durch Laboruntersuchungen. *Allgem. Forstzeitschr.* 26:443.

EYRE, S. R. 1962. *Vegetation and Soils. A World Picture.* Edward Arnold, Ltd., London. 324 pp.

FAO. 1964. Forest genetics and tree improvement. Report of the 1963 World Consultation. Unasylva 18 (2–3). 144 pp.

―――. 1970. Second world consultation on forest tree breeding. Unasylva 24(2–3). 132 pp.

FEDERER, C. A., and C. B. TANNER. 1966. Spectral distribution of light in the forest. *Ecology* 47:555–560.

FENNOSCANDIAN FORESTRY UNION. 1962. A symposium on forest land and classification of site in the Fennoscandian countries. (Translation of the paper, Skogsmark och Bonitering i de Nordiska Landerna. *Svenska Skogsvardsforeningens Tidskr.* 52:189–226.) U. S. Forest Service, Washington, D. C. 42 pp.

FIRBAS, FRANZ. 1949. *Spät- und nacheiszeitliche Waldgeschichte Mitteleuropas nördlich der Alpen. I. Allgemeine Waldgeschichte.* Verlag Gustav Fischer, Jena. 480 pp.

―――. 1950. *Spät- und nacheiszeitliche Waldgeschichte Mitteleuropas nördlich der Alpen. II. Waldgeschichte der einzelnen Landschaften.* Verlag Gustav Fischer, Jena. 256 pp.

FLACOUS, E. 1959. Revegetation of landslides in the White Mountains of New Hampshire. *Ecology* 40:692–703.

FONS, WALLACE L. 1940. Influence of forest cover on wind velocity. *J. For.* 38:481–486.

FORTESCUE, J. A. C., and G. G. MARTEN. 1970. Micronutrients: forest ecology and systems analysis. *In* DAVID E. REICHLE (ed.), *Analysis of Temperate Forest Ecosystems.* Springer-Verlag, New York.

FOSTER, R. W. 1959. Relation between site indexes of eastern white pine (*Pinus strobus*) and red maple (*Acer rubrum*). *For. Sci.* 5:279–291.

FOWELLS, H. A. 1948. The temperature profile in a forest. *J. For.* 46:897–899.

FOWLER, D. P. 1965a. Effects of inbreeding in red pine, *Pinus resinosa* Ait. II. Pollination studies. *Silvae Genetica* 14:12–23.

―――. 1965b. Effects of inbreeding in red pine, *Pinus resinosa* Ait. IV. Comparison with other Northeastern *Pinus* species. *Silvae Genetica* 14:76–81.

―――, and C. HEIMBURGER. 1969. Geographic variation in eastern white pine, 7-year results in Ontario. *Silvae Genetica* 18:123–129.

FRANKLIN, E. C. 1970. Survey of mutant forms and inbreeding depression in species of the family Pinaceae. USDA For. Serv. Res. Paper SE–61. Southeast For. Exp. Sta., Asheville, N. C. 21 pp.

FRANKLIN, JERRY F. 1965. Tentative ecological provinces within the true fir-hemlock forest areas of the Pacific Northwest. USDA For. Serv. Res. Note PNW–22. Pacific Northwest For. and Rge. Exp. Sta., Portland, Ore. 31 pp.

―――. 1966. Vegetation and soils in the subalpine forests of the southern Washington Cascade Range. Ph.D. dissertation, Washington State University, Dissertation Abstr. 27(6), No. 66–13, 558.

―――, and C. T. DYRNESS. 1969. Vegetation of Oregon and Washington. USDA For. Serv. Res. Note PNW–80. Pacific Northwest For. & Rge. Exp. Sta., Portland, Ore. 216 pp.

FRASER, D. A. 1956. Ecological studies of forest trees at Chalk River, Ontario, Canada. II. Ecological conditions and radial increment. *Ecology* 37:777–789.

―――. 1962. Tree growth in relation to soil moisture. *In* T. T. KOZLOWSKI (ed.), *Tree Growth.* The Ronald Press Co., New York.

FREELAND, R. O. 1944. Apparent photosynthesis in some conifers during winter. *Plant Physiol.* 19:179–185.

FRENZEL, B. 1968. *Grundzüge der pleistozänen Vegetationsgeschichte Nordeuropas.* Franz Steiner Verlag, Wiesbaden. 326 pp.

FRITTS, HAROLD C. 1965. Dendrochronology. *In* H. E. WRIGHT, JR., and DAVID G. FREY (eds.), *The Quaternary of the United States.* Princeton Univ. Press, Princeton, N. J.

———, D. G. SMITH, and M. A. STOKES. 1965. The biological model for paleoclimatic interpretation of Mesa Verde tree-ring series. *Amer. Antiquity* 31:101–121.

———. 1966. Growth-rings of trees: their correlation with climate. *Science* 154:973–979.

———. 1971. Dendroclimatology and dendroecology. *Quaternary Res.* 1:419–449.

———, TERENCE J. BLASING, BRUCE P. HAYDEN, and JOHN E. KUTZBACH. 1971. Multivariate techniques for specifying tree-growth and climate relationships and for reconstructing anomalies in paleoclimate. *J. App. Met.* 10:845–864.

FULLER, H. J. 1948. Carbon dioxide concentration of the atmosphere above Illinois forest and grassland. *Amer. Midl. Nat.* 39:247–249.

FULLER, W. H., STANTON SHANNON, and P. S. BURGESS. 1955. Effect of burning on certain forest soils of northern Arizona. *For. Sci.* 1:44–50.

GAISER, R. N. 1952. Readily available water in forest soils. *Proc. Soil Sci. Soc. Amer.* 16:334–338.

———, and R. W. MERZ. 1951. Stand density as a factor in estimating white oak site index. *J. For.* 49:572–574.

GARNER, W. W. 1923. Further studies in photoperiodism in relation to hydrogen-ion concentration of the cell-sap and the carbohydrate content of the plant. *J. Agr. Res.* 23:871–920.

———, and H. A. ALLARD. 1920. Effect of the relative length of day and night and other factors of the environment on growth and reproduction in plants. *J. Agr. Res.* 18:553–606.

GATES, DAVID M. 1962. *Energy Exchange in the Biosphere.* Harper & Row, Inc., New York. 151 pp.

———. 1965. Heat transfer in plants. *Sci. Amer.* 213:76–84.

———. 1968. Energy exchange between organism and environment. *In* WILLIAM P. LOWERY (ed.), *Biometeorology.* Oregon State Univ. Press, Corvallis, Ore.

———. 1970. Physical and physiological properties of plants. *In Remote Sensing, with Special Reference to Agriculture and Forestry.* National Academy of Sciences, National Res. Council, Washington, D. C.

GATES, F. C. 1914. Winter as a factor in the xerophylly of certain evergreen ericads. *Bot. Gaz.* 57:445–489.

———. 1942. The bogs of northern lower Michigan. *Ecol. Monogr.* 12:213–254.

GAUCH, H. G., JR., and R. H. WHITTAKER. 1972. Comparison of ordination techniques. *Ecology* 53:868–875.

GEHRKE, F. E., and E. C. STEINBRENNER. 1965. Soil survey methods used in mapping Weyerhaeuser Company forest lands in the Pacific Northwest. *In* CHESTER T. YOUNGBERG (ed.), *Forest-Soil Relationships in North America.* Oregon State Univ. Press. Corvallis, Ore.

GEIGER, R. 1950. *The Climate near the Ground.* Translation by M. N. STEWART and others of the 2nd German edition of *Das Klima der bodennahen Luftschicht.* Harvard Univ. Press, Cambridge, Mass. 482 pp.

GENYS, JOHN B. 1968. Intraspecific variation among 200 strains of two-year old Norway spruce. *In Proc. Eleventh Meeting, Comm. For. Tree Breeding in Canada*, pp. 195–203. MacDonald College, Quebec, Canada.

GESSEL, S. P. 1968. Progress and needs in tree nutrition research in the northwest. *In Forest Fertilization.* Tennessee Valley Authority, Muscle Shoals, Ala.

GILBERT, J. M. 1959. Forest succession in the Florentine Valley, Tasmania. *Pap. Proc. Royal Soc. Tasmania* 93:129–151.

GILMOUR, J. S. L., and J. W. GREGOR. 1939. Demes: a suggested new terminology. *Nature* 144:333–334.

GLEASON, H. A. 1926. The individualistic concept of the plant association. *Bull. Torrey Bot. Cl.* 53:7–26.

———. 1939. The individualistic concept of the plant association. *Amer. Midl. Nat.* 21:92–110.

GODWIN, G. E. 1968. The influence of wind on forest management and planning. *In* R. W. V. PALMER (ed.), *Wind Effects on the Forest.* Suppl. to Forestry, Oxford Univ. Press. London.

GODWIN, H. 1956. *The History of the British Flora.* Cambridge Univ. Press, London. 383 pp.

———, D. WALKER, and E. H. WILLIS. 1957. Radiocarbon dating and postglacial vegetational history. Scaleby Moss. *Proc. Royal Soc. London* (B) 147:352–366.

———, and E. H. WILLIS. 1959. Radiocarbon dating of the late-glacial period in Britain. *Proc. Royal Soc. London* (B) 150:199–215.

GOOD, RONALD. 1965. *The Geography of the Flowering Plants,* 3d ed. John Wiley & Sons, New York. 518 pp.

GOODELL, B. C. 1958. A preliminary report on the first year's effects of timber harvesting on water yield from a Colorado watershed. USDA Rocky Mt. For. & Rge. Exp. Sta., Sta. Paper 36. 12 pp.

———. 1967. Watershed treatment effects on evapotranspiration. *In* WILLIAM E. SOPPER and HOWARD W. LULL (eds.), *Forest Hydrology.* Pergamon Press, Inc., New York.

GORDON, ALAN G., and EVILLE GORHAM. 1963. Ecological aspects of air pollution from an iron-sintering plant at Wawa, Ontario. *Can. J. Bot.* 41:1063–1078.

GORHAM, E. and A. G. GORDON. 1960a. Some effects of smelter pollution northeast of Falconbridge, Ontario. *Can. J. Bot.* 38:307–312.

———, and A. G. GORDON. 1960b. The influence of smelter fumes upon the chemical composition of lake waters near Sudbury, Ontario, and upon the surrounding vegetation. *Can. J. Bot.* 38:477–487.

GRAHAM, SAMUEL A. 1941. Climax forests of the upper peninsula of Michigan. *Ecology* 22:355–362.

———. 1955. An ecological classification of vegetation types. Mich. For. Note 11. 2 pp.

———, ROBERT P. HARRISON, JR., and CASEY E. WESTELL, JR. 1963. *Aspens: Phoenix trees of the Great Lakes region.* Univ. Michigan Press, Ann Arbor. 272 pp.

GRANT, VERNE. 1963. *The Origin of Adaptations.* Columbia Univ. Press, New York. 606 pp.

———. 1971. *Plant Speciation.* Columbia Univ. Press, New York.

GRASOVSKY, AMIHUD. 1929. Some aspects of light in the forest. Yale For. Bull. 23. 53 pp.

GRATKOWSKI, H. J. 1956. Windthrow around staggered settings in old-growth Douglas-fir. *For. Sci.* 2:60–74.

GREENLAND, D. J., and J. M. L. KOWAL. 1960. Nutrient content of the moist tropical forests of Ghana. *Plant & Soil* 12:154–174.

GREGOR, J. W., and PATRICIA J. WATSON. 1961. Ecotypic differentiation: observations and reflections. *Evolution* 15:166–173.

GREIG-SMITH, P., M. P. AUSTIN, and T. C. WHITMORE. 1967. The application of quantitative methods to vegetation survey. I. Association-analysis and principal component ordination of rain forest. *J. Ecol.* 55:483–503.

GRIFFIN, JAMES R. 1965. Digger pine seedling response to serpentinite and non-serpentinite soil. *Ecology* 46:801–807.

GRIFFITH, A. L., and R. S. GUPTA. 1948. Soils in relation to teak with special reference to laterisation. Indian For. Bull. 141. 58 pp.

GRIFFITH, B. G., E. W. HARTWELL, and T. E. SHAW. 1930. The evolution of soils as affected by the old field white pine–mixed hardwood succession in central New England. Harv. For. Bull. 15. 82 pp.

GRIME, J. P. 1965a. Comparative experiments as a key to the ecology of flowering plants. *Ecology* 46:513–515.

———. 1965b. Shade tolerance in flowering plants. *Nature* 208:161–163.

———. 1966. Shade avoidance and shade tolerance in flowering plants. *In* RICHARD BAINBRIDGE, G. CLIFFORD EVANS, and OLIVER RACKHAM (eds.), *Light as an Ecological Factor.* Blackwell Sci. Publ., Oxford, England.

———, and D. W. JEFFREY. 1965. Seedling establishment in vertical gradients of sunlight. *J. Ecol.* 53:621–642.

GRÜGER, E. 1972. Pollen and seed studies of Wisconsinan vegetation in Illinois, U. S. A. *Geol. Soc. Am. Bull.* 83:2715–2734.

GRÜGER, J. 1973. Studies on the late Quaternary vegetation history of northeastern Kansas. *Geol. Soc. Am. Bull.* 84:239–250.

GÜNTHER, M. 1955. Untersuchungen über das Ertragsvermögen der Hauptholzarten im Bereich verschiedener Standortseinheiten der württembergischen Neckarlandes. *Mitt. Vereins forstl. Standortsk.* 4:5–31.

GUSTAFSON, FELIX G. 1943. Influence of light upon tree growth. *J. For.* 41:212–213.

GUTSCHICK, V. 1950. *Forstliche Standortskunde als Grundlage für den praktischen Waldbau.* Verlag M. & H. Schaper, Hannover. 259 pp.

HAASE, EDWARD F. 1970. Environmental fluctuations on south-facing slopes in the Santa Catalina Mountains of Arizona. *Ecology* 51:959–974.

HABECK, J. R. 1958. White cedar ecotypes in Wisconsin. *Ecology* 39:457–463.

———. 1960. Winter deer activity in the white cedar swamps of northern Wisconsin. *Ecology* 41:327–333.

HACK, JOHN T., and JOHN C. GOODLETT. 1960. Geomorphology and forest ecology of a mountain region in the central Appalachians. U. S. Geol. Surv. Prof. Paper 347. 66 pp.

HACSKAYLO, JOHN, R. F. FINN, and J. P. VIMMERSTEDT. 1969. Deficiency symptoms of some forest trees. Ohio Agr. Res. and Dev. Cent. Res. Bull. 1015. 68 pp.

HADEN-GUEST, STEPHEN, JOHN K. WRIGHT, and EILEEN M. TECLAFF (eds.). 1956. *A World Geography of Forest Resources.* Amer. Geog. Soc. Spec. Publ. 33. The Ronald Press Co., New York. 736 pp.

HAGEM, O. 1947. The dry matter increase of coniferous seedlings in winter: investigations in oceanic climate. *Medd. Vestland. Forstl. Forsokssta.* 8(1): 317 pp.

HALLIDAY, W. E. D. 1937. A forest classification for Canada. Can. Dept. Resources and Develop. Bull. 89. 56 pp.

HAMILTON, E. L. 1954. Rainfall sampling on rugged terrain. U. S. Dept. Agr. Tech. Bull. 1096. 41 pp.

HAMPF, FREDERICK E. (ed.). 1965. Site index curves for some forest species in the eastern United States. USDA For. Serv., Eastern Region. Upper Darby, Pa. 43 pp.

HANNAH, PETER R. 1969. Stemwood production related to soils in Michigan red pine plantations. *For. Sci.* 15:320–326.

HANOVER, J. W. and R. C. WILKINSON. 1970. Chemical evidence for introgressive hybridization in *Picea. Silvae Genetica* 19:17–22.

HANSEN, H. P. 1947. Postglacial forest succession, climate, and chronology in the Pacific Northwest. *Trans. Amer. Philosoph. Soc.* 37(1). 130 pp.

———. 1948. Postglacial forests of the Glacier National Park region. *Ecology* 29:146–152.

———. 1955. Postglacial forests in south central and central British Columbia. *Amer. J. Sci.* 253:640–658.

HANSON, HERBERT. 1962. *Dictionary of Ecology.* Peter Owen, London. 382 pp.

HANSON, HERBERT C. 1917. Leaf-structure as related to environment. *Amer. J. Bot.* 4:533–560.

HARE, F. KENNETH. 1950. Climate and zonal divisions of the boreal forest formation in eastern Canada. *Geogr. Rev.* 40:615–635.

HARLEY, J. L. 1939. The early growth of beech seedlings under natural and experimental conditions. *J. Ecol.* 27:384–400.

————. 1969. *The Biology of Mycorrhiza.* Leonard Hill, London. 334 pp.

————, et al. 1950–1955. The uptake of phosphate by excised mycorrhizal roots of the beech. *New Phytologist* 49:388–397; 51:56–64, 342–348; 52:124–132; 53:92–98, 240–252; 54:296–301.

HARPER, J. L. 1965. Establishment, aggression, and cohabitation in weedy species. *In* H. G. BAKER and G. L. STEBBINS (eds.), *The Genetics of Colonizing Species.* Academic Press, Inc., New York.

————. 1967. A Darwinian approach to plant ecology. *J. Ecol.* 55:247–270.

HARTMANN, FRANZ. 1952. *Forstökologie.* Verlag Georg Fromme & Co., Vienna. 461 pp.

HATCHELL, G. E., and C. W. RALSTON. 1971. Natural recovery of surface soils disturbed in logging. *Tree Planters' Notes* 22:5–9.

————, and R. R. FOIL. 1970. Soil disturbances in logging. *J. For.* 68:772–778.

HAWES, AUSTIN F. 1923. New England forests in retrospect. *J. For.* 21:209–224.

HEATH, G. W., M. K. ARNOLD, and C. A. EDWARDS. 1966. Studies in leaf litter breakdown. I. Breakdown rates among leaves of different species. *Pedobiol.* 6:1–12.

HEIKURAINEN, LEO. 1964. Improvement of forest growth on poorly drained peat soils. *Int. Rev. For. Res.* 1:39–113.

HELLMERS, HENRY. 1962. Temperature effect upon optimum tree growth. *In* THEODORE T. KOZLOWSKI (ed.), *Tree Growth.* The Ronald Press Co., New York.

————. 1966a. Temperature action and interaction of temperature regimes in the growth of red fir seedlings. *For. Sci.* 12:90–96.

————. 1966b. Growth response of redwood seedlings to thermoperiodism. *For. Sci.* 12:276–283.

————, and W. P. SUNDAHL. 1959. Response of *Sequoia sempervirens* (D. Don) Endl. and *Pseudotsuga menziesii* (Mirb. Franco) seedlings to temperature. *Nature* 184:1247–1248.

————, M. K. GENTHE, and F. RONCO. 1970. Temperature affects growth and development of Engelmann spruce. *For. Sci.* 16:447–452.

HERMANN, RICHARD K., and DENIS P. LAVENDER. 1968. Early growth of Douglas-fir from various altitudes and aspects in southern Oregon. *Silvae Genetica* 17:143–151.

HESLOP-HARRISON, J. 1964. Forty years of genecology. *Adv. Ecol. Res.* 2:159–247.

HEUSSER, CALVIN J. 1960. Late-Pleistocene environments of North Pacific North America. Amer. Geog. Soc. Spec. Publ. 35. 308 pp.

————. 1965. A Pleistocene phytogeographical sketch of the Pacific Northwest and Alaska. *In* H. E. WRIGHT, JR., and DAVID G. FREY (eds.), *The Quaternary of the United States.* Princeton Univ. Press, Princeton, N. J.

————. 1969. Late-Pleistocene coniferous forests of the Northern Rocky Mountains. *In* Center for Natural Resources (ed.), *Coniferous Forests of the Northern Rocky Mountains.* Univ. of Montana Foundation, Missoula, Mont.

HEWETSON, C. E. 1956. A discussion on the "climax" concept in relation to the tropical rain and deciduous forest. *Emp. For. Rev.* 35:274–291.

HEWLETT, JOHN D. 1967. Summary of forests and precipitation session. *In* WILLIAM E. SOPPER and HOWARD W. LULL (eds.), *Forest Hydrology.* Pergamon Press, Inc., New York.

HIBBERT, ALDEN R. 1967. Forest treatment effects on water yield. *In* WILLIAM E. SOPPER and HOWARD W. LULL (eds.), *Forest Hydrology.* Pergamon Press, Inc., New York.

HILDEBRANDT, GERD (ed.). 1971. Application of remote sensors in forestry. International Union of Forest Research Organizations, Sec. 25. Druckhaus Rombach & Co., Freiburg, i. Br., Germany. 189 pp.

HILLMAN, W. S. 1969. Photoperiodism and vernalization. *In* MALCOLM B. WILKINS (ed.), *The Physiology of Plant Growth and Development.* McGraw-Hill Book Co., Inc., New York.

HILLS, G. A. 1952. The classification and evaluation of site for forestry. Ontario Dept. Lands and For., Res. Rept. 24. 41 pp.

————. 1960. Regional site research. *For. Chron.* 36:401–423.

————, and G. PIERPOINT. 1960. Forest site evaluation in Ontario. Ontario Dept. Lands and For., Res. Rept. 42. 64 pp.

HILMON, J. B., and J. E. DOUGLASS. 1968. Potential impact of forest fertilization on range, wildlife, and watershed management. *In Forest Fertilization.* Tennessee Valley Authority, Muscle Shoals, Ala.

HODGES, J. D., and L. S. PICKARD. 1971. Lightning in the ecology of the southern pine beetle, *Dendroctonus frontalis* (Coleoptera: Scolytidae). *Canad. Entomol.* 103:44–51.

HODGKINS, EARL J. 1961. Estimating site index for longleaf pine through quantitative evaluation of associated vegetation. *Proc. Soc. Am. For. 1960,* pp. 28–32.

————. 1965. Southeastern forest habitat regions based on physiography. Auburn Univ., For. Dept. Series No. 2. 10 pp.

————. 1970. Productivity estimation by means of plant indicators in the longleaf pine forests of Alabama. *In* CHESTER T. YOUNGBERG and CHARLES B. DAVEY (eds.), *Tree Growth and Forest Soils.* Oregon State Univ. Press, Corvallis, Ore.

HOLDRIDGE, L. R. 1967. *Life Zone Ecology.* Tropical Sci. Center, San Jose, Costa Rica. 206 pp.

HOLLOWAY, JOHN T. 1954. Forests and climates in the South Island of New Zealand. *Trans. Royal Soc. New Zealand.* 82(2):329–410.

HOLSWORTH, W. N. 1960. Interactions between moose, elk, and buffalo in Elk Island National Park, Alberta. M.S. thesis, British Columbia. 92 pp.

HOOK, D. D., and JACK STUBBS. 1967. An observation of understory growth retardation under three species of oaks. USDA For. Serv. Res. Note SE–70. Southeast For. Exp. Sta., Asheville, N. C. 7 pp.

HOOVER, MARVIN D. 1953. Interception of rainfall in a young loblolly pine plantation. U. S. For. Serv., Southeast. For. Exp. Sta. Paper 21. 13 pp.

————, and CHARLES F. LEAF. 1967. Process and significance of interception in Colorado subalpine forest. *In* WILLIAM E. SOPPER and HOWARD W. LULL (eds.), *Forest Hydrology.* Pergamon Press, Inc., New York.

HOPKINS, DAVID M. (ed.). 1967a. *The Bering Land Bridge.* Stanford Univ. Press, Stanford, Calif. 495 pp.

————. 1967b. The Cenozoic history of Beringia—a synthesis. *In* DAVID M. HOPKINS (ed.), *The Bering Land Bridge.* Stanford Univ. Press, Stanford, Calif.

HORI, T. (ed.). 1953. *Studies on Fogs in Relation to Fog-preventing Forest.* Foreign Books Dept. Tanne Trading Co., Ltd., Sapporo, Hokkaido. 399 pp.

HORTON, K. W. 1956. The ecology of lodgepole pine in Alberta and its role in forest succession. For. Br. Can. Tech. Note 45. 29 pp.

————. 1959. Characteristics of subalpine spruce in Alberta. Can. Dept. Northern Affairs and Nat. Res. For. Res. Div. Tech. Note No 76. 20 pp.

HOUGH, A. F. 1936. A climax forest community on East Tionesta Creek in Northwestern Pennsylvania. *Ecology* 17:1–28.

————. 1945. Frost pocket and other microclimates in forests of the northern Allegheny plateau. *Ecology* 26:235–250.

HUBERMAN, M. A. 1943. Sunscald of eastern white pine, *Pinus strobus* L. *Ecology* 24:456–471.

HUIKARI, O. 1956. Primäärisen soistumisen osuudesta Suomen soiden synnyssa. (The part played by primary bog formation in the origin of Finnish bogs.) *Commun. Inst. For. Fenn.* 46(6). 80 pp.

HURSCH, C. R. 1948. Local climate in the Copper Basin of Tennessee as modified by the removal of vegetation. U. S. Dept. Agr. Circ. 774. 38 pp.

HUXLEY, J. S. 1938. Clines, an auxiliary taxonomic principle. *Nature* 142:219–220.

————. 1939. Clines: an auxiliary method in taxonomy. *Bijdragen tot de Dierkunde* 27:491–520.

INGESTAD, T. 1962. Macroelement nutrition of pine, spruce, and birch seedlings in nutrient solution. *Medd. Skogsforskninst. Stockh.* 51(7):1–131.

IRGENS-MOLLER, H. 1968. Geographical variation in growth patterns of Douglas-fir. *Silvae Genetica* 17:106–110.

Isaac, Leo. A. 1938. Factors affecting establishment of Douglas-fir seedlings. U. S. Dept. Agr. Circ. 486. 45 pp.

———— 1946. Fog drip and rain interception in coastal forests. U. S. For. Serv., Pac. Northwest For. Rge. Exp. Sta. Paper 34. 16 pp.

————. 1956. Place of partial cutting in old-growth stands of the Douglas-fir region. U. S. For. Serv., Pac. Northwest For. Rge. Exp. Sta. Res. Paper 16. 48 pp.

Isaak, D., W. H. Marshall, and M. F. Buell. 1959. A record of reverse plant succession in a tamarack bog. Ecology 40:317–320.

Jackson, L. W. R. 1967. Effect of shade on leaf structure of deciduous tree species. Ecology 48:498–499.

————, and R. S. Harper. 1955. Relation of light intensity to basal area of short-leaf pine (Pinus echinata) stands in Georgia. Ecology 36:158–159.

Jacobs, M. R. 1955. Growth habits of the eucalypts. Forestry and Timber Bur. (Canberra). 262 pp.

Jain, S. K., and A. D. Bradshaw. 1966. Evolution in closely adjacent plant populations. I. The evidence and its theoretical analysis. Heredity 22:407–441.

Jameson, J. S. 1965. Relation of jack pine height-growth to site in the Mixedwood Forest Section of Saskatchewan. In Chester T. Youngberg (ed.), Forest-Soil Relationships in North America. Oregon State Univ. Press, Corvallis, Ore.

Janzen, Daniel H. 1969. Seed-eaters versus seed size, number, toxicity and dispersal. Evolution 23:1–27.

————. 1970. Herbivores and the number of tree species in tropical forests. Am. Nat. 104:501–528.

Jarosenko, R. P. 1956. Smeny rastitel'nogo pokrova Zakavkaz'ja. (Natural Succession in the Vegetation of Transcaucasia.) Izdatel'stvo Akademii Nauk SSSR, Moscow and Leningrad. 242 pp.

Jenny, H. 1941. Factors of Soil Formation. A System of Quantitative Pedology. McGraw-Hill Book Co., Inc., New York. 281 pp.

Jester, J. R., and P. J. Kramer. 1939. The effect of length of day in the height growth of certain forest tree seedlings. J. For. 37:796–803.

Johnsen, T. N., Jr. 1962. One-seed juniper invasion of northern Arizona grasslands. Ecol. Monogr. 32:187–207.

Johnson, Edward A. 1967. Effects of multiple use on peak flows and low flows. In William E. Sopper and Howard W. Lull (eds.), Forest Hydrology. Pergamon Press, Inc., New York.

————, and J. L. Kovner. 1956. Effect on streamflow of cutting a forest understory. For. Sci. 2:82–91.

Johnson, Francis S. 1954. The solar constant. J. Met. 11:431–439.

Johnson, Philip L. (ed.). 1969. Remote Sensing in Ecology. Univ. Georgia Press, Athens. 244 pp.

Johnstone, W. D. 1971. Total standing crop and tree component distributions in three stands of 100-year-old lodgepole pine. In Forest Biomass Studies. Misc. Publ. 132, Life Sci. and Agr. Exp. Sta., Univ. Maine, Orono.

Jones, John R. 1969. Review and comparison of site evaluation methods. USDA For. Serv. Res. Paper RM–51. Rocky Mountain For. and Rge. Exp. Sta., Fort Collins, Colo. 27 pp.

Jorgensen, J. R., and C. S. Hodges, Jr. 1970. Microbial characteristics of a forest soil after twenty years of prescribed burning. Mycologia 62:721–726.

Katz, M. (ed.). 1939. Effect of sulfur dioxide on vegetation. Nat. Res. Counc. Canada. Publ. No. 815. 447 pp.

Keays, J. L. 1971. Complete-tree utilization, resumé of a literature review. In Forest Biomass Studies. Misc. Publ. 132, Life Sci. and Agr. Exp. Sta., Univ. Maine, Orono.

Keever, C. 1953. Present composition of some stands of the former oak, chestnut forest in the southern Blue Ridge Mountains. Ecology 34:44–54.

Kelley, A. P. 1950. Mycotrophy in Plants: Lectures on the Biology of Mycorrhizae and Related Structures. The Ronald Press Co., New York. 223 pp.

KELLOGG, L. F. 1939. Site index curves for plantation black walnut in the Central States region. Central States For. Exp. Sta., Res. Note 35. 3 pp.

KEMPERMAN, JERRY ALLEN. 1970. Study of a population of trembling aspen clones in south-central Utah. Master's thesis, University of Michigan, Ann Arbor. 42 pp.

KERFOOT, O. 1968. Mist precipitation on vegetation. For. Abstracts. 29(1):8–20.

KERSHAW, KENNETH A. 1964. Quantitative and Dynamic Ecology. American Elsevier Publishing Co., New York. 183 pp.

KHOSHOO, T. N. 1959. Polyploidy in gymnosperms. Evolution 13:24–39.

KILBURN, PAUL D. 1957. Historical development and structure of the aspen, jack pine and oak vegetation types on sandy soils in northern Lower Michigan. Ph.D. thesis, University of Michigan, Ann Arbor. 267 pp.

KINCER, J. B. 1933. Is our climate changing? A study of long-time temperature trends. Monthly Weather Rev. 61:251–259.

KING, J. E. 1966. Site index curves for Douglas-fir in the Pacific Northwest. Weyerhaeuser Forest. Paper 8. 49 pp.

KITTREDGE, JOSEPH. 1953. Influences of forests on snow in the ponderosa-sugar pine-fir zone of the central Sierra Nevada. Hilgardia 22:1–96.

KNIGHT, H. 1966. Loss of nitrogen from the forest floor by burning. For. Chron. 42:149–152.

KOCH, WERNER. 1969. Untersuchungen über die Wirkung von CO_2 auf die Photosynthese einiger Holzgewächse unter Laboratoriumsbedingungen. Flora 158B: 402–428.

KOLLMANSPERGER, F. 1956. Lumbriciden in humiden und ariden Gebieten und ihre Bedeutung für die Fruchtbarkeit des Bodens. Rapp. VI Congr. Int. Sci. Sol. (Paris) C, 293–297.

KORMANIK, PAUL P., and CLAUD L. BROWN. 1969. Origin and development of epicormic branches in sweetgum. USDA For. Serv. Res. Paper SE–54. Southeast For. Exp. Sta., Asheville, N. C. 17 pp.

KORMONDY, EDWARD J. 1969. Concepts of Ecology. Prentice-Hall, Inc., Englewood Cliffs, N. J. 209 pp.

KORSTIAN, C. F., and PAUL W. STICKEL. 1927. The natural replacement of blight-killed chestnut in the hardwood forests of the Northeast. J. Agr. Res. 34:631–648.

———, and T. S. COILE. 1938. Plant competition in forest stands. Duke Univ. School For. Bull. 3. 125 pp.

KOSKI, VEIKKO. 1970. A study of pollen dispersal as a mechanism of gene flow in conifers. Comm. Inst. For. Fenn. 70:1–78.

KOZLOWSKI, THEODORE T. 1949. Light and water in relation to growth and competition of Piedmont forest tree species. Ecol. Monogr. 19:207–231.

———. 1971. Growth and development of trees. I. Seed Germination, Ontogeny, and Shoot Growth, 443 pp. II. Cambial Growth, Root Growth, and Reproductive Growth. Academic Press, Inc., New York. 520 pp.

KRAJINA, VLADIMIR J. 1959. Bioclimatic zones in British Columbia. Botanical Series No. 1, Univ. of British Columbia. 47 pp.

KRAMER, PAUL J. 1937. Effect of variation in length of day on growth and dormancy of trees. Plant Physiol. 11:127–137.

———. 1957. Some effects of various combinations of day and night temperatures and photoperiod on the growth of loblolly pine seedlings. For. Sci. 3:45–55.

———. 1969. Plant and Soil Water Relationships: A Modern Synthesis. McGraw-Hill Book Co., Inc., New York. 482 pp.

———, and J. P. DECKER. 1944. Relation between light intensity and rate of photosynthesis of loblolly pine and certain hardwoods. Plant Physiol. 19:350–358.

———, and W. S. CLARK. 1947. A comparison of photosynthesis in individual pine needles and entire seedlings at various light intensities. Plant Physiol. 22:51–57.

———, and T. T. KOZLOWSKI. 1960. Physiology of Trees. McGraw-Hill Book Co., Inc., New York. 642 pp.

546 BIBLIOGRAPHY

KRAUSS, G. A. 1936. Aufgaben der Standortskunde. *Jahresber. deutschen Forstvereins Berlin*, pp. 319–329.

KREBS, R. D., and J. C. F. TEDROW. 1958. Genesis of red-yellow podzolic and related soils in New Jersey. *Soil Sci.* 85:28–37.

KRIEBEL, HOWARD B. 1957. Patterns of genetic variation in sugar maple. Ohio Agr. Exp. Sta. Res. Bull. 791. 56 pp.

KRUCKEBERG, A. R. 1969. The implications of ecology for plant systematics. *Taxon* 18:92–120.

KUCERA, C. L. 1959. Weathering characteristics of deciduous leaf litter. *Ecology* 40:485–487.

KÜCHLER, A. W. 1967. *Vegetation Mapping.* The Ronald Press Co., New York. 472 pp.

LACATE, D. S. (ed.). 1969. Guidelines for bio-physical land classification. Can. Dept. Fish. Forest., Can. Forest Serv., Publ. 1264. 61 pp.

LAMB, H H. 1966. Climate in the 1960's: changes in the world's wind circulation reflected in prevailing temperatures, rainfall patterns and the levels of the African lakes. *Geo. J.* 132:183–212.

LAMBERT, J. M., and W. T. WILLIAMS. 1962. Multivariate methods in plant ecology. IV. Nodal analysis. *J. Ecol.* 50:775–802.

———, and M. B. DALE. 1964. The use of statistics in phytosociology. *Adv. Ecol. Res.* 2:55–99.

LANGFORD, ARTHUR N., and MURRAY F. BUELL. 1969. Integration, identity and stability in the plant association. *Adv. Ecol. Res.* 6:83–135.

LANGLET, OLOF. 1959. A cline or not a cline—a question of Scots pine. *Silvae Genetica* 8:13–22.

———. 1963. Patterns and terms of intra-specific ecological variability. *Nature* 200:347–348.

———. 1971. Two hundred years' genecology. *Taxon* 20:653–721.

LANGNER, W. 1953. Eine Mendelspaltung bei Aurea-Formen von *Picea abies* (L.) Karst als Mittel zur Klärung der Befruchtungsverhältnisse im Walde. *Z. Forstg. Forstpflz.* 2:49–51.

LANNER, RONALD M. 1966. Needed: a new approach to the study of pollen dispersion. *Silvae Genetica* 15:50–52.

LARSON, M. M. 1967. Effect of temperature on initial development of ponderosa pine seedlings from three sources. *For. Sci.* 13:286–294.

———. 1970. Root regeneration and early growth of red oak seedlings: influence of soil temperature. *For. Sci.* 16:442–446.

LARSON, PHILIP R. 1963a. The indirect effect of drought on tracheid diameter in red pine. *For. Sci.* 9:52–62.

———. 1963b. Stem form development of forest trees. For. Sci. Monogr. 5. 42 pp.

———. 1964. Some indirect effects of environment on wood formation. *In* M. H. ZIMMERMAN (ed.), *The Formation of Wood in Forest Trees.* Academic Press, Inc., New York.

LAWRENCE, DONALD B. 1958. Glaciers and vegetation in southeastern Alaska. *Amer. Sci.* 46:81–122.

LEAF, ALBERT L. 1968. K, Mg, and S deficiencies in forest trees. *In Forest Fertilization.* Tennessee Valley Authority, Muscle Shoals, Ala.

LEAPHART, CHARLES D., and ALBERT R. STAGE. 1971. Climate: a factor in the origin of the pole blight disease of *Pinus monticola* Dougl. *Ecology* 52:229–239.

LEIBUNDGUT, HANS. 1970. *Der Wald, eine Lebensgemeinschaft.* Verlag Huber & Co., Stuttgart.

———, and HANS HELLER. 1960. Photoperiodische Reaktion, Lichtbedarf und Austreiben von Jungpflanzen der Tanne (*Abies alba* Miller). *Beiheft Zeitschr. schweiz. Forstv.* 30:185–198.

LEMIEUX, G. J. 1965. Soil-vegetation relationships in the northern hardwoods of Quebec. *In* CHESTER T. YOUNGBERG (ed.), *Forest-Soil Relationships in North America.* Oregon State Univ. Press, Corvallis, Ore.

LEMMON, PAUL E. 1955. Factors affecting productivity of some lands in the Willamette Basin of Oregon for Douglas-fir timber. *J. For.* 53:323–330.

————. 1970. Grouping soils on the basis of woodland suitability. In CHESTER T. YOUNGBERG and CHARLES B. DAVEY (eds.), *Tree Growth and Forest Soils*. Oregon State Univ. Press, Corvallis, Ore.

LEOPOLD, ESTELLA B. 1969. Late Cenozoic palynology. In ROBERT H. TSCHUDY and RICHARD A. SCOTT (eds.), *Aspects of Palynology*. John Wiley & Sons, Inc., New York.

LEYTON, L. 1952. The effect of pH and form of nitrogen on the growth of Sitka spruce seedlings. *Forestry* 25:32–40.

————. 1955. The influence of artificial shading of the ground vegetation on the nutrition and growth of Sitka spruce (*Picea sitchensis* Carr.) in a heathland plantation. *Forestry* 28:1–6.

————, and K. A. ARMSON. 1955. Mineral composition of the foliage in relation to the growth of Scots pine. *For. Sci.* 1:210–218.

LI, HUI-LIN. 1953. Present distribution and habitats of the conifers and taxads. *Evolution* 7:245–261.

LIBBY, W. J., R. F. STETTLER, and F. W. SEITZ. 1969. Forest genetics and forest-tree breeding. *Ann. Rev. Genetics* 3:469–494.

LIETH, HELMUT 1968. Continuity and discontinuity in ecological gradients and plant communities. In PIERRE DANSEREAU (ed.), The continuum concept of vegetation: responses. *Bot. Rev.* 34:253–332.

LIKENS, GENE E., and F. HERBERT BORMANN. 1972. Nutrient cycling in ecosystems. In JOHN A. WIENS (ed.), *Ecosystem Structure and Function*. Oregon State Univ. Press, Corvallis, Ore.

————, ————, N. M. JOHNSON, and R. S. PIERCE. 1967. The calcium, magnesium, potassium, and sodium budgets for a small forested ecosystem. *Ecology* 48:772–785.

————, ————, ————, D. W. FISHER, and ROBERT S. PIERCE. 1970. Effects of forest cutting and herbicide treatment on nutrient budgets in the Hubbard Brook watershed-ecosystem. *Ecol. Monogr.* 40:23–47.

LINDER, SUNE. 1971. Photosynthetic action spectra of Scots pine needles of different ages from seedlings grown under different nursery conditions. *Physiol. Plant.* 25:58–63.

LINTEAU, A. 1955. Forest site classification of the northeastern coniferous section, boreal forest region, Quebec. For. Br. Can. Bull. 118. 78 pp.

LIST, ROBERT J. 1958. Smithsonian meteorological tables. Smithsonian Inst. Pub. 4014 (rev. ed. 6). 527 pp.

LITTLE, S., and E. B. MOORE. 1949. The ecological role of prescribed burns in the pine-oak forests of southern New Jersey. *Ecology* 30:223–233.

LIVINGSTON, R. B. 1949. An ecological study of the Black Forest, Colorado. *Ecol. Monogr.* 19:123–144.

LLOYD, WILLIAM J., and PAUL E. LEMMON. 1970. Rectifying azimuth (of aspect) in studies of soil-site index relationships. In CHESTER T. YOUNGBERG and CHARLES B. DAVEY (eds.), *Tree Growth and Forest Soils*. Oregon State Univ. Press, Corvallis.

LOACH, K. 1967. Shade tolerance in tree seedlings. I. Leaf photosynthesis and respiration in plants raised under artificial shade. *New Phytol.* 66:607–621.

LOGAN, K. T. 1965. Growth of tree seedlings as affected by light intensity. I. White birch, yellow birch, sugar maple, and silver maple. Dept. For. Canada, Publ. 1121. 16 pp.

————. 1966a. Growth of tree seedlings as affected by light intensity. II. Red pine, white pine, jack pine and eastern larch. Dept. For. Canada, Publ. 1160. 19 pp.

————. 1966b. Growth of tree seedlings as affected by light intensity III. Basswood and white elm. Dept. For. Canada, Publ. 1176. 15 pp.

————. 1970. Adaptations of the photosynthetic apparatus of sun- and shade-grown yellow birch (*Betula alleghaniensis* Britt.). *Can. J. Bot.* 48:1681–1688.

————, and G. KROTKOV. 1969. Adaptations of the photosynthetic mechanism of sugar maple (*Acer saccharum*) seedlings grown in various light intensities. *Physiol. Plant.* 22:104–116.

LORENZ, RALPH W. 1939. High temperature tolerance of forest trees. Univ. Minn. Agr. Exp. Sta. Tech. Bull. 141. 25 pp.

LOWRY, WILLIAM P. 1969. *Weather and Life, An Introduction to Biometeorology.* Academic Press, Inc., New York. 305 pp.

LÜDI, W. 1954. Die Neubildung des Waldes im Lavinar der Alp La Schera im schweizerischen Nationalpark (Unterengadin). *Ergeb. wissens. Untersuch. schweiz. Nationalparks* 4(30):279–296.

LUNDEGARDH, HENRIK. 1957. *Klima und Boden in ihrer Wirkung auf das Pflanzenleben,* 5th ed. (Also English translation, 1931, Edward Arnold, Ltd., London.) Gustav Fischer Verlag, Jena. 584 pp.

LUTZ, H. J. 1928. Trends and silvicultural significance of upland forest successions in southern New England. Yale For. Sch. Bull. 22. 68 pp.

————. 1930a. Original forest composition in northwestern Pennsylvania as indicated by early land survey notes. *J. For.* 28:1098–1103.

————. 1930b. The vegetation of Heart's Content, a virgin forest in northwestern Pennsylvania. *Ecology* 11:1–29.

————. 1945. Vegetation on a trenched plot twenty-one years after establishment. *Ecology* 26:200–202.

————. 1956. Ecological effects of forest fires in the interior of Alaska. U. S. Dept. Agr. Tech. Bull. 1133. 121 pp.

————. 1959. Forest ecology, the biological basis of silviculture. Publ. Univ. Brit. Col. 8 pp.

————, and A. L. McCOMB. 1935. Origin of white pine in virgin forest stands of northwestern Pennsylvania as indicated by stem and basal branch features. *Ecology* 16:252–256.

————, and ROBERT F. CHANDLER, JR. 1946. *Forest Soils.* John Wiley & Sons, Inc., New York. 514 pp.

LYNCH, DONALD W. 1958. Effects of stocking on site measurement and yield of second-growth ponderosa pine in the Inland Empire. Intermountain For. and Rge. Exp. Sta. Res. Paper 56. 36 pp.

LYR, HORST, HANS POLSTER, and HANS-JOACHIM FIEDLER. 1967. *Gehölzphysiologie.* Gustav Fischer Verlag, Jena. 444 pp.

McANDREWS, J. H. 1966. Postglacial history of prairie, savanna and forest in northwestern Minnesota. *Torrey Bot. Club Mem.* 22(2). 72 pp.

McCLURKIN, D. C. 1953. Soil and climatic factors related to the growth of longleaf pine. U. S. For. Serv. Southern For. Exp. Sta. Occ. Paper 132. 12 pp.

————. 1967. Vegetation for erosion control in the southern coastal plain of the United States. *In* WILLIAM E. SOPPER and HOWARD W. LULL (eds.), *Forest Hydrology.* Pergamon Press, Inc., New York.

McCULLOUGH, DALE R., CHARLES E. OLSON, JR., and LELAND M. QUEAL. 1969. Progress in large animal census by thermal mapping. *In* PHILIP L. JOHNSON (ed.), *Remote Sensing in Ecology.* Univ. Georgia Press, Athens, Ga.

McDERMOTT, R. E. 1954. Seedling tolerance as a factor in bottomland timber succession. Mo. Agr. Exp. Sta. Res. Bull. 557. 11 pp.

McINTOSH, ROBERT P. 1967. The continuum concept of vegetation. *Bot. Rev.* 33:130–187.

McKELVEY, P. J. 1953. Forest colonization after recent volcanicity at West Taupo. *New Zealand J. For.* 6:435–448.

McMILLAN, C. 1956. The edaphic restriction of *Cupressus* and *Pinus* in the coast ranges of central California. *Ecol. Monogr.* 26:177–212.

McPHERSON, JAMES K., and CORNELIUS H. MULLER. 1969. Allelopathic effects of *Adenostoma fasciculatum,* "chamise," in the California chaparral. *Ecol. Monogr.,* 39:177–198.

McQUILKEN, W. E. 1940. The natural establishment of pine in abandoned fields in the Piedmont Plateau region. *Ecology* 21:135–147.

McVICKAR, J. S. 1949. Composition of white oak (*Quercus alba*) leaves in Illinois as influenced by soil type and soil composition. *Soil Sci.* 68:317–328.

MADGE, D. S. 1965. Leaf fall and litter disappearance in a tropical forest. *Pedobiol.* 5:273–288.

———. 1966. How leaf litter disappears. *New Sci.* 32(517):113–115.

MADGWICK, H. A. I., and J. D. OVINGTON. 1959. The chemical composition of precipitation in adjacent forest and open plots. *Forestry* 32:14–22.

MAGUIRE, WILLIAM P. 1955. Radiation, surface temperatures, and seedling survival. *For. Sci.* 1:277–285.

MAJOR, J. 1951. A functional, factorial approach to plant ecology. *Ecology* 32:392–412.

———. 1961. A note on the International Botanical Congress in Montreal. *Vegetatio* 10:379–382.

———. 1969. Historical development of the ecosystem concept. *In* GEORGE M. VAN DYNE (ed.), *The Ecosystem Concept in Natural Resource Management.* Academic Press, Inc., New York.

MALAC, BARRY F. 1968. Research in forest fertilization at Union Camp Corporation. *In Forest Fertilization.* Tennessee Valley Authority, Muscle Shoals, Ala.

MALIN, JAMES C. 1956. *The Grassland of North America. Prolegomena to Its History.* Publ. by the author, Lawrence, Kansas. 469 pp.

MARGAROPOULOS, PANOS. 1967. Woody revegetation as a pioneer action towards restoring of totally eroded slopes in mountainous watersheds. *In* WILLIAM E. SOPPER and HOWARD W. LULL (eds.), *Forest Hydrology.* Pergamon Press, Inc., New York.

MARR, J. W. 1948. Ecology of the forest-tundra ecotone on the east coast of Hudson Bay. *Ecol. Monogr.* 18:117–144.

MARSHALL, ROBERT. 1927. The growth of hemlock before and after release from suppression. Harv. For. Bull. 11. 43 pp.

MARSTON, R. B. 1956. Air movement under an aspen forest and on an adjacent opening. *J. For.* 54:468–469.

MARTIN, PAUL S., and BYRON E. HARRELL. 1957. The Pleistocene history of temperate biotas in Mexico and eastern United States. *Ecology* 38:468–480.

MARX, D. H. 1969a. The influence of ectotrophic mycorrhizal fungi on the resistance of pine roots to pathogenic infections. I. Antagonism of mycorrhizal fungi to root pathogenic fungi and soil bacteria. *Phytopathology* 59:153–163.

———. 1969b. The influence of ectotrophic mycorrhizal fungi on the resistance of pine roots to pathogenic infections. II. Production, identification, and biological activity of antibiotics produced by *Leucopaxillus cerealis* var. *piceina. Phytopathology* 59:411–417.

———, and C. B. DAVEY. 1969a. The influence of ectotrophic mycorrhizal fungi on the resistance of pine roots to pathogenic infections. III. Resistance of aseptically formed mycorrhizae to infection by *Phytophthora cinnamomi. Phytopathology* 59:549–558.

———, and C. B. DAVEY. 1969b. The influence of ectotrophic mycorrhizal fungi on the resistance of pine roots to pathogenic infections. IV. Resistance of naturally occurring mycorrhizae to infections by *Phytophthora cinnamomi. Phytopathology* 59:559–565.

———. 1970. The influence of ectotrophic mycorrhizal fungi on the resistance of pine roots to pathogenic infections. V. Resistance of mycorrhizae to infection by vegetative mycelium of *Phytophthora cinnamomi. Phytopathology* 60:1472–1473.

MATHER, K. 1943. Polygenic inheritance and natural selection. *Biol. Rev.* 18:32–64.

MAYCOCK, P. F., and J. T. CURTIS. 1960. The phytosociology of boreal conifer-hardwood forests of the Great Lakes region. *Ecol. Monogr.* 30:1–35.

MAZE, JACK. 1968. Past hybridization between *Quercus macrocarpa* and *Quercus gambelii. Brittonia* 20:321–333.

MEEHAN, W. R., W. A. FARR, D. M. BISHOP, and J. H. PATRIC. 1969. Some effects of clear-cutting on salmon habitat of two southeast Alaska streams. USDA For. Serv. Res. Paper PNW–82. Pacific Northwest For. and Rge. Exp. Sta., Portland, Ore. 45 pp.

MEINECKE, E. P. 1928. A camp ground policy. Report, California Dept. Nat. Res., Parks Div., Sacramento, Calif. 16 pp.

MELIN, ELIAS. 1962. Physiological aspects of mycorrhizae of forest trees. *In* THEODORE T. KOZLOWSKI (ed.), *Tree Growth.* The Ronald Press Co., New York.

MERRIAM, C. HART. 1890. Results of a biological survey of the San Francisco Mountain region and the desert of the Little Colorado, Arizona. U. S. Dept. Agr. No. Am. Fauna 3:1–136.

METTLER, LAWRENCE E., and THOMAS G. GREGG. 1969. *Population Genetics and Evolution.* Prentice-Hall, Inc., Englewood Cliffs, N. J. 212 pp.

METZ, L. J., and J. E. DOUGLASS. 1959. Soil moisture depletion under several Piedmont cover types. U. S. Dept. Agr. Tech. Bull. 1207. 23 pp.

———, THOMAS LOTTI, and RALPH A. KLAWITTER. 1961. Some effects of prescribed burning on coastal plain forest soil. U. S. For. Serv. Southeastern For. Exp. Sta., Sta. Paper 133. 10 pp.

MIKOLA, PEITSA. 1962. Temperature and tree growth near the northern timber line. *In* THEODORE T. KOZLOWSKI (ed.), *Tree Growth.* The Ronald Press Co., New York.

MILLER, DAVID H. 1956. The influence of pine forest on daytime temperature in the Sierra Nevada. *Geog. Rev.* 46:209–218.

MILLER, PAUL R. 1969. Air pollution and the forests of California. *Cal. Air Environment* 1:1–3.

MIROV, N. T. 1967. *The Genus "Pinus."* The Ronald Press Co., New York. 602 pp.

MITSCHERLICH, GERHARD. 1970. *Wald, Wachstum und Umwelt. I. Form und Wachstum von Baum und Bestand.* J. D. Sauerlander's Verlag, Frankfort. 142 pp.

———. 1971. *Wald, Wachstum und Umwelt. II. Waldklima and Wasserhaushalt.* J. D. Sauerlander's Verlag, Frankfort. 365 pp.

———, K.-G. KERN, and E. KÜNSTLE. 1963. Untersuchungen über den Kohlensauregehalt der Waldluft in Plenterwald and Fichtenreinbestand. *Allg. Forst- u. Jagdzeitschrift* 134:281–290.

MOEHRING, D. H. 1970. Forest soil improvement through cultivation. *J. For.* 68:328–331.

———, C. X. GRANO, and J. R. BASSETT. Properties of forested loess soils after repeated prescribed burns. USDA For. Serv. Res. Note SO–40. Southern For. Exp. Sta., New Orleans, La. 4 pp.

———, and IKE W. RAWLS. 1970. Detrimental effects of wet weather logging. *J. For.* 68:166–167.

MOHN, CARL A., and SCOTT S. PAULEY. 1969. Early performance of cottonwood seed sources in Minnesota. Minn. For. Res. Notes No. 207. 4 pp.

MOHR, E. C. J., and F. A. VAN BAREN. 1954. *Tropical Soils: A Critical Study of Soil Genesis as Related to Climate, Rock and Vegetation.* N. V. Uitgeverij W. van Hoeve, The Hague and Bandung. 498 pp.

MOHR, H. 1969. Photomorphogenesis. *In* MALCOLM B. WILKINS (ed.), *The Physiology of Plant Growth and Development.* McGraw-Hill Book Co., Inc., New York.

MOOSMAYER, H.-U. 1955. Die Wuchsleistungen der Fichte und Buche auf den wichtigsten Standortseinheiten im Forstamt Königsbronn (Nordostteil der Schwäbischen Alb). *Mitt. Vereins forstl. Standortsk.* 4:52–60.

———. 1957. Zur ertragskundlichen Auswertung der Standortsgliederung im Ostteil der Schwäbischen Alb. *Mitt. Vereins forstl. Standortsk. Forstpflz.* 7:3–41.

MORGENSTERN, E. K., and J. L. FARRAR. 1964. Introgressive hybridization in red spruce and black spruce. Univ. Toronto, Faculty of Forestry, Tech. Rept. No. 4. 46 pp.

MORRISON, M. E. S. 1956. Factors in the degeneration of the prehistoric woodland. *Irish Naturalists J.* (*Belfast*) 12:57–65.

MOSQUIN, THEODORE. 1966. Reproductive specialization as a factor in the evolution of the Canadian flora. *In* ROY L. TAYLOR and R. A. LUDWIG (eds.), *The Evolution of Canada's Flora.* Univ. Toronto Press. 137 pp.

MOUNT, A. B. 1969. Eucalypt ecology as related to fire. *Proc. Tall Timbers Fire*

Ecology Conference, 1969, pp. 75–108. Tall Timbers Res. Sta., Tallahassee, Fla.

MUELLER-DOMBOIS, D. 1964. The forest habitat types of southeastern Manitoba and their application to forest management. Can. J. Bot. 42:1417–1444.

MULLER, CORNELIUS H. 1966. The role of chemical inhibition (allelopathy) in vegetational composition. Bull. Torrey Bot. Club 93:332–351.

MURPHY, P. W. 1953. The biology of forest soils with special reference to the mesofauna or meiofauna. J. Soil Sci. 4:155–193.

MUTCH, ROBERT W. 1970. Wildland fires and ecosystems—a hypothesis. Ecology 51:1046–1051.

NAGEL, J. L. 1950. Changement d'essences. Schweiz. Z. Forstw. 101:95–104.

NATIONAL ACADEMY OF SCIENCES. 1971. Biochemical interactions among plants. U. S. National Comm. for the Int. Biol. Program, Natl. Acad. Sci., Washington, D. C. 134 pp.

NELSON, THOMAS C. 1955. Chestnut replacement in the southern highlands. Ecology 36(2): 352–353.

———. 1957. The original forests of the Georgia Piedmont. Ecology 38:390–397.

NEWBOULD, P. J. 1967. Methods for Estimating the Primary Production of Forests. IBP Handbook No. 2. Blackwell Sci. Publ., Oxford-Edinburgh. 62 pp.

NEWNHAM, R. M. 1968. A classification of climate by principal component analysis and its relationship to tree species distribution. For. Sci. 14:254–264.

NICHOLLS, J. L. 1959. The volcanic eruptions of Mt. Tarawera and Lake Rotomahana and effects on surrounding forests. N.Z.J. For. 8(1):133–142.

NICHOLS, GEORGE E. 1923. A working basis for the ecological classification of plant communities. Ecology 4:11–23, 154–172.

NICOD, J. 1951. Sur le rôle de l'homme dans la dégradation des sols et du tapis végétal en Basse-Provence calcaire. Rev. Geogr. Alp. 39:711–748.

NIKLES, D. G. 1970. Breeding for growth and yield. Unasylva 24(2–3):9–22.

NYYSSÖNEN, AARNE. 1971. Working group on the definition of forest land and methods of land and site classification. In Definition of forest land and methods of land and site classification. IUFRO Report, Royal College of Forestry, Stockholm.

OBERLANDER, G. T. 1956. Summer fog precipitation of the San Francisco peninsula. Ecology 37:851–852.

ODUM, EUGENE P. 1971. Fundamentals of Ecology, 3rd ed. W. B. Saunders Co., Philadelphia. 574 pp.

OGDEN, J. G. 1962. Forest history of Martha's Vineyard, Massachusetts. I. Modern and precolonial forests. Amer. Mid. Nat. 66:417–430.

———. 1966. Forest history of Ohio. I. Radiocarbon dates and pollen stratigraphy of Silver Lake, Logan County, Ohio. Ohio J. Sci. 66:387–400.

OGILVIE, R. T., and E. VON RUDLOFF. 1968. Chemosystematic studies in the genus Picea (Pinaceae). IV. The introgression of white and Engelmann spruce as found along the Bow River. Canad. J. Bot. 46:901–908.

OINONEN, E. A. 1956. Kallioiden muurahaisista ja niiden osuudesta kallioiden metsitty-miseen Etela-Suomessa. (On rock ants, and their contribution to the afforestation of rocks in south Finland.) Acta Entomologica Fennica No. 12 (Helsinki). 212 pp.

OLSON, D. F., and L. DELLA-BIANCA. 1959. Site index comparisons for several tree species in the Virginia-Carolina Piedmont. U. S. For. Serv., Southeastern For. Exp. Sta. Paper 104. 9 pp.

OLSON, JERRY S. 1958. Rates of succession and soil changes on southern Lake Michigan sand dunes. Bot. Gaz. 119:125–170.

OOSTING, H. J. 1942. An ecological analysis of the plant communities of Piedmont, North Carolina. Amer. Mid. Nat. 28:1–26.

———. 1948. The Study of Plant Communities: An Introduction to Plant Ecology. W. H. Freeman & Co., San Francisco. 388 pp.

———, and L. E. ANDERSON. 1939. Plant succession on granite rock in eastern North Carolina. Bot. Gaz. 100:750–768.

OVINGTON, J. D. 1954. A comparison of rainfall in different woodlands. *Forestry* 27:41–53.

———. 1962. Quantitative ecology and the woodland ecosystem concept. *Adv. Ecol. Res.* 1:103–192.

———. 1968. Some factors affecting nutrient distribution within ecosystems. *In* F. E. ECKARDT (ed.), *Functioning of Terrestrial Ecosystems at the Primary Production Level.* UNESCO, Natural Resources Research V., Paris.

PALLMAN, H., and E. FREI. 1943. Beitrag zur Kenntnis der Lokalklimat einiger kennzeichnender Waldgesellschaften des schweizerischen Nationalparkes. *Ergeb. wissens. Untersuch. schweiz. Nationalparkes* 1:437–464.

PARDÉ, J. 1959. Retour sur l'indice C.V.P. de Paterson. *Rev. For. Franc.* 11(1):50–53.

PARKER, J. 1953. Photosynthesis of *Picea excelsa* (*P. abies*) in winter. *Ecology* 34:605–609.

———. 1955. Annual trends in cold hardiness of ponderosa pine and grand fir. *Ecology* 36(3):377–380.

———. 1963. Cold resistance in woody plants. *Bot. Rev.* 29:123–201.

PARRIS, G. K. 1967. "Needle curl" of loblolly pine. *Plant Dis. Rep.* 51:805–806.

PATERSON, S. S. 1956. The forest area of the world and its potential productivity. Dept. Geography, Royal Univ. Göteborg. 216 pp.

———. 1959. On bonitetsbegreppet som uttryck för areell produktionsförmåga. *Svenska Skogsvårdsför. Tidsk.* 57(1):83–108.

PATRIC, JAMES H., JAMES E. DOUGLASS, and JOHN D. HEWLETT. 1965. Soil water absorption by mountain and piedmont frests. *Proc. Soil Sci. Soc.* 29:303–308.

———, and PETER E. BLACK. 1968. Potential evapotranspiration and climate in Alaska by Thornthwaite's classification. USDA For. Serv. Res. Paper PNW–71. Pacific Northwest For. and Rge. Exp. Sta., Portland, Ore. 28 pp.

PAULEY, SCOTT S. 1958. Photoperiodism in relation to tree improvement. *In* KENNETH V. THIMANN (ed.), *The Physiology of Forest Trees.* The Ronald Press Co., New York.

———, and T. O. PERRY. 1954. Ecotypic variation of the photoperiodic response in *Populus.* *J. Arnold Arbor.* 35:167–188.

PEARSON, G. A. 1914. A meteorological study of parks and timbered areas in the western yellow-pine forests of Arizona and New Mexico. *Monthly Weather Rev.* 41:1615–1629.

———. 1936. Some observations on the reaction of pine seedlings to shade. *Ecology* 17:270–276.

———. 1940. Shade effects in ponderosa pine. *J. For.* 38:778–780.

———. 1951. A comparison of the climate in four ponderosa pine regions. *J. For.* 49:256–258.

PENMAN, H. L. 1963. *Vegetation and Hydrology.* Bur. Soils, Harpenden. Tech. Commun. 53. 124 pp.

PENNINGTON, WINIFRED. 1969. *The History of British Vegetation.* English Universities Press, London. 152 pp.

PEREIRA, H. C. 1967. Summary of forests and runoff session. *In* WILLIAM E. SOPPER and HOWARD W. LULL (eds.), *Forest Hydrology.* Pergamon Press, Inc., New York.

PERRY, THOMAS O. 1964. Soil compaction and loblolly pine growth. U. S. Dept. Agr. For. Serv. Tree Planters Notes 69:9.

———. 1971. Dormancy of trees in winter. *Science* 171:29–36.

———, and CHI WU WANG. 1960. Genetic variation in the winter chilling requirement for date of dormancy break for *Acer rubrum.* *Ecology* 41:790–794.

———, HAROLD E. SELLERS, and CHARLES O. BLANCHARD. 1969. Estimation of photosynthetically active radiation under a forest canopy with chlorophyll extracts and from basal area measurements. *Ecology* 50:39–44.

PHILLIPS, J. 1931. The biotic community. *J. Ecol.* 19:1–24.

———. 1934–35. Succession, development, the climax, and the complex organism; an analysis of concepts. *J. Ecol.* 22:554–571; 23:210–246, 488–508.

PHIPPS, R. L. 1961. Analysis of five years dendrometer data obtained within three deciduous forest communities of Neotoma. Ohio Agr. Exp. Sta. Res. Circ. 105. 34 pp.

PIERPONT, GEOFFREY. 1962. The sites of the kirkwood management unit. Ontario Dept. Lands and For., Res. Rept. 47. 91 pp.

PISEK, ARTHUR, WALTER LARCHER, WALTER MOSER, and IDA PACK. 1969. Kardinale Temperaturbereiche der Photosynthese und Grenztemperaturen des Lebens der Blätter verschiedener Spermatophyten. III. Temperaturabhängigkeit und optimaler Temperaturbereich der Netto-Photosynthese. *Flora* (Abt. B) 158:608–630.

POLUNIN, NICHOLAS. 1960. *Introduction to Plant Geography.* McGraw-Hill Book Co., Inc., New York. 640 pp.

POORE, M. E. D. 1955. The use of phytosociological methods in ecological investigations. *J. Ecol.* 43:226–269.

POULSON, THOMAS L., and WILLIAM B. WHITE. 1969. The cave environment. *Science* 165:971–981.

PRESCOTT, J. A., and R. L. PENDLETON. 1952. Laterite and lateritic soils. Bur. Soil Sci. Tech. Commun. 47. 51 pp.

PYATT, D. G. 1968. Forest management surveys in forests affected by winds. *In* R. W. V. PALMER (ed.), *Wind Effects on the Forest.* Suppl. to Forestry, Oxford Univ. Press, London.

RALSTON, CHARLES W. 1964. Evaluation of forest site productivity. *Int. Rev. For. Res.* 1:171–201.

RANDOLPH, L. F., IRA S. NELSON, and R. L. PLAISTED. 1967. Negative evidence of introgression affecting the stability of Louisiana iris species. Cornell University, New York State College of Agriculture, Agricultural Exp. Sta. Memoir 398. 56 pp.

RASMUSSEN, D. I. 1941. Biotic communities of the Kaibab Plateau, Arizona. *Ecol. Monog.* 11:229–275.

RAUNKIAER, C. 1937. *Plant Life Forms.* Transl. by H. GILBERT-CARTER. Oxford Univ. Press, London. 104 pp.

RAUP, HUGH M. 1957. Vegetational adjustment to the instability of the site. *Proc. Pap. 6th Tech. Meet. Int. Union Cons. Nat. & Nat. Res.* (Edinburgh), pp. 36–48.

———, and REYNOLD E. CARLSON. 1941. The history of land use in the Harvard Forest. Harv. For. Bull. 20. 64 pp.

RAYNER, M. C., and W. NEILSON-JONES. 1944. *Problems in Tree Nutrition.* Faber & Faber, Ltd., London. 184 pp.

READ, R. A. 1952. Tree species occurrences as influenced by geology and soil on an Ozark north slope. *Ecology* 33:239–246.

REICHLE, D. E. 1971. Oak Ridge National Laboratory site proposal for analysis of the structure and function of ecosystems in the Deciduous Forest Biome. Oak Ridge National Laboratory. Research proposal, FY 1972, Oak Ridge, Tenn. 162 pp.

———, P. DUVIGNEAUD, and J. S. OLSON. 1971. International woodland synthesis symposium, a proposal. *In* T. ROSSWALL (ed.), Systems analysis in northern coniferous forests—IBP workshop. Bull. 14, Ecological Res. Comm., Swedish Natural Sci. Res. Council, Stockholm, Sweden.

REIFSNYDER, WILLIAM. 1955. Wind profiles in a small isolated forest stand. *For. Sci.* 1:289–297.

——— 1967. Forest meteorology: the forest energy balance. *Int. Rev. For. Res.* 2:127–179.

———, and HOWARD W. LULL. 1965. Radiant energy in relation to forests. USDA Agr. Tech. Bull. No. 1344. 111 pp.

REMINGTON, CHARLES L. 1968. Suture-zones of hybrid interaction between recently joined biotas. *Evolutionary Biology* 2:321–428.

RENNIE, P. J. 1955. The uptake of nutrients by mature forest growth. *Plant & Soil* 7:49–95.

———. 1962. Methods of assessing forest site capacity. *Trans. 7th Inter. Soc. Soil Sci., Comm.* IV and V, pp. 3–18.

REYNOLDS, R. R. 1940. Lightning as a cause of timber mortality. U. S. For. Serv., Southern Forest Exp. Sta. Notes 31. 4 pp.

RICH, L. R. 1959. Watershed management research in the mixed conifer type. Rocky Mt. For. & Rge. Exp. Sta., Sta. Prog. Rept. 1959.

RICHARD, F. 1953. Über die Verwertbarkeit des Bodenwassers durch die Pflanze. Mitt. schweiz. Anst. forstl. Versuchsw. 29(1):17–37.

RICHARDS, N. A., and E. L. STONE. 1964. The application of soil survey to planting site selection: an example from the Allegheny uplands of New York. J. For. 62:475–480.

RICHARDS, P. W. 1952. The Tropical Rain Forest: An Ecological Study. Cambridge Univ. Press, London. 450 pp.

RIGG, G. B. 1940, 1951. The development of sphagnum bogs in North America. Bot. Rev. 6:666–693; 17:109–131.

RITCHIE, J. C. 1957. The vegetation of northern Manitoba. Ecology 38:429–435.

ROCHE, L. 1969. Introgressive hybridization in the spruce species of British Columbia. In C. W. YEATMAN (ed.), Proc. Eleventh Meeting Com. For. Tree Breeding Canada, Part 2. Dept. Fish. and For. Canada, Ottawa.

ROCKY MOUNTAIN FOREST EXPERIMENT STATION. 1959. Research on Black Mesa. A progress report. Rocky Mountain For. Exp. Sta., Sta. Paper 41. 18 pp.

RODIN, L. E., and N. I. BAZILEVICH. 1967. Production and Mineral Cycling in Terrestrial Vegetation. Transl. ed. by G. E. FOGG. Oliver & Boyd, Edinburgh. 288 pp.

ROE, A. L. 1967. Productivity indicators in western larch forests. USDA For. Serv. Res. Note INT–59. Intermountain For. and Rge. Exp. Sta., Ogden, Utah. 4 pp.

ROE, EUGENE I. 1963. Seed stored in cones of some jack pine stands, northern Minnesota. USDA For. Serv. Res. Paper LS–1. Lake States For. Exp. Sta., St. Paul, Minn. 14 pp.

ROHRMAN, F. A., and J. H. LUDWIG. 1965. Sources of sulfur dioxide pollution. Chem. Eng. Prog. 61:59–63.

ROMBERGER, J. A. 1963. Meristems, growth and development in woody plants. USDA Tech. Bull. No. 1293. 214 pp.

ROUSSEL, L. 1948. Couvert et photometrie. (Canopy and photometry.) Bull. Soc. For. Franche-Comté 25(8):313–326.

ROWE, J. S. 1956. Uses of undergrowth species in forestry. Ecology 37:461–473.

———. 1959. Forest regions of Canada. Can. Dept. Nor. Aff. and Nat. Res., Ottawa, Bull. 123. 71 pp.

———. 1960. Can we find a common platform for the different schools of forest type classification? Silva Fennica 105:82–88.

———. 1961. The level-of-integration concept and ecology. Ecology 42:420–427.

———. 1962. Soil, site and land classification. For. Chron. 38:420–432.

———. 1964. Environmental preconditioning, with special reference to forestry. Ecology 45:399–403.

———. 1966. Phytogeographic zonation: an ecological appreciation. In ROY L. TAYLOR and R. A. LUDWIG (eds.), The Evolution of Canada's Flora. Univ. Toronto Press.

———. 1969. Plant community as a landscape feature. In K. N. H. GREENIDGE (ed.), Essays in Plant Geography and Ecology. Nova Scotia Museum, Halifax, N. S.

———. 1971. Why classify forest land? For. Chron. 47:144–148.

ROWE, R. B., and T. M. HENDRIX. 1951. Interception of rain and snow by second-growth ponderosa pine. Trans. Amer. Geophys. Union 32(6):903–908.

RUBNER, KONRAD. 1960. Die pflanzengeographischen Grundlagen des Waldbaues. Neumann Verlag, Berlin. 620 pp.

———, and F. REINHOLD. 1953. Die pflanzengeographischen Grundlagen des Waldbaues, 4th ed. Neumann Verlag, Radebeul and Berlin. 583 pp.

RUTTER, A. J. 1968. Water consumption by forests. In T. T. KOZLOWSKI (ed.), Water Deficits and Plant Growth II. Academic Press, Inc., New York.

SARVAS, RISTO. 1962. Investigations on the flowering and seed crop of *Pinus silvestris*. *Comm. Inst. For. Fenn.* 53:1–198.

———. 1967. Pollen dispersal within and between subpopulations; role of isolation and migration in microevolution of forest tree species. *Proc. XIV IUFRO Congress*, III (Sec. 22–AG 22/24): 332–345.

SATOO, TAISITIROO. 1970. A synthesis of studies by the harvest method: primary production relations in the temperate deciduous forests of Japan. *In* DAVID E. REICHLE (ed.), *Analysis of Temperate Forest Ecosystems*. Springer-Verlag, New York.

SCHAEFFER, R., and R. MOREAU. 1958. L'alternance des essences. *Bull. Soc. For. Franche-Comté* 29:1–12, 76–84, 277–288.

SCHAFFALITZKY DE MUCKADELL, M. 1959. Investigations on aging of apical meristems in woody plants and its importance in silviculture. *Det Forstl. Forsgsv. i Danmark* 25:309–455.

———. 1962. Environmental factors in development stages of trees. *In* THEODORE T. KOZLOWSKI (ed.), *Tree Growth*. The Ronald Press Co., New York.

SCHLENKER, GERHARD. 1964. Entwicklung des in Südwestdeutschland angewandten Verfahrens der forstlichen Standortskunde. *In Standort, Wald und Waldwirtschaft in Oberschwaben*, "Oberschwäbische Fichtenreviere." Stuttgart.

———. 1971. Die Auswirkungen der Laubholz- bzw. Fichtenbestockung auf den Regenwurmbesatz in Parabraunerden und Pseudogleyen des Neckarlandes. *Mitt. Vereins forstl. Standortsk. Forstpflz.* 20:60–66.

———, ULRICH BABEL, and HANS PETER BLUME. 1969. Untersuchungen über die Auswirkungen des Fichtenreinanbaus auf Parabraunerden und Pseudogleye des Neckarlandes. VII. Zusammenfassung und Folgerungen für die forstliche Standortsbewertung. *Mitt. Vereins forstl. Standortsk. Forstpflz.* 19:111–114.

SCHNEIDER, G., GHAUS KHATTAK, and JOHN N. BRIGHT. 1970. Modifying sites for the establishment of black walnut. *In* CHESTER T. YOUNGBERG and CHARLES B. DAVEY (eds.), *Tree Growth and Forest Soils*. Oregon State Univ. Press, Corvallis.

SCHOENICHER, W. 1933. *Deutsche Waldbäume und Waldtypen*. Gustav Fischer Verlag, Jena. 208 pp.

SCHÖNHAR, S. 1969. Untersuchungen über das Vorkommen von Rotfäulepilzen in Fichtenbeständen der Schwäbischen Alb. *Mitt. Vereins forstl. Standortsk. Forstpflz.* 19:20–28.

SCHRAMM, J. R. 1966. Plant colonization studies on black wastes from anthracite mining in Pennsylvania. *Trans. Amer. Phil. Soc.*, Vol. 56, Part 1. 194 pp.

SCHULMAN, EDMUND. 1956. *Dendroclimatic Changes in Semiarid America*. Univ. Ariz. Press, Tucson, Arizona. 142 pp.

SCOTT, D. R. M. 1955. Amount and chemical composition of the organic matter contributed by overstory and understory vegetation to forest soil. Yale Univ. Sch. For. Bull. 62. 73 pp.

SEBALD, O. 1964. Ökologische Artengruppen für den Wuchsbezirk "Oberer Neckar." *Mitt. Vereins forstl. Standortsk. Forstpflz.* 14:60–63.

SECREST, H. C., J. J. MACALONEY, and R. C. LORENZ. 1941. Causes of the decadence of hemlock at the Menominee Indian Reservation, Wisconsin. *J. For.* 39:3–12.

SELM, H. R. 1952. Carbon dioxide gradients in a beech forest in central Ohio. *Ohio J. Sci.* 52(4):187–198.

SHANKS, R. E. 1956. Altitudinal and microclimatic relationships of soil temperature under natural vegetation. *Ecology* 37:1–7.

SHARIK, TERRY L. 1970. Leaf flushing and terminal growth cessation in populations of yellow birch (*Betula alleghaniensis* Britton) and sweet birch (*B. lenta* L.) in the Appalachian Mountains. Ph.D. diss., University of Michigan, Ann Arbor, Mich. Univ. Microfilms, Ann Arbor, Mich., Microfilm No. 71–4727. 65 pp.

SHIRLEY, H. L. 1929. The influence of light intensity and light quality upon the growth of plants. *Amer. J. Bot.* 16:354–390.

———. 1932. Light intensity in relation to plant growth in a virgin Norway pine forest. *J. Agr. Res.* 44:227–244.

————. 1935, 1945a. Light as an ecological factor and its measurement. *Bot. Rev.* 1:355–381; 11:497–532.

————. 1945b. Reproduction of upland conifers in the Lake States as affected by root competition and light. *Amer. Mid. Nat.* 33:537–612.

SHREVE, F. 1915. The vegetation of a desert mountain range as conditioned by climatic factors. Carnegie Inst. Wash., Publ. 217. 112 pp.

————. 1922. Conditions indirectly affecting vertical distribution on desert mountains. *Ecology* 3:269–274.

SIEGELMAN, H. W. 1969. Phytochrome. *In* MALCOLM B. WILKINS (ed.), *The Physiology of Plant Growth and Development*. McGraw-Hill Book Co., Inc., New York.

SIMAK, M. 1951. Untersuchungen über den natürlichen Baumartenwechsel in schweizerischen Plenterwäldern. *Mitt. schweiz. Anst. forstl. Versuchsw.* 27:406–468.

SIRÉN, G. 1955. The development of spruce forest on raw humus sites in northern Finland and its ecology. Acta For. Fenn. 62(4). 408 pp.

SMALL, J. 1954. *Modern Aspects of pH, with Special Reference to Plants and Soils.* Bailliere, Tindall and Cox, London. 247 pp.

SMITH, CHRISTOPHER C. 1970. The coevolution of pine squirrels (*Tamiasciurus*) and conifers. *Ecol. Monogr.* 40:349–371.

SMITH, DAVID M. 1951. The influence of seedbed conditions on the regeneration of eastern white pine. Conn. Agr. Exp. Sta. Bull. 545. 61 pp.

SMITH, FREDERICK E. 1970. Analysis of ecosystems. *In* DAVID E. REICHLE (ed.), *Analysis of Temperate Forest Ecosystems*. Springer-Verlag, New York.

SOLBRIG, OTTO T. 1970. *Principles and Methods of Plant Biosystematics.* The Macmillan Co., Collier-Macmillan Canada, Ltd., Toronto. 226 pp.

SOLLINS, P. 1972. Organic matter budget and model for a southern Appalachian *Liriodendron* forest. Ph.D. thesis, University of Tennessee, Knoxville, Tenn.

SOPPER, WILLIAM E., and HOWARD W. LULL (eds.). 1967. *Forest Hydrology.* Pergamon Press, Inc., New York. 813 pp.

SPROUT, P. N., D. S. LACATE, and J. W. C. ARLIDGE. 1966. Forest land classification survey and interpretations for management of a portion of the Niskonlith provincial forest, Kamloops District, B. C. Dept. For. Canada, Publ. 1159. 34 pp.

SPURR, STEPHEN H. 1941. The influence of two *Juniperus* species on soil reaction. *Soil Sci.* 50:289–294.

————. 1945. A new definition of silviculture. *J. For.* 43:44.

————. 1951. George Washington, surveyor and ecological observer. *Ecology* 32:544–549.

————. 1952a. Origin of the concept of forest succession. *Ecology* 33:426–427.

————. 1952b. *Forest Inventory.* The Ronald Press Co., New York. 476 pp.

————. 1953. The vegetational significance of recent temperature changes along the Atlantic seaboard. *Amer. J. Sci.* 251:682–688.

————. 1954. The forests of Itasca in the nineteenth century as related to fire. *Ecology* 35:21–25.

————. 1956a. Natural restocking of forests following the 1938 hurricane in central New England. *Ecology* 37:443–451.

————. 1956b. Forest associations in the Harvard Forest. *Ecol. Monogr.* 26:245–262.

————. 1956c. Soils in relation to site index curves. *Proc. Soc. of Amer. For. Meeting,* 1955, pp. 80–85.

————. 1957. Local climate in the Harvard Forest. *Ecology* 38:37–46.

————. 1960. *Photogrammetry and Photo-interpretation.* The Ronald Press Co., New York. 472 pp.

————. 1962. Growth and mortality of a 1925 planting of *Pinus radiata* on pumice. *N.Z.J. For.* 8:560–569.

————. 1963. Growth of Douglas-fir in New Zealand. New Zealand For. Serv. For. Res. Inst. Tech. Paper 43. 54 pp.

————, and J. H. ALLISON. 1956. The growth of mature red pine in Minnesota. *J. For.* 54:446–451.

————, and A. C. CLINE. 1942. Ecological forestry in central New England. *J. For.* 40:418–420.

————, and JAMES H. ZUMBERGE. 1956. Late Pleistocene features of Cheboygan and Emmett Counties, Michigan. *Amer. J. Sci.* 254:96–109.

SQUILLACE, A. E. 1966a. Racial variation in slash pine as affected by climatic factors. USDA For. Ser. Res. Paper SE–21. Southeast. For. Exp. Sta., Asheville, N. C. 10 pp.

———— 1966b. Geographic variation in slash pine. For. Sci. Monogr. 10. 56 pp.

————. 1967. Effectiveness of 400-foot isolation around a slash pine seed orchard. *J. For.* 61:281–283.

————. 1970. Genotype-environment interactions in forest trees. *In* Papers presented at the second meeting of the working group on quantitative genetics, Sect. 22, IUFRO, Aug. 18–19, 1969, Raleigh, N. C. Pub. by Southern For. Exp. Sta. 1970.

————, and R. T. BINGHAM. 1958. Localized ecotypic variation in western white pine. *For. Sci.* 4:20–34.

————, and ROY SILEN. 1962. Racial variation in ponderosa pine. For. Sci. Monogr. 2. 27 pp.

STALFELT, M. G. 1921. Till Kännedomen om förhållandet mellan solbladens och skuggbladens kolhydratsproduktion. *Medd. Statens Skogsförsöksan.* 18:221–280.

————. 1924. Tallens och Granens Kolsyreassimilation och dess Ekologiska Betingelser. *Medd. Statens Skogsförsöksan.* 21:181–258.

————. 1935. Einfluss der Durchforstung auf die Funktion der Nadeln und auf die Ausbildung der Baumkrone bei der Fichte. *Svenska Skogsvå rdsför. Tidsk.* 33:149–176.

STANHILL, GERALD. 1970. The water flux in temperate forests: precipitation and evapotranspiration. *In* DAVID E. REICHLE (ed.), *Analysis of Temperate Forest Ecosystems.* Springer-Verlag, New York.

STEARNS, F. W. 1949. Ninety-years change in a northern hardwood forest in Wisconsin. *Ecology* 30:350–358.

STEBBINS, G. LEDYARD. 1950. *Variation and Evolution in Plants.* Columbia Univ. Press, New York. 643 pp.

————. 1966. *Processes of Organic Evolution.* Prentice-Hall, Inc., Englewood Cliffs, N. J. 191 pp.

————. 1969. The significance of hybridization for plant taxonomy and evolution. *Taxon* 18:26–35.

————. 1970. Variation and evolution in plants: progress during the past twenty years. *In* MAX K. HECHT and WILLIAM C. STEERE (eds.), *Essays in Evolution and Genetics.* Appleton-Century-Crofts, Inc., New York.

STEINBRENNER, E. C. 1951. Effect of grazing on floristic composition and soil properties of farm woodlands in southern Wisconsin. *J. For.* 49:906–910.

————. 1955. The effect of repeated tractor trips on the physical properties of forest soils. *Northwest Sci.* 29:155–159.

————. 1968. Research in forest fertilization at Weyerhaeuser Company in the Pacific Northwest. *In Forest Fertilization.* Tennessee Valley Authority, Muscle Shoals, Ala.

————, and S. P. GESSEL. 1955. The effect of tractor logging on physical properties of some forest soils of southwestern Washington. *Proc. Soil Sci. Soc. Amer.* 19:372–375.

STEVEN, H. M., and A. CARLISLE. 1959. *The Native Pinewoods of Scotland.* Oliver and Boyd, Ltd., Edinburgh. 368 pp.

STEWART, W. D. P. 1967. Nitrogen-fixing plants. *Science* 158:1426–1432.

STOATE, T. N. 1951. Nutrition of the pine. Austr. For. and Timb. Bur. Bull. 30. 61 pp.

STOECKELER, JOSEPH H. 1948. The growth of quaking aspen as affected by soil properties and fire. *J. For.* 46:727–737.

————. 1960. Soil factors affecting the growth of quaking aspen forests in the Lake States. Univ. Minn. Agr. Exp. Sta. Tech. Bull. 233. 48 pp.

STONE, E. C. 1957. Dew as an ecological factor. *Ecology* 38:407–422.

————, and H. A. FOWELLS. 1955. Survival value of dew under laboratory conditions with *Pinus ponderosa*. *For. Sci.* 1:183–188.

————, A. Y. SHACHORI, and R. G. STANLEY. 1956. Water absorption by needles of pondersoa pine seedlings and its internal redistribution. *Plant Physiol.* 31:120–126.

STONE, EARL L. 1968. Microelement nutrition of forest trees: a review. *In Forest Fertilization*. Tennessee Valley Authority, Muscle Shoals, Ala.

————. 1971. Effects of prescribed burning on long-term productivity of coastal plain soils. *In* Prescribed burning symposium proceedings. USDA For. Serv. Southeast. For. Exp. Sta., Asheville, N. C.

————, and C. MCAULIFFE. 1954. On the sources of soil phosphorous absorbed by mycorrhizal pines. *Science* 120:946–948.

STRAKA, H. 1970. *Arealkunde/Floristisch-historische Geobotanik*. Verlag Eugen Ulmer, Stuttgart. 478 pp.

STROTHMANN, R. O. 1967. The influence of light and moisture on the growth of red pine seedlings in Minnesota. *For. Sci.* 13:182–191.

SUKACHEV, V. N., and N. V. DYLIS. 1968. *Fundamentals of Forest Biogeocoenology*. Translated by J. M. MACLENNAN. Oliver and Boyd, Ltd., Edinburgh. 672 pp.

SWITZER, G. L., L. E. NELSON, and W. H. SMITH. 1968. The mineral cycle in forest stands. *In Forest Fertilization*. Tennessee Valley Authority, Muscle Shoals, Ala.

SYRACH-LARSEN, C. 1956. *Genetics in Silviculture*. Trans. by MARK L. ANDERSON. Oliver and Boyd, London. 224 pp.

TAKAHARA, S., A. KAWANA, and I. TANGE. 1955. Influence of light intensity and soil moisture on the shade-endurance in the leaves of Shirakashi seedlings, *Cyclobalanopsis myrsinaefolia* Oerst. *Bot. Mag. (Tokyo)* 68:212–215.

TALBOT, LEE M., W. J. A. PAYNE, H. P. LEDGER, LORNA D. VERDCOURT, and MARTHA H. TALBOT. 1965. The meat production potential of wild animals in Africa; a review of biological knowledge. Tech. Comm. Commonwealth Bur. Animal Breeding and Genetics No. 16. 42 pp.

TAMM, CARL OLOF. 1950. Northern coniferous forest soils: a popular survey of the phenomena which determine the productive character of the forest soils of North Sweden. Transl. from the Swedish by MARK L. ANDERSON. Scrivener Press, Oxford. 253 pp.

————. 1964. Determination of nutrient requirements of forest stands. *Int. Rev. For. Res.* 1:115–170.

TANSLEY, A. G. 1935. The use and abuse of vegetational concepts and terms. *Ecology* 16:284–307.

————. 1949. *The British Islands and their Vegetation. I.* Cambridge Univ. Press, Cambridge. 484 pp.

TARRANT, R. F. 1956a. Changes in some physical soil properties after a prescribed burn in young ponderosa pine. *J. For.* 54:439–441.

————. 1956b. Effect of slash burning on some physical soil properties. *For. Sci.* 2:18–22.

TAYLOR, ALAN R. 1969. Lightning effects on the forest complex. *In Proc. Annual Tall Timbers Fire Ecology Conference, 1969*, pp. 127–150. Tall Timbers Res. Sta., Tallahassee, Fla.

————. 1971. Lightning—agent of change in forest ecosystems. *J. For.* 69:477–480.

TAYLOR, B. W. 1957. Plant succession on recent volcanoes in Papua. *J. Ecol.* 45:233–253.

TAYLOR, T. M. C. 1959. The taxonomic relationship between *Picea glauca* (Moench) Voss and *P. engelmannii* Parry. *Madrono* 15:111–115.

TEVIS, L., JR. 1956. Pocket gophers and seedlings of red fir. *Ecology* 37:379–381.

THOMAS, WILLIAM L., JR. (ed.). 1956. *Man's Role in Changing the Face of the Earth*. Univ. Chicago Press. 1,193 pp.

THORNTHWAITE, C. W. 1941. Atlas of climatic types in the United States, 1900–1939. U. S. Dept. Agric. Misc. Pub. 421. 7 pp.

——. 1948. An approach toward a rational classification of climate. *Geog. Rev.* 38:55–94.

——, and J. R. MATHER. 1957. The water balance. Drexel Inst. Tech., Lab. Climatol., Pub. Climatol., Vol. 8(1). 86 pp.

TORKILDSEN, G. B. 1950. Om årsakene til granens dårlige gjenvekst i einstapebestand. (The cause of poor reproduction of spruce in stands with an undergrowth of bracken.) *Blyttia* 8(4):160–164.

TOUMEY, J. W. 1947. *Foundations of Silviculture upon an Ecological Basis*, 2d ed. (rev. by CLARENCE F. KORSTIAN). John Wiley & Sons, Inc., New York. 468 pp.

——, and R. KIENHOLZ. 1931. Trenched plots under forest canopies. Yale Univ. Sch. Forestry Bull. 30. 31 pp.

TRANSEAU, E. N. 1935. The prairie peninsula. *Ecology* 16:423–437.

TRESHOW, MICHAEL. 1970. *Environment and Plant Response.* McGraw-Hill Book Co., Inc., New York. 422 pp.

TRIMBLE, G. R., JR., and S. WEITZMAN. 1956. Site index studies of upland oaks in the northern Appalachians. *For. Sci.* 2:162–173.

TROEGER, R. 1960. Kiefernprovenienzversuche. I. Teil. Der grosse Kiefernprovenienzversuch im südwürttembergischen Forstbezirk Schussenried. *AFJZ* 131(3–4):49–59.

TROUSDELL, K. B., and M. D. HOOVER. 1955. A change in ground-water level after clearcutting of loblolly pine in the Coastal Plain. *J. For.* 53:493–498.

TRYON, E. H., and RUDOLFS MARKUS. 1953. Development of vegetation on century-old iron-ore spoil banks. West Va. Agr. Exp. Sta. Bull. 360. 63 pp.

——. J. O. CANTRELL, and K. L. CARVELL. 1957. Effect of precipitation and temperature on increment of yellow-poplar. *For. Sci.* 3:32–44.

TSCHUDY, ROBERT H., and RICHARD A. SCOTT (eds.). 1969. *Aspects of Palynology.* John Wiley & Sons, Inc., New York. 510 pp.

TUBBS, CARL H. 1969. The influence of light, moisture, and seedbed on yellow birch regeneration. USDA For. Serv. Res. Paper NC–27. North Central For. Exp. Sta., St. Paul, Minn. 12 pp.

——. 1970. The competitive ability of yellow birch (*Betula alleghaniensis* Britton) seedlings in the presence of sugar maple (*Acer saccharum* Marsh.) with specific references to the role of allelopathic substances. Ph.D. dissertation, Univ. of Michigan, 80 pp. Microfilm No. 71–15, 327.

TUCKER, JOHN M. 1961. Studies in the *Quercus undulata* complex. I. A preliminary statement. *Amer. J. Bot.* 48:202–208.

——, WALTER P. COTTAM, and RUDY DROBNICK. 1961. Studies in the *Quercus undulata* complex. II. The contribution of *Quercus turbinella. Amer. J. Bot.* 48:329–339.

TUKEY, H. B., JR. 1962. Leaching of metabolites from above-ground plant parts, with special reference to cuttings used in propagation. *Proc. Plant. Prop. Soc.*, pp. 63–70.

——. 1969. Implications of allelopathy in agricultural plant science. *Bot. Rev.* 35:1–16.

TUREKIAN, KARL K. (ed.). 1971. *The Late Cenozoic Glacial Ages.* Yale Univ. Press, New Haven. 606 pp.

TURRESON, GOTE. 1922a. The species and the variety as ecological units. *Hereditas* 3:100–113.

——. 1922b. The genotypical response of the plant species to the habitat. *Hereditas* 3:211–350.

——. 1923. The scope and import of genecology. *Hereditas* 4:171–176.

U. S. CORPS OF ENGINEERS. 1956. Snow hydrology. Summary report of the snow investigations. North Pac. Div., U. S. C. E., Portland, Ore. 437 pp.

U. S. DEPARTMENT OF INTERIOR. 1967. Surface mining and our environment—a special report to the nation. U. S. Govt. Printing Office, Washington, D. C.

U. S. TROPICAL FOREST EXPERIMENTAL STATION. 1951. Micro-environment significant to tree-growth in limestone region. *Carib. For.* 12(1):7–8, 24–25.

VAARTAJA, O. 1954. Temperature and evaporation at and near ground level on
certain forest sites. *Canad. J. Bot.* 32:760–783.

VAN DER HAMMEN, T., T. A. WIJMSTRA, and W. H. ZAGWIJN. 1971. The floral record of the late Cenozoic of Europe. *In* KARL K. TUREKIAN (ed.), *The Late
Cenozoic Glacial Ages.* Yale Univ. Press, New Haven.

VAN ECK, W. A., and E. P. WHITESIDE. 1963. Site evaluation studies in red pine
plantations in Michigan. *Proc. Soil Sci. Soc. Amer.* 27:709–714.

VAN HAVERBEKE, DAVID F. 1968a. A taxonomic analysis of *Juniperus* in the central
and northern Great Plains. *In* Ornamental tree and shrub improvement—the
forester's role. *Proc. Sixth Cent. States For. Tree Imp. Conf.* Carbondale, Ill.

———. 1968b. A population analysis of *Juniperus* in the Missouri River Basin.
Univ. of Nebraska Studies New Series No. 38. 82 pp.

VEGIS, A. 1964. Dormancy in higher plants. *Ann. Rev. Plant Phys.* 15:185–224.

VÉZINA, P. E. 1961. Variations in total solar radiation in three Norway spruce plantations. *For. Sci.* 7:257–264.

———, and D. W. K. BOULTER. 1966. The spectral composition of near ultraviolet and visible radiation beneath forest canopies. *Canad. J. Bot.* 44:1267–1284.

VIERECK, LESLIE A., and JOAN M. FOOTE. 1970. The status of *Populus balsamifera*
and *P. trichocarpa* in Alaska. *Canad. Field-Nat.* 84:169–173.

VISHER, STEPHEN S. 1954. *Climatic Atlas of the United States.* Harvard Univ.
Press. 403 pp.

VOGELMAN, H. W., THOMAS SICCAMA, DWIGHT LEEDY, and DWIGHT C. OVITT. 1968.
Precipitation from fog moisture in the Green Mountains of Vermont. *Ecology*
49:1205–1207.

VOIGT, G. K. 1960. Distribution of rainfall under forest stands. *For. Sci.* 6:2–10.

WAGNER, FREDERIC H. 1969. Ecosystem concepts in fish and game management.
In GEORGE M. VAN DYNE (ed.), *The Ecosystem Concept in Natural Resource
Management.* Academic Press, New York.

WAGNER, W. H., JR. 1968. Hybridization, taxonomy and evolution. *In* V. H. HEY-
WOOD (ed.), *Modern Methods in Plant Taxonomy.* Academic Press, Inc., New
York.

———. 1970. Biosystematics and evolutionary noise. *Taxon* 19:146–151.

WAHL, EBERHARD W. 1968. A comparison of the climate of the eastern United
States during the 1830's with the current normals. *Monthly Weather Rev.* 96:73–
82.

———, and T. L. LAWSON. 1970. The climate of the midnineteenth century United
States compared to the current normals. *Monthly Weather Rev.* 98:259–265.

WAHLENBERG, W. G. 1949. Forest succession in the southern Piedmont region.
J. For. 47:713–715.

WAKELEY, P. C., and J. MARRERO. 1958. Five-year intercept as site index in
southern pine plantations. *J. For.* 56:332–336.

WALLWORK, J. A. 1959. The distribution and dynamics of some forest soil mites.
Ecology 40:557–563.

WARD, R. T. 1956. The beech forests of Wisconsin—changes in forest composition
and the nature of the beech border. *Ecology* 37:407–419.

WARDLE, PETER. 1968. Engelmann spruce (*Picea engelmannii* Engel.) at its upper
limits in the Front Range, Colorado. *Ecology* 49:483–495.

WAREING, P. F. 1950. Growth studies in woody species. I. Photoperiodism in first-
year seedlings of *Pinus silvestris.* II. Effect of day-length on shoot-growth in
Pinus silvestris after the first year. *Physiol. Plant. (Copenhagen)* 3(3):258–276.

———. 1951. Growth studies in woody species. III. Further photoperiodic effects
in *Pinus silvestris. Physiol. Plant. (Copenhagen)* 4(1):41–56.

———. 1956. Photoperiodism in woody plants. *Ann. Rev. Plant Phys.* 7:191–214.

———. 1969. Germination and dormancy. *In* M. B. WILKINS (ed.), *The Physiology
of Plant Growth and Development.* McGraw-Hill Book Co., Inc., New York.

WATT, A. S. 1947. Pattern and process in the plant community. *J. Ecol.* 35:1–22.

WATTS, W. A. 1970. The full-glacial vegetation of northwestern Georgia. *Ecology* 51:17–33.

WEAVER, JOHN E., and FREDERIC E. CLEMENTS. 1938. *Plant Ecology.* 2d ed. McGraw-Hill Book Co., Inc., New York. 601 pp.

WEBB, D. A. 1954. Is the classification of plant communities either possible or desirable? *Bot. Tidsskr.* 51:362–370.

WEBB, L. J. 1959. A physiognomic classification of Australian rain forests. *J. Ecol.* 47:551–570.

———. 1968. Environmental relationships of the structural types of Australian rain forest vegetation. *Ecology* 49:296–311.

———, and J. G. TRACEY, W. T. WILLIAMS, and G. N. LANCE. 1967a. Studies in the numerical analysis of complex rain-forest communities. I. A comparison of methods applicable to site/species data. *J. Ecol.* 55:171–191.

———, ———, ———, and ———. 1967b. Studies in the numerical analysis of complex rain-forest communities. II. The problem of species-sampling. *J. Ecol.* 55:525–538.

———, ———, ———, and ———. 1970. Studies in the numerical analysis of complex rain-forest communities. V. A comparison of the properties of floristic and physiognomic-structure data. *J. Ecol.* 58:203–232.

WEBER, F. P. 1971. Applications of airborne thermal remote sensing in forestry. *In* GERD HILDEBRANDT (ed.), *Application of Remote Sensors in Forestry.* Druckhaus Rombach & Co., Freiburg, i. Br., Germany.

WECK, J. 1960. Klimaindex und forstliches Produktionspotential. *Forstarchiv.* 31(7):101–105.

———. 1961. Überprüfung der Tauglichkeit eines Klimaindex zur Bestimmung forstwirtschaftlichen Produktionspotentials. *Proc. IUFRO Congress, Vienna* 2(2): 25/3.

WEISER, C. J. 1970. Cold resistance and injury in woody plants. *Science* 169:1269–1278.

WELLNER, C. A. 1948. Light intensity related to stand density in mature stands of the western white pine type. *J. For.* 46:16–19.

WELLS, CAROL G. 1971. Effects of prescribed burning on soil chemical properties and nutrient availability. *In* Prescribed burning symposium proceedings. USDA For. Serv. Southeast. For. Exp. Sta., Asheville, N. C.

WELLS, O. O. 1964a. Geographic variation in ponderosa pine. I. The ecotypes and their distribution. *Silvae Genetica* 13:89–103.

———. 1964b. Geographic variation in pondersoa pine. II. Correlations between progeny performance and characteristics of the native habitat. *Silvae Genetica* 13:125–132.

WELLS, P. V. 1965. Scarp woodlands, transported grassland soils, and concept of grassland climate in the great plains region. *Science* 148:246–249.

WENT, FRITS W. 1957. *The Experimental Control of Plant Growth.* The Ronald Press Co., New York. 343 pp.

WENT, J. C. 1963. Influence of earthworms on the number of bacteria in the soil. *In* J. DOEKSEN and J. VAN DER DRIFT (eds.), *Soil Organisms.* North-Holland Publishing Co., Amsterdam.

WERNER, HANS. 1962. Untersuchungen über das Wachstum der Hauptholzarten auf den wichtigsten Standortseinheiten der Mittleren Alb. *Mitt. Vereins forstl. Standortsk. Forstpflz.* 12:3–52.

———. 1971. Untersuchungen über die Einflüsse des Standorts und der Bestandesverhältnisse auf die Rotfäule (Kernfäule) in Fichtenbeständen der Mittleren Alb. *Mitt. Vereins forstl. Standortsk. Forstpflz.* 20:9–49.

WERNER, JÖRG. 1964. Zur Frage der Wirkung von Fichtenmonokulturen auf staunässeempfindliche Böden. *Standort, Wald und Waldwirtschaft in Oberschwaben,* "Oberschwäbische Fichtenreviere." Stuttgart.

WERT, STEVEN L., PAUL R. MILLER, and ROBERT N. LARSH. 1970. Color photos detect smog injury to forest trees. *J. For.* 68:536–539.

WEST, R. G. 1968. *Pleistocene Geology and Biology.* Longmans, Green & Co., Ltd., London. 377 pp.

WHITE, DONALD P. 1968. Progress and needs in tree nutrition research in the Lake States and Northeast. *In Forest Fertilization.* Tennessee Valley Authority, Muscle Shoals, Ala.

WHITEHEAD, DONALD R. 1965. Palynology and pleistocene phytogeography of unglaciated eastern North America. *In* H. E. WRIGHT, JR., and DAVID G. FREY (eds.), *The Quaternary of the United States.* Princeton Univ. Press, Princeton, N. J.

————. 1967. Studies of full-glacial vegetation and climate in southeastern United States. *In* E. J. CUSHING and H. E. WRIGHT, JR. (eds.), *Quaternary Paleoecology.* Yale Univ. Press, New Haven, Conn.

WHITTAKER, R. H. 1953. A consideration of climax theory: the climax as a population and pattern. *Ecol. Monogr.* 23:41–78.

————. 1954. Plant populations and the basis of plant indication. *Angewandte Pflanzensoziologie.* 1:183–206.

————. 1956. Vegetation of the Great Smoky Mountains. *Ecol. Monogr.* 26:1–80.

————. 1960. Vegetation of the Siskiyou Mountains, Oregon and California. *Ecol. Monogr.* 30:279–338.

————. 1962. Classification of natural communities. *Bot. Rev.* 28:1–239.

————. 1966. Forest dimensions and production in the Great Smoky Mountains. *Ecology* 47:103–121.

————. 1967a. Ecological implications of weather modification. *In* R. SHAW (ed.), *Ground Level Climatology.* AAAS, Washington, D. C. Publ. 86.

————. 1967b. Gradient analysis of vegetation. *Biol. Rev.* 42:207–264.

————. 1970. *Communities and Ecosystems.* The Macmillan Co., New York. 158 pp.

————, R. B. WALKER, and A. R. KRUCKEBERG. 1954. The ecology of serpentine soils. *Ecology* 35:258–288.

————, and W. A. NIERING. 1964. Vegetation of the Santa Catalina Mountains. I. Ecological classification and distribution of species. *J. Ariz. Acad. Sci.* 3:9–34.

————, and ————. 1965. Vegetation of the Santa Catalina Mountains. II. A gradient analysis of the south slope. *Ecology* 46:429–452.

————, and ————. 1968a. Vegetation of the Santa Catalina Mountains. III. Species distributions and floristic relations on the north slope. *J. Ariz. Acad. Sci.* 5:3–21.

————, and ————. 1968b. Vegetation of the Santa Catalina Mountains, Arizona. IV. Limestone and acid soils. *J. Ecol.* 56:523–544.

————, and P. P. FEENY. 1971. Allelochemics: chemical interactions between species. *Science* 171:757–770.

————, and G. M. WOODWELL. 1968. Dimension and production relations of trees and shrubs in the Brookhaven Forest, New York. *J. Ecol.* 56:1–25.

————, and ————. 1969. Structure, production and diversity of the oak-pine forest at Brookhaven, New York. *J. Ecol.* 57:157–176.

WICHT, C. L. 1967. Summary of forests and evapotranspiration session. *In* WILLIAM E. SOPPER and HOWARD W. LULL (eds.), *Forest Hydrology.* Pergamon Press, Inc., New York.

WIERSMA, J. H. 1962. Enkele quantitative aspecten van het exotenvraagstuk. *Ned. Bosbouw Tijdschrift* 34:175–184.

————. 1963. A new method of dealing with results of provenance tests. *Silvae Genetica* 12:200–205.

WIESLANDER, A. E., and R. EARL STORIE. 1952. The vegetation-soil survey in California and its use in the management of wild lands for yield of timber, forage and water. *J. For.* 50:521–526.

————, and ————. 1953. Vegetational approach to soil surveys in wild areas. *Proc. Soil Sci. Soc. Amer.* 17:143–147.

WILDE, S. A. 1954. Reaction of soils: facts and fallacies. *Ecology* 35:89–92.

————. 1958. *Forest Soils: Their Properties and Relation to Silviculture.* The Ronald Press Co., New York. 537 pp.

————, E. C. STEINBRENNER, R. S. PIERCE, R. C. DOSEN, and D. T. PRONIN. 1953. Influence of forest cover on the state of the ground-water table. *Proc. Soil Sci. Soc. Amer.* 17:65–67.

WILL, G. M. 1959. Nutrient return in litter and rainfall under some exotic-conifer stands in New Zealand. *N. Z. Agr. Res.* 2(4):719–734.

WILLIAMS, W. T., G. N. LANCE, L. J. WEBB, J. G. TRACEY, and M. B. DALE. 1969. Studies in the numerical analysis of complex rain-forest communities. III. The analysis of successional data. *J. Ecol.* 57:515–535.

————, ————, ————, and J. H. CONNELL. 1969. Studies in the numerical analysis of complex rain-forest communities. IV. A method for the elucidation of small-scale forest pattern. *J. Ecol.* 57:635–654.

WILSON, C. C. 1948. Fog and atmospheric carbon dioxide as related to apparent photosynthetic rate of some broadleaf evergreens. *Ecology* 29:507–508.

WITKAMP, M., and D. A. CROSSLEY, JR. 1966. The role of arthropods and microflora in breakdown of white oak litter. *Pedobiol.* 6:293–303.

WOLFE, JACK A. 1971. Tertiary climatic fluctuations and methods of analysis of Tertiary floras. *Palaeogeog., Palaeoclimatol., Palaeoecol.* 9:27–57.

————, and E. B. LEOPOLD. 1967. Neogene and early Quaternary vegetation of northwestern North America and northeastern Asia. *In* D. M. HOPKINS (ed.), *The Bering Land Bridge.* Stanford Univ. Press, Stanford, Calif.

WOLFE, J. N., R. T. WAREHAM, and H. T. SCOFIELD. 1949. Microclimates and macroclimates of Neotoma, a small valley in central Ohio. *Ohio Biol. Surv. Bull.* 41. 267 pp.

WOODS, F. W. 1953. Disease as a factor in the evolution of forest composition. *J. For.* 51:871–873.

————, and R. E. SHANKS. 1957. Replacement of chestnut in the Great Smoky Mountains of Tennessee and N. Carolina. *J. For.* 55:847.

WRIGHT, H. E., JR. 1970. Vegetational history of the Central Plains. *In* WAKEFIELD DORT, JR., and J. KNOX JONES, JR. (eds.), *Pleistocene and Recent Environments of the Central Great Plains.* Univ. Press of Kansas, Lawrence, Kan.

————. 1971. Late Quaternary vegetational history of North America. *In* KARL K. TUREKIAN (ed.), *The Late Cenozoic Glacial Ages.* Yale Univ. Press, New Haven.

————, and DAVID G. FREY (eds.). 1965. *The Quaternary of the United States.* Princeton Univ. Press, Princeton, N. J. 922 pp.

WRIGHT, JONATHAN W. 1955. Species crossability in spruce in relation to distribution and taxonomy. *For. Sci.* 1:319–352.

————. 1962. Genetics of forest tree improvement. FAO Forestry and For. Prod. Studies No. 16, Rome. 399 pp.

————, and H. I. BALDWIN. 1957. The 1938 International Union Scotch pine provenance test in New Hampshire. *Silvae Genetica* 6:2–14.

————, and W. IRA BULL. 1963. Geographic variation in Scotch pine. *Silvae Genetica* 12:1–25.

————, and SCOTT S. PAULEY, R. BROOKS POLK, JALMER J. JOKELA, and RALPH A. READ. 1966. Performance of Scotch pine varieties in the North Central Region. *Silvae Genetica* 15:101–110.

————, LOUIS F. WILSON, and WILLIAM RANDALL. 1967. Differences among Scotch pine varieties in susceptibility to European pine sawfly. *For. Sci.* 13:175–181.

WRIGHT, T. W. 1955, 1956. Profile development in the sand dunes of Culbin Forest, Morayshire. *J. Soil Sci.* 6:270–283; 7:33–42.

WULFF, E. V. 1943. *An Introduction to Historical Plant Geography.* Chronica Botanica Co., Waltham, Mass. 223 pp.

YAROSHENKO, P. D. 1946. O smenakh rastitel 'nogo pokrova. (On changes in vegetational cover.) *Bot. Zh. S.S.S.R.* 31(5):29–40

YOUNG, HAROLD E. 1964. The complete tree concept—a challenge and an opportunity. *Proc. Soc. Amer. For., 1964,* pp. 231–233.

———. 1971. Biomass sampling methods for puckerbrush stands. *In Forest Biomass Studies.* Misc. Publ. 132, Life Sci. and Agr. Exp. Sta., Univ. Maine, Orono.

YOUNGBERG, CHESTER T. 1959. The influence of soil conditions, following tractor logging, on the growth of planted Douglas-fir seedlings. *Proc. Soil Sci. Soc. Amer.* 23:76–78.

——— (ed.). 1965. *Forest-Soil Relationships in North America.* Papers at Second North Am. For. Soils Conf. Oregon State Univ. Press, Corvallis. 532 pp.

———, and CHARLES B. DAVEY (eds.). 1970. *Tree Growth and Forest Soils.* Proc. Third North Am. For. Soils Conf. Oregon State Univ. Press, Corvallis. 527 pp.

ZACH, LAWRENCE W. 1950. A northern climax, forest or muskeg? *Ecology* 31:304–306.

ZACHARIAE, G. 1962. Zur Methodik bei Geländeuntersuchungen in der Bodenzoologie. *Z. Pflanzenernähr. Düng. Bodenk.* 97:224–233.

ZAHNER, ROBERT. 1955. Soil water depletion by pine and hardwood stands during a dry season. *For. Sci.* 1:258–264.

———. 1956. Evaluating summer water deficiencies. U. S. For. Serv. Southern For. Exp. Sta., Occ. Paper 150. 18 pp.

———. 1957. Field procedures for soil-site classification of pine land in South Arkansas and North Louisiana. U. S. For. Serv. Southern For. Exp. Sta., Occ. Paper 155. 17 pp.

——— 1958a. Site-quality relationships of pine forests in southern Arkansas and northern Louisiana. *For. Sci.* 4:162–176.

———. 1958b. Hardwood understory depletes soil water in pine stands. *For. Sci.* 4:178–184.

———. 1962. Loblolly pine site curves by soil groups. *For. Sci.* 8:104–110.

——. 1967. Refinement in empirical functions for realistic soil-moisture regimes under forest cover. *In* WILLIAM E. SOPPER and HOWARD W. LULL (eds.), *Forest Hydrology.* Pergamon Press, Inc., New York.

———. 1968. Water deficits and growth of trees. *In* T. T. KOZLOWSKI (ed.), *Water Deficits and Plant Growth II.* Academic Press, Inc., New York.

———, and F. W. WHITMORE. 1960. Early growth of radically thinned loblolly pine. *J. For.* 58:628–634.

———, and NED A. CRAWFORD. 1965. The clonal concept in aspen site relations. *In* CHESTER T. YOUNGBERG (ed.), *Forest-Soil Relationships in North America.* Oregon State Univ. Press, Corvallis.

———, and A. R. STAGE. 1966. A procedure for calculating daily moisture stress and its utility in regressions of tree growth on weather. *Ecology* 47:64–74.

———, and J. R. DONNELLY. 1967. Refining correlations of rainfall and radial growth in young red pine. *Ecology* 48:525–530.

ZINKE, P. J. 1959. Site quality for Douglas-fir and ponderosa pine in northwestern California as related to climate, topography, and soil. *Proc. Soc. Amer. For., 1958,* pp. 167–171.

———. 1960. The soil-vegetation survey as a means of classifying land for multiple-use forestry. *Proc. Fifth World Forestry Congress* 1:542–546.

———. 1961. Forest site quality as related to soil nitrogen content. *Trans. 7th Int. Cong. Soil Sci.* 3:411–418.

———. 1967. Forest interception studies in the United States. *In* WILLIAM E. SOPPER and HOWARD W. LULL (eds.), *Forest Hydrology.* Pergamon Press, Inc., New York.

ZOBEL, DONALD B. 1969. Factors affecting the distribution of *Pinus pungens,* an Appalachian endemic. *Ecol. Monogr.* 39:303–333.

ZOLTAI, S. C. 1965. Forest sites of site regions 5S and 4S, Northwestern Ontario. Vol. I. Ontario Dept. Lands and For. Res. Rept. 65. 121 pp.

Index